EDUCATIONAL PSYCHOLOGY 97/98

Twelfth Edition

Editor

Kathleen M. Cauley
Virginia Commonwealth University

Kathleen M. Cauley received her Ph.D. in educational studies/human development from the University of Delaware in 1985. Her research interests center on applying cognitive developmental research to school learning. Currently, she is studying children's mathematical understanding in classrooms that are implementing the National Council of Teachers of Mathematics Standards for Mathematics.

Editor

Fredric Linder
Virginia Commonwealth University

Fredric Linder received an A.B. in American civilization from the University of Miami, Florida, an M.A. in psychology from the New School for Social Research, and a Ph.D. in educational psychology from the State University of New York at Buffalo. His research and publications focus on the values, locus of control, and cognitive learning styles of students.

Editor

James H. McMillan
Virginia Commonwealth University

James H. McMillan received his bachelor's degree from Albion College in 1970, his M.A. from Michigan State University in 1972, and his Ph.D. from Northwestern University in 1976. He has reviewed and written extensively on many topics in educational psychology. His current interests are classroom assessment and school report cards.

A Library of Information from the Public Press
Dushkin/McGraw-Hill
Sluice Dock, Guilford, Connecticut 06437

Visit us on the Internet—http://www.dushkin.com

The Annual Editions Series

ANNUAL EDITIONS is a series of over 65 volumes designed to provide the reader with convenient, low-cost access to a wide range of current, carefully selected articles from some of the most important magazines, newspapers, and journals published today. ANNUAL EDITIONS are updated on an annual basis through a continuous monitoring of over 300 periodical sources. All ANNUAL EDITIONS have a number of features that are designed to make them particularly useful, including topic guides, annotated tables of contents, unit overviews, and indexes. For the teacher using ANNUAL EDITIONS in the classroom, an Instructor's Resource Guide with test questions is available for each volume.

VOLUMES AVAILABLE

Abnormal Psychology
Adolescent Psychology
Africa
Aging
American Foreign Policy
American Government
American History, Pre-Civil War
American History, Post-Civil War
American Public Policy
Anthropology
Archaeology
Biopsychology
Business Ethics
Child Growth and Development
China
Comparative Politics
Computers in Education
Computers in Society
Criminal Justice
Criminology
Developing World
Deviant Behavior
Drugs, Society, and Behavior
Dying, Death, and Bereavement

Early Childhood Education
Economics
Educating Exceptional Children
Education
Educational Psychology
Environment
Geography
Global Issues
Health
Human Development
Human Resources
Human Sexuality
India and South Asia
International Business
Japan and the Pacific Rim
Latin America
Life Management
Macroeconomics
Management
Marketing
Marriage and Family
Mass Media
Microeconomics

Middle East and the
   Islamic World
Multicultural Education
Nutrition
Personal Growth and Behavior
Physical Anthropology
Psychology
Public Administration
Race and Ethnic Relations
Russia, the Eurasian Republics,
   and Central/Eastern Europe
Social Problems
Social Psychology
Sociology
State and Local Government
Urban Society
Western Civilization,
   Pre-Reformation
Western Civilization,
   Post-Reformation
Western Europe
World History, Pre-Modern
World History, Modern
World Politics

Cataloging in Publication Data
Main entry under title: Annual Editions: Educational Psychology. 1997/98.
        1. Educational psychology—Periodicals. 2. Teaching—Periodicals. I. Cauley, Kathleen M., *comp.*; Linder, Fredric, *comp.*; McMillan, James H., *comp.* II. Title: Educational psychology.
        ISBN 0–697–37261–8   370.15′05   82–640517

Twelfth Edition

Cover Image ©1996 PhotoDisc, Inc.

Printed in the United States of America

Printed on Recycled Paper

Editors/Advisory Board

Members of the Advisory Board are instrumental in the final selection of articles for each edition of ANNUAL EDITIONS. Their review of articles for content, level, currentness, and appropriateness provides critical direction to the editor and staff. We think that you will find their careful consideration well reflected in this volume.

EDITORS

Kathleen M. Cauley
Virginia Commonwealth University

Fredric Linder
Virginia Commonwealth University

James H. McMillan
Virginia Commonwealth University

ADVISORY BOARD

Staff

Ian A. Nielsen, Publisher

To the Reader

In publishing ANNUAL EDITIONS we recognize the enormous role played by the magazines, newspapers, and journals of the *public press* in providing current, first-rate educational information in a broad spectrum of interest areas. Many of these articles are appropriate for students, researchers, and professionals seeking accurate, current material to help bridge the gap between principles and theories and the real world. These articles, however, become more useful for study when those of lasting value are carefully *collected, organized, indexed,* and *reproduced* in a *low-cost format,* which provides easy and permanent access when the material is needed. That is the role played by ANNUAL EDITIONS. Under the direction of each volume's *academic editor,* who is an expert in the subject area, and with the guidance of an *Advisory Board,* each year we seek to provide in each ANNUAL EDITION a current, well-balanced, carefully selected collection of the best of the public press for your study and enjoyment. We think that you will find this volume useful, and we hope that you will take a moment to let us know what you think.

Educational psychology is an interdisciplinary subject that includes human development, learning, intelligence, motivation, assessment, instructional strategies, and classroom management. The articles in this volume give special attention to the application of this knowledge to teaching.

Annual Editions: Educational Psychology 97/98 is presented in six units. An overview precedes each unit, explaining how the articles in the unit are related to the broader issues within educational psychology. The first unit presents issues central to the teaching role. The essays address the challenges of responding to calls for educational reform and the role of research in meeting those challenges.

The second unit, concerned with child and adolescent development, covers the cognitive, social, and emotional components of development. The articles in this unit examine the developmental implications for teachers of early childhood programs, the social forces affecting children and adolescents, and the personal and social skills needed to cope with school learning and developmental tasks.

The third unit, regarding exceptional and culturally diverse students, focuses on the learning disabled, the gifted, and multicultural education. Diverse students are different in some way and require an individualized approach to education. The articles in this unit review the characteristics of these children and suggest programs and strategies to meet their needs.

The fourth unit includes essays about theories of learning and instructional strategies. The different views of learning, such as information processing, behaviorism, and constructivist learning, represent the accumulation of years of research on the way humans change in thinking or behavior due to experience. The principles generated by each approach have important implications for teaching. These implications are addressed in a

section on instructional strategies, covering such topics as instructional methods, authentic instruction, computer-aided teaching, learning styles, and discovery methods.

The topic of motivation is perhaps one of the most important aspects of school learning. Effective teachers need to motivate their students both to learn and to behave responsibly. How to manage children and what forms of discipline to use are issues that concern parents as well as teachers and administrators. The fifth unit presents a variety of perspectives on motivating students and discusses approaches to managing student behavior.

Unit 6 reviews assessment approaches that can be used to diagnose learning and improve instruction. The focus is on grading practices and appropriate uses of standardized tests. Performance-based assessment is introduced as a promising new approach to classroom measurement.

This 12th edition of *Annual Editions: Educational Psychology* has been revised so as to present articles that are current and useful. Your responses to the selection and organization of materials are appreciated. Please fill out and return the postage-paid *article rating form* on the last page of the book.

Kathleen M. Cauley

Fredric Linder

James H. McMillan
Editors

Contents

UNIT 3

Exceptional and Culturally Diverse Students

Eight articles look at the problems and positive effects of educational programs for learning disabled, gifted, and culturally diverse children.

UNIT 4

Learning and Instruction

Twelve selections explore the important types of student/teacher interaction.

The concepts in bold italics are developed in the article. For further expansion please refer to the Topic Guide and the Index.

The concepts in bold italics are developed in the article. For further expansion please refer to the Topic Guide and the Index.

UNIT 5

Motivation and Classroom Management

Seven selections discuss student control and motivation in the classroom.

The concepts in bold italics are developed in the article. For further expansion please refer to the Topic Guide and the Index.

UNIT 6

Assessment

Six articles discuss the implications of educational measurement for the classroom decision-making process and for the teaching profession.

The concepts in bold italics are developed in the article. For further expansion please refer to the Topic Guide and the Index.

Topic Guide

This topic guide suggests how the selections in this book relate to topics of traditional concern to educational psychology students and professionals. It is useful for locating articles that relate to each other for reading and research. The guide is arranged alphabetically according to topic. Articles may, of course, treat topics that do not appear in the topic guide. In turn, entries in the topic guide do not necessarily constitute a comprehensive listing of all the contents of each selection.

TOPIC AREA	TREATED IN	TOPIC AREA	TREATED IN
Action Research	3. Using Action Research to Assess Instruction	Constructivism	2. Six National Goals 27. Caring Classroom's Academic Edge 29. Problem Based Learning 32. Choices for Children 37. Creating a Constructivist Classroom Atmosphere
At-Risk Behavior	10. Developmental Tasks of Early Adolescence 11. At-Risk Students and Resiliency		
Behaviorism	23. Rewards of Learning 24. Rewards versus Learning 25. Sticking Up for Rewards	Creativity	30. Investing in Creativity
		Criterion-Referenced	40. Making the Grade 41. Creating Tests Worth Taking
Child/Adolescent Development	5. Learning through "Play" as Well as "Work" in the Primary Grades 6. Moral Child 7. Early Childhood Programs That Work for Children from Economically Disadvantaged Families 8. Helping Children Become More Prosocial 9. Caring for Others and Being Cared For 10. Developmental Tasks of Early Adolescence 11. At-Risk Students and Resiliency	Critical Thinking	29. Problem Based Learning
		Disabilities	12. When Your Child Is Special 13. Holistic Approach to Attention Deficit Disorder
		Discipline	30. Choices for Children 37. Creating a Constructivist Classroom Atmosphere 38. Why Violence Prevention Programs Don't Work—and What Does
Classroom Climate	25. Caring Classroom's Academic Edge	Diverse Students	18. "All Kids Can Learn"
Classroom Management	35. From Negation to Negotiation 36. Images of Management for Learner-Centered Classrooms	Early Childhood	5. Learning through "Play" as Well as "Work" in the Primary Grades 7. Early Childhood Programs That Work for Children from Economically Disadvantaged Families 8. Helping Children Become More Prosocial
Cognitive Development	5. Learning through "Play" as Well as "Work" in the Primary Grades 6. Moral Child		
Cognitive Learning	20. Remembering the Forgotten Art of Memory 22. Thinking Maps 29. Problem Based Learning	Educational Reform	2. Six National Goals 41. Creating Tests Worth Taking
		Family Structure	6. Moral Child 7. Early Childhood Programs That Work for Children from Economically Disadvantaged Families 10. Developmental Tasks of Early Adolescence
Cognitive Maps	22. Thinking Maps		
Collaborative Learning	28. Framework for Culturally Responsive Teaching		
Computer-Assisted	31. How K–12 Teachers Are Using Computer Networks		

Perspectives on Teaching

The teaching-learning process in school is enormously complex. Many factors influence pupil learning—such as family background, developmental level, prior knowledge, motivation, and, of course, effective teachers. Educational psychology investigates these factors to better understand and explain student learning. We begin our exploration of the teaching-learning process by considering the teaching role.

In the first article, Jeffrey Aceto describes the teacher's role through the eyes of a first-time substitute teacher. He finishes his first day with a renewed admiration for the many talents required of full-time teachers.

Aceto, however, sees only the surface features of a school day. As the selection by Constance Kamii, Faye Clark, and Ann Dominick suggests, our philosophy of teaching can have an enormous influence over the way we conceive of the teaching role. These authors expound a constructivist perspective on the goals in *America 2000*. They argue that developing both moral and intellectual autonomy in children ought to be our overarching goal. If we adopt the goal of autonomy, then classroom practices will change in significant ways.

Another less obvious aspect of the teaching role is the systematic effort to improve. The next two articles address two useful activities to support pedagogical change. Peggy Raines and Linda Shadiow argue that reflection on teaching helps teachers change in ways that are driven by their own theories of teaching. Then, as the teacher maps out a plan for improvement, engaging in action research—or systematic inquiry—will enable her or him to document the effects of that plan. Carole Shulte Johnson and Inga Kromann-Kelly illustrate how teachers should conduct an action research project to improve the classroom learning environment. The authors describe five basic questions to guide the development of action research projects. The five questions determine (1) the question to answer in the study; (2) the data that are relevant; (3) how the data will be collected; (4) how the data will be analyzed; and (5) what implications can be drawn from the data. As the professional development schools envisioned by the Holmes Group (a consortium of research institutions) and others are established, teacher research may become a professional expectation.

Educational psychology is a resource for teachers that emphasizes disciplined inquiry, a systematic and objective analysis of information, and a scientific attitude toward decision making. The field provides information for decisions that are based on quantitative and qualitative studies of learning and teaching rather than on intuition, tradition, authority, or subjective feelings. It is our hope that this aspect of educational psychology is communicated throughout these readings, and that as a student you will adopt the analytic, probing attitude that is part of the discipline.

While educational psychologists have helped to establish a knowledge base about teaching and learning, the unpredictable, spontaneous, evolving nature of teaching suggests that the best they will ever do is to provide concepts and skills that teachers can adapt for use in their classrooms. The issues raised in this unit about the impact of the reform movement on teachers help us understand the teaching role and its demands. As you read articles in other units, consider the demands they place on the teaching role as well.

Looking Ahead: Challenge Questions

Describe several of the roles teachers are expected to perform.

As educational reform progresses, what new demands will it place on teachers?

How does research, either teacher research or formal educational research, improve teaching?

UNIT 1

A Piece of Cake

Mr. Aceto describes his first day as a substitute teacher in an elementary school. Would he do it again? Absolutely! Would he consider doing it for a living? Not a chance!

Jeffrey T. Aceto

JEFFREY T. ACETO is a civil engineer with DeLuca Hoffman Associates, Inc., consulting engineers, in South Portland, Me.

Illustration by Brenda Grannan

RECENTLY I found myself nearing 30 and an unemployed college graduate. So when a friend urged me to try substitute teaching, I thought, Why not? How could it possibly be difficult? I'm a mature, well-adjusted adult, and they'd only be little kids. Besides, the day would be a short seven hours. It would be a piece of cake!

Arriving at school on a crisp autumn morning, I find the scene reminiscent of my own youth. School buses unloading kids in colorful jackets who clutch homework, books, and lunch boxes. My own lunch is the sole content of my briefcase, and it occurs to me that after 20 years I've only traded my metal lunch box for a leather one.

The assistant principal greets me warmly and assures me the day will go smoothly. "Just follow your instructions, and everything will be fine," she says. Sure, I think. Piece of cake.

I find my classroom spotless and orderly, with clean chalkboards and the desks and chairs lined up neatly. Student work and seasonal displays adorn the walls. A paper turkey with necktie feathers watches me warily from the back wall. Not a bad room, I think, although the teacher I'm replacing has spelled *calendar* wrong. That's a bad sign, I think, but I shrug it off.

The children begin to flood into the room. At least, I assume that these are my students. I realize that I'm largely at their mercy with regard to who is supposed to be where and when. As they shrug off their child-sized backpacks, they turn fresh little faces toward me. It is a scene a grandparent would love. At first they are reluctant to speak to me, but soon I am bombarded with questions and comments: "Where is Mrs. Smith? Are you Mr. Smith? How long will you be here?"

I can see the realization dawning on them that what they have here is a rare bird, indeed: a substitute teacher — and a man, to boot. This guy is fresh meat. The class quickly reaches a silent consensus: today is a good day for raising some hell.

"Just" follow the instructions, and everything will be okay, the assistant principal had said. Here, Christian, "just" go in there and take on those lions. Hail, Caesar, we who are about to die salute thee! Let the games begin. I confidently announce that it is time for math and ask them to take out their books. Immediately there is a flurry of activity that Federal Express would admire.

Have you ever tried to wrestle an octopus? One boy is fighting with another, and a girl is writing on the chalkboard. Someone has just gone out the door, and half a dozen girls are crooning over a troll catalogue.

Names are the first minor crisis. I have no idea who is who. I look up to the turkey for assistance, but its facial expression clearly says, "You're on your own, pal."

Great. Four years of college, and I've been reduced to babysitting on a large scale. My vocabulary for the day swiftly degenerates into versions of a few set phrases: Please sit down. Do your own work. Leave her alone. Raise your hand if you want to speak. Stay in line. I quickly discover that fact is stranger and more complicated than fiction; Schwarzenegger had it easy in *Kindergarten Cop*.

I find myself frantically scanning the instructions every five minutes or so. Are we doing what we're supposed to be doing? Is everyone in the right place? Are we falling behind or running ahead of the schedule? These instructions are my lifeline, and I tape them up — out of the students' reach — with great reverence.

An unbidden rush of thoughts cascades through my brain. Why did I wear a tie? It just gives them something to get a grip on. I've heard less noise at a University of Maine hockey game. Are fishing vessels lost at sea homing in on the roar emanating from this classroom? Are the other teachers shaking their heads in disgust at a rookie who can't control the students?

"Quiet, please" is like whistling in the wind. "Let's keep it quiet" has all the impact of a popgun on an elephant. It's time to go ballistic. "I need quiet right now or someone's going to the office!" That's better. Good job, Jeff, practice "teaching by terrorism." I'm not surprised that threats work — after all, I'm a little bit afraid of the office myself. But threats work for only about five minutes.

Soon, snack time arrives. Everything so far has been just a warm-up for the main event, as the little darlings go into a sugar-crazed frenzy. I see candy, donuts, chips, and soda; fruit, vegetables, and juice are scarcely to be found. What a great idea this is: fill them up with sugar-laden snacks; then ask them to sit quietly and read.

WE MOVE steadily through the day. There is a toothache, an earache, a nosebleed, a lost pair of glasses. Two of the worst offenders are dispatched to the office; one student has to take anti-nervousness drugs. I am assured by the veteran teachers that this qualifies as a typical day.

Recess duty is the longest 20 minutes of my life. Now I know how Custer felt. I'm surrounded by 200 little wingnuts running into, over, and through each other. "Suzie hit me!" "Johnny kissed me!" "I can't find my watch!" I resist the strong urge to seek a hiding place instead of the missing watch.

With the incessant din of children's sounds, I find myself yearning for adult companionship. I pass fellow teachers in the halls; as if we're members of a secret society, we salute one another with weary, harried looks.

The teachers' lounge has all the warmth of an unemployment office. The chairs are wooden, hard, and too heavy for most of us to move by ourselves. The teachers share the room with mimeograph machines and cast-off office equipment. Ragged notices from the union compete for bulletin board space with news of bake sales and Tupperware parties. Talk in the lounge revolves around kids with head lice, kids who aren't toilet trained, abused kids, and kids who, it is conjectured, need psychological evaluation. I've felt more relaxed during dental surgery.

The children are the centerpiece of this confusing circus, of course, and no one can spend even one day with them without encountering a few special moments. A girl whom I coax through a reading passage breaks into a broad smile when I tell her she did a great job. A few children who are clearly ignored by their parents and starved for attention give me big hugs at the end of the day. I notice a chubby, plain girl who is ignored by the rest of the children. She reads aloud a story she has written. "Once-upon-a-time stories are stories of beautiful places where you will never

go," she reads. It's the saddest thing I've ever heard; she's 8 years old, and already she's decided that she can never go to beautiful places.

I realize that this teaching stuff is more than babysitting. Trying to encourage youngsters like her is truly an important, even noble, cause.

"You're the best teacher in the world! Are you coming back tomorrow?" All day long they've been running through the halls, talking out in class, and using the restricted art supplies. They're pulling fast ones on me, but it doesn't matter. My sole goal is to end the day with the same number of warm, breathing bodies with which it began.

The end of the day arrives at last. A bus number is garbled over the intercom, there's a final rush to the door, and, suddenly, the quiet and stillness are deafening. The room looks as if it has been visited by a division of Patton's tanks. Desks and chairs are strewn about; the wastebaskets are overflowing. The carpeted floor is a collage of paper, candy wrappers, crayons, a half-eaten donut, an escaped earring, and one blue sock. That last item troubles me a bit. The turkey droops from the wall and appears to be laughing at me. One of the paper decorations hanging from the ceiling suddenly comes unglued and drifts to the floor.

It's time to put the day into perspective, I think. This was a class of "normal" kids. I didn't have those with fetal alcohol syndrome or those who have been abused. Everything was in my favor. There will be janitors to clean up after us, and there were other teachers to take charge of music, physical education, library, and special needs. I had a detailed plan and a schedule of what to do. The buses ran on time, and no gangs stalked the halls. I didn't have to deal with any parents or committees. And yet I feel as if I have just run a marathon.

The insignificant events of this, my first day in elementary education, are just a sampling of business as usual. I am now doubly impressed by the commitment and talents required of full-time teachers. I no longer condemn Mrs. Smith for her spelling error. I'm so tired that I have trouble finding my car after just one brief, seven-hour day.

Would I do it again? Absolutely. Piece of cake. Would I consider doing this for a living? Not a chance!

The Six National Goals

A Road to Disappointment

The people who set goals for education seldom take into account scientific knowledge about how children acquire knowledge and moral values — and the six national goals formulated in 1990 are no exception, these authors charge.

....

CONSTANCE KAMII,
FAYE B. CLARK, AND
ANN DOMINICK

CONSTANCE KAMII is a professor in the Department of Curriculum and Instruction at the University of Alabama, Birmingham; FAYE B. CLARK is an assistant professor in the School of Education, Samford University, Birmingham; and ANN DOMINICK is a fourth-grade teacher at Shades Cahaba Elementary School, Homewood, Ala.

MANY FACTORS can be cited to explain the meager results of the reform efforts of the past decade. The quick-fix approach to accountability that led only to attempts to raise test scores and increase graduation requirements and a variety of other reasons have been mentioned in recent years. Many people are calling for bolder, fundamental, systemic changes, especially changes that bring true innovation into the classroom. A factor seldom mentioned is the need for coherent goals that are based on the best scientific theory available today about how human beings acquire knowledge and moral values. Such goals are of the utmost importance in education reform because, if our objectives are poorly conceived, the rest of our efforts will be misdirected.

Goals in education are usually defined by groups of people who have the power to decide what outcomes are desirable. The people who set these goals seldom take into account scientific knowledge about how children acquire knowledge and moral values. They usually formulate goals based on tradition and on their own values and priorities. The six national goals that were formulated by President Bush and the National Governors' Association are no exception.[1]

In contrast to our political leaders, Jean Piaget started out by conceptualizing only one broad aim for education — the development of autonomy.[2] Our purpose here is to argue that, unless we have a set of goals coherently formulated with autonomy as the overall aim, the results of the second decade of reform will once again be disappointing. Piaget's conception of autonomy as the aim of education was a result of his application of his theory, constructivism, which is a scientific theory supported by 60 years of research all over the world.[3]

Since autonomy in the Piagetian sense means something different from what we often understand by the term, we will first explain what Piaget meant by autonomy. Then we will discuss autonomy as the aim of education — and the drastic changes in classroom practices that this goal entails. We will also point out the inadequacies of the six national goals.

PIAGET AND AUTONOMY

In common parlance, autonomy means the *right* of an individual or group to be self-governing. When we speak of Palestinian autonomy, we are referring to this kind of political right. In Piaget's theory, however, autonomy refers not to the right but to the *ability* of an individual to be self-governing — in the moral as well as in the intellectual realm. Autonomy is the ability to think for oneself and to decide between right and wrong in the moral realm and between truth and untruth in the intellectual realm by taking all relevant factors into account, independently of rewards or punishments. The opposite of autonomy in the Piagetian sense is heteronomy. Heteronomous people are governed by someone else because they are unable to think for themselves.

Moral autonomy. An extreme example of moral autonomy is the struggle of Martin Luther King, Jr., to obtain civil rights for African Americans and others. King was autonomous enough to take relevant factors into account and to conclude that the laws discriminating against African Americans were unjust and immoral. Convinced of the need to make justice a reality, he fought to end the discriminatory laws in spite of the police, jails, dogs, fire hoses, and threats of assassination. Morally autonomous people are not governed by rewards and punishments.

An extreme example of moral heteronomy is the affair of the Watergate cover-up. The perpetrators went along with what they knew to be morally wrong to reap the rewards that President Nixon could bestow on those who helped in the cover-up.

 From *Phi Delta Kappan*, May 1994, pp. 672-677.

In *The Moral Judgment of the Child*, Piaget cited more commonplace examples of autonomy and heteronomy.[4] He interviewed children between the ages of 6 and 14 and asked them, for example, why it is bad to tell lies. Young heteronomous children replied, "Because you get punished when you tell lies." Piaget asked, "Would it be okay to tell lies if you were not punished for them?" The young children answered yes. Their judgment of matters of right and wrong was obviously governed by others.

Piaget also made up many pairs of stories and asked children which one of the two children in the stories was the worse. The following is an example of such a pair.

> A little boy . . . goes for a walk in the street and meets a big dog who frightens him very much. So then he goes home and tells his mother he has seen a dog that was as big as a cow.

> A child comes home from school and tells his mother that the teacher had given him good marks, but it was not true; the teacher had given him no marks at all, either good or bad. Then his mother was very pleased and rewarded him.[5]

Young children systematically manifested the morality of heteronomy by saying that it was worse to say, "I saw a dog as big as a cow." Why was it worse? Because dogs are never as big as cows, and adults do not believe such stories. Older, more autonomous children, however, tended to say that it was worse to say, "The teacher gave me good marks" *because* this lie is more believable. For more autonomous children, a believable lie is worse than one that is so outlandish that people will not be deceived.

All babies are born helpless and neither autonomous nor heteronomous. But young children are initially dependent on adults and, therefore, become heteronomous. Ideally, they become increasingly autonomous as they grow older. As they become more autonomous, they become less heteronomous. In other words, to the extent that children become able to govern themselves, they are governed less by other people.

In reality, however, human development does not happen in this ideal way. Most people do not attain their potential, and many stop developing at a low level. This observation can easily be confirmed in our daily lives. Newspapers are filled with stories about corruption in government and dishonesty in business practices, as well as with items dealing with drug trafficking, theft, assault, and murder.

The important question for parents and teachers is, What causes certain children to become more autonomous than others? Piaget's answer to this question was that adults reinforce children's heteronomy when they use rewards and punishments, thereby hindering the development of autonomy. By refraining from using rewards and punishments and by instead exchanging points of view with children, we can foster the development of autonomy, he said.

For example, if a child tells a lie, an adult could punish the child by saying, "No dessert tonight." Alternatively, the adult could look the child straight in the eye, with both affection and skepticism, and say, "I *really* can't believe what you are saying because . . . (state the reason). And when you tell me something next time, I am not sure I'll be able to believe you. . . . I want you to go to your room (or seat) and think about what you might do to be believed next time." Children want to be trusted, and, when they are confronted with this kind of statement, they are likely, over time, to come to the conclusion that it is best for people to deal honestly with each other.

In general, punishment leads to three possible outcomes. The first outcome is a weighing of risks. Children who are punished will learn to calculate their chances of getting caught the next time and to weigh the price they might have to pay against their chances of getting caught. The second possible outcome is, interestingly, the opposite of the first one: blind obedience. Sensitive children will do anything to avoid being punished. Thus by completely conforming to the rules, they give the impression that punishment works. The third outcome of punishment derives from the second: revolt. Many "model" children surprise everyone by beginning to cut classes, to take drugs, and to engage in other acts that characterize delinquency. Their reason for switching to these behaviors is that they are tired of living for their parents and teachers and think that the time has come for them to start living for themselves.

Piaget was realistic enough to say that it is sometimes necessary to impose restrictions on children. However, he made an important distinction between *punishment* and *sanctions by reciprocity*. Depriving the child of dessert for telling a lie is an example of a punishment, because the relationship between the lie and dessert is completely arbitrary. Telling children that we cannot believe what they said and sending them away to think about how they can be believed next time is an example of a sanction by reciprocity. Sanctions by reciprocity are directly related to the act that we want to discourage and to the adult's point of view. They have the effect of motivating the child to construct rules of conduct from within, through the coordination of viewpoints. Other examples of sanctions by reciprocity — such as excluding the child from the group, depriving the child of the thing he or she has misused, and having the child make restitution — can be found in *The Moral Judgment of the Child* and in *Young Children Reinvent Arithmetic*.[6]

Piaget's theory about how children acquire moral values is fundamentally different from traditional theories and from common sense. In the traditional view, the child is believed to acquire moral rules and values by *internalizing* them from the environment. According to Piaget, children acquire moral convictions not by absorbing them directly from the environment but by *constructing* them from the inside, through the exchange of points of view with people who are close and important to them. For example, no child is taught that it is okay to tell lies if one is not punished for them. Yet young children construct this belief as they try to make sense out of what adults say and do. Fortunately, they continue to construct other relationships, and many children ultimately conclude that lies are bad even if one is not punished for them.

The exchange of viewpoints between adults and children fosters the development of autonomy by enabling the children to consider relevant factors, such as other perspectives. When children can take relevant factors into account, especially other people's rights and feelings, they construct from within the rule of treating others as they wish to be treated by them. A person who has constructed this conviction from within cannot lie in situations like the Watergate affair — no matter what reward may be offered.

Many behaviorists and others believe that punishment is bad because it is negative and that rewards are positive and good. However, rewards do not make children any more autonomous than punishment. Children who help their parents only to get money and those who fill out worksheets only to get stickers are governed by someone else, just as much as those who behave well only to avoid being punished.

Money, candy, and stickers are rewards because they are attractive objects used to manipulate or control children. By contrast, honest praise and expressions of appreciation are part of human relationships involving the exchange of points of view. Just as it is necessary to express disbelief when a child is not telling the truth, it is desirable to communicate our pleasure and appreciation when children behave in especially praiseworthy ways. Praise is thus different from rewards, such as money and stickers, but it too can be used in insincere, manipulative ways. Praise can thus degenerate into a reward, just as an expression of disbelief can turn into an angry, punitive act.

Autonomy is often confused with adopting a laissez-faire attitude. However, when one takes such relevant factors into account as the rights and feelings of other people, one is not free to break promises, tell lies, or act inconsiderately or irresponsibly.

Intellectual autonomy. In the intellectual realm, too, autonomy means the ability to govern oneself by being able to take relevant factors into account in deciding what is true or untrue. Copernicus provides an extreme example of intellectual autonomy. (The same applies to inventors of any other revolutionary theory.) Copernicus invented the heliocentric theory when nearly everybody else believed that the sun revolved around the earth. He was ridiculed off the stage but was autonomous enough to remain convinced of his own idea. An intellectually heteronomous person, by contrast, believes unquestioningly what he or she is told, including illogical conclusions, slogans, and propaganda.

A more common example of intellectual autonomy is the case of a child who used to believe in Santa Claus. When she was about 6, she surprised her mother by asking, "How come Santa Claus uses the same wrapping paper as we do?" Her mother's explanation satisfied her for a few minutes, but she soon came up with the next question: "How come Santa Claus has the same handwriting as Daddy?" This child had her own way of thinking, which was different from what she had been taught.

According to Piaget, the child acquires knowledge in a way similar to the way a child acquires moral values: by *constructing* knowledge from within, rather than by internalizing knowledge directly from the environment. Children may accept what they are told for a time, but they are not passive vessels that merely hold what is poured into their heads. Children construct knowledge by creating and coordinating relationships. When the child described above put Santa Claus into a relationship with everything else she knew, she began to feel that something was wrong somewhere. When children are not convinced by what they are told, they rack their brains to make sense of these "facts."

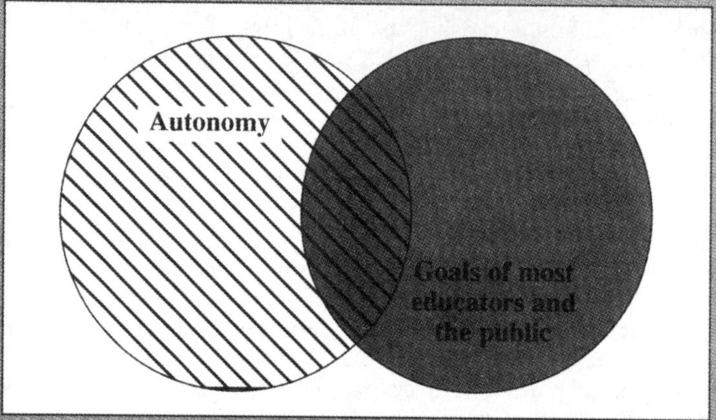

Unfortunately, children are not encouraged to think autonomously in school. Teachers use rewards and punishments in the intellectual realm to get children to give "correct" responses. An example of this practice is the use of worksheets. For example, in first-grade arithmetic, if a child writes "$4 + 4 = 7$," most teachers mark this answer wrong. The result of this kind of teaching is that children become convinced that only the teacher (or someone else) knows which answers are correct. Furthermore, when we walk around a first-grade classroom while children are working on worksheets and stop to ask individual children how they arrived at particular answers, they typically react by grabbing their erasers — even when their answers are perfectly correct! Already many children have learned to distrust their own thinking. Children who are thus discouraged from thinking critically and autonomously will construct less knowledge than those who are confident and do their own thinking.

If a child says that $4 + 4 = 7$, a better reaction is to refrain from correcting him or her and inquire instead, "How did you get 7?" Children often correct themselves as they try to explain their reasoning to someone else. The child who tries to explain his or her reasoning has to decenter in order to make sense to the other person. Trying to coordinate his or her point of view with that of another person makes the child think critically, and this often leads to a higher level of thinking.

Another way of dealing with a child's correct or incorrect answer to $4 + 4$ is to ask the class, "Does everybody agree?" The exchange of points of view among peers stimulates critical thinking, which leads to a higher level of reasoning. In the following section, we argue that we must replace the conformity and obedience that are now valued in schools with an education that emphasizes the honest, critical exchange of viewpoints.

AUTONOMY AS THE AIM OF EDUCATION

Figure 1 is our interpretation of the relationship of autonomy, the goal Piaget set for education, to the goals of most educators and the public. In the circle on the right, labeled "goals of most educators and the general public," we would put those goals that resulted in our memorizing words and their definitions just to pass one test after another. All of us who succeeded in school achieved this success by memorizing an enormous num-

Figure 1. Autonomy Versus Traditional Goals

Autonomy

Goals of most educators and the public

ber of words without necessarily understanding them or caring about them. The shaded part also includes the moral heteronomy that schools generally reinforce by using rewards and punishments.

A more accurate label for the circle on the right would have been "heteronomy." However, we did not use that label because today's educators do not consciously set out to foster children's heteronomy. Indeed, most educators (to say nothing of the general public) have not even heard of autonomy and heteronomy. Nevertheless, they unwittingly manipulate children with rewards and punishments, thereby reinforcing children's heteronomy.

In the intersection with the circle labeled "autonomy," we put those things we learned in school but did not forget after the test. The ability to read and write, to do basic arithmetic, to read maps and charts, and to situate events in history are examples of what we learned in school that we did not forget after cramming for tests. The little bit of moral autonomy we have managed to build came mostly from our homes, but schools have also made a contribution to this development. *When fostering moral and intellectual autonomy becomes our aim, educators will work hard to increase the area of overlap between the two circles.*

The six national education goals for the year 2000 were conceived within the circle on the right in Figure 1. There is nothing new in these six goals. Everybody agrees on the values they endorse. However, because they are not guided by an overall goal based on scientific theory, the six goals are fragmentary, sometimes contradictory, and conspicuous in their lacunae.

Goal 2 — increasing the graduation rate to 90% — would be easily fulfilled if autonomy were the aim of education and if schools were better adapted to today's students. All adolescents want to become competent and socially respectable, but they drop out of school when classes seem irrelevant and coercive. If high school curricula were relevant and interesting to students, we would find it unnecessary to preach the value of a high school diploma.

The aims of Goal 3 — demonstrating competency in challenging subject matter and being prepared for responsible citizenship — are already included within the idea of autonomy as the aim of education, but they are conceptualized differently. A teacher whose aim is to foster autonomy does not teach English,

mathematics, science, history, and so on merely to prepare students for "responsible citizenship, further learning, and productive employment in our modern economy." Intellectual pursuits should enable individuals to make sense of the world and to become competent human beings. Of course, competent individuals are likely to be good citizens and good workers, and educators need to pay closer attention to what sense individuals are making of the world during each hour in every subject.

Goal 4 — to be first in the world in math and science — would be eliminated because mathematics and science are already included in Goal 3, and being first in the world is not a valid goal for education. Our goal should be to turn out young people who can make sense of mathematics and science and who like these subjects. Another reason for eliminating Goal 4 is that it contradicts Goal 2. If 90% of the students stayed in high school, it would certainly not be possible to be "first in the world in mathematics and science achievement" by the year 2000.

Goal 5 — dealing with adult literacy and lifelong learning — would be eliminated, too, because literacy and "knowledge and skills" are already included in Goal 3. Goal 5 makes us wonder whether the governors viewed it as a special goal for the part of the student population that traditionally consists of low achievers.

Goal 6 — that schools be safe, orderly, and free of drugs and violence — would also be eliminated if autonomy were the aim of education because individuals who can take relevant factors into account do not take drugs or resort to violence. The statement that every school in America "will offer a disciplined environment" also reveals a traditional way of thinking. Schools cannot *offer* a disciplined environment. A disciplined environment has to be *created from within* by students and teachers — together.

The lacunae in the six national goals are conspicuous. Nowhere in the formulation of these goals is any attention paid to young people's sense of self, to their relationships with other human beings, or to their making sense of the world, or to their mastering of their environment by becoming creative problem solvers.

The social and moral qualities necessary for successful employment, such as dependability, initiative, and a sense of responsibility, are totally absent from the

six national goals. These qualities are part of autonomy, which is prevented from developing in most schools and in many homes today. Since heteronomous parents raise heteronomous children, public schools must assume a major role in breaking the cycle of heteronomy.

In a multicultural society, autonomy as the aim of education has the special advantage of not specifying the particular values that we want youngsters to have. We cannot predict, for example, whether an autonomous child will have the values and priorities associated with an environmentalist or those that characterize an industrialist. While we cannot predict what specific virtues and aspirations the child will have, we can be sure of two things about all autonomous people: 1) they will have thought deeply about the factors relevant to any decision, and 2) through exchanging viewpoints, they will have constructed certain basic values, such as taking the rights and feelings of others into account, negotiating solutions in situations of conflict, and basing decisions on what is morally right rather than on anticipated rewards or punishments.

AUTONOMY IN CLASSROOM LIFE

Classrooms today are all too often heteronomous environments in which teachers control children and push them through uninspiring textbooks. Below we specify and illustrate three practices that can be observed throughout the day when the teacher's aim is to develop autonomy in children.

1. *Encouraging children to make decisions and to enforce their own rules.* The traditional role of the teacher is to control children by telling them what to do and by giving them ready-made rules. But children who are always controlled by others can only learn to be controlled. If we want children to be able to make their own decisions and to feel responsible for those decisions, it is best to allow them to make decisions from an early age. For example, a third-grade teacher asked her class to decide how many minutes each student should be allotted to give an oral book report. The children initially decided on 10-minute reports. Then they considered relevant factors, such as the fact that this would take a total of three hours and 40 minutes for the 22 students in the class. Deciding that this was much too long, they next considered five minutes and finally settled

on three-minute reports. Having to make such a decision also made for an excellent math lesson, motivated by a genuine need to know.

Children often make exactly the same rules and decisions that the teacher would have made. However, the fact that children have made a rule or decision makes an enormous difference in their commitment to it. Children tend to understand and respect the rules they make. In the course of making a rule, they also come to know that *their* opinions are respected, and they are then more likely to respect the opinions of others, including adults.

To cite another example, teachers often announce that they will give a lower grade or a zero to a paper that is turned in late. By contrast, a teacher whose aim is the development of children's autonomy presents the problem to the class and asks for suggestions about the best way to deal with the problem. The group may make the same rule as the teacher, but this rule will have been constructed by the group out of a personally felt need of its members. Someone may even ask the person whose paper was late, "Do you want me to call you in the evening to make sure you're doing your homework?" The very fact of participating in such a discussion helps children take relevant factors into account as they learn how to make good decisions. Whole-class discussions are much more powerful in motivating students from within than the rewards and punishments teachers usually use.

2. *Fostering intrinsic motivation.* Traditional teaching tries to transmit knowledge through well-organized, "objective," and uninspiring textbooks, with assistance from tests, grades, and other forms of rewards and punishments. The result is that most of us remember such terms as cosine and neutron and such names as the Second Continental Congress. However, we may have only the vaguest notion of what these words mean.

Constructivism, a scientific theory, coupled with the development of autonomy as the aim of education, recognizes that human beings have an intrinsic desire to make sense of the world and that they learn best when they are personally curious, deeply involved, or in a social situation that requires them to take and defend a position. As Piaget pointed out, children work hard when they have intriguing questions to answer and problems to solve. If teaching truly appealed

to the human desire to make sense of things, the memorization and the rewards and punishments used today would become outdated. Nor would we forget most of what we "learned" in school.

To take an example from the teaching of American history, a teacher whose goal is children's development of autonomy might ask students to prepare for a debate. With respect to the Second Continental Congress, for instance, a good debate might be between a position in sympathy with the loyalists (loyal to the British Crown) and a position opposing them. Students would have to be extremely well-informed, logical, and critical to participate in such a debate. They might, for example, read biographies of such figures as John Adams, Joseph Galloway, and Thomas Jefferson and come to know the uncertainties and agonies each individual faced as well as the façades and strategies each employed under various circumstances. Having to coordinate subjective perspectives in a debate makes history much more alive and unforgettable than does the "objective," dull textbook. If children are allowed to change sides in the middle of a debate, this especially motivates them to understand both sides of an issue.

3. *Encouraging children to exchange viewpoints.* An essential part of Piaget's theory is the importance of social interaction for the construction of knowledge and moral values. In fact, Piaget pointed out that science has been constructed over the centuries through the exchange of points of view among scientists. Science is a social enterprise.[7]

Let us return to the example given above of 4 + 4. If in response to the answer "8" the teacher refrains from saying, "That's right," but asks instead, "Does everybody agree?" the class has to come to its own conclusion through the exchange of ideas. If a child says that 4 + 4 = 7, the teacher should also ask if everybody agrees and encourage the subsequent debate. Children *will* arrive at the truth in mathematics if they debate long enough, because nothing is arbitrary in mathematics. In traditional classrooms, the teacher's role is to reinforce correct answers and to correct wrong ones. But children stop thinking and debating when the teacher assumes the responsibility of judging which answer is correct.

If the reader asks any fourth-grader why he or she works from left to right in long division but not in addition, subtraction, and multiplication, the answer

is likely to be: "That's the way the teacher told us to do it." In most elementary schools today, mathematics is taught with intellectual heteronomy as the unintended goal of education. If long division were taught through honest, critical debate about each step, there would be no need for all the repetition and worksheets that are now endlessly imposed on children.[8]

A similar situation exists in the social/moral realm. In the case of a conflict between two children in class, traditional teachers tell the parties to "stop it" and to pay attention to the lesson. The result is often that the conflict continues when the teacher's back is turned. A teacher whose aim is autonomy is likely to tell the students to step away from the group to negotiate a solution. If negotiation (the exchange of viewpoints) is encouraged from an early age, children become surprisingly good about settling their disputes.

If two kindergartners are fighting over a toy, for example, traditional teachers preach the virtue of sharing and specify how the toy will be shared. A teacher who fosters the development of autonomy, however, may say to the children, "I don't know what to do, but what I do know how to do is to keep the toy for you until *you* decide on a fair way to solve this problem." As noted earlier, children often decide that neither of them should get the toy. This outcome may be the same as the adult's taking the toy away because they "don't know how to play nicely with it." From the standpoint of the development of the children's autonomy, however, there is a world of difference between their making the decision and an adult's imposition of the same decision.

Most educators and most of the public today think that the hour for English is only for English, that the hour for math is only for math, and so on. They also view the drug problem, AIDS, teenage pregnancies, and violence as separate issues, to be dealt with apart from academic subjects. However, drug abuse, unsafe sex, and violence are all symptoms of heteronomy. As noted earlier, children who can take relevant factors into account do not take drugs or resort to violence to settle conflicts. In the classroom, students develop or are prevented from developing intellectually as well as socially and morally. And the intellectual and social/moral domains are inseparable. A classroom cannot foster the development of autonomy in the intellectual realm while suppressing it in the social and moral realms.

Traditional education begins with a list of desired outcomes and seeks to produce results through the use of pep talks and the promise or threat of rewards or punishments. Piaget's theory, constructivism, coupled with the idea of autonomy as the aim of education, reflects the belief that the education of human beings requires a much deeper, longer-range perspective that is different from the mindset necessary to produce quality cars.

Education that aims to produce autonomy is better suited for life in a democracy than traditional education, which fosters conformity. A long-lasting, successful democracy requires informed, autonomous citizens who consider relevant factors in voting for laws and representatives who make those laws. Autonomy goes far beyond equipping youngsters with "the knowledge and skills necessary to compete in a global economy." If all the public schools in the United States educated children for autonomy during every hour of the 13 years the children are in school, the nation's prisons would be less crowded, the federal deficit and the drug problem would be more amenable to control, and we would be working more positively to solve many of our human and social problems.

1. *America 2000: An Education Strategy* (Washington, D.C: U.S. Government Printing Office, 1991), pp. 62-66.

2. Jean Piaget, *To Understand Is to Invent* (1948; reprint, New York: Viking, 1973).

3. For example, the experiments described in Jean Piaget and Alina Szeminska, *The Child's Conception of Number* (1941; reprint, London: Routledge and Kegan Paul, 1952) have been replicated in Africa, Asia, Australia, North America, and South America.

4. Jean Piaget, *The Moral Judgment of the Child* (1932; reprint, New York: Free Press, 1965).

5. Ibid., p. 148.

6. Ibid.; and Constance Kamii, *Young Children Reinvent Arithmetic* (New York: Teachers College Press, 1985).

7. Jean Piaget and Rolando Garcia, *Psychogenesis and the History of Science* (1983; reprint, New York: Columbia University Press, 1989).

8. For further detail on a constructivist approach to primary arithmetic within the context of autonomy as the overall goal, readers should refer to the following books and videotapes by Constance Kamii, published by Teachers College Press, New York, N.Y.: *Young Children Reinvent Arithmetic* (1985); *Young Children Continue to Reinvent Arithmetic, 2nd Grade* (1989); *Young Children Continue to Reinvent Arithmetic, 3rd Grade* (in press); *Double-Column Addition: A Teacher Uses Piaget's Theory* (videotape, 1989); *Multiplication of Two-Digit Numbers: Two Teachers Using Piaget's Theory* (videotape, 1990); and *Multidigit Division: Two Teachers Using Piaget's Theory* (videotape, 1990).

Using Action Research To Assess Instruction

Carole Schulte Johnson and Inga Kromann-Kelly

Carole Schulte Johnson is a faculty member in the Department of Elementary and Secondary Education, at Washington State University, in Pullman, Washington. Inga Kromann-Kelly is a faculty member in the Department of Teaching and Learning, at Washington State University, in Pullman, Washington.

For years teachers have used self assessment as one way to improve the learning environment in their classrooms. Such assessment, however, tended to be of a private, nonsystematic nature and often was not clearly focused on a central question. Today more and more teachers are developing and experiencing an organized approach to classroom inquiry, known as action research, a concept which has evolved over the past several years. This approach entails stepping back from the immediate concern in order to gain a broader perspective on a problem; then collecting, analyzing, and interpreting data on the basis of a defined plan, and often sharing the results with professional colleagues.

Rather than formulating complex research procedures, perhaps best left to experts, we recommend beginning action research by answering these five basic questions: 1) What is the main question I am interested in pursuing? 2) What data are relevant? 3) What specific data will be collected, and how? 4) How will the data be analyzed? 5) What interpretations or implications can be drawn from the data?

THE QUESTION

Teachers often have several questions they wish to explore; however, in order to keep the research manageable you as a teacher embarking on action research need to decide your basic or most important question. Limited questions related to what you are doing in your classroom, such as "Are my students learning from this strategy?" or "What strategies do students use most successfully in perform-

ing some particular task?" work well for action research. For example, suppose we are interested in learning more about our students' attitude toward reading. We realize that various elements of the literacy program probably affect those attitudes so our basic question could be "How do the students feel about the different methods and materials used in the literacy program?"

COLLECTING DATA

Data can be gathered from transactions/interactions, products and cued or structured responses. Figure 1, while not all inclusive, suggests various sources of data within each category.

Triangulation of data (using at least three different data sources) is recommended. The value of using triangulation is in analyzing the question from several different viewpoints. For instance, one data set could be from each of the three categories on the chart or from two of the three categories. If only three data sources are used, it is recommended that no more than one cued or structured response source be included since these data usually are collected only at specific points of time, thus limiting the information to the context of those times.

When the different data sources are congruent, the acceptance of the results is strengthened. Conflicting data raise questions such as: Should other types of data sets have been used? Should some data sources carry more weight—for example, were the cued responses too structured or answered to please the teacher? Would it be valuable to refine or do additional research on this question?

We make decisions regarding the specific data to collect on the basis of its importance in seeking answers to the question and also the feasibility of collecting and analyzing it. In general, quantifiable data take less time to collect and analyze; however, meaningful data are not always readily quantifiable. While importance and feasibility are basic, other aspects are considered. Using excessive class, student and/or teacher time is avoided by collecting data from ongoing class activities such as journals and portfo-

From *Reading Horizons*, Vol. 35, No. 3, 1995, pp. 199-208. © 1995 by Western Michigan University, Kalamazoo, MI. Reprinted by permission.

Figure 1
Data Sources

	From Teacher	From Students
Transactions/ Interactions	Field/observation/anecdotal notes	Video/audio tapes
	Video/audio tapes	
Products		Written products
		Artifacts
		Open-ended interviews
		Open-ended conferences
Cued/Structured Responses	Ratings	Tests
	Checklists	Questionnaires
	Tally of behaviors	Attitude measures
		Structured interviews
		Structured conferences
		Writing/work samples
		Checklists
		Ratings
		Logs

lios, the taping of class or small group activities as well as from brief cued or structured responses.

Unless individual conferences are part of the ongoing program and the data to be collected a normal part of the conferences, they may not be a feasible source of information. However, if a second person is available or only a small subset of students is involved, individual conferences become a possibility.

Another consideration is that students may tell teachers what they think the teacher wants to hear when cued or structured responses are obtained face-to-face. Responses on paper may be similarly biased, but such data-gathering instruments are generally viewed as providing a degree of anonymity.

When teacher observations are used, consideration is given to how structured and systematic they will be. Ways to provide structure include using a checklist of behaviors (e.g., answering, volunteering, getting out of seat) and keeping a tally of the number of times a behavior occurs, or by describing behavior at set time intervals. Audio/videotaping of an on-going class activity is an example of an unstructured observation. Systematic observations are made on a regular basis such as daily or weekly. The data can be taped; however, if teacher notes

are used, it is recommended they be written daily. Less systematic observations are those noted occasionally, when the teacher has time or when something strikes the teacher as important to note.

When writing notes, we need to remind ourselves that we see what we expect, so there is danger of bias. For example, as teachers, we know that certain of our students love to read while others do not. Thus, in examining attitudes, we are more inclined to note student behaviors which confirm what we already believe than those which conflict with our expectations.

Each source of data requires decisions on the part of the teacher. With materials such as journals, portfolios, or tapes, you decide what data to include and then structure the class or group so it can be collected. When a checklist or questionnaire is involved, you decide its content and how students (or teacher) will respond. Among the possibilities for such instruments are open ended questions or statements, items for the respondent to check off, or some type of rating system.

If you use a rating scale, you need to decide whether it will be an even numbered scale, thus avoiding a neutral position, or an odd numbered one which includes it. A two or three point scale is simpler for students in the primary grades; a five to seven point scale is common in upper grades and has the advantage of identifying subtle differences. Common terms for labeling points on a scale are *agree/disagree, like most/like least,* or 1 *(very low)* to 5 *(highest)*.

A simple format is helpful. Present the ratings at the top of the page; then list the items below with a blank for the number rating in front of each item. With instruments such as this, it is important to remind the students that you really want to know what they think so their opinions can be considered in making decisions about materials or procedures. From whom will student data be collected—the entire class, a small group or groups of students, individuals or some combination? For our research on student attitudes, we prefer information from the class rather than from selected representative students. The latter may well provide the spectrum of attitudes regarding reading, but not its strength related to specific methods or materials.

In examining student attitudes toward reading, the feelings of students constitute important and relevant data. To collect such information, we might use informal teacher observations, preferably collected on a regular basis, and student records of books and pages read daily and brief comments or reactions to what they have read. All of these items are easily obtained as a normal part of classroom activity.

Additionally, we would include a questionnaire asking students to rate what they think about each of the different literacy materials and activities used in the program. If many items are included, the questionnaire can be divided into several parts. Class discussion of the results would provide a useful source of additional information. Neither activity would take an inordinate amount of time and the findings could result in an improved curriculum. Our questionnaire requires limited teacher preparation time since it only involves developing a list of the materials and activities used, deciding their order as well as the kind of rating scale to use, and formatting the instrument.

ANALYZING AND INTERPRETING DATA

When analyzing data, teachers may want information about the class as a whole, about individual children, or about certain subgroups. Subgroups might include students at certain achievement levels, such as above grade level, at grade level, students with special needs, boys at different achievement levels, or girls at different ones. When data are kept for each student, teachers can decide at any time what individuals or subgroups they may wish to study.

Some of the data teachers gather are quantifiable and can be analyzed without the use of statistics. Under some circumstances, statistical analyses show significance with only small differences in raw data, and such results may not be particularly useful. For example, knowing the

percent of the class rating an item *very low* or *highest* may be more important for your consideration in curriculum change. Again, it is the teacher who must interpret the data and decide what is meaningful. What do the results mean in your classroom? How do they answer your original question? Were they what you expected? Any surprises? What was successful or not successful?

Our questionnaire regarding student opinion about materials and activities can best be summarized with tables for the class and for each subgroup. We would list the materials and activities in a column with the ratings listed across the top. Then for each item, the percent choosing the rating is listed.

To interpret the tables, we would consider the class or group distribution across the continuum: Were responses concentrated at one end of the continuum? Were there gross differences such as a large group at each end of the continuum, or was there a fairly even distribution across it? If the distribution is mainly at one end, we would decide what percent of the class or group to consider significant in our decision making: it might be 40 percent, $1/3$, $1/4$ or whatever we feel is appropriate. For example, if 40 percent of students rate something *very low* while few or no students rate it *highest*, or the reverse, that clearly is important information.

Data which are not readily quantifiable, such as that from logs, journals, informal observations, conferences or tapes of class activities, are usually reviewed by teachers so they can pull out what appear to be trends, major ideas, or important elements related to the question at hand. If these data are collected over a period of time, or if the material is extensive, it will need to be reviewed periodically, and preferably over a time frame which allows for reflection. This is an important and valuable process because it often leads to further insights and refinements. In general, for non-quantified data, we would review all the categories and subcategories and draw conclusions related to the original question. The conclusions may be firm or tentative. In either case, it is important to consider whether data from other sources agree with it. Informal observations, anecdotal notes, and class discussion of results are used to confirm, disconfirm or raise questions about findings from the rest of the data.

In the case of our question about students' attitudes, we would review teacher observations and anecdotal notes as well as student logs for indication of feelings about reading, positive, negative, or general reactions indicating that students are or are not involved with their reading. While we would start with categories such as *positive* and *negative*, as the data collection grows we would expect subcategories to develop. For example, we might subcategorize aspects related to writing, to self-selected reading, to assigned reading, or to informational reading. Categories are flexible and can change as we continue to review the data. Which categories make sense and help answer the question? How do these data fit with the results of the questionnaire?

Finally, we would review the data as a whole. What is supported by all data sources? What is partially supported? Is anything not supported? What conclusions do you draw?

We piloted a questionnaire in a fourth grade class which used both trade books and children's literature. The results indicated that boys and girls were quite similar in their high and low ratings, as were the readers who were mature, on-grade level or special needs readers. However, when we looked at the groups of items rated *high* or *low*, we noticed those rated *low* tended to be the type of activities associated with the basal while those rated *high* were those traditionally considered enrichment activities. In terms of materials, with the exception of the special needs readers, all rated using literature books higher than using basals. The students in the class willingly informed us why they responded as they did. In general, the special needs readers felt they could handle the grade level basal but with literature books they had trouble keeping pace with others in their groups, and in some cases with the vocabulary as well.

Since there was nothing in teacher notes or student logs to contradict this, we would use literature books as the core of the literacy program, avoiding "basalizing" them by incorporating writing and enrichment activities similar to those suggested by Yopp and Yopp (1992). In selecting and gathering books related to themes or units, we would seek to include books special needs readers would feel successful in using. Then while implementing this program, we'd probably start a new action research project concentrating on the special needs readers.

CONSIDERATIONS FOR INVOLVEMENT IN ACTION RESEARCH

There are four important factors to consider in planning action research. First, action research requires additional planning time. However, useful and successful projects can be accomplished without consuming an inordinate amount of additional time. Second, action research is improved when teachers discuss the five questions with colleagues because the interaction provides a supportive environment which helps clarify and solidify thinking regarding the project. Sharing ideas and suggestions, whether for the same question or different ones, can be valuable. Colleagues not involved in action research also can provide helpful insights.

Third, teachers undertaking action research should be aware that expectations affect what we see and how we interpret data. Triangulation of data is helpful as are our awareness of this effect, discussion with others as the research evolves, and an effort on our part to be open to alternative explanations as well as to surprises in the data. Finally, teachers can use the results of action research in their classrooms. Action research can improve the teaching/learning process in classrooms by reinforcing, modifying and/or changing perceptions based solely on more informal techniques such as non-systematic observations.

REFERENCES

Yopp, R. H., & Yopp, H. K. (1992). *Literature-based reading activities.* Boston: Allyn and Bacon.

Reflection and Teaching: The Challenge of Thinking Beyond the Doing

PEGGY RAINES and LINDA SHADIOW

She soon discovered that knowing something and teaching it are as different as dreaming and waking.

—May Sarton, *The Small Room*

Preservice teachers embarking on their student teaching semester often express the belief that sustained day-to-day classroom experience is exactly what they will need to complete their "knowledge" of teaching. In a more sophisticated but similar vein, teachers who return to a university for advanced coursework or for professional development nod their heads approvingly during discussions of the benefits of "reflective teaching" and then agree that as a natural part of their planning for teaching, they indeed are all "reflective practitioners." The two words *reflection* and *practice* are a part of everyone's general vocabulary, so it is easy to reduce the complexities and challenges of the phrase to something like "thinking about the doing." Because no one wants to be accused of *not* thinking about the doing, educators—whether novice or veteran—are usually unanimous about their being reflective practitioners.

One consequence of this automatic agreement—that by virtue of being a teacher one is already a reflective teacher—can be an unproductive superficiality: "reflection with no experience is sterile and generally leads to unworkable conclusions, while experience with no reflection is shallow and at best leads to superficial knowledge" (Posner 1989, 22). The challenge for educators is to move beyond the literal meaning of this seemingly simplistic phrase—reflective teacher—to an understanding of its pedagogical implications, which encompass (1) a respect for teachers' ongoing profes-

sional growth (beyond learning more "things to do"), (2) a mutually beneficial dialogue between elements of one's theory and practice (beyond a simple recounting of one's successes), and (3) a potential for more critically deliberative classroom practices.

The concepts of *reflection*, *reflective teaching*, and *reflective practitioner* have gained much recent attention in the professional education literature, but a cursory reading can overlook frequent references to the work of John Dewey (and others), which provided a substantive base for reflective practices. Although a comparison of the first paragraphs of many of these teacher-as-thinker articles illustrates the observation that "there is no generally accepted definition of these concepts" (Korthagen 1993, 133), the substantive aims share a theoretical foundation that, if ignored, suggests at best a partial use and at worst a misuse of a powerful concept for teachers using their own work as "text." The term *reflective teacher* in its theoretical context is more likely to provide teachers with a sense of the mindfulness and thoughtfulness from which a list of promising reflective practices is drawn and with a glimpse of the deliberative pedagogy to which it can lead. A teacher's "'intelligent practice' in a classroom . . . develops *in action* rather than by application of rules learned outside the context of practice" (Russell and Johnston 1988, 1). Teachers' "intelligent action" is subsequently strengthened through the "development of the *capacity for self-directed learning*" so teachers emerge as their own teacher educators (Korthagen 1993, 136).

Reflective Action and Routine Action

The distinction between *reflective action* and *routine action* is one that respects teachers as professionals whose technical expertise goes beyond the application of pedagogical "treatments." Understanding this distinction can help teachers to penetrate the superficial agreement that can come too quickly and easily when, in either preser-

---

Peggy Raines is an assistant professor and Linda Shadiow is a professor, both at the Center for Excellence in Education, Northern Arizona University, Flagstaff.

From *The Clearing House*, May/June 1995, pp. 271-274. © 1995 by the Helen Dwight Reid Educational Foundation. Reprinted by permission of Heldref Publications, 1319 Eighteenth Street, NW, Washington, DC 20036-1802.

vice or inservice, teachers are asked about their use of reflective practice. One current writer, in fact, characterizes routine action and its reliance on thinking about methods in absence of context as "magical" because of the powers ascribed to their use (Bartolome 1994). The well-intentioned frenzy for identifying more and better ways of doing things, he says, constitutes a "methods fetish," and Lilia Bartolome agrees with Donaldo Macedo (1994) that an anti-methods pedagogy is more likely to encourage critical (or reflective) action. In 1933, Dewey made this same distinction and likened routine action to the stream of consciousness that accompanies everyday experience, in which the ends are taken for granted but the means for getting to those ends may be problematic (the goal or desired outcome of this routine action is unexamined and any procedural deviation can be tinkered with to improve the likelihood of the desired end). Reflective action, on the other hand, entails "active, persistent, and careful consideration of any belief or supposed form of knowledge in the light of the grounds that support it and the further conclusions to which it leads" (Dewey 1933, 9). In this sense, reflection is not a point of view but rather a process of deliberative examination of the interrelationship of ends, means, and contexts.

Vivian Gussin Paley engages in this reflective action in her book *White Teacher* (1979), in which she stands both within and above the stream of consciousness of her kindergarten teaching in a classroom with a diverse student population. She observes the children and the differences between what she expects of them and what their actions are, and then she critically questions (as Dewey's work suggests) the reliability and worth and value of the predetermined "ends" in order to validate, redirect, or modify both ends and means. In the preface to a later book, *Molly Is Three* (1986), Paley describes the inherent challenge of this level of reflection: "It is not easy to wait and listen. In my haste to display the real world, I offer the children solutions to unimagined problems. My neatly classified bits and pieces clamor for attention. . . . I try to stand aside . . . "(xv).

Fifty years after Dewey identified three attitudes—open-mindedness, responsibility, and wholeheartedness—that characterize reflective practice (attitudes evident in Paley's accounts), other writers are reiterating that reflective practice is "neither a solitary nor meditative process . . . . [It is] a challenging, demanding, and often trying process that is most successful as a collaborative effort" (Osterman and Kottkamp 1993, 19). Dewey defined *open-mindedness* as "an active desire to listen to more sides than one; to give heed to the facts from whatever source they come; to err in the beliefs that are dearest to us" (29). *Responsibility* he viewed as being a deliberative consideration of the consequences of actions, and *wholeheartedness* he equated with an abiding commitment to open-mindedness and responsibility. Taken together, these attitudes have much in common with the "believing

and doubting game" that Peter Elbow writes about in *Embracing Contraries* (1986)—an acceptance that "certainty evades us" (254)—and with the need to examine our certainty in order to move to a more thorough and substantive level of understanding.

The resulting reflective action, Dewey maintained, moves teachers away from impulsive and routine activity; reflective action thus places inquiry, not response, in the foreground. Such inquiry-oriented teaching places the teacher-as-*learner* in a prominent position while at the same time it challenges the teacher to delve deeper into the "doing" of teaching. Donald Schon (1983) voices the conviction that "competent practitioners usually know more than they can say" (viii), and teachers like Vivian Paley demonstrate that when deliberative reflection gives voice to one's knowing and not knowing, professional growth and development accelerates; thus reflection has the potential to benefit both the teacher and the taught. This view echoes the distinctions of "knowledge telling" and "knowledge transforming" (Bereiter and Scardamalia 1987), but it places an internal, rather than external, audience in the foreground.

Problem Solving and Problem Setting

The artificial but pervasive dichotomy of theory and practice presents an obstacle for viewing reflective practice as a powerful contributor to a teacher's professional development. Building partly on Dewey's notion of reflection, Schon (1983) proposes a reorganization of the way we think about professional practice and the relationship between theory and practice. He criticizes the still-prevailing model of technical rationality: "According to the model of Technical Rationality—the view of professional knowledge which has most powerfully shaped both our thinking about the professions and the institutional relations of research, education and practice—professional activity consists in instrumental problem solving made rigorous by the application of scientific theory and technique" (21).

Selection of a technique from a broad professional repertoire based solely on the matching of sets of pre-identified characteristics can serve to elevate teaching rituals, tradition, and decontextualized authority to unrealistic levels. On the other hand, actions based solely on intuition and one's own biography can result in an equally isolated (and idiosyncratic) approach. The potential for professional growth comes, in Schon's view, from a persistent and rigorous acknowledgment of both spheres, "a dialogue of thinking and doing through which I become more skillful" (1987, 31). One vehicle for engaging in this dialogue is the distinction between problem *solving* and problem *setting*:

> In real world practice, problems do not present themselves to the practitioner as given. They must be constructed from the materials of problematic situations that are puzzling, troubling, uncertain. When we set the problem, we select what we will treat as "things" of the situation, we set

the boundaries of our attention to it, and we impose upon it a coherence which allows us to say what is wrong and in what directions the situation needs to be changed. Problem setting is a process in which interactively, we name the things to which we will attend and frame the context in which we will attend to them. (Schon 1983, 40)

Problem setting demands a broader view than problem solving. In teachers' published accounts of their own growth, many, like Paley, engage in more than problem identification and, in fact, end up re-orienting their views of what a "problem" is and what theory and practice can both contribute to any kind of resolution. In *Uptaught* (1970), an account of his uneasiness with college teaching, Ken Macrorie provides a record of the reflection that led to changes in his approach to teaching (later developed as a text, *Writing to be Read*); similarly, Peter Elbow recounts his reflective journey in *Embracing Contraries* and in many ways places his earlier text, *Writing without Teachers* (1973), in the realm of problem setting; poet Richard Hugo shares a view of his growth and reflection as a teacher of creative writing in *Triggering Town* (1979); teacher educator William Ayers explores the intertwining of his own teaching, learning, and parenting in *To Teach: The Journey of a Teacher* (1993). It is not by accident that touchstones such as these were written by teachers of writing, people who are more practiced at putting a voice to the reflective process. These and other books, however, allow individual teachers (preservice or inservice) or groups of teachers from any grade or subject matter to eavesdrop on another educator's process of reflection. A newly developed group of educational cases (*Case Studies for Teacher Problem Solving* by Silverman, Welty, and Lyon [1992]; *Diversity in the Classroom: A Casebook for Teachers and Teacher Educators* by Shulman and Mesa-Bains [1993]) can be used in inservice sessions to help teachers develop skills in problem setting and recognizing the distinctions that Schon makes. The cases themselves can be used superficially where limited discussion is presumed to constitute "reflective practice." Basing case discussions primarily on one's experiences as a teacher and learner can deify experience, however, and the result is "telling" with little likelihood of "transforming" one's pedagogy (McAnnich 1993).

Books such as these also illustrate another distinction that belies the more simplistic definition of reflection. Schon differentiates between reflection-in-action and reflection-on-action (1983). Reflection-in-action is formative in that it is a part of the interactive phase of teaching in the presence of students. It is usually stimulated by some unpredictableness that prompts the teacher to respond with on-the-spot restructuring, spontaneous re-evaluation of past experiences, or deliberate testing of past knowledge in order to arrive at a solution to the immediate problem. Reflection-on-action happens at another level where a teacher engages in revising experiences and knowledge, in reformulating foundational structures

on which he or she bases classroom practice. This is not unlike Dewey's distinction between routine and reflective practice, but it seeks to make the two interdependent.

Doing and Thinking About the Doing

Experience in the absence of reflection is unstable (Schon 1983) because it contributes little to the deliberative development that is a part of the potential of reflective practice:

> When we go about the spontaneous, intuitive performance of the actions of everyday life, we show ourselves to be knowledgeable in a special way. Often we cannot say what it is we know. When we try to describe it we find ourselves at a loss, or we produce descriptions that are obviously inappropriate. Our knowing is ordinarily tacit, implicit in our patterns of action and in our feel for the stuff with which we are dealing. It seems right to say that our knowing is *in* our action. (49)

Reflecting on this knowing-in-action is what identifies a master teacher, according to Schon. This is the "dialogue of the thinking and doing," the reflexive interchange between the immediate and the reflective that Schon has called reflection-in-action. The doing (teaching) is accompanied by a co-existing "thinking about the doing" (knowing-in-action), and then there are deliberate opportunities to think both about and beyond the doing (reflection-in-action).

Teachers, curriculum specialists, or professional development personnel who want to engage in reflection will be assisted by the recent work of several researchers and theorists. Freema Elbaz (1988), in her experiences with teachers examining their own knowledge, initially found that "autobiographical writing, combined with other types of writing, work on metaphors and imagery, and group discussion, enhanced teachers' awareness of their situations" (180). Later, Elbaz found that it was important for teachers to generate and exchange different views in a group process and to envision concrete alternative courses of action if they are to become self-sustaining in the reflective process. Henry Giroux's work explores the dialogue both within one's self as well as within one's context; his book *Teachers as Intellectuals: Toward a Critical Pedagogy of Learning* (1988) forges a persuasive description of the transformative potential that occurs when we combine the "language of critique with the language of possibility" (134).

Reflective practitioners often need help in developing observation skills and must be provided with opportunities for analyzing teaching (Wildman and Niles 1987). Necessary attitudes and resources, such as time and collegial support for nurturing reflection, are essential. Daily or weekly logs or some such method of recording events and personal reactions are effective tools for facilitating initial reflection. These and other reflective opportunities such as seminars, discussions, or reviews are needed to encourage reflection in and on action. Within the context of assessment, some districts and states are seeking the formalization of teaching portfolios that document action, thought, and thought-in-action for teachers seeking status as master teachers or for career ladder advancement. The National Board of Professional Teaching Standards is pursuing an evaluation process that will include components encompassing such reflection.

Thinking Both About and Beyond the Doing

In a far more structured way, the work of Gary Fenstermacher and Virginia Richardson has focused on skills that develop a "practical rationality," which they trace to the work of Aristotle and define as "a process of thought that ends in an action or an intention to act" (102). They criticize the calls for reflective practice as being "murky" and imprecise in that "it is not enough to provide answers [to why one teaches as one does]" but that "it is also important that the answers accord with a reasonable and morally defensible conception of what it means to educate a fellow human being" (101).

Reflective teaching is a concept that can, under the press of large class sizes, increasing extracurricular responsibilities, and vociferous calls for technical reform, be set aside as something so inherent in the profession of teaching as to not need deliberate attention or support. On the contrary, however, reflective practice goes beyond just thinking about one's teaching and opens doors to professional growth and collaboration that can contribute to teachers' having a clearer and more substantive role in reform, both locally and nationally. Thinking about teaching practices is only the beginning; describing perceived classroom successes and failures is an initial step. Reflection, in the most potent sense of the word, involves searching for patterns in one's thinking about classroom practices and interrogating the reasons for one's labeling some lessons as successes or failures; it challenges one not to stop with thinking *about* the doing.

During her first year of university teaching, the main character in the May Sarton novel *The Small Room* is faced with the realization that "knowing something and teaching it are as different as dreaming and waking" (44). Thinking-*beyond*-the-doing challenges teachers at all levels to learn from a more deliberate wakefulness about how and why we teach as we do and then to use what we discover about ourselves to benefit the students whom we teach.

REFERENCES

Ayers, W. 1993. *To teach: The journey of a teacher.* New York: Teachers College Press.

Bartolome, L. 1994. Beyond the methods fetish: Towards a humanizing pedagogy. *Harvard Educational Review* 64(2): 173–94.

Bereiter, C., and M. Scardamalia. 1987. *The psychology of written composition.* Hillsdale, N.J.: Lawrence Erlbaum.

Dewey, J. 1933. *How we think.* Boston: D. C. Heath.

Elbaz, F. 1988. Critical reflection on teaching: Insights from Freire. *Journal of Education for Teaching* 14(2): 171–81.

Elbow, P. 1973. *Writing without teachers.* New York: Oxford University Press.

———. 1986. *Embracing contraries: Explorations in learning and teaching.* New York: Oxford University Press.

Fenstermacher, G. D., and V. Richardson. 1993. The elicitation and reconstruction of practical arguments in teaching. *Journal of Curriculum Studies* 25(2): 101–14.

Giroux, H. 1988. *Teachers as intellectuals: Toward a critical pedagogy of learning.* New York: Bergin and Garvey.

Hugo, R. 1979. *Triggering town: Lectures and essays on poetry and writing.* New York: W. W. Norton.

Korthagen, F. A. J. 1993. The role of reflection in teachers' professional development. In *Teacher professional development: A multiple perspective approach,* edited by L. Kremar-Hayon, H. C. Vonk, and R. Fessler, 133–45. Amsterdam/Lisse: Swets & Zeitlinger, B. V.

Macedo, D. 1994. Preface. In *Conscientization and resistance,* edited by P. McLaren and C. Lankshear. New York: Routledge.

Macrorie, K. 1970. *Uptaught.* New York: Hayden.

———. 1984. *Writing to be read.* New Jersey: Boynton/Cook.

McAninch, A. R. 1993. *Teacher thinking and the case method: Theory and future directions.* New York: Teachers College Press.

Osterman, K. F., and R. B. Kottkamp. 1993. *Reflective practice for educators.* Newbury Park, Calif.: Corwin Press.

Paley, V. 1979. *White teacher.* Cambridge, Mass.: Harvard University Press.

———. 1986. *Molly is three.* Chicago: University of Chicago Press.

Posner, G. 1989. *Field experience: Methods of reflective teaching.* New York: Longman.

Russell, T., and P. Johnston. 1988. Teacher reflection on practice. Paper presented at the meeting of the American Educational Research Association, New Orleans, April 5–9.

Sarton, M. 1961. *The small room.* New York: W. W. Norton.

Schon, D. 1983. *The reflective practitioner.* New York: Basic Books.

———. 1987. *Educating the reflective practitioner.* San Francisco: Jossey-Bass.

Shulman, J., and A. Mesa-Bains. 1993. *Diversity in the classroom: A casebook for teachers.* New Jersey: Research for Better Schools and Lawrence Erlbaum.

Silverman, R., W. Welty, and S. Lyon. 1992. *Case studies for teacher problem solving.* New York: McGraw-Hill.

Wildman, T. M., and J. A. Niles. 1987. Reflective teachers: Tensions between abstractions and realities. *Journal of Teacher Education* 38(4): 25–31.

Development

- Childhood (Articles 5–8)
- Adolescence (Articles 9–11)

The study of human development provides us with knowledge of how children and adolescents mature and learn within the family, community, and school environments. Educational psychology focuses on description and explanation of the developmental processes that make it possible for children to become intelligent and socially competent adults. Psychologists and educators are presently studying the idea that biology as well as the environment influence cognitive, personal, social, and emotional development and involves predictable patterns of behavior.

Jean Piaget's theory regarding the cognitive development of children and adolescents is perhaps the best known and most comprehensive. According to this theory, the perceptions and thoughts that young children have about the world are often quite different from those of adolescents and adults. That is, children may think about moral and social issues in a unique way. Children need to acquire cognitive, moral, and social skills in order to interact effectively with parents, teachers, and peers. If human intelligence encompasses all of these skills, then Piaget may have been correct in saying that human development is the child's intelligent adaptation to the environment.

Today the cognitive, moral, social, and emotional development of children takes place in a rapidly changing society. A child must develop positive conceptions of self within the family as well as at school in order to cope with the changes and become a competent and socially responsible adult. In the essay "Learning through 'Play' as well as 'Work' in the Primary Grades," Jane Perlmutter and Louise Burrell present ways in which teachers can provide children with appropriate experiences that enhance their development. The selections "The Moral Child" and "Helping Children Become More Prosocial: Ideas for Classrooms" discuss the moral and social skills of children. The article by Frances Campbell and Karen Taylor describes early childhood intervention programs that work. Adolescence brings with it the ability to think abstractly and hypothetically and to see the world from many perspectives. Adolescents strive to achieve a sense of identity by questioning their beliefs and tentatively committing to self-chosen goals. Their ideas about the kinds of adults they want to become and the ideals they want to believe in sometimes lead to conflicts with parents and teachers. Adolescents are also sensitive about espoused adult values versus adult behavior. This unit discusses the cognitive, social, and emotional changes that confront adolescents and also suggests ways in which the family and school can help meet the needs of adolescents.

Looking Ahead: Challenge Questions

What early childhood programs have long-term benefits for economically disadvantaged children?

How can parents and teachers provide children and adolescents with experiences that promote their cognitive, moral, social, and emotional development?

Describe the developmental tasks adolescents face. What historical and cultural changes may put some youth at risk? What is meant by *resiliency*?

What can adolescents tell us about their perceptions of caring?

UNIT 2

Learning through "Play" As Well As "Work" in the Primary Grades

Jane C. Perlmutter with Louise Burrell

Jane C. Perlmutter, Ed.D., is an associate professor of early childhood education at Western Carolina University in Cullowhee, North Carolina. She has worked collaboratively with Louise Burrell for many years in Louise's primary classrooms.

Louise Burrell, M.A. Ed., is now a second-grade teacher at Cullowhee Valley Elementary School. She has been teaching for more than 30 years.

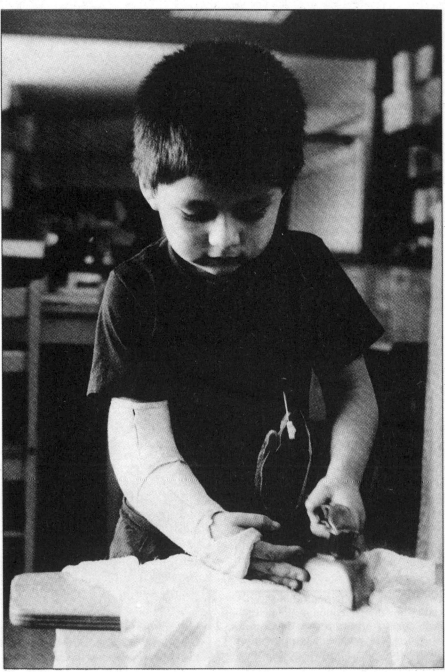

© Elisabeth Nichols

A visitor to Mrs. Burrell's class is struck by the level of purposeful activity as kindergarten and first- and second-grade children all share work and play in a room full of learning materials. While a first-grade child is in the woodworking center building a small bed to be used for book sharing, a second grader saws purposefully. Across the room a 5-year-old and a 7-year-old are engrossed in a computer game. Several children shop in the creative play center. Another child working on "investigations" estimates and then checks his classmate's weight, using bathroom scales. Other children write in their journals or on planning pads. The teacher and the assistant confer with individual children and check their reading progress. In such a busy, exciting place where children can be observed both playing and working, the lines between work and play become blurred.

Mrs. Burrell's class is unusual because there are few primary classrooms where one may observe kindergarten, first-, and second-grade children in one class *or* in groups playing and making choices of activities (King 1987). In many primary classrooms, recess is the only officially sanctioned, voluntary play left for children.

The relationship of children's play to various aspects of children's development has been studied intensively, especially over the last several decades (Rubin, Fein, & Vandenberg 1983). Most of the research on children's play has focused on preschool populations (Bergen 1987) and provides evidence that play is related to the development of preschool children's language, social competence, creativity, and problem-solving abilities (Athey 1987; Rogers & Sawyer 1988).

Children's perceptions of the differences between work and play change as they move from kindergarten into elementary school (King 1987). King asked kindergarten and elementary children about play and work in school. She found that kindergarten children call what the teacher tells them to do "work" and what they choose to do "play." Older elementary children will call a teacher-directed activity "play" if it is "fun." All children designate outside recess time as "playtime."

Currently, there is considerable debate in the field of early childhood education about developmentally appropriate practices for young children. In the primary grades, many people call for a return to a child-sensitive approach to teaching and learning (Morrison 1991). Play is part of this approach (Fromberg 1987). The debate deals with the balance between child-chosen activity and teacher-assigned ac-

We Studied Play in a Mixed-Age Primary Class

Mrs. Burrell's class is a combination kindergarten, first, and second grade in a K–8 school in Cullowhee, North Carolina. The school, adjacent to the campus of Western Carolina University, is one of five elementary schools in the Jackson County school district. The surrounding area is primarily rural, the people strongly rooted in the mountain Appalachian heritage. Students in Mrs. Burrell's class come from families associated with the university, as well as from families who have lived in the area for generations.

For the past four years, I have been participating in and observing Mrs. Burrell's classroom, while children are at work and play. The field data for this study were collected throughout the school year. Most of the observational data on children's play were collected in the fall of the year. I visited the classroom once or twice a week usually during the morning work period. A graduate student also spent approximately 20 hours a week as a participant–observer in the class. Interviews with the children about their perceptions of work and play were conducted during the spring semester.

We wanted to see what happens to play past preschool and how play fits with developmentally appropriate practice in primary grades. We wanted to describe the classroom organization in order to see how opportunities for play affect the academic climate. We were also interested in finding out how children in this type of setting perceive their work and play. A variety of types of data were collected, including the following:

• field notes on children's play and on interactions between children and teachers;

• notes taken during large-group times for planning and sharing;

• records of conferences between children and teachers;

• informal interviews with children as they did their work;

• notes about our helping out as children measured sand and water, sawed through big pieces of wood, wrote stories, sewed designs, made birthday cards, and all the other things children were busy doing; and

• individual interviews with the children about their perceptions of the classroom, the activities they did, and the differences between work and play.

tivity or, as some children might see it, between play and work.

Do first and second graders still play? Our observations confirm what most parents of primary school children know, that primary children are still accomplished pretenders and builders. Their play is creative and full of drama. Wars fought in the sand table reflected conflicts happen-

ing in the Middle East. Children shopped, took care of babies, became animals, and flew airplanes. What from a distance appeared to be a water-measuring activity was also two girls making a magic potion. Obviously, creative play and building with blocks are not just for kindergarten children.

Does the play of primary children differ from that of preschool children? With older children even more than with younger children, the play is often difficult to assign to neat categories. For example, building may overlap with games played with rules. The play of two children with an inclined plane and cars in the block center illustrates the difficulty of categorization. The children were conducting "slow" races to see which car could be pushed down the ramp most slowly. They recorded scores and pretended to be driving. They were building with the blocks, pretending, making up and playing a game. This was also a response to the day's math assignment, which was to make up and record a game with rules.

Observing children's play allowed us to peek into their private worlds of fantasy. In dramatic play, particularly in the sand, water, and blocks centers, the stories the children created as they played often seemed to be internalized. Two children playing side by side interacted frequently. Words were exchanged, little figures moved about, but each child seemed to

> **Many people are calling for a return to child-sensitive teaching and learning in the primary grades. Play is part of this approach.**

be constructing a private story. Pretending may be becoming more of a private fantasizing. This parallels Vygotsky's notion of *inner speech* (1978) and the changes in inner speech from "out loud" to "private" that occur as children move from preschool to primary school.

Play of primary-grade children is more precise and focused than the play of most younger children. Second graders playing in sand want to have areas clearly marked and want a purpose for all of the materials. Buildings become more complex and intricate as children's abilities expand. In dramatic play a group of the same children may maintain a complex story line over several weeks.

The additional experiences that two more years of living have furnished are evident in the

play of primary children compared to younger children, as seen in the transition from dramatic play to the dramatization of plays and puppet shows. Older primary children are also likely to create more detail and accessories to accompany their plays than are kindergarten children. Plays and puppet shows are more carefully planned when older children produce them. The beauty of a multi-age class is that younger children observe older children and want to do what they are doing. Older children can help the younger ones out of difficulties. Peer tutoring happens naturally and on an as-needed basis.

How is the classroom organized? There are three different layers in the classroom. The first layer is the environment of play and learning materials, the second is the work layer or the daily assignments, and the third layer is composed of the applications to real life in projects and businesses. The layers are linked informally and most activity flows comfortably from one to the next. These layers form a learning web that supports integrated learning, formal and informal.

The classroom environment itself constitutes the first layer. The room is full of raw materials for children's learning. Sand, water, clay, woodworking, junk materials for art, blocks, books, empty food containers, a cash register, dressup clothes, many kinds of writing materials, tapes with books to listen to, puppets and puppet theater—all have educational purposes. In linking

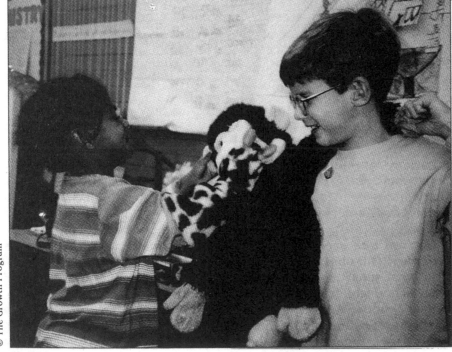

© The Growth Program

play with academics, educational materials like containers for measuring volume are placed next to small plastic figures for dramatic play. For example, playing with water and containers that hold water builds knowledge about how liquids flow and what things sink or float and what air pressure does to containers when they are turned over in the water. As another example, a displacement vessel is available for playing in the water center. The juxtaposition of play and learning materials encourages hands-on explorations that prepare children for more formal investigations and projects. This exploration leads to intuitive understandings of mathematical concepts of comparative size, volume, length, height, shapes, and patterns.

The classroom environment encourages dramatic play, which provides the context for all kinds of learning. In the Creative Play area, children play "store" and "house" and in the process count money and classify by attributes. When setting the table, a child uses one-to-one correspondence to have enough for everyone. In the store children read labels, write notes, and make grocery lists. As children construct buildings with blocks, they are adding and subtracting with concrete objects. Building means measuring and balancing. Using unit blocks, children gain intuitive understanding of fractions and division.

Out of children's spontaneous play comes the need for solving real-life problems. When a building collapses the builders must revise their thinking and solve the problem. Trying another way builds persistence and a willingness to revise and try again. Writers also must develop the same persistence and patience with the need for revision. The joy of constructive play is in the infinite possibilities of creating new things.

Play and language are intimately linked. Cooperative play

What Do the Children Call "Work" or "Play"?

We asked, "What kinds of things in your classroom are for playing and what things are for working?" The children tended to categorize the activities that they chose in the classroom environment as "play." As Laura said, "Centers are for playing, but actually everything in our class is work." The children most often identified creative play, blocks, and sand as "for play," although the blocks that stick together are to be counted and measured and thus are for work. Books, cooking, clay, and the computer were also mentioned as "play." One child said that sand is "sort of workish but fun, too." How a material is categorized appears to depend on what the child is doing with the material. This may be why several children said that blocks and sand are for working and playing. If the child measures the sand, that child is working, but if the child has a war in the sand table, he is probably playing. In the teacher's mind, in each case, the child is gaining valuable concrete experiences with raw materials.

Cooking was called "work" by some children and "play" by others. One child said, "Then there's one center that you pretty much have to work in or you'll be thrown out of . . . that would be cooking. 'Cause you can't be messing around with the stove and messing around with food." Woodworking has work in the title, so it must be work. Joshua got very specific about the work and play possibilities in woodworking. "Woodworking is kinda like a hobby. Woodworking would be like a beginner's thing for carpenters. And we work with wood, we measure, we do stuff like that, and then it can be play 'cause sometimes you nail stuff together and . . . don't measure." Dates on the calendar, writing, and reading were labeled "work." "When you read," described another child, "it'd be working 'cause you have to record it."

provides constant opportunities for oral language to develop. Two children building a fort or playing store must discuss and organize their efforts with words as well as actions. Puppet shows and other dramatic productions challenge children to plan and organize. Writing a script gives real reasons for writing. If a child wants friends to take part in a puppet show, she must write clearly enough to be understood.

The arrangement of materials in the various centers and the daily need to put things in order create real-life sorting and classifying problems. The children are responsible for maintaining the environment. Guided practice in classification happens every day when blocks are organized by size or science materials by function.

What kinds of work do these children do? The second layer in the classroom is composed of the daily assignments. Although the teacher respects the children's need for self-directed play activity, she also sets high standards for work the children must do. The children are responsible for completing certain work tasks every day. Even though there is a great deal of child choice in deciding how to accomplish the tasks and children help plan the parameters of each assignment, the tasks are still determined by the teacher. When the children are asked to tell about the work in the classroom, they talk about their journals, planning pads, investigations, and reading logs. All of these are done in blank books with open-ended assignments. All of the children are given a topic, but each child handles it differently and often uses different materials. Most of the children show a strong sense of responsibility for getting their work done. Many mention "getting all of their work done" as a source of pride.

According to Erikson (1963), a central task of primary children is to develop a sense of industry. Most 5-, 6-, and 7-year-olds want to work and to feel successful in their work. Big kids who ride on the bus, and big brothers and sisters, all go to school and work all day and have homework all night. Being a big kid means to have plenty of work to do. Completed work can be a badge of honor and brings with it the feeling of self-fulfillment and accomplishment.

How does Mrs. Burrell help the children integrate their work and play? Mrs. Burrell thinks children learn when they play, as do many theorists and play researchers. She tries to help children use their play in their work. One example of the integration of work and play is found in the formal mathematics activities for the class, called "investigations." Children help develop challenges to find ways to measure, graph, add, or record in a variety of situations. Often investigations are tied to activities and materials normally termed "play." For example, Mrs. Burrell tells the children, "Construct something in the block area and record what you've used in your construction." This open-ended assignment could be completed by listing the sizes and shapes of the blocks used.

Some children use tally marks, while others make a chart. Other investigations might involve going to the water center and finding out how many measured cups are in different containers. Students plan solutions, try them out, and record in writing what they have done. During sharing time, they report on their activities. One person's ideas often spark others to consider the problem from a different angle. "That's wonderful! How else could you try it?" is frequently heard.

Through recording and sharing, children become more self-aware of the learning processes involved in building with blocks and playing in sand or water. Having to plan for, record, and report on play activities ties play to academic learning. Children have real-life subject matter to write about and read to others. Not all play must be recorded by any means. But the frequent challenge to find a way to record what you have built or created ties naturally occurring constructive play to academic demands and gives purpose to reading, writing, and arithmetic.

How do these children learn responsibility? Play provides content and context for academic work. It also provides motivation for "getting your work done" so you will still have time to play. This is a worthy goal for children and adults. Balanced lives are happy lives. The children in Mrs. Burrell's class learn to balance the demands of work and play.

They must plan responsibly. This classroom would not work without clear expectations and requirements for academic work. Mrs. Burrell makes these expectations clear each morning in group time. Due dates for larger projects are marked on large calendars. Sharing times are posted. Children know what they must accomplish in the course of each day and week. This is not a laissez-faire environment. If a child does not complete the "givens," Mrs. Burrell may worry out loud that the child is tired and needs to rest in order to be able to get the work done. Usually, after a few minutes of "rest," the child asks for his work.

Key words for this class are dependability, responsibility, caring, and persistence. Mrs. Burrell relates class work to real-world responsibilities. Grownups have to go to work each day. They have to pay their light bills, or they will have no power. All through life, responsibility accompanies freedom. In this class, freedom to explore in centers is tied to completing the tasks for which you are responsible.

Accepting responsibility and organizing time for accomplishing tasks are vital skills that develop as children are allowed to decide what to do first, then next, and next, and then last. One day during a morning sharing time, Tim admitted that he had not completed his investigations from the day before. The other

> **The current debate about what is or is not developmentally appropriate in the primary grades deals, in part, with the balance between child-chosen activity and teacher-assigned activity.**

children were asked what should be done if work was not completed. They answered in unison, "Do it the next day!" Mrs. Burrell assured him that she would remember to call on him first during the afternoon sharing time so he would have a chance to finish his work. Friendly, respectful accountability encourages children to complete their assignments on time. Children are taught not to make excuses and not to blame others for things that happen. They learn to reach into themselves to find the solutions to problems. Forgetting to do a task one day means finding a way to solve the problem of completing double assignments the next day.

How does children's work and play relate to the real world of grownups and work? The link of classroom responsibility to real-world responsibility is part of the third and final layer in the classroom, which Mrs. Burrell calls "applications." Projects that the children plan and execute are a part of this level. Through projects children pull together the skills learned in daily play and work (levels one and two) and apply them to topics that interest them. Children work alone or together on subjects they choose. For example, a second-grade girl and a kindergarten boy decided to find out about dolphins. They began by writing down what they knew and what they wanted to find out. They found books, read about dolphins, made models with various art materials, and wrote about what they learned. They also presented their project to the whole class.

Cooking in the classroom, selling the food, keeping track of the money, saving for classroom needs are other real-life applications. Through these activities dramatic play becomes simulation of real-world businesses. Children work and play at being producers and consumers. Since

© The Growth Program

part of the real world is holding a job, in this class the children apply for positions, such as cleaning up a center, writing for the newsletter, or handling money for the bank. The dramatic play we see in kindergarten becomes more serious and more closely approximates adult roles when second graders are in charge.

How does play relate to motivation and management? Motivation and apathy are two central issues that plague educators today. Many teachers use grades, stickers, or other forms of external reinforcement to induce children to complete work and to do

the best they can. In this classroom, children's work is treated with respect and receives honest and constructive feedback. Both in individual conferences and in group sharing times, work is scrutinized. Work that shows thought and creativity is appreciated. Areas in which changes would help the finished product are pointed out. When work is done in blank books, there are few wrong answers. Children are encouraged to evaluate their own work rather than to wait for others to sit in judgment. Through work that is tied to play, children's love of learning is fostered. They learn to reach out

The additional experiences that two more years of living have furnished are evident in the play of primary children compared to younger children, as seen in the transition from dramatic play to the dramatization of plays and puppet shows. Older primary children are also likely to create more detail and accessories to accompany their plays than are kindergarten children.

for more knowledge. Through an emphasis on persistence, they learn not to give up quickly.

Ironically, many teachers fear a classroom in which children move around and select activities because they assume chaos will ensue. King (1987) categorizes elementary school play as instrumental (games and fun activities with specific academic focus), recreational (recess), or illicit (fooling around, acting up). Illicit play often happens when the teacher's back is turned. Children use illicit play as a way to make contact with friends or to keep from doing work tasks that they may regard as irrelevant. According to King, illicit play provides children a sense of control and autonomy in a teacher-dominated situation. Thus, in a traditional classroom, play may be seen as the enemy. In Mrs. Burrell's child-sensitive class, play is an accepted part of children's lives and is assumed to help carry the academic agenda forward.

True discipline comes from within. In order to learn self-control and self-discipline, children must be allowed to be in charge of themselves. Learning to be a self-disciplined person is a long-term project, but helping children develop independent thought in a community of learners removes many discipline problems common to more teacher-controlled situations.

From a teacher's point of view, plenty of play opportunities means that little time is wasted in trying to keep small bodies unnaturally still in seats. For many children, having to sit still for long periods of time takes so much concentration that they can not attend to the academic work tasks at hand. Active playtimes allow for increased concentration during work times. The children in this class find comfortable individual rhythms for their work and play. After the morning group discussions, the children are told to go to work. Having been well trained in the purposes of courtesy, they get up in an orderly fashion and disperse quickly to all parts of the classroom. The attentive listener often hears comments from some children, for instance, "I'm going to do all my work first so I'll be able to play this afternoon." Other children start with the sand table or the blocks before settling down to journal writing or investigations.

The smooth transitions from group time to individual work are the result of careful planning, training, and monitoring of the work that is accomplished. At the beginning of the year, the children go on "field trips" around the room to discuss appropriate behaviors in each area. The children themselves generate guidelines for working and playing together in the small space that is their classroom. All guidelines spell out clear purposes. The overriding principle is that of consideration for other people. Caring, respect, and courtesy make the class into a very functional family group.

How does play provide a context for assessing children's progress? In grades one and two, the North Carolina educational system uses a checklist format for continuous teacher monitoring of children's progress through observation of their performance. Mrs. Burrell finds the children's play, as well as their work, an excellent context for evaluating the development of their concepts and skills. The children are often unaware that the teacher or the assistant is making note of what they are doing. Watching several children playing with Cuisenaire rods, Mrs. Burrell is able to check their use of patterns and symmetry. Listening to children pretending allows teachers to assess oral language skills. Thus, play is a context in which the teacher can see what a child can do.

Summary

Children do continue to play in primary school when the opportunity is provided. Their play is rich, creative, and more complex than that of younger children. Work and play intertwine throughout the layers of the classroom. Children learn while playing and play while learning, and the combination helps them learn to manage time responsibility. One clear message comes through in talking to these children: the reason school is a pleasure rather than a pain is the choices involved and the play opportunities available.

What do primary children learn when they work and play in school in a child-sensitive classroom? They learn responsibility, organization, how to enjoy themselves and still be task oriented. As they play together, oral language skills are honed in ways that would not be possible through traditional classroom talk. Play for primary children, like play for preschool children and play for adults, is about possibilities. Playful people are risk takers whose thinking is open ended and whose minds are creative.

What are the teaching implications of tying play and work together? Teachers anxious to maintain developmentally appropriate classrooms would do well to provide plenty of time and materials for a class full of work and play. Having children responsible for organizing their time "to get everything done and still play in centers" helps train them for future organizing of life, work, and leisure. Giving children choices at 5, 6, and 7 prepares them for major choices at 15, 16, and 17—and 27. A child who learns at 7 to say, "No, I can't play right now, I have to finish my journal," may be the child who can manage time well as a first-year college student. Children need to learn that their actions have consequences. Children need to be able to balance the demands of responsibilities and relaxation. We all need healthy doses of work and play.

References

Athey, I. 1987. The relationship of play to cognitive, language and moral development. In *Play as a medium for learning and development: A handbook of theory and practice,* ed. D. Bergen, 81–101. Portsmouth, NH: Heinemann.

Bergen, D. 1987. Stages of play development. In *Play as a medium for learning and development: A handbook of theory and practice,* ed. D. Bergen, 49–66. Portsmouth, NH: Heinemann.

Erikson, E. 1963. *Childhood and society.* New York: Norton.

Fromberg, D.P. 1987. Play. In *The early childhood curriculum: A review of current research,* ed. C. Seefeldt, 35–74. New York: Teachers College Press.

King, N.R. 1987. Elementary school play: Theory and research. In *School play: A source book,* eds. J.H. Block & N.R. King, 143–65. New York: Garland.

Morrison, G.S. 1991. *Early childhood education today.* 3rd ed. New York: Merrill.

Rogers, C.S., & J.K. Sawyer. 1988. *Play in the lives of children.* Washington, DC: NAEYC.

Rubin, K.N., G.G. Fein, & B. Vandenberg. 1983. Play. In *Handbook of child psychology. Vol. 4, Socialization, personality and social development,* eds. E.M. Hetherington & P.H. Mussen, 698–774. New York: Wiley.

Vygotsky, L.S. 1978. *Mind in society: The development of higher psychological processes,* eds. M. Cole, V. Dan-Steiner, S. Scribner, & E. Souberman. Cambridge, MA: Harvard University Press.

THE MORAL CHILD

We're at ground zero in the culture wars: how to raise decent kids when traditional ties to church, school and community are badly frayed

Only in contemporary America could selecting a family anthology be considered a political act. On one cultural flank is famous Republican moralist William Bennett's bestselling *Book of Virtues,* a hefty collection of tales, fables and poems celebrating universal virtues such as courage, compassion and honesty. Side by side with the Bennett tome in many bookstores is Herbert Kohl and Colin Greer's *A Call to Character,* a similar assemblage of proverbs and stories organized around equally cherished values. No one could blame the casual browser for arbitrarily grabbing one or the other. But it's not a casual choice. These two volumes represent a fundamental and acrimonious division over what critics call the most pressing issue facing our nation today: how we should raise and instruct the next generation of American citizens.

The differences between the two volumes of moral instruction aren't even that subtle, once you're familiar with the vocabulary of America's culture war. Both agree on qualities of character like kindness and responsibility. But look deeper: Is unwavering patriotism more desirable than moral reasoning? Does discretion trump courage, or the

other way around? Read the *Book of Virtues* to your children and they'll learn about valor from William Tell and Henry V at Agincourt. Read from *A Call to Character* and their moral instructors will be Arnold Lobel's decidedly unheroic but very human Frog and Toad. The former has sections devoted to work, faith and perseverance; the latter, playfulness, balance and adaptability. It's not just semantics or moral hairsplitting. These dueling miscellanies symbolize a much wider struggle for the hearts and minds of America's kids.

Beyond the hearth. Child rearing has always been filled with ambiguities. But while parents once riffled through their Dr. Spock and other how-to manuals for helpful perspectives on toilet training and fussy eaters, today the questions and concerns seem to have moved beyond the scope of child psychology and the familiar hearthside dilemmas. The issue for today's parents is how to raise decent kids in a complex and morally ambiguous world where traditional tethers to church, school and neighborhood are badly frayed. Capturing the heightened concerns of thousands of parents from around the country gathering at the Lincoln Memorial for this week's Stand for Children, one 41-year-old mother ob-

WIMP OR BULLY?

Your 5-year-old has been in a fistfight. Although another child was clearly the aggressor, your son dominated the older boy in the end. You experience mixed feelings: pride that your son is not a wimp, but concern about the escalating use of violence to resolve childhood disputes.

EXPERTS' VIEW

This is a common dilemma, experts say, and one that genuinely has two sides. Parents should always try first to teach a child that there are lots of ways to resolve conflict harmoniously and that reason and compromise are more effective than duking it out. Kids should also be taught that the distinction between wimp and aggressor is a false one. But if the choice is being a victim or not, children need to learn to stand up for themselves. Says psychologist William Damon: "Even young children can handle some complexity. You may not use the words 'justifiable self-defense,' but kids can grasp the idea."

serves about raising her teenage daughter: "It's not just dealing with chores and curfews. That stuff's easy. But what do you do when the values you believe in are being challenged every day at the high school, the mall, right around the corner in your own neighborhood?"

It is a sign of how high the stakes have risen that both first lady Hillary Rodham Clinton and former Vice President Dan Quayle weighed in this year with new books on proper moral child rearing. Both are motivated by fear that the moral confusion of today's youth could be deleterious to our democracy, which draws its sustenance and vitality from new generations of competent and responsible citizens. There's a sense of desperation in current writing about moral parenting, a sense that, as one psychologist puts it, improper child rearing has become a "public health problem" requiring urgent attention. Some lawmakers and public officials are even agitating for creation of a national public policy on the cultivation of private character.

The perceived threat to the commonwealth varies, of course, depending on one's political perspective. Critics on the right view moral relativity and indulgent parenting as the cause of today's moral confusion and call for the rediscovery of firmness, regimentation, deference and piety to counter our culture's decline. Those on the left are alarmed at what they see as a wave of simplistic nostalgia gaining force in the country: In their view, it is a bullying reformation designed to mold moral automatons incapable of genuine judgment or citizenship.

Morality's bedrock. The split is political, not scientific. Psychological understanding of moral development is actually quite sophisticated and consistent. For example, decades of research leave little doubt that empathy—the ability to assume another's point of view—develops naturally in the first years of life. Parents, of course, know this just from casual observation. Even infants show unmistakable signs of distress when another child is hurt or upset, and rudimentary forms of sympathy and helping—offering a toy to a distraught sibling, for example—can be observed in children as young as 1. Most psychologists who study empathy assume that the basic skill is biologically wired, probably created along with the bonds of trust that an infant forms with a caretaker, usually the mother. The task for parents is not so much a matter of teaching empathy as not quashing its natural flowering.

Building blocks. Empathy is the bedrock of human morality, the emotional skill required for the emergence of all other moral emotions—shame, guilt, pride

and so forth. Almost every form of moral behavior imaginable—from doing chores responsibly to sacrificing one's life for a cause—is inconceivable without it. Yet empathy is not enough. A second crucial building block of morality is self discipline, and psychologists have some solid evidence about how this moral "skill" is nurtured.

Most parents tend to adopt one of three general "styles" of interacting with their kids, each style a different combination of three basic factors: acceptance and warmth (vs. rejection), firmness (vs. leniency) and respect for autonomy (vs. control). How parents combine these traits sends very different messages to their children, which over time are "internalized" in such character traits as self-esteem, self-control, social competence and responsibility—or, of course, in the absence of those traits.

There is little doubt about what works and what doesn't. In fact, says Temple University child psychologist Laurence Steinberg, author of a new study called *Beyond the Classroom*, extensive research over many years shows that parents who are more accepting and warm, firmer about rules and discipline and more supportive of their child's individuality produce healthier kids: "No research has ever suggested that children fare better when their parents are aloof than when they are accepting, when their parents are lenient rather than firm, or when their parents are psychologically controlling, rather than supportive of their psychological autonomy."

Psychologists call this ideal parenting style "authoritative" parenting, a middle ground between "autocratic" and "permissive" parenting, both of which tend to produce untoward consequences for children in terms of both competence and integrity. The need to control children appears to be especially damaging to self-discipline. "Parents who are high in control," Steinberg says, "tend to value obedience over independence. They are likely to tell their children that young people should not question adults, that their opinions count less because they are children, and so on. Expressions of individuality are frowned upon in these families and equated with signs of disrespect."

The best con men, of course, combine self-discipline with a keen ability to read others' thoughts and feelings. Morality requires more—specifically, the ability to think about such things as justice and fairness and ultimately to act on those thoughts. According to the late psychologist Lawrence Kohlberg of Harvard Uni-

versity, people pass through six fairly inflexible "stages" or moral reasoning, beginning with a childlike calculation of self-interest and ending with the embodiment of abstract principles of justice. The ability to think logically about right and wrong, Kohlberg believed, was essential to the development of complete moral beings: Moral habits and emotions alone, he argued, were inadequate for dealing with novel moral dilemmas or when weighing one value against another, as people often must do in real life.

Moral identity. Psychologists emphasize the importance of young children's "internalizing" values, that is, absorbing standards that are then applied in different times, places or situations. In a recently published study called *Learning to Care*,

SHAME AND RIDICULE

Your 6-year-old's teacher punishes him by making him wear a dunce cap. That strikes you as archaic and severe, but the teacher insists a bit of shame helps teach old-fashioned manners.

EXPERTS VIEW

Psychologists no longer believe that shame and guilt are the stuff of neurosis. In fact, most now are convinced that morality cannot develop without these fundamental moral emotions. But public ridicule is more likely to produce humiliation and anger than healthy contrition. Parents should talk privately with the teacher to see if there are gentler and less demeaning ways to make misbehaving children feel shame.

Princeton sociologist Robert Wuthnow argues that teenagers basically need to go through a second experience of internalization if they are to become caring adults. Just as young children absorb and integrate a rudimentary understanding of kindness and caring from watching adult models, adolescents need to witness a more nuanced form of caring, to absorb "stories" of adult generosity and self-sacrifice. That way, they see that involvement is a real possibility in a world where so much caring has been institutionalized.

Similarly, a recent study suggests that people who have chosen lives of lifelong, passionate commitment have had more opportunities than most people to develop appropriate trust, courage and responsible imagination. There is no such thing as a "Gandhi pill," Lesley College Prof. Laurent Parks Daloz and his colleagues write in the new book *Common Fire,* but there are commonly shared experiences: a parent committed to a cause, service opportunities during adolescence, cross-cultural experiences, a rich mentoring experience in young adulthood. Often, the authors conclude, the committed differ from the rest of us only by having more of these experiences, and deeper ones.

Force of habit. Of course, cultural battles rarely reflect the complexity of human behavior, and the current debate about proper moral child rearing has a black-and-white quality. As Bennett writes in his introduction to the *Book of Virtues,* moral education involves "explicit instruction, exhortation, and training. Moral education *must* provide training in good habits." But critics charge that such preoccupation with drill and habit suggests a dark and cynical view of human nature as a bundle of unsavory instincts that need constant squelching and reining in. In theology, it's called original sin; in psychological terms, it's a "behaviorist" approach, conditioning responses—or habits—which eventually become automatic and no longer require the weighing of moral options. The opposing philosophy—drawing from the romanticism of Jean Jacques Rousseau, psychology's "human potential" movement and the "constructivist" movement in education—emphasizes the child's natural empathy and untapped potential for reasoning.

The Clinton and Quayle volumes show how simplistic psychology can make for unsophisticated public philosophy. There's no question that the first lady's *It Takes a Village* is informed by an overriding respect for children as essentially competent beings who need nurturance to blossom. But critics see Clinton's optimism as dewy eyed and unrealistic, too much akin to the self-esteem movement and a "child centered" parenting style that allows kids to become morally soft. Quayle's *The American Family,* by contrast, endorses control and punishment as "a way to shape behavior toward respect and obedience." He notes approvingly that the five healthy families he studied reject the counsel of "prominent child experts," including the well-document-

ed finding that spanking and other forms of physical coercion teach violence rather than values.

Quayle's analysis is only one of many calls to return to a time when children knew their proper place and society was not so disorderly. Perhaps the strongest prescription is *The Perversion of Autonomy* by psychiatrist Willard Gaylin and political theorist Bruce Jennings, both of New York's Hastings Center for Bioethics. The book is a gleeful celebration of the value of coercion. In the view of these authors, the manifest vulgarities of liberal society justify and demand a serious rollback of the civil rights era; for the good of society, it follows, children require early and decisive flattening.

There is little question that the worst of New Age gobbledygook makes the cultural left an easy target for attack. One parent tells the story of when her 6-year-old was caught stealing at school. She met with the teacher, hoping together they could come up with a strategy to make it clear that stealing was unacceptable. But the teacher's response astonished her: "We don't use the word *stealing* here," she said. "We call it *uncooperative behavior.*" Few defend such foolish excesses of the self-esteem movement. But progressives argue they are aberrations used to attack liberal parenting and pedagogy. It's naive to focus on examples of indulgence, they argue, when if anything our culture is a child-hating culture, with family policies to match.

Classroom politics. This same ideological tug of war can be observed in the nation's schools, specifically in battles over the so-called character education movement. Only a few years old, the movement is fairly diverse, in some schools involving a specific packaged curriculum and reading materials, in others more of a philosophy or administrative style. But the general idea has captured the attention of the White House and Congress, both of which are searching for an appropriate federal role in promoting basic decency. Lawmakers have lent their symbolic support by endorsing "National Character Counts Week." The Department of Education has funded a few pilot programs and will soon fund a few more. And next week, President Clinton will address a joint White House-congressional conference on character building, the third such meeting sponsored by this administration.

Many states have also created character education requirements, and by conservative estimate, hundreds of schools and districts have adopted strategies for addressing morals and civic virtue. Precisely because of the diversity of philosophies that fall under the rubric "char-

acter education," experts say, parents need to be aware of what the term means in their own child's classroom.

For example, some schools have adopted conservative models that tend to emphasize order, discipline and courage—what Boston University educator Kevin Ryan labels the "stern virtues," as opposed to "soft" or easy virtues like compassion and self-esteem. Such programs don't shy away from unfashionable ideas like social control and indoctrination, says University of Illinois sociologist Edward Wynne, a guiding light of this approach and coauthor, with Ryan, of *Reclaiming Our Schools.*

ORDER AND SQUALOR

Your 12-year-old daughter's bedroom is a pigsty. You worry that a disorderly room means a disorderly mind, but your husband says it's more important not to violate her personal space.

EXPERTS VIEW

Experts are divided. Some come down firmly on the side of orderliness as an important habit and a lesson in family obligation. They dismiss the personal space argument as New Age nonsense. Others do not consider it a moral issue at all but an aesthetic one. Even adults differ: Some don't bother to make their beds, while others are fastidious. It's an issue for negotiation, which is a life skill that teenagers should learn.

Wynne calls for a return to the "great tradition in education," that is, the transmission of "good doctrine" to the next generation. Because of the "human propensity for selfishness," Wynne encourages schools to use elaborate reward systems, including "ribbons, awards and other signs of moral merit." The model also emphasizes group sports and pep rallies as effective ways to elevate school spirit. Variations of this reward-and-discipline model emphasize drilling in a prescribed set of values, often focusing on a "virtue of the month."

Programs based on the stern virtues

also tend to emphasize institutional loyalty and submission of the individual to the larger community. Ryan points to Roxbury Latin, a 350-year-old private boys' school in Boston, as an example of this approach. The school subscribes to an unambiguous set of Judeo-Christian values—honesty, courtesy and respect for others, according to the catalog. It attempts to inculcate these values through a classical curriculum, through mandatory, sermonlike "halls" and

CODES AND CREATIVITY

Your son is dismissed from school because his pierced ear violates the dress code. You argue with the principal that the earring is a form of self-expression, but he insists societies need rules.

EXPERTS VIEW

Some psychologists consider it unconscionable to place a child in the center of a culture war. The most crucial issue, they argue, is for parents and other authority figures to present kids with a united moral front. But psychologist Michael Schulman disagrees: "It could be an opportunity for a valuable lesson in choosing life's battles: Is this an important one? If so, what's the most effective strategy for social change?"

through formal and casual interactions between teachers (called "masters") and students. No racial, ethnic or religious student organizations are permitted, in order to encourage loyalty to the larger school community. According to Headmaster F. Washington Jarvis, an Episcopal priest, Roxbury Latin's view of human nature is much like the Puritan founders': "mean, nasty, brutish, selfish, and capable of great cruelty and meanness. We have to hold a mirror up to the students and say, 'This is who you are. Stop it.' "

Roxbury Latin teaches kids to rein in their negative impulses not with harsh discipline, however, but with love and security of belonging. Displays of affection are encouraged, according to Jar-

vis, and kids are disciplined by being made to perform (and report) good deeds—a powerful form of behavior modification. Students are rebuked and criticized when they stray, but criticism is always followed by acts of caring and acceptance. Whenever a student is sent to Jarvis's office for discipline, the headmaster always asks as the boy leaves, "Do I love you?"

Ethical dilemmas. At the other end of the spectrum are character education programs that emphasize moral reasoning. These, too, vary a great deal, but most are derived at least loosely from the work of Kohlberg and other stage theorists. Strict Kohlbergian programs tend to be highly cognitive, with students reasoning through hypothetical moral dilemmas and often weighing conflicting values in order to arrive at judgments of right and wrong. A classic Kohlbergian dilemma, for example, asks whether it's right for a poor man to steal medicine to save his dying wife. Even young children tend to justify dishonesty in this situation, but only adults do so based on a firmly held principle of what's unchallengeably right. Kohlbergian programs are also much more likely to have kids grapple with controversial social dilemmas, since it's assumed that the same sort of moral logic is necessary for citizens to come to informed decisions on the issues of the day—whether gay lifestyles ought to be tolerated in the U.S. Navy, for example.

Variations in programs on strict moral reasoning are generally based on a kind of "constructivist" model of education, in which kids have to figure out for themselves, based on real experiences, what makes the other person feel better or worse, what rules make sense, who makes decisions. Kids actively struggle with issues and from the inside out "construct" a notion of what kind of moral person they want to be. (Advocates of moral reasoning are quick to distinguish this approach from "values clarification," a 1960s educational fad and a favorite whipping boy of conservative reformers. Values clarification consisted of a variety of exercises aimed at helping kids figure out what was most important to them, regardless of how selfish or cruel those "values" might be. It's rarely practiced today.)

The Hudson school system in Massachusetts is a good example of this constructivist approach. The program is specifically designed to enhance the moral skills of empathy and self-discipline. Beginning in kindergarten, students participate in role-playing exercises, a series of readings about ethical

dilemmas in history and a variety of community service programs that have every Hudson student, K through 12, actively engaged in helping others and the community. Environmental efforts are a big part of the program: Kindergartners, for instance, just completed a yearlong recycling project. The idea, according to Superintendent Sheldon Berman, is for children to understand altruism both as giving to the needy today and as self-sacrifice for future generations. By contrast, the conservative "Character Education Manifesto"

MEDIA AND MORES

You allow your kids to watch certain R-rated videos, but you can't preview each one. Your 13-year-old argues: "I'm not going to become an ax murderer just because I watch a movie, Dad."

EXPERTS' VIEW

It's true he won't become an ax murderer, but he might absorb some distorted lessons about uncaring sexuality—if you're not around to discuss the differences between fantasy and reality. It's OK to question and reject social codes like movie ratings, psychologists say, but if you do, you must substitute meaningful discussion of sex, violence and censorship.

states explicitly: "Character education is *not* about acquiring the right *views*," including "currently accepted attitudes about ecology."

Needless to say, these philosophical extremes look very different in practice. Parents who find one or the other more appealing will almost certainly have different beliefs about human behavior. But the best of such programs, regardless of ruling philosophy, share in one crucial belief: that making decent kids requires constant repetition and amplification of basic moral messages. Both Roxbury Latin and Hudson, for example, fashion themselves as "moral communities," where character education is woven into the basic fabric of the school and reflected in every aspect of the school day.

Community voices. This idea is consistent with the best of moral development theory. According to Brown University developmental psychologist William Damon, author of *Greater Expectations,* "Real learning is made up of a thousand small experiences in a thousand different relationships, where you see all the facets of courage, caring and respect." Virtue-of-the week programs will never work, Damon contends, because they lack moral dimension and trivialized moral behavior. Children can handle moral complexity, he says, and sense what's phony. "Kids need a sense of purpose, something to believe in. Morality is not about prohibitions, things to avoid, be afraid of or feel guilty about."

Building this sense of purpose is a task beyond the capacity of most families today. The crucial consistency of a moral message requires that kids hear it not only from their parents but from their neighbors, teachers, coach, the local policeman. Unfortunately, Damon says, few do. The culture has become so adversarial that the important figures in a child's life are more apt to be at one another's throats than presenting a unified moral front. Litigiousness has become so widespread that it even has a name, the "parents' rights movement." More than ever before, parents see themselves primarily as advocates for their children's rights, suing schools over every value conflict. In a New York case now making its way through the courts, for example, parents are suing because they object to the school district's community service requirement.

Moral ecology. The irony of postmodern parenting, writes sociologist David Popenoe in *Seedbeds of Virtue,* is that just when science has produced a reliable body of knowledge about what makes decent kids, the key elements are disintegrating: the two-parent family, the church, the neighborhood school and a safe, nurturing community. Popenoe and others advocate a much broader understanding of what it means to raise a moral child today—what communitarian legal theorist Mary Ann Glendon calls an "ecological approach" to child rearing, which views parents and family as just one of many interconnecting "seedbeds" that can contribute to a child's competency and character.

Hillary Clinton borrowed for her book title the folk wisdom, "It takes a village to raise a child." It's an idea that seems to be resonating across the political spectrum today, even in the midst of rough cultural strife. Damon, for example, ended his book with the inchoate notion of "youth charters," an idea that he says has taken on a life of its own in recent months. He has been invited into communities from Texas to New England to help concerned citizens identify shared values and develop plans for modeling and nurturing these values in newly conceived moral communities.

Americans are hungry for this kind of moral coherence, Damon says, and although they need help getting past their paralysis, it's remarkable how quickly they can reach consensus on a vision for their kids and community. He is optimistic about the future: "My great hope is that we can actually rebuild our communities in this country around our kids. That's one great thing about America: people love their kids. They've just lost the art of figuring out how to raise them."

BY WRAY HERBERT WITH
MISSY DANIEL IN BOSTON

SMOKE AND MIRRORS

Despite your own youthful experimentation with drugs, you're worried about your teenager's fascination with today's drug culture. He claims he's embracing the values of the '60s.

EXPERTS' VIEW

This comes up a lot, now that children of the '60s are raising their own teenagers. It's crucial to be honest, but it's also fair to explain the social context and the spirit in which drugs were being used at the time. And it's OK to say it was a mistake—it wasn't the key to nirvana. Most experts suggest focusing on health effects and illegality rather than making it a moral issue.

Early Childhood Programs That Work for Children from Economically Disadvantaged Families

Frances A. Campbell and Karen Taylor

The demand for early child care continues to increase among economically disadvantaged families as welfare reform requires mothers receiving aid to return to school or work. This is both an opportunity and a challenge for early childhood professionals. The opportunity is to design quality programs in which children from low-income families can develop to their highest potential, but the number of children affected presents an enormous challenge. What sorts of programs will maximize children's chances of growing up physically and mentally healthy?

A survey of early childhood intervention programs provided for children from low-income families was undertaken to find ways in which children or parents derived benefits

© Francis Wardle

Frances A. Campbell, Ph.D., is a senior investigator and fellow at the Frank Porter Graham Child Development Center at the University of North Carolina. She is one of the principal investigators for the Abecedarian Project and the Head Start Transition Demonstration Project.

Karen Taylor, M.R.P., is the data coordinator for the North Carolina Head Start Transition Demonstration Project, which is designed to study the effects of providing Head Start-like services to low-income children during their first few years of public school. Karen works with both the program and evaluation staffs of the transition project.

*This is one of a regular series of Research in Review columns. The column in this issue was invited by **Carol Seefeldt**, Ph.D., professor at the University of Maryland, College Park.*

and to find how long the effects lasted. Only studies that permitted scientific comparison of outcomes among children who did and did not receive services were included.

The programs surveyed differed in their timing, their intensity, and their goals. The Mobile Unit for Child Health (Gutelius et al. 1972), the Prenatal Early Infancy Project (Olds 1988), and the Yale Child Welfare Program (Provence & Naylor 1983) began working with mothers before target children were born. Programs that began working with children in infancy were the Milwaukee Project (Garber 1988), the Syracuse University Family Development Research Program (Lally, Mangione, & Honig 1988), the Abecedarian Project (Ramey & Campbell 1991), Project CARE (Wasik et al. 1990), the Brookline Early Education Project (Pierson 1988), and the Infant Health and Development Project (HIDP 1990). The Houston Parent-Child Development Center (Johnson & Walker 1991) began working with families when target infants were one. The Harlem Study (Palmer 1983) contrasted outcomes in children provided short-term intervention either as two-year-olds or three-year-olds. The Verbal Interaction Project (Levenstein, O'Hara, & Madden 1983) provided a home-based language stimulation program for two- or three-year-olds. Other programs, such as the Perry Preschool Project (Beruetta-Clement et al. 1984), the Early Training Project (Gray, Ramsey, & Klaus 1982), the Chicago Child and Parent Center and Expansion Program (Reynolds 1994), and

Almost all programs, at their intervention end points, show cognitive benefits for children who participated in the program.

Head Start (McKey et al. 1985) began working with children in preschools beginning at age three or four. Four programs were clearly more intensive, in terms of duration of intervention, than the rest. These were the Syracuse University Family Development Program, which provided care for five years, the Milwaukee Project, in which children were involved from infancy through kindergarten (age six), and Project CARE and the Abecedarian study, whose maximal intervention was provided for children from infancy through age eight. (Other Abecedarian groups had either five or three years of intervention.)

Parent components were included in many programs because of the belief that early intervention would succeed only if parents became heavily involved and they themselves made major changes (Bronfenbrenner 1974). Several programs combined home visits with center-based child care. Some provided parents with opportunities for personal development, such as job training. Others used a home-visit model alone. A few had maternal and child health as their primary objective and used nurses as their visitors, while others had social workers to provide emotional support to parents.

Because children raised in low-income families are more likely to have academic and behavior problems in school (Connell 1994; Patterson, Kupersmidt, & Vaden 1990) and because preschool intellectual levels and early language development are so strongly associated with school success, almost all early childhood programs emphasized activities to enhance children's cognitive development. Some interventionists attempted to do this through direct teaching of children in child care centers or preschools. Others modeled interactive and teaching behaviors for parents with the expectation that parents would then teach their children.

All programs had end-point evaluations when intervention was terminated, but not all have long-term data on their participants. A few followed their samples into adolescence or even young adulthood. Program outcomes were examined in terms of cognitive/academic, socioemotional, and health benefits.

Cognitive/academic outcomes

Almost all programs, at their intervention end points, show cognitive benefits for children who participated in the program. However, early disillusionment with preschool intervention for children from low-income families came when a large-scale evaluation of Project Head Start (Cicirelli 1969) showed that mean IQs of Head Start children, after only three years in school, were not significantly different from those of children who had not participated. The study that delivered this bad news was attacked on methodological grounds, with many skeptics arguing that it did not fairly assess the benefits of Head Start. To provide a definitive investigation of the effects of preschool interventions for children from low-income families, a Consortium for Longitudinal Studies was formed in which 11 investigators followed up their participants to learn how long early benefits persisted (Lazar et al. 1982). Results pooled across all 11 programs showed that statistically significant IQ differences among intervention and control subjects were largely gone after three to four years in public school, and significant differences on academic tests of reading and mathematics were gone after five to six years. On the other hand, the consortium found important, lasting benefits in terms of fewer retentions in grade and fewer placements into special education for treated children.

The consortium results have been widely cited by both critics and proponents of early intervention as supportive of their own position. Focusing on the erosion of significant IQ and academic benefits, critics conclude that lasting, positive effects of early childhood programs have not been demonstrated. Some policymakers have labeled them ill-advised and wasteful. However, not all programs included in the consortium failed to find lasting IQ or academic benefits, and a number of early childhood studies carried out since those in the consortium also have found long-lasting IQ or academic gains. In general, the most enduring IQ benefits for children were associated with child-centered programs, such as the Milwaukee and Abecedarian studies, that began very early in the life span and provided many hours of educational exposure. On the other hand, participants in the Harlem study also showed long-term IQ gains with a much shorter period of participation that began no earlier than age two. Other preschool experiences that started at age three or four, such as those in the Early Training Project, Project Head Start, and the Perry Preschool study, reported significant IQ differences when their programs ended, but these differences eroded within a few years.

To provide a definitive investigation of the effects of preschool interventions for children from low-income families, a Consortium for Longitudinal Studies was formed in which 11 investigators followed up their participants to learn how long early benefits persisted. The consortium found important, lasting benefits in terms of fewer retentions in grade and fewer placements into special education for treated children.

Socioemotional outcomes for children can be roughly grouped into three categories: behavioral adjustment, attitudes and attributions, and self-concept. Socioemotional outcomes for parents largely consisted of measures of maternal behaviors, such as affection and punitiveness.

Long-term (fifth grade or higher) academic test results or indices of school progress (retentions, placements, or graduation rates) are available for the Early Training Project, the Harlem study, the Perry Preschool Project, the Houston PCDC program, the Syracuse Family Development Program, the Milwaukee Project, and the Abecedarian study. Girls involved with the Syracuse study had higher grades than control girls in grades 7-8. Participants in the Early Training Project had fewer retentions or placements into special education, and girls who participated in this program were more likely to graduate from high school and more likely to return to school if they became teen mothers. Abecedarian subjects who received preschool services had significantly higher scores on tests of reading and math through age 15 and fewer retention and placements into special education. The Milwaukee study found no academic test-score differences after 10 years in school, but significant IQ differences persisted through age 14. All these programs contained child-centered components. The evidence thus shows that children from low-income families can derive significant and long-lasting cognitive and academic benefits from child-oriented preschool programs.

There are also reports of long-term positive effects on child IQ and academic performance from some of the more parent-oriented programs, but the evidence for long-term benefits is more mixed. Programs that emphasized parents as the mediators of treatment, such as the Mobile Unit for Child Health and the Brookline Early Edu-

cation Project, found significant child IQ or "language" benefits when their programs ended. The Verbal Interaction Project had mixed results; some, but not all, program variations resulted in significant gains for participating children. In contrast, the Family Education group from Project CARE and the Yale, Syracuse, and Houston programs did not find significant intervention/control IQ differences at their end points, although, as noted, Syracuse and Houston later found evidence of academic benefits, as also did some variations of the Verbal Interaction Project. Child IQ and academic benefits appear to have eroded quickly in the case of the Mobile Unit for Child Health (Gutelius et al. 1977).

The importance of providing young children with safer environments, better nutrition, and better dental and health care is obvious.

The evidence is also mixed on the value of continuing to provide intervention for graduates of preschool programs into public school. In their summary of findings from a Follow-Through project in a northern urban area, Seitz and colleagues (1983) found that Follow-Through children had higher IQs at the program end point than did children not in the program, and they earned higher scores on academic tests of math and general knowledge at the end of third grade. The findings through eighth grade showed that Follow-Through graduates continued to demonstrate modest positive effects. Their academic test scores declined less over the years than those of the controls, although there were some group and gender differences in this regard and positive effects were not found in all areas tested—there were none in reading, for example.

For children in the Abecedarian study, the effects of the school-age program were weaker than those of the preschool program. There was no evidence that having the three years of follow-up in the primary grades helped to maintain IQ gains even through age eight. The reading-score means through age 15 favor the group that had both preschool and school-age follow-through, but the difference between preschool graduates with and without the follow-through pro-

gram was not significant by then. The preschool effect was even stronger for mathematics; by age 15 there was no longer an advantage associated with having had the school-age program in addition to preschool (Campbell & Ramey 1995).

Socioemotional outcomes

Socioemotional outcomes for children can be roughly grouped into three categories: behavioral adjustment, attitudes and attributions, and self-concept. Socioemotional outcomes for parents largely consisted of measures of maternal behaviors, such as affection and punitiveness.

An important socioemotional benefit associated with the Prenatal/Early Infancy Program was a reduction in child abuse and neglect within families of children who participated in the program. Parents involved with the Houston program were observed to be more affectionate and less punitive with their children, and mothers treated in the Verbal Interaction Program were observed to behave more positively toward their children than did control mothers.

Where follow-up data are available, it appears that intervention/control differences in socioemotional development have generally been short-term. Head Start researchers found strong positive effects on immediate behavioral adjustment in school, but this difference dropped sharply during the first year (McKey et al. 1985). Mothers of children in the Infant Health and Development program rated their three-year-olds lower on problem behaviors than did mothers of children who did not participate, but this difference was not found when the children were five (Brooks-Gunn et al. 1994). Kindergarten observers rated children served in the Brookline program significantly higher on "social adjustment" and "use of time," compared to controls, yet an effect was not seen by second grade. Children served in the Syracuse Family Development Program were rated as superior in socioemotional functioning in kindergarten, but by first grade they sought teacher attention in negative ways.

It would be interesting, however, to have more long-term follow-up on behavioral adjustment. A follow-up of

Many such children are born to young mothers who need to finish school. For them, and for all students who will eventually become parents, there is a lack of school curricula directed toward parenthood. For teenage parents, regular school curricula could be combined with child care and parent training at school sites, benefiting both parent and child.

the Syracuse sample showed that girls who had participated in the program were more positive toward peers in adolescence. When participants in the Yale Child Welfare program were followed up after 10 years, boys who had participated in the program had better behavioral adjustment that did control boys (Seitz & Provence 1990). The Syracuse study found that program participants had fewer court records for delinquent acts, and the Perry Preschool Project found that program graduates had fewer arrests (Schweinhart & Weikart 1980).

Not all socioemotional differences associated with intervention were positive. The primary-grade teachers in the Milwaukee project described program graduates as less cooperative and less compliant than their controls. As noted, Syracuse program graduates displayed some negative behaviors toward teachers in first grade. Haskins (1985) found that primary-grade teachers rated children who had the Abecedarian preschool services higher on verbal and physical aggression than Abecedarian preschool controls.

As for attitudes, some investigators reported positive effects of early childhood programs on children's academic motivation and self-concepts. The Early Training Project, the Perry Preschool Project, and the Verbal Interaction Project found a significant difference in the proportion of program graduates who reported being proud of themselves for academic achievement, in contrast to

This brief survey of selected early childhood programs shows that providing appropriate and stimulating learning environments for young children of low-income families and supporting parents in their role benefit both parent and child. Many participants made higher academic test scores and better progress through school, as reflected in fewer retentions, fewer placements into special education, and high rates of graduation. Parents made positive changes in their own educational and employment levels and showed reductions in child abuse and neglect. Early childhood programs clearly do help overcome the barriers imposed by impoverishment.

control subjects, but this finding was mainly true of younger program graduates—it was not true for groups aged 15–19 (Lazar et al. 1982). Schwein-hart and Weikart (1980) found that their program graduates placed a higher value on education at age 15. Meta-analysis of Head Start outcomes suggest immediate, small, positive effects on both self-esteem and academic motivation, but both dropped sharply after one year in school. Academic motivation, however, appeared to make a modest recovery during the third year. Abecedarian program graduates scored more like middle-class peers on achievement attributions in the primary years (Walden & Ramey 1983), but this effect did not persist into adolescence (Campbell 1995).

> **Politicians stress the importance of "family values" but are curiously silent on urging business leaders to provide family supports.**

> **Those who are quick to discount the importance of early childhood programs have not suggested constructive alternatives.**

Health, dental, and nutritional benefits

The importance of providing young children with safer environments, better nutrition, and better dental and health care is obvious. The investigators of the Prenatal/ Early Infancy Project found a reduction in accidents and poison ingestions within homes of participating children. The better nutrition associated with Head Start resulted in both higher growth rates and higher serum levels of iron and other beneficial trace elements. There is not clear evidence of a lasting reduction in rates of illness for Head Start versus non-Head Start children, even though Head Start children had better rates of immunization. Head Start children had better dental care and more dental treatment than did non-Head Start children (McKey et al. 1985). These important outcomes are based on site-specific studies; the long-term consequences of these benefits are not known, but even if not sustained, they were clearly important in their own right at the time.

Summary

This brief survey of selected early childhood programs shows that providing appropriate and stimulating learning environments for young children from low-income families and supporting parents in their role benefit both parent and child. Many of the surveyed programs demonstrated modest but long-lasting IQ gains, and participants in many programs made higher academic test scores and better progress through school, as reflected in fewer retentions, fewer placements into special education, and high rates of graduation. Parents made positive changes in their own educational and employment levels and showed reductions in child abuse and neglect. Early childhood programs clearly do help overcome the barriers imposed by impoverishment.

No one model emerges as clearly superior to another: positive benefits were found for limited interventions as well as for the most massive. The findings imply that cognitive gains are greater when intervention begins in very early childhood, but questions remain about the socioemotional effects of this practice. With more and more children needing early care, it is essential that such care be of the highest quality. Clearly, particular attention also should be paid to socioemotional factors. More research on how best to foster healthy emotional growth in young children is needed.

There are no easy answers on best practices for children from low-income families. Many such children are born to young mothers who need to finish school. For them, and for all students who will eventually become parents, there is a lack of school curricula directed toward parenthood. For teenage parents, regular school curricula could be combined with child care and parent training at school sites, benefiting both parent and child. However, it is difficult to fit yet another subject into a

> **Business and industry could do much more for families. If child care were provided at work sites, with work schedules flexible enough to allow parents—especially breast-feeding mothers—to visit infants during the day, both parent and child would greatly benefit. Management could provide parent education classes on site, with child care continuing through the instruction period. This would support parents in their role as nurturing caregivers as well as financial providers for their children. Further, primary health and dental care could be provided at work sites. Such coordination of services could greatly enhance the health and well-being of young children.**

The message for lawmakers is plain. If parents are to work, high-quality child care must be provided from the earliest years, and programs for young children will have to be greatly expanded. Early childhood professionals can help by urging their lawmakers to support quality programs for preschoolers. Low-income families could be supported through stipends for quality child care services. Schools and businesses should be given all possible incentives for providing child care and family supports. It does make a difference.

crowded school day, and only a few states mandate curricula for parenting. Schools where child care is available are almost nonexistent.

Business and industry could do much more for families. If child care were provided at work sites, with work schedules flexible enough to allow parents—especially breast-feeding mothers—to visit infants during the day, both parent and child would greatly benefit. Management could provide parent education classes on site, with child care continuing through the instruction period. This would support parents in their role as nurturing caregivers as well as financial providers for their children. Further, primary health and dental care could be provided at work sites. Such coordination of services could greatly enhance the health and well-being of young children.

© Francis Wardle

Politicians stress the importance of "family values" but are curiously silent on urging business leaders to provide family supports. Tax incentives could be given to corporations that have family-enhancing benefit plans. Leaders in education, business, and industry will have to make a strong commitment to young children and their families for this to happen on a broad scale. Those who are quick to discount the importance of early childhood programs have not suggested constructive alternatives. Early childhood programs ultimately save taxpayer dollars in terms of reductions in the costs of education, welfare, and crime (Berrueta-Clement et al. 1984). These benefits are associated with child and family interventions provided in the preschool years. The message for lawmakers is plain. If parents are to work, high-quality child care must be provided from the earliest years, and programs for young children will have to be greatly expanded. Early childhood professionals can help by urging their lawmakers to support quality programs for preschoolers. Low-income families could be supported through stipends for quality child care services. Schools and businesses should be

given all possible incentives for providing child care and family supports. It does make a difference.

References

Berrueta-Clement, J.R., L.J. Schweinhart, W.S. Barnett, A.S. Epstein, & D.P. Weikart. 1984. *Changed lives: The effects of the Perry Preschool Program on youths through age 19.* Monographs of the High/Scope Educational Research Foundation, no. 8. Ypsilanti, MI: High/Scope.

Bronfenbrenner, U. 1974. Is early intervention effective? *Day Care and Early Education* 44 (1): 12–18.

Brooks-Gunn, J., C.M. McCarton, P.H. Casey, M.C. McCormick, C.R. Bauer, J.C. Bernbaum, J. Tyson, M. Swanson, F.C. Bennett, D.T. Scott, J. Tonascia, & C.L. Meinert. 1994. Early intervention in low-birth-weight premature infants: Results through age 5 years in the Infant Health and Development Program. *Journal of the American Medical Association* 272 (16): 1257–62.

Early childhood programs ultimately save taxpayer dollars in terms of reductions in the costs of education, welfare, and crime.

Campbell, F.A. 1995. *The development of academic self-concept and its relationship to academic performance and self-esteem: A longitudinal study of African American students.* Paper presented at biennial meeting of Society for Research in Child Development, March, Indianapolis, IN.

Campbell, F.A., & C.T. Ramey. 1995. Cognitive and school outcomes for high-risk African American students at middle adolescence: Positive effects of early intervention. *American Educational Research Journal* 32 (4): 743–72.

Cicirelli, V.G. 1969. *The impact of Head Start: An evaluation of the effects of Head Start on children's cognitive and affective development, Vol. 1.* Athens: Westinghouse Learning Corp., Ohio University.

Connell, R.W. 1994. Poverty and education. *Harvard Educational Review* 64 (2): 125–49.

Garber, H.L. 1988. *The Milwaukee Project: Prevention of mental retardation in children at risk.* Washington, DC: American Association on Mental Retardation.

Gray, S.W., B.K. Ramsey, & R.A. Klaus. 1982. *From 3 to 20: The Early Training Project.* Baltimore: University Park.

Gutelius, M.F., A.D. Kirsch, S. MacDonald, M.R. Brooks, & T. McErlean. 1977. Controlled study of child health supervision: Behavioral results. *Pediatrics* 60 (3): 294–304.

Gutelius, M.F., A.D. Kirsch, S. MacDonald, M.R. Brooks, T. McErlean, & C. Newcomb. 1972. Promising results from a cognitive stimulation program in infancy: A preliminary report. *Clinical Pediatrics* 11 (10): 585–93.

Haskins, R. 1985. Public school aggression among children with varying daycare experience. *Child Development* 56 (3): 689–703.

Infant Health and Development Program. 1990. Enhancing the outcomes of low-birthweight, premature infants: A multisite, randomized trial. *Pediatrics* 263 (22): 3035–42.

Johnson, D.L., & T. Walker. 1991. A follow-up evaluation of the Houston Parent-Child Development Center: School performance. *Journal of Early Intervention* 15 (3): 226–36.

Lally, J.R., P.L. Mangione, & A.S. Honig. 1988. The Syracuse University Family Development Research Program: Long-range impact on an early intervention with low-income children and their families. In *Annual advances in applied developmental psychology, Vol. 3. Parent education as early childhood intervention: Emerging directions in theory, research, and practice,* eds. I.E. Sigel & D.R. Powell, 79–104. Norwood, NJ: Ablex.

Lazar, I., R. Darlington, H. Murray, J. Royce, & A. Snipper. 1982. *Lasting effects of early education: A report from the Consortium for Longitudinal Studies.* Monographs of the Society for Research in Child Development Vol. 47, No. 2–3, Serial No. 195.

Levinstein, P., J. O'Hara, & J. Madden. 1983. The mother-child home program of the Verbal Interaction Program. In *As the twig is bent: Lasting effects of preschool programs,* ed. Consortium for Longitudinal Studies, 237–64. Hillsdale, NJ: Lawrence Earlbaum.

McKey, R.H., L. Condelli, H. Ganson, B.J. Barrett, C. McConkey, & M.C. Plantz. 1985. *The impact of Head Start on children, families, and communities.* Department of Health and Human Services Publication No. (OHDS) 90-31193. Washington, DC: U.S. Government Printing Office.

Olds, D. 1988. The Prenatal/Early Infancy Project. In *14 ounces of prevention: A casebook for practitioners,* eds. R.H. Price, E.L. Cowen, R.P. Lorion, & J. Ramon-McKay, 9–23. Washington, DC: American Psychological Association.

Palmer, F.H. 1983. The Harlem Study: Effects by type of training, age of training, and social class. In *As the twig is bent: Lasting effects of preschool programs,* ed. Consortium for Longitudinal Studies, 201–36. Hillsdale, NJ: Lawrence Earlbaum.

Patterson, C.J., J.B. Kupersmidt, & N.A. Vaden. 1990. Income level, gender, ethnicity, and household composition as predictors of children's school-based competence. *Child Development* 61 (2): 485–94.

Pierson, D.E. 1988. The Brookline Early Education Project. In *14 ounces of prevention: A casebook for practitioners,* eds. R.H. Price, E.L. Cowen, R.P. Lorion, & J. Ramon-McKay, 24–31. Washington, DC: American Psychological Association.

Provence, S., & A. Naylor. 1983. *Working with disadvantaged parents and their children.* New Haven, CT: Yale University Press.

Ramey, C.T., & F.A. Campbell. 1991. Poverty, early childhood education, and academic competence: The Abecedarian experiment. In *Children in poverty,* ed. A. Huston, 190–221. New York: Cambridge University Press.

Reynolds, A.J. 1994. Effects of a preschool plus follow-on intervention for children at risk. *Developmental Psychology* 30 (6): 787–804.

Schweinhart, L.J., & D.P. Weikart. 1980. *Young children grow up: The effects of the Perry Preschool Program on youth through age 15.* Monographs of the High Scope Educational Research Foundation, no. 7. Ypsilanti, MI: High/Scope.

Schweinhart, L.J., H.V. Barnes, & D.P. Weikart. 1993. *Significant benefits: The High/Scope Perry Preschool study through age 27.* Monographs of the High Scope Educational Research Foundation, no. 10. Ypsilanti, MI: High/Scope.

Seitz, V., & S. Provence. 1990. Caregiver-focused models of early intervention. In *Handbook of early childhood intervention,* eds. S. Meisels & J. Shonkoff, 400–27. New York: Cambridge University Press.

Seitz, V., N.H. Apfel, L.K. Rosenbaum, & E. Zigler. 1983. Long-term effects of projects Head Start and Follow-Through: The New Haven Project. In *As the twig is bent: Lasting effects of preschool programs,* ed. Consortium for Longitudinal Studies, 299–332. Hillsdale, NJ: Lawrence Earlbaum.

Walden, T., & C.T. Ramey. 1983. Locus of control and academic achievement: Results of a preschool intervention program. *Journal of Educational Psychology* 75 (3): 865–76.

Wasik, B.H., C.T. Ramey, D.M. Bryant, & J.J. Sparling. 1990. A longitudinal study of two early intervention strategies: Project CARE. *Child Development* 61 (6): 1682–96.

Helping Children Become More Prosocial: Ideas for Classrooms, Families, Schools, and Communities

Alice S. Honig and Donna S. Wittmer

Alice Sterling Honig, Ph.D., professor of child development at Syracuse University in Syracuse, New York, was program director for the Family Development Research Program and has authored numerous books, including Parent Involvement in Early Childhood Education *and* Playtime Learning Games for Young Children. *She directs the annual Syracuse Quality Infant/Toddler Caregiving Workshop.*

Donna Sasse Wittmer, Ph.D., is assistant professor in early childhood education at the University of Colorado in Denver. She has had extensive experience directing, training in, and conducting research in early childhood care and education programs.

Part 1 of this review of strategies and techniques to enhance prosocial development focused on techniques that teachers and parents can use with individual children or small groups of children (see Wittmer & Honig, Encouraging Positive Social Development in Young Children, *Young Children* 49 [5]: 4–12). Part 2 offers suggestions for involving whole classrooms, entire school systems, parents, and communities in creating classroom and home climates for kindness, cooperation, generosity, and helpfulness.

Child-sensitive, high-quality care in classrooms promotes prosocial behaviors

If you thought so, you were right. Here is more information to back you up. Peaceful play and cooperation are more likely to occur when teachers set up developmentally appropriate classrooms (Bredekamp & Rosegrant 1992). Staff competence and years of teacher experience are significant factors in ensuring such quality care. In one research study the more highly trained and stable the preschool staff were, the *lower* were teacher-rated and observed preschool aggression scores, despite children's varying histories of full-time or part-time nonparental care during infancy and toddlerhood (Park & Honig 1991). In another study 4-year-olds in a constructivist classroom, given many opportunities for choices and autonomous construction of attitudes, principles, and social problem-solving strategies, showed higher social-cognitive skills than their peers from another preschool program with whom they played board games (DeVries & Goncu 1990).

Children in strongly adult-directed preschool classrooms engage in less prosocial behavior than do children in classrooms that encourage more child-initiated learning and interactions (Huston-Stein, Friedrich-Cofer, & Susman 1977). In a longitudinal study of 19-year-olds who had attended either a highly adult-directed preschool or a program

© Elisabeth Nichols

From *Young Children*, January 1996, pp. 62-70. © 1996 by the National Association for the Education of Young Children. Reprinted by permission.

that emphasized child initiations much more, the teenagers who had been in the latter program were more socially competent and had fewer juvenile delinquency convictions (Schweinhart, Weikart, & Larner 1986).

Howes and Stewart (1987) discovered that children who experience high-quality child care and supportive parents acquire the *ability to decode and regulate emotional signals in peer play.* Social sensitivity to others' cues and needs is a good predictor of positive peer relations. Unfortunately, the researchers also found that families who are the most stressed choose the lowest quality child care arrangements, are the most likely to change arrangements, and have children with the lowest levels of competence during social play with peers. A community resource-and-referral agency may be the best source of materials and information to help families recognize and choose high-quality child care and to inform parents about NAEYC accreditation.

Emphasize cooperation rather than competition

Every experienced preschool teacher surely wants young children to be prepared to succeed in their school learning careers. Competitive classrooms result in some children becoming tense, fearing failure, and becoming less motivated to persist at challenging tasks. In a cooperative-interaction classroom, the emphasis is on children working together to accomplish mutual goals (Aronson, Bridgeman, & Geffner 1978). Even toddlers can work together in cooperative play. For example, if each grasps the opposite end of a towel and both coordinate efforts, they can keep a beach ball bouncing on the towel.

Every child has an essential and unique contribution to make

to class learning. One teaching tool has been called the "jigsaw technique" because the teacher provides each child with one piece of information about a lesson; then the children must work cooperatively with each other to learn all the material and information necessary for a complete presentation by the group (Aronson et al. 1978).

We have referred here only to a few studies emphasizing the positive outcomes of cooperative learning environments, but surely our readers have read about this in numerous books and articles in recent years!

Teach cooperative and conflict-resolution games and sports

Caregiver creativity in initiating group games and in devising conflict-resolution games promotes peace in the classroom (Kreidler 1984). New games and variations of traditional children's games and sports that encourage cooperation rather than competition facilitate prosocial interactions (Orlick 1982, 1985; Prutzman et al. 1988). When Musical Chairs is played so that each time a chair is taken away, the "leftover" child must find a lap to sit on rather than be forced out of the game, no child feels left out or a failure. Bos (1990) provides examples of such games. In Spider Swing one child sits on the lap of another, with legs hanging out the back of the swing. Bos calls games in which children play cooperatively together to create pleasure and fun "coaction." Why not try these and invent some of your own?

Of course, even more important than an occasional game is helping children live cooperatively in the classroom every day and resolve personal conflicts peaceably.

Set up classroom spaces and play materials to facilitate cooperative play

Arrangements of space and varieties of toys and learning materials affect whether children act more aggressively or cooperate more peacefully. A small, cluttered play area can lead to more tension and fights. A group seesaw, a tire-bouncer, or a nylon parachute encourage group cooperation because the children *need* each other to maximize their enjoyment.

In the research we reviewed, more prosocial responses were given by young children attending child care or nursery school programs when (1) a variety of age-appropriate materials were available and (2) space was arranged to accommodate groups of varying sizes (Holloway & Reichhart-Erickson 1988). Children who played with large hollow blocks and unit blocks in a large block area of their preschool learned and practiced positive social problem-solving skills rather than aggression (Rogers 1987). Yet, where preschoolers are crowded together in a narrow area with large blocks, there is greater pressure to use the blocks as missiles or pretend guns.

Classroom layout affects children's emotional security and sense of free choice in play. Combine your environmental design skills with your expertise in early childhood education to arrange class traffic patterns that maximize peaceful interactions. Think through the placement of clearly defined and well-supplied interest centers; provide unobstructed access to materials; give aesthetic attention to color and wall decorations; and decrease clutter. Arrange inviting spaces with soft cushions for children to nestle on when they need to calm down or rest when distressed.

Your executive space-planning skills can promote more comfortable feelings conducive to a more harmonious, cooperative classroom climate.

Use bibliotherapy: Incorporate children's literature to enhance empathy and caring in daily reading activities

A growing number of preschool and primary teachers do use bibliotherapy. If you do not, you may find this a good time to begin!

Choose children's literature for prosocial themes and characters that provide altruistic models. *Two Good Friends* (by Judy Delton) is the charming story of how two friends—Bear, who is messy but a fine cook, and Duck, who is tidy but a poor cook—care for each other lovingly and generously. Dr. Seuss's Horton the Elephant is that kind of prosocial character in the books *Horton Hears a Who* and *Horton Hatches an Egg*. So is the king's young page boy in Seuss's *The King's Stilts*. And so is *The Little Engine That Could,* as she chugs courageously up and over a very tall mountain to bring toys to boys and girls. Sucking his thumb vigorously, one little boy listened enraptured as his caregiver read the story of the brave little engine who did not want to disappoint the children. The child kept nodding his head and whispering to himself, "That was very nice of her! That was very nice of her!"

McMath (1989) suggests asking open-ended questions that help children think about and understand the motives and actions of storybook characters. When skilled adults read stories that feature altruistic characters, they promote children's ability to grasp socioemotional motivations and motivate children to imitate empathic and helpful responses (Dreikurs, Grunwald, & Pepper 1982). Many publishers, such as the Albert Whitman Company, provide children's books that adults can read to young chil-

dren to help them cope with and find adaptive solutions to disturbing personal concerns, such as living with family alcoholism, parental divorce, or domestic violence.

Actively lead group discussions on prosocial interactions

Some teachers focus on developing supportive classroom communities. Discussion of social interactions within the group is usually a central part of the curriculum in this kind of classroom.

Sharing increases among preschool children whose teachers give them explanations as to *why* sharing is important and *how* to share (Barton & Osborne 1978). Some second-grade teachers daily set aside brief classroom time to encourage children to discuss specific incidents in which they and their classmates were helpful and kind with one another. After one month, prosocial interactions increased about twofold among these children, compared with a randomly assigned group of control children (Honig & Pollack 1990).

As a teacher, you have learned a great deal about the individual interests and talents of your children. During show-and-tell circle times you can extend group discussion to increase children's awareness of *distributive justice*—how goods and benefits are distributed justly among people with varying needs, temperaments, talents, and troubles. Lively discussions can center around what is "fair" or not so fair. Children between 4 and 8 years old are busy learning rules for games and rules for social relations, and they are often concerned about fairness and who gets advantages. Yet, preschoolers are capable of realizing, for example, that at meal and snack times, rigid equality in distributing food would not be the best plan if one child habitu-

ally comes to school without breakfast and is very hungry.

Young children often protest if there is not strict equality in distributing goodies. Many a teacher or parent has heard the protest, "That's not fair. He got more than me!" Through discussions, children can move from a position of belief in strict equality in treat or toy distribution toward awareness of the concepts of *equity and benevolence*—that is, the idea that the special needs of others must be taken into account (Damon 1977).

Talk about taking turns and about *different* ways each child gets some special time or privilege, although not exactly the same as another receives. These talks can be especially helpful for preschoolers who are distressed because Mama is now nursing a new baby and seemingly gives lots more time and attention to the tiny new stranger. Caregiver kindness lies not only in providing extra nurturing for that preschooler during this difficult time but also in assisting all the children to think through issues of neediness and fairness. As you help children to learn about "turn taking" through group discussions, you increase their understanding of fairness. Although in some families it may be a new baby's turn to get special attention, such as nursing, preschoolers now get other kinds of special attention from parents, such as a story reading at bedtime or a chance to help with cooking, a household repair job, or some other special activity in which a baby cannot participate.

Encourage social interaction between normally developing children and children with special needs

Teachers must initiate specific friendship-building strategies when atypical children in an inclusive classroom exhibit low-level prosocial skills. Activities to promote classroom friendship are available (Fox 1980; Smith 1982; Edwards 1986; Wolf 1986). Children with disabilities need your inventive interventions to learn how to make a friend, use positive and assertive techniques to enter a play group, and *sustain* friendly play bouts with peers (Honig & Thompson 1994). Promotion of specific friendship skills to enhance the social integration of typical and atypical children requires well-planned teacher strategies and initiatives. Prosocial interactions of children with disabilities may need a boost. Some typical preschoolers also may need a boost in their sensitivity to others' difficulties *and* competencies (Gresham 1981; Honig & McCarron 1990).

More than other children, a child with a disability may need help from classmates and the teacher or extra time to finish a project. If you are making preparations to create an inclusive classroom that integrates atypical and typical children, then class discussions about fairness become particularly urgent. Children will need to talk about and struggle with a new idea: strict equal apportionment according to work done may not be the kindest or most prosocial decision in special cases. If a child with cerebral palsy and marked difficulties in hand coordination finishes far fewer placemats than the other children in a class project, she or he has tried just as hard as the others and should receive the same share of any "profits" from the class craft sale.

Develop class and school projects that foster altruism

With the help of a caring teacher, children can think about and decide on a class project to help others (Solomon et al. 1988). Some classes prominently label and display a jar in which they put pennies to donate to hungry children or to families in need at holiday time. When the jar is full, children count the money and compose a joint class letter to the organization to which they are contributing. Other class projects can arise from children's suggestions during group discussion times about troubles that faraway or nearby children are having. Prosocial projects include cleaning up the schoolyard, writing as pen pals to children in troubled lands, collecting toys or food for individuals in need, and making friends with older people during visits to a home for the aged.

Your perceptive knowledge about individuals in the class is especially useful when you encourage each child to generate personal ideas for sharing kindness and caring in her or his own family. As a group, the children may decide to draw their own "helping coupons." Each child creates a gift book with large, hand-drawn coupons. Every coupon promises a helpful act to a parent or family member. Some of the coupons could be "reading my baby sister a story," "setting the table," "sorting socks from the laundry basket into pairs," "sharing my toy cars with my brother," and "brushing my teeth all by myself while Papa puts the baby to bed." Young children dictate their helpful offers for you to write down and then illustrate the coupons with signs and pictures that remind them of what sharing or caring action their coupon represents. Children generously give the coupons to family members as personal gifts— promises of help.

Encourage cooperative in-classroom activities that require several children's joint productive efforts. Ideas include drawing a group mural, building a large boat or space station with blocks and Tinkertoys, planning and producing a puppet show, and sewing a yarn picture that has been outlined on both sides of burlap.

Move very young children with peers to the next age group

Toddlers adjust more positively to movement from one group to a slightly older group in center care when they move with peers. Howes (1987) found that children who stayed in the same child care center with the same peer group increased their proportion of complementary and reciprocal peer play more than did children who changed peer groups within their center. Continuity of quality child care and continuity of peer group relationships are important in the development of a child's feelings of security and social competence. Consider security needs and friendship patterns rather than rigid age criteria in moving young children to a new classroom.

Arrange regular viewing of prosocial media and videogames

Viewing prosocial videos and television programs increases children's social contacts as well as fosters smiling, praising, hugging (Coates, Pusser, & Goodman 1976), sharing, cooperating, turn taking, positive verbal/physical contact (Forge & Phemister 1987), and willingness to help puppies in need (Poulds, Rubinstein, & Leibert 1975). Regular viewing of prosocial television, particularly *Mister Rogers' Neighborhood*, has resulted in higher levels of task persistence, rule obedience, and tolerance of delayed gratification. Children from low-socioeconomic families who watched this program daily showed increased cooperative play, nurturance, and verbalization of feelings (Friedrich & Stein 1973). In contrast, children who were exposed to aggressive videogames donated less to needy children than did children who played prosocial videogames (Chambers 1987).

Invite moral mentors to visit the class

Damon (1988) urges teachers actively to recruit and involve *moral mentors* in the classroom. Invite individuals who have contributed altruistically to better the lives of others in the community to come in and talk about their lives and experiences. Children may be eager to nominate someone in their own family to tell about how they help others. Perhaps Aunt Esther visits a nursing home and livens up senior citizens' days. Perhaps Uncle Irving outfitted the family station wagon with a ramp so he can take people in wheelchairs to weekend ball games. Children learn to reframe their ideas about community helpfulness and personal generosity toward others in trouble if a special guest—a high school swimming star who volunteers as a coach for children with physical impairments, for example—comes to visit and talks about her or his experiences helping others.

Work closely with families for prosocial programming

Families need to know that prosocial interactions are an integral curriculum component of your child care program. As a practicing professional, you use your prosocial skills to support and affirm family members of each child in your classroom. And, of course, you know how your close contact with parents provides you with insight and more sensitive understanding of each child. Parents also need you to share your concern for and emphasis on prosocial classroom activities and goals. During informal greetings at the beginning of the day or at end-of-day pickup times, you may want to affirm how special each parent's role is

in promoting care and concern for others at home (Barnett et al. 1980). Yarrow and colleagues (in Pines 1979) revealed that parents who exhibit tender concern when their very young children experience fright or upset and who firmly discourage aggressive actions to solve squabbles have children who show very early signs of concern and empathy for others' troubles. These personal examples of "baby altruism" persist into elementary school (Pines 1979).

In interviews 10 years after graduation from a program that emphasized caring and prosocial development in outreach with families as well as in high-quality group care, teenagers and their families reported that they felt more family support, closeness, and appreciation than did control youth. Compared with members of the control group, the adolescents also had far lower rates of juvenile delinquency (Lally, Mangione, & Honig 1988).

Establish a parent resource lending library

Interested parents will appreciate being able to browse through prosocial articles in your child care facility. For example, make available a copy of Kobak's (1979) brief article on how she embeds caring and awareness of positive social interactions in all classroom activities, dialogues, and projects. Her concept of a *caring quotient* (CQ) classroom emphasizes the importance of children learning positive social interaction skills as well as intellectual (IQ) skills. Social problem solving by a class must take into consideration that the child whose problem is being brainstormed has to feel that the class members *care* about him or her as they explore ways to resolve a problem, such as chronic truancy or a book borrowed from a teacher and never returned.

Convince parents of the importance of a specific focus on prosocial as well as cognitive curriculum through displays of brief, easy-to-read reports of research articles. The Abecedarian program provides powerful research findings (Finkelstein 1982). Children who had attended this infant and preschool program that emphasized cognitive development were 15 times more aggressive with kindergarten peers than a control group of children who had not been in child care or who had attended community child care. A prosocial curriculum was then instituted for future waves of children in the program; the difference in aggression between program children and their peers in kindergarten subsequently disappeared, according to later evaluations.

Promote a bias-free curriculum

A bias-free curriculum promotes more prosocial interactions among children despite multicultural differences in ethnicity, language, or family background (Derman-Sparks & the A.B.C. Task Force 1989). Emphasize how all children and adults feel better and get a fairer chance when others treat them courteously and kindly. Children who feel that others are *more,* rather than less, similar to themselves behave more prosocially toward them (Feshbach 1978). During class meeting times, children discover how much alike they are—in having special family members they feel close to, in enjoying a picnic or an outing with family, in playing with friends, and in wanting to feel safe, well-loved, and cared about.

Require responsibility: Encourage children to care for younger children and classmates who need extra help

Anthropologists, studying six different cultures, noted that when children help care for younger siblings and interact with a cross-age variety of children in social groups in nonschool settings, then children feel more responsible for the welfare of the group and gain more skills in nurturing (Whiting & Whiting 1975).

Children should be given responsibility, commensurate with their abilities, to care for and help teach younger children or children who may need extra personal help in the classroom. In a long-term study of at-risk infants born on the island of Kauai, children who carried out such caring actions of *required helpfulness* were more likely 32 years later to be positively socially functioning as family members and as community citizens (Werner 1986).

Become familiar with structured curriculum packages that promote prosocial development

Complete program packages are available with materials and specific ideas as well as activities for enhancing prosocial behaviors in the classroom. Shure's (1992) daily lesson plans give step-by-step techniques for teaching how the feelings or wishes of one child may be the same or different from those of another child and how to challenge children to think of the consequences of their behaviors and to think up alternatives to inappropriate or hurtful behaviors in solving their social problems. *Communicating to Make Friends* (Fox 1980) provides 18 weeks of planned activities to promote peer acceptance. Dinkmeyer and Dinkmeyer's *Developing Understanding of Self and Others* (1982) provides puppets, activity cards, charts, and audiocassettes to promote children's awareness of others' feelings and social skills. The Abecedarian

program instituted *My Friends and Me* (Davis 1977) to promote more prosocial development.

Arrange Bessell and Palomares's (1973) Magic Circle lessons so that children, each day during a safe, nonjudgmental circle time, feel *secure enough to share* their stories, feelings, and memories about times they have had troubles with others, times when they have been helped by others, and times when they have been thoughtful and caring on behalf of others.

Commercial sources also provide some materials that directly support teacher attempts to introduce peace programs and conflict-resolution programs in their classrooms (e.g., Young People's Press, San Diego). Sunrise Books (Provo, Utah) is a commercial source of book and video materials for teachers and parents to promote positive discipline and conflict resolution. One book by Nelson (n.d.) features the use of class meetings, a technique that builds cooperation, communication, and problem solving so that classmates' mutual respect and accountability increase.

Watkins and Durant (1992) provide pre-K to second-grade teachers with specific classroom techniques for prevention of antisocial behaviors. They suggest the right times to *ignore* inappropriate behavior and specify other situations when the teacher must use *control*. Teachers are taught to look for signs that they may actually be rewarding socially inappropriate behavior by their responses. The use of subtle, nonverbal cues of dress, voice control, and body language are recommended in order to promote children's more positive behaviors.

Implement a comprehensive school-based prosocial program that emphasizes ethical teaching

John Gatto, a recipient of the

New York City Teacher of the Year award in 1990, admitted, "The children I teach are cruel to each other, they lack compassion for misfortune, they laugh at weakness, they have contempt for people whose need for help shows too plainly" (Wood 1991, 7).

Wood urges teachers to conceptualize a more ethical style of teaching that he calls "maternal teaching." He suggests that teachers develop a routine of morning meetings that involve greetings and cooperation, as in singing together. Children feel personally valued when they are greeted by name as they enter a school. Classes can create rules of courtesy for and with each other, and the rules should be prominently posted. Wood urges teachers to "figure out a way to teach recess and lunch . . . . When children come in from recess, the teacher often can spend another half hour of instructional time sorting out the hurt feelings and hurt bodies and hurt stories she wasn't even there to see or hear" (1991, 8). Children can be taught the power of "please" and "thank you." Role playing helps them become aware of how hurtful name-calling and verbal put-downs are. You, of course, are a powerful positive model of social courtesies as you listen to each child's ideas and give each a turn to talk at mealtime and grouptime. Help children feel all-school ownership. Flowers and tablecloths in school lunchrooms can be incentives for making lunchtime a friendly and positive experience.

Brown and Solomon (1983) have translated prosocial research for application throughout school systems. In the California Bay Area, they implemented a comprehensive program in several elementary schools to increase prosocial attitudes and behavior among the children and their families. In the program the following occur:

Suggested Books for Classroom Parents' Library

Bos, B. 1990. *Together we're better: Establishing a coactive learning environment.* Roseville, CA: Turn the Page Press.

Briggs, D. 1975. *Your child's self-esteem.* New York: Dolphin.

Crary, E. 1990. *Kids can cooperate: A practical guide to teaching problem solving.* Seattle, WA: Parenting Press.

Damon, W. 1988. *The moral child: Nurturing children's natural moral growth.* New York: Free Press.

Feshbach, N., & S. Feshbach. 1983. *Learning to care: Classroom activities for social and affective development.* Glenview, IL: Scott Foresman.

Finkelstein, N. 1982. Aggression: Is it stimulated by day care? *Young Children* 37 (6): 3–13.

Gordon, T. 1975. *Parent effectiveness training.* New York: Plume.

Honig, A. 1996. *Developmentally appropriate behavior guidance for infants and toddlers from birth to 3 years.* Little Rock, AR: Southern Early Childhood Association.

Kobak, D. 1970. Teaching young children to care. *Children Today* 8 (6–7): 34–35.

Orlick, T. 1985. *The second cooperative sports and games book.* New York: Pantheon.

Shure, M. 1994. *Raising a thinking child: Help your young child to resolve everyday conflicts and get along with others.* New York: Henry Holt.

Smith, C. 1993. *The peaceful classroom: 162 easy activities to teach preschoolers compassion and cooperation.* Mount Rainier, MD: Gryphon House.

Wolf, P., ed. 1986. *Connecting: Friendship in the lives of young children and their teachers.* Redmond, WA: Exchange Press.

Train older children as peer mediators

In some New York City schools and elsewhere in the United States, the Resolving Conflict Creatively Program (RCCP) trains fifth-graders as peer mediators to move to situations of social conflict, such as a playground fight, and help the participants resolve their problems. RCCP rules mandate that each child in a conflict be given a chance by the peer mediators to describe and explain the problem from her or his viewpoint and to try to agree on how to settle the problem. Peer mediators are trained in nonviolent and creative ways of dealing with social conflicts (RCCP, 163 Third Avenue # 239, New York, NY 10003).

Teachers of kindergarten and primary children may want to look into this. Think how much influence the "big kids" would have on *your* children!

1. Children from about age 6 onward, with adult supervision, take responsibility for caring for younger children.

2. Cooperative learning requires that children work with each other in learning teams within classes.

3. Children are involved in structured programs of helpful and useful activities, such as visiting the elderly or shut-ins, making toys for others, cleaning up or gardening in nearby parks and playgrounds.

4. Children of mixed ages engage in activities.

5. Children help with home chores on a regular basis with parental approval and cooperation.

6. Children regularly role-play situations in which they can experience feelings of being a victim *and* a helper.

7. The entire elementary school recognizes and rewards caring, helping, taking responsibility, and other prosocial behaviors, whether they occur at home or at school.

8. Children learn about prosocial adult models in films, television, and their own community. The children watch for such models in the news media and clip newspaper articles about prosocially acting persons. They also invite such models to tell their stories in class.

9. Empathy training includes children's exposure to examples of animals or children in distress, in real life or staged episodes. They hear adults comment on how to help someone in trouble, and they watch examples of helpfulness.

10. Continuity and total saturation in a school program create a climate that *communicates prosocial expectations and supports children's learning and enacting prosocial behaviors* both at home and in school.

Cherish the children: Create an atmosphere of affirmation through family/classroom/community rituals

Loving rituals—such as a group greeting song that names and welcomes each child individually every morning, or leisurely and soothing backrubs given at naptime in a darkened room—establish a climate of caring in the child care classroom.

College students who scored high on an empathy scale remembered their parents as having been empathic and affectionate when the students were younger (Barnett et al. 1980). Egeland and Sroufe (1981), in a series of longitudinal research studies, reported devastating effects from the lack of early family cherishing of infants and young children. (Of course, therapists' offices and prisons are full of people who were not loved in their early years.)

A warm smile or an arm around the shoulder lets a child know he or she is valued and cared for. Encourage children to tell something special about their relationship to a particular child on that child's birthday. Write down these birthday stories in a personal book for each child. An attitude of affirmation creates an environment in which children feel safe, secure, accepted, and loved (Salkowski 1991). Special holiday celebration times, such as Thanksgiving, Abraham Lincoln's birthday, Father's Day, and Mother's Day, offer opportunities to create ritual class activities and to illustrate ceremonies and appropriate

behaviors for expressing caring and thankfulness.

Teachers are bombarded with books and articles about the importance of developing positive self-esteem in each child and how to attempt to instill it. Many of these sources contain important and helpful ideas (see Honig & Wittmer 1992).

Sometimes children come into care from such stressful situations that it is hard for them to control their own sadness and anger. One teacher uses a "Magic Feather Duster" to brush off troubles and upsets from children. A preschooler arriving in child care aggravated and upset announces, "Teacher, I think you better get the Magic Feather

Duster to brush off all the 'bad vibes'!" After the teacher carefully and tenderly uses her magic duster, the child sighs, relaxes, and feels ready to enter into the atmosphere of a caring and peaceful classroom. Each teacher creates her or his own magic touches to help children feel secure, calm, and cooperative.

The more cherished a child is, the less likely he or she is to bully others *or* to be rejected by other children. The more nurturing parents and caregivers are—the more positive affection and responsive, empathic care they provide—the more positively children will relate in social interactions with teachers, caring adults, and peers and in coooperating with classroom learning goals, as well.

References

Aronson, E., D. Bridgeman, & R. Geffner. 1978. Interdependent interactions and prosocial behavior. *Journal of Research and Development in Education* 12 (1): 16–27.

Aronson, E., C. Stephan, J. Sikes, N. Blaney, & M. Snapp. 1978. *The jigsaw classroom.* Beverly Hills, CA: Sage.

Barnett, M., J. Howard, L. King, & G. Dino. 1980. Empathy in young children: Relation to parents' empathy, affection, and emphasis on the feelings of others. *Developmental Psychology* 16: 243–44.

Barton, E.J., & J.G. Osborne. 1978. The development of classroom sharing by a teacher using positive practice. *Behavior Modification* 2: 231–51.

Bessell, H., & U. Palomares. 1973. *Methods in human development: Theory manual.* El Cajun, CA: Human Development Training Institute.

Bos, B. 1990. *Together we're better: Establishing a coactive learning environment.* Roseville, CA: Turn the Page Press.

Bredekamp, S., & T. Rosegrant, eds. 1992. *Reaching potentials: Appropriate curriculum and assessment for young children.* Vol. 1. Washington, DC: NAEYC.

Brown, D., & D. Solomon. 1983. A model for prosocial learning: An in-progress field study. In *The nature of prosocial development: Interdisciplinary theories and strategies*, ed. D.L. Bridgeman. New York: Academic.

Chambers, J. 1987. The effects of prosocial and aggressive videogames on children's donating and helping. *Journal of Genetic Psychology* 148: 499–505.

Coates, B., H. Pusser, & I. Goodman. 1976. The influence of "Sesame Street" and "Mr. Rogers' Neighborhood" on children's social behavior in the preschool. *Child Development* 47: 138–44.

Damon, W. 1977. *The social world of the child.* San Francisco, CA: Jossey-Bass.

Damon, W. 1988. *The moral child: Nurturing children's natural moral growth.* New York: Free Press.

Davis, D.E. 1977. *My friends and me.* Circle Pines, MN: American Guidance Service.

Derman-Sparks, L., & the A.B.C. Task Force 1989. *Anti-bias curriculum: Tools for empowering young children.* Washington, DC: NAEYC.

DeVries, R., & A. Goncu. 1990. Interpersonal relations in four-year-old dyads from constructivist and Montessori programs. In *Optimizing early child care and education*, ed. A.S. Honig, 11–28. London: Gordon & Breach.

Dinkmeyer, D., & D. Dinkmeyer, Jr. 1982. *Developing understanding of self and others* (Rev. DUSO-R). Circle Pines, MN: American Guidance Service.

Dreikurs, R., B.B. Grunwald, & F.C. Pepper. 1982. *Maintaining sanity in the classroom: Classroom management techniques.* New York: Harper & Row.

Edwards, C.P. 1986. *Social and moral development in young children: Creative approaches for the classroom.* New York: Teachers College Press.

Egeland, B., & A. Sroufe. 1981. Developmental sequelae of maltreatment in infancy. *Directions for Child Development* 11: 77–92.

Feshbach, N. 1978. Studies of empathetic behavior in children. In *Progress in experimental personality research*, Vol. 8, ed. B. Maher, 1–47. New York: Academic Press.

Finkelstein, N. 1982. Aggression: Is it stimulated by day care? *Young Children* 37 (6): 3–13.

Forge, K.L., & S. Phemister. 1987. The effect of prosocial cartoons on preschool children. *Child Study Journal* 17: 83–88.

Fox, L. 1980. *Communicating to make friends.* Rolling Hills Estates, CA: B.L. Winch.

Friedrich, L.K., & A.H. Stein. 1973. *Aggressive and prosocial television programs and the natural behavior of preschool children.* Monographs of the Society for Research in Child Development, vol. 38, issue 4, no. 151. Chicago: University of Chicago Press.

Gresham, F. 1981. Social skills training with handicapped children: A review. *Review of Educational Research* 51: 139–76.

Holloway, S.D., & M. Reichhart-Erickson. 1988. The relationship of day care quality to children's free-play behavior and social problem-solving skills. *Early Childhood Research Quarterly* 3: 39–53.

Honig, A., & P. McCarron. 1990. Prosocial behaviors of handicapped and typical peers in an integrated preschool. In *Optimizing early child care and education*, ed. A.S. Honig. London: Gordon & Breach.

Honig, A., & B. Pollack. 1990. Effects of a brief intervention program to promote prosocial behaviors in young children. *Early Education and Development* 1: 438–44.

Honig, A.S., & A. Thompson. 1994. Helping toddlers with peer entry skills. *Zero to Three* 14 (5): 15–19.

Honig, A.S., & D.S. Wittmer. 1992. *Prosocial development in children: Caring, sharing, and cooperating: A bibliographic resource guide.* New York: Garland Press.

Howes, C. 1987. Social competence with peers in young children: Developmental sequences. *Developmental Review* 7: 252–72.

Howes, C., & P. Stewart. 1987. Child's play

with adults, toys, and peers: An examination of family and child care influences. *Developmental Psychology* 23 (8): 423–30.

Huston-Stein, A., L. Friedrich-Cofer, & E. Susman. 1977. The relation of classroom structure to social behavior, imaginative play, and self-regulation of economically disadvantaged children. *Child Development* 48: 908–16.

Kobak, D. 1979. Teaching children to care. *Children Today* 8 (6/7): 34–35.

Kreidler, W. 1984. *Creative conflict resolution.* Evanston, IL: Scott Foresman.

Lally, J.R., P. Mangione, & A.S. Honig. 1988. The Syracuse University Family Development Research Program: Long range impact of an early intervention with low-income children and their families. In *Parent education as early childhood intervention: Emerging directions in theory, research, and practice,* ed. D. Powell, 79–104. Norwood, NJ: Ablex.

McMath, J. 1989. Promoting prosocial behaviors through literature. *Day Care and Early Education* 17 (1): 25–27.

Nelson, J. n.d. *Positive discipline in the classroom featuring class meetings.* Provo, UT: Sunrise.

Orlick, T. 1982. *Winning through cooperation: Competitive insanity—cooperative alternatives.* Washington, DC: Acropolis.

Orlick, T. 1985. *The second cooperative sports and games book.* New York: Pantheon Press.

Park, K., & A. Honig. 1991. Infant child care patterns and later teacher ratings of preschool behaviors. *Early Child Development and Care* 68: 80–87.

Pines, M. 1979. Good samaritans at age two? *Psychology Today* 13: 66–77.

Poulds, R., E. Rubinstein, & R. Leibert. 1975. Positive social learning. *Journal of Communication* 25 (4): 90–97.

Prutzman, P., L. Sgern, M.L. Burger, & G. Bodenhamer. 1988. *The friendly classroom for a small planet: Children's creative response to conflict program.* Philadelphia: New Society.

Rogers, D. 1987. Fostering social development through block play. *Day Care and Early Education* 14 (3): 26–29.

Salkowski, C.J. 1991. Keeping the peace: Helping children resolve conflict through a problem-solving approach. *Montessori Life* (Spring): 31–37.

Schweinhart, L.J., D.P. Weikart, & M.B. Larner. 1986. Consequences of three curriculum models through age 15. *Early Childhood Research Quarterly* 1: 15–45.

Shure, M. 1992. *I can problem solve: An interpersonal cognitive problem-solving program.* Champaign, IL: Research Press.

Smith, C.A. 1982. *Promoting the social development of young children: Strategies and activities.* Palo Alto, CA: Mayfield.

Solomon, D., M.S. Watson, K.L. Delucci, E. Schaps, & V. Battistich. 1988. Enhancing children's prosocial behavior in the classroom. *American Educational Research Journal* 25 (4): 527–54.

Watkins, K.P., & L. Durant. 1992. *Complete early childhood behavior management guide.* West Nyack, NY: Center for Applied Research in Education.

Werner, E. 1986. Resilient children. In *Annual editions: Human development,* eds. H.E. Fitzgerald & M.G. Walraven. Sluice-Dock, CT: Dushkin.

Whiting, B., & J. Whiting. 1975. *Children of six cultures: A psychocultural analysis.* Cambridge, MA: Harvard University Press.

Wittmer, D., & A. Honig. 1994. Encouraging positive social development in young children, Part 1. *Young Children* 49 (5): 4–12.

Wolf, P., ed. 1986. *Connecting: Friendship in the lives of young children and their teachers.* Redmond, WA: Exchange Press.

Wood, C. 1991. Maternal teaching: Revolution of kindness. *Holistic Education Review* (Summer): 3–10.

Caring for Others And Being Cared For
Students Talk Caring in School

What can adolescents themselves tell us about their perceptions of caring? Ms. Bosworth — who was co-director of a study team that spent a year in two middle schools, exploring the indicators of caring in young adolescents — draws some answers from that experience.

Kris Bosworth

KRIS BOSWORTH is director of the Center for Adolescent Studies, Indiana University, Bloomington. She wishes to thank Gerald Smith, Maria Ferriera, Darren Smith, and Chris Jaffe for their contributions.

Illustration by Loren Long

RECENTLY, IN one mid-sized city in the Midwest, two teenagers, ages 18 and 15, fired a single shot from a stolen gun into the head of a cab driver. Following the incident, a juvenile probation officer lamented, "We're seeing an increase in kids who just don't care."

Often adults see negative, disrespectful, or violent behavior as evidence that teens simply do not care. They tend to react to adolescents as if their noncaring behavior were the norm, as if caring attitudes and behaviors were as foreign to young people as neural surgery. Thus the first approach many adults take to dealing with teens is to focus on changing the be-

haviors seen as "uncaring." In fact, strategies dealing with negative behavior dominate most schools. Programs or strategies that enhance caring values, attitudes, and behaviors by providing students with opportunities to discuss caring, to demonstrate caring to others, and to participate thoughtfully in caring relationships with peers and adults are scarce.

If adults tend to think that many young people don't care, what can adolescents themselves tell us about their perceptions of caring? In discussions of how caring manifests itself in schools and other institutions that serve young people, their opinions are often missing. What do ado-

lescents say about caring, about how they demonstrate caring, and about how they identify caring in others, particularly in their teachers? Understanding how young people view caring provides a place to begin in developing formal programs that promote and encourage caring, as well as in showing how the behaviors of adults who work with teens might support and encourage caring.

Does what adolescents say about caring have any relationship to how they behave? Although values and attitudes are important contributors to behavior, they are certainly not the only influences that determine whether a teen demonstrates caring behavior. However, valuing caring and having a positive attitude toward it are certainly steps toward exhibiting caring behavior. What values, attitudes, and understandings do teens have about caring? How can these be used to enhance the qualities of caring in school relationships?

Teachers are the brokers of caring in schools. They provide the bridge between the school and the individual. Understanding what adolescents see as caring behavior can facilitate communication between teachers and students and can help teachers model caring behavior. Hearing student voices can provide educators with a clearer understanding of approaches to enhance caring.

Before talking to teens, though, we should explore several assumptions that may influence our expectations. The first concerns gender issues. Are female adolescents better able to articulate what caring is? Are girls able to provide more sophisticated definitions of what it means to care? Such an expectation comes both from the common perception of females in this society as nurturing and caring and from some studies of adolescent girls. A finding of gender differences or lack thereof would be important in designing any programs or interventions to enhance caring in schools.

One might also expect that adolescents would be so self-absorbed (often described as "egocentric") that altruism and caring would be totally out of character for any of them, regardless of gender. Adults often describe adolescents' behavior in ways that suggest that young people scarcely recognize that anyone else exists, let alone has feelings, wants, and needs. Caring implies relationship. Indeed, some have described the relationship between the giver and the recipient of caring as reciprocal or mutual. To what extent do teens find caring to be mutual with other students or with adults?

Recently, Gerald Smith and I led a study team that spent a year in two middle schools, exploring the indicators of caring in young adolescents. One school, serving a population of 800 students, was located in the heart of a large industrial city in the Midwest. The other was located about 10 miles from that urban area and drew its student body (1,200 students) from suburban subdivisions, poor rural areas, and the inner city (as a result of a desegregation plan). In our exploration we observed about 300 classrooms over four months. We interviewed more than

100 students in the sixth, seventh, and eighth grades in the two schools.

To select students who would represent a range of caring and uncaring behavior, we asked teachers to identify their five most caring and their five most uncaring students. Although the goal in collecting these data was to identify students for the interviews, the teachers' reports can serve as crude indicators of caring behavior. The students we interviewed represented a range of early adolescents from rural, suburban, and urban areas and from low-income and middle-class families. About one-third of the adolescents interviewed were nonwhite, mostly African American.

Definition of Caring

What does it mean to care? All but four of the adolescents interviewed could clearly articulate a definition of caring and identify specific behaviors that indicated caring. A few definitions were simple synonyms, such as "loving" or "helping," but most included two or more dimensions or characteristics of caring. The teens sometimes discussed caring in terms of single acts (e.g., helping someone with schoolwork), but more often they saw caring as an integral part of relationships within their circle of intimate friends and family members, as well as in their school, their community, and the rest of the world. When asked what came to mind when they heard the word "caring," most students gave responses like these:

Bob: Doing something for somebody when they can't do it, like helping them, giving them their needs and watching over them.

Bob's definition of caring includes both specific acts, "doing something for somebody," and the more general attitude, "watching over them." Most students, regardless of grade, gender, or race, agreed with Bob that caring involved helping of some kind.

Alicia: I think of loving. Maybe appreciating the fact that somebody's different than you. If you care for them, no matter what they are or what they do wrong, then you still care for them. You appreciate who they are.

Alicia begins her explanation with a synonym, "loving," but she goes on to explain that this includes the concept of appreciating differences and a belief that caring is constant.

William: To be sure somebody knows how you feel, to have sympathy for somebody, to have feelings for somebody, to be interested about somebody.

Like many of the middle schoolers with whom we spoke, William's definition has a strong relationship component. To let someone know how you feel, communication needs to be clear and probably reciprocal. The kind of caring relationship William describes is most likely not casual, as indicated by the other ways he describes the relationship: having sympathy, having feelings, and being interested.

Tara: The way one person feels toward another person about their feelings. Like if I was injured or something and you were to come by, you wouldn't sit there and laugh at me. You'd want to try to help.

Tara elaborates on the theme of helping as part of caring. For Tara, feelings play an important role in explaining caring. She also understands what caring is not: laughing at adversity or making fun of someone.

The responses of Bob, Alicia, William, and Tara suggest the range of responses students made to our general question about what caring means. Most students identified more than one dimension or attribute when discussing what caring is. In looking at what all the students said, five themes were dominant: helping, feelings, relationships, personal values, and activities.

Helping. The most common theme to emerge from students' discussions of the concept of caring was that caring involves helping. Nearly 30% of the responses described helping of some kind. For a few students, the phrase "to help" was synonymous with "to care." When discussing caring in terms of helping, some students used concrete or specific situations. For example, friends and classmates were described as the recipients of help with schoolwork. "If a friend is having a problem with schoolwork," said one female eighth-grader, "I show them the way to do it and do an example for them or something." Similarly, a male seventh-grader said, "In class, I usually go back and explain work to them [classmates and friends], because sometimes the teacher is up front, and there's noise, and they don't understand. So I'll just go and help them out."

Besides helping classmates and friends with schoolwork, some adolescents menioned helping in other ways. "I help them [friends and family members]: when there is something that I can do that they cannot do, I do it for them," said one eighth-grade female. To another student, helping went beyond the intimate circle of friends and family: "If somebody is elderly or if somebody is just having a rough time and needs something done, all you're able to do is help them out." This suggests that there is more to caring than the mere act itself. A kind of sensitivity should guide a person's act of caring. One sixth-grade male took this helping a step further. He would "ask them what the problem is, and try to help them solve it."

Students who talked about taking care of someone or something usually referred to a concrete situation. Saying "give them their needs" or "to be cared for while you are sick" gives the impression that the relationship between the caregiver and the receiver is richer than a relationship based just on one person physically providing for another. There is a certain warmth that transcends the physical act of caring.

Providing guidance was another specific kind of helping that students identified. Thus "giving advice" becomes part of the process of trying to help someone with a problem. But giving advice must be done in a caring manner. In the words of an eighth-grade male, "When you're with somebody and they're doing something wrong, . . . you don't just go out and yell at them."

Helping a specific person with a specific task is an activity that may be easy for an adolescent to identify as caring because it is visible and because the person being cared for is easily identified. A less direct indicator of caring — such as doing a conscientious job of mowing the school lawn so that the school looks nice or attending a workshop to learn a new teaching technique — would be harder to identify. Such activities are not aimed toward a specific person and may not be evident to the student for some time after they have taken place. When asked what they do to care for others, students themselves did not identify the more subtle caring acts, such as paying attention when others speak in class or not littering, as acts of caring.

Feelings. The theme that came in second, mentioned by about one-fourth of the students, was that caring concerns feelings. An important component of feelings is empathy or "knowing how someone else feels," and the flip side of empathy is being able to "tell someone how you feel."

"Love" or "loving" was the feeling most commonly mentioned as a part of caring. Some students just offered the word "love," while others identified the recipients of love as parents or friends. A number of students, however, mentioned "loving other people." As one female seventh-grader put it, "When somebody really cares for you, they love you."

Other feelings mentioned include comforting someone by "picking them up when they are down." It could involve cheering them up by "making them laugh, making funny faces, or something." These responses reflected a one-sided relationship in which there was a caregiver and a receiver of care. Other students described a more reciprocal connection between those involved: "Let them lean on you, just like you lean on them." This is akin to having an unconditional acceptance and appreciation for another person.

Relationships. A sizable number of student responses explicitly mentioned relationships with self, family, friends, or simply "others." The relationship in and of itself was a definition of caring. For example, to a seventh-grader, caring meant simply "caring about yourself," whereas to a sixth-grade male it meant "having respect for what you have" and "taking care of what you do."

Some students associated caring with family members. "I think about my parents," said an eighth-grade female. She went on to acknowledge that they gave her a home, clothes, and shelter. This student seemed to understand the fact that her parents had chosen to care for her by taking care of her needs.

Friendship was also a synonym for caring. Although some students mentioned their particular friends, others felt that caring meant "being a friend to everybody." Interestingly, although friends play an important developmental role in the lives of young adolescents, the concept of friends and friendship was not mentioned as often as family or the more general "others."

Although early adolescence is often seen as an egocentric period, nearly one in four of the adolescents we interviewed said that caring involved a relationship with others, and many of them did not limit that relationship to those closest to them. In the words of a sixth-grader, "If more people cared, there wouldn't be that much crime on the streets."

Values. Students identified three personal values related to the concept of caring: kindness, respect, and faithfulness. When speaking of kindness as a value related to caring, most students simply said that caring involves "being nice to people" or "being kind." Those who identified respect as an important component of caring gave such examples as "not calling people names" and "not talking about other people." Because of the realities of peer relationships typical in middle schools, these simple statements describe an attitude of tolerance and consideration toward others that seems to run counter to some peer-group norms. In the words of a sixth-grade female, one respects others by "appreciating the fact that somebody's different than you."

Faithfulness is another value to live by in a caring relationship. To the students we surveyed, this meant that "someone won't just one minute be your friend and, if something better comes along, they won't just leave you behind." These students sense that real caring involves a bond that survives, as one student said, "the good and the bad times."

Activities. The theme mentioned least often as a component of caring had to do with activities; only 10% of the total number of responses mentioned activities. Three activities garnered a similar number of responses: spending time with someone, sharing, and listening. Some of these activities are single events, but most students described general activities that suggest that a caring relationship is more than one isolated instance.

For one sixth-grader, caring related to someone "spending time with you" and "taking you to places"; to another, it meant being with someone "to get to know you better." One of the assumptions underlying these responses is that each individual is content with spending time in the company of another, without the draw of entertainment or a holiday or celebration.

Sharing implies a sort of equivalence in the context of a relationship. In sharing activities it is not at all clear who is the caregiver and who is the receiver. Sharing differs from lending in that lending may be an isolated event in which no relationship outside the event is implied. Interestingly, lending school materials was never identified by students as an act of caring. "Sharing things" and "sharing with them" were the most common responses in the sharing category. One very pragmatic student equated sharing with letting others "play with my Nintendo."

Listening implied different degrees of involvement. To one sixth-grader, caring meant "somebody who listens to what you've got to say," whereas, to one seventh-grader, a caring person is "wanting to listen." To an eighth-grade female, listening is an important component in her relationships with her friends: "When they are having problems, you just sit there and listen to them."

In its simplest form, any definition of caring involves at least two people who are engaged in some sort of activity in which one person gives while the other receives, and the roles of the giver and receiver may be interchangeable at any point in a relationship or at any moment in time. When the students described what they meant by caring, however, they indicated that something more than a particular, isolated event or activity bonds two persons. "To think about people around you" and "to be interested about someone" indicate that the relationship between the caregiver and the receiver is richer than just a relationship based on helping someone with an isolated homework problem. For the adolescents we surveyed, caring arose from relationships that involved a commitment on the part of both parties.

While about 90% of the young adolescents with whom we spoke gave complex, multidimensional definitions of caring, there appeared to be some differences in the nature of those definitions. Although 69% of the females identified "helping" as a characteristic of caring, an even larger proportion of males (87%) gave responses related to the helping theme. A similar pattern occurred with the theme of "feelings": 83% of the males and 62% of the females made responses that fell into this category. There was a smaller difference in the "relationships" theme: 65% of males gave responses that fell into this category, as opposed to 56% of females. Females provided slightly more responses related to activities (31% to 24%). And similar proportions of males and females gave responses related to "personal values." These findings suggest that males and females share similar conceptions of caring. In fact, the adolescent boys with whom we spoke attributed helping and feelings to caring more often than did the girls.

When we examined each theme in relation to racial groups, we found some differences. Proportionally more nonwhite students provided responses under the themes of "relationships" and "activities," whereas a greater number of white stu-

Our observations indicated that most interactions between students or between students and their teachers were neutral.

dents provided responses under "feelings" and "personal values." We did not find differences with regard to the theme of "helping."

It appears that, for many nonwhite students, caring is more concrete and is translated through such activities as "spending time with someone," "sharing," and "listening when someone has a problem." In addition, when discussing caring, nonwhite students tended to talk about specific people. "To think about someone you really dearly care about, like your friends," said an eighth-grade female. In contrast, many white students discussed caring more abstractly and included emotions or values. "Showing respect," responded a sixth-grade female. "The way a person feels towards another person" reflects a caring attitude, replied another.

While we did notice some differences, they should not detract from the voices of most of the middle school students, who give evidence that — regardless of age, race, or gender — there is a rich and multidimensional understanding of what caring is. This understanding can serve as a basis for engaging young adolescents in activities that will enhance their comprehension of caring and help turn it into positive action.

Given the rich understanding that young adolescents have of the concept of caring, how did this understanding manifest itself in the classroom? What did teachers do to support or nurture caring in their students? Our observations indicated that most interactions between students or between students and their teachers were neutral. Each went about his or her busi-

ness without engaging in overt acts of caring or uncaring. Mostly they were pleasant and polite to one another, but the structure of the school day left little space or time for interpersonal interaction.

During class time teachers were clearly in charge, and the majority of time was devoted to traditional types of learning (lectures, workbook exercises, silent reading, viewing videos, and so on) in which caring interactions are not encouraged. In both schools we studied, there was pressure to improve scores on standardized tests administered statewide. While the teachers were not "teaching to the test," a clear goal was to improve academic performance. This goal may have influenced teachers to use the traditional learning strategies that left little time for personal interactions.

Some teachers took advantage of the times before and after school to be in the halls and to interact with students. But many teachers simply played the role of disciplinarian during these times.

Themes of caring were rarely discussed even though course content — such as study of the Holocaust — could have reasonably generated such discussion. Even such a clearly caring/helping activity as donating cans of food for the needy did not become a springboard for a discussion of caring. The focus was more on ways to increase the number of cans collected than on why the school was involved in the activity.

We saw only a few instances in which students were given the opportunity to help other students. In one case, a boy was asked to orient a new student (also a boy) to the classroom. The other cases involved free time at the end of a class. Teachers asked students who had received good grades on their tests or quizzes to help those who were studying for the retest.

Outside of the classroom, time constraints (students had less than five minutes to change classes) and structure (students had to line up to move from class to class) offered few opportunities for caring or helping. Since most students rode buses to school, they did not "hang around" after school. Thus, although these middle school students had the prerequisite understanding of what caring is, they had few chances to demonstrate it within the structure of the school day. When teachers did provide opportunities to demonstrate caring, those opportunities often favored students who were academically stronger. This tendency could lead teachers to see a false correlation between caring behavior and academic proficiency.

Caring Teachers

Although a typical school day does not offer students much opportunity to demonstrate caring, what did the students identify as caring from their teachers? When asked to describe what they would see in the classroom of a caring teacher, most students gave descriptions similar to this one from an eighth-grade male: "Everyone would be in their seats, doing work. The teacher would go around the room talking to everybody to see how they were doing [and] to answer questions. Sometimes she'd just say, 'Good job.'" In this scenario, the teacher is involved with each student, meeting the needs of each student for specific help with an academic problem or offering positive reinforcement and encouragement.

Most students had little difficulty articulating characteristics of caring teachers. Their responses can be grouped into three large categories: the most frequently identified characteristic (140 responses) had to do with classroom or teaching practices; the second most frequently mentioned category (81 responses) was nonclassroom activities, such as after-school help and guidance; and the final category (49 responses) was personal characteristics.

Teaching Practices

While some of the caring things teachers did in classrooms could be described as "good teaching" (helping with schoolwork, explaining work, and checking for understanding), others represent such personal traits as valuing individuality, showing respect, encouraging students, and being tolerant. The following paragraphs discuss these characteristics and behaviors in rank order, by the number of times students mentioned them.

Helping with schoolwork. Student descriptions of caring teachers were consistent across grades, race, and gender. A caring teacher would help students under the following conditions: "if you are stuck on a problem," "when you need it," "if you don't understand something," "when you ask a question," and "even if you don't need it." Helping students with schoolwork was the highest-ranking category for both males and females, for whites, and for all grades. It ranked second for nonwhite students. Clearly, simply helping with

schoolwork is seen as a strong indicator that a teacher cares.

Valuing individuality. Teachers who saw students as individuals in the classroom were perceived to be caring teachers by many students. The caring teachers noticed and inquired about changes in behavior; they recognized different learning styles and speeds; they sought to know students as unique human beings. Valuing individuality ranked highest among seventh- and eighth-graders and among males.

As one seventh-grade female put it, "[A caring teacher] doesn't see you as a unit; she sees each person as an individual." Another seventh-grade female said, "If you were the only person in the classroom who didn't understand it and everybody did, then he or she wouldn't doubt you for not understanding it." An eighth-grade male explained it this way: "[Caring teachers] can see problems in your schoolwork and help you with them." Or, as another seventh-grade male said, "They ask you questions about how you are doing with all your classes." One eighth-grade male said, "She wants to know what type of person you are."

Showing respect. Showing respect has several dimensions for middle schoolers. In regular classroom practice, teachers who show respect will call on students when they raise their hands and listen to what the students have to say. As one seventh-grade male said, "They treat you the way you want to be treated."

Many students described the actions of respectful, caring teachers in situations where students had made a mistake or broken a rule. For example, one sixth-grade female said, "She won't yell at you or anything like that." Another aspect of respect was "talking in a quiet voice or talking to you in private or alone" when a reprimand was needed.

Being tolerant. According to students, tolerant teachers give students second chances to make up work, to improve their behavior, or to get the right answer. One seventh-grade female eloquently described this characteristic of tolerance and equity: "Somebody who no matter what the student is, what their past was, would start off with a clean slate, just come in, make them feel good about themselves, saying, 'You're going to be one of my best students, and you will succeed in this class.' Making them know from the start that they can do it." A sixth-grade male said that this characteristic is shown by a teacher who "pays attention, not just to

one person, but to all." Another sixth-grade male said, "Let's say there's an uncaring student. A caring teacher has to care about that student, too."

Explaining work. Students report that a caring teacher does a good job of explaining the content area, particularly with regard to assignments that students must do. This category differs from helping with work in that it requires of a teacher the specific skill of making sure that all students understand rather than simply helping with specific problems of an individual student.

According to one seventh-grade female, a caring teacher "wouldn't just say, 'Do it the way you think you do it, and see if you get it right.'" Instead, a caring teacher would "explain your assignments before you do them, would explain an assignment thoroughly, would show you how to do the work before you take it home." This characteristic was identified more frequently by older students.

Checking for understanding. Teachers who display this trait are very active in the classroom. They do more than help only when a hand is raised. They interact with students and seek out students who need clarification or additional explanation. One eighth-grade male described such a teacher as "someone who walks around making sure you're understanding your work."

Encouraging. Actively encouraging students to improve is another dimension of teaching practice that a caring teacher would exhibit. Some students talked about the encouragement as a material reward, such as candy, but most students focused on the verbal encouragement that caring teachers gave. One sixth-grade female said, "She sticks up for you when she knows you did something right." A sixth-grade male said, "When you get bad grades, she says, 'You can do better than this.'"

Planning fun activities. A few students mentioned that a caring teacher provided an enjoyable classroom atmosphere and would take students on field trips and plan fun activities for them. Some students also mentioned that a caring teacher was considerate about the amount of homework given.

Nonclassroom Activities

Eighty-one responses focused on things that teachers did outside of their classroom teaching responsibilities. These responses fell clearly into three categories:

helping with personal problems, providing guidance, and going the extra mile.

Helping with personal problems. Most responses were fairly general in identifying the types of problems a caring teacher helps with or in specifying what a caring teacher does to help. For some students, just listening was sufficient. Others found that a caring teacher was much more active in problem solving. One seventh-grade female said, "If you were mad at one of your friends and you were really upset and were crying, they would probably help you guys work it out." Another seventh-grade female said, "A lot of times they can help you with problems at home or anything." An eighth-grade male mentioned that a caring teacher would help students with family problems and with problems between friends.

Looking at the distribution of these responses, it is interesting to note that males were somewhat more likely to mention help with personal problems than females. One might think of asking for and getting help with personal problems as more characteristic of females than of males, but our data show that males ranked this an important indicator of a caring teacher.

Providing guidance. The guidance category was the second most frequently mentioned topic. In this category were responses that indicated that teachers took a full, active role in providing direction, goal-setting activities, and advice. Viewed from a distance, these actions might often be seen as uncaring, for they include such things as talking to parents if a student has been disruptive. However, a high percentage of responses testified to the role that caring teachers play in providing direction and correction to students. A seventh-grade female said, "A caring teacher wants to make sure you don't get in trouble." Another seventh-grade female said, "A caring teacher doesn't let students get by with everything." An eighth-grade female described a caring teacher as one "who is always helping me decide what I want to do and where I'm going to go to college." An eighth-grade male said, "Sometimes they can be a little rough or angry with us when trying to look out for our well-being."

The frequency with which students mentioned the guidance offered by caring teachers indicated that they were perceptive about those teachers who had the best interests of students at heart — even if they took actions that could be seen by students as firm, if not actually harsh. It is significant that a large number of minor-

ity students emphasized this category of caring behavior. Indeed, it was the highest-ranked category for nonwhite students.

Going the extra mile. Students said that caring teachers would extend themselves in ways that went beyond the job description. A major caring behavior in this category was staying after school to help students with their work or to talk to them about their problems. Considering the number of students who mentioned this action, it appears that extending the school day was seen in a positive light. Although the majority of statements in this category were as vague as "Teachers that really go out of their way to make you happy" or "They're there for you to listen," a few students offered specific examples. One seventh-grade female said, "They'll take you out on their own time to help you with schoolwork and privately tutor you after school." An eighth-grade female said, "She always is available if we need help." An eighth-grade male said, "Stops fights and stuff." Another eighth-grade male reported, "She comes to every sport I play."

Personal Attributes

Forty-eight students listed personal attributes or descriptions of caring teachers that did not involve their teaching strategies or out-of-classroom activities. These attributes fell into four categories: being nice or polite, liking to help students, being success-oriented, and being involved.

Being nice/polite. Ten students representing both schools, both genders, and all grades simply said that caring teachers are "nice." Three students framed their comments negatively, saying that caring teachers are not rude or mean. Three students gave behavioral descriptions of what they meant by "nice." One seventh-grade female said that caring teachers "are always smiling and stuff." Another seventh-grade female said, "They always greet you with a smile."

Liking to help students. Willingness to assist students was seen as an important personal attribute of caring teachers. One sixth-grade female said, "They put forth a lot of effort." An eighth-grade male said, "[They are] devoted to helping you." This category is different from the previous categories of helping, in that there was no actual activity to which the students could point. The impression that teachers were willing to help was the personal attribute discussed by many student respondents.

Being success-oriented. A number of students identified caring teachers as being success-oriented. That is, they believed in their students' capabilities and wanted them to do their best and to succeed.

Being involved. Students identified being involved with students as an attribute of caring teachers. Many simply said that such teachers "are involved." Others focused on friendship. For example, a seventh-grade female said, "A caring teacher is not only a teacher but your friend, too." Other examples of involvement included setting a good example for students, trusting students, telling the truth, and "just liking kids."

Overall, students were able to identify specific behaviors and — to a lesser extent — attitudes of caring teachers. Many of these were similar to those that they identified in defining the concept of caring. However, in describing their teachers' behaviors, students depicted one-way relationships — the teacher did something (e.g., helping or listening) for the student. Students did not describe these activities as mutual or reciprocal.

Except for a few students who saw caring related to fun activities in the classroom, most students did not attribute caring to content or to curricular matters. A

> *For all groups, helping with schoolwork was the most frequently mentioned characteristic of a caring teacher.*

good lesson, an interesting unit, or bringing in an outside speaker were never offered as examples of caring on the part of a teacher. It was through personal actions and attitudes that teachers demonstrated that they cared, both in and out of the classroom. Broadly interpreted, these data say that a "caring teacher" is an interpreter or guide to learning.

Although the disparities were small, there were some differences in responses between grades, genders, and races that bear further investigation. For nonwhite

...udents, 56% ranked guidance as an in-...cator of caring. Although this guiding ...le was identified by a considerable num-...er of white students (23%), the differ-...ce between racial groups was clear. ...eachers should be aware that students ...alue and appreciate a teacher who has ...andards for student performance and is ...illing to play a role in guiding students.

For all groups, helping with school-...ork was the most frequently mentioned ...haracteristic of a caring teacher. This is ...ore important to females (58%) than to ...ales (41%). Regardless of grade or race, ...ales see what teachers do outside the ...lassroom as more closely related to car-...g than do females. Thirty-nine percent ...f the males versus 20% of the females ...w "help with problems" as an impor-...nt characteristic.

Observations

Clearly, young adolescents from a va-...ety of backgrounds have a clear under-...tanding of the complexity of the concept ...f caring. Almost all of them are able to ...rticulate a multidimensional description ...f what caring means to them and to list ...variety of activities in which they engage ...hat constitute caring. Moreover, most of ...he caring activities have a positive ori-...ntation: most teens will tell you what ...hey do that demonstrates caring (e.g., ...elping others with schoolwork), rather ...han mention activities that they avoid be-...ause such activities (e.g., spreading ru-...nors) are not caring activities.

These young adolescents see caring ...emonstrated within the context of per-...onal relationships. Caring behaviors are ...lmost exclusively described in the con-...ext of an ongoing relationship rather than ...s a single generous act, such as helping ...stranger who has fallen down in the hall-...vay or on the street. Moreover, within these ...ngoing relationships, very few young ado-...escents mentioned material forms of car-...ng, such as giving gifts. What they re-...ported as demonstrations of caring in-...olved giving time and sharing of them-...elves.

Helping was the dominant theme in all ...ur discussions with these teens about car-

ing. The central focus of both their defi-nition of caring and their description of activities that demonstrate caring is help-ing — with schoolwork and with person-al problems. The closeness of the rela-tionship between caring and helping is ex-pressed by all genders, grades, and races.

Where teachers are concerned, caring is often a one-way affair; few students re-port some reciprocal caring. Caring teach-ers are seen as teachers who help students and treat them as individuals.

These observations lead us to offer several suggestions for educators who wish to nurture caring in students. Our finding that young adolescents see caring as grounded in relationships and find it more difficult to discuss caring for others out-side their immediate circle of friends and family suggests that more people need to be included in an adolescent's circle of re-lationships. Creating caring communities by actively promoting activities and atti-tudes that help develop relationships is essential. The students we interviewed came from large schools. Large schools tend to be impersonal — and even the strategy of breaking the student body in-to smaller teams or houses, which the schools we studied employed, could be further exploited to build stronger caring communities.

Young adolescents also need the op-portunity to demonstrate caring. In our months of observations, we found that the schools offered little opportunity for most students to practice caring or to be rec-ognized or rewarded for it. Nearly all the events and activities in each school were organized and directed by adults. Both schools had community service organi-zations, but they were either very small or required a specific grade-point average of participants. The most common way stu-dents were asked to show caring was for the teacher to ask the better students to help others who were having academic difficulties. This happened rarely during our observations, and when it did, very few of the eligible students responded.

One-time acts of caring, such as food drives or neighborhood clean-up activi-ties, are important, but they are not suf-ficient for the development of caring in

young adolescents. All students need mul-tiple opportunities to engage in caring ac-tivities in caring educational communi-ties.

Students' perceptions of what a caring teacher does indicate a style of teaching that takes into consideration the needs of individual learners. The caring teacher first provides good explanations and then seeks to clarify misunderstandings. Although some students also appreciate a teacher who will help with specific problems, this is less important to students than the role of teacher as learning guide or coach.

Even within a highly structured school day, we saw numerous "missed opportu-nities" for the demonstration of caring. We observed too many classes in which teachers rarely smiled, said anything pos-itive to a student, or used a student's name other than for a reprimand. Changes in these behaviors might go a long way to-ward promoting caring and need not de-tract from the pursuit of academic goals. In a number of classes, students would seek help with a lesson or assignment on-ly from the teacher. Often students had to wait their turn for the teacher to have time to answer their questions. Because the adolescents in this study identified help-ing as a key component of caring, schools that wish to provide opportunities for ado-lescents to demonstrate caring should work to expand the pool of people who can help with schoolwork.

The school can take action to facilitate teachers' demonstration of caring to stu-dents as well. Reducing the size of schools and classrooms would allow teachers to get to know their students individually, to help them more with their work, to be-come involved with their extracurricular activities, and to interact with families. All of these are activities that students rec-ognize as caring. With institutional sup-port teachers can heed the words of their young adolescent students and model car-ing behaviors, offer students opportuni-ties to practice caring, support a widen-ing circle of relationships in which caring is more likely to be meaningful, and reg-ularly reward and affirm caring behav-iors.

Developmental Tasks of Early Adolescence: How Adult Awareness Can Reduce At-Risk Behavior

JUDITH L. IRVIN

Judith L. Irvin is an associate professor in the College of Education, Florida State University, Tallahassee. This article is drawn from her forthcoming book, Literacy and the Middle Level Student: Strategies to Enhance Learning *(Allyn and Bacon).*

At any inservice session for middle level educators, the first topic generally is "Characteristics of Young Adolescents," having to do with the physical, social, emotional, and intellectual growth and development of ten to fourteen year olds.

Although such information is important, it is somewhat incomplete. What needs to be explored in greater depth in those sessions—and by all middle level educators—are the developmental tasks of adolescence. A characteristic of early adolescents, for example, is defiance—not a pleasant trait. If looked at in broader terms, however, we see that defiance is a vehicle for the developmental task of personal autonomy.

Thus, although the developmental tasks of early adolescence more often than not are accompanied by obnoxious behaviors, it is how adults respond to those behaviors that can trigger a smooth or rocky transition into adulthood. And given that many "at risk" behaviors, such as drug and alcohol abuse and early sexual experiences, begin during early adolescence, it seems logical that success in developmental tasks and positive interactions with adults may reduce the need that some adolescents feel to engage in those behaviors.

In this article, I present a historical and cultural perspective of adolescence and discuss the developmental tasks at this period and the negative behaviors that can result from tackling those tasks. I believe that educators who understand the place of adolescence in history and society and who appreciate the behavior normally associated with the developmental tasks of that time in life will be in a good position to form positive relationships with young adolescents.

Background

Historical Perspectives

During the colonial days, the family formed the main social and economic unit of society; older children had an important and highly visible role in society and in the family. Young people were often farmed out to apprenticeships or boarding schools, and they generally functioned as adults at the tender age of fifteen or so (Modell and Goodman 1990).

In the next century, mass immigration and industrialization required keeping young people out of the labor force because of the need to provide sufficient employment for adult workers. Young people were obliged to remain in school for a longer period of time and were encouraged to attend college or vocational training beyond high school. That move had dire consequences for the teenager who, lacking an interest in formal education and biologically

From *The Clearing House*, March/April 1996, pp. 222-225. © 1996 by the Helen Dwight Reid Educational Foundation. Reprinted by permission of Heldref Publications, 1319 Eighteenth Street, NW, Washington, DC 20036-1802.

ready to assume a productive adult role in society, now was forced to continue in school or to become a "dropout" and face many negative consequences as a result. Thus prolonged formal schooling, together with a lack of adequate vocational training, appears to put non–college-bound young people at risk, as they are underprepared to assume a role in adult society.

Cultural Perspectives

Families, neighborhoods, economic conditions, and our historical era are all factors that influence a gracious or awkward transition into adulthood. Because adolescence is closely tied to the structure of and condition of adult society (Modell and Goodman 1990), many of the factors that put students at risk, in reality, reflect larger societal problems.

Family conditions, socioeconomic status, and ethnicity are all important factors in adolescent development (Feldman and Elliott 1990). Minority youth, in particular, have difficulty in school for two reasons. First, "minority youth are well aware of the values of the majority culture and its standards of performance, achievement, and beauty" (Spencer and Dornbusch 1990, 131). "Minorities whose cultural frames of reference are oppositional to the cultural frame of reference of American mainstream culture have greater difficulty crossing cultural boundaries at school to learn" (Ogbu 1992, 5). Second, the conflict between the majority culture and their own often creates tension for minority students working on the developmental task of identity.

The Myth of Storm and Stress

Perhaps because of the cumulative physical, social, and psychological changes experienced by young adolescents, adults have traditionally viewed early adolescence as a time of turbulence and disruption (Hill 1980). Recent information, however (Brooks-Gunn and Reiter 1990; Hauser and Bowlds 1990; Hillman 1991; Offer, Ostrov, and Howard 1989; Scales 1991; Steinberg 1990), clearly indicates that only a small percentage of students (less than 20 percent) exhibit signs of serious disturbance and need adult intervention. Although the changes experienced are stressful for most young people, Dorman and Lipsitz (1981) argued, adults should "distinguish between behavior that is distressing (annoying to others) and behavior that is disturbed (harmful to the young person exhibiting the behavior)" (4). When adults expect and reinforce irresponsible behavior, they may, indeed, exacerbate the occurrence.

Developmental Tasks

If most teenagers pass through adolescence relatively problem free, then why does such a negative stereotype of that age exist? It may be that parents and teachers see only the narrow picture of sometimes irritating behavior. "Even well-adjusted, intelligent, and reasonable adolescents do, on occasion, exhibit truly obnoxious behavior. . . . [T]hey are not like this all of the time, but probably all adolescents

behave this way some of the time. They can be exasperating, and adult reaction can lead to more serious problems" (Newman 1985, 636). Viewing young adolescent development from a broader perspective may help the adults who share their lives to accept, if not condone, the behaviors that result from working on the tasks before them.

Some of the most obvious developmental tasks are learning how to handle a more mature body, forming a sexual identity, continuing to progress with such abilities as reading and writing, and beginning to explore career options. Of course, developmental tasks begin in early childhood and continue through adulthood. Unique to early adolescence, however, are the new cognitive abilities of dealing with problems in more abstract ways and of considering multiple perspectives. Students are moving from the "concrete" stage (able to think logically about real experiences) to the "formal" stage (able to consider "what ifs," think reflectively, and reason abstractly). This intellectual change is gradual and may occur at different times for different students. They may even shift back and forth from the concrete to the abstract, although it is important to remember that not all young adolescents, not even all adults, achieve this capacity.

These new abilities for young adolescents represent "*potential* accomplishments rather than typical everyday thinking" (Keating 1990, 65). Most students begin the process at about age twelve and display formal thinking consistently at age fifteen or sixteen. Until that time, during early adolescence, students are practicing this new ability. Like any new skill, formal reasoning must be practiced repeatedly in a safe, encouraging environment.

Young adolescents are egocentric. But, the emerging formal thinker is, for the first time, able to consider the thoughts of others and perceive him- or herself as the object of attention of others; in fact, adolescents "assume themselves to be a focus of *most* other people's perspective *much* of the time" (Keating 1990, 71). "As adolescents develop the capacity to think about their own thoughts, they become acutely aware of themselves, their person, and ideas. As a result they become egocentric, self-conscious, and introspective" (Rice 1990, 183). As students become accustomed to that new ability, they outgrow the egocentrism so characteristic of early adolescence.

Cognitive growth and development regulate the success of the four other major developmental tasks that I will discuss here: (1) forming a personal identity or self-concept, (2) acquiring social skills and responsibility, (3) gaining personal autonomy, and (4) developing character and a set of values.

Personal Identity/Self-Concept

The development of a personal identity is not really possible until children move beyond concrete levels of thinking, enabling them to be self-conscious and introspective. The development of positive self-esteem takes reflection, introspection, comparisons with others, and a sensitivity to the opinions of other people. Those processes only become possible with the advent of formal thinking.

Self-esteem declines at age eleven and reaches a low point between twelve and thirteen (Brack, Orr, and Ingersoll 1988; Harter 1990). Students, especially girls, making the shift to large, impersonal junior high schools at grade seven seem to experience long-term negative effects on their self-esteem (Simmons and Blyth 1987), particularly because of the interruption of peer groups. "Schools that emphasize competition, social comparison, and ability self-assessment" can cause students' academic motivation and self-esteem to deteriorate (Wigfield and Eccles 1995).

Minority youth have an especially difficult time forming an identity because the values of their culture may clash with the values and standards of the dominant culture. Minority youth, however, who have successful role models and who can learn to negotiate a balance between the two value systems will develop self-esteem (Spencer and Dornbusch 1990).

In a thorough review of literature on self-esteem, Kohn (1994) questioned the value of programs designed to enhance self-esteem. Educators would do better to treat students with "respect [rather] than shower them with praise" (282) "When members of a class meet to make decisions and solve problems, they get the self-esteem building message that their voices count, they experience a sense of belonging to a community, and they hone their ability to reason and analyze" (279). A meaningful curriculum (Beane and Lipka 1986), a safe and intellectually challenging environment (Wigfield and Eccles 1995), and meaningful success experiences (Kohn 1994) lead to the long-lasting development of self-identity and positive self-esteem.

Social Skills

Socialization is an important developmental task. Savin-Williams and Berndt (1990) concluded that "students who have satisfying and harmonious friendships typically report positive self-esteem, a good understanding of other people's feelings, and relatively little loneliness" (288). Additionally, those students with harmonious friendships "tend to behave appropriately in school, are motivated to do well, and often receive high grades" (290). Adults often ridicule the time and intensity of phone conversations, frenzied note passing, and frequent broken hearts, but those interactions are "critical interpersonal bridges that move [adolescents] toward psychological growth and social maturity" (277).

A myth about the negative influence of peer groups has developed over the years. Recent research shows that young adolescents "do not routinely acquiesce to peer pressure. In fact, they are more likely to follow the advice of adults rather than peers in matters affecting their long-term future and they actually rely on their own judgment more often than that of either peers or parents" (Brown 1990, 174). Peer groups usually reinforce rather than contradict the values of parents. It is not surprising that young adolescents tend to form friendships similar to the relationships they have with their families. Brown (1990) further concluded that students "seek out the peer group best suited to

meeting their needs for emotional support and exploration or reaffirmation of their values and aspirations" (180).

Students do not select a crowd as much as they are thrust into one by virtue of their personalities, backgrounds, interests, and reputations among peers (Brown 1990). A peer group is a place for trying out roles and ideas and serves as a validation of one's value within a social unit beyond the family. Young adolescents need many opportunities to experience success in socially acceptable ways so that the peer group reinforces prosocial activities.

Autonomy

Another developmental task that sometimes leads to emotional trauma is a young adolescent's need to establish autonomy. The onset of adolescence is, no doubt, a time for major realignments in relationships with adults both at home and at school. Steinberg (1990) took a sociobiological perspective of "intergenerational conflict" (family fighting). He suggested that "bickering and squabbling at puberty is an atavism that ensures that adolescents will spend time away from the family of origin and mate outside the natal group" (269). Disagreement becomes a vehicle to inform parents about changing self-conceptions and expectations and an opportunity to shed the view that parents can do no wrong. Of course, this low-level conflict must begin with an already strong emotional bond between parents and

Although much young adolescent behavior appears rejecting, this is not the time for adults to alienate themselves from their children.

children. If relationships are not strong before puberty (and often stepchildren and stepparents have a particularly rough time), this fighting can become destructive.

We tend to treat young adolescents like children one minute, adults another. Their ambiguous status in society and their new powers of reasoning cause them frustration, which occasionally leads to their lashing out at adults. Although much young adolescent behavior appears rejecting, this is not the time for adults to alienate themselves from their children. Early separation from adults may result in an increased risk of susceptibly to negative peer influences and participation in unhealthy, even risky, behaviors.

Moral/Character Development

The development of character is intricately linked to socioemotional and cognitive growth. A new capacity for abstract thinking allows adolescents to ask the "what ifs"; social and emotional growth provide the context for the answers. "Character develops within a social web or environment" (Leming 1993, 69). Reference groups such as families, peer groups, and television are particularly important as students seek to understand their place in the world (Rice 1990). "Middle school students can be helped to think about who they are and who they want to be, to form identities as self-respecting, career minded persons" (Davis 1993, 32).

Young adolescents will acquire a value system with or without the help of parents and teachers. At a stage of development when students are emerging as reflective citizens, educators can help them to be consciously aware of constructive values, to think logically about consequences, to empathize with others, and to make personal commitments to constructive values and behavior (Davis 1993).

All young adolescents are "at risk" of not successfully completing developmental tasks and of bearing the emotional scars of inappropriate and negative interactions with adults. The socioeconomic condition of society partially shapes the experiences of youth, but societal norms and economic conditions change slowly.

Educators do, however, have control over their interactions with young adolescents. By understanding and appreciating the normal behaviors necessary to accomplish developmental tasks, they have the power to eliminate or at the very least reduce the "risk" for many young people.

REFERENCES

Beane, J. A., and R. P. Lipka. 1986. *Self-concept, self-esteem, and the curriculum.* New York: Teachers College Press.

Brack, C. J., D. P. Orr, and G. Ingersoll. 1988. Pubertal maturation and adolescent self-esteem. *Journal of Adolescent Health Care* 9: 280-85.

Brooks-Gunn, J., and E. O. Reiter. 1990. The role of pubertal processes. In *At the threshold: The developing adolescent*, edited by S. S. Feldman and G. R. Elliott, 16-53. Cambridge, Mass.: Harvard University Press.

Brown, B. B. 1990. Peer groups and peer cultures. In *At the threshold: The developing adolescent*, edited by S. S. Feldman and G. R. Elliott, 171-96. Cambridge, Mass.: Harvard University Press.

Davis, G. A. 1993. Creative teaching of moral thinking: Fostering awareness and commitment. *Middle School Journal* 24(4): 32-33.

Dorman, G., and J. Lipsitz. 1981. Early adolescent development. In *Middle grades assessment program, 4-8*, edited by G. Dorman. Carrboro, N.C.: Center for Early Adolescence.

Feldman, S. S., and G. R. Elliott. 1990. *At the threshold: The developing adolescent.* Cambridge, Mass.: Harvard University Press.

Harter, S. 1990. Self and identity development. In *At the threshold: The developing adolescent*, edited by S. S. Feldman and G. R. Elliott, 388-413. Cambridge, Mass.: Harvard University Press.

Hauser, S. T., and M. K. Bowlds. 1990. Stress, coping, and adaptation. In *At the threshold: The developing adolescent*, edited by S. S. Feldman and G. R. Elliott, 388–413. Cambridge, Mass.: Harvard University Press.

Hill, J. P. 1980. *Understanding early adolescence: A framework.* Carrboro, N.C.: Center for Early Adolescence.

Hillman, S. B. 1991. What developmental psychology has to say about early adolescence. *Middle School Journal* 23(1): 3-8.

Keating, D. P. 1990. Adolescent thinking. In *At the threshold: The developing adolescent*, edited by S. S. Feldman and G. R. Elliott, 54-90. Cambridge, Mass.: Harvard University Press.

Kohn, A. 1994. The truth about self-esteem. *Phi Delta Kappan* 76(4): 272-83.

Leming, J. S. 1993. Synthesis of research: In search of effective character education. *Educational Leadership* 51(3): 63-71.

Modell, J., and M. Goodman. 1990. Historical perspectives. In *At the threshold: The developing adolescent*, edited by S. S. Feldman, and G. R. Elliott, 93-122. Cambridge, Mass.: Harvard University Press.

Newman, J. 1985. Adolescents: Why they can be so obnoxious. *Adolescence* 10(79): 636-46.

Offer, D., E. H. Ostrov, and K. I. Howard. 1989. Adolescence: What is normal? *American Journal of Diseases of Children* 143: 731-36.

Ogbu, J. G. 1992. Understanding cultural diversity and learning. *Educational Researcher* 21(8): 5-14.

Rice, F. P. 1990. *Adolescent development: Relationships, and culture.* Boston: Allyn and Bacon.

Savin-Williams, R. C., and T. J. Berndt. 1990. Friendship and peer relations. In *At the threshold: The developing adolescent*, edited by S. S. Feldman and G. R. Elliott, 277-307. Cambridge, Mass.: Harvard University Press.

Scales, P. C. 1991. *A portrait of young adolescents in the 1990s.* Carrboro, N.C.: Center for Early Adolescence.

Simmons, R. G., and D. A. Blyth. 1987. *Moving into adolescence: The impact of pubertal change and school context.* Hawthorne, N.Y.: Aldine De Gruyter.

Spencer, M. B., and S. M. Dornbusch. 1990. Challenges in studying minority youth. In *At the Threshold: The developing adolescent*, edited by S. S. Feldman and G. R. Elliott, 123-46. Cambridge, Mass.: Harvard University Press.

Steinberg, L. 1990. Autonomy, conflict, and harmony in the family. In *At the threshold: The developing adolescent*, edited by S. S. Feldman, and G. R. Elliott, 255-76. Cambridge, Mass.: Harvard University Press.

Wigfield, A., and J. S. Eccles. 1995. Middle grades schooling and early adolescent development. *Journal of Early Adolescence* 15(1): 5-8.

At-Risk Students and Resiliency: Factors Contributing to Academic Success

JAMES H. McMILLAN and DAISY F. REED

James H. McMillan is a professor and Daisy F. Reed is an associate professor—both at the School of Education, Virginia Commonwealth University, Richmond, Virginia. Funds to support this research were received from the Metropolitan Educational Research Consortium. The views expressed are those of the authors and do not represent opinions or beliefs of the members of the consortium.

The increasingly high number of at-risk middle and high school students—those in danger of dropping out of school because of academic failure or other problems—is a major concern in education today. At-risk students show persistent patterns of under-achievement and of social maladjustment in school, leading to their failure to finish high school. Indeed, the national dropout rate averages about 25 percent (Sklarz 1989), and for minorities, that rate is higher, with an average of 30 percent leaving school before they graduate (Liontos 1991). In Texas, the dropout rate for Hispanic Americans is 45 percent. Additionally, students in urban schools have much higher dropout rates than those in other areas: in Boston, Chicago, Los Angeles, Detroit, and other major cities, dropout rates range from 40 percent to 60 percent of the total school population (Hahn 1987).

An interesting approach to helping at-risk students succeed is to examine the notion of "resilience." Despite incredible hardships and the presence of at-risk factors, some students have developed characteristics and coping skills that enable them to succeed. They appear to develop stable, healthy personas and are able to recover from or adapt to life's stresses and problems. These students can be termed *resilient* (Winfield 1991).

In one recent large-scale study, approximately 19 percent of students who could be classified as at-risk became individuals who had success in school, with positive goals and plans for the future (Peng, Lee, Wang, and Walberg 1992). What enables these resilient students to succeed academically? What can educators and other concerned citizens do to foster these qualities in the 81 percent of at-risk students who do not succeed in school? We believe that much can be learned from studying students who may be classified as at-risk but are resilient, that is, doing well in school despite the odds against them. In this article, we integrate existing literature with our own research that examines resiliency, and then suggest a model to explain resiliency that can be used to better understand why these students have been successful and what can be done to help other at-risk students.

The factors that seem to be related to resiliency can be organized into four categories: individual attributes, positive use of time, family, and school (Peng et al. 1992; McMillan and Reed 1993).

Elements of Resiliency

Individual Attributes

Resilient at-risk students possess temperamental characteristics that elicit positive responses from individuals around them. These personality traits begin in early childhood and are manifested in adolescence as students seek out new experiences and become self-reliant. This begins a cycle of positive reciprocity that enables these students to reach out to other people and expect help. Their positive attitudes are usually rewarded with helpful reactions from those around them. Thus, they come to see the world as a positive place in spite of the difficult issues with which they have to deal. Their positive attitudes include respecting others, coming to class prepared, volunteering for in- and out-of-class assignments, and knowing how to play the school game.

High intrinsic motivation and internal locus of control seem to enable resilient at-risk students to succeed. In their study of 17,000 tenth graders from low-income families, Peng et al. (1992) found that locus of control was a significant predictor of academic success—students with higher academic achievement tended to have a more in-

From *The Clearing House*, January/February 1994, pp. 137-140. © 1994 by the Helen Dwight Reid Educational Foundation. Reprinted by permission of Heldref Publications, 1319 Eighteenth Street, NW, Washington, DC 20036-1802.

rnal locus of control. They also found that successful udents had higher educational aspirations than non-re-lient students. In a qualitative study of the perceptions f academically successful at-risk students, many stu-ents spoke of satisfaction gained from experiencing suc-ess in self-fulfilling activities (McMillan and Reed 1993). hese students were motivated by a desire to succeed, to e self-starting, and to be personally responsible for their chievements. They attributed poor performance to in-rnal factors such as a lack of effort, not caring, not try-g, not studying as much as they needed to, goofing off, nd playing around; most respondents thought that poor erforming students could do better if they put in more ork and got serious about school. A strong sense of lf-efficacy is important; students see themselves as be-g successful because they have chosen to be so and give uch credit to themselves.

Resilient students have clear, realistic goals and are op-mistic about the future. They have hope, despite all the egative circumstances in their lives, and confidence that hey can achieve their long-range goals. For some stu-ents a particularly difficult experience, either direct or icarious, reinforces the importance of getting an educa-ion. These might be called "reality checks" because they eem to motivate students toward positive goals (McMil-an and Reed 1993). The reality check may have been ropping out of school, becoming pregnant, being in rug rehabilitation, or some other event or circumstance hat showed them that without an education their oppor-unities would be limited. As a result, these resilient stu-ents tend to be very mature in their explanations and oals.

Resilient students do not believe that the school, neigh-orhood, or family is critical in either their successes or ailures. They acknowledge that a poor home environ-ment can make things difficult, but they do not blame heir performance on these factors.

Positive Use of Time

In the qualitative study conducted by McMillan and Reed (1993), resilient students were asked about their obbies, activities, and participation in clubs, church, or ther organizations and about how they spend their time. t was clear that they used their time positively and were eaningfully involved in school and other activities. With some exceptions, this involvement was not in a spe-cial program or group for at-risk students or students with specific problems. This positive involvement did not leave these students with much spare time. Active in-volvement in extracurricular events at school and in other areas seems to provide a refuge for resilient stu-dents. Hobbies, creative interests, and sports help pro-mote the growth of self-esteem. Being recognized and supported for special talents is also important. In addi-tion, simply being involved in an activity considered spe-cial appears to increase self-esteem and a belief in one's ability to succeed (Geary 1988; Werner 1984; Coburn and

Nelson 1989; McMillan and Reed 1993). Such involve-ment may provide an important social-psychological sup-port system by connecting the students to others in mean-ingful ways. Success in these activities may be important in enhancing self-esteem by providing recognition and a sense of accomplishment.

Involvement in "required helpfulness" seems to be a factor in resilient students' experiences. Required help-fulness may mean volunteer work in the community, tu-toring or buddying at school, or taking care of siblings or otherwise helping at home. These activities seem to lend purpose to the difficult life of an at-risk student and serve to increase their caring about others. They realize there are people that even they can help (Werner 1984; Philli-ber 1986).

Family Factors

Most resilient at-risk students have had the opportu-nity to establish a close bond with at least one caregiver who gives them needed attention and support. A sense of trust is developed that is very important in interactions with teachers and peers. This support may be from peo-ple other than parents, such as siblings, aunts, uncles, or grandparents who become positive role models. Resilient children seem to be adept at finding these substitute care-givers, much as they are adept at eliciting positive re-sponses from many people around them (Werner 1984).

Family support seems to be an attribute of successful at-risk students. Parents of resilient students have higher expectations for their children's education. Such expecta-tions exert pressure on the children to remain engaged in school and work toward high achievement. These stu-dents are more likely to interact with parents, to have more learning materials in the home, and to be involved in out-of-school educational activities than are non-resil-ient at-risk students (Peng et al. 1992).

Interestingly, family composition seems to have no sig-nificant relationship to at-risk students' success or failure (Peng et al. 1992). Students living with both parents do not necessarily have a higher level of resiliency than stu-dents in single-parent families or other configurations. Instead, good parent-child relationships and supportive attachments appear to act as protective factors from the environment. Parents who are committed to their chil-dren provide informal counseling, support, and help in achieving success. This parental commitment lends a feel-ing of coherence to the family unit. Werner (1984) main-tains that these strong family ties help at-risk students to believe that life makes sense and that they have some con-trol over their own lives. This sense of meaning becomes a powerful motivation for many resilient at-risk students.

Finally, the educational background of parents is re-lated to student resiliency. Peng et al. (1992) found that less than 11 percent of students whose parents had less than a high school education were classified as resilient students as compared with 23 percent of students whose parents had a high school education or beyond.

School Factors

Resilient students seem to find support outside of the home environment, usually in school. They like school, in general, or at least put up with it. Most attempt to involve themselves in classroom discussions and activities. School is more than academics for these students. Most are involved in at least one extracurricular event that becomes an informal source of support. The extracurricular event not only increases involvement, belonging, and self-esteem, it also provides a network of people who have a common bond and work in cooperation with each other (Werner 1984; Coburn and Nelson 1989). Extracurricular events at school, especially sports, seem to mitigate the powerful and widespread peer pressure not to do well. Many resilient students seem to feel they must be involved with a nonacademic activity in order to "fit in" with the majority of students. This involvement maintains the resilient at-risk student's positive engagement in school (Geary 1988).

Teachers play an important role in the success of resilient students. In three qualitative studies, resilient at-risk students mentioned school staff who had taken a personal interest in them as being important to their success (Geary 1988; Coburn and Nelson 1989; McMillan and Reed 1993). Both interpersonal relations and professional competence are important to at-risk students. They cite the following interpersonal qualities of a teacher as important: being caring, having respect for them as persons and as learners, being able to get along with them, listening without being intrusive, taking them seriously, being available and understanding, helping and providing encouragement, and laughing with them. Professional behavior and competence are also important. Resilient at-risk students look for these qualities: the ability to represent and further the goals of the system and the school, a willingness to listen to the motivations behind inappropriate behavior before they discipline, fairness in grading and instruction, praise and encouragement that they can succeed, high expectations, and a willingness to get to know the students personally as well as academically (Werner 1984). Students feel that they can talk to "good" teachers and counselors about almost anything and that the teacher or counselor will listen without judging the student. These counselors and teachers "push" the students and at the same time are very supportive.

Profile of the Resilient Student

Resilient at-risk students have a set of personality characteristics, dispositions, and beliefs that promote their academic success regardless of their backgrounds or current circumstances. They have an internal locus of control and healthy internal attributions, taking personal responsibility for their successes and failures and showing a strong sense of self-efficacy. They feel that they have been successful because they have *chosen* to be successful and have put forth needed effort. Even though they wel-

come and appreciate the efforts of the significant adul[t]s in their lives, they do not see these people as being r[e]sponsible for their success or failure. They credit them[s]elves. They have positive expectations about their ab[il]ities and the future, an optimistic perspective with re[al]istic long-range goals. This strong sense of hope is a[c]companied by a belief that doing well in school is nece[s]sary to doing well in life. These students are very matu[re] in their outlook and attitudes and tend to make positi[ve] choices about how to use their time.

To develop these characteristics, resilient students ha[ve] a psychological support system that provides a safety n[et] and encouragement. This system is evident in the way th[e] students are meaningfully connected to others, in or o[ut] of school. They are actively involved in positive activiti[es] that provide a sense of support, success, and recognitio[n]. Activities such as hobbies give these students a reason t[o] feel proud and provide a solace when other aspects o[f] their lives are troubling. Involvement in both academi[c] and extracurricular activities maintains resilient student[s'] positive engagement in school.

Resilient students have adults—usually a parent (mo[re] often mother than father) and someone from the school—with whom they have trusting relationships. These adul[ts] have high expectations and provide support and encou[r]agement with firmness. Students respect these adul[ts] because they obviously care about their welfare.

Thus, there are important environmental factors th[at] contribute to the strong, resilient personalities and belie[fs] that are critical to these students. These factors are illu[s]trated with the conceptual model in figure 1. The mod[el] shows how significant relationships with adults an[d] positive use of time provide encouragement, high expe[c]tations, a psychological suport system, and recognitio[n] and accomplishment. These environmental factors influ[u]ence these students so that they develop self-efficacy, goals, personal responsibility, and so forth. It is thes[e] traits that make students resilient. The challenge t[o] schools is to provide the relationships and involvemen[t] that can foster this development.

Implications for School Personnel

The model suggests several implications for school per[-] sonnel. First, instructional strategies and techniques, a[s] well as other dimensions of the school environment[,] must be developed to promote a sense of internal locus o[f] control, self-efficacy, optimism, and a sense of persona[l] responsibility. Teachers should establish reference point[s] where achievement will be identified, and they must con[-] tinually relate success to effort and ability. Goal setting i[s] also important, particularly setting long-range goals tha[t] demonstrate the need to focus beyond one's immediat[e] interests and activities.

Second, teachers, administrators, and counselors nee[d] to be trained and encouraged to provide classroom activ[-] ities and classroom environments that stress high aca[-] demic achievement while also building students' self-es[-]

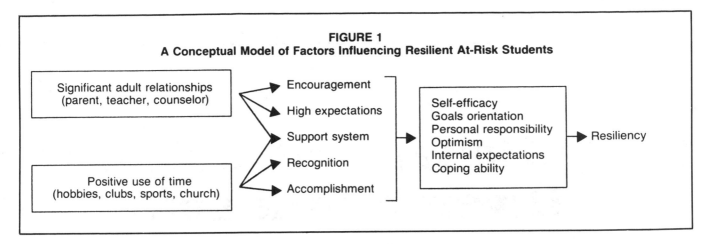

FIGURE 1
A Conceptual Model of Factors Influencing Resilient At-Risk Students

teem and self-confidence. The classroom environment should facilitate time-on-task, student interaction, student success, and positive reinforcement for desired classroom behaviors. Teachers need to be aware of the difference between high expectations and high standards. High expectations involve beliefs about what students are capable of doing and achieving, while high standards do not necessarily suggest that students can reach them. Positive experiences in school help provide students a sense of belonging, bonding, and encouragement.

In addition, extracurricular activities need to be expanded and promoted in schools where there are large populations of at-risk students. As previously mentioned, these activities increase involvement in school. However, many at-risk students will not voluntarily participate in activities because of their general feelings of disconnectedness. Teachers and administrators should develop needed programs and systematically issue personal invitations for at-risk students to join. These programs should include the usual school clubs such as drama, choir, "Future Teachers," "Future Farmers," and others, as well as support groups for various concerns such as adolescent mothers, victims of abuse, children of alcoholic parents, and children of incarcerated parents.

Third, teachers need to be provided with training and encouragement to develop relationships that benefit at-risk children. These students need teachers who are respectful, caring, honest, patient, open-minded, and firm. They also need teachers who understand learning styles, expect positive results, and recognize cultural norms and differences. Perhaps teacher education programs for preservice and inservice teachers need to offer special seminars or classes on working with at-risk populations.

Resilient students give us hope and encouragement, for it is clear that despite unfavorable odds, they have succeeded. We need to learn from them and put into practice what we have learned.

REFERENCES

Coburn, J., and S. Nelson. 1989. *Teachers do make a difference: What Indian graduates say about their school experience* (Report No. RC-017-103). Washington, D.C.: Office of Educational Research and Improvement. (ERIC Document Reproduction Service No. ED 306 071)

Geary, P. A. 1988. *"Defying the odds?": Academic success among at-risk minority teenagers in an urban high school* (Report No. UD-026-258). Paper presented at the annual meeting of the American Educational Research Association, New Orleans, La. (ERIC Document Reproduction Service No. ED 296 055)

Hahn, A. 1987. Reaching out to America's dropouts: What to do? *Phi Delta Kappan* 69(4): 256–63.

Liontos, L. B. 1991. *Trends and issues: Involving families of at-risk youth in the educational process.* ERIC Clearinghouse on Educational Management. Eugene, Oregon: College of Education, University of Oregon. ED 328946

McMillan, J. H., and D. F. Reed. 1993. A qualitative study of resilient at-risk students. Paper presented at the 1993 annual meeting of the American Educational Research Association, Atlanta.

Peng, S. S., R. M. Lee, M. C. Wang, and H. J. Walberg. 1992. Resilient students in urban settings. Paper presented at the 1992 annual meeting of the American Educational Research Association, San Francisco.

Philliber, S. 1986. *Teen outreach: Data from the second year of a national replication.* Paper presented at the 1986 annual national conference of the Children's Defense Fund, Washington, D. C.

Sklarz, D. P. 1989. Keep at-risk students in school by keeping them up to grade level. *The American School Board Journal* 176(9): 33–34.

Werner, E. E. 1984. Resilient children. *Young Children* 40(1): 68–72.

Winfield, L. A. 1991. Resilience, schooling, and development in African-American youth: A conceptual framework. *Education and Urban Society* 24(1): 5–14.

Exceptional and Culturally Diverse Students

- **Educationally Disabled (Articles 12 and 13)**
- **Gifted and Talented (Articles 14–16)**
- **Culturally and Academically Diverse (Articles 17–19)**

The Equal Educational Opportunity Act for All Handicapped Children (Public Law 94-142) gives disabled children the right to an education in the least-restrictive environment, due process, and an individualized educational program that is specifically designed to meet their needs. Professionals and parents of exceptional children are responsible for developing and implementing an appropriate educational program for each child. The application of these ideas to classrooms across the nation at first caused great concern among educators and parents. Classroom teachers whose training did not prepare them for working with the exceptional child expressed negative attitudes about mainstreaming. Special resource teachers also expressed concern that mainstreaming would mitigate the effectiveness of special programs for the disabled and would force cuts in services. Parents feared that their children would not receive the special services they required because of governmental red tape and delays in proper diagnosis and placement.

It has been more than two decades since the implementation of P.L. 94-142, which was amended by the Individuals with Disabilities Education Act (IDEA) in 1991 and introduced the term "inclusion." Many of the concerns just named have been studied by psychologists and educators, and their findings have often influenced policy. For example, research has indicated that mainstreaming is more effective when regular classroom teachers and special resource teachers work cooperatively with disabled children.

Writings in this unit concerning the educationally disabled confront many of these issues. Elaine Wilmore, in "When Your Child Is Special," describes her personal and professional experiences with exceptional children. Then, Thomas Armstrong takes a new look at attention deficit hyperactivity disorder.

Other exceptional children are the gifted and talented. These children are rapid learners who can absorb, organize, and apply concepts more effectively than the average child. They often have IQs of 140 or more and are convergent thinkers (i.e., they give the correct answer to teacher or test questions). Convergent thinkers are usually models of good behavior and academic performance, and they respond to instruction easily; teachers generally value such children and often nominate them for gifted programs. There are other children, however, who do not score well on standardized tests of intelligence because their thinking is more divergent (i.e., they can imagine more than one answer to teacher or test questions). These gifted divergent thinkers may not respond to traditional instruction. They may become bored, respond to questions in unique and disturbing ways, and appear uncooperative and disruptive. Many teachers do not understand these unconventional thinkers and fail to identify them as gifted. In fact, such children are sometimes labeled as emotionally disturbed or mentally retarded because of the negative impressions they make on their teachers. Because of the differences between these types of students, a great deal of controversy surrounds programs for the gifted. Such programs should enhance the self-esteem of all gifted and talented children, motivate and challenge them, and help them realize their creative potential. The articles in the unit subsection on gifted children consider the characteristics of giftedness, and they explain how to identify gifted students and provide them with an appropriate education.

The third subsection of this unit concerns student diversity. Just as labeling may adversely affect the disabled child, it may also affect the child who comes from a minority ethnic background where the language and values are quite different from those of the mainstream culture. The term "disadvantaged" is often used to describe these children, but it is negative, stereotypical, and apt to result in a self-fulfilling prophecy whereby teachers perceive such children as incapable of learning. Teachers should provide academically and culturally diverse children with experiences that they might have missed in the restricted environment of their homes and neighborhoods. The reports in this section address these individual differences and suggest strategies for teaching these diverse children.

Looking Ahead: Challenge Questions

What are some issues regarding the Public Law 94–142 provision calling for "least restrictive environment"?

What is meant by "full inclusion"? What are the pros and cons?

Who are the gifted and talented? How can knowledge of their characteristics and learning needs help to provide them with an appropriate education?

What cultural differences exist in our society? How can teacher expectations affect the culturally diverse child? How would multicultural education help teachers deal more effectively with these differences?

When Your Child Is Special

Decisions about where to enroll a child should come down to this: What would I do to ensure success if this were my child?

Elaine L. Wilmore

Elaine L. Wilmore is a Professor, Center for Professional Teacher Education, University of Texas at Arlington, Box 19227, Arlington, TX 76019-0227.

Everywhere you go in education today *inclusion* is the new buzzword, the new save-the-world concept. Everyone seems to have not only an opinion, but a strong opinion about allowing any physically, emotionally, or academically handicapped child, regardless of the severity, to return to the regular classroom, preferably with support.

Social reformers zealously seek to change society through the schools. In order to provide the handicapped more accessibility, they seek to abandon the traditional resource room and, teachers fear, revert to many practices commonly used prior to passage of the *Individuals with Disabilities Education Act* (P.L. 94-142 amended) in 1991. Teachers publicly protest and sign petitions.

Proponents of full inclusion, alluding to a P.L. 94-142 provision, argue that the regular classroom is the only true "least restrictive environment." They contend that all children

do better academically and socially when exposed to higher performing students, and that "normal" children need to learn how to live in a society with handicapped people. Many parents of handicapped children want their offspring in an age-appropriate educational environment for many of these same reasons.

Then there is me. I am a former classroom teacher, counselor, and principal. I am now a professor and still teach Sunday school. I am also

the mother of a handicapped child. Where does that leave me? Somewhere in between, in Peter Pan's Never-Never Land.

Brooke

Why do so many people push for inclusion?

I have a 12-year-old daughter named Brooke. Her middle name is Elaine, after me, her mom. She has long blonde hair almost to her waist. She has beautiful blue eyes and braces

Courtesy of Elaine Wilmore

Brooke and her mom study at home.

on her teeth. She has a smile from ear to ear and loves to have a friend over to spend the night. She likes to sing in the front yard while she jumps rope. She is a nice, well-behaved child who earns "Excellent" in Conduct on her report cards. She also has a great big learning disability.

School is hard for Brooke. She is academically and developmentally delayed. She was slower than her peers in learning to talk. She had difficulty learning to read. We still haven't mastered two-place long division. Fractions elicit blank stares. Even attempting much work on her grade level is a major event. Every teacher Brooke has had has been loving, cooperative, and helpful. It's not their fault Brooke is a slow learner. Her father and I work with her every night of her life just to help keep her afloat.

The Teacher's Perspective

Many mainstream educators argue that they lack the time, training, and inclination to teach handicapped students. They see it as modified baby-sitting at the expense of the rest of the class, and often feel that slow, sometimes *very* slow learners will hold back the rest of the class. In many cases, they see the presence of severely handicapped or emotionally disturbed children as a distraction at best, a major disruption at worst, impinging on the rights of the other children to a calm and safe environment.

As a former teacher, I can sympathize with teachers' typical anxieties. I prided myself in having a well-organized, structured, efficient learning environment. I also enjoyed being creative with my class, and taught the love of language and reading as life skills. I was proud that my classes were disciplined but fun, that my students scored well on standardized tests, and that parents often requested that their children be placed in my classes. I was into lots of hugs, kisses, and warm fuzzies for my students.

So how would I have reacted to having a severely handicapped child in my class? I would have to answer that

with a firm "it depends." If the child was physically able to maintain himself or herself in my room, was cooperative, and, most important, able to behave so as not to distract or threaten the safety of my other students, then great. Send that child in. I would not mind modifying, or using a totally different curriculum for the child. On the other hand, if the student's behavior negatively affected or harmed the other children, I would have a problem; that, I firmly believe, is where that person's rights end. It would be time to have another Admission, Review, or Dismissal meeting and either modify the situation or change it totally.

The Principal's Perspective

As a principal, my philosophy was the same. I was responsible for the total learning situation for our campus. Because of that, it would not have been fair to come out for or against inclusion. I was for all children having every opportunity to succeed to the best of his or her ability in a positive, supportive environment.

These decisions must be made on an individual basis. No school district should say, "We are going to full inclusion; we are getting rid of our resource rooms." Phooey! No one learning situation is perfect for *all* children. Recommendations on inclusion or anything else should be made for individual children by everyone involved in their education.

I believe parents' views should be strongly and compassionately considered. Some parents of severely or multiply handicapped children do not want their child removed from the security of the resource classroom. They feel their child is physically safe with more people who have been trained to work with his or her disabilities. Regardless of the philosophy of the district, the campus, or the special education department, those parents' wishes should be honored. Not listening to parents has been a major factor in public education's bad rap.

Of course, other parents are equally adamant that their handicapped children be placed in a regular classroom,

with support as needed. Common reasons are the desire to expose their children to good behavior and higher academic standards. Still other parents point out that the world is not segregated. They feel their children will make greater strides if they are in the mainstream. But then what?

Again, if it is possible to honor the parents' wishes and write an Individualized Education Program to make the situation work, go for it. Be reasonable with it. Write in behavioral as well as academic objectives. Allow for classroom modifications. Try from the outset to set the child up for success and a happy day. Don't expect more from a child than that child can possibly give.

I'd also try my best to provide the child with a cooperative classroom teacher who is open-minded and really wants to try to make the situation work. Teachers need to *want* the child in their room. I would never consider putting a child into a classroom in which I did not think he or she stood a reasonable chance of success.

We all want our child to be one of the rest of the kids, to have a happy, successful life.

Brooke's Challenge

For the last three years, my daughter Brooke has received assistance with math and language. Her resource teacher has become a surrogate mother to her. She sincerely loves Brooke, and Brooke returns her love. Every child with a learning disability should have a teacher as fine, efficient, and caring as Helen Nelson. And still Brooke struggles.

Next school year Brooke will be entering intermediate school. We will attempt to place her in the regular classroom and attempt content mastery. Do you know how I feel as her mother? Scared to death. What if she can't do it? What if changing classes and having so many teachers is more than she can handle? She may be 12, but maturationally she is behind. What if she can't keep up with her assignments? What if in her anxiety to bring home her math, she completely forgets her language arts and science?

What if the teachers and principal don't take good care of Brooke? What if no one looks out for my little girl? In elementary school her classroom teachers and Mrs. Nelson worked together to keep her on track and somewhat organized. Now, we won't be there as her safety net, even though we have worked hard to make her independent. She knows she is as responsible for herself, her work, and her conduct as any other student. Behavior is not a problem for Brooke. Learning is.

Reality

As a former principal, I believe teacher attitudes and perceptions are critical to successful inclusion for any child, regardless of how minor the handicap. Some teachers will welcome a handicapped child with open arms; many others will pitch a screaming fit, especially if the child placed in their classroom is emotionally disturbed or has a behavior disorder. Selling inclusion to this group will be a formidable task.

Many teachers feel overwhelmed just keeping up with their daily routine and their regular children, let alone teaching a handicapped child. They do not feel educationally, emotionally, or, sometimes, philosophically prepared to handle handicapped children in their classrooms. Even the strongest of inclusion advocates believe in providing training and support for regular education teachers. But reality intrudes. Where will the money come from? Where's the available time? Most local school districts are strapped for both. Few special education departments or district instructional specialists have the staff or expertise to provide the training classroom teachers so desperately need.

When Brooke goes off to her new school next year, I, like all the other inclusion parents, will worry, bite my fingernails, and pray a whole lot. Her father and I want Brooke to succeed so much. We'd give anything to make learning easier for her. I understand how the parents of more severely handicapped children feel. They want their children to be normal. We all want our child to be one of the rest of the kids, to experience all the joys of childhood, to have a happy, successful life. In a perfect world we wouldn't have these worries. But we don't live in a perfect world.

Which brings us back to the concept of inclusion. Is it good, or is it bad? It's both. Under the best of circumstances, it can be very, very good. With too little funding, training, or development, it can be a disaster. Like anything else, it is what we make it. One secret is in selecting the right children to use it. And that decision ultimately comes down to the child's Admission, Review, or Dismissal Committee.

Every committee must think, What if this child were my child? Think about the child's tomorrows. Think about what we do now that will affect those tomorrows. We can't afford to make mistakes.

Author's note: Since this article was written, Brooke successfully completed the 6th grade, returning to the resource classroom for math only. She is happily enjoying the 7th grade and passing all her subjects—so far! She has Content Mastery assistance when needed, which is often. I am now a professor and seek daily to teach preservice teachers the importance of opening their hearts as well as their minds in their classrooms.

A Holistic Approach to Attention Deficit Disorder

Thomas Armstrong

What do Winston Churchill and Florence Nightingale have in common? Both found inventive outlets for their boundless energy (also called *hyperactivity*). Here are some strategies for home and school that may help children labeled with ADHD to harness their talents and strengths.

Eight-year-old Billy, in the front row, will have nothing to do with my demonstration of new techniques for teaching spelling. During my visit to his elementary school classroom in upstate New York, Billy is out of his seat during most of the lesson.

When I ask the children to visualize their spelling words, however, I am amazed to see Billy return to his seat and remain perfectly still. Covering his eyes, Billy "looks" intently at his imaginary words—fascinated with the images in his mind!

Later on, I realize that something more important than a spelling lesson went on that afternoon: Billy was able to transform his external physical hyperactivity into internal mental motion—and, by internalizing his outer activity level, was able to gain control over it.

This incident occurred sometime ago but remains memorable to me. Why? Because it suggests that internal empowerment, rather than external control, is often the best way to help kids diagnosed as having ADHD (Attention Deficit Hyperactivity Disorder).

A Decidedly Unholistic Approach

Much of the work currently being undertaken in the field of ADHD looks at the issue from an external control perspective. The two interventions touted in almost all books and programs about ADHD are *medication* and *behavior modification*. While these approaches are often dramatically effective with kids labeled as having ADHD, both have troubling features that often receive scant attention.

When children receive medication, some researchers suggest that they may attribute their improved behaviors to the pills rather than to their own inner resources (Whalen and Henker 1980). Others may expect the medication to do all the work and thus neglect underlying issues that may be the true causes of a child's attention and/or behavior difficulties.

Behavior modification programs, which abound, seek to control children's behaviors through some combination of rewards, punishments, or response costs (the taking away of rewards). Some programs rely on token economy systems, while others use behavior charts, stickers, and even machines. For example, the Attention Training System sits on a child's desk and automatically awards a point every 60 seconds for on-task behavior.

THOUSANDS OF STUDIES TELL US WHAT these kids *can't* do, but few tell us what they *can* do and who they really are.

The teacher can also deduct points for bad behavior using a remote control. Students trade points for prizes and privileges.

Although behavior modification programs may influence children to change their behavior, they do it for the wrong reason—to get rewards. Such programs can discourage risk-taking, blunt creativity, decrease levels of intrinsic motivation, and even impair academic performance (Kohn 1993).

Looking at the Whole Child

What's needed is a new vision of educational interventions to reflect a deeper appreciation for the *whole child* based upon a *wellness* paradigm, rather than a deficit perspective rooted in a medical or *disease-based* model.

Most ADHD researchers and practitioners see children labeled with ADHD in terms of their deficits. Thousands of studies tell us what these kids *can't* do, but few tell us what they *can* do and who they really are. (One exception is Crammond 1994.) Where are the studies that tell us what these kids are interested in; what kinds of positive learning styles or combinations of intelligences they use successfully in the classroom; and what sorts of artistic, mechanical, scientific, dramatic, or personal contributions they can make to their schools and communities?

Such research is critical if we are going to develop sound classroom strategies that empower these kids. The above anecdote, for example, suggests that visualization may be a powerful tool. Parents and teachers tell me about cases of ADHD-labeled kids who are talented dancers, musicians, sculptors, and dramatists. The ADHD community needs to conduct research on the positive qualities of these children and what these abilities could mean in contributing to their success in the classroom and in life. Recently, for example, a teacher told me of a child who'd had a terrible time in a traditional straight-rows-of-desks environment—but who was indistinguishable from his "normal" peers in hands-on, project-based classroom activities.

Some research suggests that kids with ADHD do better in environments that are active, self-paced, and hands-on (McGuinness 1985). Video games and computers are powerful learning tools for many of these kids. In fact, their high-speed behavior and thinking lend themselves quite well to such cutting-edge technologies as hypertext and multimedia (Armstrong 1995).

Alternative Avenues
While the ADHD worldview tacitly approves of a teacher-centered, worksheet- and textbook-driven model of education (almost all of its educational suggestions are based on this kind of classroom), current research suggests that all students benefit from project-based environments in which they actively construct new meanings based upon their existing knowledge of a subject.

We need to initiate a new field of study to help children with behavior and attention difficulties—one based upon their strengths rather than their deficits. Such a field would develop assessment strategies geared toward identifying their inner capabilities. Gardner's theory of multiple intelligences (Gardner 1983) is one possible framework for developing appropriate assessment instruments to help identify such abilities (a refreshing change from the behavior rating scales and artificial performance tests currently used to assess ADHD in children). We must develop individualized educational plans (IEPs) that give more than lip service to a child's strengths and that solidly reflect, in their goals and objectives, that IEPs help the child achieve success.

Finally, interventions need to go beyond strategies such as smiley faces, points, and medications, and reflect a full sense of the child's true nature. Here are a few approaches for use at home and school that might help children identified as having ADHD.

■ *Cognitive.* Use focusing and attention training techniques (for example, meditation and visualization), self-talk skills, biofeedback training, organizational strategies, attributional skills (including the ability to attribute success to personal effort), and higher-order problem solving.

■ *Ecological.* Limit television and video games, provide appropriate spaces for learning, use music and art to calm or stimulate, find a child's best times of alertness, provide a balanced breakfast, and remove allergens from the diet.

■ *Physical.* Emphasize a strong physical education program, martial arts training, use of physical touch and appropriate movement, outdoor activities, noncompetitive sports and games, and physical relaxation techniques.

■ *Emotional.* Use self-esteem building strategies; provide positive role models and positive images of the future; employ values clarification; offer individual psychotherapy; and identify talents, strengths, and abilities.

■ *Behavioral.* Use personal contracting; immediate feedback; natural and logical consequences; and consistent rules, routines, and transitions. Involve the child in a selection of strategies.

■ *Social.* Stress effective communication skills, social skills, class meetings, family therapy, peer and cross-age tutoring, and cooperative learning.

■ *Educational.* Use computers; hands-on learning; high-stimulation learning resources; expressive arts; creativity development; and multiple intelligences, whole language, and attention-grabbing activities.

This tentative list provides a far richer storehouse of interventions than the instructional strategies given in the ADHD literature—for example, seating the child next to the teacher, posting assignments on a child's desk, maintaining eye contact, and breaking up assignments into small chunks. Such a deficit-oriented perspective gives differential treatment to the "ADHD child." Most of the above strategies, by contrast, are good for *all* children. Thus, in an inclusive classroom, the child labeled ADHD can thrive with the same kinds of nourishing and stimulating activities as everyone else and be viewed in the same way as everyone else: as a unique human being.

The Creative Roots of ADHD
Because research has long suggested that many children labeled ADHD are actually *underaroused* (Ritalin provides enough medical stimulation to bring their nervous systems to an optimal level of arousal), a strength-based approach makes more sense than a deficit-based one (Zentall 1975). By providing these kids with high-stimulation learning environments grounded in what they enjoy and can succeed in, we're essentially providing them with a kind of educa-

R e l a t e d R e a d i n g s

■ Crook, W. (1991). *Help for the Hyperactive Child.* Jackson, Tenn.: Professional Books.

■ Hartmann, T. (1993). *Attention Deficit Disorder: A Different Perception.* Lancaster, Pa.: Underwood-Miller.

■ Kurcinka, M. S. (1991). *Raising Your Spirited Child.* New York: HarperCollins.

■ Reif, S. F. (1993). *How to Reach and Teach ADD/ADHD Children.* West Nyack, N.Y.: Center for Applied Research in Education.

■ Taylor, J. F. (1990). *Helping Your Hyperactive Child.* Rocklin, Calif.: Prima Publishing.

tional psychostimulant that works as well as Ritalin but which is internally empowering rather than externally controlling.

Remember that a hyperactive child is an *active* child. These kids often possess great vitality—a valuable resource that society needs for its own renewal. Look at the great figures who transformed society, and you'll find that many of them had behavior problems or were hyperactive as children: Thomas Edison, Winston Churchill, Pablo Picasso, Nikola Tesla,[1] Charles Darwin, Florence Nightingale, and Friedreich Nietzsche (see Goertzel and Goertzel 1962). As educators, we can make a big difference in the lives of these kids if we stop getting bogged down in their deficits and start highlighting their strengths!

[1]Tesla, an electrician, invented the Tesla coil, the AC generator, and other innovations.

References

Armstrong, T. (1995). *The Myth of the ADD Child*. New York: Dutton.

Crammond, B. (1994). "Attention-Deficit Hyperactivity Disorder and Creativity: What Is the Connection?" *Journal of Creative Behavior* 28: 193–210.

Gardner, H. (1983). *Frames of Mind*. New York: Basic Books.

Goertzel, V., and M. G. Goertzel. (1962). *Cradles of Eminence*. Boston: Little, Brown.

Kohn, A. (1993). *Punished by Rewards*. Boston: Houghton Mifflin.

McGuinness, D. (1985). *When Children Don't Learn*. New York: Basic Books.

Whalen, C., and B. Henker. (1980). *Hyperactive Children: The Social Ecology of Identification and Treatment*. New York: Academic Press.

Zentall, S. (July 1975). "Optimal Stimulation as a Theoretical Basis of Hyperactivity." *American Journal of Orthopsychiatry* 45, 4: 549–563.

Thomas Armstrong is the author of seven books including *The Myth of the ADD Child: 50 Ways to Improve Your Child's Behavior and Attention Span without Drugs, Labels, or Coercion*. He can be reached at: P.O. Box 548, Cloverdale, CA 95425.

Is It Acceleration or Simply Appropriate Instruction for Precocious Youth?

John F. Feldhusen
Lanah Van Winkle
David A. Ehle

How do we arrange classroom learning experiences at a level, pace, and depth appropriate to individual students' levels of precocity and need?

How do we assess students' current levels of achievement and readiness for new material?

How do we arrange instructional conditions to place students with a teacher and curriculum material appropriate to their needs?

These questions are important to many teachers of students with special gifts and talents. Without such efforts, precocious students are often bored in school (Feldhusen & Kroll, 1991).

Robert Slavin (1990) stated the case well: "I would certainly be opposed to any plan that would `hold back' gifted children from achieving as much as they are able to accomplish" (p. 3). Yet, such is surely the school experience of many precocious youth much of the time (Westberg, Archambault, Dobyns, & Salvin, 1991). Slavin suggested that gifted programs "are most justifiable when the content of the special program represents true acceleration. Research generally does not find achievement benefits of enrichment programs" (p. 4).

We recently spoke with a junior high school student about the school reform movement. When we asked what she saw as the most serious problem with American schools today, she responded, "They won't let us learn." We thought she misunderstood the question—but as she went on, her point was clear:

> What I mean is, they seem to think they have to keep us all together all the time. That means in the subjects I'm good at I can't learn more because I'm always waiting for others to catch up. I guess if I get too far ahead I'll be doing the next year's work, but I can't understand what's wrong with that if that's what I'm ready for.

For this student it seemed so simple, and she had clearly given it much thought while she was doing all that waiting. As we reflected on her words of wisdom, two ideas emerged: She seems to be calling for "acceleration" as it is often conceptualized; and yet, the underlying philosophy that her comments reveal is not at all what we have traditionally called "acceleration."

Assessment Is Key

Effective teaching involves assessing each students' status in the curriculum sequence and posing new learning tasks slightly beyond the level already mastered (Feldhusen & Klausmeier, 1959). Good teachers have been addressing individual ability differences in this manner in their classrooms for years. In our traditional age-graded system, teachers carry a tremendous burden in planning to meet the needs of all students, one that will not lighten as long as we insist on equating "academic peer" and "age." Yet this effort becomes increasingly difficult when students vary markedly from the norm. If Julie has mastered concepts *A* and *B*, and our goal is to challenge her at a level slightly exceeding the level already mastered, does it not make sense that we should allow her to proceed to concept *C*?

What Is Acceleration?

Now comes that word—*acceleration*. Will we have to accelerate Julie before she can go on to concept *C*? Contrary to common perception, we do not have to *do* anything to Julie before she can learn advanced concepts. Julie is fine just being her own academic self, and we are here to serve her. There's nothing "accelerative" about meeting Julie's needs. If we do not meet her needs, in a sense we "decelerate" her: We hinder her learning. We agree with David Elkind (1988):

> Promotion of intellectually gifted children is simply another way of attempting to match the curriculum to the child's abilities, not to accelerate those abilities. Accordingly, the promotion of intellectually gifted children in no way contradicts the accepted view of . . . the negative effects of hurrying. Indeed, the positive effects of promoting intellectually gifted children provide additional evidence for the benefits of developmentally appropriate curricula. (p. 2)

Acceleration is a misnomer; the process is really one of bringing talented youth up to a level of instruction commensurate with their achievement levels and *readiness* so that they are properly challenged to learn the new material (Feldhusen, 1989).

Curricular Context of Acceleration

We often forget the traditional meaning of the words *acceleration* and *enrichment* when we apply them in education. Both "accelerated" and "enriched" only have meaning when used to compare two different states or situations. When we use acceleration and enrichment in the traditional educational sense, our usual reference point is the standard school curriculum. Jane is in *third* grade but is working on *fifth*-grade math; she is "accelerated" in math. Carl is planning an exploration of Mars; he is doing an "enrichment" activity in science. Adoption of a specific curriculum as a reference point, however, blurs the distinction between acceleration and enrichment. If Carl is in the second-grade enrichment program, but the space exploration activity is done by all sixth-grade students, is he doing an enrichment activity, or has he been accelerated to the sixth-grade level? Most third-grade students are learning simple single-digit multiplication; if Jane is working on three-digit multiplication, is she not doing an enrichment activity in math?

The examples of both enrichment and acceleration programs that are typically given, demonstrate the lack of a precise meaning of these concepts and the importance of relating these terms to a curriculum. The most popular subject for acceleration is math, while language arts or social studies is usually the focus of enrichment programs. It is easier to identify math instruction as being accelerated, since most students learn math concepts in a fairly structured order. On the other hand, most language arts and social studies programs are referred to as enrichment programs. They are often seen as *extended* rather than *advanced* curriculum experiences.

A Call for New Terminology

Where does this leave us? We can either change conceptions of acceleration and enrichment to reflect their commonalities and relativism, or find new terminology to better reflect the concepts involved and eliminate the confusion. Rather than talking about a program that is accelerated or enriched, why not talk about a program that focuses on *higher-level constructs*, greater appreciation of the underlying knowledge structure of a discipline, or mastery of a larger knowledge base in and associated with a field of study? These are the characteristics that differentiate an *expert* in a field from a *novice* (Johnson, Kochevar, & Zualkerman, 1992). This type of program could involve enrichment *and* acceleration; it transcends both terms to strike at the heart of the cognitive goals of gifted education. Such a program brings the content of the curriculum up to the level of the child.

If we accept the premise that gifted and talented students are precocious, doesn't it make sense to challenge them to move in the direction of more advanced learners? Coupled with strong services to meet the social and emotional needs of bright students, *a program to develop the leaders of tomorrow would result*. But what does all this mean in action in a school situation?

Providing Higher-Level Learning Opportunities

Practically, how do we go about bringing the content of the school up to the level

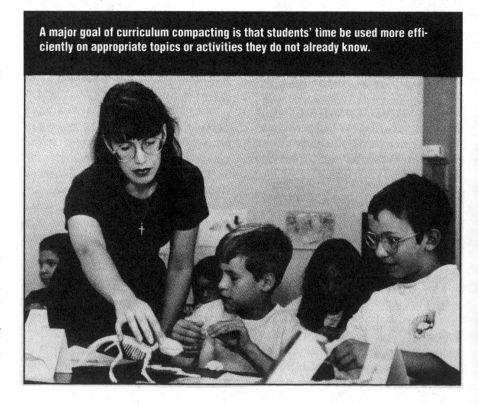

A major goal of curriculum compacting is that students' time be used more efficiently on appropriate topics or activities they do not already know.

The first step in the Diagnostic Testing followed by Prescriptive Instruction (DT-PI) model is to determine the students' current level of knowledge through appropriate tests.

of the child? First, we should not assume that a child does not know what we have not yet taught. A study by the Educational Products Information Exchange Institute (1980-81), a nonprofit educational consumer agency, revealed that 60% of the fourth graders in some of the school districts studied scored 80% or higher on a test of the content of their math texts *before* they had opened their books in September. Similar findings were reported for content tests on 4th- and 10th-grade science texts and 10th-grade social studies texts (Renzulli & Reis, 1986). Since textbooks have continued to drop in levels of difficulty over the past 10-15 years, one would not expect these percentages to be any lower today for our highly able students. We need a way to determine the exact level at which to begin appropriate instruction.

Diagnostic Testing-Prescriptive Instruction

Hoping to develop a teaching approach that would accommodate students' differing levels of knowledge as well as their rates of learning, Stanley (1978) originated the Diagnostic Testing followed by Prescriptive Instruction (DT-PI) model. Benbow (1986) developed the procedure further for use in educational programs for gifted youth. Described in simple terms, the DT-PI model has four steps:

1. Determine students' current level of knowledge through appropriate tests.

2. Identify areas of weakness by analyzing items missed on the tests.

3. Instruct the students in those areas of weakness and allow them to show mastery on a second form of the test.

4. Proceed to the next higher level and repeat Steps 1-3.

The DT-PI model of instruction has been the approach used in the Study of Mathematically Precocious Youth (SMPY) in the summer programs at The Johns Hopkins University since 1971. SMPY's longitudinal study has shown the effectiveness of such acceleration for talented youth. SMPY's most salient finding in working with 85,000 young gifted students over a 13-year period is that *school systems need far more curricular flexibility* (Benbow, 1986). Swiatek and Beubow (1991) have also conducted a 10-year follow-up of fast-paced mathematics classes and found higher achievement in classes using DT-PI methods.

Curriculum Compacting

Another technique that can be used to bring the content up to the level of the child is curriculum compacting (Reis, 1995), a system designed to adapt the regular curriculum to meet the needs of above-average students by either eliminating work that has been mastered pre-

viously or streamlining work that may be mastered at a pace commensurate with the student's ability. A major goal of curriculum compacting is that students' time be used more efficiently on appropriate topics or activities rather than completing tasks they already know. Both DP-TI and curriculum compacting strive for proficiency in the basic curriculum and then continue student learning at an appropriate level for which they are ready. The two approaches differ in that *curriculum compacting focuses on a challenging environment within the context of grade-level curriculum*, while the philosophy behind DP-TI is clearly to enable students to advance at their own pace through the scope and sequence of the curriculum.

The Bottom Line

Most teachers want their students to enjoy learning, to enjoy school, and most of all, to accomplish as much as they are capable. When their students are bored much of the school day, frustrated by repeating material they already know, and are not given the opportunity to accomplish nearly what they could, good teachers are troubled.

Each child has the right to learn new material commensurate with his or her ability and knowledge, even if other students who are ready for that material are 3 years older; age really makes no difference. If acceleration is not an accurate term, is there one? Although we are not at all convinced that we must have a word, there are some terms that appear more philosophically sound. In a recent review, Benbow (1991) made the following suggestions: "curricular flexibility," "flexible pacing," and "developmental placement."

The bottom line is that *our educational programs must respond to the abilities and readiness of individual children.* It is a sad irony that a student could say of those responsible for her education, "They won't let me learn." Let's try to loosen our dependence on the lingo of "acceleration" and "enrichment" and simply go about the business of meeting students' needs, whatever that may require. Curricular and instructional flexibility are the prerequisites. Adapting instruction to individual readiness and need is the answer.

One way to respond to the different abilities and readiness levels of individual students is through flexible curricula and instructional practices.

References

Benbow, C. P. (1986). SMPY's model for teaching mathematically precocious students. In J. S. Renzulli (Ed.), *Systems and models for developing programs for the gifted and talented* (pp. 1-26). Mansfield Center, CT: Creative Learning Press, Inc.

Benbow, C. P. (1991). Meeting the needs of gifted students through use of acceleration. In M. C. Wang, M. C. Reynolds, & H. J. Walberg (Eds.), *Handbook of special education: Research and practice: Vol. 4. Emerging Programs* (pp. 23-36). New York: Pergamon Press.

Educational Products Information Exchange Institute. (1980-81). *Educational research and development report*, 3, 4.

Elkind, D. (1988). Acceleration. *Young Children*, 43(4), 2.

Feldhusen, J. F. (1989). Synthesis of research on gifted youths. *Educational Leadership*, 46(6), 6-11.

Feldhusen, J. F., & Klausmeier, H. J. (1959). Achievement in counting and addition. *The Elementary School Journal*, 59, 388-393.

Feldhusen, J. F., & Kroll, M. D. (1991). Boredom or challenge for the academically talented. *Gifted Education International*, 7(2), 80-81.

Johnson, P. E., Kochevar, L. K., & Zualkerman, I. A. (1992). Expertise and fit: Aspects of cognition. In H. L. Pick, P. Van Den Broek, & D. C. Knill (Eds.), *Cognition: Conceptual and methodological issues* (pp. 305-331).

Washington, DC: American Psychological Association.

Reis, Sally M. (1995). *Curriculum compacting communicator, 28*(2), 1, 27-32. Mansfield Center, CT: Creative Learning Press, Inc.

Renzulli, J. S., & Reis, S. M. (1986). The enrichment triad/revolving door model: A schoolwide plan for the development of creative productivity. In J. S. Renzulli (Ed.), *Systems and models for developing programs for the gifted and talented* (pp. 216-266). Mansfield Center, CT: Creative Learning Press, Inc.

Swiatek, M. A., & Beubow, C. P. (1991). A ten-year longitudinal follow-up of participants in a fast-paced mathematics course. *Journal for Research in Mathematics Education, 22*, 138-150.

Slavin, R. E. (1990). Ability grouping, cooperative learning and the gifted. *Journal for the Education of the Gifted, 14*(1), 3-9.

Stanley, J. C. (1978). SMPY's DT-PI model: Diagnostic testing followed by prescriptive instruction. *Intellectually Talented Youth Bulletin, 4*(10), 7-8.

Westberg, K. L., Archambault, F. X., Dobyns, S. M., & Salvin, T. J. (1991). *The classroom practices observation study.* (Technical Report). Storrs, CT: The National Research Center on the Gifted and Talented.

John F. Feldhusen, Director, Gifted Education Resource Institute; *Lanah Van Winkle*, Assistant Coordinator, Shared Information Services; *David A. Ehle*, Coordinator, Gifted Education Resource Institute, Summer Residential Programs, Purdue University, West Lafayette, Indiana.

Address correspondence to John F. Feldhusen, Purdue University, 1446 Liberal Arts/Education Building, West Lafayette, IN 47907-1446 (e-mail: feldhuse@vm.cc.purdue.edu).

Meeting the Needs of Your High-Ability Students

Strategies every teacher can use

SUSAN WINEBRENNER

Do you feel you could be doing more to help your gifted and talented students achieve their potential? The four strategies described here will help you engage your most advanced students and develop the abilities of every child.

1. FIND HIDDEN ABILITIES

Student Scenario: Elizabeth

Sixth grader Elizabeth had difficulty reading and writing because of a learning disability, and didn't appear to be gifted. But when I introduced a unit on map skills, Elizabeth approached me after class and said, "You know, Mrs. Winebrenner, I know a lot about maps."

"You do? How did that happen?" I asked.

"I don't know. I just love maps."

"What do you like to do with this love of maps?"

"Well, when my family goes on a vacation, I plan our trip on the map."

"No kidding! Where did you go last year?"

"Yellowstone National Park."

"And how did you get there?"

Elizabeth proceeded to do something I'm not sure I could do—she told me how she had navigated her family to Yellowstone: highway by highway, county by county, state by state. I was amazed.

"Pretty impressive," I said. "I bet the prospect of doing a unit on map skills is not very appealing to you."

"I've thought about that."

"I'll tell you what. I'll give you the end-of-unit test

From *Instructor,* September 1994, pp. 60-65. Adapted from *Teaching Gifted Kids in the Regular Classroom: Strategies and Techniques Every Teacher Can Use to Meet the Academic Need of the Gifted and Talented* by Susan Winebrenner. © 1992 by Free Spirit Publishing. To order the book, call 800-735-7323.

tomorrow, and if you pass it with an A, you'll be able to spend your social studies time on a different activity of your choice." Elizabeth was thrilled.

Next, I offered the same deal to everyone in the class. This is something I've learned to do routinely, so that every student has the opportunity to shine.

Sixteen of my twenty-seven students volunteered to take the pretest. The pretesters knew beforehand that if they did not earn an A, their tests would not count. Two passed with A's—Elizabeth was one of them.

While the class honed their map skills, Elizabeth worked independently, creating a papier-mâché relief map of an imaginary country. Because her learning disability prevented her from writing well, I encouraged her to simply flag the population centers, the natural resources, the manufacturing centers, and so on. When she'd finished her project, she gave an interesting talk about her country that fascinated the class.

Did other students ask to do a project like Elizabeth's? Yes! And I let everyone do one as a culminating activity for the map unit, while Elizabeth acted as a consultant. Imagine the boost to Elizabeth's self-esteem when her classmates turned to her for advice.

CUSTOM-MADE LEARNING

What does Elizabeth's story tell us? It's up to teachers to determine what competencies certain students have, and give them full credit for what they already know. Then we need to decide how to modify the curriculum so that these students will learn something new. Dr. Joseph S. Renzulli of The National Research Center on the Gifted and Talented in Storrs, Connecticut, calls this process "curriculum compacting." Dr. Renzulli, author of *Schools for Talent*

Development: A Practical Plan for Total School Improvement, and Linda H. Smith developed the form that follows. Use it to record all the modifications you make for your students.

2. APPOINT RESIDENT EXPERTS
Student Scenario: Joey

Joey, a student in my fifth-grade class, was exceptional in every subject area, but his actual classroom performance left a lot to be desired. He spent most of his time daydreaming, and he seldom completed his homework, yet he always aced the tests. Joey behaved rudely during class discussions, often remarking under his breath to amuse other students.

When Joey's class was about to begin a Civil War unit, I gave him and other students whom I felt could tackle the text on their own a chance to do an independent project on the Civil War during social studies.

I dubbed them "resident experts" and told them they would be responsible for presenting a report on their topic to the class. I gave them each a list of project ideas, but they were free to choose a topic of their own. I also assured all my students that they could do an independent project at the end of the unit.

I asked each resident expert to sign an independent study contract that included the major Civil War concepts I expected them to know, activities related to these ideas, and a timetable of all class quizzes and discussions to assess their progress. (Resident experts take the quizzes and/or participate in discussions along with the other students. Those who do not earn a B or higher, or who display problematic behavior, must rejoin the class until the next quiz. If they achieve a B or higher on the next quiz, they may return to their project. If they don't, they can finish their project when the rest of the class gets school time to work on independent projects.)

You can modify these contracts to include detailed expectations about the quality of the projects you would like students to produce. A contract I designed especially for Joey is shown below.

Unlike the independent study method I used with Elizabeth, the resident-expert strategy is not based on the results of a pretest given to all students willing to give it a try. Instead, teachers use their own judgment, selecting students they feel are capable of developing an in-depth talk, performance, or display of their investigation.

THE COMPACTOR		
Joseph Renzulli & Linda H. Smith		
Student's Name:		
Areas of Strength	**Methods used to document student's mastery of a skill, competency, chapter, concept, or unit**	**Activities student will be engaged in as an alternative to the regular class activities**

EVALUATION CONTRACT
Civil War Project

For a grade of "B," use information gathered from other sources. Choose from the ideas below, or design your own with my approval:

1. Research the different types of trains and locomotives that would have been used during the Civil War era. Draw them to scale.
2. Discover the details about the lives of two famous generals, one Union and one Confederate. Comment on at least two similarities you find.
3. Learn several Civil War songs from both sides. Teach one song from each side to the class. Lead the class in a discussion of similarities and differences in the songs.

For a grade of "A," create a unique product that requires high levels of thinking. Choose from the ideas below, or design your own with my approval:

1. Draw the trains of the Civil War era on routes between the major manufacturing centers and four famous battlefields: two in the North and two in the South. Be prepared to discuss how the proximity of the battlefields to the manufacturing centers may have affected the outcome of the war.
2. Create an interview with a famous Civil War general. Include some information that was probably unknown to the general public at the time of the Civil War. Prepare a live interview where you and a friend impersonate the general and the interviewer. Come in appropriate costume.
3. Discover the role that music has played to create and maintain patriotic feelings during wartime. Illustrate your presentation with musical excerpts.

Use this space to describe your project:

#1

I am contracting for a grade of: ___A___

Student's signature: ___Joey___

3. PROVIDE A VENUE TO SHOWCASE TALENTS
Student Scenario: Alvin

Alvin was passionate about reading and writing poetry, and he had the talent to match it. But he was reluctant to share his poetry with me or his peers, and kept his work at home. In school, Alvin preferred to work alone, wary of group activities. I needed to showcase Alvin's poetic talent in a way that would make him feel more comfortable with his peers.

One Monday, I announced that Friday would be the first of many Great Friday Afternoon Events and explained how the events would work (see chart, on next page). I asked Alvin if he would like to be captain of the poetry team. "I guess so," he replied, nervously.

Within a couple of days, Alvin seemed at ease with the other team members, and the poem the team recited had lots of Alvin-like language and images. The Great Friday Afternoon Events became an effective way to have Alvin and other high-ability students work productively in heterogeneous groups, and gave all students a chance to showcase their talents.

WHO'S GIFTED?
CHARACTERISTICS TO LOOK FOR

Whom teachers consider gifted is changing as we use new tools to measure children's talents and consider a broader range of "gifts," from visual intelligence to affective abilities. (For more about evolving definitions of **giftedness, see next page.**) Nevertheless, **the partial list of** indicators below, which is organized into three different categories, will help you recognize the high-ability students in your classroom. Gifted students may exhibit many but not all of these qualities.

General
- Has an advanced vocabulary
- Possesses an outstanding memory
- Is curious about many things; asks lots of questions
- Has many interests and hobbies
- Is intense; gets totally absorbed in activities and thoughts
- Operates on higher levels of thinking than his or her age peers
- Perceives subtle cause-and-effect relationships
- Catches on quickly, then resists doing work, or works in a sloppy, careless manner
- Is sensitive to beauty and other people's feelings and emotions
- Possesses an advanced sense of justice
- Sees connections between apparently unconnected ideas and activities
- May prefer to work alone; resists cooperative learning
- May be street-smart while not doing well on school tasks

Creative Thinking
- Displays original ideas
- Is fluent in idea generation and development
- Is able to elaborate on ideas
- Values nonconformity in appearance, thought, etc.

Perfectionism
- Believes he is valued for what he can do rather than who he is
- May cry easily in frustration that her work at school can never be perfect
- Procrastinates to the point that work never even gets started
- Asks for lots of help and reassurance from the teacher

New Ways to Think About Giftedness

Carolyn Callahan, a researcher and teacher at the University of Virginia's Curry School of Education and president-elect of the National Association for Gifted Children, talks with Instructor's *Senior Associate Editor Wendy Murray about giftedness and what teachers can do to encourage the special abilities of every child.*

How has our society's conception of giftedness changed over the years?

In the past, the traditional gifted child was one who possessed exceptional reading and writing skills—a giftedness that everyone could see. This usually meant children who scored well on standardized tests, which was problematic because the tests don't accommodate children's different learning styles. New definitions of intelligence have stretched our definition of giftedness and talent. Now we know we must consider many ways of assessing how children perform, interact with their learning, and problem-solve, beyond just reading and writing, to find out who's gifted.

How can teachers unveil their students' talents?

We need to give children the opportunity to show their strengths in a variety of ways. Can students fix a toy pump? Tell a story dramatically? Create a song? Construct a model of a mathematical principle? We have to combine tests with portfolios, observations, and other performance-based assessments.

What is the most important thing a teacher can do to meet the needs of gifted students?

Differentiate the curriculum! For example, say you're planning a unit on community. Think to yourself, I have some chidren who need to learn what a community is; I have others who already know. What activities will challenge each group? While one group might explore the community of their family or the local community, the other can compare world communities.

What other strategies should teachers use?

Teach in an interdisciplinary manner, weaving math, literature, science, social studies, and so on, into whatever it is your students are exploring. Ask yourself, How can I structure this unit so that children think about and solve real-world problems?

Here's my favorite example of bringing the real world into school: One kindergarten teacher I know was teaching her class about germs—viruses and bacteria—in all sorts of interesting ways. Still, there was one child who went ten steps further. He wanted to figure out how to stop the spread of flu at school. He designed an experiment where he put up paper cups at the drinking fountain for a certain number of days and noted student absences from school during that period. Then he took the cups away, tracked the absences, and put the data on a graph that showed drinking cups cut down on the number of students absent due to colds and flus. Then he went to the PTA and got it to pay for cups! Never underestimate the learner!

THE GREAT FRIDAY AFTERNOON EVENT

Students, in four teams, present a program to class.
Teams stay intact for four weeks.
Each week, each team has a different task.
Tasks rotate until each team has done each task.

	POETRY	DECLAMATION	PLAY	NEWSCAST
	Students read or recite a poem of their choice or creation.	(Readers' Theater) Students present a dramatic reading.	Students present Readers' Theater or dramatic play.	Students broadcast a 5–10 minute radio or video show.
WEEK 1	A	B	C	D
WEEK 2	B	C	D	A
WEEK 3	C	D	A	B
WEEK 4	D	A	B	C

Teachers Who Are Good with the Gifted

A team of researchers at the National Research Center on the Gifted and Talented and I recently examined ten U.S. schools that had a reputation for meeting the needs of capable students in regular classrooms. Among other things, we wanted to find out what these successful teachers were doing right. Here's what we found.

In addition to using methods such as curriculum compacting, independent study projects, and heterogeneous-group activities requiring critical thinking, teachers who were most successful with high-ability students possessed these attributes:

● **Trust.** At a northeastern school, we observed a teacher as she showed a group of capable math students how to use protractors to measure degrees in angles. Afterward, she said, "Go through the first four pages of the next chapter. Along the way, *you* decide which problems you need to do to help you understand measurement of triangles."

● **Spontaneity.** In an urban school, a student approached her teacher, a Shakespearean play in hand.

"I know Shakespeare is not very popular at this time, but I really feel he will be appreciated again soon," she said, before asking whether she could share the play with another student. The teacher didn't miss a beat; she told her it was a great idea. This same teacher once put aside what she had planned, to take advantage of a snowstorm. When we walked into her room, students were busy determining the volume of snow that had to be plowed from the school's driveway.

● **Rapport.** One of the most memorable things we observed was watching teachers who clearly enjoy swapping ideas with colleagues. At one school, four teachers of the same grade level meet for dinner at a Mexican restaurant once a week. They refer to these evenings as Ol' Mexico night, and during these dinners they plan their unique "Enrichment Wednesdays," during which they teach special classes designed to address their students' interests. ■

—*Karen L. Westberg, Ph.D., The National Center on the Gifted and Talented, Storrs, Connecticut.*

4. REDIRECT LEADERSHIP QUALITIES

Student Scenario: Lucy

Twelve-year-old Lucy had unusual leadership abilities. She could think on her feet, persuade others to see her point of view, and inspire classmates to work as a team—when she applied herself. But too often she took the shortcut, dominating discussions and bossing other students around. She needed more structured opportunities to hone her gift for persuasion.

With Lucy in mind, I built an array of group activities into the curriculum, setting aside every Wednesday afternoon to engage in these events. Groups of kids held mock trials (we even invited in a lawyer, who ended up being a great mentor for the children),

worked together to simulate running a business, and planned a city of the future, to mention just a few.

By posing open-ended questions to groups of students (such as: If you were sent to live on a planet, what five people would you need to have along to survive?) every student gets to stretch intellectually, and students like Lucy positively blossom. Lucy relished the intellectual challenge, and her peers enjoyed the chance to make her back up her opinions with facts.

The self-assessment involved in these activities is also valuable for children of every ability who lack confidence. Students assess their own ideas and those of the group, and come to see that these evaluations are as valid as yours.

Ability Grouping: Geared for the Gifted

The anti-tracking movement has given ability grouping a bad name. The two are not the same.

Ellen D. Fiedler, Richard E. Lange, and Susan Winebrenner
From *Roeper Review*

Ellen D. Fiedler is Associate Professor, Gifted/ Talented Masters Degree Program, Northeastern Illinois University, Chicago. Richard E. Lange is Director of Gifted Education, Staff Development, and Assessment, Prospect Heights Public Schools, and Adjunct Faculty Member, College of Education, National-Louis University, Evanston, both in Illinois. Susan Winebrenner is an independent consultant in staff development.

IN the 1990s, the anti-tracking movement has suddenly become anti*ability grouping*, side effects ranging from the Regular Education Initiative for students with learning handicaps to attempts to eliminate programs for highly able or gifted students. The concern is about negative effects of locking certain students into unchallenging classes and locking them out of educational situations that stretch their minds. But, all of the relevant research and its ramifications have not been considered.

There are six common myths about appropriate educational programs for all students, including the gifted:

Myth 1:
Tracking and ability grouping are the same.
Reality:

Tracking separates students into class-size groups using their perceived ability or prior achievement. It results in students being assigned full-time to instructional groups based on a variety of criteria, including presumed ability derived from achievement test scores and teacher observations of classroom performance.

This often means a high-ability group for Teacher A, a middle-ability group for Teacher B, and a low-ability group for Teacher C. Once students are in a track, there is little movement between tracks during a school year or from one school year to another. Consistent placement in the low track leads students to disenfranchisement in a class system where there are clear differences between the "haves" and "have-nots."

Ability grouping is re-grouping students to provide curriculum aimed at a common instructional level. Elementary teachers create more homogeneous reading or math groups while teaching heterogeneous groups for most other subjects. Secondary students may be assigned to high-ability groups in areas of their strengths and to average- or low-ability groups in other subjects. Ability grouping does not imply permanently locking students out of settings that are appropriately challenging; it means placing them with others with similar learning needs for whatever length of time works best.

Myth 2:
Ability grouping is elitist.
Reality:

Most gifted educators work to develop an understanding of giftedness in the context of individual differences rather than superiority—consistent with newly emerging approaches

 From *The Education Digest*, January 1994, pp. 52-55. Condensed from *Roeper Review*, 16 (September 1993), pp. 4-7.

that consider cognitive and affective development as equally important.

Keeping one or two highly gifted students in a classroom of mixed abilities may create snobbery. Scattering gifted students through all classrooms may lead them to feel far superior to classmates and promote arrogance. Unless gifted students can be challenged by intellectual peers, the possibilities that they will develop an elitist attitude might increase.

However, when gifted students are grouped together for instruction, studying with intellectual peers may actually lower self-esteem somewhat. There is nothing so humbling as discovering other students in the group equally capable or more knowledgeable. If one goal of education is to help all students develop a realistic appraisal of their own ability, students need to measure themselves with appropriate yardsticks. Comparisons are more likely to be accurate when made with others of similar abilities.

Interestingly, educators have no qualms about identifying outstanding athletes and providing specialized programs for them. If this is not considered elitist, why should intellectual giftedness be given short shrift?

Myth 3:
Ability grouping inevitably discriminates against racial and ethnic minorities.
Reality:

Gifted educators have made great progress in refining identification methods. Widespread efforts are being made to overcome inequities of over-reliance on standardized test scores and assumptions that too often have been made about students who, although gifted, may not fit the stereotype of high achievers with positive attitudes toward school.

The direction is toward approaches that include studying student behaviors for indicators of gifted potential, with attention on training teachers to do this. Also, behavioral descriptors are used to identify other underserved populations. Preschool and kindergarten children, creative thinkers, nonproductive gifted students, and gifted students with learning disabilities and other handicaps are being screened more accurately.

Eliminating ability grouping because of inequitable identification is throwing out the baby with the bath water. Furthermore, singling out racial and ethnic minorities as the only disenfranchised group is misleading. The intent of gifted programs has not been to exclude certain populations. But identification procedures needed revision, and improved methodologies are already being implemented.

Myth 4:
Gifted students will make it on their own; grouping them by ability does not improve their learning or achievement.
Reality:

Studies confirm what gifted educators have known for years: Gifted students benefit cognitively and affectively from working with other gifted students.

Some studies indicate no increase in achievement test scores for high-ability students grouped together, but they omit gifted students. Robert Slavin's research that recommended heterogeneous grouping for all ability groups systematically omitted data from students in the top 5 percent. Such omissions can lead to dangerous overgeneralizations by interpreters.

Also consider ceiling effects: Grade-level achievement tests fail to reveal growth for students who already perform in the top percentile ranks because they have reached the ceiling of the test—the highest scores attainable for that age group. Only with instruments designed for older students can actual achievement gains be determined for students in the extreme upper range.

Another critical issue involves the goals of the gifted program and whether its purposes are actually focused on increasing academic achievement. What gifted students learn should be measured by far more comprehensive criteria than increased achievement test scores. Equally important are the development of socialization and leadership skills, experience with complex concepts and challenging learning, and opportunities to pursue topics in great depth. If such a program is more concerned with helping gifted students work together to grapple with global concerns that are complex and substan-

tive, increases in achievement test scores in specific subject areas are not appropriate for measuring success.

Myth 5:
Heterogeneously grouped cooperative learning is most effective for serving all students, including the gifted.
Reality:

The students who may learn the least in a given class are the gifted. So much of what they are asked to learn they may have already mastered. Teachers may then be tempted to use them as classroom helpers or to teach others, robbing the gifted of consistent opportunities to learn through real struggle. This can have a negative impact on them in many ways, including lowered self-esteem. Without regular encounters with challenging material, the gifted fail to learn how to learn and have problems developing study skills for future academic pursuits.

Cooperative learning is designed to be used with either homogeneous or heterogeneous groups. It seems reasonable to allow teachers the flexibility to determine which lessons lend themselves to heterogeneous cooperative learning groups and which to homogeneous cooperative learning groups and make professional decisions to place students accordingly.

Myth 6:
Having gifted students in all classrooms provides positive role models and will automatically improve the classroom climate.
Reality:

The notion that gifted students in low-ability classrooms will automatically benefit students performing at lower levels rests on questionable assumptions: that the performance discrepancies will be perceived as alterable by the less capable students; that gifted students are consistently highly-motivated high achievers who will inspire others to similar accomplishments; and that gifted students placed in low-ability or heterogeneous classrooms will continue to perform at their peak even when they lack regular opportunities to interact with intellectual peers who can stimulate their thinking. Research indicates that students model their behavior on that of others who are of similar ability and are coping well in school.

Furthermore, heterogeneous grouping may have negative side-effects on both the gifted and others. Gifted students who are a minority of one or who have only one or two classmates whose ability level approaches their own feel either odd or arrogant. If all the other students watch from the sidelines while the smart one provides all the answers, their perceptions of themselves as competent, capable learners suffer.

Equality in education does not require that all students have exactly the same experiences. Rather, education in a democracy promises that everyone will have an equal opportunity to actualize their potential, to learn as much as they can.

Education in a free society should not be a choice between equity and excellence. Providing for formerly disenfranchised groups need not take away appropriate programs from any other group. As the research clearly indicates, gifted students benefit from working together. Therefore, ability grouping for the gifted must continue. While the educational community moves toward heterogeneity for students who benefit more from working in mixed ability groups, it should not deny gifted students the right to educational arrangements that maximize their learning. The goal of an appropriate education must be to create optimal learning experiences for all.

What We Can Learn from Multicultural Education Research

Educators will be more successful if they understand five variables that matter in working with a diverse student population.

Gloria Ladson-Billings

Gloria Ladson-Billings is an Assistant Professor at the University of Wisconsin-Madison, Department of Curriculum and Instruction, 225 N. Mills St., Madison, WI 53706.

Many findings from multicultural education research can be applied in the everyday world of teachers and administrators. This observation holds regardless of whether the educators work with many students of color or with only a few.

The research shows that five areas matter a great deal in the education of a multicultural population: teachers' beliefs about students, curriculum content and materials, instructional approaches, educational settings, and teacher education. One other area—whether the race and ethnicity of teachers affects student learning—remains unclear.

Beliefs About Students Matter

To begin to see how teacher beliefs affect student achievement, imagine two new teachers. Don Wilson and Margie Stewart are starting their first year of teaching.

How teachers think about education and students makes a pronounced difference in student performance and achievement.

Don Wilson. After his first weeks of teaching in an urban school, Wilson is exhausted and uncertain about whether he chose the right profession. His class of 28 fourth graders are African Americans and Latinos. Wilson knows that they have not had many advantages, so he doesn't push them too hard. He wants his students to have fun learning. He worries, though, be-

cause many of them don't seem to be having fun or learning. Many are one or more achievement levels below national averages, and some attend school sporadically, fail to complete homework assignments, and seem unmotivated in the classroom. Although Wilson has sent several notes home expressing concern, parents have not responded. Wilson doubts that he makes any difference in the lives of his students.

Margie Stewart. The first weeks of teaching in a suburban school have been exhausting for Stewart, too, but she is enjoying herself. Of Stewart's 28 third graders, 23 are white, upper-middle-class children. Three of the remaining five are African American, and two are Mexican American (one speaks limited English). In general, the students test at or above grade level on standardized tests, but the students of color lag behind the others. Stewart is also concerned about José. Because José's English is limited, Stewart must explain everything to him four or five times, and she can seldom work with him one-on-one. She fears that he is a special needs student. Perhaps she will ask the school psychologist to test José.

The research literature suggests that how teachers like Wilson and Stewart think about education and students makes a pronounced difference in student performance and achievement (Apple 1990, Cooper 1979). Winfield (1986) found that teachers expect more from white students than from African-American students, and they expect more from middle-class students than from working- and lower-class students. Teachers often perceive African-American students from working- or lower-class backgrounds as incapable of high-quality academic work. Both Wilson and Stewart are entertaining such thoughts. They are not attributing their problems with students of color to ineffective teaching approaches.

Sometimes, unrecognized or outright racism causes teachers to hold negative beliefs about students of color. A dramatic example from a first-year teacher's journal entry:

> I hate [African-American students'] ethnic attitude and their lingo. I hate to categorize it but ... I am more comfortable with black students who act white (Birrell 1993).

Such negative attitudes toward students of color lower expectations for achievement, which lowers achievement (King and Ladson-Billings 1990, Lipman 1993).

Content and Materials Matter

Teachers who are sincerely committed to multicultural education cannot be satisfied with superficial celebrations of heroes and holidays. This approach to content trivializes multicultural education and conveys the idea that diversity issues come into play only during celebratory moments with foods, fun, and festivals.

In the multicultural festival model, teachers, students, and parents typically spend lots of time and energy preparing for an all-school activity. Students may do background research about a culture, prepare maps, and help create indigenous costumes. Parents may help to prepare various ethnic foods. On the day of the festival, members of the school

community go from class to class, visiting the various cultures, sampling the foods, and enjoying dances, songs, and arts and crafts. At the end of the day, everyone agrees that the annual event has been a great success. Then teachers and students go back to their real work.

In the transformative model, on the other hand, multicultural education is not a separate, isolated, once-a-year activity. Instead, the regular curriculum includes a range of cultural perspectives, as in the following two classroom scenarios.

In a primary classroom, the teacher reads several versions of the Cinderella story. One is the familiar European tale by the Brothers Grimm, but other versions are Chinese, Egyptian, and Zimbabwean. The teacher helps students compare the different versions. Similarities include story structure, plot development, moral and ethical dilemmas, and the use of magic. Differences include standards of beauty, settings, use of language, and specific characters. The students absorb the importance of understanding cultural differences and similarities.

In an intermediate history class, students study the African slave trade, but not solely from the perspective of the European traders. They also read a range of primary documents, like the slave narrative called *The Interesting Life of Olaudah Equiano* (it compares slavery in Africa with slavery in the Americas). In addition, the teacher introduces information about the European feudal system. The students compare the lives of enslaved people in Africa, the Americas, and medieval Europe. Finally, they generate analytical questions, such as, What is the relationship between slavery and racism? How could a nation striving for equality and justice permit slavery? Why did some people in Africa participate in the slave trade? And how does the textbook's treatment of slavery compare to primary source material?

The teacher in this class plans to do similar in-depth study when the class studies the displacement of Native Americans, the Spanish mission

system, European immigration of the 1890s, and Japanese internment. Although the transformative approach requires redesigning the curriculum, searching for additional materials, and limiting the number of topics taught, the teacher thinks the outcome is worth the effort. Students learn more content and develop a real ability to ask and answer critical questions.

The materials used in classrooms have important effects, too. As Banks' comprehensive literature review (1993a) points out, children are aware of their race and ethnicity at an early age. "If realistic images of ethnic and racial groups are included in teaching materials in a consistent, natural, and integrated fashion," Banks (1993b) concludes, all children "can be helped to develop more positive racial attitudes." Similar results are reported on gender issues (Scott and Schau 1985).

If classrooms use materials that do not portray diverse groups realistically, students are likely to develop, maintain, and strengthen the stereotypes and distortions in the traditional curriculum. Text analysis (a common form of multicultural research) indicates that textbook images and representations exclude, distort, and marginalize women, people of color, and people from lower socioeconomic echelons. A growing proportion of textbooks do include diversity, but their images and representations tend to be superficial and incorrect (Swartz 1992).

Instructional Approaches Matter

Changes to make curriculum content more equitable must be accompanied by changes that make pedagogy even-handed. To ensure "equitable pedagogy," Banks says, teachers must modify instruction to "facilitate academic achievement among students from diverse groups."

To some teachers, simultaneously dealing with the flood of new materials and modifying instructional approaches seems like an overwhelming task. These teachers think that it is all they can do to teach the new material in old ways. In other classrooms, however, teachers have

17. Multicultural Education Research

asked themselves, what one move can make to ensure that all students have opportunities for success?

For some teachers, providing more equitable pedagogy may be as simple as using more cooperative learning strategies in class. After all, cooperative learning was first developed as a way to create more equitable classroom environments (Cohen and Benton 1988, Slavin 1987).

For other teachers, equitable pedagogy will demand that they use the language and understandings that children bring to school to bridge the gap between what students know and what they need to learn (Au and Jordan 1981, Erickson and Mohatt 1982, Jordan 1985, Vogt et al. 1987). In addition, the total school context must come to accept whatever students have learned and experienced as legitimate knowledge (Irvine 1990, Ladson-Billings 1992, in press). Teachers can further these ends if they spend time in their students' community and apply in the classroom what they learned in students' homes.

Teachers may also profit by learning their students' language. A teacher who knows how to ask and answer basic questions in a second language can often make the classroom a welcoming and psychologically safe environment for speakers of that language. If a teacher becomes sufficiently fluent to teach academic content in English and a student's home language, the teacher tacitly promotes bilingualism and biliteracy (Hornberger 1988).

Educational Settings Matter

Forty years ago, the Supreme Court handed down a landmark decision, *Brown v. Board of Education,* which declared separate schools inherently unequal. Yet now, after years of hard-fought battles to desegregate the nation's schools, most students of color still attend segregated schools (Orfield 1989). Even when students go to desegregated schools, they are resegregated within the school via tracking and ability grouping (Oakes 1985).

For students of color, perhaps more devastating is the lack of access to high-quality education (Kozol 1991).

Clearly, as a society, our care and concern for student learning is differentiated along racial, class, and ethnic lines.

To grasp the impact of these inequities, imagine that our new teachers, Wilson and Stewart, were to participate in a school exchange program. Wilson's students would visit Stewart's class. Then Stewart's class would visit Wilson's. What will each setting informally teach the children?

When Wilson's students arrive at Stewart's school, they are struck by its physical beauty and space. Well-kept grounds have ample playground equipment. Inside the school, the halls gleam, and a lively buzz emanates from the various classrooms. Each brightly lighted classroom has at least one computer. The school library has several computers, CD-ROM, laser disks, and an extensive library of videotapes. The school has many special rooms: a gymnasium, a multi-purpose room, vocal and instrumental music rooms, an art room, and a room for enrichment activities. In each of the rooms is a teacher who regularly works with Stewart's students, freeing her for 45 minutes each day. She uses the time to plan, read, hold parent conferences, and do research.

When Stewart's class visits Wilson's school, they enter an old structure built in the 1920s. Its concrete yard is littered with broken glass, graffiti cover the walls, and the only piece of playground equipment is a netless basketball hoop. Inside the building, the dark halls are eerily silent, since room doors are closed and locked from the inside. There is a room where books are stored, but they are not catalogued because there is no librarian. The entire school shares one VCR and monitor. One of the two 16 mm film projectors is broken. A few filmstrips hide in various closets. The one room that does have computers, listening centers, and film loop machines is the Chapter One lab.

Here, students with literacy and mathematics deficits receive small-group instruction and skill practice for 30 to 45 minutes each day. In a corner of the multipurpose room, 12

gifted students in grades 3 to 5 meet one morning a week with a visiting gifted and talented education teacher. Classroom teachers are responsible for all other instruction, so they rarely have time to plan or confer.

What Stewart's students learn from their encounter is that Wilson's students are underprivileged, and perhaps, undeserving. The students will probably come to see inequities as normal and to equate African Americans and Latinos with poverty.

Meanwhile, Wilson's students learn that material advantages go with being white. Since Stewart's and Wilson's students are all about the same age with similar interests and abilities, the major difference that Wilson's students can see is skin color.

The few students of color in Stewart's class learn that they are very lucky. Under other circumstances, they could be at Wilson's school. Even though they may do poorly in a predominantly white school, they regard being there as a privilege.

Teacher Education Matters

If Wilson's and Stewart's students derive naive conceptions from their exchange visits, the teachers themselves also have trouble making sense of the differences. Neither teacher learned much about cultural variation during preservice preparation (Zeichner 1992, Ladson-Billings, in press).

Wilson took an ESL course, but Stewart did not, and she has José. Both Wilson and Stewart took a required human relations course, but although it presented some historical information about Native Americans, African Americans, Asian Americans, and Latinos, it was silent on European-American cultures and the role of culture in learning and achievement. Both Wilson and Stewart believed, further, that the course was designed to make them feel guilty. As a result, they silently resisted the material, and its impact on their eventual practice was sharply reduced.

As inservice teachers, Wilson and Stewart have had some opportunities to learn about multicultural education, but these have taken the form of fleeting, one-time workshops. The experiences had little or no follow-up, and no one attempted to ensure that teachers applied the new information (Sleeter 1992).

Fortunately, one of Wilson's colleagues is a graduate student who has taken several courses dealing with race, class, and gender issues. He has learned from the experiences of two teachers like Vivian Paley (1979) and Jane Elliot (Peters 1987). Wilson's colleague is impressive because he seems to manage his classes easily, and his students achieve well on tasks that go beyond worksheets and drills. Wilson plans to enroll in a multicultural education course next semester. He hopes to learn something that will help him succeed with students of color.

While Wilson is motivated to change, Stewart is not. Because she is successful with most of her students, she thinks her lack of success with students of color stems from their deficiencies. Stewart's colleagues and the parents of her white students reinforce this belief.

Does the Race and Ethnicity of Teachers Matter?

Whether teachers' race and ethnicity affect student achievement remains an open question. We know that most teachers in the United States are white and that the next largest group, African Americans, comprise less than 5 percent of all public school teachers. We also know that the majority of students in the 25 largest public school systems are students of color.

No empirical evidence, however, indicates that students of color learn better when taught by teachers of color. The most recent review of the literature on African-American teachers (King 1993) finds no connection between teacher race/ethnicity and student achievement. The positive aspect of this finding is that it makes all teachers accountable for teaching all students.

If current demographic trends hold, our student population will become more diverse, while the teaching population remains predominantly white. The implication is that if teachers are

to be effective, they will need to be prepared to teach children who are not white. If we are lucky, more teachers will follow Wilson's lead. They will know that the multicultural education research literature can help them understand themselves, their culture, and the cultures of others, and be more successful with all students.

References

Apple, M. (1990). *Ideology and Curriculum.* 2nd ed. New York: Routledge.

Au, K., and C. Jordan. (1981). "Teaching Reading to Hawaiian Children: Finding a Culturally Appropriate Solution." In *Culture and the Bilingual Classroom: Studies in Classroom Ethnography,* edited by H. Trueba, G. Guthrie, and K. Au. Rowley, Mass.: Newbury House.

Banks, J. A. (1993a). "Multicultural Education for Young Children: Racial and Ethnic Attitudes and Their Modification." In *Handbook of Research on the Education of Young Children,* edited by B. Spodek. New York: Macmillan.

Banks, J. A. (1993b). "Multicultural Education: Development, Dimensions, and Challenges." *Phi Delta Kappan* 75: 22-28.

Birrell, J. (February 1993). "A Case Study of the Influence of Ethnic Encapsulation on a Beginning Secondary School Teacher." Paper presented at the annual meeting of the Association of Teacher Educators, Los Angeles.

Cohen, E., and J. Benton. (Fall 1988). "Making Groupwork Work." *American Educator:* 10-17, 45-46.

Cooper, H. (1979). "Pygmalion Grows Up: A Model for Teacher Expectation Communication and Performance Influence." *Review of Educational Research* 49: 389-410.

Erickson, F., and G. Mohatt. (1982). "Cultural Organization and Participation Structures in Two Classrooms of Indian Students." In *Doing the Ethnography of Schooling,* edited by G. Spindler. New York: Holt, Rinehart and Winston.

Hornberger, N. (1988). "Iman Chay?: Quechua Children in Peru's Schools." In *School and Society: Teaching Content Through Culture,* edited by H. Trueba and C. Delgado-Gaitan. New York: Praeger.

Irvine, J. (1990). *Black Students and School Failure.* Westport, Conn.: Greenwood Press.

Jordan, C. (1985). "Translating Culture: From Ethnographic Information to Educational Program." *Anthropology and Education Quarterly* 16: 105-123.

King, J., and G. Ladson-Billings. (1990). "The Teacher Education Challenge in Elite University Settings: Developing

Critical Perspectives for Teaching in Democratic and Multicultural Societies." *European Journal of Intercultural Education* 1: 15-20.

King, S. H. (1993). "The Limited Presence of African-American Teachers." *Review of Educational Research* 63: 115-149.

Kozol, J. (1991). *Savage Inequalities.* New York: Crown Publishers.

Ladson-Billings, G. (1992). "Reading Between the Lines And Pages: A Culturally Relevant Approach to Literacy Teaching." *Theory into Practice* 31: 312-320.

Ladson-Billings, G. (In press). "Multicultural Teacher Education: Research, Practice, and Policy." In *Handbook of Research in Multicultural Education,* edited by J. A. Banks and C. M. Banks. New York: Macmillan.

Lipman, P. (1993). "Teacher Ideology Toward African-American Students in Restructured Schools." Doctoral diss., University of Wisconsin-Madison.

Oakes, J. (1985). *Keeping Track: How Schools Structure Inequality.* New Haven, Conn.: Yale University Press.

Orfield, G. (1989). *Status of School Desegregation 1968- 1986.* (Report of Urban Boards of Education and the National School Desegregation Research Project). Washington, D.C.: National School Boards Association.

Paley, V. (1979). *White Teacher.* Cambridge, Mass.: Harvard University Press.

Peters, W. (1987). *A Class Divided: Then and Now.* New Haven, Conn.: Yale University Press.

Scott, K. P., and C. G. Schau. (1985). "Sex Equity and Sex Bias Instructional Materials." In *Handbook for Achieving Sex Equity Through Education,* edited by S. S. Klein. Baltimore: Johns Hopkins University Press.

Slavin, R. (November 1987). "Cooperative Learning and the Cooperative School." *Educational Leadership* 45, 3: 7-13.

Sleeter, C., and C. Grant. (1988). "An Analysis of Multicultural Education in the United States." *Harvard Educational Review* 57: 421-444.

Swartz, E. (1992). "Multicultural Education: from a Compensatory to a Scholarly Foundation." In *Research and Multicultural Education: From the Margins to the Mainstream,* edited by C. Grant. London: Falmer Press.

Vogt, L., C. Jordan, and R. Tharp. (1987). "Explaining School Failure, Producing School Success: Two Cases." *Anthropology and Education Quarterly* 18: 276-286.

Winfield, L. (1986). "Teacher Beliefs Toward At-Risk Students in Inner-Urban Schools." *The Urban Review* 18: 253-267.

Zeichner, K. (1992). *Educating Teachers for Cultural Diversity.* East Lansing, Mich.: National Center for Research on Teacher Learning.

"All Kids Can Learn": Masking Diversity in Middle School

CAROL ANN TOMLINSON

Carol Ann Tomlinson is an assistant professor of educational studies, Curry School of Education, The University of Virginia, Charlottesville.

In the Northwest Territories of Canada, the aboriginal peoples build giant figures roughly in the shape of a human by piling stone upon stone. The primitive-looking shapes, called *inukshuks*, serve a dual purpose. In the heavy snows and ice fogs, they serve as guides to people trying to find their way home. In better weather, they serve as decoys to fool bears and other prey. The inukshuk is placed near a location where a bear may go for food or water. Seeing the looming, human-like form, the bear believes it to be a man and turns away from the inukshuk toward a blind where a hunter hides, waiting for the bear to be frightened and to retreat in the hunter's direction. It is an interesting paradox that inukshuks serve as both guideposts and traps.

We build educational inukshuks too. We construct them to offer us guidance in making critical decisions. Sometimes, however, we become the bear, and the inukshuk becomes our trap. One example of guide-turned-snare is our current buzz-phrase, "All kids can learn." It is particularly pervasive in educational settings, such as middle schools, which promote "educational equity."

Like all clichés, this one reflects some reality. It is invoked as a way of telling teachers not to give up on students whom we might assume to be struggling, at risk, or remedial. The cliché is problematic, however, because rather than pointing middle school educators homeward, it lures us into the dangerous assumption that what benefits one child educationally is bound to benefit others in the same way. At a time in our educational history when middle school learners are more diverse, both culturally and academically, than at any other time in the past, it validates educational practices that mask the diversity. The real problem has never been so much that middle school teachers believe that some kids *can't* learn. The real problem is that, as middle school educators, we've exhibited for decades a belief that all kids can learn the same things, in the same way, over the same time span.

Cases in Point: A Tale of Two Learners

Early in my career as a middle school teacher, I taught Golden and Jonathan during third period English. Eyes downcast and hand over his mouth, Golden whispered to me on the first day of school that he could not read. He was correct. At fifteen, he was a seventh grader who did not know the alphabet well and took a long time to grasp simple meanings, even when ideas were delivered orally or in pictures. He was a gentle boy, beautiful and persistent, and resilient in a quiet sort of way. I spent much of my time that year looking inside myself and learning from Golden how to teach reading to a fifteen-year-old and still have him feel fifteen. I was not trained to teach Golden, and I don't know that I did brilliantly with him academically, but I tried, and we cared for each other, and we both made progress in our learning.

Later that year, I discovered Jonathan. He'd been in the class all along—at the table with Golden, actually. It wasn't that I had been unaware of his physical presence. I knew he was there, interacted with him in the sort of way that's invited by the presence of 150 young bodies passing through the door each day. It was April when I discovered Jonathan's mental presence. It happened one day when Jonathan responded with a sigh to my query about whether anyone could explain what a symbol is in literature. He waited until it was clear no one else was going to answer. Then, sighing not with impatience so much as with resignation, Jonathan explained, "A symbol is a concrete representation of an abstract entity." He was right too. And it's as good a definition as I've ever read or heard. I wasn't trained to teach Jonathan either—or even to notice him. He made good grades. He was no trouble. I was grateful. In April, I discovered that my magical seventh-grade English class was as poorly suited to Jonathan as to Golden.

I concluded that year of teaching with my own two symbols clearly in mental view. They were concrete representations of the abstract reality that middle school students differ immensely and that my previous notion of developing a single lesson plan that would reach them all was unrealistic. I always believed that both Jonathan and Golden could learn. Like most other teachers, I could not have continued to show up at school without that conviction. I would be a better teacher for Golden and Jonathan if I had the opportunity to teach them today, not because I have been a recent convert to believing "all kids can learn," but because I have spent a sizable portion of my career learning to respond to the reality that students have *different* learning needs.

Neglecting Golden

I have also spent a great deal of my career as a middle school educator being dismayed at our inability at this level to embrace Jonathan and Golden simultaneously and in ways appropriate for their individual needs. For at least a decade, students like Golden have drifted through junior high or middle school compensatory classes where they were taught to read in the same standard ways that proved unsuccessful during the previous year. As teachers, we weren't hostile to these students; we just accepted them as "limited." We understood little about how school must look to them. We certainly underestimated the impact of poverty and culturally different homes—or maybe we just didn't look outside the schoolhouse door often or long enough. Nature and nurture challenged Golden's learning, and a traditional, single lens view of students and schooling aggravated the problem.

Golden is not only a symbol for me as a teacher. He is a three-dimensional case for the urgency of addressing the needs of at-risk learners in American middle schools. Powerful cases for increasing attention to at-risk learners have been made by many sensitive and convincing writers (e.g., Kozol 1991; Freedman 1990; McLaren 1989). It is clear that schooling as it is typically structured still falls short of addressing the immense needs of many of America's young who are like Golden.

Points to Ponder on Golden's Behalf

Of course there is a need for educational improvement for at-risk learners, for "educational equity." The guidepost of equity becomes a trap, however, if we assume that equity for Golden means that all middle school students must learn the same things, in the same way, over the same time span. We need to think carefully about at least three propositions in Golden's behalf as we plan for his years in middle school:

Golden's educational challenges are real. Some students like Golden contend with specific physiological impairments in the intake or the processing of information. Many like him come to middle school lacking food or affection or security. Many come to middle school with communication patterns or views of time or ways of relating to peers and adults that differ in meaningful ways from those of the majority of educators who will

work with them. The list of challenges can be long and varied. Each item on the list can affect learning in powerful ways.

Ignoring Golden's differences is damaging. Traditional school practices seldom serve Golden well. Many educators make compelling arguments for movement away from traditional schooling for *all* children. The strengths of those arguments notwithstanding, many children have at least survived traditional schooling with functional skills in place. That has not often been the case for students like Golden. It may be that the ways in which we have most poorly served previous Goldens have stemmed from our assumptions that the culture that reflects the worldview of many children accurately reflects Golden's as well, and that the ways in which many children successfully take in and process information will yield success for Golden also. Those educators who have been triumphant with students like Golden have deeply understood the students' differences and have made powerful adjustments in their responses to those differences.

Most educational generalists are currently unprepared to respond appropriately to Golden's needs. Why can't Golden read at fifteen? How do we motivate him to try again for one more year? What if his peers reject schooling as well? What can we do to make his effort worth the risk? Why doesn't he follow directions that seem clear enough to other students? How do we contend with our curriculum when Golden can't read the basic vocabulary list in the rear of the text? What do we do if his anger causes him to boil over in the classroom? Why doesn't he look us in the eye when we talk with him? Why does he seem unconcerned at turning in assignments late? How do we keep him hopeful when we also operate in the tradition of keeping a gradebook? Our understandings of educational handicaps are shallow. Our understandings of cultural diversity are sparse. Our definitions of instruction are narrow. Our sense of fairness hangs on norms. We know how to teach groups better than individuals. In middle school, regular classroom teachers may (or may not) be prepared to work on Golden's self-concept. We currently know of little to do for his sense of self-efficacy.

Rejecting Jonathan

At least in our rhetoric, middle school education in recent years has embraced Golden. The irony is that, in doing so, we seem to feel it necessary to reject Jonathan.

I happened upon a colleague in an airport recently. She is an enthusiastic educator and an effective staff developer for teachers of middle school students. As we walked down a corridor, she said she had been puzzling about the tensions that exist between middle school and gifted education and that she had discussed it with a nationally known middle school educator and leader. "I think I understand now," she said. "In middle school, we are for the underdog. Gifted kids are so far ahead.

What we are interested in is making sure the other kids catch up. Gifted kids are just so privileged. They don't need us like at-risk learners do."

Another nationally respected educator with deep middle school roots said to me recently, "Gifted education just isn't interesting. It's not important."

In a recent issue of the *Washington Post* (Denny 1994), a staff editorialist called for the abolition of special programs for gifted learners, advocating that all students be exposed to "the same challenging curriculum."

Middle school students mirror our adult rejection of high-end achievement. In our schools, notes the president of the Educational Testing Service (Anrig 1992), we apply derogatory names to our brightest students. These days, they are *nerds* or *dweebs*. Students like Jonathan understand the messages. In a recent study, such adolescents indicated that they wanted to do well in school but not exceptionally well. To do too well is to be rejected by the "in crowd." To be perceived as "a brain" is to be banished.

Points to Ponder on Jonathan's Behalf

It is not acceptable for middle school educators to deny or dismiss students like Jonathan, any more than it is to turn our interest away from Golden. There are at least three propositions that middle school educators need to consider in determining a course of action for Jonathan and his tribe:

High-end talent is a reality. Some kids learn faster than others and with a greater depth of understanding. At twelve, Greg understood the physics of black holes and of time. Ray could discuss the imagery and symbolism of Poe. Theresa was more than conversant with calculus. These youngsters once again give evidence that while it is true that all kids can learn, they learn in different ways, at different rates, with differing facility and insight. Advanced talent is not everything, but it is real. It is an important human resource.

It is okay to have talent as a learner. It is not elitist to be an advanced learner any more than it is elitist to be taller than average or a better-than-average soccer player. It is the way some kids are. Middle schools need to be in the talent development business, eager to latch onto and develop talent whenever it surfaces—and to help it surface when it does not do so on its own. If middle school does not celebrate and extend the talent of high-end learners, it is at risk as an institution. No organization grows that does not accept the challenge of those of its members who push against its ceilings and cause them to rise.

Highly talented kids need teacher assistance in developing their potential. In part, the learning capacity of students like Golden is compromised by parents, neighborhoods, teachers, or adults in society at large who fail to become mentors and advocates. Jonathan may or may not have been failed by home or neighborhood or society at large.

There are Jonathans in the most impoverished settings. Even a Jonathan from a supportive home, however, needs teachers. It is the teacher who is the keeper of knowledge, a gadfly for persistence, an encourager when the risk seems too great. Twelve-year-old Kathleen understood when she wrote a poem to her teacher:

Push me. See how far I go.
Work me 'til I drop. Then pick me up.
Open a door, and make me run to it before it closes.
Teach me so that I might learn.
But then show me the Tunnel of Experience and let me walk through it alone.
And when, near the end, I look back, and I see you in the opening with another,
I shall smile.

Points to Ponder for Both Golden and Jonathan

If middle schools are going to be good places for Jonathan and Golden, and if middle school educators are going to move past slogans to action, we must consider several propositions:

There is no time for a linear approach to student needs. We have a pattern in American schools of focusing on high-end learners to the exclusion of troubled learners for a period of time—then turning our rhetoric and practice in the direction of troubled learners, to the exclusion of advanced learners. All the while, we lament that attention to learning needs of those groups robs the "average" student. In middle school, we have been prone to embrace the at-risk learner and to alternate between irritation at, and denial of, the high-end learner. So long as schools take a sort of one-at-a-time approach to its clients, schools will fail many more children than necessary. A given child has only one passage through the middle school years. If it is not Jonathan's "turn" to be attended to and valued, or Golden's, or any other student's, we have a moral obligation to inform his parents that he is not currently "in vogue" and therefore not a priority for talent development.

"The same challenging curriculum" is a myth. The science curriculum that intrigued Greg would have stupefied most other preadolescents. Golden could not have understood *oral* renditions of Poe in seventh grade, let alone *print* versions. It seems virtually impossible that he could have understood the tapestry of symbols in Poe's works that year. Do we make "the same challenging math curriculum" one that Golden can master? One that more typical seventh graders can master? Or do we accept the calculus curriculum that challenged eleven-year-old Theresa and attempt to challenge *all* seventh graders with it? Embracing diversity is our challenge in education, not pretending singularity.

One-size-fits-all instruction is not an acceptable option. Jonathan and Golden differ significantly from each other and from many of their age-mates. If we advocate instructional arrangements in which middle schoolers are treated largely or wholly alike, we will, in the long run, be as unfair to Golden as we were in the days when we overlooked him or when we subscribed to the notion of remediation. We will also continue to assume, by comparison with the norm, that Jonathan is fine and producing high quality work. Middle school students will become discouraged or disenchanted. Middle school teachers will become weary and weighted with the guilt they carry when it is evident that they are losing students. In the end, we will, as we have in the past, revert to separate classes within a very few years.

We need to teach teachers to adjust for student differences, not trick them into doing so. Much of the argument for heterogeneity is that teachers lower expectations for students in homogeneous remedial classes. If teachers receive all students en masse, the logic goes, they automatically raise expectations for struggling learners because of the greater mass of comparatively more advanced learners. There are problems with that theory. First, such a plan will as likely *lower* expectations for students like Jonathan who were in advanced classes as it will raise them for students who were in slower-paced classes. Second, it perpetuates the idea that a single level of expectations will somehow be appropriate for all students. It skirts the more significant reality that in an increasingly diverse classroom, teachers will need to identify individual needs and respond in various ways to those needs. It is also insulting in its implications that (*a*) teachers cannot learn to adjust expectations proactively, and, therefore, (*b*) students must be moved about in ways that cause reactive teacher response.

Differentiated classrooms are a rarity. If we intend to recognize and address individual differences and needs within heterogeneous settings, we have a long way to go. Most teachers are like I was—stymied by the presence of Golden and unaware that Jonathan had any real problems. National studies indicate that little appropriate differentiation of instruction for academically diverse learners currently takes place in classrooms (Tomlinson et al., 1994; Archambault, Westberg, Brown, Hallmark, Zhang, and Emmons 1993; McIntosh, Vaughn, Schumm, Haager, and Lee 1993; Tomlinson In press). The paucity of differentiation has a multitude of causes: our own long histories as students in one-size-fits-all classrooms, our own experiences as practitioners of one-size-fits-all instruction, our general lack of preservice and inservice preparation in teaching academically diverse learners, teach-to-the-test mandates that cause us to drag all learners through the same content, over-dependence on text-driven curricula, discouraging student-teacher ratios,

choppy time blocks that invite dealing with students as a herd, and lack of administrative and policy support for the long-term change process that is required to alter habitual teaching behaviors. There is little guidance in the middle school literature that exhorts us to differentiate instruction or that offers us concrete guidance in how to do so.

Truth or Trap

Golden and Jonathan are real. Most middle school teachers have taught them. Odds are, most of us have taught them less well than they deserve because we taught them as though they were alike. We have to move beyond intoning the belief that both can learn. We know that. It's why we became teachers—why we stayed on. Rather, we need to confront the harder truths: that middle schoolers differ greatly in the ways they learn and in their learning needs; that middle school educators have to be serious students of learner differences and have to respond effectively to those differences; that single-size instruction is going to be a misfit for many middle schoolers; and that we cannot be truly effective so long as we pretend that Golden and Jonathan can flourish in a learning environment that offers them both "the same challenging curriculum."

The inukshuk is out there, stone piled upon stone. Jonathan and Golden need middle school educators who will make it a guidepost rather than a trap.

REFERENCES

Anrig, G. 1992. What we can learn from the Second International Assessment of Educational Progress. Prepared remarks for press conference. Washington, D.C. (5 February).

Archambault, F., K. Westberg, S. Brown, B. Hallmark, W. Zhang, and C. Emmons. 1993. Classroom practices used with gifted third and fourth grade students. *Journal for the Education of the Gifted* 16(2): 103–19.

Denny, S. 1994. How Fairfax fails the "normal" student. *Washington Post* (14 August): C-10.

Freedman, S. 1990. *Small victories: The real world of a teacher, her students and their high school.* New York: Harper and Row.

Kozol, J. 1991. *Savage inequalities: Children in America's schools.* New York: Crown.

McIntosh, R., S. Vaughn, J. Shumm, D. Haager, and O. Lee. 1993. Observations of students with learning disabilities in general education classrooms. *Exceptional Children* 60(3): 249–61.

McLaren, P. 1989. *Life in schools: An introduction to critical pedagogy in the foundations of education.* New York: Longman.

Tomlinson, C. In press. Deciding to differentiate instruction in middle school: One school's journey.

Tomlinson, C., E. Tomchin, C. Callahan, C. Adams, P. Pizzat-Tinnin, C. Cunningham, B. Moore, L. Lutz, C. Roberson, N. Eiss, M. Landrum, S. Hunsaker, and M. Imbeau. 1994. Practices of preservice teachers related to gifted and other academically diverse learners. *Gifted Child Quarterly* 38(3): 106–14.

Multiculturalism: Practical Considerations for Curricular Change

TONY R. SANCHEZ

Tony R. Sanchez is an assistant professor of education at Indiana University Northwest, Gary, Indiana.

Many school districts today are jumping on the multicultural bandwagon by adopting, or at least encouraging, a more divisified curriculum. Proponents of multiculturalism call for an interdisciplinary approach that draws from and spans all subject areas, an approach that I believe is the most effective. I offer here a framework designed to be useful to teachers who want to change their personal or curricular perspective from one that is "mainstream" to one that is more "diverse" and are willing to incorporate that new perspective into whatever subject matter they teach.

Unfortunately, misconstruing the purposes or definition of multicultural education, many teachers either back off from it entirely or teach about different groups sequentially, resulting in a fragmented and isolated treatment. We do the latter when we assign specific groups to specific months (Black History Month, Hispanic Heritage Month, Women's History Month). During one of these periods, the attitude is that teachers will deal with that group for thirty days (maximum) and then return to the mainstream curriculum. Multiculturalism, however, belongs within the framework of the existing curriculum.

The Teacher's Role

By exposing our students to other cultures (whether the contributions of various groups or nonmainstream perspectives of an event or concept), we help them learn about other people's lifestyles and values. This awareness in turn may alter negative, stereotypic thinking, reduce intolerance, and promote cooperation (Cohen 1986). It will also expand *your* personal horizons as well as your students'.

As an educator interested in such an outcome, what might your creed be? I suspect something like this: *Within my course I will promote the recognition and understanding of diversity, and teach respect for it. By doing so, I hope not only to provide personal enrichment but also, through my teaching and actions, to help develop positive, productive interactions and attitudes.*

To put this creed into action, you most likely will do the following: teach the perspectives of the mainstream culture (don't assume students already know them); teach the perspectives of other cultures (with the message: they're equally valid to some); and examine similarities and differences between cultures (Hernandez 1989). This last point is certainly the most challenging; *both* similarities and differences should be addressed so that your students move from merely tolerating differences to viewing them as acceptable, desirable, and valuable (Noar 1989).

Implementing a multicultural curriculum requires specific components. These include (1) a teacher willing to critically evaluate his or her personal perspectives, (2) instructional materials that provide diverse but accurate perspectives, and (3) general goals and objectives.

Analyzing Your Attitude

As the teacher, you implement and guide the questioning, reasoning, analysis, and truth-seeking in your classroom. As such, you must consider your personal attitudes toward your subject area—negative and positive—and the fact that they can't be hidden from your students. What exactly is your level of commitment to the value of diverse perspectives?

Coming to grips with your values and attitudes, changing some, and developing sensitivity to diversity will require time—and courage. It will depend on your willingness to work on your new perspective. Without this commitment, you may find yourself saying, "I'm not very comfortable with this diverse curriculum I'm trying out, but I think it's working out." What that really means is, "It's not working because I don't really believe in it." If that becomes the case, back off. Don't deceive yourself and your students. The payoff for this self-examination will be that the ugliness of prejudice, rejection, and exclusion—all results of ignorance and misinformation—will have no place in your classroom. You will be sensitizing your students not only to the mechanics of learning but also to their own worth and value. The rest of the process will be anticlimactic by comparison with this step.

Choosing Instructional Materials

In the next step of the process, you examine and select instructional materials that reflect accurate, quality (i.e., true) information. Choose materials that you're comfortable with, that won't require a radical change in your style (a change that many teachers needlessly fear).

Danger of Relying on Textbooks

Textbooks, as we know, account for most of the teaching/learning process (Sewall 1987). Furthermore, "Teachers tend to not only rely on, but believe in, the textbook as the source of knowledge" (Fitzgerald 1979).

Recent evaluations indicate that a diverse curriculum requires a change in this attitude. Various cultural/ethnic groups have brought attention to bear on the depiction of their respective cultures in textbooks (Garcia and Florez-Tighe 1986). The attitude shared by these groups can be summed up as follows: "The sole false perspective is that which claims to be the only one there is" (Gasset, cited in Smith and Otero 1982). The multicultural movement does *not* require abandonment of the mainstream perspective. This would only lead to isolated enclaves, fragmentation, and polarization. On the contrary, the movement promotes integrating a variety of perspectives, which must include the mainstream (Banks 1991).

Bias in textbooks appears in several forms, including stereotyping, omissions, distortions, overrepresentation in certain contexts, romanticized portrayals, token representations, and biased language. As educators, we need to examine and evaluate these materials in terms of content, language, and illustrations. Though textbook bias has been reduced in some quarters, it still remains, its manifestations sometimes blatant and other times subtle (Garcia and Florez-Tighe 1986).

How do we go about identifying such bias? We will need to explore, compare, contrast, question, and evaluate information from multiple sources (which may include students, peers, and the community). Eventually, we will strengthen our evaluative skills so that we can uncover discrepancies and contradictions. Analyzing and questioning the accuracy of the content we teach may represent a major departure for us, but it may also keep us from becoming "adults who believe everything they read—or read only what they wish to believe" (Klein 1985, 27). Passing on critical reading skills to our students may ultimately be our greatest legacy to them.

Guidelines for Multicultural Curriculum

Here are some basic guidelines to keep in mind as you purposively change your curricular perspective (Gaines 1992):

Go beyond a trivializing, "tourist" curriculum. A diversity curriculum is more than holidays, special months, food, and costumes. Rather, it means coming to know the values, viewpoints, and meaningful traditions that characterize individuals and groups (and you can still include food and costumes). These interpretations must be regular, built-in components of your subject area.

Go beyond tokenism. Do you enrich your class with African American or Hispanic perspectives simply because you have some black or Mexican students? Or, instead, do you employ multiple, unbiased perspectives because you recognize the value of alternative interpretations and want to promote acceptance and respect for different experiences and viewpoints? The former approach is characteristic of a teacher who doesn't really believe in or is uncomfortable with the notion of diversity in his or her subject area; the teacher's efforts will come off as phony. The latter approach characterizes a teacher who appreciates diversity.

Go beyond stereotyping. Give students continuous opportunities to examine images for accuracy. Too often a student's stereotypic perception goes unchallenged and therefore becomes solidified as truth. In this regard, you must expect to handle incidences of bias and ignorance that arise in the classroom. What should you do on such occasions? Here are four pieces of advice that I have found helpful:

1. *Don't ignore comments or questions that reflect misinformation.* Address the issue while a direct connection to the goals of the curriculum can still be made. Your silence on such matters can only be interpreted as confirmation.

2. *Don't excuse comments or questions that could be interpreted as culturally or racially insulting.* The students who are targets of such remarks (which can very quickly escalate into full-blown classroom incidents) will segregate themselves for protection—something that you didn't provide.

3. *Don't be afraid to step in to handle and clarify a situation.* Doing something on the spot is certainly preferable to doing nothing and allowing things to fester.

4. *Don't forget your commitment.* Your mission in establishing a diverse curriculum is to expand your students' knowledge so that they will develop more positive attitudes and behaviors that will enable them to interact effectively in our diverse society. Your responsibility in the mission is consistency.

Goals and Objectives

What learning outcomes should a multicultural curriculum promote? The following goals are frequently found in a diversified curriculum (Hernandez 1989; Kosmoski 1989):

To help students recognize and understand the values and experiences of one's own ethnic/cultural heritage

To promote sensitivity to diverse ethnicities/cultures through exposure to other cultural perspectives

To develop an awareness and respect for the similarities and differences among diverse groups

To identify, challenge, and dispel ethnic/cultural stereotyping, prejudice, and discrimination in behavior, textbooks, and other instructional materials

Goals are, of course, intended to be guidelines. A multicultural curriculum can only be effective when the teacher is given choices as to how to achieve such goals within his or her subject area or grade level. An inappropriate or too narrowly focused curriculum—a product of haste and pressure to conform—will likely result when teachers are not free to make those decisions. How to integrate a multicultural perspective into the curriculum rather than making it a blatant "add-on" is the main issue they face. Teachers usually approach this task by trial and error. Using a single, all-encompassing model to implement a diverse curriculum is not a good idea because no model can provide what is effective for all students at all times and under all circumstances. Rather, the teacher must systematically incorporate content and strategies in a comfortable balance. The process requires time, with the teacher "testing the waters" on a by-unit or by-lesson basis.

As an initial effort, many teachers employ a "cultural" unit or lesson in their standard monocentric curricula. It is usually additive instead of integral, but it serves the important purpose of "breaking the multicultural ice." Such an initial effort is almost always necessary to allow the educator to comfortably ease into a truly diverse curriculum.

Development and implementation of a multicultural curriculum must eventually be evaluated for effectiveness (California State Department of Education 1979). What must be assessed? Three chief components are (1) achievement; (2) student behavior; and (3) student attitudes (Hernandez 1989). Achievement, the primary focus of American education, can be fairly assessed through various conventional measures. Student behavior can be monitored and evaluated formally (questionnaires, surveys, discussion groups, reduced number of disruptive incidents) and informally (teacher observations of cooperative interactions, voluntary student participation and assistance, student willingness to explore cultural similarities and differences). Student attitudes are the most difficult to assess for change. The validity of evaluation is dependent on the instrument used and should always be interpreted with caution. Research indicates that attitude change as a goal of multicultural education is indeed feasible. Studies of the use of content and strategies to change cultural/ethnic/racial attitudes and reduce prejudice show positive results, even when complex, multiple variables, such as age, socioeconomic status, and social institutions, are involved (Sanchez 1991). Establishing the foundation for such change—through diverse content and teacher modeling—cannot guarantee positive attitude changes. As educators, however, we must be willing to take the chance that this endeavor will promote understanding, acceptance, and respect.

REFERENCES

Banks, J. A. 1991. *Teaching strategies for ethnic studies.* 5th ed. Needham Heights, Mass.: Allyn and Bacon.

California State Department of Education. 1979. *Guide for multicultural education.* Sacramento, Calif.: California State Department of Education.

Cohen, C. B. 1986. Teaching about ethnic diversity. *ERIC Digest* 32: 1–2.

Fitzgerald, F. 1979. *America revisited.* Boston, Mass.: Atlantic Monthly Press/Little, Brown.

Gaines, L. 1992. What you can do. *Creative Classroom* (Sept.): 115.

Garcia, J., and V. Florez-Tighe. 1986. The portrayal of Blacks, Hispanics, and Native Americans in recent basal reading series. *Equity and Excellence* 22(4-6): 72–76.

Hernandez, H. 1989. *Multicultural education.* Columbus, Ohio: Merrill.

Klein, G. 1985. *Reading into racism.* London: Routledge and Kegan Paul.

Kosmoski, G. J. 1989. *Multicultural education.* Chicago: Third World Press.

Noar, G. 1989. *Sensitizing teachers to ethnic groups.* Needham Heights, Mass.: Allyn and Bacon.

Sanchez, T. R. 1991. *The effects of knowledge acquisition about Blacks on the racial attitudes of White high school sophomores.* Ann Arbor, Mich.: University Microfilms, Inc.

Sewall, G. T. 1987. *American history textbooks: An assessment of quality.* New York: Columbia University, Teachers College, Educational Excellence Network.

Smith, G. R., and G. Otero. 1982. *Teaching about cultural awareness.* Denver, Col.: University of Denver, Center for Teaching International Relations.

Learning and Instruction

- Information Processing/Cognitive Learning (Articles 20–22)
- Behavioristic Learning (Articles 23–25)
- Humanistic/Social Psychological Learning (Articles 26 and 27)
- Instructional Strategies (Articles 28–31)

Learning can be broadly defined as a relatively permanent change in behavior or thinking due to experience. Learning is not a result of change due to maturation. Changes in the behavior and thinking of students result from complex interactions between their individual characteristics and environmental factors. A continuing challenge in education is understanding these interactions so that learning can be enhanced. This unit focuses on approaches within educational psychology that represent different ways of viewing the learning process and related instructional strategies. Each approach to learning emphasizes a different set of personal and environmental factors that influence certain behaviors. While no one approach can fully explain learning, each is a valuable contribution to our knowledge about the process.

The discussion of each learning approach includes suggestions for specific techniques and methods of teaching to guide teachers in understanding student behavior and in making decisions about how to teach. This unit reflects a recent emphasis on applied research conducted in schools and on constructivist theories. The relatively large number of essays on information processing/cognitive learning and instruction, as opposed to behaviorism, also reflects a change in emphasis. Behaviorism, however, remains important in our understanding of learning and instruction.

Researchers have recently made significant advances in understanding the way our minds work. Information processing refers to the way in which the mind receives sensory information, stores it as memory, and recalls it for later use. This procedure is basic to all learning, no matter what teaching approach is taken. We know that the method used in processing information determines to some extent how much and what we remember. The essays in the first subsection present fundamental principles of information processing, including important new developments in multiple intelligences.

For years, behaviorism was the best-known approach to learning. Most practicing and prospective teachers are familiar with concepts such as classical conditioning, reinforcement, and punishment, and there is no question that behaviorism has made significant contributions to understanding learning. But behaviorism has also been subject to much misinterpretation, in part because it seems so simple. In fact, the effective use of behavioristic principles is complex and demanding, as debates in the second subsection point out.

Humanistic/social psychological learning emphasizes the affective, social, moral, and personal development of students. Humanistic learning involves acceptance of the uniqueness of each individual, stressing character, feelings, values, and self-worth. To the humanist, learning is not simply a change in behavior or thinking; learning is also the discovery of the personal meaning of information. Social psychology is the study of the nature of interpersonal relationships in social situations. In education, this approach looks at teacher-pupil relationships and group processes to derive principles of interaction that affect learning. The two articles in the third subsection examine self-esteem and the emerging issue of caring.

Instructional strategies are the teacher behaviors and methods of conveying information that affect learning. Teaching methods or techniques can vary greatly, depending on objectives, group size, types of students, and personality of the teacher. For example, discussion classes are generally more effective for enhancing thinking skills than are individualized sessions or lectures. For the final subsection of the unit, major instructional strategies to illustrate a variety of approaches have been selected. First, "A Framework for Culturally Responsive Teaching" shows how collaborative and cooperative teaching methods can be used in our increasingly diverse classrooms. This is followed by John Savery and Thomas Duffy's description of a problem-based approach to teaching. Strategies to promote creative thinking are explored next. The final article examines the growing importance of technology in the classroom.

Looking Ahead: Challenge Questions

Compare and contrast the different approaches to learning. What approach do you think is best? Why? What factors are important to your answer (e.g., objectives, types of students, setting, personality of the teacher)?

What teaching strategies could you use to promote greater student retention of material? What are good ways to attract and keep students' attention? Must a teacher be an "entertainer"? Why or why not?

How can a teacher promote positive self-esteem, values, character, and attitudes? How are they related to cognitive learning? How much emphasis should be put on cultivating character or positive student interactions? How would you create a "caring" classroom? Discuss whether or not this would interfere with achievement of cognitive learning targets. Is cooperative learning feasible in the grade level and subject in which you will teach? Why or why not?

Describe some strategies for enhancing students' creative thinking. Will these strategies have a detrimental effect on student retention and problem solving?

How can technology be used productively in the classroom? What learning theories should be used as a basis for instruction that utilizes technology?

REMEMBERING THE FORGOTTEN ART OF MEMORY

THOMAS E. SCRUGGS AND MARGO A. MASTROPIERI

Thomas E. Scruggs and Margo A. Mastropieri are professors of special education at Purdue University. Their book on memory techniques is entitled Teaching Students Ways To Remember: Strategies for Learning Mnemonically, *published in 1991 by Brookline Books, Cambridge, Massachusetts.*

IN THE fifth century B.C., the Greek poet Simonides narrowly escaped death, and in so doing provided the birth of memory strategies. Reciting a poem at a banquet, Simonides was called out of the house for a message. While he was out, the building collapsed, and the diners within were crushed beyond recognition. Asked to help identify the bodies, Simonides noted that he was able to do so by remembering an image of the diners' positions at the table. This inspiration gave birth to the *Method of Loci,* the most ancient of mnemonic techniques.

Ancient Greeks and Romans placed great value on the development of memory skills, partly because the relative lack of printed materials required individuals to commit many things to memory. Throughout the Middle Ages, complex memory strategies took on religious aspects, and sometimes became associated with individuals who dabbled in magic and the occult, such as Giordano Bruno and his secret of "Shadows."

With the development of the printing press, memory skills received less and less emphasis; nonetheless, knowledge of many of these techniques survived, such as those described in 1890 by William James in his *Principles of Psychology.* For a time in American schools, memorization and recitation of inspirational passages and quotations were considered important in developing well-trained minds. Unfortunately, the act of memorizing *per se* is not usually helpful in intellectual development; further, many of the things American schoolchildren were compelled to memorize were decontextualized and therefore of little meaning in themselves. As a result, "memorizing" began to become regarded as a pointless waste of time, as it no doubt was in many cases. Further, "progressive" educators such as John Dewey began rightly to promote the facilitation of "higher-order" thinking skills over the mindless repetition of facts and passages. With the recent renewal of interest in constructivist perspectives and the rise of technological advances in information storage and retrieval, the decline of interest in memory skills has apparently become nearly complete.

With this decline in interest in memory skills, students' memory for important school content also has declined. A recent national report documented the sad fact that American students have become deficient at recall of even the most basic information about history and literature. For example, only one out of three American seventeen-year-olds could place the Civil War within the correct half-century or correctly identify the Reformation or the Magna Carta.

In this article, we wish to provide a different perspective on memory. We define memory skills as techniques for increasing the initial learning and long-term retention of important information. We argue that good memory skills are as important now as they were in Simonides' day; that memory strategy instruction has a very impor-

> *American Students have become deficient at recall of even the most basic information about history and literature.*

tant place in schools, yet unrealized; and that good instruction in memory strategies enhances, rather than detracts from, the facilitation of "higher-order" skills such as comprehension and critical thinking. Indeed, while there are many important things to learn and do in school, and learning and retaining factual information is only one component of the entire school experience, it is our contention that a strong declarative knowledge base is an absolutely critical first step to "higher-level" skills.

We also provide brief descriptions of nine strategies for promoting strong memory skills.

W E BECAME aware of the critical importance of good memory skills during the course of our work with students with learning disabilities. Many learning-disabled students have some difficulty with semantic memory, or memory for verbally presented information. Clearly, such students face enormous challenges in courses that require vast amounts of verbal information to be "memorized," such as traditionally taught social studies and science courses. In addition, learning-disabled students usually perform poorly on tests of verbal reasoning or higher-order thinking skills. One explanation why these students with average intelligence may do so poorly on verbal reasoning tasks is that they can remember little verbal information to help them on the task. And, it has been well established that content knowledge is one of the best predictors of performance on reasoning tasks. When we trained students in powerful mnemonic strategies to facilitate memory of the core content, we noticed dramatic improvements in their ability not only to remember content information but also to participate actively in classroom discussions that required thinking actively about the subject.

The relation between knowledge and thinking can be further explained by an example. In a recent national educational performance test, one item presented outlines of four birds and asked students to identify the one that probably lives close to water. Students who make effective use of their reasoning abilities could consider the characteristics of such environments, observe the four bird outlines, and correctly conclude that the long-legged bird, physically equipped for wading, was the most likely choice. However, students who remembered important information about birds and their environments could easily recognize one of the birds as a heron and immediately answer the question. Thus, what is a higher-order thinking task to a student lacking background knowledge is a simple recall task to a student possessing the relevant information. As can be seen, the "reasoning" deck is stacked against the student who has not learned, or cannot remember, critical information.

Memory is not only helpful for facilitating thought about academic subjects. One of us remembers the great difficulties he had learning to sail, until he began to master the highly specialized vocabulary associated with sailing. When terms such as *sheet, jib, starboard,* and *boom-vang* became automatic, he began to make rapid progress in sailing. Likewise, we found that students began to make greater progress in vocational skills when they began to learn and remember the specialized vocabulary associated with such areas as rough construction and electricity. Why does verbal knowledge seem to facilitate procedural knowledge, such as sailing and construction? Since we are accustomed to thinking in language, we find it difficult to reflect and elaborate on new information until the relevant language associated with this information has been acquired and remembered. So, it can be seen that a well-established verbal knowledge base is a prerequisite for critical or reflective thinking.

Although memory and attention are not the same thing, it is true that things are not likely to be remembered if they are not attended to in the first place.

Nor can computer data bases take the place of a broad background of knowledge committed to memory. We often here the refrain, "In a few years, all of this will be unnecessary. Students will wear on their arms a computer no larger than a wristwatch but powerful enough to contain all the information known to mankind." The problem with this line of thinking is that one needs a sufficient knowledge base to know *what* to call forth from the computer, to give form to the endless ocean of information. Research has shown that students who have the most firmly established knowledge base are the ones who can most easily assimilate and apply new information.

Unfortunately, it is not only students with learning disabilities who may find themselves weak in prior knowledge. Students from less-privileged economic backgrounds may come to school not having had the same background experiences as other students. Students for whom English is a second language may have more difficulty expressing their knowledge in English. Finally, if recent national reports are considered, many "ordinary" students exhibit a surprising lack of memory for basic information in school subjects. It seems, therefore, that the argument should not be *whether* to teach memory skills, but *how* memory skills can be best taught. Some recommendations are given in the section that follows.

O UR RESEARCH and experience have shown us that there are at least nine ways that teachers can greatly improve the ability of their students to remember. We will summarize these recommendations in order of complexity. The ninth method, promoting mnemonic strategy use, is the most complicated and will require the most explanation.

1. Promote Attention

Although memory and attention are not the same thing, it is true that things are not likely to be remembered if they are not attended to in the first place. This makes attention an important prerequisite to memory.

There are several methods for improving attention. The simplest include direct appeals ("Please pay attention to what I'm about to say") and follow-up ("What did I say was the assignment for tomorrow?"), and physical proximity to students who are likely not to pay attention. Other strategies for promoting attention include intensifying instruction, with enthusiastic teaching, use of high-intensity visual aids, and providing relevant activi-

---

Teachers who are expert in certain content areas may forget how difficult it is to acquire new speech sounds to represent new concepts or facts.

ties for students, rather than simple listening and note-taking. Teaching is more easily intensified by focusing on a smaller number of critical concepts than by covering a wide range of less important information.

Provide positive feedback for students when they exhibit good attending skills. For more persistent attending problems, teach self-recording of attending, e.g., by having an egg timer go off at random intervals and hav-

---

ACROSTICS AT HARVARD

SOURED, PERHAPS, by memories of the multiplication tables, college students hate the annual ritual of memorizing the geological time scale in introductory courses on the history of life. We professors insist, claiming this venerable sequence as our alphabet. The entries are cumbersome—Cambrian, Ordovician, Silurian—and refer to such arcana as Roman names for Wales and threefold divisions of strata in Germany. We use little tricks and enticements to encourage compliance. For years, I held a mnemonics contest for the best entry to replace the traditional and insipid "Campbell's ordinary soup does make Peter pale . . ." or the underground salacious versions that I would blush to record, even here. During political upheavals of the early seventies, my winner for epochs of the Tertiary (see table) read: "Proletarian efforts off many pig police. Right on!" The all-time champion reviewed a porno movie called *Cheap Meat*—with perfect rhyme and scansion and only one necessary neologism, easily interpreted, at the end of the third line. This entry proceeds in unconventional order, from latest to earliest, and lists all the eras first, then all the periods:

> *Cheap Meat* performs passably,
> Quenching the celibate's jejune thirst,
> Portraiture, presented massably,
> Drowning sorrow, oneness cursed.

The winner also provided an epilogue, for the epochs of the Cenozoic era:

> Rare pornography, purchased meekly
> O Erogeny, Paleobscene.*

When such blandishments fail, I always say, try an honest intellectual argument: If these names were arbitrary divisions in a smooth continuum of events unfolding through time, I would have some sympathy for the opposition—for then we might take the history of modern multicellular life, about 600 million years, and divide this time into even and arbitrary units easily remembered as 1-12 or A-L, at 50 million years per unit.

But the earth scorns our simplifications and becomes much more interesting in its derision. The

---

*There are two in jokes in this line: *orogeny* is standard geological jargon for mountain building; *Paleobscene* is awfully close to the epoch's actual name—Paleocene.

GEOLOGIC ERAS			
Era	Period	Epoch	Approximate number of years ago (millions of years)
Cenozoic	Quaternary	Holocene (Recent) Pleistocene	
	Tertiary	Pliocene Miocene Oligocene Eocene Paleocene	
Mesozoic	Cretaceous Jurassic Triassic		65
Paleozoic	Permian Carboniferous (Pennsylvanian and Mississippian) Devonian Silurian Ordovician Cambrian		225
Precambrian			570

The geological time scale.

history of life is not a continuum of development, but a record punctuated by brief, sometimes geologically instantaneous, episodes of mass extinction and subsequent diversification. The geological time scale maps this history, for fossils provide our chief criterion in fixing the temporal order of rocks. The divisions of the time scale are set at these major punctuations because extinctions and rapid diversifications leave such clear signatures in the fossil record. Hence, the time scale is not a devil's ploy for torturing students, but a chronicle of key moments in life's history. By memorizing those infernal names, you learn the major episodes of earthly time. I make no apologies for the central importance of such knowledge.

Excerpted with permission from Wonderful Life: The Burgess Shale and the Nature of History, *by Stephen Jay Gould (W. W. Norton & Company, 1989).*

ing students indicate whether or not they were paying attention at that moment.

William James argued, "My experience is what I agree to attend to." Promoting attending will not guarantee improvement in memory, but it is a great place to start.

2. Promote External Memory

One very simple way for students to remember things better is to learn to write them down and refer back when necessary. This is one method of "external memory," which refers to the use of any device outside the student's own mind used to enhance memory. External memory devices include writing things in notebooks, appointment books, or on cards; placing things to be remembered (e.g., books, notes, self-reminders) in prominent places where they will be noticed; and using physical prompts (e.g., a string on the finger, a watch placed on the opposite wrist), which remind students to think of or do some particular thing. One drawback to external memory is that it is not a substitute for truly remembered information, especially in test situations, in which use of such systems is usually considered cheating.

3. Increase Meaningfulness

Students remember familiar and meaningful information much more readily than non-meaningful information; and students often surprise us by what is not meaningful to them. The most usual way of increasing meaningfulness is to develop experiences with the things being learned and to relate new information in some way to things that are already known. For instance, in describing the components of levers, use see-saws, oars, rakes, and wheelbarrows as examples. Tie examples of abstractions, such as "torque," to everyday things the student already understands.

4. Use of Pictures or Imagery

Most information is more easily remembered when it is pictured. Pictures make concepts more concrete, and, therefore, more easily remembered. Pictures allow students to more easily employ their mental imagery, which also facilitates remembering. Pictures can be shown to all students simultaneously on the overhead or opaque projector. If information is only presented verbally, it is less likely to be stored in students' memories as images, and, therefore, may be more difficult for them to retrieve. If it is not possible to show pictures, describe the information clearly and concretely, and encourage students to make pictures in their minds. If they can draw their images clearly, they are more likely to remember them.

5. Minimize Interfering Information

Highlight the most important information and reduce the number of unnecessary digressions. Provide only the most highly relevant examples. Unfortunately, some textbooks present what appears to be an endless string of facts, concepts, and vocabulary for students to memorize; it has been reported that some science textbooks

Research has consistently indicated that mnemonic techniques help students perform better on comprehension tasks.

contain more vocabulary words than are found in foreign language texts! If you do rely on textbooks to cover important class information, prioritize the terminology, facts, and concepts to include those that you consider most important and provide special emphasis on this information.

6. Encourage Active Participation

Concepts are better remembered if students actively manipulate or otherwise act out instances or manifestations of these concepts. For instance, in science, students are more likely to remember about series and parallel circuits if they have actively created these circuits. In social studies, students are more likely to remember information if they assume roles in debating historical issues, such as the U.S. recognition of the Republic of Texas, or current events, such as United Nations policy in the Sudan. Students can also assume roles in historical problem solving, such as problems in pioneer bridge building.

7. Promote Active Learning

Encourage students to reason actively through new information. Promote deductive reasoning when appropriate. Ask students to draw conclusions for themselves rather than simply telling them the information. For example, rather than explaining to students why earthworms are found on the ground after a rainfall, or why the full moon rises shortly after sunset, ask questions intended to lead students to draw the correct conclusions for themselves.

8. Increase Practice and Review

Many teachers require information to be remembered for a weekly or unit test (e.g., spelling, science) but rarely monitor recall of that information after it has been tested. To promote long-term recall of previously learned information, isolate the most critical content and provide brief but regular reviews over a longer time period. Students can review this information individually, question each other with flash cards, ask questions from books, or review with the teacher as a whole class activity. Although finding even small amounts of additional time for such activities may seem unlikely, look for occasions for brief reviews before or after transitions (lunch, recess, assemblies) or while students are standing in line or doing other activities that take minimal mental energy.

9. Use Mnemonic Techniques

Mnemonics are systematic techniques designed to enhance memory, particularly memory for new vocabu-

OKAY, WHO REMEMBERS THE FIVE MAJOR DIVISIONS OF VERTEBRATES?

SCIENCE IS an area in which many students experience frustration and disappointment. There are many causes for this. Although science itself is a fascinating subject, many students may fail to become interested because they fail to learn and remember key concepts and vocabulary. Without this foundation, more advanced learning and meaningful applications are impossible. In other cases, the content may be too complex or abstract for some students to readily grasp. Many advocates of science education have stressed the importance of experiment and discovery in science learning. Nevertheless, many key concepts and vocabulary must first be learned to make later experiment and discovery meaningful.

Mnemonic techniques can be very effective in science teaching, since they help make complex content simpler, abstractions more concrete, and seemingly meaningless information more meaningful.

For example, life science, as typically taught, has much to do with the classification, organization, and description of living things. Therefore, much instruction in life science has to do with learning characteristics and taxonomies. This type of learning easily lends itself to mnemonic instruction.

Vertebrates. The study of vertebrates is a relatively easy unit in life science because students usually are familiar with many of the relevant concepts. In fact, most students are familiar with what a "backbone" is, although they may not know the meaning of the word "vertebrate." In this case, a keyword strategy is helpful in teaching this verbal label for an already-familiar concept.

"Dirt" can be used as a keyword for "vertebrate" because it sounds like the first syllable of vertebrate and can be pictured (e.g., a dirt pile). A picture then can show a backbone (or a vertebrate animal with an obvious backbone) sticking out of a pile of dirt, to help students remember this definition of vertebrate.

There are five major divisions of vertebrates: amphibians, fish, reptiles, birds, and mammals. Two of the five, fish and birds, are almost certainly familiar to students. Therefore, fish and birds can be shown in *mimetic* or representational pictures, and important concrete attributes, such as scales, fins, and feathers, can be portrayed within these mimetic pictures.

Reptiles are also familiar to many students. However, many other students may not know what reptiles are, or they may not know all the different types of reptiles, such as snakes, lizards, turtles, and crocodilians. If reptiles are as familiar to students as birds and fish, they can be presented in a mimetic picture. If they are less familiar, a keyword elaboration will be helpful. In this case, the word "tiles" could be a good keyword for reptiles, because it sounds like the second syllable for reptiles, and can be pictured. A picture depicting reptiles in some relationship to tiles, e.g., a picture of snakes, lizards, turtles, and crocodilians sitting on tiles, or with tiles for scales, or both, could be effective.

Possible keywords could be "bib" for amphibian (*amplifier* may also be good) and "camel" for mammal. "Bib" is an acceptable keyword because, although a short keyword for a long word, bib sounds very much like the accent-ed second syllable of amphibian. Camel is a particularly good keyword because a camel *is* a mammal.

Organization. Much of life science instruction involves teaching which of several types of plants or animals go together. With respect to the *vertebrates* examples, above, students may be required to "have the five types committed to memory." Once the names of these animals have become familiar, a first-letter strategy is appropriate. The first letters of the five vertebrates cannot be combined to make a "real" word, but together they do form the acronym (suggested by Roy Halleran) "FARM-B." Now, FARM-B does not convey any particular meaning to us, other than, say, an unusual name for a farm; nevertheless, with a little practice this can become a very effective mnemonic for retrieving *f*ish, *a*mphibian, *r*eptile, *m*ammal, *b*ird. To integrate this idea with the concept "vertebrate," place a picture of each animal on a pile of *dirt* (keyword for vertebrate). Also, to reinforce the keywords in the acoustically transformed animal names, show the amphibian with a *bib,* the reptile on *tiles,* and a camel for the *mammal.*

———

Excerpted from Teaching Students Ways To Remember: Strategies for Learning Mnemonically.

Types of Vertebrates = Fish, Amphibians (bib), Reptiles (tiles), Mammals (camel), Birds (FARM-B)

lary or terminology, facts, and concepts. They are most effective, and most appropriate, when used to facilitate memory of things that cannot be deduced or otherwise constructed by students. Examples include remembering the seemingly arbitrary speech sounds in new vocabulary or terminology, human conventions, or basic facts such as the number and names of continents or planets.

Teachers who are expert in certain content areas may forget how difficult it is to acquire new speech sounds to represent new concepts or facts. Mnemonics often work by impacting on retrieval of the *acoustic properties,* or sounds, of unfamiliar words. A retrieval route is constructed between the sound of the word and the underlying meaning or conceptualization. Mnemonic techniques have been studied empirically over the past two decades and have been shown to be remarkably facilitative in promoting memory objectives.

In our recent book, *Teaching Students Ways to Remember: Strategies for Learning Mnemonically* (Cambridge, MA: Brookline Books), we describe a variety of effective mnemonic techniques and provide examples of how they can be applied in classroom settings. We will provide here some examples of *keyword, pegword,* and *letter* mnemonic strategies.

Keyword strategies. Keyword strategies are employed by creating an acoustically similar proxy (the keyword) for a new vocabulary word, proper name, fact or concept, and linking the keyword to the relevant associated information through an interactive picture or image. For instance, to help students remember that ranid (rā'nid) refers to the family of typical frogs, create a keyword for ranid that sounds like ranid and is easily pictured, e.g., *rain.* Then, show the rain and the frog interacting in a picture, e.g., a *frog* in the *rain.* Then remind students, when they hear the word ranid, think of the keyword, rain, think of the picture with rain in it, think what else was in the picture, and retrieve the response, *frog.* Have students practice until they can retrieve the information backwards, i.e., frog = ranid. For another example, to help students remember that *olfactory* refers to *sense of smell,* create a keyword for olfactory, e.g., "oil factory," and show or prompt imagery of a *smelly oil factory.* Verbal elaboration is also helpful. In this case, a person could be pictured walking past a smelly oil factory, holding his nose, and commenting, "That *oil factory* is bothering my *olfactory* sense!" When students hear the word olfactory, they can think of the keyword, oil factory, think of the picture of the smelly oil factory, and remember that olfactory referred to sense of smell. Keywords can also be used to promote foreign vocabulary learning and to help remember the names of important people and places in history. In a recent investigation, we found that pictured keywords for place names (e.g., Ticonderoga = Tiger) on maps promoted better recall of historical locations than the place names alone.

Pegwords. Pegwords are rhyming proxies (one is *bun,* two is *shoe,* three is *tree,* etc.) for numbers and are used in remembering numbered or ordered information.

For example, to help students remember that a *rake* is an example of a third-class lever, show a picture of a rake leaning against a *tree* (pegword for three). To help them remember that a wheelbarrow is an example of a second-class lever, show a picture of a wheelbarrow on a *shoe* (pegword for two).

Letter strategies. Letter strategies, particularly acronyms, are the strategies most commonly used by adults to remember things in clusters or series. Most everyone knows the HOMES strategy for remembering the names of the Great Lakes or that the name ROY G. BIV can help retrieve the colors of the spectrum. Acronyms can also be combined with keywords and pegwords. For example, you can help students remember the names of countries in the World War I Central Powers Alliance by using the acronym TAG (T = Turkey, A = Austria-Hungary, G = Germany). This acronym can be linked to the Central Powers by depicting children playing TAG in Central Park (keyword for Central Powers). To remember freedoms guaranteed by the First Amendment to the Constitution, have students think of a contemporary singer who RAPS (R = religion, A = assembly and petition, P = press, S = speech). To effectively tie these freedoms to the First Amendment, portray a singer who RAPS about *buns* (pegword for one).

In addition to acronyms are acrostics, which expand rather than condense representations. One example is *My Very Educated Mother Just Served Us Nine Pizzas,"* to represent the planets in order from the Sun: Mercury, Venus, Earth, Mars, Jupiter, Saturn, Uranus, Neptune, Pluto. Another is "King Phillip's Class Ordered a Family of Gentle Spaniels," to remember the classifications Kingdom, Phylum, Class, Order, Family, Genus, and Species, in order. Letter strategies are helpful whenever information can be clustered and when the information itself is relatively familiar.

IN SPITE of their success in facilitating memory, mnemonic techniques have often been criticized for promoting simple recall at the expense of conceptual understanding. However, research has consistently indicated that mnemonic techniques do not inhibit comprehension and actually help students perform better on comprehension tasks, probably because students employing these techniques can use more information in answering questions. Of course, it is possible to remember information that is not comprehended, and it is advisable to ensure that all information to be remembered is meaningful to students and that coursework is not overloaded with excessive amounts of facts and vocabulary to be memorized. On the other hand, it is not possible to comprehend or use information that is not remembered. To address this potential problem, memory strategies are appropriate.

Good memory skills have benefited humanity for thousands of years, and no doubt will continue to do so for thousands more. Although memory objectives can certainly be overemphasized in school settings, it is time to place appropriate emphasis on the importance of memory in school learning, as well as the skills that allow us to remember effectively.

Reflections on Multiple Intelligences

Myths and Messages

Mr. Gardner discusses seven myths that have grown up about multiple intelligences and attempts to set the record straight by presenting seven complementary "realities."

HOWARD GARDNER

HOWARD GARDNER is a professor of education and co-director of Project Zero at the Harvard Graduate School of Education and an adjunct professor of neurology at the Boston University School of Medicine. For their comments on an earlier draft of this article, he wishes to thank Melissa Brand, Patricia Bolanos, Thomas Hatch, Thomas Hoerr, Mara Krechevsky, Mindy Kornhaber, Jerome Murphy, Bruce Torff, Julie Viens, and Ellen Winner. Preparation of this article was supported by the MacArthur Foundation and the Spencer Foundation.

A SILENCE OF A DECADE'S LENGTH is sometimes a good idea. I published *Frames of Mind*, an introduction to the theory of multiple intelligences (MI theory) in 1983.[1] Because I was critical of current views of intelligences within the discipline of psychology, I expected to stir controversy among my fellow psychologists. This expectation was not disappointed.

I was unprepared for the large and mostly positive reaction to the theory among educators. Naturally I was gratified by this response and was stimulated to undertake some projects exploring the implications of MI theory. I also took pleasure from—and was occasionally moved by—the many attempts to institute an MI approach to education in schools and classrooms. By and large, however, except for a few direct responses to criticisms,[2] I did not speak up about new thoughts concerning the theory itself.

In 1993 my self-imposed silence was broken in two ways. My publisher issued a 10th-anniversary edition of *Frames of Mind*, to which I contributed a short, reflective introductory essay. In tandem with that release, the publisher issued *Multiple Intelligences: The Theory in Practice*, a set of articles chronicling some of the experiments undertaken in the wake of MI theory — mostly projects pursued by colleagues at Harvard Project Zero, but also other MI initiatives.[3] This collection gave me the opportunity to answer some other criticisms leveled against MI theory and to respond publicly to some of the most frequently asked questions.

In the 12 years since *Frames of Mind* was published, I have heard, read, and seen several hundred different interpretations of what MI theory is and how it can be applied in the schools.[4] Until now, I have been content to let MI theory take on a life of its own. As I saw it, I had issued an "ensemble of ideas" (or "memes") to the outer world, and I was inclined to let those "memes" fend for themselves.[5] Yet, in light of my own reading and observations, I believe that the time has come for me to issue a set of new "memes" of my own.

In the next part of this article, I will discuss seven myths that have grown up about multiple intelligences and, by putting forth seven complementary "realities," I will attempt to set the record straight. Then, in the third part of the article, reflecting on my observations of MI experiments in the schools, I will describe three primary ways in which education can be enhanced by a multiple intelligences perspective.

In what follows, I make no attempt to isolate MI theory from MI practice. "Multiple intelligences" began as a theory but was almost immediately put to practical use. The commerce between theory and practice has been ready, continuous, and, for the most part, productive.

Myths of Multiple Intelligences

Myth 1. Now that seven intelligences have been identified, one can — and perhaps should — create seven tests and secure seven scores.

Reality 1. MI theory represents a critique of "psychometrics-as-usual." A battery of MI tests is inconsistent with the major tenets of the theory.

Comment. My concept of intelligences is an outgrowth of accumulating knowledge about the human brain and about human cultures, not the result of a priori definitions or of factor analyses of test scores. As such, it becomes crucial that intelligences be assessed in ways that are "intelligent-fair," that is, in ways that examine the intelligence directly rather than through the lens of linguistic or logical intelligence (as ordinary paper-and-pencil tests do).

Thus, if one wants to look at spatial intelligence, one should allow an individual to explore a terrain for a while and see whether she can find her way around it re-

From *Phi Delta Kappan*, November 1995, pp. 200-203, 206-209. © 1995 by Howard Gardner. Reprinted by permission.

iably. Or if one wants to examine musical intelligence, one should expose an individual to a new melody in a reasonably familiar idiom and see how readily the person can learn to sing it, recognize it, transform it, and the like.

Assessing multiple intelligences is not a high priority in every setting. But when it is necessary or advisable to assess an individual's intelligences, it is best to do so in a comfortable setting with materials (and cultural roles) that are familiar to that individual. These conditions are at variance with our general conception of testing as a decontextualized exercise using materials that are unfamiliar by design, but there is no reason in principle why an "intelligence-fair" set of measures cannot be devised. The production of such useful tools has been our goal in such projects as Spectrum, Arts PROPEL, and Practical Intelligence for School.[6]

Myth 2. An intelligence is the same as a domain or a discipline.

Reality 2. An intelligence is a new kind of construct, and it should not be confused with a domain or a discipline.

Comment. I must shoulder a fair part of the blame for the propagation of the second myth. In writing *Frames of Mind*, I was not as careful as I should have been in distinguishing intelligences from other related concepts. As I have now come to understand, largely through my interactions with Mihaly Csikszentmihalyi and David Feldman,[7] an *intelligence* is a biological and psychological potential; that potential is capable of being realized to a greater or lesser extent as a consequence of the experiential, cultural, and motivational factors that affect a person.

In contrast, a *domain* is an organized set of activities within a culture, one typically characterized by a specific symbol system and its attendant operations. Any cultural activity in which individuals participate on more than a casual basis, and in which degrees of expertise can be identified and nurtured, should be considered a domain. Thus, physics, chess, gardening, and rap music are all domains in Western culture. Any domain can be realized through the use of several intelligences; thus the domain of musical performance involves bodily-kinesthetic and personal as well as musical intelligences. By the same token, a particular intelligence, like spatial intelligence, can be put to work in a myriad of domains, ranging from sculpture to sailing to neuroanatomical investigations.

Finally, a *field* is the set of individuals and institutions that judge the acceptabil-

ity and creativity of products fashioned by individuals (with their characteristic intelligences) within established or new domains. Judgments of quality cannot be made apart from the operation of members of a field, though it is worth noting that both the members of a field and the criteria that they employ can and do change over time.

Myth 3. An intelligence is the same as a "learning style," a "cognitive style," or a "working style."

Reality 3. The concept of *style* designates a general approach that an individual can apply equally to every conceivable content. In contrast, an *intelligence*

> *The commerce between theory and practice has been continuous and mostly productive.*

---

is a capacity, with its component processes, that is geared to a specific content in the world (such as musical sounds or spatial patterns).

Comment. To see the difference between an intelligence and a style, consider this contrast. If a person is said to have a "reflective" or an "intuitive" style, this designation assumes that the individual will be reflective or intuitive with all manner of content, ranging from language to music to social analysis. However, such an assertion reflects an empirical assumption that actually needs to be investigated. It might well be the case that an individual is reflective with music but fails to be reflective in a domain that requires mathematical thinking or that a person is highly intuitive in the social domain but not in the least intuitive when it comes to mathematics or mechanics.

In my view, the relation between my concept of intelligence and the various conceptions of style needs to be worked out

empirically, on a style-by-style basis. We cannot assume that "style" means the same thing to Carl Jung, Jerome Kagan, Tony Gregoric, Bernice McCarthy, and other inventors of stylistic terminology.[8] There is little authority for assuming that an individual who evinces a style in one milieu or with one content will necessarily do so with other diverse contents — and even less authority for equating styles with intelligences.

Myth 4. MI Theory is not empirical. (A variant of Myth 4 alleges that MI theory is empirical but has been disproved.)

Reality 4. MI theory is based wholly on empirical evidence and can be revised on the basis of new empirical findings.

Comment. Anyone who puts forth Myth 4 cannot have read *Frames of Mind*. Literally hundreds of empirical studies were reviewed in that book, and the actual intelligences were identified and delineated on the basis of empirical findings. The seven intelligences described in *Frames of Mind* represented my best-faith effort to identify mental abilities of a scale that could be readily discussed and critiqued.

No empirically based theory is ever established permanently. All claims are at risk in the light of new findings. In the last decade, I have collected and reflected on empirical evidence that is relevant to the claims of MI theory, 1983 version. Thus work on the development in children of a "theory of mind," as well as the study of pathologies in which an individual loses a sense of social judgment, has provided fresh evidence for the importance and independence of interpersonal intelligence.[9] In contrast, the finding of a possible link between musical and spatial thinking has caused me to reflect on the possible relations between faculties that had previously been thought to be independent.[10]

Many other lines of evidence could be mentioned here. The important point is that MI theory is constantly being reconceptualized in terms of new findings from the laboratory and from the field (see also Myth 7).

Myth 5. MI theory is incompatible with *g* (general intelligence),[11] with hereditarian accounts, or with environmental accounts of the nature and causes of intelligence.

Reality 5. MI theory questions not the existence but the province and explanatory power of *g*. By the same token, MI theory is neutral on the question of heritability of specific intelligences, instead underscoring the centrality of genetic/environmental interactions.

Comment. Interest in *g* comes chiefly from those who are probing scholastic intelligence and those who traffic in the correlations between test scores. (Recently people have become interested in the possible neurophysiological underpinnings of *g*[12] and, sparked by the publication of *The Bell Curve*,[13] in the possible social consequences of "low *g*.") While I have been critical of much of the research in the *g* tradition, I do not consider the study of *g* to be scientifically improper, and I am willing to accept the utility of *g* for certain theoretical purposes. My interest, obviously, centers on those intelligences and intellectual processes that are not covered by *g*.[14]

While a major animating force in psychology has been the study of the heritability of intelligence(s), my inquiries have not been oriented in this direction. I do not doubt that human abilities — and human differences — have a genetic base. Can any serious scientist question this at the end of the 20th century? And I believe that behavioral genetic studies, particularly of twins reared apart, can illuminate certain issues.[15] However, along with most biologically informed scientists, I reject the "inherited versus learned" dichotomy and instead stress the interaction, from the **moment of conception, between genetic and environmental factors.**

Myth 6. MI theory so broadens the notion of intelligence that it includes all psychological constructs and thus vitiates the usefulness, as well as the usual connotation, of the term.

Reality 6. This statement is simply wrong. I believe that it is the standard definition of intelligence that narrowly constricts our view, treating a certain form of scholastic performance as if it encompassed the range of human capacities and leading to disdain for those who happen not to be psychometrically bright. Moreover, I reject the distinction between talent and intelligence; in my view, what we call "intelligence" in the vernacular is simply a certain set of "talents" in the linguistic and/or logical-mathematical spheres.

Comment. MI theory is about the intellect, the human mind in its cognitive aspects. I believe that a treatment in terms of a number of semi-independent intelligences presents a more sustainable conception of human thought than one that posits a single "bell curve" of intellect.

Note, however, that MI theory makes

> *There is no point in assuming that every topic can be effectively approached in at least seven ways.*

no claims whatsoever to deal with issues beyond the intellect. MI theory is not, and does not pretend to be, about personality, will, morality, attention, motivation, and other psychological constructs. Note as well that MI theory is not connected to any set of morals or values. An intelligence can be put to an ethical or an antisocial use. Poet and playwright Johann Wolfgang von Goethe and Nazi propagandist Joseph Goebbels were both masters of the German language, but how different were the uses to which they put their talents!

Myth 7. There is an eighth (or ninth or 10th) intelligence.

Reality 7. Not in my writings so far. But I am working on it.

Comment. For the reasons suggested above, I thought it wise not to attempt to revise the principal claims of MI theory before the 1983 version of the theory had been debated. But recently, I have turned my attention to possible additions to the list. If I were to rewrite *Frames of Mind* today, I would probably add an eighth intelligence — the intelligence of the naturalist. It seems to me that the individual who is able readily to recognize flora and fauna, to make other consequential distinctions in the natural world, and to use this ability productively (in hunting, in farming, in biological science) is exercising an important intelligence and one that is not adequately encompassed in the current list. Individuals like Charles Darwin or E. O. Wilson embody the naturalist's intelligence, and, in our consuming culture, youngsters exploit their naturalist's intelligence as they make acute discriminations among cars, sneakers, or hairstyles.

I have read in several secondary sources that there is a spiritual intelligence and, indeed, that I have endorsed a spiritual in-telligence. That statement is not true. It i[s] true that I have become interested in u[n]derstanding better what is meant by "spir[-]ituality" and by "spiritual individuals"; a[s] my understanding improves, I expect t[o] write about this topic. Whether or not i[t] proves appropriate to add "spirituality" t[o] the list of intelligences, this human ca[-]pacity certainly deserves discussion an[d] study in nonfringe psychological circle[s.]

Messages About MI in the Classroom

If one were to continue adding myth[s] to the list, a promising candidate woul[d] read: There is a single educational approac[h] based on MI theory.

I trust that I have made it clear ove[r] the years that I do not subscribe to thi[s] myth.[16] On the contrary, MI theory is i[n] no way an educational prescription. Ther[e] is always a gulf between psychologica[l] claims about how the mind works an[d] educational practices, and such a gulf i[s] especially apparent in a theory that wa[s] developed without specific educationa[l] goals in mind. Thus, in educational dis[-]cussions, I have always taken the posi[-]tion that educators are in the best posi[-]tion to determine the uses to which M[I] theory can and should be put.

Indeed, contrary to much that has bee[n] written, MI theory does not incorporate [a] "position" on tracking, gifted education[,] interdisciplinary curricula, the layout o[f] the school day, the length of the schoo[l] year, or many other "hot button" educa[-]tional issues. I have tried to encourage cer[-]tain "applied MI efforts," but in genera[l] my advice has echoed the traditional Chi[-]nese adage "Let a hundred flowers bloom.["]

And I have often been surprised and de[-]lighted by the fragrance of some of thes[e] fledgling plants — for example, the us[e] of a "multiple intelligences curriculum["] in order to facilitate communication be[-]tween youngsters drawn from different cul[-]tures or the conveying of pivotal princi[-]ples in biology or social studies through [a] dramatic performance designed and stage[d] by students.

I have become convinced, however, tha[t] while there is no "right way" to conduc[t] a multiple intelligences education, som[e] current efforts go against the spirit of m[y] formulation and embody one or more o[f] the myths sketched above. Let me men[-]tion a few applications that have jarre[d] me.

• *The attempt to teach all concepts o[r] subjects using all the intelligences.* As [I] indicate below, most topics can be powerfully approached in a number of ways. But there is no point in assuming that every topic can be effectively approached in at least seven ways, and it is a waste of effort and time to attempt to do this.

• *The belief that it suffices, in and of itself, just to go through the motions of exercising a certain intelligence.* I have seen classes in which children are encouraged simply to move their arms or to run around, on the assumption that exercising one's body represents in itself some kind of MI statement. Don't read me as saying that exercise is a bad thing; it is not. But random muscular movements have nothing to do with the cultivation of the mind . . . or even of the body!

• *The use of materials associated with an intelligence as background.* In some classes, children are encouraged to read or to carry out math exercises while music is playing in the background. Now I myself like to work with music in the background. But unless I focus on the performance (in which case the composition is no longer serving as background), the music's function is unlikely to be different from that of a dripping faucet or a humming fan.

• *The use of intelligences primarily as mnemonic devices.* It may well be the case that it is easier to remember a list if one sings it or even if one dances while reciting it. I have nothing against such aids to memory. However, these uses of the materials of an intelligence are essentially trivial. What is not trivial — as I argue below — is to think musically or to draw on some of the structural aspects of music in order to illuminate concepts like biological evolution or historical cycles.

• *The conflating of intelligences with other desiderata.* This practice is particularly notorious when it comes to the personal intelligences. Interpersonal intelligence has to do with understanding other people, but it is often distorted as a license for cooperative learning or applied to individuals who are extroverted. Intrapersonal intelligence has to do with understanding oneself, but it is often distorted as a rationale for self-esteem programs or applied to individuals who are loners or introverted. One receives the strong impression that individuals who use the terms in this promiscuous way have never read my writings on intelligence.

• *The direct evaluation (or even grading) of intelligences, without regard to context or content.* Intelligences ought to be seen at work when individuals are carry-

When I visit an "MI school," I look for signs of personalization.

ing out productive activities that are valued in a culture. And that is how reporting of learning and mastery in general should take place. I see little point in grading individuals in terms of how "linguistic" or how "bodily-kinesthetic" they are; such a practice is likely to introduce a new and unnecessary form of tracking and labeling. As a parent (or as a supporter of education living in the community), I am interested in the *uses* to which children's intelligences are put; reporting should have this focus.

Note that it is reasonable, for certain purposes, to indicate that a child seems to have a relative strength in one intelligence and a relative weakness in another. However, these descriptions should be mobilized in order to help students perform better in meaningful activities and perhaps even to show that a label was premature or erroneous.

Having illustrated some problematic applications of MI theory, let me now indicate three more positive ways in which MI can be — and has been — used in the schools.

1. *The cultivation of desired capabilities.* Schools should cultivate those skills and capacities that are valued in the community and in the broader society. Some of these desired roles are likely to highlight specific intelligences, including ones that have usually been given short shrift in the schools. If, say, the community believes that children should be able to perform on a musical instrument, then the cultivation of musical intelligence toward that end becomes a value of the school.

Similarly, emphasis on such capacities as taking into account the feelings of others, being able to plan one's own life in a reflective manner, or being able to find one's way around an unfamiliar terrain are likely to result in an emphasis on the cultivation of interpersonal, intrapersonal, and spatial intelligences respectively.

2. *Approaching a concept, subject matter, or discipline in a variety of ways.* Along with many other school reformers, I am convinced that schools attempt to cover far too much material and that superficial understandings (or nonunderstandings) are the inevitable result. It makes far more sense to spend a significant amount of time on key concepts, generative ideas, and essential questions and to allow students to become thoroughly familiar with these notions and their implications.

Once the decision has been made to dedicate time to particular items, it then becomes possible to approach those topics or notions in a variety of ways. Not necessarily seven ways, but in a number of ways that prove pedagogically appropriate for the topic at hand. Here is where MI theory comes in. As I argue in *The Unschooled Mind*, nearly every topic can be approached in a variety of ways, ranging from the telling of a story, to a formal argument, to an artistic exploration, to some kind of "hands-on" experiment or simulation. Such pluralistic approaches should be encouraged.[17]

When a topic has been approached from a number of perspectives, three desirable outcomes ensue. First, because children do not all learn in the same way, more children will be reached. I term this desirable state of affairs "multiple windows leading into the same room." Second, students secure a sense of what it is like to be an expert when they behold that a teacher can represent knowledge in a number of different ways and discover that they themselves are also capable of more than a single representation of a specified content. Finally, since understanding can also be demonstrated in more than one way, a pluralistic approach opens up the possibility that students can display their new understandings — as well as their continuing difficulties — in ways that are comfortable for them and accessible to others. Performance-based examinations and exhibitions are tailor-made for the foregrounding of a student's multiple intelligences.

3. *The personalization of education.* Without a doubt, one of the reasons that MI theory has attracted attention in the educational community is because of its

ringing endorsement of an ensemble of propositions: we are not all the same; we do not all have the same kinds of minds; education works most effectively for most individuals if these differences in mentation and strengths are taken into account rather than denied or ignored. I have always believed that the heart of the MI perspective — in theory and in practice — inheres in taking human differences seriously. At the theoretical level, one acknowledges that all individuals cannot be profitably arrayed on a single intellectual dimension. At the practical level, one acknowledges that any uniform educational approach is likely to serve only a minority of children.

When I visit an "MI school," I look for signs of personalization: evidence that all involved in the educational encounter take such differences among human beings seriously; evidence that they construct curricula, pedagogy, and assessment insofar as possible in the light of these differences. All the MI posters, indeed all the references to me personally, prove to be of little avail if the youngsters continue to be treated in homogenized fashion. By the same token, whether or not members of the staff have even heard of MI theory, I would be happy to send my children to a school with the following characteristics: differences among youngsters are taken seriously, knowledge about differences is shared with children and parents, children gradually assume responsibility for their own learning, and materials that are worth knowing are presented in ways that afford each child the maximum opportunity to master those materials and to show others (and themselves) what they have learned and understood.

Closing Comments

I am often asked for my views about schools that are engaged in MI efforts. The implicit question may well be: "Aren't you upset by some of the applications that are carried out in your name?"

In truth, I do not expect that initial efforts to apply any new ideas are going to be stunning. Human experimentation is slow, difficult, and filled with zigs and zags. Attempts to apply any set of innovative ideas will sometimes be half-hearted, superficial, even wrongheaded.

For me the crucial question concerns what has happened in a school (or class) two, three, or four years after it has made a commitment to an MI approach. Often, the initiative will be long since forgotten — the fate, for better or worse, of most educational experiments. Sometimes, the school has gotten stuck in a rut, repeating the same procedures of the first days without having drawn any positive or negative lessons from this exercise. Needless to say, I am not happy with either of these outcomes.

I cherish an educational setting in which discussions and applications of MI have catalyzed a more fundamental consideration of schooling — its overarching purposes, its conceptions of what a productive life will be like in the future, its pedagogical methods, and its educational outcomes, particularly in the context of the values of that specific community. Such examination generally leads to more thoughtful schooling. Visits with other schools and more extended forms of networking among MI enthusiasts (and critics) constitute important parts of this building process. If, as a result of these discussions and experiments, a more personalized education is the outcome, I feel that the heart of MI theory has been embodied. And if this personalization is fused with a commitment to the achievement of worthwhile (and attainable) educational understandings for all children, then the basis for a powerful education has indeed been laid.

The MI endeavor is a continuing and changing one. There have emerged over the years new thoughts about the theory, new understandings and misunderstandings, and new applications, some very inspired, some less so. Especially gratifying to me has been the demonstration that this process is dynamic and interactive: no one, not even its creator, has a monopoly on MI wisdom or foolishness. Practice is enriched by theory, even as theory is transformed in the light of the fruits and frustrations of practice. The burgeoning of a community that takes MI issues seriously is not only a source of pride to me but also the best guarantor that the theory will continue to live in the years ahead.

1. Howard Gardner, *Frames of Mind: The Theory of Multiple Intelligences* (New York: Basic Books, 1983). A 10th-anniversary edition, with a new introduction, was published in 1993.

2. Howard Gardner, "On Discerning New Ideas in Psychology," *New Ideas in Psychology*, vol. 3, 1985, pp. 101-4; and idem, "Symposium on the Theory of Multiple Intelligences," in David N. Perkins, Jack Lochhead, and John C. Bishop, eds., *Thinking: The Second International Conference* (Hillsdale, N.J.: Erlbaum, 1983), pp. 77-101.

3. Howard Gardner, *Multiple Intelligences: The Theory in Practice* (New York: Basic Books, 1993).

4. For a bibliography through 1992, see the appendices to Gardner, *Multiple Intelligences*.

5. The term "memes" is taken from Richard Dawkins, *The Selfish Gene* (Oxford: Oxford University Press, 1976).

6. See Gardner, *Multiple Intelligences*.

7. Mihaly Csikszentmihalyi, "Society, Culture, and Person: A Systems View of Creativity," in Robert J. Sternberg, ed., *The Nature of Creativity* (New York: Cambridge University Press, 1988), pp. 325-39; idem, *Creativity* (New York: HarperCollins, forthcoming); David H. Feldman, "Creativity: Dreams, Insights, and Transformations," in Sternberg, op. cit., pp. 271-97; and David H. Feldman, Mihaly Csikszentmihalyi, and Howard Gardner, *Changing the World: A Framework for the Study of Creativity* (Westport, Conn.: Greenwood, 1994).

8. For a comprehensive discussion of the notion of cognitive style, see Nathan Kogan, "Stylistic Variation in Childhood and Adolescence," in Paul Mussen, ed., *Handbook of Child Psychology*, vol. 3 (New York: Wiley, 1983), pp. 630-706.

9. For writings pertinent to the personal intelligences, see Janet Astington, *The Child's Discovery of the Mind* (Cambridge, Mass.: Harvard University Press, 1993); and Antonio Damasio, *Descartes' Error* (New York: Grosset/Putnam, 1994).

10. On the possible relation between musical and spatial intelligence, see Frances Rauscher, G. L. Shaw, and X. N. Ky, "Music and Spatial Task Performance," *Nature*, 14 October 1993, p. 611.

11. The most thorough exposition of *g* can be found in the writings of Arthur Jensen. See, for example, *Bias in Mental Testing* (New York: Free Press, 1980). For a critique, see Stephen J. Gould, *The Mismeasure of Man* (New York: Norton, 1981).

12. Interest in the neurophysiological bases of *g* is found in Arthur Jensen, "Why Is Reaction Time Correlated with Psychometric 'G'?," *Current Directions of Psychological Science*, vol. 2, 1993, pp. 53-56.

13. Richard Herrnstein and Charles Murray, *The Bell Curve* (New York: Free Press, 1994).

14. For my view on intelligences not covered by *g*, see Howard Gardner, "Review of Richard Herrnstein and Charles Murray, *The Bell Curve*," *The American Prospect*, Winter 1995, pp. 71-80.

15. On behavioral genetics and psychological research, see Thomas Bouchard and P. Propping, eds., *Twins as a Tool of Behavioral Genetics* (Chichester, England: Wiley, 1993).

16. On the many approaches that can be taken in implementing MI theory, see Mara Krechevsky, Thomas Hoerr, and Howard Gardner, "Complementary Energies: Implementing MI Theory from the Lab and from the Field," in Jeannie Oakes and Karen H. Quartz, eds., *Creating New Educational Communities: Schools and Classrooms Where All Children Can Be Smart: 94th NSSE Yearbook* (Chicago: National Society for the Study of Education, University of Chicago Press, 1995), pp. 166-86.

17. Howard Gardner, *The Unschooled Mind: How Children Learn and How Schools Should Teach* (New York: Basic Books, 1991).

Thinking Maps:
Seeing is Understanding

David Hyerle

By using visual tools that correspond to thinking processes, students can organize their ideas on paper or by computer, and—as a result—read, write, and think better.

Walk through schools these days, and you will see teachers and students using a wide array of visual tools to construct, organize, assess, and convey knowledge. Semantic maps for brainstorming, graphic organizers for structuring information, and simple maps in textbook lessons are just a few tools being used to activate student learning. While educational reformers seek to restructure schools, a gradual, but fundamental, shift has been occurring in the everyday communication in classrooms.

Over the past 20 years (and more rapidly during the past five years), teachers, administrators, curriculum designers, staff developers, and even test-makers have turned to graphic representations for showing relationships. In some states, such as Texas and North Carolina, graphic organizers are showing up on tests as formal guides to find out how students are solving problems.

My first experiences with visual tools came during the early 1980s, when I began teaching writing in an urban middle school in Oakland, California. I introduced my students to the "mind mapping" and "webbing" techniques developed by innovators such as Tony Buzan, Gabriele Rico, and teachers with the Bay Area Writing Project at the University of California at Berkeley. There was a fundamental problem, however.

Despite the wealth of knowledge my students displayed on their semantic maps, they were ultimately confused about how to further organize, analyze, and evaluate their representations. They could brainstorm exciting and imaginative ideas, but they were less capable at following through with an organized, coherent piece of writing. As a novice teacher, I began asking myself: What happens to the brain after the storm?

After the Brainstorm

I became immersed in the thinking process approach to curriculum, and later devised a language of eight related visual tools—what I call Thinking Maps (see fig. 1). These forms are designed to help K–12 students generate and organize their thoughts and ideas, either on paper or by using the software, and construct simple to complex mental models. Each Thinking Map corresponds to a single thinking process:

- *Circle map*—helps define words or things in context and presents points of view.
- *Bubble map*—describes emotional, sensory, and logical qualities.
- *Double bubble map*—compares and contrasts qualities.
- *Tree map*—shows the relationships between main ideas and supporting details.
- *Flow map*—shows events as a sequence.

- *Multi-flow map*—shows causes and effects and helps predict outcomes.
- *Brace map*—shows physical structures and part-whole relationships.
- *Bridge map*—helps to transfer or form analogies and metaphors.

Teachers are trained to introduce students to all eight maps as a related set of tools for content learning. They then show the students how to use these maps as needed, isolated or together. Teachers can do this in a short time because each map is a concrete tool rather than an abstract definition.

For example, Figure 2 shows how a 6th grader used the bubble map to understand the story, "William Tell, the Archer and the Apple," which her class in Brooklyn, New York's District 13 had read. The bubble map may look like a generic web, but it isn't. It is based on the thought process of identifying qualities using adjectives and adjective phrases. Students use it in analyzing character traits in language arts, attributes in mathematics, properties in science, and cultural traits in social studies.

The graphic configuration of each Thinking Map becomes more complex as student thinking improves and content knowledge is enriched over time. Upper elementary, secondary, and college students quickly become fluent in using the maps for complex tasks. Lower elementary students usually need several years to build up the capacity to use all the maps as interrelated tools.

Schemes for Subtler Thinking

Typically, graphic organizers are useful as isolated strategies, but using

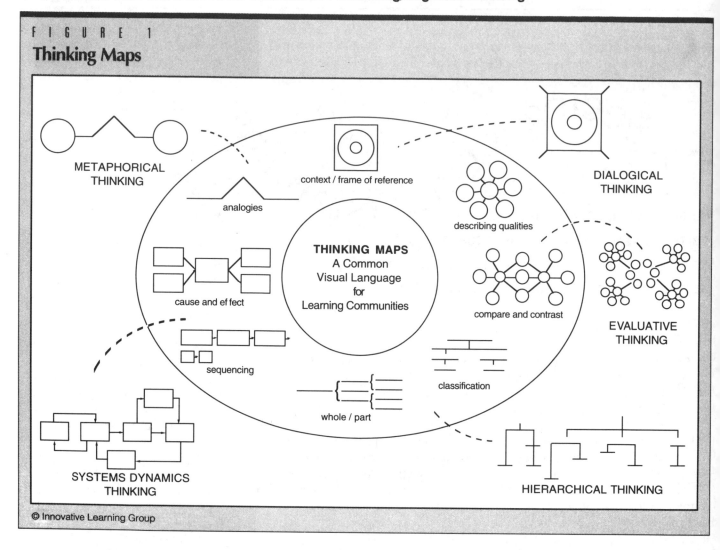

FIGURE 1

Thinking Maps

METAPHORICAL THINKING

analogies

context / frame of reference

DIALOGICAL THINKING

describing qualities

THINKING MAPS
A Common
Visual Language
for
Learning Communities

cause and effect

compare and contrast

EVALUATIVE THINKING

sequencing

classification

whole / part

SYSTEMS DYNAMICS THINKING

HIERARCHICAL THINKING

© Innovative Learning Group

a single graphic related to a specific task may not provide the student with the flexibility necessary to link strategies in more complex situations, such as in reading comprehension across disciplines and interpreting literature. For example, we may ask students to

do several things while reading—to understand the context for the story, identify qualities of a central character, compare characters, and sequence what happened. These four tasks require different thinking processes that are not necessarily linear in form.

The investigation of character traits in the William Tell story led naturally—and graphically—to a comparison of two characters, using the double bubble map. By using this map, the student began to think about comparing and contrasting qualities and how the characters are similar and different. The student also used the flow map (see fig. 3) to analyze the story's plot and see the events as a sequence.

This linking of different patterns of thinking when analyzing literature is similar to structuring information and constructing knowledge in other

content areas. Indeed, one can use visual representations as key tools for concept development and for the interpretation and assimilation of new information in every content area.

In science, for example, students use concept mapping or systems diagrams to develop mental models of scientific concepts, and teachers use it to assess students' development of concepts and misconceptions (Novak and Gowin 1984). For reading comprehension, students might receive preset text structures, such as problem-solution formats, to help them organize and summarize what they read (Armbruster 1987). New Thinking Maps software will help students quickly make connections and organize information for oral reports, social studies research, science experiments, and other projects.

Researchers have found that

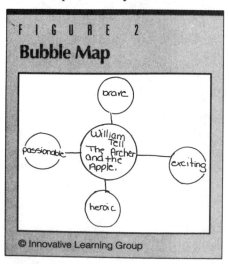

FIGURE 2

Bubble Map

brave

William Tell The Archer and the Apple.

passionate

exciting

heroic

© Innovative Learning Group

presenting selected graphic organizers on computers helps students to see the relationships between main ideas and supporting details (as in the tree map), and that this in turn leads to higher scores on reading and writing tests (Cronin et al. 1990).

In North Carolina, many elementary and junior high schools that had introduced the Thinking Maps schoolwide in 1993–94 found significant increases in holistic writing test scores over successive years (Hyerle, in press). Researchers also have found that students enjoy using graphics for networking information and constructing knowledge, thus shifting from passive to interactive learning.

In this age of information overflow and networking, students must be able to use multiple strategies to solve complex problems. In language arts, for example, students are evaluated through their responses to complex reading selections or to an array of writing prompts. In mathematics, they must solve multistep word problems. The new testing formats require them to complete varied tasks and show their work and reasoning.

Unfortunately, most students are not prepared for these layered tasks. Barbara Bell, principal of the Joe Hall Elementary School in Miami, says one reason she adopted Thinking Maps at her school was that

> it is particularly difficult to find strategies that work together to develop higher-order thinking skills.

By learning how to use Thinking Maps together, students show they can persevere and not give up in mid-problem.

Whole School Ties

In a learning community, Thinking Maps become a common visual language among students and between students and teachers—not only within content areas but also across disciplines. In the Thinking Maps transfer approach, we work with whole schools over several years. This is essential because it offers all-important continuous support for students as they move through grade levels.

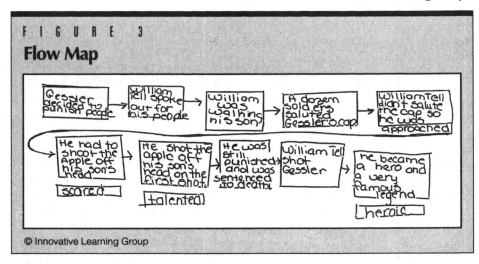

FIGURE 3
Flow Map

© Innovative Learning Group

"The key to the success of this approach," suggests Barbara Bell, "is the common thinking process, vocabulary, and visual language." She reflects on the 1993–94 school year, during which all her administrators, teachers, and 1,400 students—from kindergarten on up—began using the maps:

> The teachers embraced these maps because they were able to incorporate them directly into their everyday questioning techniques and classroom activities. Students learned the maps easily because the maps were reinforced across the whole school.

Marilyn Lawrence, director of curriculum in Brooklyn's District 13, has guided implementation of these maps in schools there. She believes it is critical that teachers be trained "to introduce and model for students how to transfer the maps across content areas," so that students can consciously use them, both independently and in cooperative groups.

Teachers at Joe Hall Elementary School participated in a year of professional development in Thinking Maps and follow-up support in the classrooms. They then met in groups, by grade. They brought their own curriculum ideas, along with student writing portfolios, including those showing work by bilingual, special education, and gifted students.

The teachers agreed that the maps had successfully helped students develop their thinking processes and their ability to organize ideas, improved the quality and quantity of

their writing, and also motivated them to learn. Further, the maps benefited the teachers by helping them organize content and assess student learning.

Significantly, the teachers who gave the maps the highest approval rating were those who worked closely with the large population of Spanish-speaking students who are learning English. They said that the common visual language for thinking enabled their students to transfer patterns of thinking from Spanish into English, to focus on learning, and to build vocabulary.

Portfolios of Change
When teachers collect Thinking Maps over time and within student portfolios, many interesting possibilities emerge. Portfolios enable students and teachers to see how learners are assimilating new knowledge into the big picture of any content area, and how thinking and content knowledge develop incrementally.

Karen Joslin, a teacher at Hurley Elementary School in Salisbury, North Carolina, reviewed the portfolios with her Title I students to decide which Thinking Maps were appropriate to include in their portfolios. In this way, she helped students evaluate what they knew and how they came to construct content knowledge using Thinking Maps with other strategies. Students become aware of how visual tools support what Arthur Costa has described as their "displayed metacognition" of patterns of thinking (in

Clarke 1991). Or, as one 3rd grader from Laurel, Mississippi, put it: "I see what I learn."

In most schools, teachers find continuous development of student thinking from grade to grade much more elusive than planning the scope and sequence of a curriculum. Yet it is this kind of reinforcement of thinking processes that helps students become independent, reflective learners. Thinking process maps of all kinds become a visual crossroads for consciously linking content with process learning.

As with any innovation in education, we have encountered obstacles along with positive changes in implementation. One of the first hurdles is gaining the commitment of a school's whole faculty to develop a schoolwide design for using these tools. But with time and visible successes, this commitment tends to come.

Success Stories

Chadbourn Elementary School in Goldsboro, North Carolina, wrote Thinking Maps into its Chapter I program to prepare students for the state's first annual assessment of 4th graders' writing in February 1993. (Nearly 90 percent of Chadbourn's students qualify for a free or low-cost lunch.) The first year, teachers systematically introduced the maps, and the second year, they helped students use the maps to organize their writing in response to test prompts.

The result? In 1992–93, the 4th graders' writing scores averaged 35 percent—the highest of the 11 district schools tested, and more than 11 percent higher than the district and state averages. In 1993–94, Chadbourn's 4th graders did even better: they finished first with a 51 percent average. This compared to 31 percent and 34 percent, respectively, for the district and state averages. This past year, Chadbourn's average shot up to 61 percent. Rarely do scores increase so significantly three years in a row.

At Another Title I school, Atlanta's Margaret Fain Elementary, reading scores on the Georgia State Test of Basic Skills rose sharply—from 29 to 69 percent. Principal Patricia Austin says Thinking Maps helped her students improve in both the reading and mathematics portions of the test.

Then there was the initial workshop at Marcelle Elementary in Mission, Texas, when a teacher specialist, Louise Esau, asked me how she could use these maps with a 4th grader named Richie, who is blind. Visual tools for the blind? I had never thought about the possibilities.

During my next visit, Esau unveiled a set of Braille Thinking Maps, some created by Richie, showing how he had used the Braille machine to pattern his ideas. Along with the raised bumps and patterns on these papers, she presented a video clip showing Richie proudly reading his Thinking Maps by hand and leading his classmates in discussing a description of a truck he had written.

After seeing and feeling this work, I had no doubt that patterns of thinking run much deeper than how we traditionally have conveyed them to students. Although we are now going beyond linear representations, we are just beginning to investigate how student-centered designs for thinking facilitate learning. And we're on the edge of seeing the implications of using visual tools for opening up the mind's eye.

References

Armbruster, B. B., T. H. Anderson, and J. Ostertag. (1987). "Does Text Structure/Summarization Instruction Facilitate Learning from Expository Text?" *Reading Research Quarterly* 22: 331–346.

Clarke, J. H. (1991). *Patterns of Thinking.* Needham Heights, Mass.: Allyn and Bacon.

Cronin, H., D. Meadows, and R. Sinatra. (1990). "Integrating Computers, Reading, and Writing Across the Curriculum." *Educational Leadership* 63, 8: 57–62.

Hyerle, D. (In press). *Visual Tools for Constructing Knowledge.* Alexandria, Va.: Association for Supervision and Curriculum Development.

Novak, J. D. and B. D. Gowin. (1984). *Learning How to Learn.* Cambridge: Cambridge University Press.

David Hyerle is Director of Curriculum and Staff Development, Innovative Learning Group, 975 Walnut St., Suite 342, Cary , NC 27511 (e-mail: ilg@valley.net).

The Rewards of Learning

To teach without using extrinsic rewards is analogous to asking our students to learn to draw with their eyes closed, Mr. Chance maintains. Before we do that, we should open our own eyes.

Paul Chance

Paul Chance (Eastern Shore Maryland Chapter) is a psychologist, writer, and teacher. He is the author of Thinking in the Classroom *(Teachers College Press, 1986) and teaches at James H. Groves Adult High School in Georgetown, Del.*

A man is seated at a desk. Before him lie a pencil and a large stack of blank paper. He picks up the pencil, closes his eyes, and attempts to draw a four-inch line. He makes a second attempt, a third, a fourth, and so on, until he has made well over a hundred attempts at drawing a four-inch line, all without ever opening his eyes. He repeats the exercise for several days, until he has drawn some 3,000 lines, all with his eyes closed. On the last day, he examines his work. The question is, How much improvement has there been in his ability to draw a four-inch line? How much has he learned from his effort?

E. L. Thorndike, the founder of educational psychology and a major figure in the scientific analysis of learning, performed this experiment years ago, using himself as subject.[1] He found no evidence of learning. His ability to draw a four-inch line was no better on the last day than it had been on the first.

The outcome of this experiment may seem obvious to us today, but it was an effective way of challenging a belief widely held earlier in this century, a belief that formed the very foundation of education at the time: the idea that "practice makes perfect."

It was this blind faith in practice that justified countless hours of rote drill as a standard teaching technique. Thorndike's experiment demonstrated that practice in and of itself is not sufficient for learning. Based on this and other, more formal studies, Thorndike concluded that prac-

tice is important only insofar as it provides the opportunity for reinforcement.

To reinforce means to strengthen, and among learning researchers *reinforcement* refers to a procedure for strengthening behavior (that is, making it likely to be repeated) by providing certain kinds of consequences.[2] These consequences, called *reinforcers,* are usually events or things a person willingly seeks out. For instance, we might teach a person to draw a four-inch line with his eyes closed merely by saying "good" each time the effort is within half an inch of the goal. Most people like to succeed, so this positive feedback should be an effective way of reinforcing the appropriate behavior.

Hundreds of experimental studies have demonstrated that systematic use of reinforcement can improve both classroom conduct and the rate of learning. Yet the systematic use of reinforcement has never been widespread in American schools. In *A Place Called School*, John Goodlad reports that, in the elementary grades, an average of only 2% of class time is devoted to reinforcement; in the high schools, the figure falls to 1%.[3]

THE COSTS OF REWARD

There are probably many reasons for our failure to make the most of reinforcement. For one thing, few schools of education provide more than cursory instruction in its use. Given Thorndike's finding about the role of practice in learning, it is ironic that many teachers actually use the term *reinforcement* as a synonym for *practice.* ("We assign workbook exercises for reinforcement.") If schools of education do not teach future teachers the nature of reinforcement and how to use it effectively, teachers can hardly be blamed for not using it.

The unwanted effects of misused reinforcement have led some teachers to shy away from it. The teacher who sometimes lets a noisy class go to recess early will find the class getting noisier before recess. If high praise is reserved for long-winded essays, students will develop wordy and redundant writing styles. And it should surprise no one if students are seldom original in classrooms where only conventional work is admired or if they are uncooperative in classrooms where one can earn recognition only through competition. Reinforcement is powerful stuff, and its misuse can cause problems.

Another difficulty is that the optimal use of reinforcement would mean teaching in a new way. Some studies suggest that maximum learning in elementary and middle schools might require very high rates of reinforcement, perhaps with teachers praising someone in the class an average of once every 15 seconds.[4] Such a requirement is clearly incompatible with traditional teaching practices.

Systematic reinforcement can also mean more work for the teacher. Reinforcing behavior once every 15 seconds means 200 reinforcements in a 50-minute period — 1,000 reinforcements in a typical school day. It also implies that, in order to spot behavior to reinforce, the teacher must be moving about the room, not sitting at a desk marking papers. That may be too much to ask. Some studies have found that teachers who have been taught how to make good use of reinforcement often revert to their old style of teaching. This is so even though the teachers acknowledge that increased use of reinforcement means fewer discipline problems and a much faster rate of learning.[5]

Reinforcement also runs counter to our Puritan traditions. Most Americans have always assumed — occasional protestations to the contrary notwithstanding — that learning should be hard work and at least slightly unpleasant. Often the object of education seems to be not so much to teach academic and social skills as to "build character" through exposure to adversity. When teachers reinforce students at a high rate, the students experience a minimum of adversity and actually enjoy learning. Thus some people think that reinforcement is bad for character development.

All of these arguments against reinforcement can be countered effectively. Schools of education do not provide much instruction in the practical use of reinforcement, but there is no reason why they cannot do so. Reinforcement can be used incorrectly and with disastrous results, but the same might be said of other powerful tools. Systematic use of reinforcement means teaching in a new way, but teachers can learn to do so.[6] A great deal of reinforcement is needed for optimum learning, but not all of the reinforcement needs to come from the teacher. (Reinforcement can be provided by computers and other teaching devices, by teacher aides, by parents, and by students during peer teaching and cooperative learning.) No doubt people do sometimes benefit from adversity, but the case for the character-building properties of adversity is very weak.[7]

However, there is one argument against reinforcement that cannot be dismissed so readily. For some 20 years, the claim has been made that systematic reinforcement actually undermines student learning. Those few teachers who make extensive use of reinforcement, it is claimed, do their students a disservice because reinforcement reduces interest in the reinforced activity.

Not all forms of reinforcement are considered detrimental. A distinction is made between reinforcement involving intrinsic reinforcers — or rewards, as they are often called — and reinforcement involving extrinsic rewards.[8] Only extrinsic rewards are said to be harmful. An *intrinsic reward* is ordinarily the natural consequence of behavior, hence the name. We learn to throw darts by seeing how close the dart is to the target; learn to type by seeing the right letters appear on the computer screen; learn to cook from the pleasant sights, fragrances, and flavors that result from our culinary efforts; learn to read from the understanding we get from the printed word; and

learn to solve puzzles by finding solutions. The Japanese say, "The bow teaches the archer." They are talking about intrinsic rewards, and they are right.

Extrinsic rewards come from an outside source, such as a teacher. Probably the most ubiquitous extrinsic reward (and one of the most effective) is praise. The teacher reinforces behavior by saying "good," "right," "correct," or "excellent" when the desired behavior occurs. Other extrinsic rewards involve nonverbal behavior such as smiles, winks, thumbs-up signs, hugs, congratulatory handshakes, pats on the back, or applause. Gold stars, certificates, candy, prizes, and even money have been used as rewards, but they are usually less important in teaching — and even in the maintenance of good discipline — than those mentioned earlier.

The distinction between intrinsic and extrinsic rewards is somewhat artificial. Consider the following example. You put money into a vending machine and retrieve a candy bar. The behavior of inserting money into a vending machine has been reinforced, as has the more general behavior of interacting with machines. But is the food you receive an intrinsic or an extrinsic reward? On the one hand, the food is the automatic consequence of inserting money and pressing buttons, so it would appear to be an intrinsic reward. On the other hand, the food is a consequence that was arranged by the designer of the machine, so it would seem to be an extrinsic reward.[9]

Though somewhat contrived, the distinction between intrinsic and extrinsic rewards has been maintained partly because extrinsic rewards are said to be damaging.[10] Are they? First, let us be clear about the charge. The idea is that — if teachers smile, praise, congratulate, say "thank you" or "right," shake hands, hug, give a pat on the back, applaud, provide a certificate of achievement or attendance, *or in any way provide a positive consequence (a reward) for student behavior* — the student will be less inclined to engage in that behavior when the reward is no longer available.

For example, teachers who offer prizes to students for reading books will, it is said, make the children less likely to read when prizes are no longer available. The teacher who reads a student's story aloud to the class as an example of excellent story writing actually makes the student less likely to write stories in the future, when such public approval is not forth-

coming. When teachers (and students) applaud a youngster who has given an excellent talk, they make that student disinclined to give talks in the future. The teacher who comments favorably on the originality of a painting steers the young artist away from painting. And so on. This is the charge against extrinsic rewards.

No one disputes the effectiveness of extrinsic rewards in teaching or in maintaining good discipline. Some might therefore argue that extrinsic rewards should be used, even if they reduce interest in learning. Better to have students who read only when required to do so, some might say, than to have students who cannot read at all.

But if rewards do reduce interest, that fact is of tremendous importance. "The teacher may count himself successful," wrote B. F. Skinner, "when his students become engrossed in his field, study conscientiously, and do more than is required of them, but *the important thing is what they do when they are no longer being taught*" (emphasis added).[11] It is not enough for students to learn the three R's and a little science and geography; they must be prepared for a lifetime of learning. To reduce their interest in learning would be a terrible thing — even if it were done in the interest of teaching them effectively.

The question of whether rewards adversely affect motivation is not, then, of merely academic or theoretical importance. It is of great practical importance to the classroom teacher.

Extrinsic rewards are said to be damaging. Are they? First, let us be clear about the charge.

More than 100 studies have examined this question.[12] In a typical experiment, Mark Lepper and his colleagues observed 3- to 5-year-old nursery school children playing with various kinds of toys.[13] The toys available included felt tip pens of various colors and paper to draw on. The researchers noted the children's inclination to draw during this period. Next the researchers took the children aside and asked them to draw with the felt tip pens. The researchers promised some children a "Good Player Award" for drawing. Other children drew pictures without receiving an award.

Two weeks later, the researchers returned to the school, provided felt tip pens and paper, and observed the children's inclination to draw. They found that children who had been promised an award spent only half as much time drawing as they had originally. Those students who had received no award showed no such decline in interest.

Most studies in this area follow the same general outline: 1) students are given the opportunity to participate in an activity without rewards; 2) they are given extrinsic rewards for participating in the activity; and 3) they are again given the opportunity to participate in the activity without rewards.

The outcomes of the studies are also fairly consistent. Not surprisingly, there is usually a substantial increase in the activity during the second stage, when extrinsic rewards are available. And, as expected, participation in the activity declines sharply when rewards are no longer available. However, interest sometimes falls below the initial level, so that students are less interested in the activity than they had been before receiving rewards. It is this net loss of motivation that is of concern.

Researchers have studied this decline in motivation and found that it occurs only under certain circumstances. For example, the effect is most likely to occur when the initial interest in the activity is very high, when the rewards used are *not* reinforcers, and when the rewards are held out in advance as incentives.[14]

But perhaps the best predictor of negative effects is the nature of the "reward contingency" involved. (The term *reward contingency* has to do with the nature of the relationship between behavior and its reward.) Alyce Dickinson reviewed the research literature in this area and identified three kinds of reward contingency:[15]

Task-contingent rewards are available for merely participating in an activity, without regard to any standard of performance. Most studies that find a decline in interest in a rewarded activity involve task-contingent rewards. In the Lepper study described above, for instance, children received an award for drawing *regardless of how they drew*. The reward was task-contingent.

Performance-contingent rewards are available only when the student achieves a certain standard. Performance-contingent rewards sometimes produce negative results. For instance, Edward Deci offered college students money for solving puzzles, $1 for each puzzle solved. The rewarded students were later less inclined to work on the puzzles than were students who had not been paid. Unfortunately, these results are difficult to interpret because the students sometimes failed to meet the reward standard, and failure itself is known to reduce interest in an activity.[16]

Success-contingent rewards are given for good performance and might reflect either success or progress toward a goal. Success-contingent rewards do not have negative effects; in fact, they typically *increase* interest in the rewarded activity. For example, Ross Vasta and Louise Stirpe awarded gold stars to third- and fourth-graders each time they completed a kind of math exercise they enjoyed. After seven days of awards, the gold stars stopped. Not only was there no evidence of a loss in interest, but time spent on the math activity actually increased. Nor was there any decline in the quality of the work produced.[17]

Dickinson concludes that the danger of undermining student motivation stems not from extrinsic rewards, but from the use of inappropriate reward contingencies. Rewards reduce motivation when they are given without regard to performance or when the performance standard is so high that students frequently fail. When students have a high rate of success and when those successes are rewarded, the rewards *do not have negative effects*. Indeed, success-contingent rewards tend to increase interest in the activity. This finding, writes Dickinson, "is robust and consistent." She adds that "even strong opponents of contingent rewards recognize that success-based rewards do not have harmful effects."[18]

The evidence, then, shows that extrinsic rewards can either enhance or reduce interest in an activity, depending

on how they are used. Still, it might be argued that, because extrinsic rewards *sometimes* cause problems, we might be wise to avoid their use altogether. The decision not to use extrinsic rewards amounts to a decision to rely on alternatives. What are those alternatives? And are they better than extrinsic rewards?

ALTERNATIVES TO REWARDS

Punishment and the threat of punishment are — and probably always have been — the most popular alternatives to extrinsic rewards. Not so long ago, lessons were "taught to the tune of a hickory stick," but the tune was not merely tapped on a desk. Students who did not learn their lessons were not only beaten; they were also humiliated: they sat on a stool (up high, so everyone could see) and wore a silly hat.

Gradually, more subtle forms of punishment were used. "The child at his desk," wrote Skinner, "filling in his workbook, is behaving primarily to escape from the threat of a series of minor aversive events — the teacher's displeasure, the criticism or ridicule of his classmates, an ignominious showing in a competition, low marks, a trip to the office 'to be talked to' by the principal, or a word to the parent who may still resort to the birch rod."[19] Skinner spent a lifetime inveighing against the use of such "aversives," but his efforts were largely ineffective. While extrinsic rewards have been condemned, punishment and the threat of punishment are widely sanctioned.

Punishment is popular because, in the short run at least, it gets results. This is illustrated by an experiment in which Deci and Wayne Cascio told students that, if they did not solve problems correctly within a time limit, they would be exposed to a loud, unpleasant sound. The threat worked: all the students solved all the problems within the time limit, so the threat never had to be fulfilled. Students who were merely rewarded for correct solutions did not do nearly as well.[20]

But there are serious drawbacks to the use of punishment. For one thing, although punishment motivates students to learn, it does not teach them. Or, rather, it teaches them only what *not* to do, not what *to* do. "We do not teach [a student] to learn quickly," Skinner observed, "by punishing him when he learns slowly, or to recall what he has learned by punishing him when he forgets, or to think logically by punishing him when he is illogical."[21]

Punishment also has certain undesirable side effects.[22] To the extent that punishment works, it works by making students anxious. Students get nervous before a test because they fear a poor grade, and they are relieved or anxious when they receive their report card depending on whether or not the grades received will result in punishment from their parents.[23] Students can and do avoid the anxiety caused by such punishment by cutting classes and dropping out of school. We do the same thing when we cancel or "forget" a dental appointment.

Another response to punishment is aggression. Students who do not learn easily — and who therefore cannot readily avoid punishment — are especially apt to become aggressive. Their aggression often takes the form of lying, cheating, stealing, and refusing to cooperate. Students also act out by cursing, by being rude and insulting, by destroying property, and by hitting people. Increasingly, teachers are the objects of these aggressive acts.

Finally, it should be noted that punishment has the same negative impact on intrinsic motivation as extrinsic rewards are alleged to have. In the Deci and Cascio study just described, for example, when students were given the chance to work on puzzles with the threat of punishment removed, they were less likely to do so than were students who had never worked under the threat of punishment.[24] Punishment in the form of criticism of performance also reduces interest in an activity.[25]

Punishment is not the only alternative to the use of extrinsic rewards. Teachers can also encourage students. Encouragement consists of various forms of behavior intended to induce students to perform. We encourage students when we urge them to try, express confidence in their ability to do assignments, and recite such platitudes as "A winner never quits and a quitter never wins."[26]

In encouraging students, we are not merely urging them to perform, however; we are implicitly suggesting a relationship between continued performance and certain consequences. "Come on, Billy — you can do it" means, "If you persist at this task, you will be rewarded with success." The power of encouragement is ultimately dependent on the occurrence of the implied consequences. If the teacher tells Billy he can do it and if he tries

and fails, future urging by the teacher will be less effective.

Another problem with encouragement is that, like punishment, it motivates but does not teach. The student who is urged to perform a task is not thereby taught how to perform it. Encouragement is a safer procedure than punishment, since it is less likely to provoke anxiety or aggression. Students who are repeatedly urged to do things at which they ultimately fail do, however, come to distrust the judgment of the teacher. They also come to believe that they cannot live up to the expectations of teachers — and therefore must be hopelessly stupid.

Intrinsic rewards present the most promising alternative to extrinsic rewards. Experts on reinforcement, including defenders of extrinsic rewards, universally sing the praises of intrinsic rewards. Unlike punishment and encouragement, intrinsic rewards actually teach. Students who can see that they have solved a problem correctly know how to solve other problems of that sort. And, unlike extrinsic rewards, intrinsic rewards do not depend on the teacher or some other person.

But there are problems with intrinsic rewards, just as there are with extrinsic ones. Sometimes students lack the necessary skills to obtain intrinsic rewards. Knowledge, understanding, and the aesthetic pleasures of language are all intrinsic rewards for reading, but they are not available to those for whom reading is a difficult and painful activity.

Often, intrinsic rewards are too remote to be effective. If a student is asked to add 3 + 7, what is the intrinsic reward for answering correctly? The student who learns to add will one day experience the satisfaction of checking the accuracy of a restaurant bill, but this future reward is of no value to the youngster just learning to add. Though important in maintaining what has been learned, intrinsic rewards are often too remote to be effective reinforcers in the early stages of learning.

One problem that often goes unnoticed is that the intrinsic rewards for academic work are often weaker than the rewards available for other behavior. Students are rewarded for looking out the window, daydreaming, reading comic books, taking things from other students, passing notes, telling and listening to jokes, moving about the room, fighting, talking back to the teacher, and for all sorts of activities that are incompatible

with academic learning. Getting the right answer to a grammar question might be intrinsically rewarding, but for many students it is considerably less rewarding than the laughter of one's peers in response to a witty remark.

While intrinsic rewards are important then, they are insufficient for efficient learning.[27] Nor will encouragement and punishment fill the gap. The teacher must supplement intrinsic rewards with extrinsic rewards. This means not only telling the student when he or she has succeeded, but also praising, complimenting, applauding, and providing other forms of recognition for good work. Some students may need even stronger reinforcers, such as special privileges, certificates, and prizes.

REWARD GUIDELINES

Yet we cannot ignore the fact that extrinsic rewards can have adverse effects on student motivation. While there seems to be little chance of serious harm, it behooves us to use care. Various experts have suggested guidelines to follow in using extrinsic rewards.[28] Here is a digest of their recommendations:

1. Use the weakest reward required to strengthen a behavior. Don't use money if a piece of candy will do; don't use candy if praise will do. The good effects of reinforcement come not so much from the reward itself as from the reward contingency: the relationship between the reward and the behavior.

2. When possible, avoid using rewards as incentives. For example, don't say, "If you do X, I'll give you Y." Instead, ask the student to perform a task and then provide a reward for having completed it. In most cases, rewards work best if they are pleasant surprises.

3. Reward at a high rate in the early stages of learning, and reduce the frequency of rewards as learning progresses. Once students have the alphabet down pat, there is no need to compliment them each time they print a letter correctly. Nor is there much need to reward behavior that is already occurring at a high rate.

4. Reward only the behavior you want repeated. If students who whine and complain get their way, expect to see a lot of whining and complaining. Similarly, if you provide gold stars only for the three best papers in the class, you are rewarding competition and should not be surprised if students do not cooperate

with one another. And if "spelling doesn't count," don't expect to see excellent spelling.

5. Remember that what is an effective reward for one student may not work well with another. Some students respond rapidly to teacher attention; others do not. Some work well for gold stars; others don't. Effective rewards are ordinarily things that students seek — positive feedback, praise, approval, recognition, toys — but ultimately a reward's value is to be judged by its effect on behavior.

6. Reward success, and set standards so that success is within the student's grasp. In today's heterogeneous classrooms, that means setting standards for each student. A good way to do this is to reward improvement or progress toward a goal. Avoid rewarding students merely for participating in an activity, without regard for the quality of their performance.

7. Bring attention to the rewards (both intrinsic and extrinsic) that are available for behavior from sources *other than the teacher*. Point out, for example, the fun to be had from the word play in poetry or from sharing a poem with another person. Show students who are learning computer programming the pleasure in "making the computer do things." Let students know that it's okay to applaud those who make good presentations so that they can enjoy the approval of their peers for a job well done. Ask parents to talk with their children about school and to praise them for learning. The goal is to shift the emphasis from rewards provided by the teacher to those that will occur even when the teacher is not present.[29]

Following these rules is harder in practice than it might seem, and most teachers will need training in their implementation. But reinforcement is probably the most powerful tool available to teachers, and extrinsic rewards are powerful reinforcers. To teach without using extrinsic rewards is analogous to asking our students to learn to draw with their eyes closed. Before we do that, we should open our own eyes.

---

1. The study is described in E. L. Thorndike, *Human Learning* (1931; reprint ed., Cambridge, Mass.: MIT Press, 1966).

2. There are various theories (cognitive, neurological, and psychosocial) about why certain consequences reinforce or strengthen behavior. The important thing for our purposes is that they do.

3. John I. Goodlad, *A Place Called School: Prospects for the Future* (New York: McGraw-Hill, 1984). Goodlad complains about the "paucity of praise" in schools. In doing so, he echoes B. F. Skinner, who wrote that "perhaps the most serious criticism of the current classroom is the relative infrequency of reinforcement." See B. F. Skinner, *The Technology of Teaching* (Englewood Cliffs, N.J.: Prentice-Hall, 1968), p. 17.

4. Bill L. Hopkins and R. J. Conard, "Putting It All Together: Superschool," in Norris G. Haring and Richard L. Schiefelbusch, eds., *Teaching Special Children* (New York: McGraw-Hill, 1975), pp. 342-85. Skinner suggests that mastering the first four years of arithmetic instruction efficiently would require something on the order of 25,000 reinforcements. See Skinner, op. cit.

5. See, for example, Bill L. Hopkins, "Comments on the Future of Applied Behavior Analysis," *Journal of Applied Behavior Analysis*, vol. 20, 1987, pp. 339-46. In some studies, students learned to double the normal rate, yet most teachers did not continue reinforcing behavior at high rates after the study ended.

6. See, for example, Hopkins and Conard, op. cit.

7. For example, Mihaly Csikszentmihalyi found that adults who are successful and happy tend to have had happy childhoods. See Tina Adler, "Support and Challenge: Both Key for Smart Kids," *APA Monitor*, September 1991, pp. 10-11.

8. The terms *reinforcer* and *reward* are often used interchangeably, but they are not really synonyms. A reinforcer is defined by its effects: an event that strengthens the behavior it follows is a reinforcer, regardless of what it was intended to do. A reward is defined by social convention as something desirable; it may or may not strengthen the behavior it follows. The distinction is important since some studies that show negative effects from extrinsic rewards use rewards that are *not* reinforcers. See Alyce M. Dickinson, "The Detrimental Effects of Extrinsic Reinforcement on 'Intrinsic Motivation,'" *The Behavior Analyst*, vol. 12, 1989, pp. 1-15.

9. John Dewey distrusted the distinction between extrinsic and intrinsic rewards. He wrote that "what others do to us when we act is as natural a consequence of our action as what the fire does to us when we plunge our hands in it." Quoted in Samuel M. Deitz, "What Is Unnatural About 'Extrinsic Reinforcement'?," *The Behavior Analyst*, vol. 12, 1989, p. 255.

10. Dickinson writes that "several individuals have demanded that schools abandon reinforcement procedures for fear that they may permanently destroy a child's 'love of learning.'" See Alyce M. Dickinson, "Exploring New Vistas," *Performance Management Magazine*, vol. 9, 1991, p. 28. It is interesting to note that no one worries that earning a school letter will destroy a student's interest in sports. Nor does there seem to be much fear that people who win teaching awards will suddenly become poor teachers. For the most part, only the academic work of students is said to be put at risk by extrinsic rewards.

11. Skinner, p. 162.

12. For reviews of this literature, see Edward L. Deci and Richard M. Ryan, *Intrinsic Motivation and Self-Determination in Human Behavior* (New York: Plenum, 1985); Dickinson, "The Detrimental Effects"; and Mark R. Lepper and David Greene, eds., *The Hidden Costs of Reward: New Perspectives on the Psychology of Human Motivation* (Hillsdale, N.J.: Erlbaum, 1978).

13. Mark R. Lepper, David Greene, and Richard E. Nisbett, "Undermining Children's Intrinsic Interest with Extrinsic Rewards," *Journal of Personality and Social Psychology*, vol. 28, 1973, pp. 129-37.

14. See, for example, Dickinson, "The Detrimental Effects"; and Mark Morgan, "Reward-Induced Decrements and Increments in Intrinsic Motivation," *Review of Educational Research*, vol. 54, 1984, pp. 5-30. Dickinson notes that studies producing negative effects are often hard to interpret since other variables (failure, deadlines, competition, and so on) could account for the findings. By way of example, she cites a study in which researchers offered a $5 reward to top performers. The study was thus contaminated by the effects of competition, yet the negative results were attributed to extrinsic rewards.

15. Dickinson, "The Detrimental Effects."

16. Edward L. Deci, "Effects of Externally Mediated Rewards on Intrinsic Motivation," *Journal of Personality and Social Psychology*, vol. 18, 1971, pp. 105-15.

17. Ross Vasta and Louise A. Stirpe, "Reinforcement Effects on Three Measures of Children's Interest in Math," *Behavior Modification*, vol. 3, 1979, pp. 223-44.

18. Dickinson, "The Detrimental Effects," p. 9. See also Morgan, op. cit.

19. Skinner, p. 15.

20. Edward L. Deci and Wayne F. Cascio, "Changes in Intrinsic Motivation as a Function of Negative Feedback and Threats," paper presented at the annual meeting of the Eastern Psychological Association, Boston, May 1972. This paper is summarized in Edward L. Deci and Joseph Porac, "Cognitive Evaluation Theory and the Study of Human Motivation," in Lepper and Greene, pp. 149-76.

21. Skinner, p. 149.

22. For more on the problems associated with punishment, see Murray Sidman, *Coercion and Its Fallout* (Boston: Authors Cooperative, Inc., 1989).

23. Grades are often referred to as rewards, but they are more often punishments. Students study not so much to receive high grades as to avoid receiving low ones.

24. Deci and Cascio, op. cit.

25. See, for example, Edward L. Deci, Wayne F. Cascio, and Judy Krusell, "Sex Differences, Positive Feedback, and Intrinsic Motivation," paper presented at the annual meeting of the Eastern Psychological Association, Washington, D.C., May 1973. This paper is summarized in Deci and Porac, op. cit.

26. It should be noted that encouragement often closely resembles reinforcement in form. One teacher may say, "I know you can do it, Mary," as Mary struggles to answer a question; another teacher may say, "I knew you could do it, Mary!" when Mary answers the question correctly. The first teacher is encouraging; the second is reinforcing. The difference is subtle but important.

27. Intrinsic rewards are more important to the maintenance of skills once learned. An adult's skill at addition and subtraction is not ordinarily maintained by the approval of peers but by the satisfaction that comes from balancing a checkbook.

28. See, for example, Jere Brophy, "Teacher Praise: A Functional Analysis," *Review of Educational Research*, vol. 51, 1981, pp. 5-32; Hopkins and Conard, op. cit.; and Dickinson, "The Detrimental Effects."

29. "Instructional contingencies," writes Skinner, "are usually contrived and should always be temporary. If instruction is to have any point, the behavior it generates will be taken over and maintained by contingencies in the world at large." See Skinner, p. 144.

Rewards Versus Learning: A Response to Paul Chance

Mr. Kohn raises some questions about Paul Chance's article in the November 1992 Kappan* and suggests that an engaging curriculum — not manipulating children with artificial incentives — offers a genuine alternative to boredom in school and to diminished motivation when school lets out.

ALFIE KOHN

ALFIE KOHN is an independent scholar living in Cambridge, Mass., who writes and lectures widely on human behavior and education. His newest book is Punished by Rewards: The Trouble with Gold Stars, Incentive Plans, A's, Praise, and Other Bribes *(Houghton Mifflin, October 1993). ©1993, Alfie Kohn.*

IN THE COURSE of offering some suggestions for how educators can help children become more generous and empathic ("Caring Kids: The Role of the Schools," March 1991), I argued that manipulating student behavior with either punishments or rewards is not only unnecessary but counterproductive. Paul Chance, taking exception to this passage, wrote to defend the use of rewards (Backtalk, June 1991). Now, following the publication of his longer brief for behaviorism ("The Rewards of Learning," November 1992), it is my turn to raise some questions — and to continue what I hope is a constructive

[*See *Annual Editions* Article 23. Ed.]

dialogue between us (not to mention a long overdue examination of classroom practices too often taken for granted).

To begin, I should mention two points where our perspectives converge. Neither of us favors the use of punishment, and both of us think that rewards, like other strategies, must be judged by their long-term effects, including what they do for (or to) children's motivation. Chance and I disagree, however, on the nature of those effects.

Rewards, like punishments, can usually get people to do what we want for a while. In that sense, they "work." But my reading of the research, corroborated by real-world observation, is that rewards can never buy us anything more than short-term compliance. Moreover, we — or, more accurately, the people we are rewarding — pay a steep price over time for our reliance on extrinsic motivators.

REWARDS ARE INHERENTLY CONTROLLING

Applied behaviorism, which amounts to saying, "Do this and you'll get that," is essentially a technique for controlling people. In the classroom, it is a way of doing things *to* children rather than working *with* them. Chance focuses on the empirical effects of rewards, but I feel obliged to pause at least long enough to stress that moral issues are involved here regardless of whether we ultimately endorse or oppose the use of rewards.

By now it is not news that reinforcement strategies were developed and refined through experiments on laboratory animals. Many readers also realize that underlying the practice of reinforcement is a theory — specifically, the assumption that humans, like all organisms, are

basically inert beings whose behavior must be elicited by external motivation in the form of carrots or sticks. For example, Alyce Dickinson, the author Chance cites six times and from whom he borrows the gist of his defense of rewards, plainly acknowledges the central premise of the perspective she and Chance share, which is that "all behavior is ultimately initiated by the external environment."[1] Anyone who recoils from this theoretical foundation ought to take a fresh look at the real-world practices that rest on it.

I am troubled by a model of human relationship or learning that is defined by control rather than, say, persuasion or mutual problem solving. Because the reinforcements themselves are desired by their recipients, it is easy to miss the fact that using them is simply a matter of "control[ling] through seduction rather than force."[2] Rewards and punishments (bribes and threats, positive reinforcements and "consequences" — call them what you will) are not really opposites at all. They are two sides of the same coin. The good news is that our options are not limited to variations on the theme of behavioral manipulation.[3]

REWARDS ARE INEFFECTIVE

The question of how well rewards *work*, apart from what they do to children's long-term motivation, is dispatched by Chance in a single sentence: "No one disputes the effectiveness of extrinsic rewards in teaching or in maintaining good discipline" (p. 203). I found myself rereading the paragraph in which this extraordinary claim appears, searching for signs that Chance was being ironic.

In point of fact, the evidence over

whelmingly demonstrates that extrinsic rewards are ineffective at producing lasting change in attitudes or even behaviors. Moreover, they typically do not enhance — and often actually impede — performance on tasks that are any more complex than pressing a bar. This evidence, which I have been sorting through recently for a book-length treatment of these issues (*Punished by Rewards*, scheduled for publication this fall), is piled so high on my desk that I fear it will topple over. I cannot review all of it here; a few samples will have to do.

Consider first the matter of behavior change. Even behaviorists have had to concede that the token economy, a form of behavior modification once (but, mercifully, no longer) popular for controlling people in institutions, doesn't work. When the goodies stop, people go right back to acting the way they did before the program began.[4] Studies have found that rewarding people for losing weight,[5] quitting smoking,[6] or using seat belts[7] is typically less effective than using other strategies — and often proves worse than doing nothing at all.

Children whose parents make frequent use of rewards or praise are likely to be less generous than their peers.[8] On reflection, this makes perfect sense: a child promised a treat for acting responsibly has been given no reason to keep behaving that way when there is no longer a reward to be gained for doing so. The implications for behavioristic classroom management programs such as Assertive Discipline, in which children are essentially bribed or threatened to conform to rules that the teacher alone devises, are painfully clear.

Rewards (like punishments) can get people to do what we want in the short term: buckle up, share a toy, read a book. In that sense, Chance is right that their effectiveness is indisputable. But they rarely produce effects that survive the rewards themselves, which is why behaviorists are placed in the position of having to argue that we need to keep the goodies coming or replace one kind of reward with another (e.g., candy bars with grades). The fact is that extrinsic motivators do not alter the attitudes that underlie our behaviors. They do not create an enduring *commitment* to a set of values or to learning; they merely, and temporarily, change what we do. If, like Skinner, you think there is nothing to humans other than what we do, then this criticism will not trouble you. If, on the

> The good news is that our options are not limited to variations on the theme of behavioral manipulation.

other hand, you think that our actions reflect and emerge from who we *are* (what we think and feel, expect and will), then you have no reason to expect interventions that merely control actions to work in the long run.

As for the effect on performance, I know of at least two dozen studies showing that people expecting to receive a reward for completing a task (or for doing it successfully) don't perform as well as those who expect nothing. The effect is robust for young children, older children, and adults; for males and females; for rewards of all kinds (including money, grades, toys, food, and special privileges). The tasks in these studies range from memorizing facts to engaging in creative problem solving, from discriminating between similar drawings to designing collages. In general, the more cognitive sophistication and open-ended thinking required, the worse people do when they are working for a reward.[9]

At first researchers didn't know what to make of these findings. (A good sign that one has stumbled onto something important is the phrase "contrary to hypothesis" in a research report.) "The clear inferiority of the reward groups was an unexpected result, unaccountable for by theory or previous empirical evidence," a pair of experimenters confessed in 1961.[10] Rewards "have effects that interfere with performance in ways that we are only beginning to understand," said Janet Spence (later president of the American Psychological Association) in 1971.[11] Since then, most researchers — with the exception of a small cadre of un-

reconstructed behaviorists — have gotten the message that, on most tasks, a Skinnerian strategy is worse than useless: it is counterproductive.

REWARDS MAKE LEARNING LESS APPEALING

Even more research indicates that rewards also undermine *interest* — a finding with obvious and disturbing implications for the use of grades, stickers, and even praise. Here Chance concedes there may be a problem but, borrowing Dickinson's analysis, assures us that the damage is limited. Dickinson grants that motivation tends to decline when people are rewarded just for engaging in a task and also when they receive performance-contingent rewards — those "based on performance standards" (Dickinson) or "available only when the student achieves a certain standard" (Chance).

But Dickinson then proceeds to invent a new category, "success-contingent" rewards, and calls these innocuous. The term means that, when rewards are given out, "subjects are told they have received the rewards because of good performance." For Chance, though, a "success-contingent" reward is "given for good performance and might reflect either success or progress toward a goal" — a definition that appears to diverge from Dickinson's and that sounds quite similar to what is meant by "performance-contingent." As near as I can figure, the claim both Dickinson and Chance are making is that, when people come away thinking that they have done well, a reward for what they have achieved doesn't hurt. On this single claim rests the entire defense against the devastating charge that by rewarding students for their achievement we are leading them to see learning as a chore. But what does the research really say?

Someone who simply glances at the list of studies Dickinson offers to support her assertion might come away impressed. Someone who takes the time to read those studies will come away with a renewed sense of the importance of going straight to the primary source. It turns out that two of the studies don't even deal with rewards for successful performance.[12] Another one actually *disproves* the contention that success-contingent rewards are harmless: it finds that this kind of reward not only undermines intrinsic motivation but is more destructive than rewards given just for engaging in the task![13]

The rest of the studies cited by Dickinson indicate that some subjects in laboratory experiments who receive success-contingent rewards are neither more nor less interested in the task than those who get nothing at all. But Dickinson curiously omits a number of *other* studies that are also set up so that some subjects succeed (or think they succeed) at a task and are presented with a reward. These studies have found that such rewards *do* reduce interest.[14]

Such a result really shouldn't be surprising. As Edward Deci and his colleagues have been pointing out for years, adults and children alike chafe at being deprived of a sense of self-determination. Rewards usually feel controlling, and rewards contingent on performance ("If you do a good job, here's what I'll give you") are the most controlling of all. Even the good feeling produced by doing well often isn't enough to overcome that fact. To the extent that information about how well we have done *is* interest-enhancing, this is not an argument for Skinnerian tactics. In fact, when researchers have specifically compared the effects of straightforward performance feedback ("Here's how you did") and performance-contingent rewards ("Here's a goody for doing well"), the latter undermined intrinsic motivation more than the former.[15]

Finally, even if all the research really did show what Dickinson and Chance claim it does, remember that outside of the laboratory people often fail. That result is more likely to be de-motivating when it means losing out on a reward, such as an A or a bonus. This Chance implicitly concedes, although the force of the point gets lost: students do not turn off from failing per se but from failing when a reward is at stake. In learning contexts free of extrinsic motivators, students are more likely to persist at a task and to remain interested in it even when they don't do it well.

All of this means that getting children to think about learning as a way to receive a sticker, a gold star, or a grade — or, even worse, to get money or a toy *for* a grade, which amounts to an extrinsic motivator for an extrinsic motivator — is likely to turn learning from an end into a means. Learning becomes something that must be gotten through in order to receive the reward. Take the depressingly pervasive program by which children receive certificates for free pizza when they

have read a certain number of books. John Nicholls of the University of Illinois comments, only half in jest, that the likely consequence of this program is "a lot of fat kids who don't like to read."

Educational psychologists such as Nicholls, Carol Dweck, and Carole Ames keep finding that when children are led to concentrate on their performance, on how well they are doing — an inevitable consequence of the use of rewards or punishments — they become less interested in *what* they are doing. ("Do we have to know this? Will it be on the test?") I am convinced that one of the primary obligations of educators and parents who want to promote a lasting commitment to learning is to do everything in their power to help students forget that grades exist.

REWARDS IGNORE CURRICULAR QUESTIONS

One last point. Chance's defense of the Skinnerian status quo might more properly have been titled "The Rewards *for* Learning." My interest is in the rewards *of* learning, a concern that requires us to ask whether we are teaching something *worth* learning. This is a question that behaviorists do not need to ask; it is enough to devise an efficient technique to reinforce the acquisition of whatever happens to be in someone's lesson plan.

Chance addresses the matter of intrinsic motivation just long enough to dismiss it as "too remote to be effective." He sets up a false dichotomy, with an abstract math problem on one side (Why would a child be motivated to learn that $7 + 3 = 10$? he wants to know) and reinforcements (the solution to this problem) on the other. Indeed, if children are required to fill in an endless series of blanks on worksheets or to memorize meaningless, disconnected facts, they may *have* to be bribed to do so. But Chance seems oblivious to exciting developments in the field of education: the whole-language movement, the emphasis on "learner-centered" learning, and the entire constructivist tradition (in which teaching takes its cue from the way each child actively constructs meaning and makes sense of the world rather than treating students as passive responders to environmental stimuli).

I invite Chance to join the campaign for an engaging curriculum that is connected to children's lives and interests, for an approach to pedagogy in which students

are given real choices about their studies and for classrooms in which they are allowed and helped to work with one another. Pursuing these approaches, no manipulating children with artificial incentives, offers a *real* alternative to boredom in school and to diminished motivation when school lets out.

---

1. Alyce M. Dickinson, "The Detrimental Effect of Extrinsic Reinforcement on 'Intrinsic Motivation,' " *The Behavior Analyst*, vol. 12, 1989, p. 12. Notice the quotation marks around "intrinsic motivation," as if to question the very existence of the phenomenon — a telltale sign of Skinnerian orthodoxy.

2. Edward L. Deci and Richard M. Ryan, *Intrinsic Motivation and Self-Determination in Human Behavior* (New York: Plenum, 1985), p. 70.

3. Behaviorists are apt to rejoin that control is an unavoidable feature of all relationships. In response I would point out that there is an enormous difference between saying that even subtle reinforcement can be controlling and asserting that all human interaction is best described as an exercise in control. The latter takes on faith that selfhood and choice are illusions and that we do only what we have been reinforced for doing. A far more defensible position, it seems to me, is that some form of human interaction are controlling and some are not. The line might not be easy to draw in practice, but the distinction is still meaningful and important.

4. "Generally, removal of token reinforcement results in decrements in desirable responses and a return to baseline or near-baseline levels of performance," as the first major review of token economies concluded. In fact, not only does the behavior fail "to generalize to conditions in which [reinforcements] are not in effect" — such as the world outside the hospital — but reinforcement programs used each morning generally don't even have much effect on patients' behavior during the afternoon! See Alan E. Kazdin and Richard R. Bootzin, "The Token Economy: An Evaluative Review," *Journal of Applied Behavior Analysis*, vol. 5, 1972, pp. 359-60. Ten years later, one of these authors — an enthusiastic proponent of behavior modification, incidentally — checked back to see if anything had changed. "As a general rule," he wrote, with an almost audible sigh, "it is still prudent to assume that behavioral gains are likely to be lost in varying degrees once the client leaves the program." See Alan E. Kazdin, "The Token Economy: A Decade Later," *Journal of Applied Behavior Analysis*, vol. 15, 1982, pp. 435-37. Others reviewing the research on token economies have come to more or less the same conclusion.

5. The only two studies I am aware of that looked at weight loss programs to see what happened when people were paid for getting slimmer found that the incentives either had no effect or were actually counterproductive. See Richard A. Dienstbier and Gary K. Leak, "Overjustification and Weight Loss: The Effects of Monetary Reward," paper presented at the annual meeting of the American Psychological Association, Washington, D.C., September 1976; and F. Matthew Kramer et al., "Maintenance of Successful Weight Loss Over 1 Year: Effects of Financial Contracts for Weight Maintenance or Participation in Skills Training," *Behavior Therapy*, vol. 17, 1986, pp. 295-301.

6. A very large study, published in 1991, recruited subjects for a self-help program designed to help people quit smoking. Three months later, those who had been offered a prize for turning in weekly prog-

ress reports were lighting up again more often than were those who had received a no-reward treatment — and even more than those who didn't take part in any program at all. In fact, for people who received both treatments, "the financial incentive somehow diminished the positive impact of the personalized feedback." See Susan J. Curry et al., "Evaluation of Intrinsic and Extrinsic Motivation Interventions with a Self-Help Smoking Cessation Program," *Journal of Consulting and Clinical Psychology*, vol. 59, 1991, p. 323.

7. A committed behaviorist and his colleagues reviewed the effects of 28 programs used by nine different companies to get their employees to use seat belts. Nearly half a million vehicle observations were made over six years in the course of this research. The result: programs that rewarded people for wearing their seat belts were the least effective over the long haul. The author had to confess that "the greater impact of the no-reward strategies from both an immediate and [a] long-term perspective . . . [was] not predicted and [is] inconsistent with basic reinforcement theory." See E. Scott Geller et al., "Employer-Based Programs to Motivate Safety Belt Use: A Review of Short-Term and Long-Term Effects," *Journal of Safety Research*, vol. 18, 1987, pp. 1-17.

8. Richard A. Fabes et al., "Effects of Rewards on Children's Prosocial Motivation: A Socialization Study," *Developmental Psychology*, vol. 25, 1989, pp. 509-15. Praise appears to have a similar detrimental effect; see Joan E. Grusec, "Socializing Concern for Others in the Home," *Developmental Psychology*, vol. 27, 1991, pp. 338-42. See also the studies reviewed in Alfie Kohn, *The Brighter Side of Human Nature: Altruism and Empathy in Everyday Life* (New York: Basic Books, 1990), pp. 201-4.

9. A complete bibliography will be available in my forthcoming book, *Punished by Rewards*. Readers unwilling to wait might wish to begin by reading Mark R. Lepper and David Greene, eds., *The Hidden Costs of Rewards* (Hillsdale, N.J.: Erlbaum, 1978), and some of Teresa Amabile's work from the 1980s documenting how rewards kill creativity.

10. Louise Brightwell Miller and Betsy Worth Estes, "Monetary Reward and Motivation in Discrimination Learning," *Journal of Experimental Psychology*, vol. 61, 1961, p. 503.

11. Janet Taylor Spence, "Do Material Rewards Enhance the Performance of Lower-Class Children?," *Child Development*, vol. 42, 1971, p. 1469.

12. In one of the studies, either money or an award was given to children just for taking part in the experiment — and both caused interest in the task to decline. See Rosemarie Anderson et al., "The Undermining and Enhancing of Intrinsic Motivation in Preschool Children," *Journal of Personality and Social Psychology*, vol. 34, 1976, pp. 915-22. In the other, a total of three children were simply praised ("good," "nice going") whenever they engaged in a task; no mention was made of how well they were performing. See Jerry A. Martin, "Effects of Positive and Negative Adult-Child Interactions on Children's Task Performance and Task Preferences," *Journal of Experimental Child Psychology*, vol. 23, 1977, pp. 493-502.

13. Michael Jay Weiner and Anthony M. Mander, "The Effects of Reward and Perception of Competency upon Intrinsic Motivation," *Motivation and Emotion*, vol. 2, 1978, pp. 67-73.

14. Chance doesn't like Deci's 1971 study, but there are plenty of others. In David Greene and Mark R. Lepper, "Effects of Extrinsic Rewards on Children's Subsequent Intrinsic Interest," *Child Development*, vol. 45, 1974, pp. 1141-45, children who were promised a reward if they drew very good pictures — and then did receive the reward, along with a reminder of the accomplishment it represented — were less interested in drawing later than were children who got nothing. See also James Garbarino, "The Impact of Anticipated Reward upon Cross-Age Tutoring," *Journal of Personality and Social Psychology*, vol. 32, 1975, pp. 421-28; Terry D. Orlick and Richard Mosher, "Extrinsic Awards and Participant Motivation in a Sport Related Task," *International Journal of Sport Psychology*, vol. 9, 1978, pp. 27-39; Judith M. Harackiewicz, "The Effects of Reward Contingency and Performance Feedback on Intrinsic Motivation," *Journal of Personality and Social Psychology*, vol. 37, 1979, pp. 1352-63; and Richard A. Fabes, "Effects of Reward Contexts on Young Children's Task Interest," *Journal of Psychology*, vol. 121, 1987, pp. 5-19. See too the studies cited in, and conclusions offered by, Kenneth O. McGraw, "The Detrimental Effects of Reward on Performance: A Literature Review and a Prediction Model," in Lepper and Greene, eds., p. 40; Mark R. Lepper, "Extrinsic Reward and Intrinsic Motivation," in John M. Levine and Margaret C. Wang, eds., *Teacher and Student Perceptions: Implications for Learning* (Hillsdale, N.J.: Erlbaum, 1983), pp. 304-5; and Deci and Ryan, p. 78.

15. Richard M. Ryan et al., "Relation of Reward Contingency and Interpersonal Context to Intrinsic Motivation: A Review and Test Using Cognitive Evaluation Theory," *Journal of Personality and Social Psychology*, vol. 45, 1983, pp. 736-50. "Rewards in general appear to have a controlling significance to some extent and thus in general run the risk of undermining intrinsic motivation," the authors wrote (p. 748).

Sticking Up for Rewards

It is ironic that honest feedback or a straightforward contingency between work and rewards should be called manipulative, while "persuasion" and "mutual problem solving" should not, Mr. Chance retorts.

. . . .

PAUL CHANCE

PAUL CHANCE (Eastern Shore Maryland Chapter) is a psychologist, writer, and former teacher. He is the author of Thinking in the Classroom *(Teachers College Press, 1986).*

IT IS DIFFICULT to know how to respond to Alfie Kohn's critique.* It is so disjointed and so full of misrepresentations of fact and theory that it is like a greased pig: one can scarcely get a grip on it, let alone wrestle it to the ground. I will illustrate what I mean with a few examples and then reply to what I believe to be Kohn's major objections.

Item: To reward, Kohn says, is to say to a student, "Do this and you'll get that." But this is only one kind of reward — and one that I specifically advised readers to avoid when possible. It is these "contractual rewards" (or incentives) that are apt to be problematic.[1] My article focused on rewards that provide feedback about performance. Such "informational rewards" reflect effort or the quality of performance (e.g., "Good try, Janet"; "Great job, Billy"). As we shall see, even researchers who criticize contractual rewards do not normally object to informational rewards.

[*See *Annual Editions* Article 24. Ed.]

Item: Kohn says that I ask, Why would a child be motivated to learn that 7 + 3 = 10? But my question was, *How* can a child learn that 7 + 3 = 10 without some sort of response from the environment? A teacher, a peer tutor, or a computer program may provide the necessary feedback, but the natural environment rarely does. This was the point of E. L. Thorndike's line experiment, described in my article.

Item: Kohn suggests that the use of rewards is manipulative and controlling. It is ironic that honest feedback or a straightforward contingency between work and rewards should be called manipulative, while "persuasion" and "mutual problem solving" should not. Students, I suspect, know the truth of the matter. As for control: a parent rewards a baby's crying when he or she offers a bottle, and the baby rewards the parent's action by ceasing to cry. Each controls the other. Students and teachers exert the same sort of reciprocal control in the classroom.[2]

Item: Nowhere do I suggest that students must "fill in an endless series of blanks on worksheets or memorize meaningless, disconnected facts," nor is there any reason to assume that the use of rewards implies such practices. The truth is that rewards are useful whether the student is memorizing dates, mastering algebra word problems, or learning to think.[3] Some sort of extrinsic reinforcement (informational reward) is usually necessary, in the early stages at least, for learning to occur efficiently.

Item: Kohn refers to "practices too often taken for granted." Evidently he believes the mythology that rewards are widely used in our schools. Yet I noted in my article that John Goodlad found that only 2% of class time is devoted to reinforcement in elementary school — and only 1% in high school.[4] Other research consistently shows that reinforcement is notable by its absence. Harold

Stevenson, for example, compared elementary classrooms in America and Asia. He found pronounced differences in the activities of teachers when students were engaged in seatwork. In half of the classes observed in the Chicago area, the teachers provided no feedback about student performance; this seldom happened in Taiwan and almost never happened in Japan.[5]

Item: I do not assume, as suggested, that "humans, like all organisms, are basically inert beings." Nor do I know any psychologist who would embrace this view. Behavioral psychologists in particular emphasize that we learn by *acting on* our environment. As B. F. Skinner put it: "[People] act on the world, and change it, and are changed in turn by the consequences of their actions."[6] Skinner, unlike Kohn, understood that people learn best in a responsive environment. Teachers who praise or otherwise reward student performance provide such an environment.

Item: Kohn implies that I consider grades a reward. In fact, I noted (as Skinner and others had before me) that grades are more often a form of punishment. Incidentally, F. S. Keller, a behaviorist, proposed a system of education that could eliminate grades. In the Keller plan, students are required to demonstrate mastery of each skill before moving to the next. Mastery of each unit in the curriculum is recorded, so grades become superfluous.[7]

Item: Kohn says that "moral issues are involved." The implication is that I and other teachers who use rewards are immoral. If it is immoral to let students know they have answered questions correctly, to pat a student on the back for a good effort, to show joy at a student's understanding of a concept, or to recognize the achievement of a goal by providing a gold star or a certificate — if this is immoral, then count me a sinner.

From *Phi Delta Kappan*, June 1993, pp. 787-790. © 1993 by Phi Delta Kappa, Inc. Reprinted by permission.

The above points illustrate, I think, the slippery nature of Kohn's critique and may lead the reader to question his scholarship and his motives for writing. I now turn to what seem to be his major criticisms of rewards.

☑ Kohn insists that rewards undermine interest in rewarded activities.[8] Notice that Kohn does not argue that *some* rewards — or *some uses of* rewards — undermine interest. There is, in his view, no such thing as a good reward. Simple feedback, praise, smiles, hugs, pats on the back, gold stars, applause, certificates of completion, public and private commendations, prizes, special privileges, money, informational rewards, and contractual rewards — they are all one to Kohn, and they are all bad.

The best-known researchers who have found rewards sometimes troublesome are Edward Deci, Richard Ryan, Mark Lepper, and David Greene. Kohn cites all four in making his case. What he does not tell us (though he must surely know it) is that all of these researchers reject his view.[9]

Deci and Ryan believe that rewards can undermine motivation if used in a controlling way. But they add, "When used to convey to people a sense of appreciation for work well done, [rewards] will tend to be experienced informationally and will *maintain or enhance intrinsic motivation*" (emphasis added).[10]

Lepper and Greene take a similar stand. They note, "If rewards provide [a student] with new information about his ability at a particular task, this may *bolster his feelings of competence and his desire to engage in that task for its own sake*" (emphasis added).[11] They add, "If a child does not possess the basic skills to discover the intrinsic satisfaction of complex activities such as reading, the use of extrinsic rewards may be required to equip him with these skills."[12]

The position taken by Deci, Ryan, Lepper, and Greene reflects the consensus among researchers who are concerned about the possible negative effects of rewards. Mark Morgan, for example, reviewed the research and wrote that "the central finding emerging from the present review is that rewards can have either undermining or enhancing effects depending on circumstances."[13] He concludes that "the evidence seems to support strongly the hypothesis that rewards that emphasize success or competence on a task enhance intrinsic motivation."[14]

☑ Kohn claims that rewards do not work. It is true that not all rewards are

> C ertain rewards (e.g., attention, positive feedback, praise) are almost always effective reinforcers when used properly.

reinforcing. Teachers must not assume that a reward will strengthen behavior merely because that is the teacher's intention. What is reinforcing for one student may not be for another. But there is overwhelming evidence that certain rewards (e.g., attention, positive feedback, praise) are almost always effective reinforcers when used properly.

In a study by Bill Hopkins and R. J. Conard, cited in my article, teachers who provided frequent feedback, praise, and other rewards saw much faster learning.[15] Students in these classes advanced at the normal rate in spelling, at nearly twice the normal rate in mathematics, and at more than double the usual rate in reading.[16] Studies showing similar gains, due at least partly to frequent use of rewards (especially feedback and praise), are easily found by those who seek them.[17]

Even contractual rewards may be useful in some circumstances. In one program, high-risk, low-income adolescents and young adults in Lafayette Parish, Louisiana, were paid $3.40 an hour to participate in a summer program of academic instruction and job training. Students gained an average of 1.2 grade levels in reading and 1.5 grade levels in math in just eight weeks.[18]

It may be the case that the Lafayette Parish students stopped reading when money was no longer available. It probably cannot be said, however, that they read less than they did before participating in the program. If students show little or no interest in an activity, it is silly to refuse to provide rewards for fear of undermining their interest in the activity — a point made by Greene and Lepper.[19]

Kohn ignores such evidence and instead cites studies on the use of contractual rewards in weight control, smoking, and seat belt programs.[20] I am (understandably, I think) reluctant to take Kohn's assessment of these programs at face value.[21] But let us assume for the sake of argument that he is right. Note that none of these programs has anything to do with the value of rewards in classroom learning. Kohn's logic is, "If rewards do not help people stop smoking, they cannot help students learn to write." By the same logic, we would have to conclude that since aspirin is of no use in treating cancer, it must not be effective in treating headache. It is a bizarre logic.

☑ The benefits of rewards, says Kohn, are only temporary. Obviously this is not true if we are speaking of academic learning: the child who learns the Pythagorean theorem at the hands of a teacher who provides frequent feedback and praise does not suddenly forget Pythagoras because his next teacher no longer pays attention to his efforts. Nor is there any reason to think that students who are paid to read become illiterate when the money runs out.

But perhaps Kohn has other kinds of learning in mind. Teachers who praise and attend to students when they are on-task will find those students spending less time staring out the window or doodling in their notebooks.[22] If the teacher abruptly stops rewarding on-task behavior, the rate of window staring and doodling will return to its previous level.[23] To conclude from this that teachers should not reward behavior is ridiculous. It is like saying that regular exercise is pointless because your muscles get flabby again when you stop exercising. The point is not to stop.

It should be noted, moreover, that one of the things we can strengthen with rewards is persistence. Once our students are on-task for short periods, we can then begin rewarding longer periods of on-task behavior. We must be careful not to raise the standard too quickly, but we can *gradually* require more from our students. Persistence at other kinds of activities can also be built up by systematically providing rewards (especially praise) for meeting successively higher standards. Many teachers do this over the course of a school year, often without realizing it.

When behavior is rewarded intermittently in this way, it tends to become stronger. That is, it becomes *less* likely to fall off when rewards are no longer available. This is a well-established phenomenon called the partial reinforcement effect (PRE). The PRE reflects the fact that, in an uncertain world, persistence often pays off.

ONE FINAL comment: I realize that this reply to Kohn's remarks will have little impact on most readers. Kohn is selling what educators want to buy — and what many of them have been buying for several decades. It is the philosophy of education that says that students must teach themselves, that the teacher's job is to let students explore and discover on their own, and that teachers can, at most, "facilitate learning."[24]

This philosophy renders the teacher essentially impotent and leads ultimately to the conclusion that, when students fail, it is their own fault.[25] If students do not learn, it is because of some deficiency in them: lack of ability, lack of motivation, hyperactivity, attention deficit disorder — we have lots of choices. The failure is never due to inadequate teaching. Learning depends, after all, on things inside the student, well out of the teacher's reach.

I reject this view. I believe that a fair reading of the research on classroom learning points to a better way. That better way includes a teacher who is actively engaged in the educational process. Such a teacher recognizes the importance of, among other things, providing students with opportunities to perform and providing consequences for that performance. Those consequences include feedback, praise, smiles, and other forms of informational reward. In certain circumstances, they may include contractual rewards. This view of education places responsibility for learning squarely on the teacher's shoulders. Perhaps that is why there is so much opposition to it.

1. B. F. Skinner was not fond of contractual rewards himself, but he agreed that they may sometimes be necessary. See B. F. Skinner, "The Contrived Reinforcer," The Behavior Analyst, Spring 1982, pp. 3-8.

2. In an Industry Week survey, about one in three employees complained about a lack of praise for their work, a fact reported in Randall Poe and Carol L. Courter, "Fast Forward," Across the Board, September 1991, p. 5. Would workers want more praise if they considered it manipulative and controlling?

3. For instance. students can learn to find logical errors in a text by reading texts containing such errors and receiving feedback and praise for their efforts. See Kent R. Johnson and T. V. Joe Layng, "Breaking the Structuralist Barrier: Literacy and Numeracy with Fluency," American Psychologist, vol. 47, 1992, pp. 1475-90. For more on the use of rewards to teach thinking, see Paul Chance, Thinking in the Classroom (New York: Teachers College Press, 1986), Ch. 9.

4. John I. Goodlad, A Place Called School: Prospects for the Future (New York: McGraw-Hill, 1984), p. 112. Goodlad argues that teachers should be taught the skills of "providing students with knowledge of their performance, and giving praise for good work" (p. 127). For the most part they are not taught these skills. Ernest Vargas notes that, "with the exception of a stray course here or there," the 1,200 colleges of education in this country offer little instruction in reinforcement and related techniques. See Ernest A. Vargas, "Teachers in the Classroom: Behaviorological Science and an Effective Instructional Technology," Youth Policy, July/August 1988, p. 35.

5. Harold W. Stevenson, "Learning from Asian Schools," Scientific American, December 1992, pp. 70-76. Stevenson suggests that the American preference for seatwork and the failure to provide feedback may be due partly to the fact that Americans teach longer hours than their Asian counterparts.

6. Quoted in James G. Holland, "B. F. Skinner (1904-1990)," American Psychologist, vol. 47, 1992, p. 667.

7. F. S. Keller, "Goodbye, Teacher . . . ," Journal of Applied Behavior Analysis, Spring 1968, pp. 79-89. See also Paul Chance, "The Revolutionary Gentleman," Psychology Today, September 1984, pp. 42-48.

8. Studies reporting a loss of interest following rewards typically involve 1) contractual rewards and 2) behavior that is already occurring at a high rate. This is, of course, a misuse of contractual rewards, since the purpose of such rewards is to boost the rate of behavior that occurs infrequently.

9. In my article, I provided guidelines for the effective use of rewards. These guidelines were drawn, in part, from the recommendations of Deci, Ryan, Lepper, and Greene.

10. Edward L. Deci and Richard M. Ryan, Intrinsic Motivation and Self-Determination in Human Behavior (New York: Plenum, 1985), p. 300.

11. David Greene and Mark R. Lepper, "Intrinsic Motivation: How to Turn Play into Work," Psychology Today, September 1974, p. 54. Elsewhere they write that "the effects of rewards depend upon the manner and context in which they are delivered." See Mark R. Lepper and David Greene, "Divergent Approaches," in idem, eds., The Hidden Costs of Reward (New York: Erlbaum, 1978), p. 208.

12. Greene and Lepper, p. 54.

13. Mark Morgan, "Reward-Induced Decrements and Increments in Intrinsic Motivation," Review of Educational Research, Spring 1984, p. 13.

14. Ibid., p. 9. Another of Kohn's sources, Teresa Amabile, also specifically defends the use of informational rewards. See Teresa Amabile, "Cashing in on Good Grades," Psychology Today, October 1989, p. 80. See also idem, The Social Psychology of Creativity (New York: Springer-Verlag, 1983).

15. Bill L. Hopkins and R. J. Conard, "Putting It

All Together: Superschool," in Norris G. Haring and Richard L. Schiefelbusch, eds., Teaching Special Children (New York: McGraw-Hill, 1975), pp. 342-85.

16. The students also enjoyed school more and were better behaved.

17. See, for example, Charles R. Greenwood et al., "Out of the Laboratory and into the Community," American Psychologist, vol. 47, 1992, pp. 1464-74; R. Douglas Greer, "L'Enfant Terrible Meets the Educational Crisis," Journal of Applied Behavior Analysis, Spring 1992, pp. 65-69; and Johnson and Layng, op. cit.

18. Steven Hotard and Marion J. Cortez, "Evaluation of Lafayette Parish Job Training Summer Remedial Program: Report Presented to the Lafayette Parish School Board and Lafayette Parish Job Training Department of Lafayette Parish Government," August 1987. Note that this research may not represent the best use of contractual rewards, since payment was only loosely contingent on performance.

19. "Clearly," they write, "if a child begins with no intrinsic interest in an activity, there will be no intrinsic motivation to lose." See Greene and Lepper, p. 54.

20. Note that Kohn cites no evidence that his own preferred techniques — persuasion and mutual problem solving — are effective in helping people lose weight, quit smoking, or use seat belts. Indeed, reward programs have been used to treat these problems precisely because persuasion and education have proved ineffective.

21. For instance, in the study on smoking that Kohn cites, the researchers note that "the incentive was not linked directly to smoking cessation." See Susan J. Curry et al., "Evaluation of Intrinsic and Extrinsic Motivation Interventions with a Self-Help Smoking Cessation Program," Journal of Consulting and Clinical Psychology, vol. 59, 1991, p. 309. The researchers rewarded participants for completing progress reports, not for refraining from smoking.

22. Teacher attention can be an effective reward for on-task behavior. See R. Vance Hall, Diane Lund, and Deloris Jackson, "Effects of Teacher Attention on Study Behavior," Journal of Applied Behavior Analysis, Spring 1968, pp. 1-12.

23. Some might argue that we should merely provide students with more interesting (i.e., intrinsically rewarding) material. While interesting learning materials are certainly desirable, it is probably unrealistic to expect that students will always have interesting material with which to work. It may therefore be desirable for them to learn to concentrate on work even when it is not particularly agreeable.

24. The roots of today's constructivist "revolution" are described in Lawrence A. Cremin, "The Free School Movement," Today's Education, September/October 1974, pp. 71-74; and in B. F. Skinner, "The Free and Happy Student," New York University Education Quarterly, Winter 1973, pp. 2-6.

25. This is apparently the prevailing view. Galen Alessi has found that school psychologists, for instance, rarely consider poor instruction the source of a student's difficulties. Instead, the student and, in a few cases, the student's parents are said to be at fault. Galen Alessi, "Diagnosis Diagnosed: A Systematic Reaction," Professional School Psychology, vol. 3, 1988, pp. 145-51.

THE TYRANNY OF SELF-ORIENTED SELF-ESTEEM

Many modern self-esteem programs emphasize a self-focus, although a focus directed on external-to-self goals may be more productive.

James H. McMillan, Judy Singh, and Leo G. Simonetta

JAMES H. McMILLAN, Ph.D., is a professor of educational studies at Virginia Commonwealth University in Richmond, Virginia. JUDY SINGH is a doctoral student in education at Virginia Commonwealth University. LEO G. SIMONETTA is an assistant professor and social psychologist at the Center for Urban Policy Research at Georgia State University in Atlanta.

I n Ryann's second-grade classroom there was a poster on one wall to celebrate each individual student. For one week during the year each student was the "special child" of the class, and the space on the poster indicated unique and valued things about the child, such as a favorite color, hobbies, or family. Students put up pictures and other items to announce publicly what they thought was good about themselves. (Ryann, daughter of one of the authors, liked being a "special child" for a week, but the parent was not as enthusiastic.)

Activities of this type are common in elementary schools, all seeking to boost the self-esteem of the students. They assume that self-esteem is the key to achievement, and in fact much evidence, both anecdotal and research-based, shows that students achieve more with self-esteem. Teachers also seem to accept self-esteem as critical for intellectual development and necessary for students to excel or even achieve needed competence in academic tasks. According to Barbara Lerner, "Teachers generally seem to accept the modern dogma that self-esteem is the critical variable for intellectual development—the master key to learning. Children . . . cannot achieve excellence, or even competence, until their self-esteem is raised."[1]

Linking self-esteem to success and overall well-being is so well accepted that there are many institutes, foundations, task forces, and centers dedicated to promoting self-esteem programs. For example, there is the California Task Force to Promote Self-Esteem and Personal and Social Responsibility, the Center for Self-Esteem, the National Council for Self-Esteem, and the Foundation for Self-Esteem.[2] In addition, an increasing number of books, monographs, audio- and videocassettes stress developing self-esteem, as well as "how to" programs for teachers at all levels. The fundamental idea is that once educators focus on improving students' self-esteem, not only will behavior and achievement improve, but students also will be more satisfied, better adjusted, and happier. The assumption is that concentrating on enhancing self-esteem will produce these positive outcomes.

But is it possible, with the best of intentions, to overemphasize self-esteem with self-oriented activities? What are we teaching our children by encouraging and reinforcing a self-focus, and what are its long-term consequences? Since the mid-'60s, psychology has transformed our way of thinking about explanations for people's behaviors, shifting from out-

What are we teaching our children by encouraging and reinforcing a self-focus, and what are its long-term consequences?

side the self (behaviorism) to within the self. The psychologist Martin Seligman terms our current culture one of "maximal selfs," in which the individual should be gratified, fulfilled, self-actualized, and in control.[3] Seligman argues that this revolutionary change has caused increased depression, hopelessness, and other personal difficulties because of the dual burden of high expectations and self-control. Since the focus is on ourselves as being responsible, and on an expectation that we will be most content and happy if we concentrate on what is best for us, coping with failure to reach our expectations becomes difficult. If Seligman is correct, many facets of current self-esteem programs may be based on fundamentally flawed and misdirected theory. In this article the theory of self-oriented self-esteem programs will be reviewed, with illustrations of suggested practices based on this theory and the results that can be expected from this approach. An alternative theory will be recommended, with suggested practices.

Self-oriented Self-esteem

Many self-esteem programs fundamentally encourage students to think more about themselves, to be more introspective and self-oriented. The idea is that the self can be enhanced by focusing on it positively. Barbara Lerner refers to this as "feel-good-now self-esteem."[4] Jack Canfield, a well-known advocate of self-esteem

enhancement, has suggested several strategies for the classroom that emphasize introspection: 1) assume an attitude of 100 percent responsibility by getting students to think about what they are saying to themselves; 2) focus on the positive—"I spend a lot of my time having students recall, write about, draw, and share their past experiences"; 3) learn to monitor your self-talk by replacing negative thoughts with positive—"I can learn to do anything I want, I am smart, I love and accept myself the way I am"; and 4) identify your strengths and weaknesses.[5]

A popular self-esteem book for educators suggests enhancing self-esteem with one or more of the following: improving self-evaluation skills; developing a sense of personal worth; reflecting on self-esteem; thinking of oneself in positive terms; discovering reasons the individual is unhappy; or examining sources of and influences on self-esteem. Their emphasis is on enhancing students' positive self-perceptions.[6] Such ideas are often implemented in classroom activities that teach students introspective thinking: for example, keeping a journal about themselves and indicating "what I like best about myself";[7] teaching a unit entitled "I Am Great" that emphasizes their individuality through self-portraits, silhouettes of themselves, "who am I," and "coat of arms" exercises;[8] and programs such as Developing Understanding of Self and Others (DUSO), Toward Affective Development, and Dimensions of Personality. Some less-complex programs simply encourage student self-talk with phrases such as "I'm terrific" or "I'm great." All these activities or programs are designed to promote self-acceptance and self-awareness, to help students become aware of their unique characteristics, and to "put children in touch with themselves."[9]

Although these are well-intentioned programs, their encouragement of self-introspection may distort a normal, healthy perspective about oneself into self-importance, self-gratification, and ultimately selfishness. If

the message is that "me" is most important, will selfishness be viewed as normal and expected? Are we making a virtue of self-preoccupation? If so, such "selfism" may have negative consequences. As William Damon points out, "A young mind might too readily interpret a blanket incantation toward self-esteem as a lure toward self-centeredness."[10] Damon believes that placing the child at the center of the universe is psychologically dangerous because "...it draws the child's attention away from the social realities to which the child must adapt for proper character development."[11] Children taught to place themselves first care most for their own personal experiences, and in doing so they do not learn how to develop respect for others. According to Lerner, the feel-good-now variety of self-esteem eventually leads to unhappiness, restlessness, and dissatisfaction.[12] Finally, Seligman argues that our obsession with self is responsible for an alarming increase in depression and other mental difficulties,[13] and it is well-documented that such problems result from rumination and obsessive thinking about oneself.[14]

There are other negative consequences of overemphasizing self-oriented self-esteem. For most students, and surely young children, the idea of self-esteem is abstract and hard to understand. Generalized statements such as "you're valued," or "you're great," or "you're special" have no objective reality. They are simply holistic messages that, untied to something tangible and real, have little meaning.[15] Teachers making such statements will lose credibility because children are adept at discerning valid feedback from such vague generalizations. Students may develop a skepticism toward and distrust of adults, or even worse may learn to tune them out entirely, as the teacher "shades the truth ... [with] ... empty rhetoric, transparent flattery, bland distortions of reality."[16] By trying to bolster self-esteem with messages that are not "entirely" true, teachers inadvertently undermine the trust of the child. For students who already have a low self-esteem, such statements reinforce a noncaring attitude from adults. From the perspective of children, caring adults "tell it like it is" and don't hide the truth—they don't cover up or make things up that aren't true.

In contrast, there is ample evidence that our mental health improves as we forget ourselves and focus on activities that are not self-oriented. Often we are most happy when we are so involved in outside pursuits that we don't think about ourselves. This leads us to an alternative theoretical foundation for self-esteem: the notion that healthy self-esteem results not from self-preoccupation and analysis but just the opposite—from **not** being self-oriented but being occupied by interests and pursuits external to self. Indeed, many self-esteem enhancement programs appear to be based on this idea.

Accomplishment and External-to-Self-oriented Self-esteem

As an alternative to the self-orientation approach, we suggest that a healthy esteem results not from self-preoccupation and analysis but from activities that result in meaningful accomplishment or have an external-to-self orientation. Accomplishment means that self-esteem is enhanced as children work hard to meet externally set, reasonable standards of achievement. Lerner calls this "earned" self-esteem: "Earned self-esteem is based on success in meeting the tests of reality—measuring up to standards—at home and in school. It is necessarily hard-won, and develops slowly, but is stable and long-lasting, and provides a secure foundation for further growth and development. It is not a precondition for learning but a product of it."[17]

Achieving meaningful success in schoolwork enhances self-esteem after many years of meeting standards and demands. A foundation for self-esteem based on tangible evidence is internalized by students because it makes sense to them in their social environment. Internally meaningful

Accomplishment means that self-esteem is enhanced as children work hard to meet externally set, reasonable standards of achievement.

performance and accomplishment can be attributed to ability and effort. Such internal attributions underlie a sense of self-efficacy so that the child becomes confident in being a capable learner. Striving for achievement also directs children's thinking off themselves and on something external to themselves. This change in thinking orientation determines self-esteem programs that theoretically are diametrically opposed to self-oriented programs.

Recently there have been signs that psychologists may be changing their views about the emphasis on selfism to enhance self-esteem. Seligman maintains that many have lost a sense of commitment to larger entities outside themselves—country, church, community, family, God, or a purpose that transcends themselves. Without these connections people are left to find meaning and fulfillment in themselves.[18] The negative consequences of de-emphasizing other people, groups, community, and the larger society include vandalism, violence, racial tensions, high divorce rates, and drug abuse. Some psychologists attribute the growth of the "me" generation and selfish behavior to the emphasis on individuality and related themes.[19] Others argue that schools should promote selflessness by emphasizing group welfare over individuals, involvement rather than iso-

lation, and self-denial rather than self-centeredness.

These authors suggest that student well-being is best enhanced by pursuits that take attention away from self, in which one gets "lost." Such pursuits could include a hobby; a concern for helping others; having a purpose or cause bigger than oneself; submitting to duty or to a role in community; or academic success following meaningful effort. The hypothesis is that self-esteem is a byproduct of successful external-to-self experiences. The more success a student has in such activities, the stronger his or her own self-esteem will be.

From a social-psychological perspective, participating constructively with others is necessary for positive self-esteem. As stated by Damon:

> Growing up in large part means learning to participate constructively in the social world. This in turn means developing real skills, getting along with others, acquiring respect for social rules and legitimate authority, caring about those in need, and assuming social responsibility in a host of ways. All of these efforts necessarily bring children out of themselves. They require children to orient themselves toward other people and other people's standards.[21]

By focusing outside themselves children learn respect for others and an objective reference for acquiring a stable and meaningful sense of themselves. It is the outward focus that forms the foundation for self-esteem.

Some examples of self-esteem programs appear to be based on this external-to-self hypothesis. One is a successful program in which students are involved in an art project structured to enhance a feeling of belonging and accomplishment. Self-esteem is improved by involving students in meaningful group activity, not by self-introspection.[22] Another program reports that children acquire self-esteem from successful experiences and appropriate feedback in motor skill development.[23] Several other programs also stress successful achievement in affecting self-esteem.[24] In each case the program involves students in some meaningful activity, rather than focusing on themselves.

Conclusion

Clearly, educators need to concentrate their efforts on improving students' self-esteem. The important question is: How should this be done? We have suggested that approaches emphasizing meaningful achievement and external-to-self pursuits will result in more healthy self-esteem than programs that are self-oriented. Teachers and administrators need to design programs directing student attention away from the self, not toward it. Paradoxically, positive self-esteem develops as students forget about self-esteem, focus on external pursuits, and obtain positive feedback following meaningful involvement and effort

Teachers and administrators need to design programs directing student attention away from the self, not toward it.

1. Barbara Lerner, "Self-esteem and Excellence: The Choice and the Paradox," *American Educator* 9 (1985): 10-16.

2. Jack Canfield, "Improving Students' Self-esteem," *Educational Leadership* 48 (1990): 48-50.

3. Martin E. P. Seligman, "Boomer Blues: With Too Great Expectations, the Baby-Boomers Are Sliding into Individualistic Melancholy," *Psychology Today* 22 (1988): 50-55.

4. Lerner, "Self-esteem and Excellence."

5. Canfield, "Improving Students' Self-esteem."

6. James A. Beane and Richard P. Lipka, *Self-concept, Self-esteem, and the Curriculum* (Boston: Allyn and Bacon, 1984).

7. Anne E. Gottsdanker-Willenkens and Patricia Y. Leonard, "All about Me: Language Arts Strategies to Enhance Self-Concept," *Reading Teacher* 37 (1984): 801-802.

8. Richard L. Papenfuss, John D. Curtis, Barbara J. Beier, and Joseph D. Menze, "Teaching Positive Self-concepts in the Classroom," *Journal of School Health* 53 (1983): 618-620.

9. Frederic J. Medway and Robert C. Smith, Jr., "An Examination of Contemporary Elementary School Affective Education Programs," *Psychology in the Schools* 15 (1978): 266.

10. William Damon, "Putting Substance into Self-Esteem: A Focus on Academic and Moral Values," *educational HORIZONS* (fall 1991):13.

11. Ibid., 17.

12. Lerner, "Self-esteem and Excellence."

13. Seligman, "Boomer Blues."

14. Thomas J. Lasley and John Bregenzer, "Toward Selflessness," *Journal of Human Behavior and Learning* 3 (1986): 20-27.

15. Damon, "Putting Substance into Self-esteem."

16. Ibid., 15.

17. Lerner, "Self-esteem and Excellence," 13.

18. Martin E. P. Seligman, *Learned Optimism: The Skill to Conquer Life's Obstacles, Large & Small* (New York: Random House, 1990).

19. Sami I. Boulos, "The Anatomy of the 'Me' Generation," *Education* 102 (1982): 238-242.

20. Lasley and Bregenzer, "Toward Selflessness."

21. William Damon, "Putting Substance into Self-esteem," 16-17.

22. Marilee M. Cowan and Faith M. Clover, "Enhancement of Self-concept through Disciplined-based Art Education," *Art Education* 44 (1991): 38-45.

23. Linda K. Bunker, "The Role of Play and Motor Skill Development in Building Children's Self-confidence and Self-esteem," *Elementary School Journal* 91 (1991): 467-471.

24. David L. Silvernail, *Developing Positive Student Self-concept* (Washington, D.C.: National Education Association, 1987).

The Caring Classroom's Academic Edge

Catherine C. Lewis, Eric Schaps, and Marilyn S. Watson

The Child Development Project has shown that when kids care about one another—and are motivated by important, challenging work—they're more apt to care about learning.

At Hazelwood School in Louisville, Kentucky, pairs of students are scattered around a 2nd–3rd grade classroom. Heads bent together, students brainstorm with their partners why Widower Muldie, of the book *Wagon Wheels*, left his three sons behind when he set off across the wilderness in search of a home site. Although this story of an African-American pioneer family is set in the rural America of more than 100 years ago, these inner-city students have little trouble diving into the assignment: Write a dialogue between Johnnie and Willie Muldie, ages 11 and 8, who are left in charge of their 3-year-old brother.

Teacher Laura Ecken sets the stage:

Let's imagine that we're Johnny and Willie. It's the first night all alone without daddy. We've put little brother to bed, and we're just sitting up talking to each other.

A Salinas, California, student looks to her older "buddy" for help.

Before students launch into their work, Ecken asks the class to discuss "ways we can help our partners." The children demonstrate remarkable forethought about how to work together: "Disagree without being mean." "If your partner says something that don't fit, then work it into another part." "Let your partner say all they want to say."

Over the next hour, students become intensely interested in figuring out what the Muldie boys might have said to each other. The teacher offers no grade or behavioral reward for this task, nor is any needed. Students are friendly, helpful, and tactful, but also determined to write the best dialogue they know how. In one partnership, John says, "We could talk about how much we miss daddy." Cynthia counters: "But daddy's only been gone for a day." After a few exchanges on this point, John and Cynthia agree to talk about "how much we're *going* to miss daddy." In another partnership, Barry makes use of a strategy suggested by a classmate in the preceding discussion: "How about if we use your idea to 'help me hunt for food' later, because right now we're talking about how the boys feel." Students seem remarkably comfortable questioning and expressing disagreement; the easy camaraderie extends to the many partnerships that cross racial and gender lines.

Fruits of Community

That children at Hazelwood School care about learning and about one another seems perfectly natural. But it didn't just happen. The school's staff has worked very hard over the past five years to create what they call "a caring community of learners"—a community whose members feel valued, personally connected to one another, and committed to everyone's growth and learning. Hazelwood's staff—and educators at other

Do students view their classmates primarily as collaborators in learning, or as competitors in the quest for grades and recognition?

From *Educational Leadership*, September 1996, pp. 16-21. © 1996 by Catherine C. Lewis, Eric Schaps, and Marilyn S. Watson. Reprinted by permission.

© Blake McHugh/Developmental Studies Center

Child Development Project (CDP) schools across the country—believe that creating such a community is crucial to children's learning and citizenship. A growing body of research suggests they are right.

At schools high in "community"—measured by the degree of students' agreement with statements such as "My school is like a family" and "Students really care about each other"—students show a host of positive outcomes. These include higher educational expectations and academic performance, stronger motivation to learn, greater liking for school, less absenteeism, greater social competence, fewer conduct problems, reduced drug use and delinquency, and greater commitment to democratic values (Battistich et al., in press; Bryk and Driscoll 1988; Hom and Battistich 1995).

Our approach in the Child Development Project is to take research findings about how children learn and develop—ethically, socially, and intellectually—and translate them into a comprehensive, practical program with three facets: (1) a classroom program that concentrates on literature-based reading instruction, cooperative learning, and a problem-solving approach to discipline; (2) a school-

wide program of community building and service activities; and (3) a family involvement program.

We originally developed these approaches in collaboration with teachers in California's San Ramon and Hayward school districts. We then extended them, beginning in 1991, to six additional districts nationwide (Cupertino, San Francisco, and Salinas in California; Dade County, Florida.; Jefferson County, Kentucky; and White Plains, New York). In both the original and extension sites, students in CDP schools were studied and compared with students in matched non-project schools (Solomon et al. 1992).

Everything about schooling—curriculum, teaching method, discipline, interpersonal relationships—teaches children about the human qualities that we value.

Five Principles to Practice

How exactly do Child Development Project schools become "caring communities of learners"? They adhere to five interdependent principles, striving for the following.

1. Warm, supportive, stable relationships. Do all members of a school community—students, teachers, staff, parents—know one another as people? Do students view their classmates primarily as collaborators in learning, or as competitors in the quest for grades and recognition? Teachers at our CDP schools carefully examine their approaches, asking, "What kind of human relationships are we fostering?" They recast many old activities.

For example, at one California elementary school, the competitive science fair has become a hands-on family science night that draws hundreds of parents. With awards eliminated, parents are free to focus on the pleasures of learning science with their children. A Dade County, Florida, elementary school removed the competitive costume contest from its Halloween celebration, so that children could enjoy the event without worrying about winners and losers. Other schools took the competition out of PTA membership drives, refocusing them to emphasize participation and celebration of the school's progress.

Teachers also added or redesigned many academic and nonacademic activities so that students could get to know one another and develop a feeling of unity and shared purpose as a class and school. "A big change for me is that on the first morning of school, the classroom walls are blank—no decorations, no rules," explains a teacher from California. Like many of her Child Development Project colleagues, she involves students in interviewing classmates and creating wall displays about "our class" that bring children closer together.

In the first class meetings of the year, students discuss "how we want to be treated by others," and "what kind of class we want to be." From these discussions emerge a few simple principles—"be kind," "show respect," "do

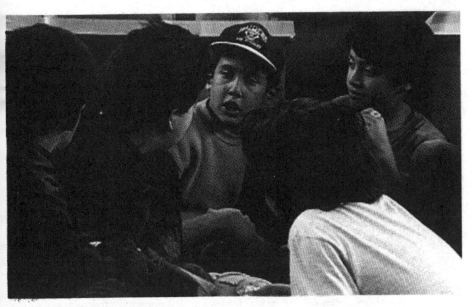

Students work harder, achieve more, and attribute more importance to schoolwork in classes in which they feel liked, accepted, and respected by the teacher and fellow students.

our best"—that are remarkably similar across diverse schools.

Says one teacher,

When you invest time up front in having the kids get to know one another, the picked-on child never has a chance to emerge. Kids find out that they share the same favorite food, hobby, or whatever; they see one another as human beings. The child who might have been the nerd in previous years never gets seen

that way because classmates remember that that child's favorite food is McDonald's hamburgers, too.

2. Constructive learning. Children naturally try to make sense of the world—to figure out how magnets work or why friends help. Good teaching fosters these efforts to understand, but also hones them, helping children become ever more skillful, reflective, and self-critical in their pursuit of knowledge. How can teachers support and extend children's natural efforts to learn?

First, educators can provide a coherent curriculum, organized around important concepts, rather than a

potpourri of isolated facts. Second, educators can connect the curriculum with children's own natural efforts to make sense of the world. Children should see mathematics, for example, as a powerful means for understanding the world, not as arbitrary principles that apply only within classroom walls. When children see how the ideas and skills of school help them understand and act upon the world—how they are genuinely useful—they begin to practice these academic skills throughout their home and school lives.

Third, lessons can be set up so that children must weigh new information against what they already know, work through discrepancies, and construct a new understanding. When children make discoveries, struggle to find explanations, and grapple with evidence and views that differ from their own, they are likely to reach more profound levels of understanding than they can achieve through simple rote learning. The students at Hazelwood School who wrote a dialogue between the Muldie boys were constructive learners in all these senses.

Like other books in our project's literature-based program, *Wagon Wheels* pursues important issues: What experiences have shaped the lives of diverse Americans? How have acts of principle, courage, and responsibility shaped history, and how do they shape our own daily lives? These issues are explored not just in literature and social studies, but in class meetings, problem solving, and in many other ways.

In addition, to make sense of an experience that happened long ago, Ecken's students needed to draw on both school learning and their own experiences. Would being left without parents and in charge of a younger brother feel any different in 1878 than in 1994? Finally, the task of writing a dialogue challenged students to take the perspective of the boys in the story and to reconcile their thinking with their partner's perspective.

3. An important, challenging curriculum. In an era of rapid technological change, certain skills and habits are likely to remain important— thoughtful reading, self-critical reflection, clear communication, asking productive questions. But the de facto curriculum defined by commercial textbooks and standardized tests often emphasizes something much less enduring—isolated subskills and piecemeal knowledge. Like Jere Brophy and Janet Alleman (1991), we believe that curriculum development must "be driven by major long-term goals, not just short-term coverage concerns." These goals should be broadly conceived to include children's development as principled, humane citizens.

Numerous critiques of the curriculum in this country argue that it sells children short by presenting material that is too simple and too easily mastered— for example, basal readers whose barren language and shallow ideas offer little reason to read. That a more challenging curriculum is more compelling to children, even so-called slow learners, is a tenet underlying some recent interventions (Hopfenberg 1993).

4. Intrinsic motivation. What kind of schooling produces eager, lifelong learners? Certainly not schooling that relies on the power of extrinsic rewards—prizes, honors, grades, and so forth. In fact, studies show that these can actually undermine children's interest in learning (Lepper and Greene 1978). Awarding prizes for creating science projects, reading books, running laps, or a host of other worthwhile ends can diminish interest in the activity itself by focusing children's

5. Attention to social and ethical dimensions of learning. Everything about schooling—curriculum, teaching method, discipline, interpersonal relationships—teaches children about the human qualities that we value. As students discuss the experiences of African-American families like the Muldies, they grow ethically and socially. This growth stems from the

promote children's responsible behavior in the long run. Teachers engage children in shaping the norms of their class and school, so that they see that these norms are not arbitrary standards set by powerful adults, but necessary standards for the well-being of everyone. Teachers also help children develop collaborative approaches to resolving conflicts, guiding them to think about the values needed for humane life in a group. Playground disputes become opportunities for students to learn about the needs and perspectives of other students, and to practice skills of nonviolent problem solving.

Faced with a competitive, skill-and-drill curriculum, educationally less-prepared children may preserve their self-esteem by reducing their efforts.

© Blake McHugh/Developmental Studies Center

Finally, teachers look at the many programs, special events, parent-supported activities, and policies of the school through the lens of social and ethical development. Do these activities help children understand the values that sustain democratic society? Do they give students many opportunities to develop and practice qualities that we want them to have as adults—responsibility, collaboration, tolerance, commitment to the common good, courage to stand up for their beliefs, and so on?

Synergy of Academic and Social Goals

It is common to think of the academic and social goals of schooling as a hydraulic—to imagine that fostering one undermines the other. But when schools attend to all five elements described above, they create environments where children care about one another and about learning.

For example, students work harder, achieve more, and attribute more importance to schoolwork in classes in which they feel liked, accepted, and respected by the teacher and fellow students. Warm, supportive relationships also enable students to risk the

attention on the reward, and by implying that the task is not inherently worthwhile (Kohn 1993). As one sage commentator quipped, "If we want children to read books, we should offer them books as a reward for eating pizzas, not pizzas for reading books."

To minimize extrinsic rewards, educators need a curriculum that is worth learning and a pedagogy that helps students see why it is worth learning. The students writing a dialogue between the Muldie boys were motivated by the task itself. *Wagon Wheels* raised issues of timeless importance, and the teacher took care to introduce the book in a way that piqued students' curiosity and helped them make personal connections to the book.

content they encounter, the experience of working with classmates, and the reflection following partner work on their difficulties and successes working with others.

Child Development Project teachers scrutinize disciplinary approaches not just for whether they help children behave in the short run, under an adult's surveillance, but whether they

To minimize extrinsic rewards, educators need a curriculum that is worth learning and a pedagogy that helps students see why it is worth learning.

new ideas and mistakes so critical to intellectual growth. It is no coincidence that, to create an environment in which students can discuss classmates' incorrect solutions to math problems, Japanese teachers spend a great deal of time building friendships among children and a feeling of classroom unity.

Schools that provide an important, challenging curriculum, and help children connect it to their own efforts to understand the world, become allies in children's quest for competence—and teachers in those schools have a head start in being seen as supportive, valued adults.

A shift away from competition, rewards, and punishments helps all students—not just the high-achievers—feel like valued members of the classroom community. Faced with a competitive, skill-and-drill curriculum, educationally less-prepared children may preserve their self-esteem by reducing their efforts. They may psychologically withdraw from the classroom or school community, leaving it powerless to influence their social, ethical, or intellectual development (Nicholls 1989).

The caring classroom is not one that avoids criticism, challenge, or mistakes. Parker J. Palmer (1983) has written:

A learning space needs to be hospitable not to make learning painless but to make the painful things possible... things like exposing ignorance, testing tentative hypotheses, challenging false or partial information, and mutual criticism of thought. [None of these] can happen in an atmosphere where people feel threatened and judged.

Like a family, the caring classroom provides a sense of belonging that allows lively, critical discussions and risk-taking.

Countering Conventional Wisdom

We think relatively few American schools have managed to sustain a simultaneous focus on students' social, ethical, and intellectual development. What will it take to achieve this on a much broader scale? First, it will take changes in thinking; the agenda we have proposed runs counter to much

> # When children see how the ideas and skills of school help them understand and act upon the world—how they are genuinely useful—they begin to practice these skills throughout their home and school lives.

current conventional wisdom in education.

Such changes cannot be expected to come quickly or easily. Because adults, too, are constructive learners, they need the same five conditions that children do. School improvement hinges on a sense of community and collaboration among teachers, conditions that enable teachers to risk changing practice and to admit and learn from mistakes.

At the schools participating in the Child Development Project, teachers spend up to 30 days over three years in staff development. The schools have worked consciously to build strong personal connections among staff members. They do this through social events, shared planning and reflection, and often by meeting regularly in "learning partnerships" of two to four teachers to discuss their efforts to reshape practice. In an era of tight budgets, such time for adult learning is difficult to obtain.

Finally, we need to recognize that community and learning are interdependent and must be pursued in context. This means that it is not enough to ask whether a new science curriculum increases students' mastery of important scientific concepts; we must also ask whether it fosters their capacity to work with fellow students, their intrinsic interest in science, and their recognition that science depends upon both collaboration and honesty. This is a big picture to keep in focus. Educators who have traditionally worked in isolation from one another—specialists in subject matter, pedagogy, school climate, motivation—must help one another to keep it in perspective.

References

Battistich, V., D. Solomon, D. Kim, M. Watson, and E. Schaps. (In press).

"Schools as Communities, Poverty Levels of Student Populations, and Students' Attitudes, Motives, and Performance." *American Education Research Journal.*

Brophy, J., and J. Alleman. (1991). "Activities as Instructional Tools: A Framework for Analysis and Evaluation." *Educational Researcher* 20, 4: 9–23.

Bryk, A. S., and M. E. Driscoll. (1988). *The School as Community: Theoretical Foundations, Contextual Influences, and Consequences for Students and Teachers.* Madison, Wisconsin: National Center on Effective Secondary Schools.

Hom, A., and V. Battistich. (April 1995). "Students' Sense of School Community as a Factor in Reducing Drug Use and Delinquency." Presentation to the 1995 American Educational Research Association Annual Meeting.

Hopfenberg, W. (1993). *The Accelerated Schools.* San Francisco: Jossey-Bass.

Kohn, A. (1993). *Punished by Rewards: The Trouble with Gold Stars, Incentive Plans, A's, Praise, and Other Bribes.* Boston: Houghton Mifflin.

Lepper, M. R., and D. Greene. (1978). *The Hidden Costs of Reward: New Perspectives on the Psychology of Human Motivation.* Hillsdale, N.J.: Lawrence Erlbaum Associates.

Nicholls, J. (1989). *The Competitive Ethos and Democratic Education.* Cambridge, Mass.: Harvard University Press.

Palmer, P. J. (1983). *To Know as We Are Known: A Spirituality of Education.* San Francisco: HarperCollins.

Solomon, D., M. Watson, V. Battistich, E. Schaps, and K. Delucchi. (1992). "Creating a Caring Community: A School-Based Program to Promote Children's Prosocial Development." In *Effective and Responsible Teaching: The New Synthesis,* edited by E. Oser, J. L. Patty, and A. Dick. San Francisco: Jossey-Bass.

Catherine C. Lewis is the Formative Research Director, **Eric Schaps** is President, and **Marilyn S. Watson** is Program Director, of the Developmental Studies Center, 2000 Embarcadero, Suite 305, Oakland, CA 94606-5300.

A Framework for Culturally Responsive Teaching

Research has shown that no one teaching strategy will consistently engage all learners. The key is helping students relate lesson content to their own backgrounds.

Raymond J. Wlodkowski and Margery B. Ginsberg

To be effective in multicultural classrooms, teachers must relate teaching content to the cultural backgrounds of their students. According to the research, teaching that ignores student norms of behavior and communication provokes student resistance, while teaching that is responsive prompts student involvement (Olneck 1995). There is growing evidence that strong, continual engagement among diverse students requires a holistic approach— that is, an approach where the how, what, and why of teaching are unified and meaningful (Ogbu 1995).

To that end, we have developed a comprehensive model of culturally responsive teaching: a pedagogy that crosses disciplines and cultures to engage learners while respecting their cultural integrity. It accommodates the dynamic mix of race, ethnicity, class, gender, region, religion, and family that contributes to every student's cultural identity. The foundation for this approach lies in theories of intrinsic motivation.

Before we outline our framework for culturally responsive teaching, we will address the bond of motivation and culture, and analyze some of the social and institutional resistance to teaching based on principles of intrinsic motivation. Understanding these relationships provides a clearer view of the challenges we must overcome if we are to genuinely transform teaching and successfully engage all students.

Motivation Is Inseparable from Culture

Engagement is the visible outcome of motivation, the natural capacity to direct energy in the pursuit of a goal. Our emotions influence our motivation. In turn, our emotions are socialized through culture—the deeply learned confluence of language, beliefs, values, and behaviors that pervades every aspect of our lives. For example, one person working at a task feels frustrated and stops, while another person working at the task feels joy and continues. Yet another person, with an even different set of cultural beliefs, feels frustrated at the task but continues with increased determination. What may elicit that frustration, joy, or determination may differ across cultures, because cultures differ in their definitions of novelty, hazard, opportunity, and gratification, and in their definitions of appropriate responses. Thus, the response a student has to a learning activity reflects his or her culture.

While the internal logic as to why a student does something may not coincide with that of the teacher, it is, nonetheless, present. And, to be effective, the teacher must understand that perspective. Rather than trying to know *what to do to* students, we must work with students to interpret and deepen their existing knowledge and enthusiasm for learning. From this viewpoint, motivationally effective

From *Educational Leadership*, September 1995, pp. 17-21. © 1995 by Raymond J. Wlodkowski and Margery B. Ginsberg. Reprinted by permission.

teaching *is* culturally responsive teaching.

Locked in Mid-Century

Most educators with whom we have worked would agree that there is a strong relationship between culture and motivation, and that it only makes sense to understand a student's perspective. Why, then, do we have such difficulty acting this way in the classroom?

One major reason is that we feel very little social pressure to act otherwise. The popular media and structural systems of education remain locked in a deterministic, mechanistic, and behavioristic orientation toward human motivation.

If one were to do a content analysis of national news broadcasts and news magazines for the last 40 years to identify the most widely used metaphor for motivation, "the carrot and the stick"—reward and punish, manipulate and control—would prevail. As a result, our national consciousness assumes there are many people who need to be motivated by other people.

The prevailing question, "How do I motivate them?" implies that "they" are somehow dependent, incapable of self-motivation, and in need of help from a more powerful "other." In this sense, the "at-risk" label acts to heighten our perception of students as motivationally dysfunctional, and increases our tendency not to trust their perspective. The fact that an inordinately high number of "at-risk" students are poor and people of color should cause us to reflect on how well we understand motivation. Thoughtful scholars have suggested that this label now serves as a euphemism for "culturally deprived" (Banks 1993).

Secondary education is influenced a great deal by the practices of higher education, and both levels tend to follow the precepts of extrinsic reinforcement. Teaching and testing practices, competitive assessment procedures, grades, grade point averages, and eligibility for select vocations and colleges form an interrelated system. This system is based on the assumption that human beings will strive to learn when they are externally rewarded for a specific behavior or punished for lack of it.

Schools and colleges successfully educate a disproportionately low number of low-income and ethnic minority students (Wlodkowski and Ginsberg 1995). Because the importance of grades and grade point averages increases as a student advances in school, it is legitimate to question whether extrinsic motivation systems are effective for significant numbers of students across cultures. We can only conclude that, as long as the educational system continues to relate motivation to learn with external rewards and punishments, culturally different students will, in large part, be excluded from engagement and success in school.

Changing Consciousness About Motivation

It is part of human nature to be curious, to be active, to initiate thought and behavior, to make meaning from experience, and to be effective at what we value. These primary sources of motivation reside in all of us, across all cultures. When students can see that what they are learning makes sense and is important, their intrinsic motivation emerges.

We can begin to replace the carrot and stick metaphor with the words "understand" and "elicit"; to change the concept of motivation from reward and punishment to communication and respect. We can influence the motivation of students by coming to know their perspective, by drawing forth who they naturally and culturally are, and by seeing them as unique and active. Sharing our resources with theirs, working together, we can create greater energy for learning.

Intrinsic systems of motivation can accommodate cultural differences.

> What may elicit frustration, joy, or determination may differ across cultures, because cultures differ in their definitions of novelty, hazard, opportunity, and gratification.

Theories of intrinsic motivation have been successfully applied and researched in areas such as cross-cultural studies (Csikszentmihalyi and Csikszentmihalyi 1988); bilingual education (Cummins 1986); and education, work, and sports (Deci and Ryan 1985). Ample documentation across a variety of student and regional settings suggests that noncompetitive, informational evaluation processes are more effective than competitive, controlling evaluation procedures (Deci et al. 1991, Deci and Ryan 1991).

A growing number of educational models, including constructivism and multiple intelligences theory, are based on intrinsic motivation. They see student perspective as central to teaching. Unfortunately, educators must often apply these theories within educational systems dominated by extrinsic reinforcement, where grades and class rank are emphasized. And, when extrinsic rewards continue to be the primary motivators, intrinsic motivation is dampened. Those students whose socialization accommodates the extrinsic approach surge ahead, while those students—often the culturally different—whose socialization does not, fall behind. A holistic, culturally responsive pedagogy based on intrinsic motivation is needed to correct this imbalance.

An Intrinsic Motivational Framework

We propose a model of culturally responsive teaching based on theories of intrinsic motivation. This model is respectful of different cultures and is capable of creating a common culture that all students can accept. Within this framework, pedagogical alignment—the coordination of approaches to teaching that ensure maximum consistent effect—is critical. The more harmonious the elements of teaching are, the more likely they are to evoke, encourage, and sustain intrinsic motivation.

The framework names four motivational conditions that the teacher and students continuously create or enhance. They are:

1. Establishing inclusion—creating a learning atmosphere in which students and teachers feel respected by and connected to one another.

2. Developing attitude—creating a favorable disposition toward the learning experience through personal relevance and choice.

3. Enhancing meaning—creating challenging, thoughtful learning experiences that include student perspectives and values.

4. Engendering competence—creating an understanding that students are effective in learning something they value.

These conditions are essential to developing intrinsic motivation. They are sensitive to cultural differences. They work in concert as they influence students and teachers, and they happen in a moment as well as over a period of time.

Culturally Responsive Teaching

Let us look at an actual episode of culturally responsive teaching based on this motivational framework. It occurs in an urban high school social science class with a diverse group of students and an experienced teacher.

At the start of a new term, the teacher wants to familiarize students with active research methods. She will use such methods throughout the semester, and she knows from previous experience that many students view research as abstract, irrelevant, and oppressive work.

After reflecting on the framework, her teaching goal, and her repertoire of methods, she randomly assigns students to small groups. She encourages them to discuss any previous experiences they may have had in doing research as well as their expectations and concerns for the course. Each group then shares its experiences, expectations, and concerns as she records them on the chalkboard. In this manner, she is able to understand her students' perspectives and to increase their connection to one another and herself *(motivational condition: establishing inclusion).*

The teacher explains that most people are researchers much of the time, and she asks the students what they would like to research among themselves. After a lively discussion, the class decides to investigate and predict the amount of sleep some members of the class had the previous night. This experience engages student choice, increases the relevance of the activity, and contributes to the favorable disposition emerging in the class *(motivational condition: developing attitude).* The students are learning in a way that includes their experiences and perspectives.

Five students volunteer to serve as subjects, and the other students form research teams. Each team must develop a set of observations and questions to ask the volunteers. (They cannot ask them how many hours of sleep they had the night before.) After they ask their questions, the teams rank the five volunteers from the most to the least amount of sleep. When the volunteers reveal the amount of time they slept, the students discover that no research team was correct in ranking more than three students.

Students discuss why this outcome may have occurred, and consider questions that might have increased their accuracy, such as, "How many hours of sleep do you need to feel rested?" Collaborative learning, hypothesis testing, critical questioning, and predicting heighten the engagement, challenge, and complexity of this process for the students *(motivational condition: enhancing meaning).*

These procedures encourage and model equitable participation for all students.

After the discussion, the teacher asks the students to write a series of statements about what this activity has taught them about research. Students then break into small groups to exchange their insights. Self-assessment helps the students to gain, from an authentic experience, an understanding of something they may value *(motivational condition: engendering competence).*

This snapshot of culturally responsive teaching illustrates how the four motivational conditions constantly influence and interact with one another. Without establishing inclusion (small groups to discuss experiences) and developing attitude (students choosing a relevant research), the enhancement of meaning (research teams devising hypotheses) may not have occurred with equal ease and energy; and the self-assessment to engender competence (what students learned from their perspective) may have had a dismal outcome. According to this model of teaching, all the motivational conditions contribute to student engagement.

Norms, Procedures, and Structures

Although the above event actually occurred, it may sound like a fairy tale because everything worked smoothly. In reality, teaching situations often become fragmented by the competing needs and interests of a diverse student body. All too often, we use educational

FIGURE 1

Four Conditions Necessary for Culturally Responsive Teaching

1. Establish Inclusion

Norms:

■ Emphasize the human purpose of what is being learned and its relationship to the students' experience.

■ Share the ownership of knowing with all students.

■ Collaborate and cooperate. The class assumes a hopeful view of people and their capacity to change.

■ Treat all students equitably. Invite them to point out behaviors or practices that discriminate.

Procedures: Collaborative learning approaches; cooperative learning; writing groups; peer teaching; multi-dimensional sharing; focus groups; and reframing.

Structures: Ground rules; learning communities; and cooperative base groups.

2. Develop Positive Attitude

Norms:

■ Relate teaching and learning activities to students' experience or previous knowledge.

■ Encourage students to make choices in content and assessment methods based on their experiences, values, needs, and strengths.

Procedures: Clear learning goals; problem solving goals; fair and clear criteria of evaluation; relevant learning models; learning contracts; approaches based on multiple intelligences theory; pedagogical flexibility based on style; and experiential learning.

Structure: Culturally responsive teacher/student/parent conferences.

3. Enhance Meaning

Norms:

■ Provide challenging learning experiences involving higher order thinking and critical inquiry. Address relevant, real-world issues in an action-oriented manner.

■ Encourage discussion of relevant experiences. Incorporate student dialect into classroom dialogue.

Procedures: Critical questioning; guided reciprocal peer questioning; posing problems; decision making; investigation of definitions; historical investigations; experimental inquiry; invention; art; simulations; and case study methods.

Structures: Projects and the problem-posing model.

4. Engender Competence

Norms:

■ Connect the assessment process to the students' world, frames of reference, and values.

■ Include multiple ways to represent knowledge and skills and allow for attainment of outcomes at different points in time.

■ Encourage self-assessment.

Procedures: Feedback; contextualized assessment; authentic assessment tasks; portfolios and process-folios; tests and testing formats critiqued for bias; and self-assessment.

Structures: Narrative evaluations; credit/no credit systems; and contracts for grades.

Based on Wlodkowski, R. J., and M. B. Ginsberg. (1995). *Diversity and Motivation: Culturally Responsive Teaching.* San Francisco: Jossey-Bass.

norms and procedures that are contradictory. The result is that we confuse students and decrease their intrinsic motivation. For example, consider the teacher who uses cooperative learning yet gives pop quizzes; or who espouses constructivist learning yet grades for participation; or who abhors discrimination yet calls mainly on boys during class discussions.

In an effort to help educators avoid such errors of incoherence, we have compiled educational norms, procedures, and structures that are effective from a motivational as well as multicultural perspective (see fig. 1). Together, they provide an integrated system of teaching practices for our model of culturally responsive teaching. They are categorized according to the motivational conditions of the framework:

Norms are the explicit values espoused by the teacher and students. *Procedures* are learning processes that carry out the norms. *Structures* are the rules or binding expectations that support the norms and procedures.

Teaching in a way that respects diversity is challenging, of course. Consider the following case example. The *norm* that Mr. Clark, a U.S. history teacher, is aiming for is "sharing the ownership of knowing." The topic is the notion of cultural pluralism, and, later, the roles that our socioeconomic backgrounds play in our lives. Clark uses the *procedures* of collaborative learning and critical questioning to facilitate student comprehension of the concepts of "melting pot," "social class," and other terms.

Clark asks the class to first brainstorm words that are associated with culture. Students volunteer "language," "ethnicity," "gender," "religion," "food preference," and so forth. In pairs, students then talk to their partner about ways in which they believe they are culturally similar and distinct from each other.

After 15 minutes, the teacher asks students to note three observations about the concept of culture. The most prevalent response is that "we were surprised at how much we have in

When students can see that what they are learning makes sense and is important, their intrinsic motivation emerges.

common." Clark indicates that he sees this as well. He asks the class, "If we have such commonality, why do some groups of people in the United States have such difficulty becoming economically secure?" Note what happen as students struggle over whose perceptions are the most accurate.

First student: Some have more difficulty because of discrimination, because people have prejudices against people whose skin is a different color from theirs.

Second student: I don't think it's that simple. Look how many people of color are doing well. We've got generals, mayors, and corporation executives. There's a black middle class and they are economically secure.

Third student: Yeah, that might be so, but it isn't as many people as you think. The newspapers just make a big deal about minorities succeeding.

Clark's ground rules *(structure)* for this conversation endorse honesty in offering opinions and forbid putdowns, so the tone of this exchange is respectful. Interest in the topic intensifies as a result of the exchange.

Clark acknowledges the different points of view and asks the class: "What questions might provide insights or clarify the differences between these viewpoints?" The class breaks into small groups after which Clark records the suggested questions. Some that emerge:

1. Which ethnic groups are most

economically successful? Least successful?

2. What proportion of each ethnic group is lower income, middle income, upper income?

3. Are more people of color economically successful today than 20 years ago? 100 years ago?

4. What is the relationship of educational opportunity to income status?

5. Do middle- and upper-class African Americans and Latinos encounter more discrimination than do European Americans?

6. Is there a difference in the quality of family and community support among middle- and upper-income African Americans, European Americans, and Latinos?

As a result of the discussion, students begin to see how the viewpoints about race and socioeconomic backgrounds are part of a broad and complex picture. The difference of opinion has become a stimulus for deeper learning. Students then divide into three groups: one to conduct library research of relevant documents and studies; one to read and analyze relevant biographies and autobiographies; and one to interview community members who represent different cultures.

A Holistic Approach

For culturally different students, engagement in learning is most likely to occur when they are intrinsically motivated to learn. This motivational framework provides a holistic and culturally responsive way to create,

plan, and refine teaching activities, lessons, and assessment practices.

References

Banks, J. A. (1993). "Multicultural Education: Historical Development, Dimensions, and Practice." In *Review of Research in Education, Vol. 19*, edited by L. Darling-Hammond. Washington, D.C.: American Educational Research Association.

Csikszentmihalyi, M., and I. S. Csikszentmihalyi. (1988). *Optimal Experience: Psychological Studies of Flow in Consciousness.* New York: Cambridge University Press.

Cummins, J. (1986). "Empowering Minority Students: A Framework for Intervention." *Harvard Educational Review* 56, 1: 18–36.

Deci, E. L., and R. M. Ryan. (1991). "A Motivational Approach to Self: Integration in Personality." In *Nebraska Symposium on Motivation: Vol. 38. Perspectives on Motivation*, edited by R. Dienstbier. Lincoln: University of Nebraska Press.

Deci, E. L., and R. M. Ryan. (1985). *Intrinsic Motivation and Self-Determination in Human Behavior.* New York: Plenum.

Deci, E. L., R. J. Vallerand, L. C. Pelletier, and R. M. Ryan. (1991). "Motivation and Education: The Self-Determination Perspective." *Educational Psychologist* 26, 3 and 4: 325–346.

Ogbu, J. U. (1995). "Understanding Cultural Diversity and Learning." In *Handbook of Research on Multicultural Education*, edited by J. A. Banks and C. A. M. Banks. New York: Macmillan.

Olneck, M. R. (1995). "Immigrants and Education." In *Handbook of Research on Multicultural Education*, edited by J. A. Banks and C. A. M. Banks. New York: Macmillan.

Wlodkowski, R. J., and M. B. Ginsberg. (1995). *Diversity and Motivation: Culturally Responsive Teaching.* San Francisco: Jossey-Bass.

Raymond J. Wlodkowski is an Educational and Psychological Consultant, 6033 Jay Rd., Boulder, CO 80301. **Margery B. Ginsberg** is Research Associate, RMC Research Corporation, Writer Square, Ste. 540, 1512 Larimer St., Denver, CO 80202.

Problem Based Learning: An Instructional Model and Its Constructivist Framework

John R. Savery
Thomas M. Duffy

John R. Savery is a Ph.D. candidate in Instructional Systems Technology at Indiana University. His dissertation research is examining issues of learner ownership in a problem based, cooperative learning environment. He has recently joined the DLS Group in Denver, Colorado, as a senior instructional designer.

Thomas M. Duffy is Professor of Instructional Systems Technology and in Language Education at the School of Education, Indiana University, and director of the under-graduate Corporate and Community Education Program. His interests are in the design of learner-centered learning environments with particular design emphasis on technology supports and a research emphasis on the collaborative practical reasoning process.

It is said that there's nothing so practical as good theory. It may also be said that there's nothing so theoretically interesting as good practice.[1] This is particularly true of efforts to relate constructivism as a theory of learning to the practice of instruction. Our goal in this article is to provide a clear link between the theoretical principles of constructivism, the practice of instructional design, and the practice of teaching. We will begin with a basic characterization of constructivism, identifying what we believe to be the central principles in learning and understanding. We will then identify and elaborate on eight instructional principles for the design of a constructivist learning environment. Finally, we will examine what we consider to be one of the best exemplars of a constructivist learning environment—Problem Based Learning, as described by Barrows (1985, 1986, 1992).

[1]This succinct statement was noted in Gaffney & Anderson (1991).

Constructivism

Constructivism is a philosophical view on how we come to understand or know. It is, in our mind, most closely attuned to the pragmatic philosophy of Richard Rorty (1991). Space limitations for this article prevent an extensive discussion of this philosophical base, but we would commend to the interested reader the work of Rorty (1991) as well as vonGlasersfeld (1989). We will characterize the philosophical view in terms of three primary propositions:

1. Understanding is in our interactions with the environment. This is the core concept of constructivism. We cannot talk about what is learned separately from how it is learned, as if a variety of experiences all lead to the same understanding. Rather, what we understand is a function of the content, the context, the activity of the learner, and, perhaps most importantly, the goals of the learner. Since understanding is an individual construction, we cannot share understandings, but rather, we can test the degree to which our individual understandings are compatible. An implication of this proposition is that cognition is not just within the individual, but rather it is a part of the entire context, i.e., cognition is distributed.

2. Cognitive conflict or puzzlement is the stimulus for learning and determines the organization and nature of what is learned. When we are in a learning environment, there is some stimulus or goal for learning—the learner has a purpose for being there. That goal is not only the stimulus for learning, but it is a primary factor in determining what the

From *Educational Technology*, September/October 1995, pp. 31-38. © 1995 by Educational Technology Publications, Inc. Reprinted by permission.

learner attends to, what prior experience the learner brings to bear in constructing an understanding, and, basically, what understanding is eventually constructed. In Dewey's terms, it is the "problematic" that leads to and is the organizer for learning (Dewey, 1938; Roschelle, 1992). For Piaget it is the need for accommodation when current experience cannot be assimilated in existing schema (Piaget, 1977; vonGlasersfeld, 1989). We prefer to talk about the learner's "puzzlement" as being the stimulus and organizer for learning, since this more readily suggests both intellectual and pragmatic goals for learning. The important point, however, is that it is the goal of the learner that is central in considering what is learned.

3. Knowledge evolves through social negotiation and through the evaluation of the viability of individual understandings. The social environment is critical to the development of our individual understanding as well as to the development of the body of propositions we call knowledge. At the first, or individual level, other individuals are a primary mechanism for testing our understanding. Collaborative groups are important because we can test our own understanding and examine the understanding of others as a mechanism for enriching, interweaving, and expanding our understanding of particular issues or phenomena. As vonGlasersfeld (1989) has noted, other people are the greatest source of alternative views to challenge our current views and hence to serve as the source of puzzlement that stimulates new learning. The second role of the social environment is to develop a set of propositions we call knowledge. We seek propositions that are compatible with our individual constructions or understanding of the world. Thus, facts are facts because there is widespread agreement, not because there is some ultimate truth to the fact. It was once a fact that the earth was flat and the sun revolved around the earth. More recently, it was fact that the smallest particles of matter were electrons, protons, and neutrons. These were facts because there was general agreement that the concepts and principles arising from these views provided the best interpretation of our world. The same search for viability holds in our daily life. In both cases, concepts that we call knowledge do not represent some ultimate truth, but are simply the most viable interpretation of our experiential world (see Resnick, 1987). The important consideration in this third proposition is that all views, or all constructions, are not equally viable. Constructivism is not a deconstructivist view in which all constructions are equal simply because they are personal experiences. Rather, we seek viability, and thus we must test understandings to determine how

adequately they allow us to interpret and function in our world. Our social environment is primary in providing alternative views and additional information against which we can test the viability of our understanding and in building the set of propositions (knowledge) compatible with those understandings (Cunningham, Duffy, & Knuth, 1991). Hence we discuss social negotiation of meaning and understanding based on viability.

Instructional Principles

The constructivist propositions outlined above suggest a set of instructional principles that can guide the practice of teaching and the design of learning environments. All too often when we discuss principles of teaching we hear the retort, "But we already do that..." While that assertion may well be accurate, too often the claim is based on the principle in isolation rather than in the context of the overall framework. Indeed, everyone "does" collaborative groups; the real issue is what the goal is in using collaborative groups, since that determines the details of how they are used and how they are contextualized in the overall instructional framework.

We think Lebow (1993) has hit upon a strategy for summarizing the constructivist framework in a way that may help with the interpretation of the instructional strategies. He talks about the shift in values when one takes a constructivist perspective. He notes that:

> ...traditional educational technology values of replicability, reliability, communication, and control (Heinich, 1984) contrast sharply with the seven primary constructivist values of collaboration, personal autonomy, generativity, reflectivity, active engagement, personal relevance, and pluralism. (1993, p. 5)

We agree with Lebow and would propose that this value system serve to guide the reader's interpretation of our instructional principles as well as the interpretation of the problem based learning environment we will describe. The instructional principles deriving from constructivism are as follows:

1. Anchor all learning activities to a larger task or problem. That is, learning must have a purpose beyond, "It is assigned." We learn in order to be able to function more effectively in our world. The purpose of any learning activity should be clear to the learner. Individual learning activities can be of any type—the important issue is that the learner clearly perceives and accepts the relevance of the specific learning activities in relation to the larger task complex (Cognition & Technology Group at Vanderbilt, 1992; Honebein, Duffy, & Fishman, 1993).

2. Support the learner in developing ownership for the overall problem or task. Instructional programs typically specify learning objectives and perhaps even engage the learner in a project, assuming that the learner will understand and buy into the relevance and value of the problem (Blumenfeld, Soloway, Marx, Krajcik, Guzdial, & Palincsar, 1991). Unfortunately, it is too often the case that the learners do not accept the goal of the instructional program, but rather simply focus on passing the test or putting in their time. No matter what we specify as the learning objective, the goals of the learner will largely determine what is learned. Hence, it is essential that the goals the learner brings to the environment are consistent with our instructional goals.

There are two ways of doing this. First, we may solicit problems from the learners and use those as the stimulus for learning activities. This is basically what happens in graduate schools when qualifying exams require the student to prepare publishable papers in each of several domains (Honebein *et al.*, 1993). Scardamalia and Bereiter (1991) have shown that even elementary students can initiate questions (puzzlements) that can serve as the foundation of learning activities in traditional school subject matter. In essence, the strategy is to define a territory and then to work with the learner in developing meaningful problems or tasks in that domain. Alternatively, we can establish a problem in such a way that the learners will readily adopt the problem as their own. We see this strategy in the design of the Jasper series for teaching mathematics (Cognition & Technology Group at Vanderbilt, 1992) and in many simulation environments.[2] In either case, it is important to engage the learner in meaningful dialogue to help bring the problem or task home to that learner.

3. Design an authentic task. An authentic learning environment does *not* mean that the fourth grader should be placed in an authentic physics lab, nor that he or she should grapple with the same problems with which adult physicists deal. Rather, the learner should engage in scientific activities which present the same "type" of cognitive challenges. An authentic learning environment is one in which the cognitive demands, i.e., the thinking required, are consistent with the cognitive demands in the environment for which we are preparing the learner (Honebein *et al.*, 1993). Thus, we do not want the learner to learn about history but rather to engage in the construction or use of history in ways that a historian or a good citizen would. Similarly, we do not want the learner to study science—

memorizing a text on science or executing scientific procedures as dictated—but rather to engage in scientific discourse and problem solving (see Bereiter, 1994; Duffy, in press; Honebein *et al.*, 1993). Allowing the problem to be generated by the learner, an option discussed above, does not automatically assure authenticity. It may well require discussion and negotiation with the learner to develop a problem or task which is authentic in its cognitive demands and for which the learner can take ownership.

4. Design the task and the learning environment to reflect the complexity of the environment they should be able to function in at the end of learning. Rather than simplifying the environment for the learner, we seek to support the learner working in the complex environment. This is consistent with both cognitive apprenticeship (Collins, Brown, & Newman, 1989) and cognitive flexibility theory (Spiro *et al.*, 1992) and reflects the importance of context in determining the understanding we have of any particular concept or principle.

5. Give the learner ownership of the process used to develop a solution. Learners must have ownership of the learning or problem-solving process as well as ownership of the problem itself. Frequently, teachers will give students ownership of the problem, but dictate the process for working on that problem. Thus, they may dictate that a particular problem solving or critical thinking methodology be used or that particular content domains be "learned." For example, in some problem based learning frameworks, the problem is presented along with the learning objectives and the assigned readings related to the problem. Thus, the student is told what to study and what to learn in relation to the problem. Clearly, with this pre-specification of activities, the students are not going to be engaged in authentic thinking and problem solving in that domain. Rather than being a stimulus for problem solving and self-directed learning, the problem serves merely as an example. The teacher's role should be to challenge the learner's thinking—not to dictate or attempt to proceduralize that thinking.

6. Design the learning environment to support and challenge the learner's thinking. While we advocate giving the learner ownership of the problem and the solution process, it is not the case that *any* activity or *any* solution is adequate. Indeed, the critical goal is to support the learner in becoming an effective worker/thinker in the particular domain. The teacher must assume the roles of consultant and coach. The most critical teaching activity is in the questions the teacher asks the learner in that consulting and coaching activity. It is essential that the teacher *value as well as*

---

[2]Let us hasten to add that many simulation environments are not designed to engage the learner in the problems they are addressing. This is a design issue, not a natural component of a particular instructional strategy.

challenge the learner's thinking. The teacher must not take over thinking for the learner by telling the learner what to do or how to think, but rather teaching should be done by inquiring at the "leading edge" of the learner's thinking (Fosnot, 1989). This is different from the widely used Socratic method wherein the teacher has the "right" answer and it is the student's task to guess/deduce through logical questioning that correct answer. The concept of a learning scaffold and the zone of proximal development, as described by Vygotsky (1978), is a more accurate representation of the learning exchange/interaction between the teacher and the student.

Learners use information resources (all media types) and instructional materials (all media types) as sources of information. The materials do not teach, but rather support the learners' inquiry or performance. This does not negate any kind of instructional resource—it only specifies the reason for using the resource. Thus, if domain specific problem solving is the skill to be learned, then a simulation which confronts the learner with problem situations within that domain might be appropriate. If proficient typing is required for some larger context, certainly a drill and practice program is one option that might be present.

7. Encourage testing ideas against alternative views and alternative contexts. Knowledge is socially negotiated. The quality or depth of one's understanding can only be determined in a social environment where we can see if our understanding can accommodate the issues and views of others and to see if there are points of view which we could usefully incorporate into our understanding. The importance of a learning community where ideas are discussed and understanding enriched is critical to the design of an effective learning environment. The use of collaborative learning groups as a part of the overall learning environment we have described provides one strategy for achieving this learning community (CTGV, 1994; Cunningham, Duffy, & Knuth, 1991; Scardamalia *et al.*, 1992). Other projects support collaboration by linking learners over electronic communication networks as they work on a common task; e.g., CoVis (Edelson & O'Neil, 1994), LabNet (Ruopp *et al.*, 1993), provide an alternative framework.

8. Provide opportunity for and support reflection on both the content learned and the learning process. An important goal of instruction is to develop skills of self-regulation—to become independent. Teachers should model reflective thinking throughout the learning process and support the learners in reflecting on the strategies for learning as well as what was learned (Clift, Houston, & Pugach, 1990; Schön, 1987).

In the next section we will explore how these eight instructional principles are realized in the problem-based learning approach.

Problem Based Learning

The instructional design principles, implemented within the framework of the values outlined by Lebow (1993), can lead to a wide variety of learning environments. A number of environments reflecting these principles are described in Duffy and Jonassen (1992) and Duffy, Lowyck, and Jonassen (1993). Further, the elaboration and application of these principles to specific contexts is described in Brooks and Brooks (1993), Duffy (in press), and Fosnot (1989). In our own examination of learning environments, however, we have found one application that seems to us to almost ideally capture the principles—the problem based learning model of Howard Barrows (1985, 1992).

Problem Based Learning (PBL), as a general model, was developed in medical education in the mid-1950's, and since that time it has been refined and implemented in over sixty medical schools. The most widespread application of the PBL approach has been in the first two years of medical science curricula, where it replaces the traditional lecture based approach to anatomy, pharmacology, physiology etc.. The model has been adopted in an increasing number of other areas, including business schools (Milter & Stinson, 1994), schools of education (Bridges & Hallinger, 1992; Duffy, 1994); architecture, law, engineering, social work (Boud & Feletti, 1991); and high school (Barrows & Myers, 1993).

As with any instructional model, there are many strategies for implementing PBL. Rather than attempting to provide a general characterization of PBL, we would like to focus on Barrows' model (Barrows, 1992) to provide a concrete sense of the implementation of this process in medical school. First we will present a general scenario, using the medical environment as the focus, and then examine some of the key elements in some detail.

When students enter medical school, typically they are divided into groups of five, and each group is assigned a facilitator. The students are then presented a problem in the form of a patient entering with presenting symptoms. The students' task is to diagnose the patient and to provide a rationale for that diagnosis and a recommended treatment. The process for working on the problem is outlined in Figure 1. The following paragraphs cover the highlights of that process.

The students begin the problem "cold"—they do not know what the problem will be until it is presented. They discuss the problem, generating hypotheses based on whatever experience or knowledge they have, identifying relevant facts in the case, and identifying learning issues. The learning issues are topics of any sort deemed of potential relevance to this problem and which the group members feel they do not understand as well as they should. A session is not complete until each student had an opportunity to verbally reflect on his or her current beliefs about the diagnosis (i.e., commit to a temporary position), and assume responsibility for particular learning issues that were identified. Note that there are no pre-specified objectives presented to the students. The students generate the learning issues (objectives) based on their analysis of the problem.

After the session, the students all engage in self-directed learning. There are no assigned texts. Rather, the students are totally responsible for gathering the information from the available medical library and computer database resources. Additionally, particular faculty are designated to be available as consultants (as they would be for any physician in the real world). The students may go to the consultants, seeking information.

After self-directed learning, the students meet again. They begin by evaluating resources—what was most useful and what was not so useful. They then begin working on the problem with this new level of understanding. Note that they do not simply tell what they learned. Rather, they use that learning in re-examining the problem. This cycle may repeat itself if new learning issues arise—problems in the medical school program last anywhere from a week to three weeks.

Milter and Stinson (1994) use a similar approach in an MBA program at Ohio University, and there the problems last between five and eight weeks (see also Stinson, 1994). In our own implementation, we are using one problem that lasts the entire semester. Of course, in the MBA program and in our own, the problems have multiple sub-problems that engage the students.

Assessment at the end of the process is in terms of peer- and self-evaluation. There are no tests in the medical school curriculum. The assessment includes evaluation (with suggestions for improvement) in three areas: self-directed learning, problem solving, and skills as a group member. While the students must pass the Medical Board exam after two years, this is outside of the curriculum structure.[3] However, tests as part of the PBL curriculum are not precluded. For example, one

[3]PBL students do as well as traditional students in a variety of discipline areas on standard or Board qualifying exams. The PBL students seem to retain their knowledge longer after the exam than students in traditional classes (Boud & Feletti, 1991; Bridges & Hallinger, 1992).

STARTING A NEW CLASS
1. Introductions
2. Climate Setting (including teacher / tutor role)

STARTING A NEW PROBLEM
1. Set the problem.
2. Bring the problem home (students internalize problem)
3. Describe the product / performance required
4. Assign tasks (Scribe 1 at the board, Scribe 2 copying from the board, and reference person)

IDEAS (Hypotheses)	FACTS	LEARNING ISSUES	ACTION PLAN
Students' conjectures regarding the problem--may involve causation, effect, possible resolutions, etc.	A growing synthesis of information obtained through inquiry, important to the hypotheses generated	Students' list of what they need to know or understand in order to complete the problem task	Things that need to be done in order to complete the problem task

5. Reasoning through the problem
What you do with the columns on the board

IDEAS (Hypotheses)	FACTS	LEARNING ISSUES	ACTION PLAN
Expand / focus	Synthesize & re-synthesize	Identify / justify	Formulate plan

6. Commitment as to probable outcome (although much may need to be learned)
7. Learning issue shaping/assignment
8. Resource identification
9. Schedule follow-up

PROBLEM FOLLOW-UP
1. Resources used and their critique
2. Reassess the problem
What you do with the columns on the board

IDEAS (Hypotheses)	FACTS	LEARNING ISSUES	ACTION PLAN
Revise	Apply new knowledge and re-synthesize	Identify new (if necessary)	Redesign decisions

PERFORMANCE PRESENTATION

AFTER CONCLUSION OF PROBLEM
1. Knowledge abstraction and summary (develop definitions, diagrams, lists, concepts, abstractions, principles)
2. Self-evaluation (followed by comments from the group)
   - reasoning through the problem
   - digging out information using good resources
   - assisting the group with its tasks
   - gaining or refining knowledge

Figure 1. The Problem Based Learning process.

Taken from Barrows and Myers (1993).

---

high school teacher we know who uses the PBL approach designs traditional tests based on what the students have identified as learning issues. Thus, rather than a pre-specification of what is to be learned, the assessment focuses on the issues the learners have identified.

That is an overview of the process in the medical school. Now we will comment on a few of the critical features.

Learning goals. The design of this environment is meant to simulate, and hence engage the learner in, the problem solving behavior that it is hoped a practicing physician would be engaged in. Nothing is simplified or pre-specified for the learner. The facilitator assumes a major role in modeling the metacognitive thinking associated with the problem solving process. Hence this is a cognitive apprenticeship environment with scaffolding designed to support the learner in developing the metacognitive skills.

Within the context of this cognitive apprenticeship environment, there are goals related to self-directed learning, content knowledge, and problem solving. To be successful, students must develop the self-directed learning skills needed in the medical field. They must be able to develop strategies for identifying learning issues and locating, evaluating, and learning from resources relevant to that issue. The entire problem solving process is designed to aid the students in developing the hypothetico-deductive problem solving model which centers around hypothesis generation and evaluation. Finally, there are specific content learning objectives associated with each problem. Since the students have responsibility for the problem, there is no guarantee that all of the content area objectives will be realized in a given problem. However, any given content objective occurs in several problems, and hence if it does not arise in one, it will almost certainly arise in one of the other problems.

Problem Generation. There are two guiding forces in developing problems. First, the problems must raise the concepts and principles relevant to the content domain. Thus, the process begins with first identifying the primary concepts or principles that a student must learn. Milter and Stinson working in the MBA program and Barrows working with medical education polled the faculty to identify the most important concepts or principles in their area. This, of course, generates considerable debate and discussion—it is not a matter of a simple survey. In developing high school PBL curricula, Myers and Barrows (personal communication) used the learning objectives identified by the state for grade and content domains.

Second, the problems must be "real." In the medical school, the patients are real patients. Indeed, Barrows worked with the presenting physician in gathering the details on the case. Milter and Stinson in the MBA program use problems such as "Should AT&T buy NCR?" These problems change each year so as to address current business issues. At the high school level, Myers and Barrows have developed problems such as:

- Do asteroids in space pose a problem, and if so, what should we be doing about it?
- What caused the flooding in the Midwest in 1993 and what should be done to prevent it in the future?

We are still developing problems and sub-problems for our Corporate and Community Education program. One of the problems currently being developed relates to the numerous PCB sites around Bloomington,

Indiana, and the general public apathy about cleaning up these sites. The problem is basically:

- What do citizens need to know about the PCB problem and how should that information be presented to encourage them to be active citizens in the discussion?

There are three reasons why the problems must address real issues. First, because the students are open to explore all dimension of the problem, there is real difficulty in creating a rich problem with a consistent set of information. Second, real problems tend to engage learners more—there is a larger context of familiarity with the problem. Finally, students want to know the outcome of the problem—what is being done about the flood, did AT&T buy NCR, what was the problem with the patient? These outcomes are not possible with artificial problems.

Problem Presentation. There are two critical issues involved in presenting the problem. First, if the students are to engage in authentic problem solving, then they must own the problem. We have been learners with the Asteroid Problem and we have been facilitators in two contexts: with a group of high school students and with a group of our peers who were attending a workshop to learn about constructivism. In all three cases, the learners were thoroughly engaged in the problem. Frankly, we were amazed at the generality across these disparate groups. In presenting this problem, we used a 10-minute video that described asteroids and showed the large number of sites on earth where they have hit and the kind of impact they can have (the diamond fields in South Africa, the possibility that an asteroid caused the extinction of dinosaurs, Crater Lake, etc.) We also talked about recent near misses—one in Alabama within the last year and one three years ago that could have hit Australia or Russia. Thus, the problem clearly has potential cataclysmic effects (we have past history) and it is a current real problem (we have had near misses quite recently).[4] This step in the PBL process of "bringing the problem home" is critical. The learners must perceive the problem as a real problem and one which has personal relevance. Of course, also central is the fact that the learners have ownership of the problem—they are not just trying to figure out what *we* want.

A second critical issue in presenting the problem is to be certain that the data presented do not highlight critical factors in the case. Too often when problems are presented, the only information that is provided is

---

[4]The potential value of real-world problems in terms of sustained learning and potential impact on interest in the news is illustrated in terms of the 1994 collisions of asteroids with Jupiter. Once having engaged in the asteroid "problem," news concerning asteroid events takes on considerably greater significance.

the key information relevant to the desired solution (end-of-chapter "problems" are notorious for this). Either the case must be richly presented or presented only as a basic question. For example, Honebein, Marrero, Kakos-Kraft, and Duffy (1994) present all of the medical notes on a patient, while Barrows (1985) provides answers generated by the presenting physician to any of 270 questions the learners might ask. In contrast, Milter and Stinson (1994) present only a four-word question and rely on natural resources to provide the full context.

Facilitator Role. In his discussion of the tutorial process, Barrows states:

> The ability of the tutor to use facilitory teaching skills during the small group learning process is the major determinant of the quality and the success of any educational method aimed at (1) developing students' thinking or reasoning skills (problem solving, metacognition, critical thinking) as they learn, and (2) helping them to become independent, self-directed learners (learning to learn, learning management). Tutoring is a teaching skill central to problem-based, self-directed learning. (1992, p. 12)

Throughout a session, the facilitator models higher order thinking by asking questions which probe students' knowledge deeply. To do this, the facilitator constantly asks "Why?" "What do you mean?" "How do you know that's true?" Barrows is adamant that the facilitators' interactions with the students be at a metacognitive level (except for housekeeping tasks) and that the facilitator avoid expressing an opinion or giving information to the students. The facilitator does not use his or her knowledge of the content to ask questions that will lead the learners to the "correct" answer.

A second tutor role is to challenge the learners' thinking. The facilitator (and hopefully the other students in this collaborative environment) will constantly ask: "Do you know what that means? What are the implications of that? Is there anything else?" Superficial thinking and vague notions do not go unchallenged. During his introduction of the Asteroid Problem, Barrows noted for the group that saying nothing about another member's facts or opinions was the same as saying "I agree." Similarly, the responsibility for a flawed medical diagnosis was shared by everyone in the group. During the first few PBL sessions, the facilitator challenges both the level of understanding and the relevance and completeness of the issues studied. Gradually, however, the students take over this role themselves as they become effective self-directed learners.

Conclusion

Our goal in this article was to present PBL as a detailed instructional model and to show how PBL is

consistent with the principles of instruction arising from constructivism. We sought to provide a clear link between theory and practice. Some of the features of the PBL environment are that the learners are actively engaged in working at tasks and activities that are authentic to the environment in which they would be used. The focus is on learners as constructors of their own knowledge in a context similar to that in which they would apply that knowledge. Students are encouraged and expected to think both critically and creatively and to monitor their own understanding, i.e., function at a metacognitive level. Social negotiation of meaning is an important part of the problem-solving team structure and the facts of the case are only facts when the group decides they are.

PBL, as we have described it, contrasts with a variety of other problem or case based approaches. Most case based learning strategies (Williams, 1992) use cases as a means for testing one's understanding. The case is presented after the topic is covered in order to help test understanding and support synthesis. In contrast, in PBL, all of the learning arises out of consideration of the problem. From the start, the learning is synthesized and organized in the context of the problem.

Other case approaches simply use the case as a concrete reference point for learning. Learning objectives and resources are presented along with the case. These approaches use the case as an "example" and are not focused on developing the metacognitive skills associated with problem solving or with professional life. The contrast is perhaps that the PBL approach is a cognitive apprenticeship focusing on both the knowledge domain and the problem solving associated with that knowledge domain or profession. Other problem approaches present cases so that critical attributes are highlighted, thus emphasizing the content domain, but not engaging the learner in authentic problem solving in that domain.

Finally, this is not a Socratic process, nor is it a kind of limited discovery learning environment in which the goal for the learner is to "discover" the outcome the instructor *wants*. The learners have ownership of the problem. The facilitation is not knowledge driven; rather, it is focused on metacognitive processes.

References

Barrows, H. S. (1985). *How to design a problem based curriculum for the preclinical years.* New York: Springer Publishing Co.

Barrows, H. S. (1986). A taxonomy of problem based learning methods. *Medical Education, 20,* 481–486.

Barrows, H. S. (1992). *The tutorial process.* Springfield, IL: Southern Illinois University School of Medicine.

Barrows, H. S., & Myers, A. C. (1993). *Problem based learning in secondary schools.* Unpublished monograph.

Springfield, IL: Problem Based Learning Institute, Lanphier High School, and Southern Illinois University Medical School.

Bereiter, C. (1994). Implications of Postmodernism for science, or, science as progressive discourse. *Educational Psychologist, 29*, 3–12.

Blumenfeld, P. C., Soloway, E., Marx, R. W., Krajcik, J. S., Guzdial, M., & Palincsar, A. (1991). Motivating project-based learning: Sustaining the doing, supporting the learning. *Educational Psychologist, 26* (3&4), 369–398.

Boud, D., & Feletti, G. (Eds.) (1991). *The challenge of problem based learning*. New York: St. Martin's Press.

Bridges, E., & Hallinger, P. (1992). *Problem based learning for administrators*. ERIC Clearinghouse on Educational Management, University of Oregon.

Brooks, J. G., & Brooks, M. G. (1993). *In search of understanding: The case for constructivist classrooms*. Alexandria, VA: Association for Supervision and Curriculum Development.

Brown, J. S., Collins, A., & Duguid, P. (1989). Situated cognition and the culture of learning. *Educational Researcher, 18(1)*, 32–42.

Clift, R., Houston, W., & Pugach, M. (Eds.), (1990). *Encouraging reflective practice in education*. New York: Teachers College Press.

Cognition & Technology Group at Vanderbilt. (1992). Technology and the design of generative learning environments. In T. M. Duffy & D. H. Jonassen (Eds.), *Constructivism and the technology of instruction: A conversation*. Hillsdale, NJ: Lawrence Erlbaum Associates. Originally in *Educational Technology*, 1991, *31*(5).

Cognition & Technology Group at Vanderbilt. (1994). From visual word problems to learning communities: Changing conceptions of cognitive research. In K. McGilly (Ed.), *Classroom lessons: Integrating cognitive theory and classroom practice*. Cambridge, MA: MIT Press/Bradford Books.

Cohen, E. (1994). Restructuring the classroom: Conditions for productive small groups. *Review of Educational Research, 64*, 1–35.

Collins, A., Brown, J. S., & Newman, S. E. (1989). Cognitive apprenticeship: Teaching the crafts of reading, writing, and mathematics. In L.B. Resnick (Ed.), *Knowing, learning, and instruction: Essays in honor of Robert Glaser* (pp. 453–494). Hillsdale, NJ: Lawrence Erlbaum Associates.

Cunningham, D. J., Duffy, T. M., & Knuth, R. A. (1991). The textbook of the future. In C. McKnight, A. Dillon, & J. Richardson (Eds.), *Hypertext: A psychological perspective*. London: Horwood Publishing.

Dewey, J. (1938). *Logic: The theory of inquiry*. New York: Holt and Co.

Duffy, T. M. (1994). *Corporate and community education: Achieving success in the information society*. Unpublished paper. Bloomington, IN: Indiana University.

Duffy, T. M. (in press). *Strategic teaching frameworks: An instructional model for complex, interactive skills*. To appear in C. Dills & A. Romiszowski (Eds.), *Instructional development*. Englewood Cliffs, NJ: Educational Technology Publications.

Duffy, T. M., & Jonassen, D. H. (Eds.) (1992). *Constructivism and the technology of instruction: A conversation*. Hillsdale, NJ: Lawrence Erlbaum Associates.

Duffy, T. M., Lowyck, J., & Jonassen, D. H. (Eds.) (1993). *Designing environments for constructivist learning*. Berlin: Springer-Verlag.

Edelson, D., & O'Neil, K. (1994). *The CoVis collaboratory notebook: Computer support for scientific inquiry*. Paper presented at the annual meeting of the American Educational Research Association, New Orleans.

Fosnot, C. T. (1989). *Enquiring teachers, enquiring learners. A Constructivist approach to teaching*. New York: Teachers College Press.

Gaffney, J. S., & Anderson, R. C. (1991). Two-tiered scaffolding: Congruent processes of teaching and learning. In E. H. Hiebert (Ed.), *Literacy for a diverse society: Perspectives, practices, & policies*. New York: Teacher College Press.

Honebein, P., Duffy, T. M., & Fishman, B. (1993). Constructivism and the design of learning environments: Context and authentic activities for learning. In T. M. Duffy, J. Lowyck, & D. H. Jonassen (Eds.), *Designing environments for constructivist learning*. Berlin: Springer-Verlag.

Honebein, P., Marrero, D. G., Kakos-Kraft, S., & Duffy, T. M. (1994). *Improving medical students' skills in the clinical care of diabetes*. Paper presented at the annual meeting of the American Diabetes Association, New Orleans.

Johnson, D. W., & Johnson, R. T., (1990). Cooperative learning and achievement. In S. Sharan (Ed.), *Cooperative learning: Theory and practice*. New York: Praeger.

Kagan, S. (1992). *Cooperative learning*. San Juan Capistrano, CA: Kagan Cooperative Learning.

Lebow, D. (1993). Constructivist values for systems design: Five principles toward a new mindset. *Educational Technology Research and Development, 41*, 4–16.

MacDonald, P. J. (1991). Selection of health problems for problem-based curriculum. In D. Boud & G. Feletti (Eds.), *The challenge of problem based learning*. New York: St. Martin's Press.

Milter, R. G., & Stinson, J. E. (1994). Educating leaders for the new competitive environment. In G. Gijselaers, S. Tempelaar, & S. Keizer S. (Eds.), *Educational innovation in economics and business administration: The case of problem-based learning*. London: Kluwer Academic Publishers.

Piaget, J. (1977). *The development of thought: Equilibrium of cognitive structures*. New York: Viking Press.

Resnick, L. B. (1987). Learning in school and out. *Educational Researcher, 16*, 13–20.

Rorty, R. (1991). *Objectivity, relativism, and truth*. Cambridge: Cambridge University Press.

Roschelle, J. (1992). *Reflections on Dewey and technology for situated learning*. Paper presented at annual meeting of the American Educational Research Association, San Francisco.

Ruopp, R., Gal, S., Drayton, B., & Pfister, M. (Eds.) (1993). *LabNet: Toward a community of practice*. Hillsdale, NJ: Lawrence Erlbaum Associates.

Scardamalia, M., & Bereiter, C. (1991). Higher levels of agency for children in knowledge building: A challenge for the design of new knowledge media. *The Journal of the Learning Sciences, 1*, 37–68.

Scardamalia, M., Bereiter, C., Brett, C., Burtis, P. J., Calhoun, & Lea, N. S. (1992). Educational applications of a networked communal database. *Interactive Learning Environments, 2,* 45–71.

Schön, D. A. (1987). *Educating the reflective practitioner.* San Francisco: Jossey-Bass.

Slavin, R. (1990). *Cooperative learning: Theory, research, and practice.* Boston: Allyn and Bacon.

Spiro, R. J., Feltovich, P. L., Jacobson, M. J., & Coulson, R. L. (1992). Cognitive flexibility, constructivism, and hypertext: Random access for advanced knowledge acquisition in ill-structured domains. In T. M. Duffy & D. H. Jonassen (Eds.), *Constructivism and the technology of instruction: A*

conversation. Hillsdale, NJ: Lawrence Erlbaum Associates. Originally in *Educational Technology,* 1991, *31*(5).

Stinson, J. E. (1994). *Can Digital Equipment survive?* Paper presented at the Sixth International Conference on Thinking, Boston, MA.

Williams, S. M., (1992) Putting case-based instruction into context: Examples from legal and medical education. *Journal of the Learning Sciences, 2,* 367–427.

vonGlasersfeld, E. (1989). Cognition, construction of knowledge, and teaching. *Synthese, 80,* 121–140.

Vygotsky, L. S. (1978) *Mind in Society: The development of higher psychological processes.* Cambridge MA: Harvard University Press.

Investing in CREATIVITY: Many Happy Returns

Robert J. Sternberg

Through 12 strategies grounded in the psychology of creativity, teachers can awaken the creative impulse in their students—and in themselves.

Alice is brilliant, but she doesn't have a drop of creative talent in her. Barbara is wonderfully creative, but she does terribly on standardized ability tests.

How many times have we, as teachers, administrators, or parents, heard remarks like these? And how many times have we concluded that abilities, like hieroglyphics, are etched in stone, as inexplicable and immutable as those peculiar markings?

Although there is considerable research literature on the development of critical thinking (for example, Baron and Sternberg 1987, Costa 1985, Nickerson 1994, Nickerson et al. 1985), much less has been written about creative thinking potentials. Yet creative thinking is every bit as malleable as critical thinking.

From my own experience, I know that the overwhelming majority of teachers want to encourage creativity in their students (and in themselves), but often are not sure how to go about it. To help, I will offer a dozen strategies that teachers and administrators may use to encourage creativity. These strategies follow from a psychological theory of creativity—the investment theory (Sternberg and Lubart 1995).

This theory holds that creatively gifted people share a number of characteristics, including certain styles of thinking, motivation, and the right environment. It is consistent, however, with many theories of creativity that teachers would do well to read (for example, Amabile 1983, Boden 1992, Gardner 1994, Ghiselin 1985, Gruber 1981, John-Steiner 1987, Schank 1988, Sternberg 1988a).

Buying Low and Selling High

Like good investors, creative thinkers buy low and sell high. That is, they propose ideas that are like undervalued stocks, ideas that are often summarily rejected by the public at large, and viewed by others as odd, counterproductive, or even foolish. Many people simply do not realize—and often do not want to realize—that these ideas may be valid and perhaps superior to the way they think. They may realize, however, that creative people tend to be somewhat oppositional in nature, and they may find this tendency annoying or even downright offensive.

At any rate, the innovators "invest" in these ideas, bring them to fruition, and attempt to convince others of their worth. Once they succeed in this, they sell high—that is, they leave the idea to others and move on to the next unpopular idea.

In this view, then, creativity is as much an attitude toward life as it is a particular ability. And it is just this kind of creativity that we often see in young children. It is only in older children and adults that it so often is absent, not because they lack the potential, but because creativity has been suppressed by socialization that encourages conformity.

A Three-Way Balance

Viewed another way, creativity requires the application and balancing of three types of abilities—the synthetic, the analytic, and the practical—all of which can be developed

© Jim Richards

(Sternberg 1985, 1988b; Sternberg and Lubert 1995). As educators, we need to promote the attitude that all three of these skills are important.

■ *Synthetic ability* is what we typically think of as creativity: the ability to go beyond the given to generate novel and interesting ideas. Good synthetic thinkers see connections others don't see—they *synthesize*.

■ *Analytic ability* is what we typically think of as critical thinking: the ability to analyze and evaluate ideas, recognizing the good ones, working out their implications, and perhaps testing them.

■ *Practical ability* is the ability to translate theory into practice, to abstract ideas into practical accomplishments. In any organization—schools included—there are entrenched ideas about how things

Creativity is as much an attitude toward life as it is a particular ability.

should be done. The investment theory implies that good ideas do not just sell themselves, but that we must convince others of their worth. A practical thinker also recognizes which of his or her ideas may or may not have an audience at that school.

Strategies by the Dozen

Now to apply our theory to the classroom. Here are 12 strategies that teachers and administrators may use to make students, staff—and themselves—more creative.

1. Serve as a role model for creativity. This is the single most powerful way of developing creativity in your students or staff. Children develop creativity not when you tell them to do so, but when you show them how. Just ask yourself: What teachers do I remember best and which ones most influenced me? You will probably not name those who crammed the most content into their lectures, but instead, those whose ways of thinking and acting you have emulated in your own life. Most likely, they are teachers who balanced content with how to think with and about that content.

2. Encourage questioning of assumptions. We all tend to have assumptions about the way things are or must be. Often, we do not even realize we hold these notions because many of the people we know share them. Creative people not only question assumptions but also lead others to question them as well. (When Copernicus said the Earth revolves around the sun, the statement was viewed as preposterous.)

Teachers can be role models in this respect. Years ago, my 7th grade social studies teacher, Mr. Ast, asked whether there was anyone in the class who did not know what social studies was. When his question was met by silence, he asked us to figure out what social studies really meant. We spent two days examining, questioning, and, in some cases, changing our assumptions about something we thought we knew for sure. The discussion went far beyond mere definition, however, forcing us to question what social phenomena are and how people might go about studying such phenomena.

3. Allow mistakes. Every once in a while, a great thinker comes along—a Freud, a Piaget, a Chomsky, or even an Einstein—and shows us a new way to think. These people were able to make the contributions they made only because they allowed themselves and their collaborators to make mistakes.

Schools, though, tend to be unforgiving of mistakes. When children hand in workbooks with errors, their errors are often marked with a large and pronounced *X*. When they answer a question incorrectly, some teachers pounce on them for not having read or understood the material, and their classmates often snicker. In hundreds of ways, children learn that it's not all right to make mistakes. As a result, they become afraid to err, and thus to risk the kind of independent and sometimes flawed thinking that can lead to creativity. They begin to suppress their natural creativity when, both literally and figuratively, they increasingly are asked to draw within the lines of the coloring book.

4. Encourage sensible risk-taking. When you buy low and sell high, you take a risk. Creative people are *sensible* risk-takers, but in taking risks, they sometimes make mistakes. Schools, for the most part, discourage risk-taking, and children learn early how the system works: To succeed, you must get high grades, and to get high grades, you've got to stay on the straight and narrow.

When my daughter, Sara, was in 3rd grade, her class was studying the planets. The children were to dress up as astronauts and pretend to fly to Mars. Sara wanted to dress up as a Martian and meet the astronauts when they arrived. The teacher, however, told her she couldn't do that because space probes had shown there were no Martians. Lesson: Don't take the risk.

5. Design creative assignments and assessments. If a teacher gives only multiple-choice tests, children will learn quickly enough what is valued—no matter what you say to the contrary. To encourage creativity, you need to include in your assignments and tests at least some opportunities for creative thought. On a psychology test, for example, I may ask students to recognize the basic tenets of theories of depression. But in addition, I will ask them to synthesize these existing theories and produce a new theory by integrating the others with their own ideas. I don't expect perfection, just a serious creative effort.

The same principle can be applied in any course:

■ English—students write short stories, poems, or alternative endings to existing stories.

■ Social studies—students put themselves in the shoes of great historical figures and explain what decisions they would have made, and why. Or, they might speculate on aspects of the future history of the world.

■ Science—students propose their own intuitive theories of phenomena, then design simple experiments or do independent research to support those theories.

■ Mathematics—students invent their own word problems or systems of enumeration or measurement.

■ Foreign languages—students create skits about events in a foreign country, simulating not just the language but the customs.

6. Let students define problems themselves. Allow students to choose their own topics for papers or presentations, and their own ways of solving problems. And sometimes, when they learn they have made the wrong choice, let them choose again. In my courses, I often require several brief papers, and for at least three of these I allow students to choose their own topics, subject to my approval. My only reason for requesting approval is to make sure the topic is in some way relevant to what we are teaching, and that it has at least some chance of leading to a successful product.

7. Reward creative ideas and products. It's not enough to talk about the value of creativity; students are used to teachers and others who say one thing and do another. When I assign papers, I tell my students up front that I will look for the usual things, namely, knowledge, analytical skills, and good writing. But I also tell them that I will look for and reward creativity. The question is not whether I agree with what they say, but whether they go beyond what they have heard or read and come up with new ideas that synthesize others' ideas and their own ways of thinking.

Some teachers complain that they cannot as objectively grade creative responses as they can multiple-choice or short-answer tests. And at one level, they are correct; there *is* some sacrifice of objectivity. But our research and that of others (for example,

Amabile 1983) shows that evaluators are remarkably consistent in assessing creativity. Moreover, our main goal in assessment ought to be instruction—another opportunity for students to learn.

8. Allow time to think creatively. We are a society in a hurry. We love fast-food; we rush from one place to another. To say that someone is quick is one way of saying that person is

smart (see Sternberg 1985)—a sure indication of our values.

In school, our standardized tests tend to present large numbers of problems (usually multiple-choice) to complete in a very short time. Even if someone were allowed to think creatively, how would they find the time? If you stuff questions into exams, or give children so many homework assignments that they scarcely have time to complete any of them, you'll preclude any creative thinking. Contrary to popular myth, most creative insights do not come in a flash; people require time to understand a problem and to toss it around in their heads.

9. Encourage tolerance of ambiguity. Historically in the United States, we have tended to cast matters in black and white. A given country is all good or all bad; an education idea works or doesn't work. But creative ideas, even when worked out, may have their pluses and minuses. Further, the creative process takes time and tends to be uncomfortable: you want the solution now, but have only half of it. Without the time or ability to tolerate ambiguity, you may jump to a less than optimal solution.

10. Point out that creative thinkers invariably face obstacles. Because they have defied the crowd, they are often viewed with suspicion and

perhaps disdain and derision. The question is, will that person persevere in the face of resistance? As a new assistant professor, I gave one of my first colloquiums at an organization that valued—and had a vested interest in—conventional ideas about intelligence. I foolishly believed that they would welcome new ideas. Wrong! The point was not whether my ideas were correct or incorrect—they were

In hundreds of ways, children learn that it's not all right to make mistakes. As a result, they become afraid to risk independent thinking.

different, and my audience simply was not willing to listen.

11. Be willing to grow. Once a person has a major creative idea, it is easy to spend the rest of a career following up on that one idea. It is frightening to contemplate that the next idea may not be as good as this one, or that the success to which you have become accustomed may fade with the next idea. So we stop being creative and become complacent.

Complacency also comes with expertise: we think we know all there is to know, but often are the last to see that the world has passed us by. As teachers and administrators, we are all susceptible to becoming victims of our own expertise—to becoming entrenched in ways of thinking that may have worked for us in the past, but that will not necessarily work for us in the future. Being creative involves a willingness to step outside the boxes that we and others have created for ourselves.

12. Recognize that creative thinkers need to find nurturing environments (See especially Csikszentmihalyi 1988, Gardner 1994). This is as important to the teacher as it is to the student: we all need to find a setting in which our unique creative contributions are rewarded instead of punished. The same lesson, student product, or idea for school reform that praised in one place may be evaluated in another.

This last point goes back to the need to translate ideas into accomplishments. We need to help our students—and ourselves—find a balance among the three components of creativity—the ability to synthesize or see connections among ideas, to analyze ideas, and also to put ideas into practice. This creative *attitude* is at least as important as any creative thinking skills (Schank 1988).

References

Amabile, T. M. (1983). *The Social Psychology of Creativity*. New York: Springer-Verlag.

Baron, J. B., and R. J. Sternberg, eds. (1987). *Teaching Thinking Skills*. New York: Freeman.

Boden, M. (1992). *The Creative Mind: Myths and Mechanisms*. New York: BasicBooks.

Costa, A. L, ed. (1985). *Developing Minds: A Resource for Teaching Thinking*. Alexandria, Va.: Association for Super-vision and Curriculum Development.

Csikszentmihalyi, M. (1988). "Society, Culture, and Person: A Systems View of Creativity." In *The Nature of Creativity*, edited by R. J. Sternberg, pp. 325–339. New York: Cambridge University Press.

Gardner, H. (1994). *Creating Minds*. New York: BasicBooks.

Ghiselin, B., ed. (1985). *The Creative Process: A Symposium*. Berkeley, Calif.: University of California Press.

Gruber, H. (1981). *Darwin on Man: A Psychological Study of Scientific Creativity* (2nd ed.). Chicago: University of Chicago Press.

John-Steiner, V. (1987). *Notebooks of the Mind: Explorations of Thinking*. New York: Harper and Row.

Nickerson, R. S. (1994). "The Teaching of Thinking and Problem Solving." In *Thinking and Problem Solving*, edited by R. J. Sternberg, pp. 409–449. San Diego: Academic Press.

Nickerson, R. S., D. N. Perkins, and E. E. Smith. (1985). *The Teaching of Thinking*. Hillsdale, N.J.: Erlbaum.

Schank, R. C. (1988). *The Creative Attitude*. New York: Macmillan.

Sternberg, R. J. (1985). *Beyond IQ*. New York: Cambridge University Press.

Sternberg, R. J., ed. (1988a). *The Nature of Creativity*. New York: Cambridge University Press.

Sternberg, R. J. (1988b). *The Triarchic Mind*. New York: Viking-Penguin.

Sternberg, R. J., and T. I. Lubart. (1995). *Defying the Crowd: Cultivating Creativity in a Culture of Conformity*. New York: Free Press.

Author's note: Development of this article was supported by a grant under the Javits Act Program, administered by the Office of Educational Research and Improvement, U.S. Department of Education. The article does not necessarily represent U.S. government positions or policies, and no official endorsement should be inferred.

Robert J. Sternberg is IBM Professor of Psychology and Education, Department of Psychology, Yale University, P.O. Box 208205, New Haven, CT 06520-8205 (e-mail: sterobj@yale.vm).

How K–12 Teachers Are Using Computer Networks

[Internet Use in Schools: Observations and Issues]

Jon M. Peha

Jon M. Peha is Assistant Professor, Carnegie Mellon University, Department of Engineering and Public Policy, and Department of Electrical and Computer Engineering, Pittsburgh, PA 15213-3890 (http://www.ece.cmu.edu/afs/ece/usr/peha/peha.htm/)

A Carnegie Mellon University study, conducted in conjunction with the Pittsburgh Public Schools, looks at technology present and technology future.

[Proponents in both government and the telecommunications industry have fueled a growing interest in connecting schools to various regional, national, and international computer networks. Educators must now determine how these networks can be integrated into class room curricula, and how this affects school systems. Ultimately, we must also evaluate the potential benefits, and determine whether they justify the expense. While it is too soon to offer definitive answers to these difficult questions, this paper will present a few pieces of the puzzle. It will describe a wide range of promising classroom activities involving computer networks. Based on feedback from those involved and from direct observation, this paper will describe some of the apparent effects, including both potential benefits

and pitfalls to be avoided. It will also discuss how school systems might provide preparation and support for teachers.] By almost any measure, the world's largest computer network is the Internet. The Internet evolved from a U.S. Defense Department communications system to become an interconnected collection of more than 46,000 independent networks, public and private, around the world (National Science Foundation 1995). Now serving millions of users worldwide, its growth is rapid and exponential.

[Consequently, we focus on programs that bring Internet access to schools.] In 1993, the Pittsburgh Public Schools began such a program, in partnership with the Pittsburgh Supercomputer Center and the University of Pittsburgh, and with funding from the National Science Foundation. At that time, Carnegie Mellon University began a four-month project to aid the Pittsburgh Public Schools in their new endeavor, which was known as Common Knowledge Pittsburgh.

To observe the uses of the Internet in Pittsburgh, our research group surveyed and/or interviewed approximately 45 educators in various positions throughout the school system. Of that number, 24 teachers and 4 librarians from 4 schools attended a professional development workshop on Internet use in classrooms. Of the 28, 14 completed surveys about the effectiveness of that program. We also interviewed students.

In addition, we made numerous observations in one of the four schools participating in the first year of the project, an elementary school in a low income area of Pittsburgh. A comparable number of schools have come online each subsequent year (Carnegie Mellon University 1994).

To catalog what other teachers outside of Pittsburgh were doing with the Internet, we compiled responses from a questionnaire addressed to educators who use the Internet via relevant newsgroups and e-mail distribution lists. We received 21 responses describing 34 distinct classroom activities. Given the small sample size and a method of distributing questionnaires that naturally favors frequent Internet users, our statistics are not terribly meaningful. Our questionnaire was deliberately unstructured, however, to enable recipients to elaborate on their experiences and to share insights about using the Internet. We also conducted unstructured interviews with educators who were using the Internet. To supplement these data, we studied descriptions from the printed literature of roughly 40 classroom activities.

How Students Are Using Computers
Before looking at what we found occurring in classrooms, let's define a few key terms. For many years, three types of traffic have dominated the Internet:

The teachers who responded to our questionnaire offered several ways to overcome difficulties in introducing the Internet in a K–12 curriculum.

■ With *electronic mail*, the most popular tool at all grade levels, a user can quickly send a message to any other user or specified group of users. E-mail can also reach mass audiences when used in conjunction with:

— distribution lists, made up of e-mail addresses of people with shared interests (a list of educational distribution lists is available via anonymous FTP [see below] from nic.umass.edu); or

— newsgroups, also called electronic bulletin boards, where any user interested in a topic may read about it much the same way one reads personal e-mail.

■ *File transfers* (FTPs) allow a user to copy a file (which can contain text, software, pictures, and music) from, or to, another computer system. With a variation, anonymous FTP, a user can copy files without the need for password privileges.

■ *Telnet* allows a user to log onto a remote computer as if it were in the same room. For example, one might telnet onto a system because it has capabilities that the local system lacks.

A number of important tools have also developed in recent years that facilitate the search for information on the Internet, such as Gopher, Archie, Veronica, Mosaic, and, more recently, Netscape. Obviously, such tools are useful only if the network contains useful information. (There is no way to describe all of the resources available on the Internet; see Resources box for five examples.)

The classroom activities that we observed, that educators shared with us, or that we read about in the literature fall into the following broad categories that build on these capabilities.

1. Students send their work to some other party for evaluation or response. The network provides a high-tech postal service, but with no cost per letter, minimal hassle, and most important, a negligible time for the message to reach its destination, which enables meaningful interaction. With pen pal programs, younger students write e-mail messages about themselves and their interests to peers in distant places. There is strong mo-

tivation for students to write good letters because, as one teacher put it, "A good letter writer generally receives good letters." Older students exchange more complex material like stories and artwork, sometimes critiquing one another's work.

Other programs provide a forum to learn about distant events and different ways of life. In one example, inner-city elementary school students corresponded with Native American peers who live on a reservation. E-mail is also sometimes written in a foreign language to both motivate and help students learning that language.

The Internet makes possible communication between students and older students or professionals as well. Some students send their writing samples to professional writers for feedback; others correspond with professional engineers for help with independent science projects. Still other activities link [disabled] students with big brothers and sisters, for example, or connect students from schools where few go on to college with their older counterparts who are in college.

2. Group projects enable students at different locations to collaborate on activities. For example, students can cooperate on tasks like taking temperature and barometric measurements for a weather project or surveying garbage around their schools for an environmental project. Because many of these projects are experimental in nature, students engage in meaningful exploratory science with a large body of data. They gather information locally, and then pool data from around the world. Although they spend a relatively small amount of time collecting their part of the data, students understand how all of the data were collected, and have a sense

of ownership. Other projects show students the value of working in groups, because each classroom is bound to produce ideas that improve the group's solution.

3. Students exploit remote data sources and processing capabilities on the network. Most often, the Internet serves as an enormous library with extraordinary search capabilities. With the growing popularity of new browsing tools, such activities are likely to become more common. The Internet's remote processing capabilities can also be valuable. For example, students can run computationally intensive scientific simulations on a powerful remote computer that cannot be run on the school's inexpensive equipment. Such simulations can also replace expensive (or dangerous) laboratory equipment in the school.

Many educators told us that the Internet allows them to tap information sources on their discipline or on teaching in general, and to correspond with other educators around the world with similar interests. As one teacher said, "When I get the information I'm seeking, I can incorporate some of the activities in my lessons, also advancing my own professionalism."

Figure 1 is a breakdown of activities described in responses to our questionnaire. Although these results are not statistically significant, they do dispel the myth that computers and networks are just for math and the sciences.

How the Internet Benefits the Classroom

Two-thirds of the respondents to our questionnaire said that a primary benefit of the Internet is making students aware that they are part of a global community. Others commented that the Internet gives students a wide variety of resources, stimulates thinking, and improves computer literacy.

From our many observations in the inner-city elementary school in Pittsburgh, an important benefit of using this technology is enthusiasm. Whenever the Internet teacher walked into the room, students appeared hopeful that it would be their turn to use the Internet. Teachers even threatened to revoke a student's computer privileges as a punishment for disruptive behavior. As for teachers, their enthusiasm was unmistakable in both direct interviews and survey responses.

The Internet and other information technology in the classroom, of course, do much more than boost enthusiasm or expand information resources. Internet use fundamentally alters the roles of teachers and students. For example, when students write to impress a pen pal or a distant expert, the teacher is no longer the sole judge of quality, and grades are less of a motivating factor than in traditional classrooms. In addition, many activities require students to work in teams. When students spend class time browsing the Internet rather than listening to a teacher's lecture, they encounter more diverse expert opinions, work more independently, and proceed at their own pace. In fact, we observed that students experiencing computer problems were more likely to consult peers than the teacher. Throughout this process, the teacher becomes more of a facilitator, helping students find information and, more important, figure out what to do with it.

There is also potential to change the role of parents with this technology. For example, during parents' nights, students may be able to teach their parents something new about computers or networks. Doing so can greatly boost a student's self-esteem. Because familiarity with information technology can lead to jobs, schools may also want to expand their efforts to train neighborhood adults after school hours.

When parents have access to this technology at home or at work, they can become more closely involved in

FIGURE 1

How K–12 Teachers Use Computers

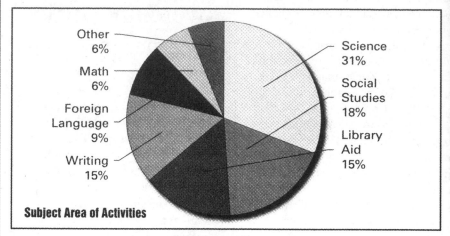

Subject Area of Activities

- Other 6%
- Math 6%
- Foreign Language 9%
- Writing 15%
- Science 31%
- Social Studies 18%
- Library Aid 15%

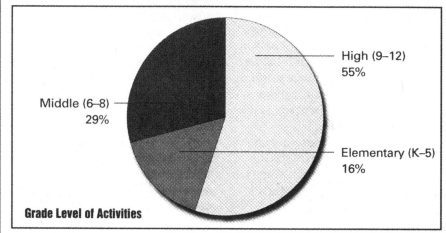

Grade Level of Activities

- High (9–12) 55%
- Middle (6–8) 29%
- Elementary (K–5) 16%

their children's education. Many parents already have Internet access at work. Thirty-five percent of U.S. households now have computers, and those with children are more likely to have computers than those without, even families on a somewhat limited budget. Of households with children and total annual incomes under $30,000, 30 percent have computers. Given that consumer spending on home computers now exceeds spending on televisions, these percentages should continue to rise quickly (Negroponte 1995). All it takes is a telephone line and a modem to connect a home computer to the network. More important, because there will always be parents without home computers, some states and municipalities are bringing network capabilities to all of their

citizens. In Seattle, for example, even the homeless will be able to communicate over the network by getting an account from the city, using it in libraries and other public buildings.

How to Overcome Difficulties

The teachers who responded to our questionnaire offered several ways to overcome difficulties in introducing the Internet in a K–12 curriculum. Four suggestions in particular surfaced frequently:

1. Be specific about expectations and objectives. By providing deadlines for activities and for intermediate milestones, teachers can keep students moving in the right direction.

2. Search the Internet yourself before asking students to. As one teacher said, "Know what to look for in advance, so you and your students will not be disappointed."

3. Allow ample time. "Realize that it will take twice as much time as you have budgeted," suggested one teacher. Another offered, "Have students work in groups to speed up the process."

4. Establish a commitment with other parties involved in an activity. As one teacher urged, "There is nothing worse than getting a project organized or planning one into your lesson plans and then no mail arrives from your partners or people start dropping out."

Teachers also identified three difficulties not entirely within their control. First, 40- to 50-minute class periods limit students' ability to engage in unstructured tasks. Allowing time for longer activities, therefore, may require creative structuring of the school day. Second, some teachers must overcome a lack of hardware, telephone lines, or accounts. Finally, lack of time for teachers to explore the Internet is a problem. The Internet's resources are vast, and the tools change from year to year. Keeping up is not easy. Things will improve when more principals and others understand the value of the Internet, and the importance of teacher time spent exploring it.

Probably the most disturbing problem came out in direct interviews with teachers who were not part of the Pittsburgh project. Not only are rewards for innovative teachers often small, but some principals and teachers actually discourage resourceful teachers from disrupting the status quo. The reasons for such opposition may include two fears: that benefits will be small and not worth the effort, and that benefits will be great, so other teachers will be expected to keep up.

Although our respondents did not mention the next problem, it has the potential to seriously disrupt efforts to bring the Internet to classrooms. Students using the Internet, like students wandering the Library of Congress, may look at something their parents would prefer they not see—for

---

Resources Available on the Internet: Some Examples

1. The Educational Resources Information Center (ERIC) provides information on curriculums, professional development, teaching methods, and educational materials. Telnet to acsnet.syr.edu, login: suvm, userid: suinfo. An ERIC gopher is also available.

2. The NASA Spacelink offers an interactive database with lesson plans, science activities, and NASA flight information. Telnet to spacelink.msfc.nasa.gov; username: newuser.

3. Digital images highlighting the photography of the Smithsonian Institution are available via anonymous FTP from photo1.si.edu.

4. Worldwide meteorological data (including forecasts, records, and storm warnings) are available. Telnet to hurricane.ncdc.noaa.gov, login: storm; password: research.

5. The Library of Congress Information System (LOCIS) contains more than 15 million catalog records. Telnet to locis.loc.gov; no password is necessary.

---

example, sexually explicit material. Topics like drugs, politics, religion, abortion, and homosexuality may also stir controversy.

In June 1995, the U.S. Senate attempted to address a part of this problem by approving an amendment to the telecommunications bill that would prohibit the flow of "indecent" material (not limited to pornography) on the Internet. Aside from the serious civil rights implications of such censorship, it would not even prevent the distribution of pornography on this network of millions of users around the world, any one of whom can provide such information.

In April 1995, the Washington State legislature found a more drastic solution to protect minors from objectionable material: they made it illegal to give minors Internet access. (An even more effective solution would be to prohibit minors from learning to read.) The governor vetoed the bill.

Schools can take some precautions—for example, not carrying obviously troublesome newsgroups on local servers. And new information-filtering tools are coming. There is really no way, however, to prevent a bright, determined student from finding something he or she wants to see. Constant teacher supervision is one solution, but it is time-consuming and would deter curious exploration.

The best approach is to develop a

written policy stating what does and does not constitute acceptable student usage of the Internet. In general, Internet usage should relate to coursework. Both students and parents must agree to this policy before gaining access. While such a strategy does not prevent abuse, it does make it easier to revoke the privileges of students who violate the policy, and it brings parents into the discussion from the beginning.

About Teacher Preparation and Support

Before adopting the Internet, a school system must determine how much preparation and ongoing support to provide. Two-thirds of the respondents to our questionnaire survived without any formal training, relying instead on printed literature and experimentation, or as one person described it, "blood, sweat, and tears."

Common Knowledge Pittsburgh developed a professional development workshop for teachers and librarians that participants generally found quite successful. The primary goal was to give them the problem-solving skills to become explorers of the Internet, rather than teaching them facts or rote methods. Because Internet tools and resources are constantly changing, teachers must have the ability to adapt—a view echoed by several respondents to our questionnaire.

The workshop, held in June 1993,

provided 24 teachers and 4 librarians with 13 hours of instruction over two and a half days. Participants worked in pairs to promote brainstorming and to make the task less intimidating. They used a variety of tools ranging from newsgroups to Gopher, and explored resources that workshop organizers thought might be useful, like the NASA library (see box, Resources Available on the Internet: Some Examples). To test their newfound skills, they participated in a scavenger hunt for information on the Internet.

After this session, workshop organizers helped participants set up borrowed school computer equipment in their own homes to experiment during the summer. Finally, the workshop reconvened in August for 10 hours of additional instruction over a two-day period. In addition to learning more about the Internet, participants discussed possible lesson plans.

As noted earlier, 14 workshop participants responded to our survey. Every respondent agreed that the teaching methods were effective; only one person did not yet feel capable of teaching the Internet to students, with two people unsure. All found the workshop informative, and almost all would recommend it to a colleague.

Because a primary goal of this workshop was to encourage exploration, that issue deserves special consideration. After a few months into the school year, nearly half of the participants had done three or more Gopher searches in the week we surveyed them, but two people indicated that they were no longer exploring the Internet. Despite the popularity of the workshop, participants indicated that they learned only about half of the information on the Internet from workshop instructors. That finding would seem to corroborate the importance of independent exploration.

How would the Pittsburgh educators improve the workshop? They were about evenly split on the need for more step-by-step instruction time, but expressed a pressing need for more exploration time.

Because one can't afford to stop learning about the Internet, ongoing support may also be important. In answer to the questionnaire we sent to network users around the world, teachers indicated that Internet guides, newsgroups, and distribution lists are very helpful. Personal support is also needed at times.

In Pittsburgh, teachers turned to their fellow teachers most often, with the centralized support staff a close second. This finding is important because widescale adoption is possible only if teachers help one another; a centralized support staff can't be everywhere.

When asked about other kinds of ongoing technical assistance, teachers who responded to the questionnaire most often mentioned classroom visits by Internet instructors, monthly meetings of Internet users, and online support.

The Future

Teachers have only begun to exploit existing capabilities of network technology in schools. Indeed, the majority of classroom activities that we've observed use only Internet tools that are more than two decades old, like basic e-mail. As noted, tools such as Mosaic and Netscape greatly facilitate the process of finding information on the Internet.

People are also experimenting with more interactive applications. For example, the Internet has been used for person-to-person video teleconferences, and to broadcast part of a Rolling Stones concert live.

Moreover, new networks are coming based on ATM (asynchronous transfer mode) technology. Although such things are possible to a limited degree on the Internet, ATM networks

are better able to support applications where intermittent disruptions are noticeable to the user, like using a telephone, playing interactive games with a distant player, or controlling a laboratory experiment at a remote site. ATM networks can also transmit data at a rapid rate, allowing users to watch broadcast-quality video or better on demand, to quickly retrieve a series of images from the space shuttle's tele-

> To reduce installation costs, new schools should be wired for computers and networks when they are built, just as commercial office spaces are.

scope or the complete works of Shakespeare, or to use sophisticated visualization tools to watch changing weather patterns in the area. Recently, North Carolina deployed a statewide ATM network to which schools will have access.

Although the growth of Internet use in classrooms is encouraging, schools have not been keeping up with any of the commercial sectors in adopting new information technology—so it is not clear whether technical advances alone will be beneficial for learning. An obvious obstacle is money. However, 97 percent of American schools already have some computers (Wheland 1995), and adding a low-speed Internet connection is no more expensive than adding a telephone line. Still, many of these computers are not integrated into the curriculum in a meaningful way, other than one designed specifically to teach about computers. While funding is certainly an issue—and more conclusive proof is needed that money spent on Internet access is more beneficial than money spent elsewhere—increased funding alone is unlikely to lead to productive use of information technology.

To truly exploit these advances, technology and innovation must permeate the culture of education. Teachers should be exposed to technology early in their careers, and should be actively encouraged to keep up on continual advances. To reduce installation costs, new schools should be wired for computers and networks when they are built, just as commercial office spaces are. Districts should hire staff who can help schools build and troubleshoot computer and network systems. Teachers must be given freedom and encouragement to experiment with technology.

Common Knowledge Pittsburgh, now operating in 14 schools, is currently funded through December 1997. The Pittsburgh Public Schools

are showing that more teachers will choose to bring technology into the classroom when given both resources and encouragement.

References

Carnegie Mellon University. (1994). "The Internet in K–12 Education." Pittsburgh: Carnegie Mellon University.

National Science Foundation. (April 26, 1995). "NSF-MCI Background on the Internet/NSFnet." NSF Press Release.

Negroponte, N. (February 11, 1995). "homeless@info.hwy.net." *New York Times*, A15.

Wheland, R. (February 1995). U.S. Department of Education, personal communications.

Author's note: To order "The Internet in K–12 Education," send $12.40, or $16.60 from outside the U.S., to Department Receptionist, Department of Engineering and Public Policy, Carnegie Mellon University, Pittsburgh, PA 15213.

Jon M. Peha is Assistant Professor, Carnegie Mellon University, Department of Engineering and Public Policy, and Department of Electrical and Computer Engineering, Pittsburgh, PA 15213-3890 (e-mail: peha@ece.cmu.edu).

Motivation and Classroom Management

- Motivation (Articles 32–34)
- Classroom Management and Discipline (Articles 35–38)

The term *motivation* is used by educators to describe the processes of initiating, directing, and sustaining goal-oriented behavior. Motivation is a complex phenomenon, involving many factors that affect an individual's choice of action and perseverance in completing tasks. Furthermore, the reasons why people engage in particular behaviors can only be inferred; motivation cannot be directly measured.

Several theories of motivation, each highlighting different reasons for sustained goal-oriented behavior, have been proposed. We will discuss three of them: behavioral, humanistic, and cognitive. The behavioral theory of motivation suggests that an important reason for engaging in behavior is that reinforcement follows the action. If the reinforcement is controlled by someone else and is arbitrarily related to the behavior (such as money, a token, or a smile), then the motivation is extrinsic. In contrast, behavior may also be initiated and sustained for intrinsic reasons such as curiosity or mastery.

Humanistic approaches to motivation are concerned with the social and psychological needs of individuals. Humans are motivated to engage in behavior to meet these needs. Abraham Maslow, a founder of humanistic psychology, proposes that there is a hierarchy of needs that directs behavior, beginning with physiological and safety needs and progressing to self-actualization. Other important needs that influence motivation are affiliation and belonging with others, love, self-esteem, influence with others, recognition, status, competence, achievement, and autonomy.

The dominant view of motivation in the educational psychology literature is the cognitive approach. This set of theories proposes that our beliefs about our success and failure affect our expectations and goals concerning future performance. Students who believe that their success is due to their ability and effort are motivated toward mastery of skills. Students who blame their failures on inadequate abilities have low self-efficacy and tend to set ability and performance goals that protect their self-image. Alfie Kohn, in the first selection, argues that one important way to help eliminate student apathy is to allow students to make decisions about their own learning. Kohn provides a rationale for incorporating more opportunities for student choice in the classroom. Next, Deborah Stipek echoes the importance of allowing children to set their own goals. She also discusses other techniques to encourage more effort on academic tasks. Finally, Rachel Collopy and Theresa Green describe how one elementary school has changed in response to the dramatic findings of achievement goal theory. The school they created emphasizes learning rather than relative ability.

No matter how effectively students are motivated, teachers always need to exercise management of behavior in the classroom. Classroom management is more than controlling the behavior of students or disciplining them following misbehavior. Instead, teachers need to initiate and maintain a classroom environment that supports successful teaching and learning. The skills that effective teachers use include preplanning, deliberate introduction of rules and procedures, immediate assertiveness, continual monitoring, consistent feedback to students, and specific consequences.

The first three articles of the next subsection describe the most current thinking about the new forms of classroom management that will be required to meet the needs of learning-centered classrooms. H. James McLaughlin argues that teachers need to shift from management metaphors of obedience to negotiation. In "Images of Management for Learner-Centered Classrooms," Catherine Randolph and Carolyn Evertson suggest that the management of instruction and the management of behavior become enmeshed in learning-centered classrooms. Their metaphor for classroom management is orchestration. Then, practical principles that create a socio-moral atmosphere appropriate for a learning-centered classroom are explained by Rheta DeVries and Betty Zan in their article.

The last selection in this unit addresses a disciplinary issue facing educators today: violence in schools. David Johnson and Roger Johnson argue that violence prevention needs to focus on helping students resolve conflicts in appropriate ways, such as using peer mediation. The adults in schools, too, need to model constructive ways to resolve conflicts by eliminating corporal punishment.

Looking Ahead: Challenge Questions

Discuss several ways to motivate both at-risk and typical students. What difference is there?

How are motivation and classroom management related?

How are classroom management and discipline different? Discuss whether discipline can be developed within students, or whether it must be imposed by teachers. Support your argument with data derived from your reading.

Choices for Children:
Why and How to Let Students Decide

The key to transforming student apathy into student engagement, Mr. Kohn suggests, may be as simple as allowing students to make decisions about their learning.

....

ALFIE KOHN

ALFIE KOHN, who writes and lectures widely on education and human behavior, lives in Cambridge, Mass. His books include Punished by Rewards: The Trouble with Gold Stars, Incentive Plans, A's, Praise, and Other Bribes *(Houghton Mifflin, 1993), a newly revised edition of* No Contest: The Case Against Competition *(Houghton Mifflin, 1992), and* The Brighter Side of Human Nature *(Basic Books, 1990).*

The essence of the demand for freedom is the need of conditions which will enable an individual to make his own special contribution to a group interest, and to partake of its activities in such ways that social guidance shall be a matter of his own mental attitude, and not a mere authoritative dictation of his acts.

— John Dewey
Democracy and Education

EDUCATORS ARE painfully well acquainted with the phenomenon known as "burnout." Some days it seems that the bulbs have gone out in most faculty lounges and administration buildings. But what if, hypothetically speaking, this syndrome also affected students?

How would *they* talk and act? Teachers around the country to whom I have put this question immediately suggest such symptoms as disengagement and apathy — or, conversely, thoughtlessness and aggression. Either tuning out or acting out might signal that a student was burning out. In both cases, he or she would presumably just go through the motions of learning, handing in uninspired work and counting the minutes or days until freedom.

Of course, no sooner is this sketch of a hypothetical student begun than we recognize it as a depiction of real life. The fact is that students act this way every day. But now let us ask what we know from research and experience in the workplace about the cause of burnout. The best predictor, it turns out, is not too much work, too little time, or too little compensation. Rather, it is powerlessness — a lack of control over what one is doing.

Combine that fact with the premise that there is no minimum age for burnout, and the conclusion that emerges is this: much of what is disturbing about students' attitudes and behavior may be a function of the fact that they have little to say about what happens to them all day. They are compelled to follow someone else's rules, study someone else's curriculum, and submit continually to someone else's evaluation. The mystery, really, is not that so many students are indifferent about what they have to do in school but that any of them are not.

To be sure, there is nothing new about the idea that students should be able to participate, individually and collectively, in making decisions. This conviction has long played a role in schools designated as progressive, democratic, open, free, experimental, or alternative; in educational philosophies called developmental, constructivist, holistic, or learner centered; in specific innovations such as whole-language learning, discovery-based science, or authentic assessment; and in the daily practice of teachers whose natural instinct is to treat children with respect.

But if the concept is not exactly novel, neither do we usually take the time to tease this element out of various traditions and examine it in its own right. Why is it so important that children have a chance to make decisions about their learning? How might this opportunity be provided with regard to academic matters as well as other aspects of school life? What limits on students' right to choose are necessary, and what restrictions compromise the idea too deeply? Finally, what barriers might account for the fact that students so rarely feel a sense of self-determination today? A close inspection of these issues will reveal that the question of choice is both more complex and more compelling than many educators seem to assume.

SEVERAL years ago, a group of teachers from Florida traveled to what was then the USSR to exchange information and ideas with their Russian-speaking counterparts. What the Soviet teachers most wanted from their guests was guidance on setting up and running democratic schools. Their questions on this topic were based on the assumption that a country like the United States, so committed to the idea of democracy, surely must involve children in decision-making processes from their earliest years.

The irony is enough to make us wince. As one survey of American schools after another has confirmed, students are rarely invited to become active participants in their own education.[1] Schooling is typically about doing things *to* children, not working *with* them. An array of punishments and rewards is used to enforce compliance with an agenda that students rarely have any opportunity to influence.

Think about the rules posted on the wall of an elementary school classroom, or the "rights and responsibilities" pamphlet distributed in high schools, or the moral precepts that form the basis of a values or character education program. In each case, students are almost never involved in deliberating about such ideas; their job is basically to do as they are told.

Moreover, consider the conventional response when something goes wrong (as determined, of course, by the adults). Are two children creating a commotion instead of sitting quietly? Separate them. Have the desks become repositories for used chewing gum? Ban the stuff. Do students come to class without having done the reading? Hit them with a pop quiz. Again and again, the favorite motto of teachers and administrators seems to be "Reach for the coercion" rather than engaging children in a conversation about the underlying causes of what is happen-

ing and working together to negotiate a solution.

Earlier this year, the principal of a Brooklyn high school told a *New York Times* reporter that he lived by "a simple proposition: This is my house, I'm 46 years old. A 15-year-old is not going to dictate to me how this school is run."[2] But even educators who recoil from such a frank endorsement of autocracy may end up acting in accordance with the same basic principle. I have met many elementary teachers, for example, who make a point of assuring students that "this is *our* classroom" — but proceed to decide unilaterally on almost everything that goes on in it, from grading policy to room decor.

As for the content of instruction, the educators who shape the curriculum rarely bother to consult those who are to be educated. There is plenty of enthusiasm about reforms such as outcome-based education but little concern about bringing students into the process of formulating the outcomes. There is spirited debate about "school choice" — an arrangement in which districts are compelled to compete for the business of parent-consumers — but much less talk about how much choice students have concerning what happens in their classrooms. Indeed, spontaneous, animated conversations about topics of interest to children, when they are allowed to occur at all, are soon snuffed out in order that the class can return to the prescribed lesson plan.

THE RATIONALE

To talk about the destructive effects of keeping students powerless is to describe the benefits of having a sense of self-determination.[3] Five such benefits seem particularly compelling.

1. Effects on general well-being. Many different fields of research have converged on the finding that it is desirable for people to experience a sense of control over their lives. These benefits reach into every corner of human existence, starting with our physical health and survival. One series of studies has shown that people who rarely become ill despite having to deal with considerable stress tend to be those who feel more control over what happens to them.[4] In another well-known experiment, nursing home residents who were able to make decisions about their environment not only became happier and more active but were

Those who feel more control over what happens to them rarely become ill despite high levels of stress.

also more likely to be alive a year and a half later than were other residents.[5]

The psychological benefits of control are, if anything, even more pronounced. All else being equal, emotional adjustment is better over time for people who experience a sense of self-determination; by contrast, few things lead more reliably to depression and other forms of psychological distress than a feeling of helplessness.[6] (One recent study showed this was true in an educational setting: distress was inversely related to how much influence and autonomy teachers said they had with respect to school policy.[7]) Whereas rewards and punishments are notably ineffective at maintaining behavior change,[8] people are likely to persist at doing constructive things, like exercising, quitting smoking, or fighting cavities, when they have some choice about the specifics of such programs.[9] Laboratory experiments have also shown that individuals are better able to tolerate unpleasant sensations like noise, cold, or electric shock when they know they have the power to end them.[10]

Children are no exception to these rules, the studies show. One-year-old infants had fun with a noisy mechanical toy if they could make it start; it was less interesting, and sometimes even frightening, if they had no control over its action.[11] Elementary students had higher self-esteem and a greater feeling of academic competence when their teachers bolstered their sense of self-determination in the classroom.[12]

2. Effects on behavior and values. One is repeatedly struck by the absurd spectacle of adults insisting that children need to become self-disciplined or lamenting that "kids just don't take responsibility for their own behavior" — while spending their days ordering children around. The truth is that, if we want children to *take* responsibility for their own behavior, we must first *give* them responsibility, and plenty of it. The way a child learns how to make decisions is by making decisions, not by following directions. As Constance Kamii has written,

> We cannot expect children to accept ready-made values and truths all the way through school, and then suddenly make choices in adulthood. Likewise, we cannot expect them to be manipulated with reward and punishment in school, and to have the courage of a Martin Luther King in adulthood.[13]

In fact, an emphasis on following instructions, respecting authority (regardless of whether that respect has been earned), and obeying the rules (regardless of whether they are reasonable) teaches a disturbing lesson. Stanley Milgram's famous experiment, in which ordinary people gave what they thought were terribly painful shocks to hapless strangers merely because they were told to do so, is not just a comment about "society" or "human nature." It is a cautionary tale about certain ways of teaching children. Indeed, an emphasis on obedience, with all the trappings of control that must be used for enforcing it, typically fails even on its own terms: children are less likely to comply with a rule when they have had no role in inventing or even discussing it. And if our goals are more ambitious — if we want children to make good values their own over the long haul — then there is no substitute for giving them the chance to become actively involved in deciding what kind of people they want to be and what kind of classroom or school they want to have.

To talk about the importance of choice is also to talk about democracy. At present, as Shelley Berman of Educators for Social Responsibility has drily noted, "We teach reading, writing, and math by [having students do] them, but we teach democracy by lecture."[14] I believe it is time to call the bluff of every educator who claims to prize democratic principles. Anyone who truly values democracy ought to be thinking about preparing students to participate in a democratic culture — or to transform a culture *into* a democracy, as the case may be. The only way this can happen, the only way children can acquire both the skills of decision making and the inclination to use them, is if we maximize their experiences with choice and negotiation.[15]

Ultimately, even virtues that appear to be quite different from an orientation toward participation or a capacity to make intelligent decisions turn out to depend on these things. For example, like many others, I am concerned about how we can help children to become generous, caring people who see themselves as part of a community.[16] But these values simply cannot be successfully promoted in the absence of choice. A jarring reminder of that fact was provided by a man who recalled being "taught that my highest duty was to help those in need" but added that he learned this lesson in the context of how important it was to "obey promptly the wishes and commands of my parents, teachers, and priests, and indeed of all adults. . . . Whatever they said was always right." The man who said that was Rudolf Höss, the commandant of Auschwitz.[17] A commitment to helping is important, but if the environment in which such values are taught emphasizes obedience rather than autonomy, all may be lost.

3. *Effects on academic achievement.* Every teacher who is told what material to cover, when to cover it, and how to evaluate children's performance is a teacher who knows that enthusiasm for one's work quickly evaporates in the face of being controlled. Not every teacher, however, realizes that exactly the same thing holds true for students: deprive them of self-determination and you have likely deprived them of motivation. If learning is a matter of following orders, students simply will not take to it in the way they would if they had some say about what they were doing. Not long ago, in a 10th-grade geometry class whose teacher collaborates with students to decide about curriculum and grades, a student explained to me that being able to make such choices "leads to learning rather than just remembering."

The evidence to support that view is so compelling that it is frankly difficult to understand how anyone can talk about school reform without immediately addressing the question of how students can be given more say about what goes on in their classes. The classic Eight-Year Study, which should be required reading for everyone with an interest in education, provided data on this point more than half a century ago. After 30 high schools were encouraged to develop innovative programs whose "essential value was democracy,"[18] researchers found that the graduates of those schools did better in college than a matched comparison group from traditional schools. In fact, the students who were most successful tended to come from the schools that had departed most significantly from the conventional college-prep approach — the approach currently lauded by those calling for higher standards, more accountability, and getting back to basics.

Subsequent research has confirmed the conclusion:

• When second-graders in Pittsburgh were given some choice about their learning, including the chance to decide which tasks they would work on at any given moment, they tended to "complete more learning tasks in less time."[19]

• When high school seniors in Minneapolis worked on chemistry problems without clear-cut instructions — that is, with the opportunity to decide for themselves how to find solutions — they "consistently produced better write-ups of experiments" and remembered the material better than those who had been told exactly what to do. They put in more time than they had to, spending "extra laboratory periods checking results that could have been accepted without extra work." Some of the students initially resisted having to make decisions about how to proceed, but these grumblers later "took great pride in being able to carry through an experiment on their own."[20]

• When preschoolers in Massachusetts were allowed to select the materials they used for making a collage, their work was judged more creative than the work of children who used exactly the same materials but did not get to choose them.[21]

• When college students in New York State had the chance to decide which of several puzzles they wanted to work on and how to allot their time to each of them, they were a lot more interested in working on such puzzles later than were students who were told what to do.[22]

• When teachers of inner-city black children were trained in a program designed to promote a sense of self-determination, the students in these classes missed less school and scored better on a national test of basic skills than those in conventional classrooms.[23]

• When second-graders spent the year in a math classroom where textbooks and rewards were discarded in favor of an emphasis on "intellectual autonomy"

— that is, where children, working in groups, took an active role in figuring out their own solutions to problems and were free to move around the classroom on their own initiative to get the materials they needed — they developed more sophisticated reasoning skills without falling behind on basic conceptual tasks.[24]

The evidence goes on and on. At least one recent study has found that children given more "opportunity to participate in decisions about schoolwork" score higher on standardized tests;[25] other research shows that they are more likely than those deprived of autonomy to continue working even on relatively uninteresting tasks.[26] There is no question about it: even if our only criterion is academic performance, choice works.

In a way, this conclusion shouldn't be surprising. Putting aside the value of particular programs that give students more discretion about what they are doing, the irrefutable fact is that students always have a choice about whether they will learn. We may be able to force them to complete an assignment, but we can't compel them to learn effectively or to care about what they are doing. The bottom line is that "teaching requires the consent of students, and discontent will not be chased away by the exercise of power."[27] No wonder that expanding the realm in which the learner's consent is sought tends to enhance learning.

4. *Effects on teachers.* Despite attitudinal barriers to creating democratic classrooms and schools, which I will discuss later, educators who are willing to share power may well find that they benefit directly from doing so. One's job becomes a good deal more interesting when it involves collaborating with students to decide what is going to happen. As one fifth-grade teacher in upstate New York explained,

I've been teaching for more than 30 years, and I would have been burned out long ago but for the fact that I involve my kids in designing the curriculum. I'll say to them, "What's the *most* exciting way we could study this next unit?" If we decide their first suggestion isn't feasible, I'll say, "Okay, what's the *next* most exciting way we could study this?" They always come up with good proposals, they're motivated because I'm using their ideas, and I never do the unit in the same way twice.[28]

Teachers also benefit in other ways from allowing students to be active participants in their learning. In such a classroom, according to the researchers involved in the second-grade math project described above, the teacher is "freed from the chore of constantly monitoring and supervising the children's activity and [is] able to give her full attention to . . . interacting with the children" as they work.[29]

5. *Intrinsic value.* Finally, it needs to be said that allowing people to make decisions about what happens to them is inherently preferable to controlling them. It is more respectful and consistent with basic values to which most of us claim to subscribe. Apart from the skills that will be useful for students to have in the future, they ought to have a chance to choose in the present. Children, after all, are not just adults-in-the-making. They are people whose current needs and rights and experiences must be taken seriously. Put it this way: students should not only be trained to live in a democracy when they grow up; they should have the chance to live in one today.[30]

CHOOSING IN PRACTICE

Because quite a few programs and practices in which children can make meaningful choices have been described elsewhere, I will offer only a sampling of the ways this basic idea can be implemented. These suggestions can be grouped according to whether they are primarily concerned with academic decisions or with social and behavioral ones.

Academic issues. The four key realms in which students can make academic decisions are what, how, how well, and why they learn. *What* they learn is the most straightforward of these. Student participation here can range from choosing where in an assigned text to start reading to deciding what course to take. In between these examples is the question of what is to be read, not only by individual students but by the class as a whole. "Here are five books that the supply store has in stock," a fourth-grade teacher may say to the class. "Why don't you flip through them during your free time this week, and we'll decide together on Friday which one to read next." (Of course, if students are not reading stories at all but making their way through worksheets and workbooks, basals and primers and dittos, then their capacity to par-

> *Every day ought to include at least one block of time in which children can decide what to do.*

ticipate in their education has been significantly curtailed from the start.)

Teachers may not always have the discretion to let students participate in deciding what topic to study. But even when compelled to teach a certain lesson, a teacher might open up a discussion in which members of the class try to figure out together why someone apparently thought the subject was important enough to be required. The next step would be to connect that topic to students' real-world concerns and interests. When teachers have themselves decided for one reason or another to exclude students from the selection of the subject matter, there is still room to give them choices about the specific questions within a general topic to be explored. A teacher might begin any unit, for example, by inviting children to discuss what they already know about the subject and what they would like to know.

The question of *how* students learn embraces a great many issues — beginning with whether to work alone, in small groups, or as a class — and including such incidental matters as where students will sit (or lie) while they work. (One teacher swears that achievement in her class improved markedly as soon as she gave students the right to find a favorite reading place and position.) And there are other choices as well: if a student has written a story, she ought to be able to decide whether or not to read it aloud and, if so, whether to answer her classmates' questions about it afterward and, if so, whom to call on.

Every day ought to include at least one block of time in which children can decide individually what to do: get a head start on homework, write in one's journal, work on an art project, or read a library book. Creative writing assignments offer plenty of opportunity for decisions to be made by the writers themselves. In expressing an idea or responding to a lesson, children sometimes can be allowed to decide what medium or genre they will use — whether they want to write a poem, an essay, or a play or do a collage, painting, or sculpture. Mathematics lessons can be guided by quantitative issues of interest to students.

The entire constructivist tradition is predicated on the idea of student autonomy, which is to say, the chance for students to view learning as something "under their control rather than as disembodied, objectified, subject matter."[31] The same can be said about some (but not all) models of cooperative learning. One version, devised by Shlomo Sharan and his colleagues and known as Group Investigation, is based on the idea of active participation throughout the process. Students break a subject into specific questions, sort themselves into groups to explore these questions, plan and conduct an investigation, and figure out how to share what they have learned with the rest of the class.[32]

To talk about *how well* a student is doing is to raise the complicated issues of assessment and evaluation, the improvement of which has lately been of increasing concern to educators. But a key consideration in changing these systems, beyond whether judgments are based on sufficiently rich measures of student achievement, is the extent to which students themselves are involved in the process. Obviously, the chance to pick one of three possible essay questions for one's final paper does not begin to get at what is important here. Students ought to help determine the criteria by which their work will be judged and then play a role in weighing their work against those criteria. This achieves several things at once: it gives students more control over their education, it makes evaluation feel less punitive, and it provides an important learning experience in itself. Students can derive enormous intellectual benefits from thinking about what makes a story interesting, a mathematical proof elegant, or an argument convincing. More traditional approaches to testing can also be improved if students are consulted

about what the test ought to cover and when it ought to be given; there is no need for teachers to decide these things on their own.

Last, and most frequently overlooked, is the need to involve students in talking about *why* they are learning. Few aspects of education are more important than the "participation of the learner in the formation of the purposes which direct his activities in the learning process," as Dewey put it.[33] Children should be given a voice not only about the means of learning but also the ends, the why as well as the what. Even very young children are "curriculum theorists," according to John Nicholls, and there may be no better use of classroom time than a sustained conversation following someone's challenge: "Why do we gotta do this stuff?"[34]

Social and behavioral issues. School is about more than intellectual development; it is about learning to become a responsible, caring person who can make good choices and solve problems effectively. Thus educators must think about ways of helping students to take an active part in decisions that are only indirectly related to academics.

Is it necessary to raise one's hand before talking or to line up before walking through the school? How much noise is too much? How should the furniture be arranged in our room? Where might we take a field trip? These are the sorts of questions that children should be encouraged to ponder and argue about. In considering what kind of classroom or school each person wants to have, the point is to reach consensus on general guidelines or principles, not to formulate a list of rules. (Specific admonitions tend to invite legalistic thinking about their application and a preoccupation with enforcement that emphasizes punishment over problem solving.) Moreover, this process goes well beyond, and may even exclude, the practice of voting. What we want to promote are talking and listening, looking for alternatives and trying to reach agreement, solving problems together and making meaningful choices. Voting, which is an exercise in adversarial majoritarianism, often involves none of these acts. It may be the least objectionable method when a quarter of a billion people must govern themselves, but classroom teachers can do better.[35]

A structured opportunity for members of a class or school to meet and make decisions provides several advantages: it helps children feel respected by making

it clear that their opinions matter; it builds a sense of belongingness and community; and it contributes to the development of social and cognitive skills such as perspective taking (imagining how the world looks to someone else), conflict resolution, and rational analysis.[36] Few contrasts in education are as striking as that between students participating in such meetings, taking responsibility for deciding how they want their classroom to be, and students sitting in rows, having been bribed or threatened into complying with an adult's rules.

Thus, when problems develop, the adage for teachers to keep in mind is "Bring the kids in on it." This approach may call for a class meeting in the case of a conflict involving a number of students, or, when only one or two are directly concerned, it could mean a conversation just with them. If a child is daydreaming and failing to complete assignments, or if two children cannot seem to be anywhere near each other without becoming nasty, the most successful (and respectful)[37] solutions are those that emerge after the teacher asks, "What do you think we can do about this?"

REASONABLE LIMITS

A number of writers and teachers who resist giving children the chance to make decisions have justified their opposition by erecting an enormous straw man called "absolute freedom" and counterposing it to the status quo. Since most of us do not relish the idea of children spending their time at school doing anything they please, deprived of structure or adult guidance, we are encouraged to settle for the controlling practices that now exist.

Not only is this a classic false dichotomy, but virtually every influential proponent of choice for students — as well as the programs that have put the idea into effect — proceeds from the assumption that there are indeed limits on the capacity and right of children to decide. The scary specter of laissez-faire liberty that shows up in the rhetoric of traditionalists is not easy to locate in the real world. Nearly every essay on education by John Dewey, the father of progressive schooling, stresses the importance of adult guidance and derides the idea of "leaving a child to his own unguided fancies."[38] Even A. S. Neill, whose Summerhill school and philosophy lie at the outer edges of serious discussion about the issue, distinguished sharply between freedom and license, emphasizing repeatedly that "a child should not be permitted to violate the personal rights of others."[39] All reasonable adults, meanwhile, acknowledge that safety concerns will necessitate placing constraints on certain kinds of actions.

While agreement exists at a general level about the need to restrict students' choice, however, there is far less consensus about when and how to do so. The issues most frequently raised in support of such restrictions are not as simple as they first appear. Take the question of *age*. It goes without saying that a 16-year-old can approach a decision in a more sophisticated way than a 6-year-old and therefore can usually be entrusted with more responsibility. But this fact is sometimes used to justify preventing younger children from making choices that are well within their capabilities. Moreover, the idea that we must wait until children are mature enough to handle responsibilities may set up a vicious circle: after all, it is experience with decisions that helps children become capable of handling them.[40]

A second rationale for restricting choice is *time*: if students were entitled to make decisions about, and had to agree on, everything they did, there would be no time to do anything else. True enough, and yet the heuristic value of such discussions is often overlooked in the rush to get on with the "real" lesson. In class meetings, for example, teachers would do well to remember that, at least to some extent, *the process is the point*. The idea isn't just to make a choice, reach a decision, and move on.

Of course, it is still true that there won't be time to hash out every matter; sometimes a teacher will need to request that students just do something. But a democratic approach doesn't demand that everything *is* actively chosen, only that it *can* be. As Deborah Meier has said, what matters is not whether a given issue is discussed but that it is discussable. Unavoidable time constraints should not be used to rationalize avoidable authoritarian practices.

Third, the importance of choice is often weighed against the fact that children need some *structure or limits* for their behavior, if not for their learning. Once again, this point may be accurate but does not justify much of what educators actually do. "The critical question," as Thomas Gordon has put it, "is not *wheth-*

er limits and rules are needed . . . but rather *who* sets them: the adults alone or the adults and kids — together."[41] Before depriving children of choice, then, an educator is obliged to demonstrate not that they need some structure but that there is some reason to exclude them from helping to shape that structure. The crucial difference between structures and limits, on the one hand, and control and coercion, on the other, has generally gone unrecognized.[42]

Fourth, and possibly most compelling, is the caution that the right to choose must give way to the needs and preferences of *other people*. Even the minimalist sort of liberalism articulated by Neill (in which one's connection to others is limited to not violating their rights) implies that people cannot do whatever they want. A more ambitious commitment to the value of community would seem to restrict choice even more severely. While each child ought to have more opportunity to make decisions than is typically allowed in American classrooms, such decisions must take into account their impact on the other people in the room. This may not feel like a burdensome restriction once a child has internalized a concern about others' well-being — but, strictly speaking, one person's freedom to choose is always compromised by a set of obligations to others. At a recent town meeting of the long-standing experimental school-within-a-school program at Brookline (Massachusetts) High School, one student remarked that someone's choice to show up in class without having done the reading assignment adversely affects the quality of discussion for everyone. "It's not just 'You get out what you put into it,' " another girl added. "It's 'You get out what the class puts into it' " — and vice versa.

On closer examination, however, it seems clear that what must occasionally be restricted is not choice but *individual* choice. (It is an interesting reflection on our culture that we tend to see these as interchangeable.) To affirm the importance of community does not at all compromise the right to make decisions, per se, or the importance of involving everyone in a class or school in such a process. In fact, we might say that it is the integration of these two values, community and choice, that defines democracy.

I THINK we can conclude that, while some legitimate limits to the right to choose can be identified, the most commonly cited reasons for those

limits may not automatically justify restrictions. But this discussion also raises questions about a conventional response to the matter of appropriate limits. Many people, understandably impatient with an either/or choice in which the possibilities are limited to freedom and its absence, assert that we need to find a happy medium between these two poles. This seems facile. For one thing, such a pronouncement offers no guidance about where on that continuum we should set up camp. For another, it overlooks the fact that the sensible alternative to two extremes may not be an intermediate point but a different way of thinking about the issue altogether. The interesting question here, for example, is not how *much* adults should limit the power of children to make decisions, but *how* they should get involved.

In a broad sense, that involvement may consist of suggesting the tasks, teaching the skills, supplying the resources — in short, providing the conditions under which students can choose productively and learn effectively. The teacher's role is to be a facilitator, but, as Carolyn Edwards points out, this doesn't mean to " 'mak[e] smooth or easy,' but rather to 'stimulate' [learning] by making problems more complex, involving, and arousing."[43] Notice the implication here: a democratic classroom is not one where the teacher has less work to do. There is no zero-sum game in which more responsibility for the children means less for the adults. Helping students to participate effectively takes talent and patience and hard work. "I'm in control of putting students in control," one teacher told me — a responsibility that demands more of an educator than simply telling students what to do.

Notice also that this role for the teacher does not always amount to being a voice for moderation or mainstream values — a conservative counterweight to students' reckless impulses. If, for example, children have been raised to assume that anyone who does something wrong must be forced to suffer a punitive consequence, they will be likely, left to their own devices, to spend their time deciding what should be done to a rule breaker. Here, the teacher might intervene to guide the discussion away from "Which punishment?" and toward the more radical question of whether an entirely different response — "Something has gone wrong; how can we solve this problem?" — might be more productive.

On a range of issues, adults can participate — and circumscribe children's choices — in fundamentally different ways. To wit:

• The teacher and the students may take turns at deciding something, each choosing on alternate weeks, for example, which book to read next. Or the responsibility can rotate between individual students, cooperative learning groups, the whole class, and the teacher.

• The teacher may offer suggestions and guidance, questions and criticism, but leave the final choice to students. Thus I have heard a third-grade teacher advise her students that it might not be a good idea to go outside for recess on a day when there is slush on the ground but then make it clear that it is up to each child to make the final decision for him- or herself. A high school teacher, meanwhile, suggests that it might make sense for the whole class to talk about the homework together but offers them the option of discussing it in small groups if they prefer.

• The teacher can narrow the number of possibilities from which students are permitted to choose. He or she may want to do this to make sure that any material or text a student works with is likely to be of educational value and of approximately the right level of challenge. (On the other hand, neither of these goals always requires restricting children's choice.[44] And even when the teacher does decide to limit their options, she should explain her rationale for doing so and remain open to reasonable additions to her list. As a general rule, it is more important for children to have the chance to *generate* different possibilities than merely to select one possibility from among those that have been set before them.[45])

• The teacher may provide the parameters according to which decisions can be made, perhaps specifying the goal that has to be reached but inviting students to figure out how they want to get there. For example, "It's important to me that no one in here feels scared that other people will laugh at him for saying something stupid. How do you think we can prevent that from happening?" Or, "I need some way at the end of this unit to see how much you understand. Think of a way you might be able to demonstrate what you've learned."

• A decision does not have to be thought of as something that teachers either make or turn over to students. In-

stead, it can be negotiated together. The emphasis here is on shared responsibility for deciding what gets learned and how the learning takes place. This process can become a lesson in itself — an opportunity to make arguments, solve problems, anticipate consequences, and take other people's needs into account — as well as a powerful contribution to motivation.

WHILE well-meaning educators may offer very different prescriptions regarding the nature and scope of students' participation in decision making, I believe that certain ways of limiting participation are basically deceptive and best described as "pseudochoice." It is disturbing to find these tactics recommended not only by proponents of blatantly controlling classroom management programs, such as Assertive Discipline, but also by critics of such programs who purport to offer an enlightened alternative.

In the first version of pseudochoice, a student is offered a choice that is obviously loaded. "You can finish your math problems now or you can stay in during recess. Which would you prefer?" The problem here is not just that the number of options has been reduced to two, but that the second one is obviously something no student would select. The teacher is really saying, "Do what I tell you or you'll be punished," but he is attempting to camouflage this conventional use of coercion by pretending to offer the student a choice.

In a variation of this gambit, the student is punished after disobeying the teacher's command, but the punishment is presented as something the student asked for: "I see you've chosen to miss recess today." The appeal of this tactic is no mystery: it appears to relieve the teacher of responsibility for what she is about to do to the child. But it is a fundamentally dishonest attribution. Children may choose not to complete a math assignment,* but they certainly do not

---

*Even this assumption needs to be questioned, since a young child may lack the capacity for rational decision making or impulse control that is implicit in the suggestion that he made a choice. If so, the child needs help in developing these faculties, not punishment accompanied by blame. I have heard some teachers reply to this point by insisting that, if students are permitted to make choices, they must "take responsibility" for making a bad one. This approach, however, assumes that "taking responsibility" for a poor decision means being made to suffer for it rather than being part of a nonpunitive problem-solving process.

choose to miss recess; teachers do that *to* them. To the injury of punishment is added the insult of a kind of mind game whereby reality is redefined and children are told, in effect, that they chose to be punished. This gimmick uses the word *choice* as a bludgeon rather than giving children what they need, which is the opportunity to participate in making real decisions about what happens to them.[46]

Another kind of pseudochoice purports to let a student or a class make a decision even though there is only one choice that will be accepted. I recently heard a well-known educator and advocate for children reminisce about her experiences as a teacher. Recalling a student of hers who frequently and articulately challenged her authority, she commented with a smile, "I had to be a better negotiator than she was." This remark suggests that what had taken place was not negotiation at all but thinly disguised manipulation. As Nel Noddings has written, "We cannot enter into dialogue with children when we know that our decision is already made."[47]

If students are informed that they have made the "wrong" decision and must try again, they will realize they were not truly free to choose in the first place. But the last, and most insidious, variety of pseudochoice tries to prevent students from figuring this out by encouraging them to think they had a say when the game was actually rigged. The "engineering of consent," as it has been called, seems to offer autonomy while providing "the assurance of order and conformity — a most seductive combination. Yet its appearance and its means should be understood for what they really are: a method of securing and solidifying the interests of those in power."[48] This description by educator James Beane might have been inspired by the behavior of politicians, but it is no less applicable to what goes on in schools. If we want students to learn how to choose, they must have the opportunity to make *real* choices.

BARRIERS

If we are to act on the arguments and evidence supporting the value of making students active participants in their education, we need to understand why more educators haven't already done so. I think the barriers to giving students more choice fall into three categories: structural impediments, resistance by teachers and resistance by the students themselves.

Structural impediments. Classroom teachers frequently protest that they would love to open up the decision-making process but for the fact that a significant number of decisions are not theirs to give away or even to make themselves. Highly controlling schools and school districts may leave teachers very little discretion about either curricular or disciplinary issues. As Dewey noted, classrooms characterized by demands for "sheer obedience to the will of an adult" may sometimes imply a "situation [that] almost forced [that arrangement] upon the teacher," such as an absence of democracy or community among the educators themselves.[49] Even if controlling structures do not literally remove options from teachers, they may create a climate in which teachers do to children what is done to them. Often, teachers subject to rigid directives from above may find it easier not "to resist administrators but to increase controls on their students."[50]

Resistance by teachers. While structural constraints are sometimes very real, they can also be used as excuses to with-

> *Parting with power is not easy, if only because the results are less predictable without control.*

hold power from students that teachers in any case are not inclined to share. The traditional instructional model sees the teacher as the king or queen of the classroom, and the fact is that monarchs do not always abdicate gracefully. On the basis of my own years as a teacher as well as my conversations with scores of others in the profession, I would argue that there is a certain reassurance and satisfaction to be taken from making unilateral decisions. No wonder many teachers who express relief at having "a good class this year" use the word *good* as parents of a newborn might talk about having "a good

baby" — that is, one who is quiet, docile, and little trouble to manage.

Popular books about classroom life, as well as workshops and other forms of guidance offered to educators, typically take for granted that a teacher must secure control of the class. Hence the use of curricular materials, including basals and worksheets, that have the effect of keeping order.[51] And hence the popularity of manipulative measures such as punishments and rewards: their use can be traced back to the belief that there are exactly two possibilities: control or chaos. When students are allowed to make decisions, it is therefore only about matters that don't threaten the teacher's reign. More than once I have heard teachers pride themselves on letting students choose "when I don't really care what they end up with" — which is, of course, a far cry from a democratic process that helps students to become responsible decision makers.

If challenged, defenders of classroom autocracy may insist that a teacher must get control of the class *first* in order that students can be helped to become good learners and good people. Whether this is a sincerely held belief or just a rationalization for holding on to power, it is simply wrong. Control not only is unnecessary for fostering academic motivation; it undermines its development, substituting reluctant compliance for the excitement that comes from the experience of self-determination. Likewise for the nonacademic realm: as one group of social scientists put it, the emphasis on control "endanger[s] the long-term enterprise of socialization itself."[52]

This is no mere academic speculation. Watch what happens when a teacher concerned about maintaining control of his classroom walks away for a few minutes or is absent for a day: the class is likely to erupt, just as a child raised by parents who emphasize strict discipline is apt to misbehave when he is away from home. It is in classrooms (and families) where participation is valued above adult control that students have the chance to learn *self*-control — and are more likely to keep working when the teacher or parent isn't around.

There is nothing surprising about the fact that teachers resist being told what they can teach and how they must manage their classrooms. The astonishing fact is that so many of these teachers treat their students in exactly the way they themselves find so offensive. Whatever

the reason for this discrepancy, though, students must be permitted to make substantive decisions about learning and living together, and this will not happen until teachers and administrators understand that *control can't be the goal* — or even a technique. This recognition, in turn, may require reconsidering basic beliefs about human nature and motivation. A teacher convinced that children are egocentric little terrors who must be forced to attend to other people's needs is likely to prefer a model of tight control.[53] And control, in turn, produces exactly the sort of antisocial behavior that such a teacher expects, confirming the view that such tactics are needed.

Sometimes, however, the main barrier to giving children choices is a simple lack of gumption. Parting with power is not easy, if only because the results are less predictable than in a situation where we have control. Asking students to decide about even the simplest issues can be scary. An elementary teacher once told me how difficult it was for her to leave the classroom walls bare when her students showed up on the first day of school. If she had already decorated them, she realized, it was really *her* room they were entering. But it took several years before she found the courage to bring them into the process, a decision that ultimately made an enormous difference in how the children felt about coming to school — and also occasioned a natural and eagerly received lesson on fractions so that the students could measure and tack up the construction paper that they had chosen for *their* walls.

Student resistance. Finally, and most discouragingly, teachers sometimes find that their willingness to let students make decisions is met with an apparent reluctance on the part of the students. This is really not so surprising, given that most of them have been conditioned to accept a posture of passivity at school and sometimes at home. After a few years of being instructed to do what you're told, it is disconcerting to be invited — much less expected — to take responsibility for the way things are.[54]

This resistance takes three primary forms. The first is simply *refusing*: "That's your job to decide," students may protest. The second is *testing*: offering outrageous suggestions or responses to see if the teacher is really serious about the invitation to participate. The third is *parroting*: repeating what adults have said or guessing what this adult probably wants to hear. (Thus a fifth-grader asked to suggest a guideline for class conduct may recite, "We should keep our hands and feet to ourselves.")

The key question is how we respond to these maneuvers. It can be tempting to conclude that students are either unable to handle the responsibility of making decisions or unworthy of having it. But our challenge is to persevere. As Selma Wassermann has written,

> I have heard teachers give it up after a single attempt, saying, "Children cannot behave responsibly," then remove all further opportunity for students to practice and grow in their responsible behavior. I have also heard teachers say, "Children cannot think for themselves," and proceed thereafter to do children's thinking for them. But these same teachers would *never* say, "These children cannot read by themselves," and thereafter remove any opportunity for them to learn to read.[55]

Specifically, the comment "That's your job" provides a teachable moment, a chance to engage students in a conversation about their experiences with being controlled and about when they have found learning to be most exciting. Outlandish ideas can be met with a sense of humor but also taken seriously: a student who is asked how school could be improved and replies that all the books should be thrown away may be saying something about her experience of the curriculum that we ignore at our peril. Finally, in the case of parroting, it can be hard even to recognize this tactic as a form of resistance — or as something undesirable. Getting our ideas to come out of their mouths is a ventriloquist's trick, not a sign of successful participation and student autonomy. It represents an invitation to ask students about their experiences with saying what they knew would please an adult and how different that feels from taking the risk of making a suggestion that someone might not like — and then emphasizing that the latter is what we are looking for here.

Of course, whether the last point is true — whether we really are looking for students who take risks and make decisions — is the first question that each of us must answer. The structural and attitudinal barriers erected by educators often seem impregnable, with the result that students continue to feel powerless and, to that extent, burned out. For decades, prescriptions have been offered to en-hance student motivation and achievement. But these ideas are unlikely to make much of a difference so long as students are controlled and silenced. It is not "utopian" or "naive" to think that learners can make responsible decisions about their own learning; those words best describe the belief that any group of people will do something effectively and enthusiastically when they are unable to make choices about what they are doing.

1. For example, see Charles E. Silberman, *Crisis in the Classroom: The Remaking of American Education* (New York: Random House, 1970); John I. Goodlad, *A Place Called School: Prospects for the Future* (New York: McGraw-Hill, 1984); Linda McNeil, *Contradictions of Control: School Structure and School Knowledge* (New York: Routledge and Kegan Paul, 1986); and the observations of William Glasser in much of his work.

2. Felicia R. Lee, "Disrespect Rules," *New York Times Education Life*, 4 April 1993, p. 16.

3. Strictly speaking, as such thinkers as Jean-Paul Sartre and Viktor Frankl have pointed out, people are never entirely powerless. Deborah Meier applies this observation to an education context: "Even devalued and disrespected people remain powerful, but they are forced to exercise their powers in odd, distorted, and limited ways. . . . Children have been exercising their powers for years, without the formal right to do so. Ditto for teachers . . . [who] sabotage reforms — the best and the worst — when they feel imposed upon and helpless." See "The Kindergarten Tradition in the High School," in Kathe Jervis and Carol Montag, eds., *Progressive Education for the 1990s: Transforming Practice* (New York: Teachers College Press, 1991), pp. 140-41.

4. Suzanne C. Kobasa and her colleagues found that control, together with a deeply felt commitment to one's activities and the tendency to perceive change as a positive challenge, contributed to a profile of "hardiness" that provides significant protection against illness. See, for example, "Stressful Life Events, Personality, and Health: An Inquiry into Hardiness," *Journal of Personality and Social Psychology*, vol. 37, 1979, pp. 1-10. See also Robert A. Karasek et al., "Job Characteristics in Relation to the Prevalence of Myocardial Infarction in the U.S. Health Examination Survey (HES) and the Health and Nutrition Examination Survey (HANES)," *American Journal of Public Health*, vol. 78, 1988, pp. 910-16.

5. Judith Rodin and Ellen J. Langer, "Long-Term Effects of a Control-Relevant Intervention with the Institutionalized Aged," *Journal of Personality and Social Psychology*, vol. 35, 1977, pp. 897-902. In another study, nursing home residents who were able to control (or at least predict) when a student would come visit them were not only happier and more hopeful but also physically healthier than those who received the same number of visits but on a random schedule. See Richard Schulz, "Effects of Control and Predictability on the Physical and Psychological Well-Being of the Institutionalized Aged," *Journal of Personality and Social Psychology*, vol. 33, 1976, pp. 563-73.

6. Martin Seligman's research on helplessness is central to this field of study. For a review of the relevant studies by him and others, see Shelley E. Taylor, *Positive Illusions: Creative Self-Deception and the Healthy Mind* (New York: Basic Books, 1989).

7. See Elizabeth Tuettemann and Keith F. Punch, "Teachers' Psychological Distress: The Ameliorating Effects of Control over the Work Environment," *Educational Review*, vol. 44, 1992, pp. 181-94.

8. See Alfie Kohn, *Punished by Rewards: The Trouble with Gold Stars, Incentive Plans, A's, Praise, and Other Bribes* (Boston: Houghton Mifflin, 1993).

9. Women who were told they could choose the particulars of an exercise program at a health club were more likely to continue attending over six weeks (and to declare their willingness to keep coming after that) than were women who were told their program was simply assigned to them — even though they, too, were actually assigned activities on the basis of the preferences they had expressed. See Carol E. Thompson and Leonard M. Wankel, "The Effects of Perceived Activity Choice upon Frequency of Exercise Behavior," *Journal of Applied Social Psychology*, vol. 10, 1980, pp. 436-43. A smoking cessation program that "focused attention on the individual's own efforts in smoking cessation" was more successful than one in which people followed a set of guidelines. See Judith M. Harackiewicz et al., "Attributional Processes in Behavior Change and Maintenance: Smoking Cessation and Continued Abstinence," *Journal of Consulting and Clinical Psychology*, vol. 55, 1987, pp. 372-78. Adolescent girls (but not boys) were more likely to continue using an anticavity fluoride rinse for nearly half a year when they were invited to make decisions about how the program was designed and monitored. See Joseph A. Burleson et al., "Effects of Decisional Control and Work Orientation on Persistence in Preventive Health Behavior," *Health Psychology*, vol. 9, 1990, pp. 1-17.

10. This research has been reviewed and evaluated by Suzanne C. Thompson, "Will It Hurt Less If I Can Control It? A Complex Answer to a Simple Question," *Psychological Bulletin*, vol. 90, 1981, pp. 89-101.

11. Megan R. Gunnar-Vongnechten, "Changing a Frightening Toy into a Pleasant Toy by Allowing the Infant to Control Its Actions," *Developmental Psychology*, vol. 14, 1978, pp. 157-62.

12. Richard M. Ryan and Wendy S. Grolnick, "Origins and Pawns in the Classroom: Self-Report and Projective Assessment of Individual Differences in Children's Perceptions," *Journal of Personality and Social Psychology*, vol. 50, 1986, pp. 550-58.

13. Constance Kamii, "Toward Autonomy: The Importance of Critical Thinking and Choice Making," *School Psychology Review*, vol. 20, 1991, p. 387. In fact, the lessons of conformity that Kamii finds troubling are those that concern academic activities (such as having to "learn mathematics through blind obedience"), not just behavior.

14. Shelley Berman, "The Real Ropes Course: The Development of Social Consciousness," *ESR Journal*, 1990, p. 2. The authors of a classic text on high school teaching comment wryly that the American motto could be: "Let's have education *for* democracy, but let's be careful about democracy *in* education!" See Jean Dresden Grambs and John C. Carr, *Modern Methods in Secondary Education*, 4th ed. (New York: Holt, Rinehart & Winston, 1979), p. 71.

15. Citing several sources, Joseph D'Amico concludes that "children who have experiences in a school where they participate in making decisions are more likely to be . . . motivated to make decisions both in and out of school." See "Reviving Student Participation," *Educational Leadership*, October 1980, pp. 44-46.

16. See Alfie Kohn, "Caring Kids: The Role of the Schools," *Phi Delta Kappan*, March 1991, pp. 496-506.

17. Höss is quoted in Alice Miller, *For Your Own Good: Hidden Cruelty in Child-Rearing and the*

Roots of Violence (New York: Farrar, Straus & Giroux, 1984), pp. 67-68.

18. Kathy Irwin, "The Eight Year Study," in Jervis and Montag, eds., p. 59. For a more comprehensive description of the study, see Wilford M. Aiken, *The Story of the Eight-Year Study* (New York: Harper, 1942); and Dean Chamberlin et al., *Did They Succeed in College?* (New York: Harper, 1942).

19. Margaret C. Wang and Billie Stiles, "An Investigation of Children's Concept of Self-Responsibility for Their School Learning," *American Educational Research Journal*, vol. 13, 1976, pp. 159-79. Unfortunately, task completion was the only outcome measured in this study.

20. Robert G. Rainey, "The Effects of Directed Versus Non-Directed Laboratory Work on High School Chemistry Achievement," *Journal of Research in Science Teaching*, vol. 3, 1965, pp. 286-92.

21. Teresa M. Amabile and Judith Gitomer, "Children's Artistic Creativity: Effects of Choice in Task Materials," *Personality and Social Psychology Bulletin*, vol. 10, 1984, pp. 209-15.

22. Miron Zuckerman et al., "On the Importance of Self-Determination for Intrinsically-Motivated Behavior," *Personality and Social Psychology Bulletin*, vol. 4, 1978, pp. 443-46. On the relation between choice and task involvement, see also John G. Nicholls, *The Competitive Ethos and Democratic Education* (Cambridge: Harvard University Press, 1989), p. 169.

23. Richard deCharms, "Personal Causation Training in the Schools," *Journal of Applied Social Psychology*, vol. 2, 1972, pp. 95-113.

24. For a description of the classroom structure in this yearlong experiment, see Erna Yackel et al., "Small-Group Interactions as a Source of Learning Opportunities in Second-Grade Mathematics," *Journal for Research in Mathematics Education*, vol. 22, 1991, pp. 390-408. For a discussion of the results, see Paul Cobb et al., "Assessment of a Problem-Centered Second-Grade Mathematics Project," *Journal for Research in Mathematics Education*, vol. 22, 1991, pp. 3-29.

25. Ann K. Boggiano et al., "Helplessness Deficits in Students: The Role of Motivational Orientation," *Motivation and Emotion*, vol. 16, 1992, pp. 278-80. Informal reports from other researchers suggest that a more typical result from an intervention of this sort is an enhancement of conceptual thinking skills (along with intrinsic motivation and other psychological and social benefits) but no change on standardized test scores, which probably is a reflection on how little these scores really mean. It should be sufficient to be able to show people who care about these scores that giving students more choice about their learning has no detrimental effect on their performance on machine-scored tests while bringing about a variety of other advantages.

26. Three studies to this effect are cited in John Condry, "Enemies of Exploration: Self-Initiated Versus Other-Initiated Learning," *Journal of Personality and Social Psychology*, vol. 35, 1977, p. 466.

27. John Nicholls and Susan P. Hazzard, *Education as Adventure: Lessons from the Second Grade* (New York: Teachers College Press, 1993), p. 76.

28. Richard Lauricella is quoted in Thomas Lickona, *Educating for Character: How Our Schools Can Teach Respect and Responsibility* (New York: Bantam, 1991), p. 148. Presumably he does not mean to suggest that every aspect of a unit must be taught differently from one year to the next, only that an element that is changed on the basis of students' suggestions within a predictable structure can be invigorating for a teacher.

29. Yackel et al., p. 401.

30. This point is made forcefully by David Char-

noff, "Democratic Schooling: Means or End?," *High School Journal*, vol. 64, 1981, pp. 170-75.

31. Paul Cobb et al., "Young Children's Emotional Acts While Engaged in Mathematical Problem Solving," in D. B. McLeod and V. M. Adams, eds., *Affect and Mathematical Problem Solving: A New Perspective* (New York: Springer-Verlag, 1989), p. 129.

32. See Yael Sharan and Shlomo Sharan, *Expanding Cooperative Learning Through Group Investigation* (New York: Teachers College Press, 1992). At its best, cooperative learning "gives students an active role in deciding about, planning, directing and controlling the content and pace of their learning activities. It changes the students' role from recipients of information to seekers, analyzers and synthesizers of information. It transforms pupils from listeners into talkers and doers, from powerless pawns into participant citizens empowered to influence decisions about what they must do in school." See Shlomo Sharan, "Cooperative Learning: Problems and Promise," *The International Association for the Study of Cooperation in Education Newsletter*, December 1986, p. 4.

33. John Dewey, *Experience and Education* (1938; reprint, New York: Collier, 1963), p. 67.

34. See Nicholls and Hazzard, esp. pp. 182-84.

35. Sometimes elementary school students are asked to put their heads down when they raise their hands to register a preference. This strikes me as an apt metaphor for the whole enterprise of voting. "Who thinks we should take our field trip to the museum? Who prefers the zoo? Okay, the zoo wins, 15 to 12." About the best that can be said for this exercise is that it didn't take very long. Children have learned precious little about how to solve a problem, accommodate other people's preferences, or rethink their initial inclinations. Moreover, 12 children are now unlikely to feel very excited about the upcoming field trip. The same analysis applies on a schoolwide basis. The usual student council apparatus is deficient on three counts: most students are excluded from direct participation in decision making, some students are turned into losers since the representatives are chosen in a contest, and the council has little real power in any case. Educators interested in democratic values will discourage voting whenever possible; as the political philosopher Benjamin Barber has cogently argued, it is "the least significant act of citizenship in a democracy." See *Strong Democracy: Participatory Politics for a New Age* (Berkeley: University of California Press, 1984), p. 187.

36. My own thinking on how class meetings might be structured has been influenced primarily by the work of the Child Development Project, whose writings on the topic have not been published. I would, however, recommend two other useful and very practical discussions of class meetings: William Glasser, *Schools Without Failure* (New York: Harper and Row, 1969), chaps. 10-12; and Lickona, chap. 8.

37. "Democracy in the classroom . . . begins simply: with respect for the child as a person, someone who has a point of view and a right and a need to express it." See Thomas Lickona and Muffy Paradise, "Democracy in the Elementary School," in Ralph Mosher, ed., *Moral Education: A First Generation of Research and Development* (New York: Praeger, 1980), p. 325.

38. The quotation is from Dewey's *The School and Society* (Chicago: University of Chicago Press, 1990), p. 130.

39. "In Summerhill, a child is *not* allowed to do as he pleases," Neill added. See *Summerhill* (New York: Hart, 1960), pp. 308, 348.

40. On this point, see Lickona and Paradise, p. 323.

41. Thomas Gordon, *Teaching Children Self-Discipline* (New York: Times Books, 1989), p. 9.

42. This distinction is offered frequently in the work

of Edward Deci and Richard Ryan. It seemed to be lost on several teachers at an alternative school program I visited recently who maintained that, because today's students come from less structured home environments or are more conservative, it is appropriate to give them fewer choices about their learning.

43. Carolyn Edwards, "Partner, Nurturer, and Guide," in Carolyn Edwards et al., eds., *The Hundred Languages of Children: The Reggio Emilia Approach to Early Childhood Education* (Norwood, N.J.: Ablex, 1993), p. 157.

44. Indeed, children whose curiosity has not been killed by the use of rewards or other extrinsic controls typically select tasks of the right difficulty level for themselves. This finding "suggests that at least part of the teacher's difficult problem of matching tasks to children can be solved by providing children with more choices than they are typically offered." See Fred W. Danner and Edward Lonky, "A Cognitive-Developmental Approach to the Effects of Rewards on Intrinsic Motivation," *Child Development*, vol. 52, 1981, p. 1050.

45. A related restriction on choice that may be employed excessively is the practice of preventing students from altering an activity once they have selected it. They can choose, in other words, only among tasks that must be performed in a rigidly prescribed manner. Some critics have argued that this is a weakness of the Montessori method.

46. A nice discussion of this misuse of the idea of choice can be found in Vincent Crockenberg, "Assertive Discipline: A Dissent," *California Journal of Teacher Education*, vol. 9, 1982, esp. pp. 65-70.

47. Nel Noddings, *The Challenge to Care in Schools* (New York: Teachers College Press, 1992), p. 23.

48. James A. Beane, *Affect in the Curriculum: Toward Democracy, Dignity, and Diversity* (New York: Teachers College Press, 1990), p. 35.

49. Dewey, *Experience and Education*, p. 55.

50. McNeil, p. 9. This phenomenon is not limited to schools, of course. There is evidence from the corporate world that the middle managers most likely to act in an autocratic fashion toward those below them in the hierarchy are those who are restricted and controlled themselves. See Rosabeth Moss Kanter, *Men and Women of the Corporation* (New York: Basic Books, 1977), pp. 189-90.

51. Despite the claim that discipline is "instrumental to mastering the content," the truth is often just the reverse: "many teachers . . . maintain discipline by the ways they present course content." The reduction of teaching to the transfer of disconnected facts and skills is the means; keeping a tight grip on student behavior is the end. See McNeil, pp. 157-58.

52. Phyllis C. Blumenfeld et al., "Teacher Talk and Student Thought," in John M. Levine and Margaret C. Wang, eds., *Teacher and Student Perceptions* (Hillsdale, N.J.: Erlbaum, 1983), p. 147.

53. A survey of more than 300 parents found that those who inclined toward a negative view of human nature were more likely to prefer an authoritarian approach to child rearing. See Lawrence O. Clayton, "The Impact upon Child-Rearing Attitudes of Parental Views of the Nature of Humankind," *Journal of Psychology and Christianity*, vol. 4, no. 3, 1985, pp. 49-55. For an argument that the data do not support this negative view of human nature, see Alfie Kohn, *The Brighter Side of Human Nature: Altruism and Empathy in Everyday Life* (New York: Basic Books, 1990).

54. On this point, see Seth Kreisberg, "Educating for Democracy and Community," *ESR Journal*, 1992, p. 72; and Rheta DeVries, *Programs of Early Education: The Constructivist View* (New York: Longman, 1987), p. 379.

55. Selma Wassermann, "Children Working in Groups? It Doesn't Work!," *Childhood Education*, Summer 1989, p. 204.

Motivating Underachievers:
Make them *want* to try

DEBORAH STIPEK

Deborah Stipek was an associate professor of education at UCLA when she wrote this article.

SOONER OR LATER, AN UNDER-achiever will challenge your teaching skill—and your patience—with unfinished assignments, complaints, and excuses. Maybe you'll try to coax the child into working harder. Maybe you'll enlist the aid of parents. Maybe you'll search for special projects to pique the child's interest. And maybe none of these tactics will succeed.

Laziness, boredom, and apathy don't explain the behavior of all underachieving students. For many smart kids who fail, *not* trying simply makes more sense than the alternative. Take Melanie and Jeff, for example.

Melanie, an intelligent 2nd grader, rarely hands in homework. And when given an in-class assignment, she invariably whines, "That's too hard" or "I can't do this" until her teacher comes to help. On tests, Melanie often "consults" her classmates' papers.

Jeff, on the other hand, would never cheat on a test or seek help from a teacher or classmate. But the 6th grader is often conspicuously inattentive in class. And "bad luck" keeps him from completing a surprising number of tasks, particularly ones dealing with new material. He leaves books necessary for doing homework at school. He loses assignments on the bus. Sometimes during a test his pen runs out of ink, and he wastes valuable time rummaging through his desk to find another.

Why try?
Both Jeff and Melanie pay a price for their lack of effort: bad grades, reprimands from their teachers, detentions. Yet both persist in their behavior. Why? The answer is deceptively simple: These kids see the benefits of not trying as outweighing the costs.

Melanie is sure she *can't* do the assigned work, regardless of how hard she tries. Since effort or apathy will lead to the same end—failure—putting forth the least effort possible is perfectly logical. So Melanie continues to rely on teachers and classmates to get her through.

Unlike Melanie, Jeff isn't convinced that he can't do his schoolwork. But he has serious doubts. Since Jeff desperately wants to believe that he's intelligent and competent, and wants others to believe this too, he's afraid to try hard and fail. So for Jeff also, *not* trying—and flaunting his lack of effort—makes sense. It allows him to hold on to a self-image of competence.

Stubborn beliefs
For students like Jeff and Melanie, beliefs about personal ability and the costs and benefits of

effort can be difficult to change. For example, when Melanie *does* do well on an assignment or test, she's likely to attribute her success to the teacher's help, an easy task, or good luck. So occasional successes won't necessarily bolster her self-confidence. What really needs to be changed is her belief that no amount of effort will improve her chances of succeeding. Similarly, Jeff needs to be persuaded that making mistakes isn't a sign of stupidity or incompetence, but a natural part of the learning process. Only then will trying make sense.

Encouraging effort

The following guidelines will help you make sure that the benefits of trying outweigh those of not trying—for *all* your students.

1. Make sure that assigned tasks are realistic, so that all students can complete them if they really try. When your class contains kids with vastly different skill levels, this isn't easy. But you can use such techniques as teaching in small, flexible groups; creating cooperative work groups or setting up a peer teaching program; and preparing different assignments for different skill levels. To alleviate the additional burden this places on you, have your students check some of their own or one another's assignments. This also gives students a sense of responsibility for their own learning.

2. Focus students' attention on their own progress, not on their classmates' performance. When students measure their success by their peers' performance, those who don't do as well are bound to feel like failures. Base grades and rewards on mastery or improvement, not on relative performance. Reward the child who reduced his spelling errors from 50 percent to 20 percent just as enthusiastically as you reward the child who invariably gets all the words right. Put papers that show improvement, not just the best papers, on the bulletin board. Consider marking workbook exercises with a check mark if they're correct but making no mark if they're not. Have the student continue to work on the exercises until all have received a check mark. This allows kids many opportunities to improve their performance without any negative evaluation.

3. Reward effort, whatever the outcome. Tell your students that in learning, as in any endeavor, setbacks are inevitable. But effort and perseverance *do* pay off. Praise kids when they make progress, not just when they get everything right. If only success is praised, some students may become demoralized when their efforts don't lead to immediate mastery—which is a likely outcome when they're studying new material. And when a student does immediately master a new skill, take care not to be overly enthusiastic. Otherwise, you'll risk sending the message that you really do value brilliance rather than diligence, and slower kids may become discouraged.

4. Give every student opportunities to demonstrate competence in class. Consider setting aside a few minutes each week for kids to demonstrate an unusual—and nonacademic—skill. For example, ask your teeny Houdini to show off some sleight of hand, or your fledgling "Bird" to play a saxophone solo. This way, even academically weak students will get a good dose of self-confidence.

5. Allow students to set their own goals. (Of course, you need to make sure that these goals are realistic but challenging.) For example, encourage a child who consistently fails the weekly math quiz to set a goal for next week's quiz (say, getting two more problems correct). Have the child record the goal and his actual performance on a chart. This will give the child a concrete picture of his own progress and will foster personal responsibility. It will also reinforce the importance of perseverance.

Using Motivational Theory with At-Risk Children

Rachel Buck Collopy
and Theresa Green

Rachel Buck Collopy is a doctoral student, Combined Program in Education and Psychology, 1400 School of Education, University of Michigan, Ann Arbor, MI 48109. **Theresa Green** is Principal, Rawsonville Elementary School, 3110 Grove Rd., Ypsilanti, MI 48198.

Rawsonville Elementary is a neighborhood school near Detroit, where the automotive industry is the major employer. Recent layoffs have affected many families in the area, and more than half of the school's 480 students receive reduced or free lunch. Of the district's six elementary schools, Rawsonville has been identified as most in need of Chapter 1 services. For years, the school improvement team had worked hard to improve student motivation and learning. Yet, something was still missing. The number of at-risk and under-achieving students entering the school continued to increase.

At the same time, a group of researchers at the University of Michigan had been testing a theory of student motivation known as achievement goal theory (see Maehr and Midgley 1991, Maehr and Pintrich 1991). Their work confirmed what other studies had indicated: The goals that students pursue have a powerful influence on the quality of their learning. Schools, through their policies and practices, give strong messages to students about how success is defined within their walls. As collaborative partners, the faculty at Rawsonville Elementary and the researchers at the University of Michigan

aimed to create a school where the emphasis was on learning rather than on relative ability.

> **Rawsonville Elementary used achievement goal theory to create a learner-centered school, where success is measured not by relative ability but by individual accomplishment.**

Emphasizing Achievement, Not Ability

Often in schools where students adopt ability goals, students come to believe that success is defined in terms of how they do in comparison to others. Implicit in the comparative definition of success is the belief that some students are smart, some are average, and some are dumb. The goal becomes trying to look smart—or at least not to look dumb. Mistakes and failure, because they indicate lack of ability, are threats to a child's self-esteem (Covington 1984). Students who adopt ability goals are more likely to avoid challenging tasks and to give up in the face of difficulty (Elliott and Dweck 1988).

In contrast, learning goals define success in terms of developing skills, expanding knowledge, and gaining understanding. Success means being able to do something you could not do before. When students adopt learning goals, they take on more challenging tasks, persist longer, are less debili-

tated by mistakes and failure, and use higher-level thinking skills than when they focus on ability goals (See Ames 1992 for a review of research).

As partners in a three-year collaboration, we aimed to make Rawsonville a school where the emphasis was on learning rather than on relative ability. Achievement goal theory does not mandate policies and practices. Rather, practitioners use it as a framework to develop consistent, integrated policies and practices that are appropriate to the needs and strengths of their students, staffs, and communities. The issues of most urgent concern to teachers were our starting point.

Photos courtesy of Theresa Green

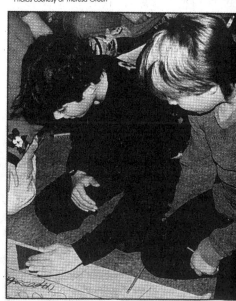

In cooperative groups, students learn spatial awareness using tangrams.

FIGURE 1

Rawsonville Elementary School's Principles of Recognition

1. Recognize individual student effort, accomplishment, and improvement.

2. Give all students opportunities to be recognized.

3. Give recognition privately whenever possible.

4. Avoid using "most" or "best" for recognizing or rewarding, as in "best project" or "most improved." These words usually convey comparisons with others.

5. Avoid recognizing on the basis of absence of mistakes. For example, avoid giving awards for students who get "fewer than five words wrong on a spelling test."

6. Avoid using the same criteria for all students. For example, avoid giving an award to "all students who get an *A* on the science test, or all students who do four out of five projects."

7. Recognize students for taking on challenging work or for stretching their own abilities (even if they make mistakes).

8. Recognize students for coming up with different and unusual ways to solve a problem or approach a task.

9. Try to involve students in the recognition process. What is of value to them? How much effort do they feel they put in? Where do they feel they need improvement? How do they know when they have reached their goals?

10. It's OK to recognize students in various domains (behavior, athletics, attendance), but every student should have the opportunity to be recognized *academically*.

11. Try to recognize the quality of students' work rather than the quantity. For example, recognizing students for reading a lot of books could encourage them to read easy books.

12. Avoid recognizing grades and test scores. This takes the emphasis away from learning and problem solving.

13. Recognition must be real. Do not recognize students for accomplishing something they have not really accomplished, for improving if they have not improved, or for trying hard if that is not the case.

Creating Learning-Focused Classrooms

Having heard a lot about the long-term negative effects of retaining students, Rawsonville's teachers were eager to find alternatives to retention. Their early discussions focused on add-ons of financial, human, and material resources. Then, two teachers suggested fundamentally changing the structure of the classroom. If several grades were taught together, they proposed, children would focus on their own improvement and progress at their own developmental pace.

A flood of questions followed. More than just the ages of students would be different in these classrooms. All areas of schooling—from curriculum, materials, and scheduling to teaching methods, classroom management, and evaluation—needed to be reconsidered. Together, we gathered information from experts in other schools and universities. We discussed the obstacles to change. Most important, we confronted our assumptions about the way learning and schooling had to be conducted and began to dream about how it could be.

As the learning-focused, multi-age classrooms began to take shape, it became clear that high- as well as low-achieving students would benefit from the proposed changes:

■ Students would stay with the same teacher for at least two years.

■ The approach to instruction would be interdisciplinary and thematic.

■ Students would progress at their own speed—focusing on meeting learning objectives, not following a lockstep curriculum.

■ The learning-focused classrooms would take advantage of the variety of skill levels through peer tutoring, cooperative learning, and inter-age cooperation.

■ Report cards would reflect progress and mastery rather than emphasizing comparative performance with letter grades.

Four teachers decided to pilot the classrooms during 1990–91. At the beginning, they were understandably anxious about possible student failures. By the end of the first year, however, they reported that students were more willing to participate in learning activities, more enthusiastic about learning, and showed greater concern for the learning of classmates. Now, half of Rawsonville's classrooms contain children of two or three grade levels.

Developing a learning-focused environment for children did not stop at the doorway of multi-age classrooms. The theoretical framework of achievement goal theory can be used to redesign single-age classrooms, too. Since Rawsonville's self-renewal began five years ago, the teachers of single-age classrooms have also moved toward an emphasis on improvement, understanding, and effort. Teachers now share methods and techniques that encourage students to adopt learning goals across all classrooms.

School change, of course, is about more than just changing classrooms. Classrooms exist within schools and are affected by the policies and practices of the wider school culture. The efforts of an individual teacher to emphasize learning goals can be undermined by school policies that emphasize relative ability and comparative performance.

Abandoning the Honor Roll

As her understanding of achievement goal theory increased, Rawsonville's principal realized that the traditional honor roll defined the goal of learning as outperforming others, not improving regardless of relative performance. Each term, only a small group of students received honor roll certificates. In addition to serving as a disincentive for the children who never received the certificates, the honor roll also discouraged high-achieving children from trying challenging tasks.

The principal's decision to eliminate the honor roll started a firestorm of controversy. Many teachers felt that they had lost a carrot to urge students to try hard; they also pointed out that many parents took pride in the honor roll certificates. As they searched for ways to recognize children in a learning-focused manner, teachers came up with Rawsonville's Principles of Recognition. Instead of dictating uniform recognition policies and practices, these principles serve as guidelines that respect the professionalism, creativity, and personal style of teachers (see fig. 1).

Other schoolwide recognition policies were also guided by the new prin-

Peer tutoring, cooperative learning, and inter-age cooperation are hallmarks of the learning-focused classroom.

ciples. As an alternative to making the honor roll, every upper elementary student now receives a certificate recognizing him or her for an area of improvement, accomplishment, and effort. Similarly, at the 5th grade awards ceremony, every graduate is applauded for an accomplishment. In the past, only a handful of students were recognized for their achievements—and often these students received several awards. By the fifth or sixth time a student went up to collect an award, other students would groan instead of applaud.

The faculty at Rawsonville Elementary have also redesigned other schoolwide policies and practices in line with a more learning-focused environment. Rather than emphasizing rewards and punishments, discipline procedures now focus on teaching children to become problem solvers. The use of mini-lessons on conflict resolution and peer mediation, for

example, has lessened discipline problems more than rewarding the "good" and punishing the "bad" ever did.

After the three-year collaboration with the University of Michigan formally ended, Rawsonville sought out a second collaborative relationship with another nearby university with the goal of increasing students' computer literacy. Staff have implemented classroom computer use within the framework of achievement goal theory. Teachers now view computers as a way to help all children—not just slow learners or gifted students—learn problem-solving and reasoning skills.

Continuing the Effort

Rawsonville Elementary's approach is but one example of how to put achievement goal theory into practice. Other schools may decide to focus on other pressing issues or design solutions that are theoretically consistent

Rather than emphasizing rewards and punishments, discipline procedures now focus on teaching children to become problem solvers.

with, but superficially different from, Rawsonville's. What is important is the theoretical perspective, the philosophical underpinnings, that these changes in practice exemplify.

Today, because a large proportion of children entering Rawsonville is still considered at risk, the faculty's commitment to the course they have set has become more important than ever. At the beginning of each school year, the principal and teachers review the changes they made and discuss the rationale behind them. Teachers have taken over the researchers' role of questioning: Will every child benefit from this experience? What message will this give about the goal of learning? What does this say about what is valued at this school?

Now that we know that achievement goal theory can be put into practice, what difference has it made? Teachers have reported improved attendance, increased enthusiasm for learning, and decreased discipline problems. As one teacher said, "I could never go back to teaching the way I did before." Referring to students' improved attitude toward learning, a 20-year veteran wrote:

Some students became so interested in some aspect of classwork that they did correlating activities on their own at home. Children brought in books, magazines, newspapers, and artifacts that pertained to areas of study. They wrote plays, drew pictures, and made dioramas.... During our study of Japan, one little boy got so interested in haiku that he borrowed my books on it and began writing it—in school and at home. His mom reported that he was driving them "cuckoo" with his "haiku."

Parents are very supportive of these efforts to change. Through formal and informal feedback, they report that their children have become more confident, more willing to take on challenges, more excited about school, and better at working independently and with others. About her son, one parent wrote on a survey that she saw "great improvement in all areas—from a student who was failing and had low self-esteem to an interested, highly motivated *learner*!"

One clear example stands out of the extent to which the school community has embraced the changes brought about by achievement goal theory. At

a recent PTO meeting, two parents suggested adding competitive rewards to an annual school event. Other parents told them that Rawsonville is not about winning and losing. It is about every child having access to the same enriching and educational experiences. It is about *learning*.

References

Ames, C. (1992). "Classrooms: Goals, Structures, and Student Motivation." *Journal of Educational Psychology* 84, 3: 261–271.

Covington, M. V. (1984). "The Self-Worth Theory of Achievement Motivation: Findings and Implications." *Elementary School Journal* 85: 5–20.

Elliott, E. S., and C. S. Dweck. (1988). "Goals: An Approach to Motivation and Achievement." *Journal of Personality and Social Psychology* 54: 5–12.

Maehr, M. L., and C. Midgley. (1991). "Enhancing Student Motivation: A Schoolwide Approach." *Educational Psychologist* 26, 3 & 4: 399–427.

Maehr, M. L., and P. R. Pintrich. (1991). *Advances in Motivation and Achievement, Vol. 7.* Greenwich, Conn.: JAI Press.

Authors' note: An earlier version of this paper was presented at the annual meeting of the American Educational Research Association, Atlanta, 1993. This work was supported in part by grants from the Office of Educational Research and Improvement. The opinions expressed, however, are those of the authors and do not represent OERI policy.

This collaboration would not have been possible without Carol Midgley and Martin Maehr of the University of Michigan and the teachers of Rawsonville Elementary School.

From Negation to Negotiation: Moving Away from the Management Metaphor

H. James McLaughlin

H. James McLaughlin formerly taught middle grades Social Studies and Mathematics. He conducts research about multi-age grouping and issues related to caring and controlling, and collaborates with teachers to do team action research.

ABSTRACT

The purpose of this article is to critique the prevailing metaphor of classroom management. The article depicts three perspectives on classroom relationships that offer differing aims: obedience, responsibility, and solidarity. First, the purposes and uses of authority within an obedience perspective are examined. Then follows a description of recent efforts to widen the interpretation of the classroom management metaphor by shifting the focus from obedience to responsibility. Subsequently, the author discusses how teacher educators might perceive classrooms and schools as sites of negotiation between teachers and students. The purposes, realms, and limits of negotiating are examined, and ideas about how to enact negotiation are presented. A summary section explores the implications of a negotiatory perspective for teacher educators and researchers.

All metaphors about teaching and learning are legitimated within philosophical systems and corresponding political stances, and they serve the interests of certain people. "Classroom management" has long been the predominant metaphor for establishing relations of authority. In its most benign form (Brown, 1933; Sears, 1928), the classroom management of generations ago meant altering the environment to encourage learning, practicing democratic principles rather than relying on teacher autocracy, and balancing punishments with positive incentives. Alter the language, along with the dated cultural references, and Brown's open-ended, wide-ranging casebook of

classroom management problems could be in print today. But alongside such accounts of the need for a democratic management, there have always been denunciations of student misbehavior and concomitant calls for greater obedience. At a societal level, the modern management metaphor mirrors a centuries-old movement to enact discipline and gain control over the individual. The term "management" accurately reflects a preoccupation with scientific efficiency and bureaucratic political control at the school level. Principals are no longer "lead teachers," but are middle-level managers.

At the classroom level, the management idea covers a lot of territory (Charles, 1989; Doyle, 1986; Duke & Meckel, 1984; and Emmer, Evertson, Sanford, Clements, & Worsham, 1989, offer extended explanations of approaches to classroom management). There is a broader definition that may entail organizing (keeping track of one's materials, establishing seating charts, and maintaining an accurate and up-to-date grading system), planning (utilizing a variety of instructional techniques), knowing students, evaluating oneself, and maintaining a positive attitude (Reed, 1991). But a significant segment of the education literature has described management in terms of rules, disciplinary actions, and other means of shaping students' actions.

The purpose of this article is to critique the prevailing metaphor of classroom management. The article depicts three perspectives on classroom relationships that encompass differing aims: obedience, responsibility, and solidarity. First, I examine the purposes and uses of authority within an "obedience perspective." Then I describe recent efforts to widen the interpretation of how to establish viable classroom relationships by shifting the focus from obedience to responsibility. Subsequently, there is a discussion of how we might perceive classrooms and schools as sites of negotiation between teachers and students. The purposes, realms, and limits of negotiating are described, and ideas about how to enact negotiation are presented. A summary section explores the implications of a negotiatory perspective for teacher educators and researchers.

From *Action in Teacher Education*, Spring 1994, pp. 75-85. © 1994 by the Association of Teacher Educators. Reprinted by permission.

THE OBEDIENCE PERSPECTIVE

A major purpose of authority—and the uses of power—in the obedience perspective is to maintain adult control over younger people. Teachers are to concern themselves with the most efficient means of control. The focus on efficiency is shown by an astonishing claim in the midst of a debate over the importance of student obedience:

> Without obedience and adult-formed structure, random forces will control student learning. This fosters inefficiency at best and, at worst, error. . . . Simply put, there *is* no task without clear and explicit teacher control, no matter how the control is manifest, and there is no "time on task" unless there is student obedience to that control (Zern, 1991, p. 7, author's emphasis).

In the preceding account, classroom management is a matter of *teacher behaviors* and not student actions. Learning tasks and structures are fashioned independent of student actions or concerns, and students are supposed to learn only what the teacher proposes. It is the professional version of 18th century aristocratic *noblesse oblige:* teachers should not share power with students because doing so constitutes legitimate authority in teaching; rather, students may learn something of interest to them or may offer a few suggestions about class rules because teachers are big-hearted and it fits their plans. Obedience is meant to result in greater time-on-task and efficiency.

Over the last decade "Assertive Discipline" has been the primary purveyor of the obedience perspective. Assertive Discipline places a strong emphasis on teachers taking charge, on being strong. Questions about its merits have swirled through the pages of leading educational journals. Has research proven this discipline program effective? How should we account for the views of practitioners in assessing program effectiveness? What are the unintended outcomes or hidden curriculum of Assertive Discipline? A recent exchange centered on such questions (McCormack, 1989; Render et al., 1989). The major research or anecdotal evidence for effectiveness included whether teachers, students and administrators perceived it as effective; whether disciplinary referrals of students decreased; and whether "off-task behavior" abated. Should teacher or administrator satisfaction with a program provide the sole evidence of its effectiveness? Is that sort of outcome related to greater student learning of important knowledge, or simply to stronger control by someone in assumed authority? Debates in journals will not resolve these issues.

There have been many criticisms of the obedience perspective on the grounds that it does not address the need for student input, it may exacerbate confrontations with students, it fails to teach students how to be responsible, it decreases teacher flexibility by pressuring teachers to publicly treat all students the same, and it is relatively ineffective anyway (Curwin & Mendler, 1988, 1989; Denscombe, 1985; Evans, Corsini, & Gazda, 1990; Jones, 1991; Lickona, 1991). Proponents of Assertive Discipline have denied the program's singular focus on obedience, and have asserted that the approach encourages students to be "self-managers" (Canter, 1989). But Assertive Discipline still embodies the supposition that self-control is born of unyielding obedience to adult domination, and that

student responsibility is engendered by the teacher's rules and consequences. The obedience perspective is flawed, but not because students should have the license to do whatever they wish in classrooms. There is no argument that some forms of social control are necessary for any classroom interaction to benefit the participants. The problem is that an obedience perspective incorporates a series of unexamined assumptions about the nature of power and control in classrooms and schools. The following five assumptions characterize certain myths of teacher control in classrooms.

Control is a classroom matter

Apple (1990), Foucault (1979), and Popkewitz (1987) painted with a broad brush the changing meanings of educational control from a societal standpoint. Denscombe (1985) has concentrated on the institutional contexts of control in schools. In Denscombe's analysis, teachers assume that classroom control is a prime duty because of prior experiences as students, the failure of teacher education to challenge assumptions, and their socialization as new teachers (p. 53). Control is also deemed necessary because of schools' social and physical organization, particularly the influence of classroom autonomy and isolation. The implicit demand for quiet, order and stillness in classrooms emanates from administrators, other teachers, and students themselves, and not just from classroom dynamics.

There exists a consensus about the aims of control, so we ought to concentrate on the means of control.

This assumed consensus is apparent in articles written by behavior management advocates (e.g., Schockley & Sevier, 1991). As I will point out shortly, the assumptions about aims are being challenged by those promoting education for responsibility and for solidarity.

Control is non-negotiated because power is assumed by the teacher's position and not conferred by students.

Glasser (1990) has articulately challenged this assumption. He talks of "boss-managers" who expect obedience and "lead-managers" who understand that real power is conferred by students when their basic needs are met. In traditional behavioral versions of classroom management, students may help to establish rules at the start of a school year, but the ongoing enforcement of those rules often is not cast as a series of negotiations over the exercise of power in the classroom—which I believe it is.

Control is basically non-curricular, and "classroom management" is differentiated from "instruction."

Denscombe (1985) posited that there are three kinds of teacher strategies which explicitly or implicitly aim to reduce teachers' reliance on personal charismatic authority and minimize uncertainty: domination, classwork management and co-optation. "Domination" strategies, which involve direct commands for compliance, fit neatly within the obedience perspective. The two other strategies assert control in less obtrusive ways. "Classwork management" relies on limited, teacher-led instructional strategies to maintain authority (such as recitation), and on group management strategies where the intention is to "keep 'em busy" and to utilize the threat of work or testing to control students' actions. "Co-optation" is achieved when students participate in sports, school committees and the like. "[T]he democratization tends to be illusory and is geared primarily to securing a certain commitment on the part of pupils to the existing social order" (p. 111). On a classroom level, teachers might use humor or a cultural identification with students to gain the students' personal commitment to class activities. Each of these strategies reflects how control is socially constructed in classrooms, even as school and societal contexts exert powerful effects. Denscombe's ideas about classwork management and co-optation relate instruction and management. McNeil (1987) and others have shown the workings of curricular control through the narrowing of content and the limiting of questioning. There is no sense in divorcing how one establishes and nurtures classroom relationships from how one teaches; the former is part-and-parcel of the latter.

Problems that threaten control are thought to reside in individual students, and so ought to be resolved through encounters with a student or a family.

There is a grievous lack of attention paid to the social nature of how one defines a "problem." Problems occur when individuals interact in a certain arena, and thus they reside within situated social systems (Purkey & Strahan, 1986, pp. 25–29). The contexts that Denscombe (1985) and others have described let us see that problems are socially and contextually defined, according to what is considered "normal" in a certain setting, and that the same actions could be labeled differently in another circumstance.

THE RESPONSIBILITY PERSPECTIVE

The responsibility perspective, which is often perceived by its proponents as a form of classroom management, offers a challenge to the behavior management metaphor that underlies an obedience perspective. Curwin and Mendler (1988) have aptly described the responsibility perspective. Its purpose is to teach students to take responsibility for their behavior. They can learn to be responsible if they are treated with dignity, if the teacher employs logical consequences, and if the teacher understands the relationship between good teaching and good discipline. The student learns that "I cause my own outcomes. I have more than one alternative behavior in any situation. I have the power to choose the best alternative" (p. 26). The authors are disdainful of a "packaged method" and supportive of a "caring classroom environment" (p. 31).

The promises and problems associated with the responsibility perspective can be found in many summaries: Evans, Corsini, & Gazda's "Individual Education" (1990); Glasser's "Control

Theory" (1990); Kohn's "Caring Schools" (1991); Lickona's "Educating for Character" (1991); Purkey & Strahan's "Positive Discipline" (1986); and Schaps & Solomon's "Developmental Discipline" (1990). Seldom do the writings on responsibility address the complex contexts of schooling and classrooms (Lickona, 1991, pp. 323–347 and 395–420, presents an exception, although the author does not account for culture, gender or social class as contexts of control and socialization). Discussions of the history and politics of control are rarely broached.

The purpose of classroom management within this perspective is most commonly to promote individual behavioral and attitudinal change—what could be labeled "self-discipline." Authors in this vein reject overt coercion, de-emphasize struggles over control, and emphasize individual choice-making and mutual respect (see examples in Curwin & Mendler, 1988, pp. 102–109). Lists of goals such as "responsibility, respect, resourcefulness, and responsiveness" (Evans, Corsini, & Gazda, 1990) or "trust, intentionality, respect, and optimism" (Purkey & Strahan, 1986) are promoted. Rewards and consequences are demoted in favor of efforts to intrinsically motivate students. Whatever consequences are enforced should be "natural" and "logical" (with hats off to Dreikurs Cassel, 1972).

In this perspective I applaud the emphasis on engendering students' self-discipline through teachers' caring acts. I also think that throughout this literature on responsibility there seems an uneasy peace between centering on responsibility for oneself (an emphasis that is quite pronounced in Evans, Corsini, & Gazda, 1990), and focusing more on group processes and responsibility for others (especially Kohn, 1991; Schaps & Solomon, 1990; and the numerous practical examples in Lickona, 1991). This is because in some cases there are *really two* potentially complementary purposes being discussed: responsibility and solidarity. Legitimate authority depends on establishing solidarity with and among students, through classroom negotiations. The next section of the article discusses the contexts, purposes, and practices of negotiation.

NEGOTIATION AND THE CREATION OF LEGITIMATE AUTHORITY

The tensions of establishing legitimate authority

For teachers today, issues of authority and control are dealt with through numerous inservice programs that purport to show them how to be better classroom "managers" and how to deal with discipline problems in a more efficient and positive manner. "Teacher as manager" is highlighted, and the idea of "teacher as negotiator" is generally ignored. Even so, good teachers are not simply well-meaning but unwitting institutional managers. Most teachers with whom I have taught and talked over the years wish to enact legitimate authority by encouraging varying levels of student participation. In doing so, they experience an important tension in teaching. *Tension* derives from the Latin "tendere," meaning "to stretch." Tension is the state of being stretched tight and made taut; or in another light, the balance maintained in an artistic work between opposing forces or elements (Webster's). Frequently, tension is interpreted in negative terms. The teacher may feel stretched to the point of breaking because of an inability to control events in the classroom, or to maintain a caring approach to students. Such tensions are certainly present, but I want also to examine the positive form of tension, as a balance between differing (though not always opposing) forces.

In this case, I believe there are two sorts of tensions teachers feel. One is between the desire to care for students and the hope to control the environment and students' actions. The other tension is between a focus on individual responsibilities and a focus on group solidarity. Solidarity "involves the rapport established through social interaction or the feeling that the interaction is proceeding on the basis of some shared interest" (Bowers & Flinders, 1989, p. 141). Many teachers seek to legitimate their authority—and thus their uses of power—by balancing acts of caring and controlling, along with individual and shared interests (McLaughlin, 1991).

Facing up to these tensions compels teachers to understand and utilize various forms of *negotiation,* which is one aspect of caring for students. Negotiation is the basis for establishing "power with" students, rather than simply "power over" them (Kreisberg, 1992). It is built on a desire to determine shared interests, an ability to confer about decisions to be made and curricular ideas to be plumbed, and a willingness to face up to conflict and then shape a compromise. There are important questions to be asked about whose interests are shared in classrooms, and about how issues of gender, culture, and social class arise in these discussions. I will now pose a series of questions concerning the purposes, realms and limits of negotiation.

Purposes of negotiation: Why do we negotiate?

Kohn (1991) stated that two of the approaches to changing students' behaviors and attitudes are "encouraging commitment to values" ("to help that child see himself or herself as the kind of person who is responsible and caring") and "encouraging the group's commitment to values" (to help the child internalize the value of community) (p. 501). Schaps and Solomon (1990) noted how children are motivated by "belonging and contributing" (p. 39), and Glasser (1990) spoke of children's needs for "power and belonging" (p. 54). Those comments and others signal the need for schools to balance the goals of individual responsibility and group solidarity. Negotiation cannot work without an individual commitment which incorporates a sense of responsibility for oneself. Nor can negotiation work without a sense of social responsibility which enables shared interests to be sought and conflicts to be directly faced. Negotiatory acts are a form of power sharing that represents the teacher's caring commitment to democratic governance and an exploration of alternative forms of social control.

Realms of negotiation: What is negotiable? How do we negotiate?

Not everything in a classroom or school is negotiable. On a schoolwide level, such practices as grading, holding classes in scheduled 50-minute periods, responding to bells, doing fire drills, and the like are nearly inescapable aspects of much institutional work. There *are* numerous ways in which teachers might agitate for broad institutional changes, in addition to the common struggles over salary or working conditions. But the focus of this section lies on classroom interactions.

In the classroom a teacher can ignore students, encourage them, negotiate in one form or another, or try to directly control without negotiation. A common principle of classroom action is to ignore what appears to be peripheral and to control what seems seriously disruptive. All else could be deemed negotiable. Often, the realms of negotiation are perceived to encompass those times when students misbehave, when they reject one's "invitations" to participate in a positive manner (Purkey & Strahan, 1986, pp. 21–22). Another way to mark the boundaries is to conceive of "discipline" as "cooperative planning and problem solving" about matters of procedures, pedagogy and "housekeeping" (Kohn, 1991, p. 504). Matters of discipline and control are curricular and non-curricular, and the possible realms of negotiation are vast. I will now describe examples of how a teacher might negotiate in three classroom realms: setting rules and goals, developing curriculum, and organizing classroom activities.

Setting Rules and Goals

Much has been written on how to develop rules and procedures collaboratively. Curwin and Mendler (1988) talk of a "social contract" in classrooms (pp. 47–64), Lickona (1991) details a "cooperative approach to rule-setting" (pp. 112–134), and Glasser (1990) holds that "lead-managers have minimal rules" which are derived through discussion (pp. 122–127). Sarason (1971) thinks of rule-setting as a matter of governance, one among many "constitutional issues" (pp. 175–178).

The aforementioned authors have offered numerous fine ideas to engage students in the negotiation of rules. There are also efforts to negotiate when conflicts arise between students, or between student and teacher. In Schaps and Solomon's "developmental discipline," the children "work collaboratively with the teacher to develop solutions to discipline problems" (1990, p. 39). Conflict resolution, a term referring to a range of formal negotiatory processes, is being enacted in scores of schools. Lickona (1991) gives examples of how teachers use "class meetings" to discuss classroom problems (pp. 143–147) and depicts several programs and information sources (286–299).

In addition to the teacher-directed approaches above, peer mediation has shown promise. The "Dispute Management in the Schools" project involved a cooperative venture between a university and school district (Araki & Takeshita, 1991). Researchers found that 95 percent of the disputes between students resulted in agreements that were still in effect a year later. "The project also revealed that all ethnic groups subscribe equally to the conflict management process, and that mediators need not be of the same ethnic group, sex, or position of influence as the disputants to be effective" (p. 36).

One more comment on this topic. Issues of gender, social status, and ethnicity should not be ignored during formal negotiations to resolve conflicts. Shook's descriptions of "ho'oponopono" (1985), a traditional Hawai'ian family problem-solving process, point out the cultural assumptions in mediation practices. There is more to be considered about the cultural and political assumptions of teacher- or peer-directed mediation.

In addition to rules and disputes, class goals can also be negotiated. Lickona (1991) detailed how some teachers have expanded students' roles in decision-making, which includes setting goals for the class. There needs to be more research and personal descriptions of the nature of teachers' and students' goals, and how the sometimes-conflicting goals might be negotiated.

Developing Curriculum

Teacher and students can cooperatively determine the topics for an upcoming curriculum unit. Beane (1990) has challenged the dominant subject-centered curriculum and proposed that an integrated curriculum center on students' personal concerns and vital social issues. Though Beane did not fully develop the planning process, in his scheme students' interests would be represented and a negotiatory process would be included in teachers' plans.

Curriculum is not a disembodied set of materials; it consists of the plans a teacher creates in advance and then continually re-creates in classroom interactions with students. A program called "Touchstones" encourages student leadership and participation in discussions by employing strategies to develop a group "where the students listen to and speak with one another, where every utterance is not mediated by the teacher" (Comber, Zeiderman, & Maistrellis, 1989, p. 40). Discussions are instances when students can negotiate with a teacher about the substance and the direction of the curriculum. Altering the forms and purposes of teacher questioning serves to further negotiation, if we will see it in that light.

Organizing Classroom Activities

The physical organization and appearance of classrooms can be subjected to negotiatory questions. What part can students play in establishing and maintaining the environment? Too many classrooms have no area in which to read, to draw, to put up student work. How can *they* be in the classroom, through a recognition of their accomplishments and their interests?

Organization also refers to the grouping of students. Regular whole-group seating arrangements or shifting arrangements for class activities can be negotiated. Grant and Sleeter (1989) made a good point that teachers may allow students to group themselves and think it participatory, when in fact it simply reproduces the social groupings stratified by gender, social class, and ethnic group. Perhaps we should seat students according to our notions of breaking down socially-sanctioned group stratifications. The widespread use of cooperative learning has been accompanied by just such an emphasis on controlled heterogeneous grouping to assure gender and ethnic balance in groups. Here is where control and caring collide: teachers must make

judgments whether it is more caring and educative to control the grouping of students, or to allow students to group themselves.

There is another aspect of cooperative learning that relates to negotiation. When students collaborate, they negotiate with each other in both obvious and subtle ways to determine leadership and to shape the outcomes of the activity. Why not include as part of the class's curriculum a clear focus on how groupwork operates as a form of negotiation, and then engage students in activities to learn how to negotiate with each other? This would constitute a kind of conflict resolution on an everyday basis. During small group work the teacher also negotiates with students regarding such matters as the goals of the group, the time limits of the activity, or the level of sound that is "allowable" before students are disturbed. These can be defined as teachers' unilateral decisions, or as matters that must be gauged by taking into account students' judgments.

The Limits and Risks of Negotiating

Creating a democratic, negotiatory classroom is a worthy aim, and there are many ways to do that. Kreisberg (1992) described how a teacher transformed his classroom into a place where community, shared decision making, cooperative learning, and individual and group problem solving were central themes of the year. Yet, teachers do not negotiate everything. There are times when control is enacted by the teacher in order to unilaterally establish order. The earlier discussion of who should compose classroom seating indicated a rationale for limiting negotiation, in that instance. There are numerous other situations where legitimate authority does not rule out unilateral, non-negotiated social control. Bowers (1987) warned us not to conceptualize emancipation as "the progressive stripping away of external forms of authority, responsibility, and embeddedness" (p. 77). Noblit's (1993) account of a teacher's ethical uses of power portrayed someone who projected moral authority. The teacher developed collective classroom rituals and routines (pp. 28–30) and engaged in "reciprocal negotiation" (p. 37), yet she did not abrogate her power to steer the curriculum and the interactions in ways that seemed to be right for children. Perhaps the central questions to ask oneself are "When will I *not* negotiate? Why not?" An exploration of the limits of negotiation would get at one's basic values and aims as a teacher.

Negotiation involves risks. Teachers who make their actions in any way accountable to students may risk maintaining control (Denscombe, 1985, p. 108). This is why "Don't smile until Christmas," "Start out tough and then you can always lighten up later," and other hackneyed phrases still have currency. These axioms are intended to scare new teachers away from idealistic notions of negotiating with students. Democracy will be discussed and not displayed. And the axiom-wielders are right, in one sense. If a teacher has no carefully considered plan for how to define and respond to students' interests, no serious scheme concerning when to ignore, encourage, negotiate or unilaterally control, then problems will multiply. Students have been socialized into restricted images of teachers, and they often rebel when asked to remake the images. Teachers must think deeply about how to establish legitimate authority and about the complexity of classroom negotiations.

IMPLICATIONS FOR TEACHER EDUCATORS

Learning how to negotiate with students—*to have power with*—is what caring teachers long have practiced. It is incumbent upon teachers at every level to think seriously about what constitutes our legitimate authority, to examine the purposes and realms of negotiation, and to consider also the institutional and personal limits and risks we face. Teacher educators are challenged to think about these matters on two levels: with regard to teaching prospective teachers, and with regard to their own practice. How will we address the ideas of authority and power, and the aims of obedience, responsibility, and solidarity, with our teacher education students? What concrete examples of classroom-level negotiations can we provide? Can we discuss these matters with practicing teachers and enlist their aid in helping prospective teachers to grapple with perplexing questions? And what about our own teaching? What are our purposes with regard to obedience, responsibility, and solidarity? What will we negotiate, and what are the limits and risks in doing so? Current efforts by teacher educators to engage in action research on their practice highlight some methodological paths to follow. By asking challenging questions about others' practice and our own, we can reconstitute the management metaphor of school relationships. By taking actions based on our tentative answers, we will move away from behavioral negation, toward enacting negotiation.

REFERENCES

Apple, M. W. (1990). *Ideology and curriculum.* New York: Routledge.

Araki, C. T., & Takeshita, C. (1991). Students helping students: Dispute management in the schools. *NASSP Bulletin,* November, 31–37.

Beane, J. (1990). *From rhetoric to reality.* Columbus, OH: National Middle School Association.

Bowers, C. A. (1987). *Elements of a post-liberal theory of education.* New York: Teachers College Press.

Bowers, C. A., & Flinders, D. J. (1990). *Responsive teaching.* New York: Teachers College Press.

Brown, E. J. (1933). *Everyday problems in classroom management.* Boston: Houghton Mifflin.

Canter, L. (1989). Assertive Discipline—More than names on the board and marbles in a jar. *Phi Delta Kappan, 71*(1), 57–61.

Charles, C. M. (1989). *Building classroom discipline.* New York: Longman.

Comber, G., Zeiderman, H., & Maistrellis, N. (1989). The Touchstones Project: Discussion classes for students of all abilities. *Educational Leadership, 46*(6), 39–42.

Curwin, R. L., & Mendler, A. N. (1988). *Discipline with dignity.* Alexandria, VA: Association for Supervision and Curriculum Development.

Curwin, R. L., & Mendler, A. N. (1989). We repeat, let the buyer beware: A response to Canter. *Educational Leadership, 46*(4), 83.

Denscombe, M. (1985). *Classroom control.* London: George Allen Unwin.

Doyle, W. (1986). Classroom organization and management. In M. C. Wittrock (Ed.), *Handbook of research on teaching* (3rd ed., pp. 392–431). New York: Macmillan.

Dreikurs, R., & Cassel, P. (1972). *Discipline without tears: What to do with children who misbehave.* New York: Hawthorne.

Duke, D. L., & Meckel, A. M. (1984). *Teacher's guide to classroom management.* New York: Random House.

Evans, T. D., Corsini, R. J., & Gazda, G. M. (1990). Individual education and the 4Rs. *Educational Leadership, 48*(1), 52–56.

Foucault, M. (1979). *Discipline and punish: The birth of the prison.* New York: Vintage.

Glasser, W. (1990). *The quality school.* New York: Harper Row.

Grant, G., & Sleeter, C. (1989). *After the school bell rings.* London: Falmer.

Jones, V. (1991). Resolved: That researchers and intellectuals grossly undervalue the importance of simple student obedience in the classroom (Con). *Curriculum Review, 31*(3), 6, 9–11, 12.

Kohn, A. (1991). Caring kids: The role of the schools. *Phi Delta Kappan, 72*(7), 496–506.

Kreisberg, S. (1992). *Educating for democracy and community: Toward the transformation of power in our schools.* Cambridge, MA: Educators for Social Responsibility.

Lickona, T. (1991). *Educating for character.* New York: Bantam.

McCormack, S. (1989). Response to Render, Padilla, and Krank: But practitioners say it works! *Educational Leadership, 46*(6), 77–79.

McLaughlin, H. J. (1991). Reconciling care and control: Authority in classroom relationships. *Journal of Teacher Education, 42*(3), 182–195.

McNeil, L. M. (1988). *Contradictions of control.* New York: Routledge.

Noblit, G. (1993). Power and caring. *American Educational Research Journal, 30*(1), 23–38.

Popkewitz, T. S. (1987). The formation of school subjects and the political contexts of schooling. In T. S. Popkewitz (Ed.), *The formation of the school subjects* (pp. 1–24). London: Falmer.

Purkey, W. W., & Strahan, D. B. (1986). *Positive discipline: A pocket of ideas.* Columbus, OH: National Middle School Association.

Reed, D. F. (1991). Effective classroom managers in the middle school. *Middle School Journal, 23*(1), 16–21.

Render, G. F., Padilla, J. M., & Krank, H. M. (1989). What research really shows about Assertive Discipline. *Educational Leadership, 46*(6), 72–75.

Sarason, S. B. (1971). *The culture of the school and the problem of change.* Boston: Allyn Bacon.

Schaps, E., & Solomon, D. (1990). Schools and classrooms as caring communities. *Educational Leadership, 48*(3), 38–42.

Schockley, R., & Sevier, L. (1991). Behavior management in the classroom: Guidelines for maintaining control. *Schools in the Middle, 1*(2), 14–18.

Sears, J. B. (1928). *Classroom organization and control.* Boston: Houghton Mifflin.

Shook, E. V. (1985). *Ho'oponopono: Contemporary uses of a Hawai'ian problem-solving process.* Honolulu, HI: University of Hawai'i Press.

Zern, D. (1991). Resolved: That researchers and intellectuals grossly undervalue the importance of simple student obedience in the classroom (Pro). *Curriculum Review, 31*(3), 6–9, 11–12.

Images of Management for Learner-Centered Classrooms

Catherine H. Randolph and Carolyn M. Evertson

Catherine Randolph is Research Assistant Professor, Department of Teaching and Learning, Peabody College, Vanderbilt University. Her interests include writing instruction and understanding classrooms as social and cultural settings.
Carolyn Evertson is chair of the Department of Teaching and Learning and Professor of Education, Peabody College, Vanderbilt University. She has authored numerous articles and books on classroom management and instruction.

ABSTRACT

This essay seeks to identify images of classroom management that are compatible with current images of learning, using scenes from one learner-centered classroom as examples. The increased complexity of classrooms with learning orientations demands more complex views of classroom management, and broader definitions of what "good management" entails. While many tasks of managing work-oriented settings and learning-oriented settings overlap, teachers in learning-centered classrooms must place additional emphasis on examining the social and academic task demands they create, and their implications for definitions of learning. Examples from a writing class illustrate how a model of learning may guide management decisions, and how management decisions may contribute to a definition of learning that is constructed in a classroom over time.

As teacher educators prepare preservice teachers for new models of learning, we must also provide new models of management that are compatible with these models of learning. We know that classroom management is the number one concern of practitioners, particularly new teachers (Veenman, 1984). However, we are lacking in images of management that match the images of learning communities we present. Most studies of classroom management have looked at classrooms where academic tasks and activities were fairly routinized and predictable. Relatively little research has examined different instructional contexts (e.g., whole language settings, inquiry-oriented mathematics, etc.) and what kinds of managerial decisions and teacher actions are required to enact academic tasks in these settings (Edelsky, Draper, & Smith, 1983). Therefore, prospective and novice teachers are likely to carry one set of images with them from their content methods courses (e.g., students working together, interacting freely, actively engaging in learning activities), and another set from their management coursework and textbooks (e.g., students in straight rows, guided step-by-step by teacher directions). In this paper, we seek to match images of learning and images of classroom management, arguing for a much closer conceptual link between content and instruction. In the process, it will become evident that the term "management" must take on a new set of meanings for all participants; in fact, it may be more useful to abandon the term altogether, in favor of one more reflective of teachers' roles in learning communities.

NEW IMAGES OF LEARNING

Management actions communicate information to students about the knowledge and participation that are valued in a particular setting. Our first task, then, must be to determine the kinds of messages about knowledge and participation we want to communicate. The messages sent by management actions must be consistent with the kinds of learning we want to encourage. In the current climate of school reform there are clear calls for teaching problem-solving and higher order thinking skills, integrating learning experiences within and across subject areas, and implementing multiple tasks (Resnick, 1987). The Council of Chief State School Officers (CCSSO, 1990) describes the movement: "Schools, previously asked to ensure the development of basic skills, are now required to teach all students a new, broad range of cognitive skills. . . . This new demand on schools is nothing less than a call for the democratization of thinking" (p. 2). Teachers' management decisions must facilitate such thinking and problem-solving.

The metaphors we use to conceptualize classrooms and classroom events shape our thinking, as they provide frame-

From *Action in Teacher Education*, Spring 1994, pp. 55-64. © 1994 by the Association of Teacher Educators. Reprinted by permission.

works for what is possible in these settings. By far the most prevalent metaphor of the past, that of a workplace, has cast classrooms as settings similar to factories. The goal of a factory is production, and students are engaged in a "performance for grades exchange" (Becker, Geer, & Hughes, 1968). When operating within a factory metaphor, it is possible to conceptualize classroom management as the close supervision of laborers, with the intent of discouraging any divergence from plans that have been carefully structured to lead to predictable outcomes. However, if the contemporary calls for redesigning schools where learning for understanding and new models of the learner are paramount (e.g., Marshall, 1992), our images of classrooms and what occurs there must change from that of workplace or factory to that of learning place.

Marshall (1990) captures the argument by distinguishing between classrooms with work orientations and classrooms with learning orientations. While "the goal in a work setting is to produce a tangible, externally visible product or service for the benefit (profit) of the employer . . .the major goal in learning settings is . . .the acquisition or construction of knowledge or skills that are of benefit to the learner . . ." (p. 98). Thus, when we change our metaphor for classrooms, we refocus our thinking from the needs of "management" (for example, high productivity in terms of output of completed papers) to the needs of the "learner," which may imply more time for study, reflection, or discussion, and less paperwork. Instead of an agenda that is communicated from teacher/manager to student/worker, control over the classroom agenda is shared between teacher/facilitator and student/learner, as jointly negotiated goals are developed.

NEW IMAGES OF MANAGEMENT

To facilitate the activities of learning settings, teachers must operate with learning-oriented images of management. Such metaphors for management must replace the work-oriented models that have dominated past thinking. Learning-oriented settings are likely to be much more complex than work settings in terms of the variety and flexibility of activities that are offered. Some disagreement exists about how much direct teacher control is required to manage this complexity. One argument (Doyle, 1986) suggests that classrooms with complex organization will require more direct management and control than simpler settings. However, Marshall (1990) and Cohen and Lotan (1990) contend that, instead of *more* teacher control, settings where small groups of students use a variety of materials and procedures for high level conceptual learning will

Table 1
Possible Definitions of Management Terms in Different Classroom Settings

Management Concept	Work-Oriented Classroom	Learning-Oriented Classroom
Task	Listen, follow directions, generate correct responses, answer questions	Listen, follow directions, modify directions, explore, challenge answers, generate directions, generate questions, generate correct responses
On-Task	During a listening task: Sit quietly, ask questions During seatwork: Write independently (usually silently), remain in seat	During a listening task: Sit quietly, ask questions, propose alternatives During seatwork: Discuss with peers, share ideas, move to most appropriate location for gaining needed information (library, resource materials area, etc.)
Achievement	Emphasis is on accurately repeating/reconstructing information given by the teacher and/or text; standardized (mostly objective) tests	Emphasis is on using information from teacher, text, personal experience, research to generate creative or novel approaches, information, products. Individual (mostly subjective) measures
A "Well-Managed" Class	Quiet, cooperative, smoothly functioning, little ambiguity about tasks or expectations, little conflict, "a well-oiled machine"	Noisy, cooperative, smoothly functioning, more ambiguous tasks and expectations, high potential for conflict or disagreement, "a bee-hive of activity"
A "Good" Manager	Explicit, aware, reflective, directive, minimizes divergence from plan	Explicit, aware, reflective, less directive, recognizes/encourages divergence from plan

require a different *kind* of teacher control. They argue that when complex instructional strategies are required, it is most efficacious for the teacher to delegate authority to students or groups of students, rather than attempting to supervise a multitude of overlapping tasks directly. According to Marshall (1990, p. 5), "Direct supervision is more appropriate to simpler routine tasks of the assembly-line variety."

Teachers in learner-oriented classrooms observed and identified by Marshall (1988) were more likely to use proactive, preventive management strategies; in the work-oriented setting, teachers were more likely to emphasize work completion. Another finding potentially important for understanding the management patterns in these classrooms was a difference in authority relationships, which were less hierarchical in the learning settings; Marshall (1990) described them as "authoritative rather than authoritarian" (p. 99).

Clearly the need for effective management exists in both work settings and learning settings. In both cases, smooth, well-running classrooms where time, space, and materials are used efficiently maximize the opportunities students have to engage material in a meaningful way. The difference can be identified by defining terms such as "efficient" and "well-running" in classrooms where "engaging material in a meaningful way" is also defined differently. Table 1 illustrates some possible differences between management in work-oriented classrooms and management in learning-oriented classrooms. As the table illustrates, when conceptions of learning and desired learning outcomes change, management must also change in order to be compatible with the new model.

Table 1 lists management concepts that recur in the literature on classroom management (task, on-task, etc.), along with possible definitions in work-oriented vs. learning-oriented classrooms. As the table shows, management demands in a learning-oriented classroom are significantly different from those in a work-oriented classroom. As long as curriculum is conceived of as something that is delivered from teacher to students, management must be conceived of as a tool for student control, a way of getting students quiet, in their seats, and ready to receive information. If, however, we believe curriculum is actively constructed by all of the participants in a setting, then the purpose of management becomes to facilitate active inquiry and collaboration among students. In a learning setting, the well-managed classroom will not necessarily be the quiet classroom, and on-task behavior is likely to look quite different than it does in a work setting. "Good" managers in both settings will be reflective. However, their reflections are likely to focus on different issues, about which they will come to different conclusions.

Thus far we have argued that, given current definitions of learning, new models of management will be necessary. This argument, however, does not in itself provide us with an understanding of what these new models of management will look like in operation. In the next section of this paper, we will present some images of management taken from one learning setting, and will discuss the kinds of management decisions and actions that are required in the creation of such images.

SEEING MANAGEMENT IN A LEARNER-CENTERED CLASSROOM

The following image comes from a classroom in which the teacher's explicit concern was to create a learner-centered environment. It is drawn from a year-long ethnographic study that examined interactions in an upper-elementary school writing class (Randolph, 1993). The study addressed questions about the nature of classroom interaction in the writers' workshop. The teacher, Ms. Cooper[1], taught writing to three groups of fifth and sixth grade students using a writers' workshop format. Over the course of a complete school year, Randolph observed and participated in Ms. Cooper's writing classes daily, documenting activities through field notes and audio tapes. Observations were supplemented by interviewing the teacher and students formally and informally, and by collecting documents such as student writing and class handouts provided by the teacher.

In general, a writers' workshop involves students working at their own paces, generating their own topics, sharing writing with each other at various stages of drafting and revision, and providing feedback to their peers. The approach claims to empower students by giving them ownership over their own work. Paralleling this claim of student power and ownership is a charge to teachers to redefine their roles in the classroom. Teachers are advised to "adopt more the role of a learner and less the role of a teacher" (Elbow, 1973, p. ix), and to function more as a "member or chair than as the sole source of knowledge and power" (Fulwiler, 1987, p. 143). These charges echo the characteristics of Marshall's metaphor of classrooms as "learning settings;" an example taken from such a setting, then, provides one image of what management could look like under these conditions.

This example comes from one of the last days of the school year, as students were sharing final drafts of writing projects they had been involved in during the previous six weeks.

It is early June, and students are sharing the products of the last writing unit, "Speechwriting." Jackson stands at the front of the room; Ms. Cooper sits in the back corner. Between them, groups of students seated at tables are facing Jackson, listening.

Jackson presents his speech on the Kennedy assassination, arguing that the assassin could not possibly have been working alone. At the end of the speech, Ms. Cooper comments on one of the conspiracy theories he has mentioned. Renee nods as Ms. Cooper speaks, then turns to Jackson with a questioning look: does Ms. Cooper's opinion agree with Jackson's research?

The discussion between Ms. Cooper and Jackson continues, with each contributing and modifying hypotheses about what really happened to JFK.

Ms. Cooper then asks the class for comments and questions. Students respond, directing their statements to Jackson. He leads the discussion, calling on and responding to his peers.

Jackson puts down the construction-paper map he has been using during his speech and turns to the chalkboard. Students follow his every move as he diagrams JFK's parade route, the grassy knoll, and the probable paths of the shots fired.

As the discussion continues, Ms. Cooper gets up and leaves the room to run an errand. There is no reaction from students; Jackson manages the discussion without interruption until she returns.

This picture of management may look like no management at all—management *in absentia*. When seen in the context of an entire year of writing class, however, the complexity of Ms. Cooper's long-term management activity becomes visible. The interaction pattern of the last day of class must be viewed as the product of a year's worth of messages about the social and academic expectations of writing class. Ms. Cooper's management across the year was a process of interacting with students, content, and tasks to build a set of shared beliefs about knowledge, teaching, learning, and studenting. Beliefs held in this setting included: knowledge comes from both students and teacher; the teacher is also a learner; learning involves drawing on past and present experiences; and studenting includes leading discussions as well as participating in them (Randolph, 1993). In this example, Ms. Cooper was able to delegate to students one aspect of management, guidance of a group discussion; this delegation reflected a year-long framework of definitions of knowledge and power that had been established through management and instructional decisions.

In this scene from the last day of writing class, students naturally turned to Jackson with their questions about the Kennedy assassination, just as he naturally acted as the knowledge expert. Jackson took on such typically teacher functions as managing the discussion by calling on the next speaker and answering questions. The reaction of the rest of the class demonstrated that his actions were within the accepted norms of the classroom. Students acknowledged the speaker's right to take on the teacher role by raising their hands and waiting to respond until called on by Jackson. Physically, they turned toward him, not toward Ms. Cooper.

Ms. Cooper was able to participate in the discussion as a learner, without taking back the authority Jackson had adopted; Renee turned to Jackson to question Ms. Cooper's contribution, rather than accepting Ms. Cooper's argument over Jackson's. Significantly, no change in the discussion occurred when Ms. Cooper left the room. The teaching and discussion management functions had been taken on by Jackson to the point that the class could operate smoothly without her, at least for a short period. Clearly Ms. Cooper taught more than writing to this class; the students also learned something about how to learn, with or without the teacher's presence.

Thus far, we have argued that models of learning must be used to define models of management in a given classroom. The converse is also true: a teacher's management decisions contribute to the definition of learning that is constructed in a particular classroom over time. Management behaviors carry messages about what "counts" as knowledge in this setting, about whose ideas are of worth, and about where knowledge comes from. The next section of this paper will examine how this process occurred in Ms. Cooper's classroom.

DEVELOPING BELIEFS ABOUT LEARNING THROUGH MANAGEMENT

One area of study that has contributed to our understanding of classroom processes is research on classroom communication. This work focuses on both the student and the teacher as active mediators and constructors of the learning environment, identifying what students need to understand to participate in class lessons, how teachers orchestrate that participation, and how norms, rules, and expectations are signaled and resignaled across time. As students and teachers negotiate the social and academic demands of classroom tasks, beliefs about knowledge and learning are communicated and constructed. The social demands of a task (who can talk to whom, when, how, and for what purposes) and the academic demands (the cognitive requirements of the task) both contribute to a definition of learning. Thus, management of the social demands of classroom activities is interwoven with the academic demands of content. Management is not a precondition for content instruction; it carries messages about content, and must be considered along with content as plans and activities are developed.

As classroom interaction patterns are defined, they in turn define knowledge in the classroom. Consider, for example, typical discourse patterns in a traditional classroom (Mehan, 1979). The teacher initiates an interaction by asking a question (usually a question to which s/he already knows the answer) and nominating a student to respond. Following the student response, the teacher evaluates it as correct/acceptable or incorrect/unacceptable, either directly ("Yes, good answer") or indirectly (moving on to the next question or asking the class, "Is that right?"). The pattern is an efficient discussion management technique for teachers, allowing them to control pace and student involvement. As a management technique, however, it is not devoid of content. A particular view of knowledge and of the classroom is built through such interactions when they are repeated over time. In these interactions, knowledge (including knowledge of the right answer) is something the teacher has, and the teacher controls access to it. The emphasis in such interactions is on "right" answers, or the answers for which the teacher is looking, regardless of whether they seem "right" to students.

Another example from Ms. Cooper's class illustrates how her management decisions contributed to students' definitions of learning. The challenge for Ms. Cooper was how to manage this highly student-centered pedagogy. Her management decisions, as expressed through her management of classroom talk, had the potential to support or to hinder the construction of a definition of writing as a process, and of the writing class as a student-centered learning environment. The academic and social demands of one activity, which participants called *Generating Characteristics,* illustrate how management and curriculum intersect in the real world of the classroom, and how together they help to define the classroom as a learning community.

Generating Characteristics took place during the first week or two of every unit. The teacher announced a genre that would be the topic of study for the unit; for example, the first unit was Children's Story. Students' first task in the unit was to bring in a favorite children's story to share with the class. As stories were shared, the teacher led the group in generalizing from each story the characteristics that were representative of all children's stories. In the children's story, characteristics included "words are simple," "not too long," "predictable," "not a lot of print on a page." Students then used the characteristics derived from the models to begin writing their own children's stories.

The following example is taken from a *Generating Characteristics* discussion in the third unit, as students studied Myths and Fables.

Ms. Cooper: What can we say about the characteristics of the morals? . . . [several exchanges of talk are omitted]

Maybe we need to explain what a lesson or moral is—how to be a better person. I'm going to put that up, unless you all have objections.

Laurie: They're trying to prevent you from making mistakes.

Ms. Cooper writes on the chalkboard: STORIES ARE USED TO HELP YOU BECOME A BETTER PERSON AND NOT MAKE MISTAKES.

Tim: I disagree; sometimes some of the things are wrong.

Hillary: Can be [wrong].

Ms. Cooper: Yes. [She changes "ARE" to "CAN BE" in the sentence on the board; it now reads, STORIES CAN BE USED TO HELP YOU BECOME A BETTER PERSON AND NOT MAKE MISTAKES.]

Ms. Cooper initiated a discussion of morals, and after a few false starts, which have been omitted here, Laurie was able to supply an appropriate response. Ms. Cooper incorporated Laurie's contribution into the characteristic the teacher had contributed and was already writing on the chalkboard. So far, the discussion appears to be fairly traditionally teacher-centered. The nature of the interaction changed as Tim questioned the characteristic that was the joint construction of the teacher and Laurie. By disagreeing, Tim took on the evaluation of the characteristic that had been developed, moving Ms. Cooper into the role of co-collaborator with Laurie. Tim used as evidence for his position the models that had been provided and shared by his peers. The acceptance of his evaluation supported the validity of students' earlier contributions to the class's shared knowledge base, and indicated that the teacher's response was as open to evaluation as any other participant's.

The pattern of talk described here illustrates both management and instruction. The academic content of the task, defining morals, was presented within a particular set of understandings about the roles teacher and student may take as they participate in class discussion. While the teacher appeared at first to be acting in the traditional teacher role at the center of the interaction, by initiating and evaluating student contributions, Tim's comment contributed to a different understanding of typical interaction patterns in this classroom. His evaluative contribution, and the class's acceptance of it, highlighted the way control over the creation and evaluation of knowledge was shared among teacher and students.

Together, the academic and social demands of the *Generating Characteristics* activity contributed to a definition of writing class as a place where students and teacher learn together, rather than a place where students memorize what the teacher tells them. What counts as knowledge in writing class is defined as what is jointly created there through class discussion, rather than what the teacher brings in to give to students. Because of the close match in messages between the academic and social demands of the *Generating Characteristics* activity, both contributed to a definition of writing as student-centered.

CONCLUSIONS AND IMPLICATIONS FOR TEACHER EDUCATION

Throughout this paper we have argued that the task for us as educators is to make sure that our images of classroom management support our images of learning. We have presented one set of images here, from a single learner-centered setting. Using the term "management" to describe these images seems inappropriate. The term management lends itself well to images of a teacher actively directing student activity; Ms. Cooper's activities described here seem to be of a different kind. The concept of management, as part of a work-place metaphor for classrooms, is essentially teacher-centered, while the classroom described above appears to be student-centered to the extent that it functions at times even without the teacher's presence. The term "orchestration" is one alternative that seems more compatible with such learner-oriented classrooms.

We realize that the argument that we can broaden our conception of management by thinking of it as orchestration does not provide us with practical steps for orchestrating learner-oriented classrooms. While we cannot provide a list of how-tos here, we would like to propose some ways of thinking as starting points. First, it is important to realize that changing our images of management does not mean forgetting all that we know about creating order. As we have already argued, many tasks of managing work-oriented settings and orchestrating learning-oriented settings overlap. The same needs exist for making expectations clear, for purposeful room arrangement, and for rules and procedures that are carefully constructed and taught. In the learner-centered classroom, however, special additional emphasis must be placed on explicit awareness of the social and academic task demands being created, and on their implications for learning. Specifically, we as teachers must ask ourselves: What is being learned in this classroom?

- What are the *social task demands*; for example, who can talk to whom, about what, when, where, in what ways and for what purposes? What self-management or group management skills will students need to have in order to accomplish these tasks? Are these skills they have already mastered, or are they new?
- What are the *academic task demands*; for example, what must be known, understood, and/or created to enhance learning?

- What is the match between the *social task demand* and the *academic task demand* of each planned event? Do both the social and the academic task demands facilitate and support the construction of desired definitions of learning?

Such thinking about management requires a conceptualization of management that goes beyond present practice and toward the realm of educational possibility. Teacher educators must facilitate such questioning and reflection as they discuss the orchestration of classroom events with their students. Most importantly, teacher education programs cannot divorce discussion of classroom management from discussion of content instruction, because any such split suggests that management and content are separate, rather than unavoidably interwoven. Instead, the task of teacher education must be to assist preservice teachers in constructing images and definitions of management that are compatible with and inseparable from the images and definitions of learning they will seek to encourage in their classrooms.

REFERENCES

Becker, H., Geer, B., & Hughes, E. (1968). *Making the grade: The academic side of college life.* New York: Wiley.

Cohen, E. G. & Lotan, R. A. (1990). Teacher as supervisor of complex technology. *Theory into Practice, 29*(2), 78–84.

Council of Chief State School Officers. (1990). *Restructuring learning for all students: A policy statement by the Council of Chief State School Officers on improved teaching of thinking.* Washington, DC: Author.

Doyle, W. (1986). Classroom organization and management. In M. C. Wittrock (Ed.), *Handbook of research on teaching* (3rd ed., pp. 392–431). New York: Macmillan.

Edelsky, C., Draper, K., & Smith, K. (1983). Hookin' 'em in at the start of school in a 'whole language' classroom. *Anthropology and Education Quarterly, 14*(4), 257–281.

Elbow, P. (1973). *Writing without teachers.* London: Oxford University Press.

Fulwiler, T. (1987). *Teaching with writing.* Upper Montclair, NJ: Boynton-Cook.

Marshall, H. H. (1988). Work or learning: implications of classroom metaphors. *Educational Researcher, 17*(9), 9–16.

Marshall, H. H. (1990). Beyond the workplace metaphor: Toward conceptualizing the classroom as a learning setting. *Theory into Practice, 29*(2), 94–101.

Marshall, H. H. (Ed.). (1992). *Redefining student learning: Roots of educational change.* Norwood, NJ: Ablex.

Mehan, H. (1979). *Learning lessons: Social organization and the classroom.* Cambridge, MA: Harvard University Press.

Randolph, C. H. (1993). *An ethnographic study of classroom interaction and literacy learning in a fifth/sixth grade writing class.* Unpublished doctoral dissertation, Vanderbilt University, Nashville, TN.

Resnick, L. (1987). *Education and learning to think.* Washington, DC: National Academy Press.

Veenman, S. (1984). Perceived needs of beginning teachers. *Review of Educational Research, 54*(2), 143–178.

NOTE

1. All names in examples are pseudonyms.

Creating a Constructivist Classroom Atmosphere

Rheta DeVries and Betty Zan

Every classroom has a socio-moral atmosphere that either hinders or promotes children's development. Consider the following transcripts from classrooms in which the teachers promote very different attitudes toward rules and create very different classroom atmospheres.

We present these two very different approaches to helping children remember rules as reflecting very different sociomoral atmospheres that influence children's development in different ways.

Rheta DeVries, Ph.D., is director of the Regents' Center for Early Developmental Education and professor of curriculum and instruction at the University of Northern Iowa. A former teacher, Rheta DeVries is the author of numerous books and articles on constructivist education and regularly conducts workshops for teachers.

Betty Zan, M.A., is a research fellow at the Regents' Center for Early Developmental Education at the University of Northern Iowa. A doctoral candidate in developmental psychology at the University of Houston, she has written and conducted numerous workshops on constructivist education with Rheta DeVries.

Classroom 1 (kindergarten):

The teacher is across the room talking to an adult who has come to the door. The children are sitting in a semicircle, waiting for her to return. Some children are engaged in skirmishes with each other—hitting, kicking, and yelling at each other—while other children are telling them to stop. One child gets up to tell the teacher. The teacher returns.

Teacher: OK, scoot back. Salisha? Leanne, would you sit down? Everybody's eyes up here. *(Raises voice.)* Eyes up here, right now!

Jamal *(to another child):* Move.

Teacher: No! You sit right where you are. Legs crossed. And if you want to pout, Jamal, that's fine, you just go ahead and pout. *(Glares at Jamal.)* Now, I am not, *at all*—Odetta, up here *(meaning, "Look at me")*—happy with the behavior you have had today. I'm not happy.

When I turn my back to talk to another teacher, you know what you're supposed to be doing, and you know what you're not supposed to be doing. Shondra, you, for one, are not supposed to be back there. *(Glares at Shondra.)* You're never allowed in that back row. You get here next to Linda. You're not supposed to be talking when I'm talking to someone else. You're not supposed to be talking when I'm talking, Shondra. You are *never* supposed to touch anyone.

We're going over these rules, again. *(Points to bulletin board with rules.)* "Number 1: Use your quiet voice." *(Uses an accusing tone.)* You all were talking out loud. You're supposed to use your quiet voice at all times. When you're at your seats, when you're answering me, when I tell you in the lunch room that you can talk to each other, you use your quiet voice.

Jamal, if you're pouting, you had better turn around and face me when you pout. Turn around, unless you want to go in where David was *(to the principal's office, to be disciplined)*.

"Number 2: Raise your hand to talk." Did I see any hands in the air? Did I? No. There wasn't one hand in the air. "Number 3: Keep your hands, feet, and objects to yourself." I've seen more tapping and more hitting and more kicking going on today than I ever want to see the rest of the year. Sarah, what's the problem?

Sarah *(complaining):* Nicole keeps on scooting . . . *(unintelligible).*

Teacher: Nicole, you scoot over and you don't move. You pretend you're a statue. You don't move. You don't touch her, your elbow doesn't touch her. Scoot it over. That way everybody is happy. *(To another child),* What's the matter with you?

Jason: Can I read rule 4?

Teacher: No. I will read rule 4, thank you. "Number 4 is, Work quietly." That also means sit quietly. That means when I'm talking, we're quiet. Now, the rest of the day we're going to practice these rules *perfectly*. I don't want to hear one person talk without her hand up. I don't want to see one person touch another person. Now, get your eyes on me.

Jamal, you're through pouting now, get your eyes on me and have your legs Indian style. Now, more on our farm unit. *(The teacher continues with the lesson that had been interrupted.)*

From *Young Children*, November 1995, pp. 4-13. © 1995 by the National Association for the Education of Young Children. Reprinted by permission.

Classroom 2 (prekindergarten):

The teacher and children have gathered in a circle for morning grouptime. The teacher has a list of rules that the children had dictated to her the week before.

Teacher: Before we get started with morning circle, do you remember what these are about? These rules?

Carter: No.

Teacher: These are rules that you guys told me to write. You told me the words, and I wrote your words down. They talk about how we want to be treated in our classroom. Do you remember that? Because some people were doing some hurting of feelings and of bodies, and we wrote these words so that people would know how to be friends in class. Do you remember what these are about?

Nan: The rules [are] about so we can make happy children, and some kids are not following them.

Teacher: That is exactly it. Let's read them again so you can remember what they are. *(Points to the written rules.)* This one is "Call them their name. Don't call them 'naughty girl' or 'naughty boy'."

Greg: That's Nan's *(meaning Nan suggested the rule).*

Teacher: So people want to be called their own name. OK.

Nan: Zina didn't call me my name.

Teacher: "Use their words. And if the words don't work, go get the teacher." If the words don't work, can you pinch and then go tell the teacher?

Children: No!

Teacher: If your words don't work, can you hit them and then go get the teacher?

Children: No!

Teacher: Donald, if your words don't work and somebody kicks you, can you kick them back?

Donald: No, I don't kick back.

Teacher: What do you do?

Hank: Go tell the teacher.

Donald: You know what happened outside today? Ben throwed sand in my mouth.

Teacher: Really? What did you do?

Donald: I told the teacher.

Teacher: Did the teacher help you to talk to Ben?

Donald: Yes.

Teacher: That's important. This one says, "Friendly hands and friendly words." So we want to use friendly hands and friendly words. Hey, you know what we could do? We could practice friendly hands.

Greg: What is that?

Teacher: You cross your hands over. *(Demonstrates.)* Now hold the hand of the person next to you. *(They all join hands in a circle.)* Now shake. Just a gentle shake. That's the biggest handshake. That's friendly hands, huh?

Aaron: Marcus doesn't have his hands crossed.

Teacher: That's OK. Now this one says, "No hitting."

Wally: I did that *(meaning he suggested that rule).*

Teacher: Do you guys remember those rules?

Children: Yeah!

Teacher: What do you think? Do you think we can remember them during outside time and during activity time?

Children: Yeah!

What do we mean by sociomoral atmosphere?

By *sociomoral atmosphere* we refer to the entire network of interpersonal relations in a classroom. This includes the child's relationship with the teacher, with other children, with academics, and with rules. In our recent book, *Moral Classrooms, Moral Children* (DeVries & Zan 1994), we describe the constructivist approach to social and moral education, exemplified by the transcript of the second teacher.

Constructivist education is a developmentally appropriate approach to early education, inspired by Piaget's theory that the child constructs knowledge, intelligence, personality, and social and moral values. This approach has been defined in terms of activities that appeal to children's interests, encourage experimentation in the physical world, and foster perspective taking and cooperation in the social world (DeVries & Kohlberg 1990). However, constructivist education is not just a set of activities. Implementing constructivist education in its most essential aspect involves more than activities, materials, and classroom organization.

The first principle of constructivist education is that a sociomoral atmosphere must be cultivated in which respect for others is continually practiced. In this sense, constructivist education is an approach to moral as well as intellectual education. Some people believe that the school should not be concerned with moral education but should focus on teaching academics or promoting intellectual development.

The problem with this view is that schools *do* influence moral development, whether they intend to or not. Teachers cannot avoid communicating moral messages as they take stands on rules and behavior and provide information about what is good and bad, right and wrong. The challenge is to relate to children and engage them in activities in which they construct their own moral convictions about relations with others.

In this article we point out the unavoidable moral aspect of schooling and describe the teacher–child relationship in a constructivist classroom. Then we specifically address how the constructivist teacher creates a cooperative sociomoral atmosphere in conducting grouptime, using cooperative alternatives to discipline, dealing with conflict, providing for activity time, engaging children in clean up, and promoting academics.

The teacher–child relationship

Constructivist classrooms are characterized by mutual, or two-way, respect between teacher and children. This philosophy contrasts with that found in most classrooms, in which respect is one-way only—children are expected to respect the teacher. Mutual respect can be discussed in terms of a particular type of teacher–child relationship that is essential to a constructivist classroom.

Our guide to the constructivist teacher–child relationship comes from Piaget's (1932) distinction between two types of morality, corresponding to two types of adult-child relationships, one that promotes children's development and one that retards it.

1. The first type of morality is a morality of obedience.

Piaget called this "heteronomous" morality, because it means following rules made by others. Therefore, the individual who is heteronomously moral follows moral rules given by others out of obedience to authority—simply ac-

cepting, conforming to, and following external rules without question.

2. The second type of morality is "autonomous."

By autonomy, Piaget did not mean simple independence in doing things for oneself without help. Rather, the individual who is autonomously moral follows moral rules of the self, rules that emerge out of internal feelings of necessity about how to treat others.

Certainly most developmentally oriented educators would not support a goal of purely obedience-based morality for children but rather want children to believe with personal conviction in such basic moral values as respect for others. Without beliefs that arise from personal conviction, children will not be likely to follow moral rules—especially in the absence of authority. Nevertheless, educators often manage children in ways that promote obedience rather than autonomy. In many schools the sociomoral atmosphere requires children to be submissive and conforming, at the expense of initiative, autonomy, and reflecting thinking.

Constructivist teachers respect children by upholding children's rights to their feelings, ideas, and opinions. These teachers use their authority selectively and refrain from using power unnecessarily. In this way they give children the opportunity to develop personalities characterized by self-confidence, respect for self and others, and active, inquiring, creative minds.

Grouptime

For many teachers, grouptime may be the most challenging time of the day. When it goes well, everyone feels as if they are a part of a caring community. Children participate in class rituals; share their feelings, discoveries, and accomplishments with each other;

and make decisions that affect their life in the classroom. The teacher must exercise subtle leadership to guide this process. Without leadership, grouptime can quickly deteriorate into chaos. With too much leadership, grouptime becomes teacher-directed instruction. The teacher must strike a delicate balance.

Rule making and decision making

A unique characteristic of constructivist education is that responsibility for decision making is shared by everyone in the class community. The teacher turns over to the children much of the power to decide how to run the class. Inviting children to make rules and decisions is one way the teacher can reduce adult authority and promote children's self-regulation.

Children also practice expressing their ideas in a clear and acceptable way so that everyone can understand and decide whether to agree. Children have the possibility of taking the perspective of the group as a whole community.

Rules are an ever-present part of every child's experience in school. Whether explicit and written or implicit and verbal, rules are a necessary part of life in a classroom. If children's experiences with rules are to contribute to their moral and social development, the teacher must consider carefully how to work with children in relation to rules.

The two examples at the beginning of this article deal with classroom rules. The first example came from videotape data collected as a part of a comparison study of sociomoral atmosphere and children's sociomoral development in classrooms reflecting different theories of learning and development (see DeVries, Haney, & Zan 1991 for a fuller description of the study). In this classroom the rules pertain mostly to behaviors, and the teacher does not discuss the reasons for these rules.

Every classroom has a sociomoral atmosphere that either hinders or promotes children's development.

The second example was taken from videotape data collected at the Human Development Laboratory School at the University of Houston. In this classroom the teacher's focus is on the reasons for the rules, based on consideration for others' feelings. In the first classroom the teacher wrote all of the rules at the beginning of the year and presented them to the children. In the second classroom the children made the rules in response to problems with hitting and name calling.

As we try to illustrate with the second example, it is not necessary to give children ready-made rules. With the teacher's careful guidance, children can suggest rules, although the rules may not take the form the teacher would have given them. Occasions for rule making may include the need for guidelines to make the classroom a happy place and the need for solving a particular classroom problem (for example, when some children think it is unfair when other children do not help with clean up).

In discussions about rules, the teacher can emphasize the reasons for the rules. When children make the rules themselves in response to problems they experience in the classroom, they are more likely to take ownership of the rules. They are also more likely to feel the necessity of following the rules and to share in the responsibility for enforcing the rules with each other.

Children's rules—in their own words and, when possible, in their own handwriting—should be available in some written form (a rule book illustrated by children, a list posted on the wall, etc.) in the classroom. Then, when break-

downs do occur (and they will), the constructivist teacher can refer to the rules *that the children have made* and emphasize that the moral authority of the classroom comes not from the teacher but from the children themselves.

When teachers offer children opportunities to make certain (carefully selected) decisions about what happens in their classroom (for example, which of two books to read, where to go on an upcoming field trip, or what foods to serve at a class party), children feel a sense of community and shared responsibility for what takes place in their classroom.

Voting

When children have differing opinions about classroom decisions, teachers can introduce children to voting. Voting offers excellent opportunities for children to exchange and defend points of view, listen to others' points of view, and decide issues fairly. (The astute teacher will see in voting numerous opportunities for lessons in oral and written language and math, as well.) Through many experiences of voting, even 4-year-olds can eventually construct the idea of equality as they see each person's opinion valued and given equal weight in the decision-making process.

Voting may be conducted in various ways, but we advise against

asking young children to raise hands. This method presents numerous problems. Often children tire of holding up their hands, so hands droop and the teacher must exhort children to keep their hands raised until he or she can count them all. Many children who do not fully understand the process may vote for every option, provoking other children to complain that it is not fair for some children to vote twice.

Finally, when the teacher counts the hands, children may not be sure that *their* hands were seen and counted. In short, children have difficulty following the process, and much of the value of voting is lost. The teacher should choose a voting process that children can follow and understand, such as polling children by going systematically around the circle and writing each child's name under the choice, or allowing children to cast ballots.

Social and moral dilemma discussions

Grouptime offers opportunities for the teacher to engage children's moral reasoning by conducting social and moral discussions. Everyday life in the classroom often provides material for these discussions, such as when something happens that children believe is not fair.

Children's literature also can provide material for discussing social and moral dilemmas. For example, in *Dr. DeSoto* by William Steig (1982), the mouse dentist (Dr. DeSoto) takes pity on a fox with a toothache, even though his policy is not to treat cats and other animals dangerous to mice. The fox clearly plans to eat Dr.

Perhaps the most distinguishing characteristic of a constructivist approach to academics is the teacher's respect for children's errors.

The first principle of constructivist education is that a sociomoral atmosphere must be cultivated in which respect for others is continually practiced.

DeSoto and his wife, but the clever mice trick him by using a "secret formula" (glue) on his teeth that they say will prevent further toothaches. In discussing this situation, the teacher can raise the question of whether it is OK for the mice to trick the fox by gluing his mouth closed.

When conducting moral discussions of this story with 4- and 5-year-olds, we observed that most children defend the mice. However, one child took the perspective of the fox and worried that, with his mouth glued shut, the fox would starve. One very advanced 4-year-old took the perspective of the entire town and argued that it is OK to glue the fox's teeth shut because if the fox ate the mice, there would be no one to fix teeth! These experiences of perspective taking contribute especially to children's construction of moral judgment.

Cooperative alternatives to discipline

The constructivist approach to "discipline" does not consist of controlling and punishing children in order to socialize them. Rather, we work *with* children as they gradually figure out how to relate to others in mutually satisfying ways. This does not mean that teachers are permissive and children run wild. On the contrary! Constructivist teachers are quite active in their search for alternatives to discipline that emphasize the natural and logical consequences of the misdeed and the resulting break in the social bond. When an object is broken, other people are deprived of its use and may be angry or sad. Whenever

possible, the person who broke the object is given an opportunity to make restitution by repairing or replacing the object. When someone lies, others may feel that they no longer can trust the one who told the lie. The rift in the social bond then requires repair.

It goes without saying that children must value these social bonds in order to want to repair them. This makes close, caring relationships between children, as well as between teacher and child, an integral component of the constructivist sociomoral atmosphere.

Conflict and its resolution

Conflicts are inevitable in any classroom where children interact freely. Rather than trying to prevent conflicts, the constructivist teacher uses conflicts between children in the interactive classroom as opportunities to help children recognize the perspectives of others and learn how to develop solutions that are acceptable to all parties. Teachers can support children's conflict resolution by stating the problem in terms the children can understand, helping children verbalize feelings and desires to each other and to listen to each other, and inviting children to suggest solutions. These principles are illustrated in the boxed example above.

We recognize that conflict resolution is not unique to constructivist education. However, the constructivist perspective may be unique in welcoming conflict and its resolution as important parts of the curriculum and not just

viewing conflict as a problem to be managed. Piaget's work leads to the recognition that conflict resolution is not just a skill but that it undergoes developmental change involving coming to recognize and figure out how to reconcile different points of view.

Activity time

Activity time (or center time) is perhaps the most important period of the day in a constructivist classroom. The objective of activity time in a constructivist classroom is that children will be intellectually, socially, and morally active and more and more self-regulating. For example, in a sinking-and-floating activity, the constructivist teacher asks children to reflect on why some objects sink and some objects float, encourages children to consider contradictory opinions, and supports the search for knowledge drawn from observation and experimentation.

In the course of acting on objects and discussing results, children "read" the results of an experiment and have the opportunity to accept these results even if they predicted something different. The teacher also asks children to reflect on how to take turns with an activity, helps them become conscious that many children want this privilege at the same time, and suggests that they try to figure out ways to satisfy everyone. When constructivist teachers refuse to be all-knowing or all-powerful, they open the way for children to struggle with issues themselves and not rely solely on adults for guidance.

Classroom activities long associated with the child development approach in early education include pretend play, block building and other construction activities, art, and reading and writing. Other activities unique to constructivist education are group games (Kamii & DeVries 1980)

We Can Help Children Solve Social Problems

Hector has placed a small ladder across the hole of the box serving as the beanbag target. Marcel does not want the ladder there.

Teacher: I'm sorry. I can't hear your words. Can you tell me again?

Hector: (Inaudible.)

Teacher: Oh, then to make it more exciting, you put that there? Is it harder to throw in there, or easier?

Hector: (Inaudible.)

Teacher: Well, Marcel, do you think that would be a fun way to play with it?

Marcel: (Inaudible.)

Teacher: Oh, Hector says it makes it fun for him.

Marcel: It makes it bad.

Teacher: Well, why don't you tell Hector about that? What would you like to tell him about it?

Marcel: I don't know.

Teacher: Well, what do you think we should do, because Hector likes to play with it that way?

Marcel: (Shrugs shoulders, says something inaudible.)

Teacher: Hector, Hector, you know what? *(Sits on floor be-side Hector.)* I see that we have a problem. You know what the problem is? *(Hector continues to play with ladder and does not seem to be listening.)* Hector, can you hear my words? I see that you would like to play with this. *(Takes ladder.)* Marcel says that he would *not* like to play with this. So what should you guys do?

Hector: I want him to play . . . *(inaudible).*

Teacher: Marcel, can you hear his idea? What is your idea, Hector?

Marcel: (Inaudible.)

Teacher: Did you hear his idea?

Marcel: Um hmm. After we put it away . . . *(inaudible).*

Teacher: Hector, can you hear Marcel's idea?

Hector: Yeah.

Teacher: Let's listen to it. What is your idea, Marcel?

Marcel: I said . . . .

Hector: (Throws beanbag; seems not to be listening.)

Teacher: Hector, let's listen to Marcel's idea because I heard that he had an idea. *(Teacher takes beanbag.)* Hector, we'll take just a minute out from play-ing with the beanbags so that we can hear the other idea. What was that other idea, Marcel?

Marcel: After you put it away, then you could get it out again.

Teacher: Oh, does that sound like a good idea?

Hector: No, I want to do it like this.

Teacher: Hector wants to do it right now.

Marcel: Well, he may play for two more seconds with that red thing *(points to ladder)*, and then I'll . . . *(points to hole and ladder)*. Well, maybe we could share, I don't know.

Teacher: Maybe you could share? Do you think you could share, Hector? Marcel said that would work.

Hector: (Inaudible.)

Teacher: OK! You know what, when you guys give it a try, let me know if you need any help, but I'll bet you can figure it out. *(Upon observing a cooperative attitude, and thinking the boys can work it out, she leaves.)*

Hector and Marcel succeed in playing together, tossing the bean-bag at the hole. Marcel accepts the ladder propped across the hole.

and physical-knowledge activities (Kamii & DeVries 1978/1993). In constructivist classrooms, activi-ties are planned with children's interests in mind, and children are regularly consulted about what they want to know and do. New opportunities can be intro-duced at grouptime, with sugges-tions about possible purposes children might want to pursue. "Remember that you said you wanted to learn about bubbles? I put some pipe cleaners and soapy water in the messy center so you can experiment and figure out how to make wands that form good bubbles."

The constructivist teacher al-lows children to choose freely their activities and playmates. In-tervening sparingly while allow-ing children to exercise initiative, the teacher assesses children's reasoning and engages with chil-dren to encourage them to test out their ideas. "What kind of shape do you think your square wand will make?" Some children expect the square wand to make a square bubble and spontane-ously announce this prediction.

Peer interaction is encouraged by referring children to other children for help, supporting ne-gotiation when tensions arise, and promoting friendly, shared experiences.

Clean-up time

Some early childhood teachers regard clean-up time as one of the most difficult times of the day and solve clean-up problems by doing all the cleaning in their classrooms themselves. How-ever, constructivist teachers use clean-up time to promote the de-

Constructivist teachers respect children by upholding children's rights to their feelings, ideas, and opinions. These teachers use their authority selectively and refrain from using power unnecessarily. In this way they give children the opportunity to develop personalities characterized by self-confidence, respect for self and others, and active, inquiring, creative minds.

velopment of children's feelings of responsibility. Care for the classroom is moral when it is motivated by consideration and fairness toward everyone in the classroom community.

By encouraging children to take responsibility for the care of their classroom, teachers turn the moral authority over to children, thereby promoting the development of children's self-regulation. Problems with clean up inevitably provide opportunities for teachers to lead discussions that help children reflect on the practical and moral reasons for clean up. "Did anybody notice that some children were just walking around during clean-up time? Does anybody have any ideas about what we should do about clean-up time?"

Academics

A misconception about constructivist education is that because it includes play, it does not include academics. In fact, constructivist teachers are serious-minded about children's construction of knowledge about literacy, numeracy, science, social studies, and fine arts. We want to emphasize that academic learning in a constructivist classroom occurs in the context of the sociomoral atmosphere we describe here. It is not possible to understand the constructivist approach to academics without first understanding the constructivist sociomoral atmosphere.

The problem for the constructivist teacher in approaching any academic content is to distinguish what must be *constructed* from what must be *instructed*. Piaget's distinction among three kinds of knowledge aids the teacher in making this distinction. When a topic involves knowledge of physical objects (for example, which objects float and sink), the teacher encourages children to act on objects and reflect on the reactions. When a topic is arbitrary or conventional in nature (such as that Christmas is on December 25 and that the letter *A* is called "a"), the teacher does not hesitate to inform children. Because all content involves logico-mathematical knowledge, the teacher encourages children to put things into relationships (for example, that heavy objects seem to sink and light objects seem to float—but not always), make comparisons and generalizations, and test their hypotheses.

Perhaps the most distinguishing characteristic of a constructivist approach to academics is the teacher's respect for children's errors. This respect results in children feeling free to express their honest reasoning without fear of being wrong. The constructivist teacher accepts children's incorrect or partially correct ideas as necessary to the constructive process that ends eventually (but by no means immediately) in correct knowledge. For example, when a 4- or 5-year-old insists that the dots on a die will be visible in its shadow, the teacher knows that the child will not be convinced by be-

ing told otherwise. The teacher thus refrains from correcting the child, instead creating opportunities for the child to experiment and find out by observing the die's shadow.

Similarly, the teacher may observe a child making a logical error when counting spaces in a board game. That is, the child rolls the die and counts as "1" the space occupied (on which he or she landed on the previous turn) rather than moving to the next space. Recognizing that the child is convinced of the correctness of this strategy (due to not having separated ordinality from cardinality, to not having integrated zero in the ordinal sequence, and to not linking the turns of play), the teacher refrains from correcting the child's counting. Rather, the constructivist teacher provides a die with only ones and twos, so that the child will count "1" and go nowhere! Feelings of contradiction will lead children eventually to correct their own logic.

Creating active situations

The constructivist integration of academics involves the creation of active situations in which children pursue their own interests and purposes. As Dewey ([1913] 1975) pointed out almost a century ago (and as probably most people can attest to in their everyday lives), people always invest more time, energy, and attention in what interests them. When a child's purpose is to play a certain path game, interest in reading rules, counting, and writing words and numerals is spontaneous. When children want to cook, they are inspired to try to figure out what the recipe says.

Young children are more mentally active when they are physically active in trying to figure out how to do something. Physical-knowledge activities involving the movement of objects (elementary physics) and changes in objects (elementary chemistry) inspire children to construct knowledge about the physical world. Using a ball on a string (as a pendulum bob) to knock down a target inspires children to construct knowledge about spatial and causal relations. "Do you think you can knock over the target if I put it here (out of the range of the pendulum)?" Experimenting with using different amounts of flour, water, and oil to make playdough inspires children to construct knowledge about the influence of each substance on the playdough's consistency: "What can you add to make your playdough less gooey?"

Fostering social interaction

The constructivist approach to academics also involves fostering social interaction around specific academic content. Social life is filled with communication needs. Writing and reading numerals, counting, and calculating are necessary in a variety of activities. Children can write the names and prices of items on a menu for a pretend restaurant, add numbers when keeping score in group games such as bowling, and learn to write others' names to address valentines.

Emphasizing self-regulation and reflection

The constructivist approach to academics emphasizes self-regulation and reflection that leads to understanding, self-confidence, and an attitude of questioning

The only way for us to live together successfully as a human species is to figure out how to deal with diversities of all sorts.

and critical evaluation. It motivates children to think about causes, implications, and explanations of physical and logical phenomena as well as social and moral phenomena. We therefore see the development of morality and intelligence as interconnected and argue that life in a moral classroom also promotes children's intellectual development. We caution, however, that it is possible to establish a cooperative sociomoral atmosphere with inadequate attention to academics. The best teaching of academics is laid on a foundation of understanding how children construct knowledge.

Conclusion

The practical principles of teaching discussed in this article rest on a foundation laid by John Dewey and other pioneers in progressive education. While some of our sociomoral activities are not entirely new, constructivist education provides new rationales and practices rooted in research-based theory. With this theoretical framework, old activities are enriched and new possibilities emerge.

The kind of sociomoral attitudes that we discuss can develop very early. Children's evident capacities suggest that educators should build on these attitudes at least from age 4. Our research demonstrates that children from classrooms characterized by a constructivist sociomoral atmosphere are more advanced in their sociomoral development, resolve more of their conflicts, and enjoy more friendly interactions with their peers than do children from more authoritarian classroom atmospheres (DeVries, Haney, & Zan 1991; DeVries,

Reese-Learned, & Morgan 1991).

The only way for us to live together successfully as a human species is to figure out how to deal with diversities of all sorts. If young children learn to do this in their small classroom group, perhaps they will be able to expand it to larger groups in society. By giving children at an early age opportunities to develop sociomoral competence, we may avoid their development into adults who know only how to mindlessly submit to or rebel against the rules of people in power. By fostering early sociomoral development of children, we may put them on the path to becoming the kinds of adults who can take up the responsibilities of democratic citizenship and work toward equity in human relationships.

References

DeVries, R., J. Haney, & B. Zan. 1991. Sociomoral atmosphere in direct-instruction, eclectic, and constructivist kindergartens: A study of teachers' enacted interpersonal understanding. *Early Childhood Research Quarterly* 6: 449–71.

DeVries, R., & L. Kohlberg. 1987/1990. *Constructivist early education: Overview and comparison with other programs.* White Plains, NY: Longman, 1987. Reprint, Washington, DC: NAEYC.

DeVries, R., H. Reese-Learned, & P. Morgan. 1991. Sociomoral development in direct-instruction, eclectic, and constructivist kindergartens: A study of children's enacted interpersonal understanding. *Early Childhood Research Quarterly* 6: 473–517.

DeVries, R., & B. Zan. 1994. *Moral classrooms, moral children: Creating a constructivist atmosphere in early education.* New York: Teachers College Press.

Dewey, J. [1913] 1975. *Interest and effort in education.* Edwardsville, IL: Southern Illinois University Press.

Kamii, C., & R. DeVries. 1978/1993. *Physical knowledge in preschool education: Implications of Piaget's theory.* New York: Teachers College Press.

Kamii, C., & R. DeVries. 1980. *Group games in early education: Implications of Piaget's theory.* Washington, DC: NAEYC.

Piaget, J. [1932] 1965. *Moral judgment of the child.* London: Free Press.

Steig, W. 1982. *Doctor DeSoto.* New York: Farrar, Straw & Giroux, A Sunburst Book.

Why Violence Prevention Programs Don't Work—and What Does

David W. Johnson and Roger T. Johnson

David W. Johnson is Professor of Educational Psychology, and **Roger T. Johnson** is Professor of Curriculum and Instruction, University of Minnesota, Cooperative Learning Center, 202 Pattee Hall, 150 Pillsbury Drive, S.E., Minneapolis, MN 55455-0298.

The best school programs in conflict resolution tend to follow six key principles.

"Joshua was chasing Octavia. He pushed her down, and she kicked him."

"Danielle is going to beat up Amber after school. They were spitting in each other's faces and calling each other names."

"Tom shoved Cameron up against the lockers and threatened him. Cameron said he's going to bring a knife to school tomorrow to get even."

Schools are filled with conflicts. The frequency of clashes among students and the increasing severity of the ensuing violence make managing such incidents very costly in terms of time lost to instructional, administrative, and learning efforts.

If schools are to be orderly and peaceful places in which high-quality education can take place, students must learn to manage conflicts constructively without physical or verbal violence. The following six principles may be helpful to schools that are trying to accomplish this goal.

1. Go beyond violence prevention to conflict resolution training.

To curb violence among students, many schools have implemented violence prevention programs. Some schools focus on anger management and general social skills. Others invite guest speakers (for example, police officers) to school, employ metal detectors, or ask police to patrol the school. Still others show videotapes of violent encounters and structure discussions around how fights start and alternative ways to manage aggression.

The proliferation of such programs raises the question: Do they work? In a review of three popular violence prevention curriculums—Violence Prevention Curriculum for Adolescents, Washington [D.C.] Community Violence Prevention Program, and Positive Adolescent Choices Training—Webster (1993) found no evidence that they produce long-term changes in violent behavior or decrease the risk of victimization. The main function of such programs, Webster argues, is to provide political cover for school officials and politicians.

In their survey of 51 violence prevention programs, Wilson-Brewer and colleagues (1991) found that fewer than half of the programs even claimed to have reduced levels of violence, and few had any data to back up their claims. Tolan and Guerra (in press), after reviewing the existing research on violence prevention, concluded that (1) many schools are engaged in well-intentioned efforts without any evidence that the programs will work, and (2) some programs actually influence relatively nonviolent students to be more violence-prone.

Why don't violence prevention programs work? Here are a few possible reasons.

1. Many programs are poorly targeted. First, they lump together a broad range of violent behaviors and people, ignoring the fact that different people turn to violence for different reasons. Second, few programs focus on the relatively small group of children and adolescents who commit most of the acts of serious violence. In our studies of a peer mediation program in inner-city schools, for example, we found that less than 5 percent of students accounted for more than one-third of the violent incidents in the school (Johnson and Johnson 1994a).

2. The programs provide materials

Few violence prevention programs focus on the relatively small group of children and adolescents who commit most of the acts of serious violence.

but don't focus on program implementation. Many programs assume that (a) a few hours of an educational intervention can "fix" students who engage in violent behavior, (b) a few hours of training can prepare teachers to conduct the program, and (c) no follow-up is needed to maintain the quality of the program. In other words, the programs ignore the literature on successful innovation within schools (Johnson and Johnson, in press) and, therefore, are often poorly implemented.

3. Proponents of violence prevention programs confuse methods that work in neighborhoods with those that work in schools. Conflicts on the street often involve macho posturing, competition for status, access to drugs, significant amounts of money, and individuals who have short-term interactions with one another. The school, on the other hand, is a cooperative setting in which conflicts involve working together, sharing resources, making decisions, and solving problems among students who are in long-term relationships. Different conflict resolution procedures are required in each setting. Street tactics should not be brought into the school, and it is naive and dangerous to assume that school tactics should be used on the street.

4. Many programs are unrealistic about the strength of the social forces that impel children toward violence. To change the social norms controlling street behavior requires a broad-based effort that involves families, neighbors, the mass media, employers, health care officials, schools, and government. Schools do not have the resources to guarantee health care, housing, food, parental love, and hope for the future for each child. Educators cannot eliminate the availability of guns (especially semi-automatic handguns), change the economics of the

drug trade (and other types of crime), or even reduce the dangers of walking to and from school. Because there is a limit to what schools can do in reducing violence among children and adolescents outside of school, violence prevention programs should be realistic and not promise too much.

Initiating a violence prevention program will not reduce the frequency of violence in schools and in society as a whole. While violence does need to be prevented, programs that focus exclusively on violence prevention may generally be ineffective. Schools must go beyond violence prevention to conflict resolution training.

2. Don't attempt to eliminate all conflicts.

The elimination of violence does not mean the elimination of conflict. Some conflicts can have positive outcomes (Johnson and Johnson 1991, 1992). They can increase achievement, motivation to learn, higher-level reasoning, long-term retention, healthy social and cognitive development, and the fun students have in school. Conflicts can also enrich relationships, clarify personal identity, increase ego strength, promote resilience in the face of adversity, and clarify how one needs to change.

It is not the presence of conflict that is to be feared but, rather, its destructive management. Attempts to deny, suppress, repress, and ignore conflicts may, in fact, be a major contributor to the occurrence of violence in schools. Given the many positive outcomes of conflict, schools need to teach students how to manage conflicts constructively.

3. Create a cooperative context.

The best conflict resolution programs seek to do more than change individual students. Instead, they try to transform

the total school environment into a learning community in which students live by a credo of nonviolence.

Two contexts for conflict are possible: cooperative and competitive (Deutsch 1973, Johnson and Johnson 1989). In a competitive context, individuals strive to win while ensuring their opponents lose. Those few who perform the best receive the rewards. In this context, competitors often misperceive one another's positions and motivations, avoid communicating with one another, are suspicious of one another, and see the situation from only their own perspective.

In a cooperative context, conflicts tend to be resolved constructively. Students have clear perceptions of one another's positions and motivation, communicate accurately and completely, trust one another, and define conflicts as mutual problems to be solved. Cooperators typically have a long-term time orientation and focus their energies both on achieving mutual goals and on maintaining good working relationships with others.

Students cannot learn to manage conflicts constructively when their school experience is competitive and individualistic. In such a context, constructive conflict resolution procedures are often ineffective and, in fact, may make the students who use them vulnerable to exploitation. Instead, schools should seek to create a cooperative context for conflict management, which is easier to do when the majority of learning situations are cooperative (Johnson and Johnson 1989, Johnson et al. 1993).

4. Decrease in-school risk factors.

Three factors place children and adolescents at risk for violent behavior. The first is academic failure. One way that schools can promote higher achievement and greater competence in using higher-level reasoning by students is to emphasize cooperative learning more than competitive or individualistic learning (Johnson and Johnson 1989). The more students know and the greater their ability to analyze situations and think through decisions, the better able they will be to envision the consequences of their actions, respect differing viewpoints, conceive of a variety of strategies for dealing with conflict, and engage in creative problem solving.

A second factor that puts children and adolescents at risk for violent and destructive behavior is alienation from schoolmates. In order to create an infrastructure of personal and academic support, schools need to encourage long-term caring and committed relationships. Two procedures for doing so are (1) using cooperative base groups that last for a number of years (Johnson et al. 1992, 1993); and (2) assigning teams of teachers to follow cohorts of students through several grades, instead of changing teachers every year (Johnson and Johnson 1994a).

Third, children and adolescents who have high levels of psychological pathology are more at risk for violent and destructive behavior than students who are psychologically well adjusted. David Hamburg, the president of Carnegie Corporation, states that reversing the trend of violence among the young depends on teaching children how to share, work cooperatively with others, and help others. The more children and adolescents work in cooperative learning groups, the greater will be their psychological health, self-esteem, social competencies, and resilience in the face of adversity and stress (Johnson and Johnson 1989).

In summary, schools must not overlook the in-school factors that place students at risk for engaging in violence and other destructive ways of managing conflicts. Anything that allows students to fail, remain apart from classmates, and be socially inept and have low self-esteem, increases the probability that students will use destructive conflict strategies.

5. Use academic controversy to increase learning.

To show students that conflicts can have positive results, schools should make academic controversies an inherent and daily part of learning situations. It is unclear whether cognitive, social, and moral development can take place in the absence of conflict. Academic *controversy* exists when one student's ideas, information, conclusions, theories, and opinions are incompatible with those of another, and the two seek to reach an agreement (Johnson and Johnson 1992).

For example, teachers can assign students to cooperative learning groups of four, divided into two pairs. One pair is assigned a pro position on an issue and the other pair, the con position. Each pair prepares a persuasive presentation (consisting of a thesis statement, rationale, and conclusion) to convince the other side of the position's validity. The two pairs then meet, and each side presents the best case possible for its position. Afterward, during an open discussion, students refute the opposing position (by discrediting the information and/or the inductive and deductive logic used) while rebutting criticisms of their position. At the same time, they try to persuade the other pair to change their minds. Next, a perspective reversal occurs in which each pair presents the best case possible for the opposing position. Finally, after trying to view the issue from both perspectives simultaneously, the students drop all advocacy and come to a consensus about their "best reasoned judgment" based on a synthesis of the two positions.

Over the past 25 years, we have conducted numerous studies on academic controversy. Similar to cooperative learning, academic controversy results in increased student achievement, critical thinking, higher-level reasoning, intrinsic motivation to learn, perspective-taking, and a number of other important educational outcomes (Johnson and Johnson 1979, 1992).

6. Teach all students how to resolve conflicts constructively.

Most of the diverse conflict resolution programs present in schools are either cadre or total student body programs. In the *cadre approach,* a small number of students are trained to serve as peer mediators for the entire school. While this approach is relatively easy and inexpensive to implement, having a few peer mediators with limited training is not likely to decrease the severity and frequency of conflicts in a school.

In the *total student body approach,* every student learns how to manage conflicts constructively by negotiating agreements and mediating their schoolmates' conflicts. The responsibility for peer mediation is rotated throughout the entire student body (or class) so that every student gains experience as a mediator. A disadvantage of this approach is the time and commitment required by the faculty. The more students who are trained how to negotiate and mediate, however, the greater the number of conflicts that will be managed constructively in the school.

An example of the total student body approach is the *Teaching Students to Be Peacemakers Program,* which we have implemented in several countries (Johnson and Johnson 1991). We conceive the training as a 12-year spiral curriculum in which each year students learn increasingly sophisticated negotiation and mediation procedures.

The negotiation procedure consists of six steps. Students in conflict: (1) define what they want, (2) describe their feelings, and (3) explain the reasons underlying those wants and feelings. Then the students: (4) reverse perspectives in order to view the conflict from both sides, (5) generate at least three optional agreements with maximum benefits for both parties, and (6) agree on the wisest course of action.

The mediation procedure consists of four steps: (1) stop the hostilities, (2) ensure that the disputants are committed to the mediation process, (3) facilitate negotiations between the disputants, and (4) formalize the agreement.

Once the students complete negotiation and mediation training, the school (or teacher) implements the Peacemakers Program by selecting two students as mediators each day. It is the actual experience of being a mediator that best teaches students how to negotiate and resolve conflicts. In addition to using the procedures, students receive additional training twice a week for the rest of the school year to expand and refine their skills.

Until recently, very little research validating the effectiveness of conflict resolution training programs in schools has existed. Over the past five years, we have conducted seven studies in six different schools in both suburban and urban settings and in two different countries (Johnson and Johnson 1994b). Students in 1st through 9th grades were involved in the studies. We found that before training, most students had daily conflicts, used destructive strategies that tended to escalate the conflict, referred the majority of their conflicts to the teacher, and did not know how to negotiate. After training, students could apply the negotiation and mediation procedures to actual conflict situations, as well as transfer them to nonclassroom and nonschool settings, such as the playground, the lunchroom, and at home. Further, they maintained their knowledge and skills throughout the school year.

Given the choice of using a "win-lose" or a "problem-solving" negotiation strategy, virtually all untrained students used the former, while trained students primarily chose the problem-solving approach. In addition, students who were taught the negotiation procedure while studying a novel during an English literature unit not only learned how to negotiate, but performed higher on an achievement test on the novel than did students in a control group, who spent their entire time studying the novel. This study represents a model of how to integrate conflict resolution training into an academic class.

After their training, students generally managed their conflicts without involving adults. The frequency of student-student conflicts teachers had to manage dropped 80 percent, and the number of conflicts referred to the principal was reduced by 95 percent. Such a dramatic reduction of referrals of conflicts to adults changed the school discipline program from arbitrating conflicts to maintaining and supporting the peer mediation process.

Knowing how to negotiate agreements and mediate schoolmates' conflicts empowers students to regulate their own behavior. Self-regulation is a central and significant hallmark of cognitive and social development. Using competencies in resolving conflicts constructively also increases a child's ability to build and maintain high-quality relationships with peers and to cope with stress and adversity.

In short, training only a small cadre of students to manage conflicts constructively and to be peer mediators will not change the way other students manage their conflicts. For this reason, schools must teach all students skills in negotiation and mediation.

Making the Future a Better Place

Every student needs to learn how to manage conflicts constructively. Without training, many students may never learn how to do so. Teaching every student how to negotiate and mediate will ensure that future generations are prepared to manage conflicts constructively in career, family, community, national, and international settings.

There is no reason to expect, however, that the process will be easy or quick. It took 30 years to reduce smoking in America. It took 20 years to reduce drunk driving. It may take even longer to ensure that children and adolescents can manage conflicts constructively. The more years that students spend learning and practicing the skills of peer mediation and conflict resolution, the more likely they will be to actually use those skills both in the classroom and beyond the school door.

References

Deutsch, M. (1973). *The Resolution of Conflict*. New Haven, Conn.: Yale University Press.

Johnson, D. W., and R. Johnson. (1979). "Conflict in the Classroom: Controversy and Learning." *Review of Educational Research* 49, 1: 51–61.

Johnson, D. W., and R. Johnson. (1989). *Cooperation and Competition: Theory and Research*. Edina, Minn.: Interaction Book Company.

Johnson, D. W., and R. Johnson. (1991). *Teaching Students to Be Peacemakers*. Edina, Minn.: Interaction Book Company.

Johnson, D. W., and R. Johnson. (1992). *Creative Controversy: Intellectual Challenge in the Classroom*. Edina, Minn.: Interaction Book Company.

Johnson, D. W., and R. Johnson. (1994a). *Leading the Cooperative School*. 2nd ed. Edina, Minn.: Interaction Book Company.

Johnson, D. W., and R. Johnson. (1994b). *Teaching Students to Be Peacemakers: Results of Five Years of Research*. Minneapolis: University of Minnesota, Cooperative Learning Center.

Johnson, D. W., and R. Johnson. (In press). "Implementing Cooperative Learning: Training Sessions, Transfer to the Classroom, and Maintaining Long-Term Use." In *Staff Development for Cooperative Learning: Issues and Approaches*, edited by N. Davidson, C. Brody, and C. Cooper. New York: Teachers College Press.

Johnson, D. W., R. Johnson, and E. Holubec. (1992). *Advanced Cooperative Learning*. 2nd ed. Edina, Minn.: Interaction Book Company.

Johnson, D. W., R. Johnson, and E. Holubec. (1993). *Cooperation in the Classroom*. 6th ed. Edina, Minn.: Interaction Book Company.

Tolan, P., and N. Guerra. (In press). *What Works in Reducing Adolescent Violence: An Empirical Review of the Field*. Denver: Center for the Study of Prevention of Violence, University of Colorado.

Webster, D. (1993). "The Unconvincing Case for School-Based Conflict Resolution Programs for Adolescents." *Health Affairs* 12, 4: 126–140.

Wilson-Brewer, R., S. Cohen, L. O'Donnell, and I. Goodman. (1991). "Violence Prevention for Young Adolescents: A Survey of the State of the Art." Eric Clearinghouse, ED356442, 800-443-3742.

Assessment

In which reading group does Jon belong? How do I construct tests? How do I know when my students have mastered the course objectives? How can I explain test results to Mary's parents? Teachers answer these questions, and many more, by applying principles of assessment. Assessment refers to procedures for measuring and recording student performance and constructing grades that communicate to other levels of proficiency or relative standing. Assessment principles constitute a set of concepts that are integral to the teaching-learning process. Indeed, a significant amount of teacher time is spent in assessment activities, and with more accountability has come a greater emphasis on assessment.

Assessment provides a foundation for making sound evaluative judgments about students' learning and achievement. Teachers need to use fair and unbiased criteria in order to assess student learning objectively and accurately and make appropriate decisions about student placement. For example, in assigning Jon to a reading group, the teacher will use his test scores as an indication of his skill level. Are the inferences from the test results valid for the school's reading program? Are his test scores consistent over several months or years? Are they consistent with his performance in class? The teacher should ask and then answer these questions so that he or she can make intelligent decisions about Jon. On the other hand, will knowledge of the test scores affect the teacher's perception of classroom performance and create a self-fulling prophecy? Teachers also evaluate students in order to assign grades, and the challenge is to balance "objective" test scores with more subjective, informally gathered information. Both kinds of evaluative information are necessary, but both can be inaccurate and are frequently misused.

The first article in this unit examines assessment principles in the context of large-scale and classroom assessment of young children. Next, "Making the Grade: What Benefits Students?" reviews teachers' grading practices and procedures that benefit student learning and lead to accurate conclusions and reporting. Teachers also need to differentiate between criterion-referenced grading for minimal objectives and the use of norms to evaluate achievement.

The next two essays discuss performance-based, "authentic" assessment. This form of assessment has great potential to integrate measurement procedures with instructional methods more effectively and to focus student learning on the application of thinking and problem-solving skills in real-life contexts. A related form of assessment, using portfolios, is described in "Planning for Classroom Portfolio Assessment."

In the last article, Blaine Worthen and Vicki Spandel review the characteristics and limitations of standardized aptitude tests. They provide suggestions for appropriate use of results from such tests.

Looking Ahead: Challenge Questions

What are some important principles for assessing young children? How is the purpose of the assessment related to these principles?

Many educators believe that schools should identify the brightest, most capable students. What are the assessment implications of this philosophy? How would low-achieving students be affected?

What is the essential difference between criterion-referenced and norm-referenced testing? What factors should be considered when deciding which approach to use?

What principles of assessment should teachers adopt for their own classroom testing? Is it necessary or feasible to develop a table of specifications for each test? How do we know if the tests teachers make are reliable and if valid inferences are drawn from the results?

How can teachers grade thinking skills such as analysis, application, and reasoning? How should objectives for student learning and grading be integrated? What are some grading practices to avoid? Why?

What are appropriate teacher uses of standardized test scores? What common mistakes do teachers make when interpreting these scores?

UNIT 6

The Challenges of Assessing Young Children Appropriately

In the past decade, testing of 4-, 5-, and 6-year-olds has been excessive and inappropriate. Given this history of misuse, Ms. Shepard maintains, the burden of proof must rest with assessment advocates to demonstrate the usefulness of assessment and to ensure that abuses will not recur.

Lorrie A. Shepard

LORRIE A. SHEPARD is a professor of education at the University of Colorado, Boulder. She is past president of the National Council on Measurement in Education, past vice president of the American Educational Research Association, and a member of the National Academy of Education. She wishes to thank Sharon Lynn Kagan, M. Elizabeth Graue, and Scott F. Marion for their thoughtful suggestions on drafts of this article.

PROPOSALS to "assess" young children are likely to be met with outrage or enthusiasm, depending on one's prior experience and one's image of the testing involved. Will an inappropriate paper-and-pencil test be used to keep some 5-year-olds out of school? Or will the assessment, implemented as an ordinary part of good instruction, help children learn? A governor advocating a test for every preschooler in the nation may have in mind the charts depicting normal growth in the pediatrician's office. Why shouldn't parents have access to similar measures to monitor their child's cognitive and academic progress? Middle-class parents, sanguine about the use of test scores to make college-selection decisions, may be eager to have similar tests determine their child's entrance into preschool or kindergarten. Early childhood experts, however, are more likely to respond with alarm because they are more familiar with the complexities of defining and measuring development and learning in young children and because they are more aware of the widespread abuses of readiness testing that occurred in the 1980s.

Given a history of misuse, it is impossible to make positive recommendations about how assessments could be used to monitor the progress of individual children or to evaluate the quality of educational programs without offering assurances that the abuses will not recur. In what follows, I summarize the negative history of standardized testing of young children in order to highlight the transformation needed in both the substance and purposes of early childhood assessment. Then I explain from a measurement perspective how the features of an assessment must be tailored to match the purpose of the assessment. Finally, I describe differences in what assessments might look like when they are used for purposes of screening for handicapping conditions, supporting instruction, or monitoring state and national trends.

Note that I use the term *test* when referring to traditional, standardized developmental and pre-academic measures and the term *assessment* when referring to more developmentally appropriate procedures for observing and evaluating young children. This is a semantic trick that plays on the different connotations of the two terms. Technically, they mean the same thing. Tests, as defined by the *Standards for Educational and Psychological Testing*, have always included systematic observations of behavior, but our experience is with tests as more formal, one-right-answer instruments used to rank and sort individuals. As we shall see, assessments might be standardized, involve paper-and-pencil responses, and so on, but in contrast to traditional testing, "assessment" implies a substantive focus on student learning for the purpose of effective intervention. While *test* and *assessment* cannot be reliably distinguished technically, the difference between these two terms as they have grown up in common parlance is of symbolic importance. Using the term *assessment* presents an opportunity to step away from past practices and ask why we should try to measure what young children know and can do. If there are legitimate purposes for gathering such data, then we can seek the appropriate content and form of assessment to align with those purposes.

Negative History of Testing Young Children

In order to understand the negative history of the standardized testing of young children in the past decade, we need to understand some larger shifts in curriculum and teaching practices. The distortion of the curriculum of the early grades dur-

From *Phi Delta Kappan*, November 1994, pp. 206-212. © 1994 by Phi Delta Kappa, Inc. Reprinted by permission.

ing the 1980s is now a familiar and well-documented story. Indeed, negative effects persist in many school districts today.

Although rarely the result of conscious policy decisions, a variety of indirect pressures — such as older kindergartners, extensive preschooling for children from affluent families, parental demands for the teaching of reading in kindergarten, and accountability testing in higher grades — produced a skill-driven kindergarten curriculum. Because what once were first-grade expectations were shoved down to kindergarten, these shifts in practice were referred to as the "escalation of curriculum" or "academic trickle-down." The result of these changes was an aversive learning environment inconsistent with the learning needs of young children. Developmentally inappropriate instructional practices, characterized by long periods of seatwork, high levels of stress, and a plethora of fill-in-the-blank worksheets, placed many children at risk by setting standards for attention span, social maturity, and academic productivity that could not be met by many normal 5-year-olds.

Teachers and school administrators responded to the problem of a kindergarten environment that was increasingly hostile to young children with several ill-considered policies: raising the entrance age for school, instituting readiness screening to

hold some children out of school for a year, increasing retentions in kindergarten, and creating two-year programs with an extra grade either before or after kindergarten. These policies and practices had a benign intent: to protect children from stress and school failure. However, they were ill-considered because they were implemented without contemplating the possibility of negative side effects and without awareness that retaining some children and excluding others only exacerbated the problems by creating an older and older population of kindergartners.[1] The more reasonable corrective for a skill-driven curriculum at earlier and earlier ages would have been curriculum reform of the kind exemplified by the recommendations for developmentally appropriate practices issued by the National Association for the Education of Young Children (NAEYC), the nation's largest professional association of early childhood educators.[2]

The first response of many schools, however, was not to fix the problem of inappropriate curriculum but to exclude those children who could not keep up or who might be harmed. Readiness testing was the chief means of implementing policies aimed at removing young children from inappropriate instructional programs. Thus the use of readiness testing increased dramatically during the 1980s

and continues today in many school districts.[3]

Two different kinds of tests are used: developmental screening measures, originally intended as the first step in the evaluation of children for potential handicaps; and pre-academic skills tests, intended for use in planning classroom instruction.[4] The technical and conceptual problems with these tests are numerous.[5] Tests are being used for purposes for which they were never designed or validated. Waiting a year or being placed in a two-year program represents a dramatic disruption in a child's life, yet not one of the existing readiness measures has sufficient reliability or predictive validity to warrant making such decisions.

Developmental and pre-academic skills tests are based on outmoded theories of aptitude and learning that originated in the 1930s. The excessive use of these tests and the negative consequences of being judged unready focused a spotlight on the tests' substantive inadequacies. The widely used Gesell Test is made up of items from old I.Q. tests and is indistinguishable statistically from a measure of I.Q.; the same is true for developmental measures that are really short-form I.Q. tests. Assigning children to different instructional opportunities on the basis of such tests carries forward nativist assumptions popular in the 1930s and

Illustration by Kay Salem

1940s. At that time, it was believed that I.Q. tests could accurately measure innate ability, unconfounded by prior learning experiences. Because these measured "capacities" were thought to be fixed and unalterable, those who scored poorly were given low-level training consistent with their supposedly limited potential. Tests of academic content might have the promise of being more instructionally relevant than disguised I.Q. tests, but, as Anne Stallman and David Pearson have shown, the decomposed and decontextualized prereading skills measured by traditional readiness tests are not compatible with current research on early literacy.[6]

Readiness testing also raises serious equity concerns. Because all the readiness measures in use are influenced by past opportunity to learn, a disproportionate number of poor and minority children are identified as unready and are excluded from school when they most need it. Thus children without preschool experience and without extensive literacy experiences at home are sent back to the very environments that caused them to score poorly on readiness measures in the first place. Or, if poor and minority children who do not pass the readiness tests are admitted to the school but made to spend an extra year in kindergarten, they suffer disproportionately the stigma and negative effects of retention.

The last straw in this negative account of testing young children is the evidence that fallible tests are often followed by ineffective programs. A review of controlled studies has shown no academic benefits from retention in kindergarten or from extra-year programs, whether developmental kindergartens or transitional first grades. When extra-year children finally get to first grade, they do not do better on average than equally "unready" children who go directly on to first grade.[7] However, a majority of children placed in these extra-year programs do experience some short- or long-term trauma, as reported by their parents.[8] Contrary to popular belief that kindergarten children are "too young to notice" retention, most of them know that they are not making "normal" progress, and many continue to make reference to the decision years later. "If I hadn't spent an extra year in kindergarten, I would be in __ grade now." In the face of such evidence, there is little wonder that many early childhood educators ask why we test young children at all.

Principles for Assessment And Testing

The NAEYC and the National Association of Early Childhood Specialists in State Departments of Education have played key roles in informing educators about the harm of developmentally inappropriate instructional practices and the misuse of tests. In 1991 NAEYC published "Guidelines for Appropriate Curriculum Content and Assessment in Programs Serving Children Ages 3 Through 8."[9] Although the detailed recommendations are too numerous to be repeated here, a guiding principle is that *assessments should bring about benefits for children, or data should not be collected at all.* Specifically, assessments "should not be used to recommend that children stay out of a program, be retained in grade, or be assigned to a segregated group based on ability or developmental maturity."[10] Instead, NAEYC acknowledges three legitimate purposes for assessment: 1) to plan instruction and communicate with parents, 2) to identify children with special needs, and 3) to evaluate programs.

Although NAEYC used *assessment* in its "Guidelines," as I do, to avoid associations with inappropriate uses of tests, both the general principle and the specific guidelines are equally applicable to formal testing. In other words, tests should not be used if they do not bring about benefits for children. In what follows I summarize some additional principles that can ensure that assessments (and tests) are beneficial and not harmful. Then, in later sections, I consider each of NAEYC's recommended uses for assessment, including national, state, and local needs for program evaluation and accountability data.

I propose a second guiding principle for assessment that is consistent with the NAEYC perspective. *The content of assessments should reflect and model progress toward important learning goals.* Conceptions of what is important to learn should take into account both physical and social/emotional development as well as cognitive learning. For most assessment purposes in the cognitive domain, content should be congruent with subject matter in emergent literacy and numeracy. In the past, developmental measures were made as "curriculum free" or "culture free" as possible in an effort to tap biology and avoid the confounding effects of past opportunity to learn. Of course, this was an impossible task because a child's ability to "draw a triangle"

or "point to the ball on top of the table" depends on prior experiences as well as on biological readiness. However, if the purpose of assessment is no longer to sort students into programs on the basis of a one-time measure of ability, then it is possible to have assessment content mirror what we want children to learn.

A third guiding principle can be inferred from several of the NAEYC guidelines. *The methods of assessment must be appropriate to the development and experiences of young children.* This means that — along with written products — observation, oral readings, and interviews should be used for purposes of assessment. Even for large-scale purposes, assessment should not be an artificial and decontextualized event; instead, the demands of data collection should be consistent with children's prior experiences in classrooms and at home. Assessment practices should recognize the diversity of learners and must be in accord with children's language development — both in English and in the native languages of those whose home language is not English.

A fourth guiding principle can be drawn from the psychometric literature on test validity. *Assessments should be tailored to a specific purpose.* Although not stated explicitly in the NAEYC document, this principle is implied by the recommendation of three sets of guidelines for three separate assessment purposes.

Matching the Why and How Of Assessment

The reason for any assessment — i.e., how the assessment information will be used — affects the substance and form of

> *The intended use of an assessment will determine the need for normative information or other means to support the interpretation of results.*

the assessment in several ways. First, the degree of technical accuracy required depends on use. For example, the identification of children for special education has critical implications for individuals. Failure to be identified could mean the denial of needed services, but being identified as in need of special services may also mean removal from normal classrooms (at least part of the time) and a potentially stigmatizing label. A great deal is at stake in such assessment, so the multifaceted evaluation employed must have a high degree of reliability and validity. Ordinary classroom assessments also affect individual children, but the consequences of these decisions are not nearly so great. An inaccurate assessment on a given day may lead a teacher to make a poor grouping or instructional decision, but such an error can be corrected as more information becomes available about what an individual child "really knows."

Group assessment refers to uses, such as program evaluation or school accountability, in which the focus is on group performance rather than on individual scores. Although group assessments may need to meet very high standards for technical accuracy, because of the high stakes associated with the results, the individual scores that contribute to the group information do not have to be so reliable and do not have to be directly comparable, so long as individual results are not reported. When only group results are desired, it is possible to use the technical advantages of matrix sampling — a technique in which each participant takes only a small portion of the assessment — to provide a rich, in-depth assessment of the intended content domain without overburdening any of the children sampled. When the "group" is very large, such as all the fourth-graders in a state or in the nation, then assessing a representative sample will produce essentially the same results for the group average as if every student had been assessed.

Purpose must also determine the content of assessment. When trying to diagnose potential learning handicaps, we still rely on aptitude-like measures designed to be as content-free as possible. We do so in order to avoid confusing lack of opportunity to learn with inability to learn. When the purpose of assessment is to measure actual learning, then content must naturally be tied to learning outcomes. However, even among achievement tests, there is considerable variability in the degree of alignment to a specific curriculum. Although to the lay person "math is math" and "reading is reading," measurement specialists are aware that tiny changes in test format can make a large difference in student performance. For example, a high proportion of students may be able to add numbers when they are presented in vertical format, but many will be unable to do the same problems presented horizontally. If manipulatives are used in some elementary classrooms but not in all, including the use of manipulatives in a mathematics assessment will disadvantage some children, while excluding their use will disadvantage others.

Assessments that are used to guide instruction in a given classroom should be integrally tied to the curriculum of that classroom. However, for large-scale assessments at the state and national level, the issues of curriculum match and the effect of assessment content on future instruction become much more problematic. For example, in a state with an agreed-upon curriculum, including geometry assessment in the early grades may be appropriate, but it would be problematic in states with strong local control of curriculum and so with much more curricular diversity.

Large-scale assessments, such as the National Assessment of Educational Progress, must include instructionally relevant content, but they must do so without conforming too closely to any single curriculum. In the past, this requirement has led to the problem of achievement tests that are limited to the "lowest common denominator." Should the instrument used for program evaluation include only the content that is common to all curricula? Or should it include everything that is in any program's goals? Although the common core approach can lead to a narrowing of curriculum when assessment results are associated with high stakes, including everything can be equally troublesome if it leads to superficial teaching in pursuit of too many different goals.

Finally, the intended use of an assessment will determine the need for normative information or other means to support the interpretation of assessment results. Identifying children with special needs requires normative data to distinguish serious physical, emotional, or learning problems from the wide range of normal development. When reporting to parents, teachers also need some idea of what constitutes grade-level performance, but such "norms" can be in the form of benchmark performances — evidence that children are working at grade level — rather than statistical percentiles.

To prevent the abuses of the past, the purposes and substance of early childhood assessments must be transformed. Assessments should be conducted only if they serve a beneficial purpose: to gain services for children with special needs, to inform instruction by building on what students already know, to improve programs, or to provide evidence nationally or in the states about programmatic needs. The form, substance, and technical features of assessment should be appropriate for the use intended for assessment data. Moreover, the methods of assessment must be compatible with the developmental level and experiences of young children. Below, I consider the implications of these principles for three different categories of assessment purposes.

Identifying Children with Special Needs

I discuss identification for special education first because this is the type of assessment that most resembles past uses of developmental screening measures. However, there is no need for wholesale administration of such tests to all incoming kindergartners. If we take the precepts of developmentally appropriate practices seriously, then at each age level a very broad range of abilities and performance levels is to be expected and tolerated. If potential handicaps are understood to be relatively rare and extreme, then it is not necessary to screen all children for "hidden" disabilities. By definition, serious learning problems should be apparent. Although it is possible to miss hearing or vision problems (at least mild ones) without systematic screening, referral for evaluation of a possible learning handicap should occur only when parents or teachers notice that a child is not progressing normally in comparison to age-appropriate expectations. In-depth assessments should then be conducted to verify the severity of the problem and to rule out a variety of other explanations for poor performance.

For this type of assessment, developmental measures, including I.Q. tests, continue to be useful. Clinicians attempt to make normative evaluations using relatively curriculum-free tasks, but today they are more likely to acknowledge the fallibility of such efforts. For such difficult assessments, clinicians must have specialized training in both diagnostic assessment and child development.

When identifying children with special needs, evaluators should use two general strategies in order to avoid confounding the ability to learn with past opportunity to learn. First, as recommended by the National Academy Panel on Selection and Placement of Students in Programs for the Mentally Retarded,[11] a child's learning environment should be evaluated to rule out poor instruction as the possible cause of a child's lack of learning. Although seldom carried out in practice, this evaluation should include trying out other methods to support learning and possibly trying a different teacher before concluding that a child can't learn from ordinary classroom instruction. A second important strategy is to observe a child's functioning in multiple contexts. Often children who appear to be impaired in school function well at home or with peers. Observation outside of school is critical for children from diverse cultural backgrounds and for those whose home language is not English. The NAEYC stresses that "screening should never be used to identify second language learners as 'handicapped,' solely on the basis of their limited abilities in English."[12]

In-depth developmental assessments are needed to ensure that children with disabilities receive appropriate services. However, the diagnostic model of special education should not be generalized to a larger population of below-average learners, or the result will be the reinstitution of tracking. Elizabeth Graue and I analyzed recent efforts to create "at-risk" kindergartens and found that these practices are especially likely to occur when resources for extended-day programs are available only for the children most in need.[13] The result of such programs is often to segregate children from low socioeconomic backgrounds into classrooms where time is spent drilling on low-level prereading skills like those found on readiness tests. The consequences of dumbed-down instruction in kindergarten are just as pernicious as the effects of tracking at higher grade levels, especially when the at-risk kindergarten group is kept together for first grade. If resources for extended-day kindergarten are scarce, one alternative would be to group children heterogeneously for half the day and then, for the other half, to provide extra enrichment activities for children with limited literacy experiences.

Classroom Assessments

Unlike traditional readiness tests that are intended to predict learning, classroom assessments should support instruction by modeling the dimensions of learning. Although we must allow considerable latitude for children to construct their own understandings, teachers must nonetheless have knowledge of normal development if they are to support children's extensions and next steps. Ordinary classroom tasks can then be used to assess a child's progress in relation to a developmental continuum. An example of a developmental continuum would be that of emergent writing, beginning with scribbles, then moving on to pictures and random letters, and then proceeding to some letter/word correspondences. These continua are not rigid, however, and several dimensions running in parallel may be necessary to describe growth in a single content area. For example, a second dimension of early writing — a child's ability to invent increasingly elaborated stories when dictating to an adult — is not dependent on mastery of writing letters, just as listening comprehension, making predictions about books, and story retellings should be developed in parallel to, not after, mastery of letter sounds.

Although there is a rich research literature documenting patterns of emergent literacy and numeracy, corresponding assessment materials are not so readily available. In the next few years, national interest in developing alternative, performance-based measures should generate more materials and resources. Specifically, new Chapter 1 legislation is likely to support the development of reading assessments that are more authentic and instructionally relevant.

For example, classroom-embedded reading assessments were created from ordinary instructional materials by a group of third-grade teachers in conjunction with researchers at the Center for Research on Evaluation, Standards, and Student Testing.[14] The teachers elected to focus on fluency and making meaning as reading goals; running records and story summaries were selected as the methods of assessment.

But how should student progress be evaluated? In keeping with the idea of representing a continuum of proficiency, third-grade teachers took all the chapter books in their classrooms and sorted them into grade-level stacks, 1-1 (first grade, first semester), 1-2, 2-1, and so on up to

fifth grade. Then they identified representative or marker books in each category to use for assessment. Once the books had been sorted by difficulty, it became possible to document that children were reading increasingly difficult texts with understanding. Photocopied pages from the marker books also helped parents see what teachers considered to be grade-level materials and provided them with concrete evidence of their child's progress. Given mandates for student-level reporting under Chapter 1, state departments of education or test publishers could help develop similar systems of this type with sufficient standardization to ensure comparability across districts.

In the meantime, classroom teachers — or preferably teams of teachers — are left to invent their own assessments for classroom use. In many schools, teachers are already working with portfolios and developing scoring criteria. The best procedure appears to be having grade-level teams and then cross-grade teams meet to discuss expectations and evaluation criteria. These conversations will be more productive if, for each dimension to be assessed, teachers collect student work and use marker papers to illustrate continua of performance. Several papers might be used at each stage to reflect the tremendous variety in children's responses, even when following the same general progression.

Benchmark papers can also be an effective means of communicating with parents. For example, imagine using sample papers from grades K-3 to illustrate expectations regarding "invented spelling." Invented spelling or "temporary spelling" is the source of a great deal of parental dissatisfaction with reform curricula. Yet most parents who attack invented spelling have never been given a rationale for its use. That is, no one has explained it in such a way that the explanation builds on the parents' own willingness to allow successive approximations in their child's early language development. They have never been shown a connection between writing expectations and grade-level spelling lists or been informed about differences in rules for first drafts and final drafts. Sample papers could be selected to illustrate the increasing mastery of grade-appropriate words, while allowing for misspellings of advanced words on first drafts. Communicating criteria is helpful to parents, and, as we have seen in the literature on performance assessment, it also helps children to understand what is expected and to become better at assessing their own work.

Monitoring National and State Trends

In 1989, when the President and the nation's governors announced "readiness for school" as the first education goal, many early childhood experts feared the creation of a national test for school entry. Indeed, given the negative history of readiness testing, the first thing the Goal 1 Technical Planning Subgroup did was to issue caveats about what an early childhood assessment must *not* be. It should not be a one-dimensional, reductionist measure of a child's knowledge and abilities; it should not be called a measure of "readiness" as if some children were not ready to learn; and it should not be used to "label, stigmatize, or classify any individual child or group of children."[15]

However, with this fearsome idea set aside, the Technical Planning Subgroup endorsed the idea of an early childhood assessment system that would periodically gather data on the condition of young children as they enter school. The purpose of the assessment would be to inform public policy and especially to help "in charting progress toward achievement of the National Education Goals,

Beginning in 1998-99, a representative sample of 23,000 kindergarten students will be assessed and then followed through grade 5.

and for informing the development, expansion, and/or modification of policies and programs that affect young children and their families."[16] Assuming that certain safeguards are built in, such data could be a powerful force in focusing national attention and resources on the needs of young children.

Unlike past testing practices aimed at evaluating individual children in comparison with normative expectations, a large-scale, nationally representative assessment would be used to monitor national trends. The purpose of such an assessment would be analogous to the use of the National Assessment of Educational Progress (NAEP) to measure major shifts in achievement patterns. For example, NAEP results have demonstrated gains in the achievement of black students in the South as a result of desegregation, and NAEP achievement measures showed gains during the 1980s in basic skills and declines in higher-order thinking skills and problem solving. Similar data are not now available for preschoolers or for children in the primary grades. If an early childhood assessment were conducted periodically, it would be possible to demonstrate the relationship between health services and early learning and to evaluate the impact of such programs as Head Start.

In keeping with the precept that methods of assessment should follow from the purpose of assessment, the Technical Planning Subgroup recommended that sampling of both children and assessment items be used to collect national data. Sampling would allow a broad assessment of a more multifaceted content domain and would preclude the misuse of individual scores to place or stigmatize individual children. A national early childhood assessment should also serve as a model of important content. As a means to shape public understanding of the full range of abilities and experiences that influence early learning and development, the Technical Planning Subgroup identified five dimensions to be assessed: 1) physical well-being and motor development, 2) social and emotional development, 3) approaches toward learning, 4) language usage, and 5) cognition and general knowledge.

Responding to the need for national data to document the condition of children as they enter school and to measure progress on Goal 1, the U.S. Department of Education has commissioned the Early Childhood Longitudinal Study: Kindergarten Cohort. Beginning in the 1998-99 school year, a representative sample of 23,000 kindergarten students will be assessed and then followed through grade 5. The content of the assessments used will correspond closely to the dimensions recommended by the Technical Planning Subgroup. In addition, data will be collected on each child's family, communi-

ty, and school/program. Large-scale studies of this type serve both program evaluation purposes (How effective are preschool services for children?) and research purposes (What is the relationship between children's kindergarten experiences and their academic success throughout elementary school?).

National needs for early childhood data and local needs for program evaluation information are similar in some respects and dissimilar in others. Both uses require group data. However, a critical distinction that affects the methods of evaluation is whether or not local programs share a

Fearing that "assessment" is just a euphemism for more bad testing, many early childhood professionals have asked, Why test at all?

common curriculum. If local programs, such as all the kindergartens in a school district, have agreed on the same curriculum, it is possible to build program evaluation assessments from an aggregation of the measures used for classroom purposes. Note that the entire state of Kentucky is attempting to develop such a system by scoring classroom portfolios for state reporting.

If programs being evaluated do not have the same specific curricula, as is the case with a national assessment and with some state assessments, then the assessment measures must reflect broad, agreed-upon goals without privileging any specific curriculum. This is a tall order, more easily said than done. For this reason, the Technical Planning Subgroup recommended that validity studies be built into the procedures for data collection. For example, pilot studies should verify that what children can do in one-on-one assessment settings is consistent with what they can do in their classrooms, and assessment methods should always allow children more than one way to show what they know.

Conclusion

In the past decade, testing of 4-, 5-, and 6-year-olds has been excessive and inappropriate. Under a variety of different names, leftover I.Q. tests have been used to track children into ineffective programs or to deny them school entry. Prereading tests held over from the 1930s have encouraged the teaching of decontextualized skills. In response, fearing that "assessment" is just a euphemism for more bad testing, many early childhood professionals have asked, Why test at all? Indeed, given a history of misuse, the burden of proof must rest with assessment advocates to demonstrate the usefulness of assessment and to ensure that abuses will not recur. Key principles that support responsible use of assessment information follow.

• No testing of young children should occur unless it can be shown to lead to beneficial results.

• Methods of assessment, especially the language used, must be appropriate to the development and experiences of young children.

• Features of assessment — content, form, evidence of validity, and standards for interpretation — must be tailored to the specific purpose of an assessment.

• Identifying children for special education is a legitimate purpose for assessment and still requires the use of curriculum-free, aptitude-like measures and normative comparisons. However, handicapping conditions are rare; the diagnostic model used by special education should not be generalized to a larger population of below-average learners.

• For both classroom instructional purposes and purposes of public policy making, the content of assessments should embody the important dimensions of early learning and development. The tasks and skills children are asked to perform should reflect and model progress toward important learning goals.

In the past, local newspapers have published readiness checklists that suggested that children should stay home from kindergarten if they couldn't cut with scissors. In the future, national and local assessments should demonstrate the richness of what children do know and should foster instruction that builds on their strengths. Telling a story in conjunction with scribbles is a meaningful stage in literacy development. Reading a story in English and retelling it in Spanish is evidence of reading comprehension. Evidence of important learning in beginning mathematics should not be counting to 100 instead of to 10. It should be extending patterns; solving arithmetic problems with blocks and explaining how you got your answer; constructing graphs to show how many children come to school by bus, by walking, by car; and demonstrating understanding of patterns and quantities in a variety of ways.

In classrooms, we need new forms of assessment so that teachers can support children's physical, social, and cognitive development. And at the level of public policy, we need new forms of assessment so that programs will be judged on the basis of worthwhile educational goals.

---

1. Lorrie A. Shepard and Mary Lee Smith, "Escalating Academic Demand in Kindergarten: Counterproductive Policies," *Elementary School Journal*, vol. 89, 1988, pp. 135-45.

2. Sue Bredekamp, ed., *Developmentally Appropriate Practice in Early Childhood Programs Serving Children from Birth Through Age 8,* exp. ed. (Washington, D.C.: National Association for the Education of Young Children, 1987).

3. M. Therese Gnezda and Rosemary Bolig, *A National Survey of Public School Testing of Pre-Kindergarten and Kindergarten Children* (Washington, D.C.: National Forum on the Future of Children and Families, National Research Council, 1988).

4. Samuel J. Meisels, "Uses and Abuses of Developmental Screening and School Readiness Testing," *Young Children,* vol. 42, 1987, pp. 4-6, 68-73.

5. Lorrie A. Shepard and M. Elizabeth Graue, "The Morass of School Readiness Screening: Research on Test Use and Test Validity," in Bernard Spodek, ed., *Handbook of Research on the Education of Young Children* (New York: Macmillan, 1993), pp. 293-305.

6. Anne C. Stallman and P. David Pearson, "Formal Measures of Early Literacy," in Lesley Mandel Morrow and Jeffrey K. Smith, eds., *Assessment for Instruction in Early Literacy* (Englewood Cliffs, N.J.: Prentice-Hall, 1990), pp. 7-44.

7. Lorrie A. Shepard, "A Review of Research on Kindergarten Retention," in Lorrie A. Shepard and Mary Lee Smith, eds., *Flunking Grades: Research and Policies on Retention* (London: Falmer Press, 1989), pp. 64-78.

8. Lorrie A. Shepard and Mary Lee Smith, "Academic and Emotional Effects of Kindergarten Retention in One School District," in idem, pp. 79-107.

9. "Guidelines for Appropriate Curriculum Content and Assessment in Programs Serving Children Ages 3 Through 8," *Young Children*, vol. 46, 1991, pp. 21-38.

10. Ibid., p. 32.

11. Kirby A. Heller, Wayne H. Holtzman, and Samuel Messick, eds., *Placing Children in Special Education* (Washington, D.C.: National Academy Press, 1982).

12. "Guidelines," p. 33.

13. Shepard and Graue, op. cit.

14. The Center for Research on Evaluation, Standards, and Student Testing is located on the campuses of the University of California, Los Angeles, and the University of Colorado, Boulder.

15. *Goal 1: Technical Planning Subgroup Report on School Readiness* (Washington, D.C.: National Education Goals Panel, September 1991).

16. Ibid., p. 6.

Making the Grade: What Benefits Students?

Thomas R. Guskey

Thomas R. Guskey is Professor of Education Policy Studies and Evaluation, College of Education, University of Kentucky, Lexington, KY 40506.

Although the debate over grading and reporting practices continues, today we know which practices benefit students and encourage learning.

Charged with leading a committee that would revise his school's grading and reporting system, Warren Middleton described his work this way:

> The Committee On Grading was called upon to study grading procedures. At first, the task of investigating the literature seemed to be a rather hopeless one. What a mass and a mess it all was! Could order be brought out of such chaos? Could points of agreement among American educators concerning the perplexing grading problem actually be discovered? It was with considerable misgiving and trepidation that the work was finally begun.

Few educators today would consider the difficulties encountered by Middleton and his colleagues to be particularly surprising. In fact, most probably would sympathize with his lament. What they might find surprising, however, is that this report from the Committee on Grading was published in 1933!

The issues of grading and reporting on student learning have perplexed educators for the better part of this century. Yet despite all the debate and the multitude of studies, coming up with prescriptions for best practice seems as challenging today as it was for Middleton and his colleagues more than 60 years ago.

Points of Agreement

Although the debate over grading and reporting continues, today we know better which practices benefit students and encourage learning. Given the multitude of studies—and their often incongruous results—researchers do appear to agree on the following points:

1. Grading and reporting aren't essential to instruction. Teachers don't need grades or reporting forms to teach well. Further, students don't need them to learn (Frisbie and Waltman 1992).

Teachers do need to check regularly on how students are doing, what they've learned, and what problems or difficulties they've experienced. But grading and reporting are different from checking; they involve judging the adequacy of students' performance at a specific time. Typically, teachers use checking to diagnose and prescribe and use grading to evaluate and describe (Bloom et al. 1981).

When teachers do both checking and grading, they become advocates as well as judges—roles that aren't necessarily compatible (Bishop 1992). Finding a meaningful compromise between these dual roles makes many teachers uncomfortable, especially those with a child-centered orientation (Barnes 1985).

2. No one method of grading and reporting serves all purposes well. Grading enables teachers to communicate the achievements of students to parents and others, provide incentives to learn, and provide information that students can use for self-evaluation. In addition, schools use grades to identify or group students for particular educational paths or programs and to evaluate a program's effectiveness (Feldmesser 1971, Frisbie and Waltman 1992). Unfortunately, many schools attempt to address all of these purposes with a single method and end up achieving none very well (Austin and McCann 1992).

Letter grades, for example, briefly describe learning progress and give some idea of its adequacy (Payne 1974). Their use, however, requires abstracting a great deal of information into a single symbol (Stiggins 1994). In addition, the cut-off between grade categories is always arbitrary and difficult to justify. If scores for a grade of *B* range from 80 to 89, students at both ends of that range receive the same grade, even though their scores differ by nine points. But the student with a score of 79—a one-point difference—receives a grade of *C*.

The more detailed methods also have their drawbacks. Narratives and checklists of learning outcomes offer specific information for documenting progress, but good narratives take time to prepare, and—not surprisingly—as

Teachers don't need grades or reporting forms to teach well. Further, students don't need them to learn.

teachers complete more narratives, their comments become increasingly standardized. From the parents' standpoint, checklists of learning outcomes often appear too complicated to understand. In addition, checklists seldom communicate the appropriateness of students' progress in relation to expectations for their level (Afflerbach and Sammons 1991).

Because one method won't adequately serve all purposes, schools must identify their primary purpose for grading and select or develop the most appropriate approach (Cangelosi 1990). This process often involves the difficult task of seeking consensus among several constituencies.

3. Regardless of the method used, grading and reporting remain inherently subjective. In fact, the more detailed the reporting method and the more analytic the process, the more likely subjectivity will influence results (Ornstein 1994). That's why, for example, holistic scoring procedures tend to have greater reliability than analytic procedures.

Subjectivity in this process, however, isn't always bad. Because teachers know their students, understand various dimensions of students' work, and have clear notions of the progress made, their subjective perceptions may yield very accurate descriptions of what students have learned (Brookhart 1993, O'Donnell and Woolfolk 1991).

When subjectivity translates into bias, however, negative consequences can result. Teachers' perceptions of students' behavior can significantly influence their judgments of scholastic performance (Hills 1991). Students with behavior problems often have no chance to receive a high grade because their infractions overshadow their

performance. These effects are especially pronounced in judgments of boys (Bennett et al. 1993). Even the neatness of students' handwriting can significantly affect a teacher's judgment (Sweedler-Brown 1992).

Training programs can help teachers identify and reduce these negative effects and lead to greater consistency in judgments (Afflerbach and Sammons 1991). Unfortunately, few teachers receive adequate training in grading or reporting as part of their preservice experiences (Boothroyd and McMorris 1992). Also, few school districts provide adequate guidance to ensure consistency in teachers' grading or reporting practices (Austin and McCann 1992).

4. Grades have some value as rewards, but no value as punishments. Although educators would undoubtedly prefer that motivation to learn be entirely intrinsic, the existence of grades and other reporting methods are important factors in determining how much effort students put forth (Chastain 1990, Ebel 1979). Most students view high grades as positive recognition of their success, and some work hard to avoid the consequences of low grades (Feldmesser 1971).

At the same time, no studies support the use of low grades as punishments. Instead of prompting greater effort, low grades usually cause students to withdraw from learning. To protect their self-image, many students regard the low grade as irrelevant and meaningless. Other students may blame themselves for the low mark, but feel helpless to improve (Selby and Murphy 1992).

Sadly, some teachers consider grades or reporting forms their "weapon of last resort." In their view, students who don't comply with

requests suffer the consequences of the greatest punishment a teacher can bestow: a failing grade. Such practices have no educational value and, in the long run, adversely affect students, teachers, and the relationship they share. Rather than attempting to punish students with a low mark, teachers can better motivate students by regarding their work as incomplete and requiring additional effort.

5. Grading and reporting should always be done in reference to learning criteria, never on the curve. Using the normal probability curve as a basis for assigning grades typically yields greater consistency in grade distributions from one teacher to the next. The practice, however, is detrimental to teaching and learning.

Grading on the curve pits students against one another in a competition for the few rewards (high grades) distributed by the teacher. Under these conditions, students readily see that helping others will threaten their own chances for success (Johnson et al. 1979, Johnson et al. 1980). Learning becomes a game of winners and losers—with most students falling into the latter category (Johnson and Johnson 1989). In addition, modern research has shown that the seemingly direct relationship between aptitude or intelligence and school achievement depends upon instructional conditions, not a probability curve.

When the instructional quality is high and well matched to students' learning needs, the magnitude of this relationship diminishes drastically and approaches zero (Bloom 1976). Moreover, the fairness and equity of grading on the curve is a myth.

Learning Criteria

When grading and reporting relate to learning criteria, teachers have a clearer picture of what students have learned. Students and teachers alike generally prefer this approach because it seems fairer (Kovas 1993). The types of learning criteria usually used for grading and reporting fall into three categories:

■ *Product criteria* are favored by advocates of performance-based

A Look Back at Grading Practices

Although student assessment has been a part of teaching and learning for centuries, grading is a relatively recent phenomenon. The ancient Greeks used assessments as formative, not evaluative, tools. Students demonstrated, usually orally, what they had learned, giving teachers a clear indication of which topics required more work or instruction.

In the United States, grading and reporting were virtually unknown before 1850. Back then, most schools grouped students of all ages and backgrounds together with one teacher. Few students went beyond the elementary education offered in these one-room schoolhouses. As the country grew—and as legislators passed compulsory attendance laws—the number and diversity of students increased. Schools began to group students in grades according to their age, and to try new ideas about curriculum and teaching methods. Here's a brief timeline of significant dates in the history of grading:

Late 1800s: Schools begin to issue progress evaluations. Teachers simply write down the skills that students have mastered; once students complete the requirements for one level, they can move to the next level.

Early 1900s: The number of public high schools in the United States increases dramatically. While elementary teachers continue using written descriptions to document student learning, high school teachers introduce percentages as a way to certify students' accomplishments in specific subject areas. Few educators question the gradual shift to percentage grading, which seems a natural by-product of the increased demands on high school teachers.

1912: Starch and Elliott publish a study that challenges percentage grades as reliable measures of student achievement. They base their findings on grades assigned to two papers

written for a first-year English class in high school. Of the 142 teachers grading on a 0 to 100 scale, 15 percent give one paper a failing mark; 12 percent give the same paper a score of 90 or more. The other paper receives scores ranging from 50 to 97. Neatness, spelling, and punctuation influenced the scoring of many teachers, while others considered how well the paper communicated its message.

1913: Responding to critics—who argue that good writing is, by nature, a highly subjective judgment—Starch and Elliott repeat their study but use geometry papers. Even greater variations occur, with scores on one paper ranging from 28 to 95. Some teachers deducted points only for wrong answers, but others took neatness, form, and spelling into account.

1918: Teachers turn to grading scales with fewer and larger categories. One three-point scale, for example, uses the categories of Excellent, Average, and Poor. Another has five categories (Excellent, Good, Average, Poor, and Failing) with the corresponding letters of A, B, C, D, and F (Johnson 1918, Rugg 1918).

1930s: Grading on the curve becomes increasingly popular as educators seek to minimize the subjective nature of scoring. This method rank orders students according to some measure of their performance or proficiency. The top percentage receives an A, the next percentage receives a B, and so on (Corey 1930). Some advocates (Davis 1930) even specify the precise percentage of students to be assigned each grade, such as 6–22–44–22–6.

Grading on the curve seems fair and equitable, given research suggesting that students' scores on tests of innate intelligence approximate a normal probability curve (Middleton 1933).

As the debate over grading and reporting intensifies, a number of

schools abolish formal grades altogether (Chapman and Ashbaugh 1925) and return to using verbal descriptions of student achievement. Others advocate pass-fail systems that distinguish only between acceptable and failing work (Good 1937). Still others advocate a "mastery approach": Once students have mastered a skill or content, they move to other areas of study (Heck 1938, Hill 1935).

1958: Ellis Page investigates how student learning is affected by grades and teachers' comments. In a now classic study, 74 secondary school teachers administer a test, and assign a numerical score and letter grade of A, B, C, D, or F to each student's paper. Next, teachers randomly divide the tests into three groups. Papers in the first group receive only the numerical score and letter grade. The second group, in addition to the score and grade, receive these standard comments: A—Excellent! B—Good work. Keep at it. C—Perhaps try to do still better? D—Let's bring this up. F—Let's raise this grade! For the third group, teachers mark the score and letter grade, and write individualized comments.

Page evaluates the effects of the comments by considering students' scores on the next test they take. Results show that students in the second group achieved significantly higher scores than those who received only a score and grade. The students who received individualized comments did even better. Page concludes that grades can have a beneficial effect on student learning, but only when accompanied by specific or individualized comments from the teacher.

—*Thomas R. Guskey*

Source: H. Kirschenbaum, S. B. Simon, and R. W. Napier, (1971), *Wad-ja-get? The Grading Game in American Education,* (New York: Hart).

approaches to teaching and learning. These educators believe grading and reporting should communicate a summative evaluation of student achievement (Cangelosi 1990). In

other words, they focus on what students know and are able to do at that time. Teachers who use product criteria often base their grades or reports exclusively on final examina-

tion scores, overall assessments, or other culminating demonstrations of learning.

■ *Process criteria* are emphasized by educators who believe product criteria don't provide a complete picture of student learning. From their perspective, grading and reporting should reflect not just the final results but also *how* students got there. Teachers who consider effort or work habits when reporting on student learning are using process criteria. So are teachers who take into consideration classroom quizzes, homework, class participation, or attendance.

■ *Progress criteria*, often referred to as "improvement scoring" and "learning gain," consider how much students have gained from their learning experiences. Teachers who use progress criteria look at *how far* students have come rather than where they are. As a result, scoring criteria may become highly individualized.

Teachers who base their grading and reporting procedures on learning criteria typically use some combination of the three types (Frary et al. 1993; Nava and Loyd 1992; Stiggins et al. 1989). Most researchers and measurement specialists, on the other hand, recommend using product criteria exclusively. They point out that the more process and progress criteria come into play, the more subjective and biased grades become (Ornstein 1994). How can a teacher know, for example, how difficult a task was for students or how hard they worked to complete it? If these criteria are included at all, most experts recommend they be reported separately (Stiggins 1994).

Practical Guidelines

Despite years of research, there's no evidence to indicate that one grading or reporting method works best under all conditions, in all circumstances. But in developing practices that seek to be fair, equitable, and useful to students, parents, and teachers, educators can rely on two guidelines:

■ *Provide accurate and understandable descriptions of learning.* Regardless of the method or form used, grading and reporting should communicate effectively what students have learned, what they can do, and whether their learning status is in line with expectations for that level. More

than an exercise in quantifying achievement, grading and reporting must be seen as a challenge in clear thinking and effective communication (Stiggins 1994).

■ *Use grading and reporting methods to enhance, not hinder, teaching and learning.* A clear, easily understood reporting form facilitates communication between teachers and parents. When both parties speak the same language, joint efforts to help students are likely to succeed. But developing such an equitable and understandable system will require the elimination of long-time practices such as averaging and assigning a zero to work that's late, missed, or neglected.

Averaging falls far short of providing an accurate description of what students have learned. For example, students often say, "I have to get a *B* on the final to pass this course." Such a comment illustrates the inappropriateness of averaging. If a final examination is truly comprehensive and students' scores accurately reflect what they've learned, why should a *B* level of performance translate to a *D* for the course grade?

Any single measure of learning can be unreliable. Consequently, most researchers recommend using several indicators in determining students' grades or marks—and most teachers concur (Natriello 1987). Nevertheless, the key question remains, "What information provides the most accurate depiction of students' learning at this time?" In nearly all cases, the answer is "the most current information." If students demonstrate that past assessment information doesn't accurately reflect their learning, new information must take its place. By continuing to rely on past assessment data, the grades can be misleading about a student's learning (Stiggins 1994).

Similarly, assigning a score of zero to work that is late, missed, or neglected doesn't accurately depict learning. Is the teacher certain the student has learned absolutely nothing, or is the zero assigned to punish students for not displaying appropriate responsibility (Canady and Hotchkiss

1989, Stiggins and Duke 1991)?

Further, a zero has a profound effect when combined with the practice of averaging. Students who receive a single zero have little chance of success because such an extreme score skews the average. That is why, for example, Olympic events such as gymnastics and ice skating eliminate the highest and lowest scores; otherwise, one judge could control the entire competition simply by giving extreme scores. An alternative is to use the median score rather than the average (Wright 1994), but use of the most current information remains the most defensible option.

Meeting the Challenge

The issues of grading and reporting on student learning continue to challenge educators today, just as they challenged Middleton and his colleagues in 1933. But today we know more than ever before about the complexities involved and how certain practices can influence teaching and learning.

What do educators need to develop grading and reporting practices that provide quality information about student learning? Nothing less than clear thinking, careful planning, excellent communication skills, and an overriding concern for the well being of students. Combining these skills with our current knowledge on effective practice will surely result in more efficient and more effective reporting.

References

Afflerbach, P., and R. B. Sammons. (1991). "Report Cards in Literacy Evaluation: Teachers' Training, Practices, and Values." Paper presented at the annual meeting of the National Reading Conference, Palm Springs, Calif.

Austin, S., and R. McCann. (1992). "'Here's Another Arbitrary Grade for your Collection': A Statewide Study of Grading Policies." Paper presented at the annual meeting of the American Educational Research Association, San Francisco.

Barnes, S. (1985). "A Study of Classroom Pupil Evaluation: The Missing Link in Teacher Education." *Journal of Teacher Education* 36, 4: 46–49.

Bennett, R. E., R. L. Gottesman, D. A. Rock, and F. Cerullo. (1993). "Influence of Behavior Perceptions and Gender on

Teachers' Judgments of Students' Academic Skill." *Journal of Educational Psychology*, 85: 347–356.

Bishop, J. H. (1992). "Why U.S. Students Need Incentives to Learn." *Educational Leadership* 49, 6: 15–18.

Bloom, B. S. (1976). *Human Characteristics and School Learning*. New York: McGraw-Hill.

Bloom, B. S., G. F. Madaus, and J. T. Hastings. (1981). *Evaluation to Improve Learning*. New York: McGraw-Hill.

Boothroyd, R. A., and R. F. McMorris. (1992). "What Do Teachers Know About Testing and How Did They Find Out?" Paper presented at the annual meeting of the National Council on Measurement in Education, San Francisco.

Brookhart, S. M. (1993). "Teachers' Grading Practices: Meaning and Values." *Journal of Educational Measurement* 30, 2: 123–142.

Canady, R. L., and P. R. Hotchkiss. (1989). "It's a Good Score! Just a Bad Grade." *Phi Delta Kappan* 71: 68–71.

Cangelosi, J. S. (1990). "Grading and Reporting Student Achievement." In *Designing Tests for Evaluating Student Achievement*, pp. 196–213. New York: Longman.

Chapman, H. B., and E. J. Ashbaugh. (October 7, 1925). "Report Cards in American Cities." *Educational Research Bulletin* 4: 289–310.

Chastain, K. (1990). Characteristics of Graded and Ungraded Compositions." *Modern Language Journal*, 74, 1: 10–14.

Corey, S. M. (1930). "Use of the Normal Curve as a Basis for Assigning Grades in Small Classes." *School and Society* 31: 514–516.

Davis, J. D. W. (1930). "Effect of the 6-22-44-22-6 Normal Curve System on Failures and Grade Values." *Journal of Educational Psychology* 22: 636–640.

Ebel, R. L. (1979). *Essentials of Educational Measurement* (3rd ed.). Englewood Cliffs, N.J.: Prentice Hall.

Feldmesser, R. A. (1971). "The Positive Functions of Grades." Paper presented at the annual meeting of the American Educational Research Association, New York.

Frary, R. B., L. H. Cross, and L. J. Weber. (1993). "Testing and Grading Practices and Opinions of Secondary Teachers of Academic Subjects: Implications for Instruction in Measurement." *Educational Measurement: Issues and Practices* 12, 3: 23–30.

Frisbie, D. A., and K. K. Waltman. (1992). "Developing a Personal Grading Plan." *Educational Measurement: Issues and Practices* 11, 3: 35–42.

Good, W. (1937). "Should Grades Be Abolished?" *Education Digest* 2, 4: 7–9.

Heck, A. O. (1938). "Contributions of Research to Classification, Promotion, Marking and Certification." Reported in *The Science Movement in Education (Part II), Twenty-Seventh Yearbook of the National Society for the Study of Education*. Chicago: University of Chicago Press.

Hill, G. E. (1935). "The Report Card in Present Practice." *Education Methods* 15, 3: 115–131.

Hills, J. R. (1991). "Apathy Concerning Grading and Testing." *Phi Delta Kappan* 72, 2: 540–545.

Johnson, D. W., and R. T. Johnson. (1989). *Cooperation and Competition: Theory and Research*. Endina, Minn.: Interaction.

Johnson, D. W., L. Skon, and R. T. Johnson. (1980). "Effects of Cooperative, Competitive, and Individualistic Conditions on Children's Problem-Solving Performance." *American Educational Research Journal* 17, 1: 83–93.

Johnson, R. H. (1918). "Educational Research and Statistics: The Coefficient Marking System." *School and Society* 7, 181: 714–116.

Johnson, R. T., D. W. Johnson, and M. Tauer. (1979). "The Effects of Cooperative, Competitive, and Individualistic Goal Structures on Students' Attitudes and Achievement." *Journal of Psychology* 102: 191–198.

Kovas, M. A. (1993). "Make Your Grading Motivating: Keys to Performance-Based Evaluation." *Quill and Scroll* 68, 1: 10–11.

Middleton, W. (1933). "Some General Trends in Grading Procedure." *Education* 54, 1: 5–10.

Natriello, G. (1987). "The Impact of Evaluation Processes On Students." *Educational Psychologists* 22: 155–175.

Nava, F. J. G., and B. H. Loyd. (1992). "An Investigation of Achievement and Nonachievement Criteria in Elementary and Secondary School Grading." Paper presented at the annual meeting of the American Educational Research Association, San Francisco.

O'Donnell, A., and A. E. Woolfolk. (1991). "Elementary and Secondary Teachers' Beliefs About Testing and Grading."

Paper presented at the annual meeting of the American Psychological Association, San Francisco.

Ornstein, A. C. (1994). "Grading Practices and Policies: An Overview and Some Suggestions." *NASSP Bulletin* 78, 559: 55–64.

Page, E. B. (1958). "Teacher Comments and Student Performance: A Seventy-Four Classroom Experiment in School Motivation." *Journal of Educational Psychology* 49: 173–181.

Payne, D. A. (1974). *The Assessment of Learning*. Lexington, Mass.: Heath.

Rugg, H. O. (1918). "Teachers' Marks and the Reconstruction of the Marking System." *Elementary School Journal* 18, 9: 701–719.

Selby, D., and S. Murphy. (1992). "Graded or Degraded: Perceptions of Letter-Grading for Mainstreamed Learning-Disabled Students." *British Columbia Journal of Special Education* 16, 1: 92–104.

Starch, D., and E. C. Elliott. (1912). "Reliability of the Grading of High School Work in English." *School Review* 20: 442–457.

Starch, D., and E. C. Elliott. (1913). "Reliability of the Grading of High School Work in Mathematics." *School Review* 21: 254–259.

Stewart, L. G., and M. A. White. (1976). "Teacher Comments, Letter Grades, and Student Performance." *Journal of Educational Psychology* 68, 4: 488–500.

Stiggins, R. J. (1994). "Communicating with Report Card Grades." In *Student-Centered Classroom Assessment*, pp. 363–396. New York: Macmillan.

Stiggins, R. J., and D. L. Duke. (1991). "District Grading Policies and Their Potential Impact on At-risk Students." Paper presented at the annual meeting of the American Educational Research Association, Chicago.

Stiggins, R. J., D. A. Frisbie, and P. A. Griswold. (1989). "Inside High School Grading Practices: Building a Research Agenda." *Educational Measurement: Issues and Practice* 8, 2: 5–14.

Sweedler-Brown, C. O. (1992). "The Effect of Training on the Appearance Bias of Holistic Essay Graders." *Journal of Research and Development in Education* 26, 1: 24–29.

Wright, R. G. (1994). "Success for All: The Median Is the Key." *Phi Delta Kappan* 75, 9: 723–725.

Creating Tests Worth Taking

The Director of Research at CLASS provides questions, criteria, and suggestions for test designers who want to engage students as well as evaluate their performance.

GRANT WIGGINS

Grant Wiggins is the Director of Research and Programs for the Center on Learning, Assessment, and School Structure (CLASS), 39 Main St., Geneseo, NY 14454. These design ideas derive from the work of CLASS in Frederick County, Md.; South Orange-Maplewood, N.J.; Urbandale, Iowa.; and with faculties in Monroe, Orange, Suffolk, Ulster, and Wayne counties, N.Y.

Should a test be enticing? I think so. And should tests more often be authentic simulations of how knowledge is tested in adult work and civic settings? Many of us believe so. "Performance assessment" calls upon test makers to be creative designers then, not just technicians.

In performance assessment the design issues resemble those facing the architect. There is ground to be covered (the syllabus), there are the logistics of making the design fit the site (making large-scale assessment work in the school), and there are building codes (psychometric norms) and town elders (school board members and district testing directors) to worry about. But designers have typically avoided another, more basic obligation: the need to serve the users — in this case, students and teachers. The clients must "own" the design; form must follow function. The more the tasks (like the house) fit seamlessly with both the environment and the client's aspirations, the better the design and the result.

In this article I offer some proven design tips, tools, and criteria for fashioning assessment tasks that are more enticing, feasible, and defensible — tests worth taking.

Questions and Criteria

Designers of performance assessments should use the following key questions as a tool to guide the design process:

• What kinds of essential tasks, achievements, habits of mind, or other valued "masteries" are falling through the cracks of conventional tests?

• What are the core performances, roles, or situations that all students should encounter and be expected to master?

• What are the most salient and insightful discriminators in judging actual performances?

• What does genuine mastery of each proposed assessment task look like? Do we have credible and appropriate exemplars to anchor our scoring system? Have we justified standards so they are more than local norms?

• Are the test's necessary constraints — imposed on help available from others, access to resources, time to revise, test secrecy, prior knowledge of standards —authentic?

• Do our assessment tasks have sufficient depth and breadth to allow valid generalizations about overall student competence?

• Have we ensured that the test will not be corrupted by well-intentioned judges of student work?

• Who are the audiences for assessment information, and how should assessment be designed, conducted, and reported to accommodate the needs of each audience? When are audit-tests appropriate and inappropriate?

These questions can be summarized and reframed to produce eight basic design criteria:

1. Assessment tasks should be, whenever possible, authentic and meaningful — worth mastering.

2. The set of tasks should be a valid sample from which apt generalizations about overall performance of complex capacities can be made.

3. The scoring criteria should be authentic, with points awarded or taken off for essential successes and errors, not for what is easy to count or observe.

4. The performance standards that anchor the scoring should be genuine benchmarks, not arbitrary cut scores or provincial school norms.

5. The context of the problems should be rich, realistic, and enticing — with the inevitable constraints on access to time, resources, and advance knowledge of the tasks and standards appropriately minimized.

6. The tasks should be validated.

7. The scoring should be feasible and reliable.

8. Assessment results should be reported and used so that *all* customers for the data are satisfied.

The suggestions and observations that follow offer further assistance to would-be designers.

Choosing What to Test

Choose exit outcomes or areas of the curriculum that now tend to fall through the cracks of conventional testing. Typical tests, even demanding ones, tend to overassess student "knowledge" and underassess student "know-how with knowledge" — that is, intellectual performance. Auditing local tests with Bloom's taxonomy as criteria, for example, shows that synthesis is infrequently assessed at present, and is *inherently resistant* to assessment by multiple-choice tests because it requires "production of a unique communication" that bears the stamp of the student.[1]

Faculties should also consider their institutional "customers." What kinds of tasks must our *former* students master? Here, for example, is a question from a freshman final exam in European history at a prestigious college; it suggests how even our better students are often ill-prepared for real intellectual tasks:

> Imagine yourself Karl Marx, living half a century later. Write a brief evaluation of the programs of the Fabian socialists and the American reformers such as T. Roosevelt to present to the Socialist International.

Think of the knowledge to be tested as a tool for fashioning a performance or product. Successful task design requires making the essential material of a course a *necessary means* to a successful performance *end.* Example: a 5th grade teacher assesses geography knowledge by having his students devise a complete itinerary, map, and travel packet for their favorite rock group's world tour, within certain budget, logistical, cultural, and demographic restrictions.

Another example: students are asked to design a museum exhibit around a theme studied in a history course, selecting from many real or facsimile artifacts; required to justify what is both included and excluded in the exhibit; and must seek funding from a "foundation" of teachers and peers for the exhibit.

We want to know: Can the student use knowledge and resources effectively, *to achieve a desired effect?* This is the question Bloom and his colleagues argued was at the heart of synthesis. These tasks should only be judged well done to the extent that the content is well used.

Designing the Tasks

Contextualize the task. The aim is to invent an authentic simulation, and like all simulations, case studies, or experiential exercises, the task must be rich in contextual detail. A context is rich if it supports multiple approaches, styles, and solutions and requires good judgments in achieving an effective result. One must please a real audience, make a design actually work, or achieve an aesthetic effect that causes pride or dismay in the result.

The test may be a contrivance, but it needn't *feel* like one.[2] Consider professional training and testing. Doctors and pilots in training confront situations that replicate the challenges to be later faced. Business and law students learn by the case method, fully immersed in the facts of real past cases. A context is realistic to the extent that we so accept the premises, constraints, and "feel" of the challenge that our desire to master it makes us lose sight of the extrinsic factors and motives at stake — namely that someone is evaluating us. In just this way, for example, putting out a school newspaper for a journalism course doesn't feel contrived.

Here's an example of how a teacher's attempt to design a performance task evolved as a concern for context was introduced. The original task, in a global studies course, required students to design a trip to China or Japan. But what kind of trip? For what customers? With what constraints of budget or time? The teacher then refined the task so that each student had a $10,000 budget for **designing a month-long, cultural-exchange trip for students their age. Still, the purpose is too abstract.** What must the tour designers accomplish? Are they trying to design a tour in the abstract or really attract tour-takers? The students were finally charged to be travel agents who develop an extensive brochure and research the cost and logistical information using a computer reservations system.

There is no such thing as performance-in-general. To understand what *kind* and *precision* of answer fits the problem at hand, the student needs contextual detail: it clarifies the desired result, hence the criteria and standards. Too many measurement tasks have an acceptable margin of error that is arbitrary. Are we measuring body temperature or roasts in the oven? It matters. The task's standard of performance (desired precision or quality of product) should be apparent. In fact, an important oversight by the global studies teacher was her failure to give the students model tour brochures.[3]

Aim to design "meaningful" tasks — not the same as "immediately relevant or practical" tasks. An assessment task will be meaningful to the extent that it provokes thought and thus engages the student's interest. But a task can be engaging without being of apparent, immediate usefulness. Whether it be mysteries, debates, mock trials, putting on plays — or, for that matter, Nintendo — students clearly respond to "irrelevant" but real challenges. What do such tasks have in common? Designers need to conduct better

empirical studies to discover the tasks that tap those twin intellectual needs: *our urge for efficacy and our need for meaningful connections.*

This caution about meaning vs. relevance is particularly warranted to avoid turning important theoretical problems into crude utilitarian ones. Many genuine problems do not have obvious practical value, but they nonetheless evoke interest and provide insight into student abilities. Consider two such problems, one in geometry and one in history/English:

We all know the Pythagorean theorem: $A^2 + B^2 = C^2$; but does it have to be a square that we draw on each leg? Suppose we drew the same shape on each leg; would the areas on A and B add up to the area on C? Find other shapes that make the equation work, too, and try to derive a more general formula of the theorem.[4]

You and your colleagues (groups of 3 or 4) have been asked to submit a proposal to write a U.S. history textbook for middle school students. The publishers demand two things: that the book hit the most important things, and that it be interesting to students. Because of your expertise in 18th-century American history, you will provide them a draft chapter on the 18th century, up to but not including the Revolution, and "field tested" on some middle school students. They also ask that you fill in an "importance" chart with your response to these questions: (1) Which event, person, or idea is most important in this time period, and why? (2) Which of three sources of history — ideas, people, events — is most important? You will be expected to justify your choices of "most important" and to demonstrate that the target population will likely be interested in your book.

Design performances, not drills. A test of many items (a drill) is not a test of knowledge in use. "Performance" is not just doing simplistic tasks that cue us for the desired bit of knowledge. It entails "putting it all together" with good judgment; good judgment cannot be tested through isolated, pat drills. As one teacher put it to me a few years ago: "The

trouble with kids today is that they don't know what to do when they don't know what to do." She is right — and a prime reason is that tests rarely put students in an authentic performance situation, where *thinking,* not just an obvious bit of knowledge, is required.

The designer's aim, then, is to avoid inventing a new round of (this time, hands-on) isolated items. Rather, we should consider the difference between drilled ability vs. performance ability and ask: *What is the equivalent of the game or recital in each subject matter?* What does the "doing" of mathematics, history, science, art, language use, and so forth, look and feel like in context? What are the projects and other kinds of synthesizing tasks performed all the time by professionals, consumers, or citizens that can be adapted to school use?

Such tasks are always "higher-order," and we would do well to use Lauren Resnick's criteria in our search for better-designed assessments. Higher-order thinking

- is *nonalgorithmic* — that is, the path of action is not fully specified in advance;
- is *complex*, with the total path not visible from any single vantage point;
- *often yields multiple solutions*, each with costs and benefits;
- involves *nuanced judgment* and interpretation;
- involves the *application of multiple criteria*, which sometimes conflict with one another;
- often involves *uncertainty*, because not everything that bears on the task is known;
- involves *self-regulation* of the thinking process, rather than coaching at each step;
- involves *imposing meaning*, finding structure in apparent disorder;
- is *effortful*, with considerable mental work involved.[5]

It may help to think of this problem as the search for larger, more interrelated but complex chunks of content to build tasks around. What, for example, might be 8 to 10 important performance tasks in a subject that effectively and efficiently "map" the essential content? Vocational programs usually grapple well with this problem by casting the course objectives as a set of increasingly complex tasks to be mastered, in which the student in the last task(s) must literally put it all together, for example, build a house in carpentry.

Refine the tasks you design by building them backwards from the models and scoring criteria. A complex task is not a vague task, with the objective or specifications unknown. All real-world performers know the target and the standards, not just their task in advance; such knowledge guides their training and

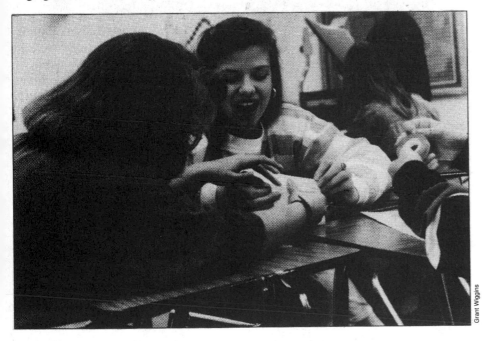

Grant Wiggins

rehearsals. Students should never have to wonder "Is this right?" "Am I finished?" "How am I doing?" "Is this what you want?" In a "real" problem the task is ill-structured but well-defined: the goal, specifications, or desired effect is known, but it is not obvious how to meet it. Knowing the *requirements of task mastery* — the "specs" — means the student must be habituated by testing to think of mastery as control over the *knowable* essentials, not as calculated cramming and good guesses. This requires providing the student with scoring criteria and models of excellent performance or production as part of instruction. (Think of diving and

debate.) Such practice is the norm throughout Carleton, Ontario, where students work from "exemplar booklets" to practice grading student work — in the same way now reserved for judges in our assessments.

"What does mastery at the task look like? What will we be able to properly infer from the collected student work?" These become the *key* questions to ask in the challenge of taking a basic idea and making a valid performance-assessment task out of it (as opposed to an instructional task). The questions properly focus on judging anticipated results and move away from design that produces merely pleasant or interesting work.

Scoring Considerations

Score what is most important for doing an effective job, not what is easiest to score. The scoring rubrics should represent generalizations about the traits found in an array of actual performances. But too often we resort to scoring what is easiest — or least controversial — to observe. A fine task can be rendered inauthentic by such bogus criteria.

Two key questions for setting up a scoring system therefore are: "What are the most salient characteristics of each level or quality of response?" and "What are the errors that are

most *justifiable* for use in lowering a score?" Obvious successes and errors (such as those that relate to spelling or computation) are not necessarily the most accurate indicators of mastery or its absence.[6] Too many essay scoring systems reward students for including merely *more* arguments or examples; quantity is not quality, and we teach a bad lesson by such scoring practices.

When possible, scoring criteria should rely on descriptive language, not evaluative and/or comparative language such as "excellent" or "fair." Judges should know specifically where in performance to look and what to look for. The ACTFL foreign language proficiency guidelines and the Victoria, Australia, "Literacy Profiles" are perhaps the best examples available of such empirically grounded criteria.[7] Teachers may also want to have students analyze a task and help devise the scoring system. This builds ownership of the evaluation, makes it clear that judgments need not be arbitrary, and makes it possible to hold students to higher standards because criteria are clear and reasonable.

"Benchmark" the standards for performance to ensure that your scoring standards are wisely chosen and suited to wider-world or next-level demands. Standard-setting for performance involves selecting exemplary samples of performance or production. The challenge is to avoid using local age-grade norms; the solution is to equate our exit-level standards at desirable colleges or professions. That advice, of course, begs a more fundamental question: Whose view of excellence should count? It is at least prudent to equate local standards of scoring to some credible wider-world or next-level standard—something routinely done in the performing arts, athletics, and vocational education.[8] *And, every so often, refer to next-level standards when scoring the work of younger students.* (I believe Illinois was the first state to assess both 6th and 8th grade writing samples against 8th grade exemplars, for instance.)

6. ASSESSMENT

Administering the Assessments

Since constraints always exist in testing, make them as authentic as possible. The question is not "Should there be constraints in testing?" but rather "When are constraints authentic, and when are they inauthentic?" It is often a matter of degree, but the principle needs to be maintained and defended.

Constraints facing the designer of authentic assessment tasks typically involve access or restrictions to the following resources: (1) time (including time to prepare, rethink, and revise), (2) reference material, (3) other people (including access to peers, experts, the test designer, and/or the judge), and (4) prior knowledge of the tasks and how they will be assessed (the issue of test security). The question then becomes: What are *appropriate* limits on the availability of these resources?

Traditional testing, because it involves indirect proxies for performance, requires numerous inauthentic constraints to preserve validity. The validity of most multiple-choice tests, for example, is compromised if questions are known in advance or if reference material can be consulted during the test. These habits of administration run deep; they seem obviously required. But what of the validity issues raised by denying students access to basic resources? Just what is being tested when the student cannot predict the historical periods or books that will be assessed, or cannot consult resources while writing?

We need not keep textbooks and other materials from students if the task is genuinely authentic. For example, in many of Connecticut's performance tasks in mathematics, the key formulas are given to the student as background to the problem. And why not allow the student to bring notes to the exam? A physics teacher I know allows students to bring an index card to the exam with anything on it; the card often reveals more about the student's knowledge than the exam answers!

Too little time for performing is not always the key issue either. Is the

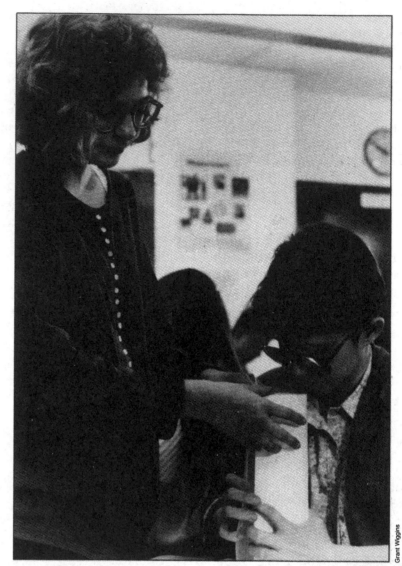

Grant Wiggins

limiting of the test to *one sitting* authentic? If writing is indeed revision, for example, why not allow writing assessment to occur over three days, with each draft graded? Many districts now do so, including Jefferson County, Kentucky, and Cherry Creek, Colorado.[9]

I am not arguing that the student should have unlimited time and access in testing.[10] Let us ask: What kinds of constraints authentically simulate or replicate the constraints and opportunities facing the performer in context? What kinds of constraints tend to bring out the best in apprentice performers and producers?

Develop a written, thorough protocol that details how the task should be administered — especially so judges will know the proper limits of their interventions to student acts, comments, or questions. It is incred-

ibly easy to invalidate performance assessment by varying the instructions, the amount of assistance provided, and the depth of responses given to inevitable student questions. Determining beforehand what is acceptable response and intervention by adults is essential; test administrators must receive standard verbal responses for delicate situations, confusions, or problems that arise.

And don't forget that kids can do the darndest things with directions that aren't thought through. In a hands-on science experiment that asked whether "the sun" heated up different colored liquids at different rates, a student did not use the heat lamp provided, moved all his equipment to the window, saw it was a cloudy day, and wrote "no."

Make the tasks maximally self-sustaining and the record-keeping obligation mostly the student's. Many educators who have never seen large-scale performance assessment cannot fathom how all students can be efficiently and effectively assessed. But they assume that the teacher will have to guide activity every step of the way and record massive amounts of information simultaneously. Thoughtful preparation, designed to make the assessment self-running, frees the teacher to be a perceptive judge.

Creating a Tool Kit

Develop a districtwide "tool kit" of exemplary tasks, task templates, and design criteria for assessment tasks. Not all of us are good designers, but why should we have to be? Teachers can help their colleagues by providing a sampler of tasks and task templates. Kentucky has done this at the statewide level, providing dozens of tasks and task ideas to teachers as part of the new state performance-based assessment system. We should consider including not only current examples of model assessment tasks, but traditional performance-based challenges such as debates, treasure hunts, mysteries, design competitions, historical reenactments, science fairs, Odyssey of the Mind tasks, Scout Merit Badges, student-run banks and stores, and so forth.

The mathematics performance assessment team of the Connecticut Department of Education has identified the following types of problems as central to its work:

- Given data on graphs, write a story that represents the data or graph.
- Given headlines or claims with background data, explain whether or not the claims are reasonable.
- Given student work containing common errors, write a response to the student.
- Given equations or number facts, write a problem that the equations or facts could solve.
- Given trends or sample data, make and justify predictions.
- Given consumer- or job-related buying, selling, or measuring situations, solve a problem.
- Given multiple or competing interpretations of given data, justify each interpretation.

Job roles provide ample opportunities for task designers to create simulations. Here are some suggestions.

- Museum curator: design museum exhibits; compete for "grant" money.
- Engineer or surveyor: bid and meet specs for largest-volume oil container; build a working roller coaster; map or survey a region around school or in the building.
- Ad agency director: design advertising campaigns, book jackets, or blurbs for books read in class.
- Psychologist/sociologist: conduct surveys, perform statistical analyses, graph results, write newspaper articles on the meaning of results.
- Archaeologist: determine the culture or time frame of a mystery artifact or person.
- Newspaper editor and writer: write articles and editorials set in the studied historical time.
- Policy analyst: predict the future in a country being studied.
- Product designer: conduct research, design ad campaign, present proposal to panel.
- Job interviewee: present portfolio and try to get "hired" for a specific job related to skills of current course (interview conducted by other students or teacher).
- Expert witness to Congress: testify on behalf of or against advertising claims, regulation of children's TV, or current policy issue.
- Commercial designer: Propose artwork for public buildings.

Piloting and Reporting

Always pilot some or all of the test. Assessment design is like software design: one can *never* accurately and fully anticipate the naive user's response. A first design may not fit the purpose or maximally evoke the desired knowledge; a prompt might result in irrelevant responses that are nonetheless appropriate or reasonable to the student; the logistical constraints of a context can turn out to be more daunting than anticipated; the judges may be too self-interested in the results or insufficiently trained. A pilot is the only way to find out, even if it involves only a tiny sample of performers. And the de-bugging requires a *naive* "guinea pig" — a teacher from a different subject or a few students — if the hidden problems in the goal, directions, or procedures are to be found.

You are what you report: Make sure that your report cards, transcripts, and district accountability reports relate achievement and progress to essential performance tasks and exit-level standards. Few transcripts reflect achievement in reference to outcomes. They tend to certify that tests were passed on each isolated packet of content instead of documenting what the student can do and to what level of performance. Further, a one-shot test cannot validly assess many important capacities, as the phrases "habits of mind" or "consistency of performance" suggest. Grading and reporting thus need to move toward scoring that provides a "progress" measure — that is, work scored against exit-level performance standards. And no worthy performance is reducible to one aggregate score. Every student ought to have the equivalent of a baseball card — many different kinds of abilities measured and a brief narrative report — if we are seriously interested in accurately documenting and improving complex performance.

Assessment's Role in School Reform

An underlying premise of this kind of assessment reveals why I believe that assessment reform is the Trojan horse of real school reform. We badly need better definitions of mastery or *understanding* to guide assessment design, curriculum design, and teacher job descriptions and performance appraisal. Circling "correct" answers to problems only test makers care about is not "knowing," nor is it the aim of teaching. Authentic tests provide a stimulating challenge instead of an onerous obligation.

Perhaps more important for school restructuring is the need to build local

Horace's School: Redesigning the American High School

Theodore R. Sizer
Boston:
Houghton Mifflin Company, 1992

This book is a valuable tool for a school in the midst of a major assessment/restructuring process. Presented as an extended case study centering around the fictional teacher, Horace Smith, the book follows Horace through a series of restructuring committee meetings he is chairing at Franklin High School.

The meetings accurately capture the blend of tedium and excitement characteristic of the committee process. Flowing from the discussions of what it means to be well educated and how to best provide this education are several examples of "exhibitions." These are the means whereby students demonstrate their understanding of ideas and skills underlying the school's newly devised program. The exhibitions provide readers Sizer's best examples of performance assessments for high school students.

Interspersed with Sizer's commentary is his narrative. It is here I found him at his best. The chapter "Policy and Power" is as cogent and heartfelt a statement about reform as I have read.

The book draws from years of research and the author's work with the Coalition of Essential Schools. Sizer delineates the Coalition's "nine common principles," which recognize there is no one way for a good school to look or proceed. Likewise, there are no shortcuts in the restructuring process, especially as it seeks to challenge the underlying principles of our current schools. This book sheds light on the reform process and helps clarify the challenge. The rest is up to us.

Available from Houghton Mifflin Company, Two Park St., Boston, MA 02108, for $19.95 (paperback).

— *Reviewed by Stephen Garger, University of Portland, Portland, Oregon.*

educator capacity and interest in quality assessment.[11] Genuine faculty empowerment is impossible without deep ownership of local standards and measures. Farming all these problems out to distant "experts" is a grave mistake — one rarely made in any other country. Good teaching is inseparable from good assessing. It may well be that experts can design more rigorous tests, and that correlational/predictive validities exist in standardized tests. But schooling we can be proud of and held genuinely accountable for demands more locally useful, authentic, and enticing assessments.

---

[1]Bloom, (1954), pp. 163, 175. Serious would-be test designers would do well to reread the *text* of the taxonomy, not just the Appendix/list, as well as the follow-up handbook developed by Bloom, Madaus, and Hastings, (1981).

[2]"The student should [have] freedom from excessive tension . . . be made to feel that the product of his efforts need not conform to the views of the instructor . . . [and] have considerable freedom of activity . . . [including] freedom to determine the materials or other elements that go into the final product." In Bloom, (1954), p. 173.

[3]See Linn, Baker, and Dunbar, (1991), for further discussion of validity design issues.

[4]I have watched half a dozen classes immerse themselves in this problem and beg to continue when time ran out.

[5]From Resnick (1987).

[6]Describing key errors and using them in the rubric is a *very different* matter than building them into test answers as "distractors."

[7]A related issue that emerges in designing rubrics (and thus far unaddressed by measurement experts) is the difference between the degree of difficulty of the task and the desired quality of the performance — a distinction made in New York's music performance assessments.

[8]See Wiggins (1991).

[9]Yes, yes, I know the issue is *really* one of cheating. Let the teacher "sign off" on the papers, then, certify authorship, as they do in Australia and now in Vermont.

[10]Though many New York State tests do allow the student what amounts to unlimited time — all day — given the shortness of the test. And certifiably learning disabled students are allowed unlimited time on the SATs as well as many state achievement tests.

[11]See Stiggins (1991).

References and Readings

Bloom, B. S., ed. (1954). *Taxonomy of Educational Objectives: The Classification of Educational Goals; Handbook I: The Cognitive Domain.* New York: Longman Publishers.

Bloom, B. S., G. F. Madaus, and J. T. Hastings. (1981). *Evaluation to Improve Learning.* New York: McGraw-Hill. [A major revision of *Handbook on Formative and Summative Evaluation of Student Learning.* (1971). McGraw-Hill].

Linn, R. L., E. L. Baker, and S. B. Dunbar. (November 1991). "Complex, Performance-Based Assessment: Expectations and Validation Criteria." *Educational Researcher* 20, 8: 15-21.

Mitchell, R. (1992). *Testing for Learning: How New Approaches to Evaluation Can Improve American Schools.* New York: The Free Press.

National Council of Teachers of Mathematics. (Forthcoming). *Mathematics Assessment: Myths, Models, Good Questions, and Practical Suggestions.* Reston, Va.: NCTM.

Resnick, L. (1987). *Education and Learning to Think.* Washington, D.C.: National Academy Press.

Schwartz, J. L., and K. A. Viator, eds. (1990). "The Prices of Secrecy: The Social, Intellectual, and Psychological Costs of Testing in America." A Report to the Ford Foundation. Education Technology Center, Cambridge, Mass.: Harvard Graduate School of Education.

Stiggins, R. (March 1991). "Assessment Literacy." *Phi Delta Kappan* 72, 7: 534-539.

Victoria Ministry of Education. (1990). *Literacy Profiles: Handbook.* Victoria, Australia. [Distributed in the U. S. by TASA, Brewster, N.Y.]

Wiggins, G. (February 1991). "Standards, Not Standardization: Evoking Quality Student Work." *Educational Leadership* 48, 5:18-25.

Wiggins, G. (June 1990). "Finding Time." *Basic Education* 34, 10.

Wiggins, G. (May 1989). "A True Test: Toward More Authentic and Equitable Assessment." *Phi Delta Kappan* 70, 9: 703-713.

Wiggins, G. (April 1989). "Teaching to the (Authentic) Test." *Educational Leadership* 46, 7: 41-47.

Performance Assessment

The Realities That Will Influence the Rewards

**Carol Anne Pierson
and Shirley S. Beck**

Carol Anne Pierson is Associate Professor and Assistant Dean of Education, University of Central Arkansas, Conway. Shirley S. Beck is Assistant Professor, Department of Curriculum and Instruction, Southwest Texas State University, San Marcos.

As educators continually strive to improve evaluation methods, performance assessment has grown in popularity and use. Performance assessment is an authentic way to acquire accurate information about students' performance and comprehension (Perrone, 1991). Its appeal may be related to the growing need for local decision-making about student progress and instructional programs, as well to the interest in outcome-based education. Extensive debate about this type of assessment is carried on in education journals, professional meetings and education policy discussions. "Expert" perceptions of the "movement" range from skepticism to a belief that it is the solution to all of education's ills (Arter, 1991; Cizek, 1991).

At best, performance assessment could be the key to restructuring schools for higher standards and improved accountability. At the very least, it adds an expanded dimension to education assessment. At worst, performance assessment could become another promising idea tossed on the junk heap of discarded innovations if care is not taken to really understand its nature and limitations. As more schools move toward performance assessment for student evaluations, teachers and particularly administrators must become knowledgeable users.

Performance assessment is not a totally new idea. It is a common form of assessment in fields such as medicine and law. Industry uses performance assessment to make promotion decisions. Performance assessment was once the most common form of assessment in education, prior to the widespread use of standardized tests (Perrone, 1991). And it has been used regularly in such subjects as physical education, music and art.

> *At best, performance assessment could be the key to restructuring schools for higher standards and improved accountability.*

Language arts teachers, in particular, have embraced the concept of performance assessment, perhaps because they have been using performance testing to varying degrees for many years (i.e., to evaluate essays, speeches, book reports and various forms of oral reading). Their cry to legitimize teacher observations of students engaged in actual literacy tasks is being heard and supported by other teachers, administrators, governors and legislators. Performance assessment of reading and writing is becoming a reality in many classrooms across the United States.

As the "movement" generates increased enthusiasm and optimism, more and more administrators are seeking help to establish performance assessment procedures not only for reading and English programs, but also for other content areas, such as math and science. The authors, as assessment consultants, have discovered that enthusiasm for and acceptance of performance assessment often exceed knowledge about its nature and complexity. As they wrestle with the task of helping administrators develop environments and structures for moving toward performance assessment, the authors have identified three basic and critical questions that often go unanswered when schools rush to jump on the performance assessment bandwagon:

- What exactly is performance assessment?

- What advice is available from experts and the research?
- What issues and concerns must be addressed?

What Exactly Is Performance Assessment?

Few discussions of performance assessment clearly define the phrase. The authors found Berk's (1986) operational definition to be a fair and concise representation of current beliefs about performance assessment. He defines performance assessment as "the process of gathering data by systematic observation for making decisions about an individual" (p. ix). Stiggins and Bridgeford (1986) establish three criteria for a performance assessment. First, students must apply knowledge they have acquired. Second, students must complete a clearly specified task within the context of either a real or simulated exercise. Third, the task or completed product must be observed

Spontaneous assessment grows out of teachers' day-to-day intuitive observations and judgments . . .

and rated with respect to specified criteria in accordance with specified procedures, requiring students to actually demonstrate proficiency.

Stiggins and Bridgeford make a very important distinction between spontaneous and structured performance assessments. Spontaneous assessment grows out of teachers' day-to-day intuitive observations and judgments in the classroom. On the other hand, structured performance assessment must meet standards for reliability and validity and is systematically designed and planned for specific purposes. It uses clearly designed and specified scoring criteria and assesses very well-defined behaviors. Structured performance assessment is

the type most performance assessment experts want us to understand.

An example of the critical distinction between structured and unstructured assessments can be found in portfolio assessment. Many articles about portfolio assessment of writing, in particular, do not suggest rigorous criteria for the selection and analysis of portfolio entries. Gathering a collection of student products is certainly a legitimate task for a teacher or school. It must be understood, however, that an unstructured collection provides no data for analysis or comparison. If performance assessment is to become a viable alternative to conventional testing, it must be rigorous. Standards for selection and analysis must be a part of every performance assessment.

Cizek (1991) makes a distinction between indirect and direct measures of student assessment. He suggests that conventional paper-and-pencil tests are indirect measures of what students know about a topic, whereas performance tests are direct measures of students' ability to employ that knowledge during an actual task. Performance assessment goes beyond measuring what students *know* to measuring what students can *do* or *apply*.

What Advice Is Available from Experts and the Research?

Structured performance assessment has been used for decades in business, industry, fine arts and sports. The actual sales record, product, play and game are recognized as legitimate means of assessing knowledge and ability to perform. Managing, supervising, directing and coaching focus on end products or performances. Structured performance assessment is not new to academic subjects, but it has not always been considered as "legitimate" a form of assessment as so-called objective or norm-referenced tests. Performance assessment is more likely to develop into a long-lived innovation if we pay heed to the following five suggestions offered by assessment experts and researchers.

- First, the use of performance assessment in other fields alerts us to the necessity of carefully and clearly describing and analyzing the tasks students will be expected to perform. Commenting on the business sector, Nathan and Cascio (1986) state, "A job analysis is necessary for showing the job-relatedness of all performance appraisal methods and is the basis for the performance standards fed back to employees" (p. 33). This same process must be applied to education. Analysis of the task that the student is to perform is a critical factor in making performance assessment a viable measurement. We cannot construct a list of criteria or a means of rating that criteria if we have not first determined what we expect students to produce.

- Second, all reliability, validity, administration and scoring standards relevant to conventional forms of assessment must also be applied to performance assessment (Brandt, 1992). Unless performance assessment is rigorous, its usefulness will be questioned. We must be wary of the misconception that any alternative assessment will automatically be a better assessment (Arter, 1991). Articles advocating portfolio assessment, for example,

Unless performance assessment is rigorous, its usefulness will be questioned.

often do not include detailed criteria for selecting and evaluating portfolio entries (Rief, 1990) and may lead practitioners to believe that evaluation can be accomplished simply by collecting and describing samples of student work.

■ Third, Grant Wiggins suggests that in order for structured performance assessment to be useful, models must be created and criteria and standards must be set (Brandt, 1992). Education does not have to invent this wheel. Established models in art, music, drama, speech and athletics may help educators develop new models appropriate for academic subjects. A significant step was taken in 1985 when a joint committee composed of representatives from American Educational Research Association, American Psychological Association and National Council on Measurement in Education established a set of standards for educational and psychological measurement that included performance assessment standards (AERA/APA/NCME Joint Committee, 1985). These standards are an excellent place for schools to begin their search for appropriate models. States such as Colorado have taken the lead in establishing

… evidence gathered from other professions … indicates performance assessment is much more transferable to real world tasks.

models that can be tested and revised to meet local needs (Gilbert, 1990).

■ Fourth, education professionals need to recognize and respond to factors that may impede further development and use of performance assessment. Developing strategies and structures for dealing with these factors may be as important as developing the new assessment instruments themselves. Speed and low cost were two attractive features of conventional tests.

Performance tests, however, are much more time-consuming to construct and administer (Maeroff, 1991). Developing, administering and scoring performance assessments are labor-intensive tasks, and the teachers who develop these new instruments will require released time. The cost of performance assessments will necessarily be weighed against their usefulness. Widespread support, as well as funding, will be the essentials that keep performance assessment from being discarded as a nonviable innovation.

■ Finally, we must be aware that the performance assessment movement in education is really still in its infancy and the body of definitive research is very small. Nor do we have clear research evidence to determine if students who do poorly on conventional tests will do appreciably better on performance tests. Furthermore, there is insufficient research evidence to establish a clear link between re-

(John Ferraro/The Shore Line Times)

As a method for extending performance assessment, proper use of the computer in a learning situation provides another tool for tracking, in a very individualized way, the progress of a student.

sults of performance assessment and effective functioning in college or on the job. We can, however, use evidence gathered from other professions that indicates performance assessment is much more transferable to real world tasks. Educators must continue to share what they know about the state of performance assessment if this form of evaluation is to become increasingly useful.

What Issues and Concerns Must Be Addressed?

Issues and concerns specific to the unique applications of performance assessment in education must be addressed carefully and systematically. As more and more districts move toward performance assessment, more and more issues and concerns about the design and use of the new tests will be raised. The questions generated by the following issues do not yet have "right" answers, or even general agreement on possible answers. Performance assessment cannot move ahead, however, until education planners at least come up with answers that are appropriate to their local situations.

The authors have identified four major issues and related questions that are most frequently discussed in the literature and must be answered before performance assessment can be implemented.

ISSUE 1: Establishing Standards for Performance Testing
- Is the assigned task worthy of being assessed?
- Is the end product clearly defined through models of acceptable products?
- Are the criteria for administering and scoring the test precise and clear?
- Do the scoring rubrics, or guidelines and procedures, accurately represent the agreed-upon criteria?
- Who will decide on the criteria? Will parents and students be a part of these decisions?

- How will criteria and standards be conveyed to all stakeholders (teachers, administrators, students, parents, the political community, others)?

ISSUE 2: Assuring Precision of Performance Assessment Instruments
- Is a performance test the best way to assess the behavior under consideration?
- Are uniform operational definitions available for all terms used? For example, the term "composite portfolio" has several definitions in the literature and in practice. One definition must be agreed upon if this term is to be used in a local proposal.
- How carefully structured is the relationship between the performance assessment and other tests in use (predictive validity)? For example, if college admission is a concern for a school district, will its high school writing test predict success on SATs?
- How do the criteria to be judged match the rating items, the prompt and the end product (content validity for observable behavior, construct validity for abstract concepts)? For example, if the end product and the criteria of a speech test were focused on persuasive ability while the prompt required the student to give an informational speech, the content validity of the assessment would be questionable.
- Are the performance assessment tasks related to and transferable to real world tasks (ecological validity)? For example, reading assessment tasks that involve narrative text may not be related to technical types of reading demanded in the workplace (Quellmalz, 1986).
- Will all raters who administer the performance tests achieve a reasonable degree of concur-

rence or inter-rater reliability?
- Will multiple samples be assessed to achieve a more reliable view of performance?
- Will the performance instrument be systematically critiqued and revised as needed?

ISSUE 3: Using Performance Assessment Scores and Results
- How will performance assessment results be translated into grades for report cards, etc. (Jongsma, 1991)?
- How will performance assessment results be used to affect classroom decisions and instructional practices?
- Will performance assessment results be used to describe individual achievement, group performance or both?
- Will performance assessment results be used in concurrence with conventional test results?
- Will the performance assessment become the new high-stakes test?

ISSUE 4: Training Personnel To Use Performance Assessments
- Are personnel who will design, administer and interpret the performance instruments knowledgeable about assessment—are they assessment literate (Stiggins, 1991)?
- Who will train personnel to administer the assessments?
- How will quality training programs be guaranteed?
- Who will train students to interpret performance assessment feedback or participate in self-assessment?

Some Final Thoughts
As knowledge and understanding of learning continue to grow, the need for more flexible and diverse measurements will only increase. Performance assessment is a promising addition to the traditional tools. If this new tool is to fulfill its promise, performance assessment must be understood and used re-

sponsibly. Educators' professional judgments may finally achieve the legitimacy and worth they deserve, provided their assessment expertise grows as well. It is the authors' hope that educators will not leave the development of this new assessment tool solely to testing companies or so-called experts, but will strive to become experts themselves.

References

AERA/APA/NCME Joint Committee. (1985). *Standards for educational and psychological testing*. Washington, DC: American Psychological Association.

Arter, J. (1991). *Performance assessment: What's out there and how useful is it really?* Portland, OR: Northwest Regional Educational Lab. (ERIC Document Reproduction Service No. ED 333 051)

Berk, R. A. (Ed.). (1986). *Performance assessment*. Baltimore, MD: The Johns Hopkins University Press.

Brandt, R. (1992). On performance assessment: A conversation with Grant Wiggins. *Educational Leadership, 49*, 35-41.

Cizek, G. J. (1991). Innovation or enervation? Performance assessment in perspective. *Phi Delta Kappan, 72*, 695-699.

Gilbert, J. C. (1990). *Performance-based assessment resource guide*. Denver, CO: Colorado Department of Education. (ERIC Document Reproduction Service No. ED 327 304)

Jongsma, K. S. (1991). Rethinking grading practices. *The Reading Teacher, 45*, 318-320.

Maeroff, G. I. (1991). Assessing alternative assessment. *Phi Delta Kappan, 73*, 272-281.

Nathan, B. R., & Cascio, W. F. (1986). Technical and legal standards. In R. A. Berk (Ed.), *Performance assessment* (pp. 1-50). Baltimore, MD: The John Hopkins University Press.

Perrone, V. (Ed.). (1991). *Expanding student assessment*. Alexandria, VA: Association for Supervision and Curriculum Development.

Quellmalz, E. S. (1986). Writing skills assessment. In R. A. Berk (Ed.), *Performance assessment* (pp. 492-509). Baltimore, MD: The John Hopkins University Press.

Reif, L. (1990). Finding the value in evaluation: Self-assessment in a middle school classroom. *Educational Leadership, 47*, 24-29.

Stiggins, R. J. (1991). Assessment literacy. *Phi Delta Kappan, 72*, 534-539.

Stiggins, R. J., & Bridgeford, N. J. (1986). In R. A. Berk (Ed.), *Performance assessment* (pp. 469-492). Baltimore, MD: The Johns Hopkins University Press.

PLANNING FOR CLASSROOM
PORTFOLIO
ASSESSMENT

Diana V. Lambdin
and Vicki L. Walker

Diana Lambdin teaches at Indiana University in Bloomington, IN 47405-1006. Her special interests include problem solving, curriculum development, assessment and evaluation, and writing to learn mathematics. Vicki Walker teaches middle school mathematics at Louisville Collegiate School, Louisville, KY 40207. She is interested in alternative methods of assessment, particularly portfolio assessment.

Three years ago, the mathematics teachers from grades 4–12 in our school met for two weeks during the summer for an in-service program related to assessment and decided to begin using portfolios with our students in the fall. I was enthusiastic, although I had no idea at that time how drastically my approach to assessment—and to teaching in general—would change as a result of the portfolio decision.

In the three years since that assessment meeting, I've struggled with learning how to use portfolios for classroom assessment and discovered many tips toward planning for their use. Among the most important things that I've learned are (*a*) the importance of having a clear

This article, although written in the first person singular, is actually a collaborative effort of the two authors, who shared equally in its conceptualization and writing. The authors became acquainted in 1990 when Louisville Collegiate School requested that mathematics educators at Indiana University give them some advice about bringing their mathematics teaching more in line with the NCTM's curriculum and evaluation standards. Frank Lester suggested the use of portfolio assessment as a catalyst for change. He and Diana Lambdin consulted with the Collegiate teachers for several years as they worked through the process of establishing the use of portfolio assessment in all their mathematics classes, grades 4–12. In 1992, the state of Kentucky began mandating the use of portfolios in mathematics assessment. For a related article see "Implementing the K–4 Mathematics Standards in Kentucky" in the November 1993 issue.

idea of the reason for assigning students to compile portfolios; (*b*) the importance of establishing workable routines for managing the production, organization, and storage of the portfolios; and (*c*) the importance of giving students clear guidance about expectations for their portfolios.

> Portfolios are more than student folders.

Why Use Portfolios?

The mathematics teachers in my school established certain goals for our use of students' portfolios. First, we were looking for a better way to assess the whole

child than just relying on test scores. Second, and perhaps most important, we wanted to help students develop better self-assessment skills and become less reliant on the grades we assign to their work. Third, we wanted to establish a better means of communication among students, parents, and teachers about the kinds of mathematical learning taking place in our classrooms.

These were lofty goals. Although it seemed that portfolios could help us attain them, early on it was not clear exactly how. In retrospect, I realize that I really had very little idea at first what good portfolios should look like, much less how I intended to manage or evaluate them. I discussed the portfolio project with my students during the first weeks of school and sent home a letter informing their parents, but for quite a while, I was actually just feeling my way along. As the year went on, the students and I all raised questions about portfolios, shared thoughts, and communicated about mathematics (and about what we thought demonstrated mathematical learning), and gradually a clearer picture developed. **Table 1,** taken from guidelines distributed in 1992 by the Kentucky Department of Education as part of an Educational Reform Act mandating the use of portfolios in mathematics assessment, furnishes an overview of the philosophy of portfolio assessment that I have gradually come to espouse. Although the process of searching for meaning has been important to my own growth as a professional, I might have been able to grow more quickly and efficiently had I realized certain things. In this article, I share some of the insights I've gained about portfolio assessment. (Resources I've found especially useful are listed in the **Bibliography**.)

TABLE 1

Mathematics-portfolio philosophy

A workable mathematics-portfolio philosophy—

- supports a method of evaluation that allows students to demonstrate their strengths rather than their weaknesses;
- values a variety of learning styles;
- values mathematics as a subject that requires careful and thoughtful investigation;
- promotes self-assessment and students' confidence in mathematics;
- encourages students to communicate their understandings of mathematics with a high level of proficiency;
- promotes a vision of mathematics that goes beyond correct answers; and
- emphasizes the role of the student as the active mathematician and the teacher as the guide.

(Adapted from Kentucky Department of Education [1992, 1–4])

Portfolios Are Not the Same as Folders

In the beginning, I tended to equate portfolios with student folders in my mind. I'd often kept folders containing examples of students' work and conference comments, and I initially thought that was more or less what the portfolios would be like. I now realize that a very important element was missing in that conception of the portfolio process—the element of self-evaluation. In the portfolio process that has evolved in my classroom, students are much more in control when putting together their portfolios than they ever were with my old folders. Developing a portfolio involves reflection, writing, and self-critiquing in an effort to present a composite picture of oneself. This approach makes a portfolio much different from simply being a collection of sample pieces of a student's work.

Deciding what kind of envelopes or folders to use as portfolios and where to store them seemed at first to be relatively minor details, but I later realized that such routine decisions can have important implications. The department had decided that students would keep a *working portfolio* (a manila file folder) and a *permanent portfolio* (a dark blue, card-stock accordion-style folder). Throughout the grading period, students placed those papers they were considering as possible portfolio entries in their working portfolio, which served as a sort of holding tank for their selections. At the end of each grading period, students reevaluated their work and made the final selections to transfer to their permanent portfolio. During the first year, all the portfolios were kept in storage boxes that tended to float around my classroom, depending on where space was available at any given moment. When it came time for a class period devoted to working on portfolios, the storage boxes were pulled out usually from underneath a mass of papers, books, and dust.

> Portfolios can improve communication with students and parents.

Looking back, I can see that something was fundamentally wrong with my whole approach toward the management of the portfolios. The idea of having a working portfolio and a permanent portfolio was, and remains, an essential part of my portfolio procedures. Yet my early method of managing the working portfolios meant that portfolio selection was just one more thing to fit into all the many instructional activities I must orchestrate. In that first year, whenever the end of a grading period approached, I scrambled to squeeze in class time for portfolio work and processing. As the portfolios were dug out, I proclaimed to my classes that we all needed to value this process of compiling portfolios. Students were instructed to choose papers that would demonstrate their competencies and their insights. After the first grading period, when many portfolios appeared to be random selections of papers, I required students to attach a comment to each piece telling why they had chosen it for their portfolio. I pleaded that they reflect thoughtfully about their mathematical endeavors and hoped they would turn in masterpieces of mathematical revelation. Then I was extremely disappointed when many portfolios consisted primarily of computational work with comments such as "I chose this because it is neat" or "I chose this because I got all the right answers." Because I had talked about demonstrating good problem solving and displaying mathematical thinking and because I had set aside what I felt to be very valuable instructional time for students to select portfolio pieces and to write comments about them, I had naively assumed that my students would share my expectations about what constituted thoughtful reflection. That first year I sat at my desk facing a huge mound of blue folders, upset not only because most of my students' choices seemed to be off target and their reflections rather shallow but also because I had no earthly idea what I should do to evaluate the portfolios.

Tips for Getting Started with Portfolio Assessment

What seems obvious to me now is that by keeping portfolios in storage boxes and only pulling them out occasionally, I was inadvertently conveying a message to my students about the value of the portfolios that was quite contrary to my preachings. By stressing portfolio work only at the end of each grading period, I was defeating my own goal of having my students invest themselves in a process of self-reflection that would culminate in a product called a portfolio. I never imagined that I was instilling anything but positive ideas about maintaining portfolios in my students. Yet, little by little, I began to realize some important adjustments that needed to be made.

6. ASSESSMENT

Portfolios need to be accessible

First of all, I rearranged things in my room, purchased some inexpensive shelves, and made a permanent home for the portfolios. At present the shelves are located in the front of my room, the area is clearly labeled "Portfolios," and student samples and selection guidelines are posted on the wall directly above the shelves. Since the portfolios are visible and accessible every day, they are tended to more consistently. They are now an integral part of my classroom and of its activities.

Students need guidance in labeling and choosing

Getting my students to label their portfolio selections clearly is a challenge. I expect not just names and page numbers but also dates, assignment titles, and descriptions that clarify what the work is all about. I did not ask for this information initially, and consequently, I did not get it. As I began to give students more specific guidelines about how to label their entries, I began to see marked improvements in their portfolio work. Moreover, I believe my students began to be much more aware of the range of activities in which we were involved and the reasons we were doing these different types of work.

Initially I gave students key phrases for the types of items I expected to go into their portfolios: for example, *favorite piece, best effort, most improved, awesome problem-solving work.* I supplied self-stick notes on which they were to indicate the reasons for their selections; the notes were to be attached to the corresponding pieces. Some students spent considerable time thinking about which pieces of their work might qualify for inclusion in their portfolio and why. Most students, however, just raced through their notebooks and their working portfolios grabbing things they thought might fit the bill. Those who just wanted to get finished fast tended to focus primarily on superficial aspects like neatness and correctness and on computational tasks, rather than reflecting on the thinking they had done in solving nonroutine problems.

The many changes I have made in my guidelines for portfolio selections and portfolio writings have convinced me that I will probably continue to make adjustments with each passing year, but I can share some ideas about what I do currently. I give my students written guidelines about the different types of work to include in their portfolios (see **tables 2** and **3**). I also supply a handout of "thinking questions" for them to work through before preparing the written reflections that I now require to accompany each entry (see **table 4**). (These written reflections have replaced the self-stick notes, which I decided were too small and informal for my purposes.) In general, my goal is to guide students through a process of reflecting, and then writing, about why they've chosen specific pieces—in particular, what they've learned from the activities or work that they select and what kind of connections they can make between this work and other school topics or other aspects of

---

TABLE 2

Mathematics-portfolio entries

A complete portfolio will include—

- a completed table of contents;
- a letter to the reviewer written by the student that describes the portfolio;
- five best entries reflective of the topics studied and the activities completed in the course.

Each entry must include the original question, task, or problem posed; a title; the date; and the student's name. Entries must be in the same order as listed in the Table of Contents and must be numbered accordingly. If an entry is in the category of photographs, audiotapes, videotapes, or computer disks, then the entry must be accompanied by a brief paragraph describing the activity and its rationale.

(Adapted from Kentucky Department of Education [1992, 1–4])

TABLE 3

Mathematics-portfolio entry types

Writing
This type of entry includes journal entries, mathematics autobiographies, explanations, reflections, justifications, and so on.

Investigations or Discovery
This type of entry can be described as an exploration that leads to understanding of mathematical ideas or to the formulation of mathematical generalizations. Examples include gathering data, examining models, constructing arguments, and performing simulations.

Application
This type of entry is to include the selection and use of concepts, principles, and procedures to solve problems in a well-grounded, real-world context.

Interdisciplinary
This type of entry demonstrates the use of mathematics within other disciplines.

Nonroutine Problems
This type of entry includes problems for which the solution or strategies are not immediately evident. This category may include mathematical recreations such as puzzles and logic problems.

Projects
This type of entry includes activities that extend over a period of days and requires a formal presentation of the material learned. This category may include research projects, designs, constructions, and original computer programs.

Note: A portfolio entry may fall into more than one of the foregoing types.

(Adapted from Kentucky Department of Education [1992, 1–4])

Students Need Guidance in Being Reflective

I never realized before I began using portfolios the importance of giving students opportunities to categorize, edit, critique, and analyze their own work and the work of other students, so that they can develop an intuitive sense of what constitutes quality. Projecting transparencies of students' work for whole-class discussion about mathematical content and quality of work has now become a common instructional activity in my class. My students seem to benefit considerably from these whole-class discussions. Similarly, I have learned a lot about which areas of my instruction have made sense to them and on which topics they have remained confused. As we have begun to spend more time analyzing and processing material in class, my students and I have both become more engaged in reflecting on the value of various activities. Even though I had included problem-solving activities, writing tasks, group work, and special project work in

---

TABLE 4

Portfolio "thinking questions"

Please think through these questions carefully as you begin finalizing your portfolio selections and preparing your written summaries.

- What activity or mathematical topic was involved?
- How did the activity help you learn something new?
- What did you learn from this experience?
- Can you describe any connections between the activity and other subject areas or real-life situations?
- Would you do anything differently if you had more time?
- What strategies did you use? (What did you *think* as you worked through the task?)
- What mathematical skills were used in your solution process?
- How would you rate your overall performance related to the activity?
- What are your areas of strength in mathematics?
- What goals have you set for yourself in mathematics?

---

their lives. (See **fig. 1** for an example of one student's work on an assignment involving estimation and her rationale for including that work in her portfolio.)

lio now has a definite beginning and end and a clearer vision-at-a-glance of what it contains and what message it is meant to convey. Furthermore, the table of contents allows for easier perusal on my part and has saved me a great deal of time during my evaluation process.

> At first I did not know how to evaluate portfolios.

A table of contents is essential

I now require students to have a table of contents for their portfolios, and I have seen remarkable improvement in their portfolios since doing so. Offering students help in preparing a table of contents is fairly easy, yet extremely critical. I generally display a sample table of contents on the overhead projector (see **fig. 2**) so that students can take notes on the format. Since I've required a table of contents, I get far fewer portfolios that are just piles of papers with fragmented thoughts attached. Students seem to be more thorough regarding the layout of their work and the overall appearance of their portfolio, perhaps because they have more of a sense of a completed project. Each portfo-

---

TABLE 5

Selected peer-evaluation portfolio reflections

Activity: Students engaged in partner conferences to discuss their portfolio selections, give advice to one another, and comment on stand-out selections

1. When I looked at the portfolio selections with Shawn, I noticed a lot of things I could have done better on. For instance, on my problem-solving section I did not do so good because it was the beginning of the year and I had not really gotten into school yet.

2. I worked with Jeff today. He helped me see many things about my papers but most of all he helped pick my best work. This is "How many books are in the library?" This work shows reasoning, estimation, observations, and many others things. This is why this work stands out so well. It shows what my work was. This was also challenging and exciting to me. Even though my estimation was 5600 and the actual was 19,000, I still think my reasoning and attitude towards this project was very good.

3. Today I worked with Andrew. He helped me see the things I was doing wrong. I had a codecracker which didn't show a lot but he helped me see how to make it work. He told me to add an explanation about it for it to fit. I think a standout piece is my million's project. It shows everything I need. It has the original problem plus it shows all my work. It has an explanation about the problem and what we did.

4. One piece of work I think I did super was the "Buckets of Trouble." Even though the explanation wasn't perfect, it showed what our group had done and had pictures to show strategies and the solution. This was a standout piece, and was a fun experiment too. Our group had to work with cups to visualize what we were doing and if it would work.

5. Today I conferenced with Jenny. She pointed out that some of my work needed explanation and helped me choose another piece of work that helps make my portfolio stand out. We chose the Library Book project. The piece was neat, colorful, and had a wonderful explanation!

FIGURE 1

Student work with portfolio reflection

Portfolio paragraph

Anne
5-25-93

I chose my "books in the library" project for an entry because it shows my work and has a clear explanation of the process I used. I enjoyed this project because we got to work our own way and find the answer alone. This project taught me to collect data, organize it, and to understand what I did enough to put it in words. Even though my answer whasn't very exact I feel that for the beginning of the year it is pretty good.

Anne
9/16/92

Books in the Library

When I began the Library Books project I thought there might be 400 books. First of all I counted 3 shelves—1 full, 1 medium, and 1 with barely any. Next I avraged them. After that I counted the number of shelves upstairs and multiplied the average amount of books per shelf by the number of shelves. Then I went downstairs and counted the books on the spinners, counted the books in the Kiddie Library, and counted all the books on the downstairs shelves. The total amount of books in the libiary is ...

26,057

This is how I got my answer:

Upstairs: 51 per shelf
×198 shelves
10,098 on the shelves
+ 97 countertop
10,195

Downstairs:
961 Kiddie Room
14,770 all shevles
9 atlases
+ 122 spinners
15,862

Downstairs 10,195
+15,862
26,057 total

Upstairs

---

my classes for years, I was surprised to discover that many of my students had never thought about the distinctions among these types of learning activities. A case in point is one student who chose only computational selections for his portfolio and justified his selections with the statement that he had spent a lot of time working the "problems." Time spent was what made them problem *solving* for him.

Whole-class discussions prompt reflection.

In addition to having the whole class share and discuss examples presented on the overhead projector, I frequently engage students in peer-evaluation activities. I pair students or have them work in small groups to make portfolio selections and record comments about their selections. This type of activity may involve having students respond to some important questions I've placed on the overhead projector or may occur at the end of a particular unit when I ask students to summarize the main ideas related to the unit. (See **table 5** for some examples of students' writing from a peer-evaluation activity.)

I involve students in peer-evaluation activities a couple of times a month. During such activities, I am able to circulate around the room, take note of valuable comments I hear, make informal assessments of students, and exchange thoughts with small groups or individuals about the type or quality of work they've completed. In this manner, my instructional style and my assessment procedures have become more unified, and portfolio selection is no longer a one-day activity at the end of each marking period. The primary goal of my peer-evaluation activities is that the students spend time thinking about, and sharing their ideas related to, mathematics. The additional benefits of such activities are that students become more aware of what they have studied and what they have learned, I gain valuable insights

---

FIGURE 2

Sample portfolio table of contents

NAME _____

GRADE _____

DATE _____

TABLE OF CONTENTS

Title of Entry	Date Completed	Page
1. Will All Quadrilaterals Tessellate?	15 Nov. 1991	1
2. Buckets of Trouble	27 Oct. 1991	3
3. M&M Probability	16–18 Mar. 1992	5
4. Statistical Project on Immigration	2–12 Feb. 1992	8
5. My Sixth-Grade Mathematics Experience	19 Apr. 1992	10

---

about my instruction, and the entire portfolio-assessment process becomes an integral part of all that we do.

Portfolio Evaluation

Evaluating student portfolios is very time consuming. I have found it easier to handle if I evaluate one class of portfolios at a time rather than try to grade all classes at once. The letter grade that I assign to each portfolio is included as part of the overall grade for the marking period and is based on three things: the diversity of selections, written reflections about selections, and the organization of the portfolio. Note that I do not grade portfolios on the quality of the selections included (homework, group work, writing assignments, tests, etc.) because many of these have already been graded. Thus, it is possible for a student who gets below-average grades on the mathematics work to receive a better portfolio grade than a student with very high grades on her or his work if the former portfolio is more thoughtfully chosen and carefully documented than the latter.

I use a two-step procedure for portfolio assessment. First I read through all the portfolios and sort them into three piles: *excellent, satisfactory,* and *needs improvement.* Then I go back through each pile and assign a score to each portfolio by using a five-point scale (1–5) for each of my three categories (selection, reflection, and organization). Assigning these points is a difficult, fairly subjective, process. But I try to set general guidelines ahead of time.

When assigning points for the selection category, I consider the diversity of the entries, the time periods represented (work should be represented from throughout the school year thus far), and the overall appropriateness of the selections. Points assigned for reflection are based on the students' written reflections about their choices. I consider clarity of thought, analysis of the problem or the mathematical concepts being displayed, use of complete sentences, legibility, and overall quality of the reflections. The category for organization involves the more technical aspects of the portfolio, such as whether it contains a table of contents, has all its pieces correctly ordered and labeled, and includes the required parental signature. I generally assign five points per category for those portfolios that show excellent work, three points for those that are satisfactory, and one point for those needing improvement. (Four points and two points are assigned, as needed, for work that seems to fall in between.) For example, a student might receive four points for diversity of selection, three points for written reflections, and five points for organization, for a total of twelve points (of fifteen possible) for the portfolio.

The final step of the evaluation process involves writing personal comments to each student about the strengths and weaknesses of his or her portfolio. Although this writing takes a great deal of my time, it greatly enhances my communication with my students and reinforces the value I place on reflection and on written expression.

Portfolios Facilitate Communication

Using portfolios has changed my communication with students and their parents in ways I had never considered before. For example, portfolios now serve as a powerful tool in parent-teacher or student-teacher conferences. As we examine together examples of such things as group work, problem solving, or written reflections, I can clarify my goals for such assignments, we can compare this type of work with more traditional textbook assignments, and students can ask questions or try to clarify thoughts that they might not have expressed well on paper. Valuable student-teacher communication also takes place through portfolio writings in which students are

> Portfolios have to be accessible all the time.

assigned to share their reactions to class activities or assignments and to reflect on their personal goals for mathematics learning. (**Fig. 3** presents an example of a student's reflection on his personal strengths and weaknesses in mathematics.)

Student-parent communication has also benefited from my use of portfolios, especially since I began requiring parental signatures on the portfolios and encouraging input from parents on students' selections. During my second year of using portfolios I began sending home a newsletter at the end of each grading period to summarize the major topics and ideas that had been covered in class. The newsletter not only has helped me review important ideas with my students as they prepare their portfolios but has facilitated student-parent communication about what has been stressed in class and why.

FIGURE 3

Student self-reflection

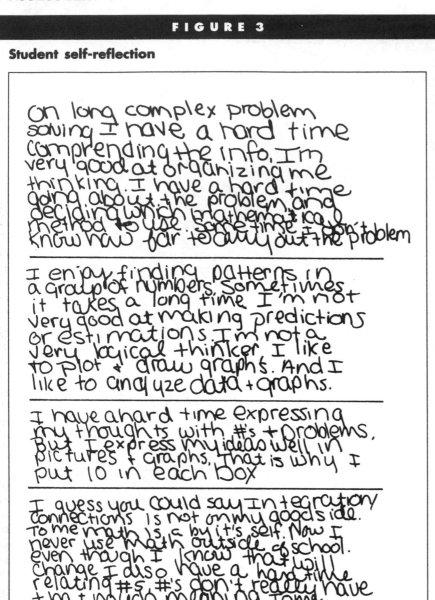

On long complex problem solving I have a hard time comprending the info. I'm very good at organizing me thinking. I have a hard time going about the problem and deciding which mathematical method to use. Some time I don't know how far to carry out the problem

I enjoy finding patterns in a group of numbers. Sometimes it takes a long time I'm not very good at making predictions or estimations. I'm not a very logical thinker. I like to plot + draw graphs. And I like to analyze data + graphs.

I have a hard time expressing my thoughts with #'s + problems. But I express my ideas well in pictures + graphs. That is why I put 10 in each box

I guess you could say Integration connections is not on my good side. To me math is a by it's self. Now I never use math outside of school. even though I know that will change. I also have a hard time relating #'s. #'s don't really have that much meaning to me.

Some Final Thoughts

Portfolio assessment has helped me and my students make progress toward a number of the goals recommended by the NCTM's *Curriculum and Evaluation Standards for School Mathematics* (1989).

My students are more thoughtful about what mathematics they are studying and why. They seem to be developing a better understanding of what is meant by problem solving and mathematical reasoning, less often resorting to the blind applica-

tion of computational algorithms when confronted with problems. In making portfolio selections, my students are learning to look for connections among mathematics topics (and between mathematics and other aspects of their lives), and they are learning to take personal responsibility for self-assessment. In writing their portfolio reflections, they are improving their abilities to communicate about mathematical ideas and about their own personal strengths and weaknesses.

I must admit, quite honestly, that portfolio assessment is time-consuming and labor-intensive for teachers, especially those who have many students. But careful planning and establishment of routines can eliminate much wasted effort and will make the job easier to do. I have found the results well worth it. Since using portfolios with my classes, I have no doubt that my students are learning more mathematics, and that has always been my ultimate goal.

Bibliography

Kentucky Department of Education. *Kentucky Mathematics Portfolio: Teacher's Guide.* Frankfort, Ky.: The Department, 1992.

Mumme, Judith. *Portfolio Assessment in Mathematics.* Santa Barbara, Calif.: University of California, 1990. (A publication from the California Mathematics Project.)

National Council of Teachers of Mathematics. *Curriculum and Evaluation Standards for School Mathematics.* Reston, Va.: The Council, 1989.

Petit, Marge. *Getting Started: Vermont Mathematics Portfolio—Learning How to Show Your Best!* Cabot, Vt.: Cabot School, 1992.

Stenmark, Jean Kerr, ed. *Assessment Alternatives in Mathematics: An Overview of Assessment Techniques That Promote Learning.* Berkeley: University of California, 1989.

———. *Mathematics Assessment: Myths, Models, Good Questions, and Practical Suggestions.* Reston Va.: National Council of Teachers of Mathematics, 1991.

Vermont Portfolio Committee. *The Vermont Mathematics Portfolio: What It Is, How To Use It.* Montpelier, Vt.: Vermont Department of Education, 1991.

Putting the Standardized Test Debate in Perspective

When used correctly, standardized tests do have value, but they provide only part of the picture and have limits—which we must understand and work to improve.

BLAINE R. WORTHEN AND VICKI SPANDEL

Blaine R. Worthen is Professor and Chair, Research and Evaluation Methodology Program, Utah State University, Psychology Department, Logan, UT 84322. **Vicki Spandel** is Senior Research Associate, Evaluation and Assessment Program, Northwest Regional Educational Laboratory, 101 S.W. Main St., Portland, OR 97204.

Are the criticisms of educational testing valid, or do most of the objections stem from the fact that such tests are often misused? By far the most common type of standardized test is the norm-referenced test—that in which a student's performance is systematically compared with the performance of other (presumably) similar students. Minimum competency and criterion-referenced tests—those that measure student performance against established criteria—can also be standardized. However, not coincidentally, most criticism has been leveled at standardized, norm-referenced tests.

Criticisms of Standardized Tests

Among the current criticisms, a few stand out as most pervasive and most bothersome to those who worry over whether to support or oppose standardized testing. In this article, we'll look at seven of the most common criticisms.

Criticism #1: Standardized achievement tests do not promote student learning. Critics charge that standardized achievement tests provide little direct support for the "real stuff" of education, namely, what goes on in the classroom. They do nothing, critics contend, to enhance the learning process, diagnose learning problems, or provide students rapid feedback.

True, standardized tests do paint student performance in broad brush strokes. They provide general performance information in content areas like math or reading—as the test developers have defined these areas. They do not, nor are they *meant* to, pick up the nuances of performance that characterize the full range of a student's skill, ability, and learning style. Of course, we hope that standardized test results are only a small portion of the assessment information a teacher relies on in making academic decisions about students or curriculum. Good classroom assessment begins with a teacher's own observations and measurement of what students are gaining from instruction every day. Standardized testing can never replace that teacher-centered assessment. But it *can* supplement it with additional information that may help clarify a larger picture of student performance.

Criticism #2: Standardized achievement and aptitude tests are poor predictors of individual students' performance. While some tests may accurately predict future performances of *groups*, critics of testing argue that they are often inaccurate predictors of *individual* performance. Remember Einstein flunked 6th grade math, the critics point out eagerly. Clearly, no test can tell everything. If standardized tests were thousands of items long and took days to administer, they'd probably be better predictors than they are now. But remember—there are predictions and predictions. When a person passes a driver's test, we can't say she'll never speed or run a red light. Similarly, when a child scores well on a standardized reading test, that doesn't mean we can kick back and say, "Well, he's a terrific reader, all right. That's how it will always be." Ridiculous. Maybe he felt extra confident. Maybe the test just happened to touch on those things he knew well. But if we look at *all* the students with high scores and *all* those with low scores, we can safely predict more reading difficulties among students with low scores.

What all this means is that in a standardized test we have the best of

From *Educational Leadership,* February 1991, pp. 65-69. © 1991 by the Association for Supervision and Curriculum Development.

one world—a measure that is relatively accurate, pretty good at what it does, but necessarily limited in scope.

Because there are so many drivers to be tested and only a finite amount of time, we cannot test each driver in every conceivable driving situation; and, similarly, we cannot measure all we might like to measure about a child's reading skills without creating a standardized test so cumbersome and complex no one would want to use it. The world of testing is, to a large extent, a world of compromise.

Criticism #3: The content of standardized achievement tests is often mismatched with the content emphasized in a school's curriculum and classrooms. Because standardized tests are intended for broad use, they make no pretense of fitting precisely and equally well the specific content being taught to 3rd graders in Salt Lake City's public schools and their counterparts at the Tickapoo School downstate. Instead, they attempt to sample what is typically taught to *most* 3rd graders in *most* school districts. The result is a test that reflects most curriculums a little, but reflects none precisely. For most users, there are big gaps—whole lessons and units and months of instruction skimmed over or left out altogether. Or the emphasis may seem wrong—too much attention to phonics, not enough on reading for meaning, perhaps. Again, the problem is the size of the test. We simply cannot cover in 10 or 20 test items the richness and diversity that characterize many current curriculums.

Criticism #4: Standardized tests dictate or restrict what is taught. Claims that standardized tests dominate school curriculums and result in "teaching to the test" are familiar and can be leveled at any type of standardized testing that has serious consequences for the schools in which it is used. On the surface it may seem inconsistent to claim that standardized tests are mismatched with what is taught in the schools and at the same time to complain that the tests "drive the curriculum." But those two allegations are not necessarily at odds. The first is grounded in a fear that in trying to represent everyone somewhat, standardized tests will wind up representing no one really well; the second arises from the consequent fear that everyone will try to emulate the ge-

neric curriculum suggested by the test content. This doesn't have to happen, of course.

Further, to the extent it does happen, it seems absurd to blame the test. The question we really need to be asking is "How are decisions about curriculum content being made?" There's often considerable fuzziness on that issue. Here's one sobering note:

Achievement test batteries are designed around what is thought to be the content of the school curriculum as determined by surveys of textbooks, teachers, and other tests. Textbooks and curriculums are designed, on the other hand, in part around the content of tests. One cannot discern which side leads and which follows; each side influences the other, yet nothing assures us that both are tied to an intelligent conceptualization of what an educated person ought to be.[1]

Criticism #5: Standardized achievement and aptitude tests categorize and label students in ways that cause damage to individuals. One of the most serious allegations against published tests is that their use harms students who are relentlessly trailed by low test scores. Call it categorizing, classifying, labeling (or mislabeling), or whatever, the result is the same, critics argue: individual children are subjected to demeaning and insulting placement into categories. The issue is really twofold: (1) tests are not infallible (students can and do change and can also be misclassified); and (2) even when tests *are* accurate, categorization of students into groups that carry a negative connotation may cause more harm than any gain that could possibly come from such classification.

Published tests, critics claim, have far too significant an effect on the life choices of young people. Some believe that achievement and intelligence tests are merely convenient and expedient means of classifying children and, in some cases, excluding them from regular education. But here again, it's important to raise the question of appropriate use. Even if we agree that it's okay to classify some children in some cases for some purposes, we must still ask whether standardized tests provide sufficient information to allow for intelligent decisions. We must also ask whether such tests provide any really useful information not already available from other sources.

Here's something to keep in mind too. Some test results rank student along a percentile range. For instance, a student with a percentile ranking of 75 on a reading test may be said to have performed better than 75 percent of the other students who took the same test. But a difference in performance on even *one test item* could significantly raise or lower that percentile ranking. Knowing this should we classify students on the basis of standardized tests? That probably depends on the consequences on whether the information is appropriate and sufficient for the decision at hand, and on whether there is any corroborating evidence. Suppose we identify talented and gifted students on the basis of standardized math and reading tests. We ought, then, to at least be able to show that high performance on those tests is correlated directly with high probability of success in the talented and gifted program.

Criticism #6: Standardized achievement and aptitude measures are racially, culturally, and socially biased. Perhaps the most serious indictment aimed at both norm-referenced and minimum competency tests is that they are biased against ethnic and cultural minority children. Most published tests, critics claim, favor economically and socially advantaged children over their counterparts from lower socioeconomic families. Minority group members note that many tests have disproportionately negative impact on their chances for equal opportunities in education and employment. We must acknowledge that even well-intentioned uses of tests can disadvantage those unfamiliar with the concepts and language of the majority culture producing the tests. The predictable result is cultural and social bias—failure of the test to reflect or take into account the full range of the student's cultural and social background.

A conviction that testing is biased against minorities has led some critics to call for a moratorium on testing and has also prompted most of the legal challenges issued against minimum competency tests or the use of norm-referenced standardized tests to classify students. It is tempting, in the face of abuses, to outlaw testing. But simplistic solutions rarely work well. A more conservative, and far more chalenging, solution is to improve our tests, to build in the sensitivity to cultural differences that would make them fair for all—and to interpret results with an honest awareness of any bias not yet weeded out.

Making such an effort is crucial, if one stops to consider one sobering thought. Assume for the moment that there *is* a bit of cultural bias in college entrance tests. Do away with them, right? Not unless you want to see college admission decisions revert to the still more biased "Good Old Boy" who-knows-whom type of system that excluded minorities effectively for decades before admissions tests, though admittedly imperfect, provided a less biased alternative.

Criticism #7: Standardized achievement and aptitude tests measure only limited and superficial student knowledge and behaviors. While test critics and supporters agree that tests only sample whatever is being tested, critics go on to argue that even what is measured may be trivial or irrelevant. No test items really ask "Who was buried in Grant's Tomb?" but some are nearly that bad.

They don't have to be. The notion that multiple choice tests can tap only recall is a myth. In fact, the best multiple choice items can—and do—measure students' ability to analyze, synthesize information, make comparisons, draw inferences, and evaluate ideas, products, or performances. In many cases, tests are improving, thanks in large part to critics who never give up.

Better Than the Alternatives

No test is perfect, and taken as a whole, educational and psychological measurement is still (and may always be) an imperfect science. Proponents of standardized tests may point to psychometric theory, statistical evidence, the merits of standardization, the predictive validity of many specific tests, and objective scoring procedures as arguments that tests are the most fair and bias-free of any procedures for assessing learning and other mental abilities. But no well-grounded psychometrician will claim that tests are flawless, only that they are enormously useful.

What do they offer us that we couldn't get without them? Comparability, for one thing. Comparability in the context of the "big picture," that is. It isn't very useful, usually, for one

teacher to compare his or her students' performance with that of the students one room down and then to make decisions about instruction based on that comparison. It's too limited. We have to back away to get perspective. This is what standardized test results enable us to do—to back off a bit and get the big, overall view on how we can answer global questions: In *general*, are 3rd graders learning basic math? Can 6th graders read at the predefined level of competency?

Thus, such tests will be useful to us if we use them as they were intended and do not ask them to do things they were never meant to do, such as giving us a microscopic view of an individual student's range of skills.

Appropriate Use Is the Key

On their own, tests are incapable of harming students. It is the way in which their results can be misused that is potentially harmful. Critics of testing often overlook this important distinction, preferring to target the instruments themselves, as if they were the real culprits. That is rather like blaming the hemlock for Socrates' fate. It is palpable nonsense to blame all testing problems on tests, no matter how poorly constructed, while absolving users of all responsibility—not that bad tests should be condoned, of course. But even the best tests can create problems if they're misused. Here are some important pitfalls to avoid.

1. *Using the wrong tests.* Schools often devise new goals and curriculum plans only to find their success being judged by tests that are not relevant to those goals or plans yet are imposed by those at higher administrative levels. Even if district or state level administrators, for example, have sound reasons for using such tests at *their* level, that does not excuse any school for allowing such tests to be the *only* measures of their programs. Teachers and local administrators should exert all the influence they can to see that any measures used are appropriate to the task at hand. They can either (1) persuade higher administrators to select new standardized achievement or minimum competency measures that better match the local curriculum or (2) supplement those tests with measures selected or constructed specifically to measure what the school is attempting to accomplish.

Subtle but absurd mismatches of purpose and test abound in education. Consider, for instance, use of statewide minimum competency tests to make interschool comparisons, without regard for differences in student ability. Misuse of tests would be largely eliminated if every test were carefully linked with the decision at hand. And if no decision is in the offing, one should question why *any* testing is proposed.

2. *Assuming test scores are infallible.* Every test score contains possible error; a student's *observed* score is rarely identical to that student's *true* score (the score he or she would have obtained had there been no distractions during testing, no fatigue or illness, no "lucky guesses," and no other factors that either helped or hindered that score). Measurement experts can calculate the probability that an individual's *true* score will fall within a certain number of score points of the *obtained* score. Yet many educators ignore measurement error and use test scores as if they were highly precise measures.

3. *Using a single test score to make an important decision.* Given the possibility of error that exists for every test score, how wise is it to allow crucial decisions for individuals (or programs) to hinge on the single administration of a test? A single test score is too suspect—in the absence of supporting evidence of some type—to serve as the sole criterion for *any* crucial decision.

4. *Failing to supplement test scores with other information.* Doesn't the teacher's knowledge of the student's ability count for anything? It should. Though our individual perceptions as teachers and administrators may be subjective, they are not irrelevant. Private observations and practical awareness of students' abilities can and should supplement more objective test scores.

5. *Setting arbitrary minimums for performance on tests.* When minimum test scores are established as critical hurdles for selection and admissions, as dividing lines for placing students, or as the determining factor in awarding certificates, several issues become acute. Test validity, always important, becomes crucial; and the minimum standard itself must be carefully scrutinized. Is there any empirical evidence that the minimum standard is

set correctly, that those who score higher than the cutoff can be predicted to do better in subsequent academic or career pursuits? Or has the standard been set through some arbitrary or capricious process? Using arbitrary minimum scores to make critical decisions is potentially one of the most damaging misuses of educational tests.

6. *Assuming tests measure all the content, skills, or behaviors of interest.* Every test is limited in what it covers. Seldom is it feasible to test more than a sample of the relevant content, skills, or traits the test is designed to assess. Sometimes students do well on a test just because they happen to have read the *particular* chapters or studied the *particular* content sampled by that test. Given another test, with a different sampling of content from the same book, the students might fare less well.

7. *Accepting uncritically all claims made by test authors and publishers.* Most test authors or publishers are enthusiastic about their products, and excessive zeal can lead to risky and misleading promises. A so-called "creativity test" may really measure only verbal fluency. A math "achievement" test administered in English to a group of Inuit Eskimo children (for whom English is a second language) may test understanding of English much more than understanding of math.

8. *Interpreting test scores inappropriately.* The test score *per se* tells us nothing about *why* an individual obtained that score. We watched the SAT scores fall year after year, but there was nothing in the scores themselves to tell us *why* that trend was downward. There turned out, in fact, to be nearly as many interpretations of the trend as there were interpreters.

A student's test *score* is not a qualitative evaluation of performance, but rather, a mere numeric indicator that lacks meaning in the absence of some criteria defining what constitutes "good" or "bad" performance.

9. *Using test scores to draw inappropriate comparisons.* Unprofessional or careless comparisons of achievement test results can foster unhealthy competition among classmates, siblings, or even schools because of ready-made bases for comparisons, such as grade-level achievement. Such misuses of tests not only potentially harm both

the schools and the children involved, but also create an understandable backlash toward the tests, which should have been directed toward those who misused them in this way.

10. *Allowing tests to drive the curriculum.* Remember that *some* individual or group has selected those tests, for whatever reason. If a test unduly influences what goes on in a school's curriculum, then someone has allowed it to override priorities that educators, parents, and the school board have established.

11. *Using poor tests.* Why go to the effort of testing, then employ a poorly constructed or unreliable measure—especially if a better one is at hand? Tests can be flawed in a multitude of ways, from measuring the wrong content or skills (but doing it well) to measuring the correct content or skills (but doing it poorly). Every effort should be made to obtain or construct the best possible measures.

12. *Using tests unprofessionally.* When educational tests are used in misleading or harmful ways, inadequate training of educators is often at fault. When test scores are used to label children in harmful ways, the fault generally lies with those who affix the labels—not with the test. When scores are not kept confidential, that is the fault of the person who violated the confidence, not the test maker. In short, as educators, we have a serious ethical obligation to use tests *well*, if we use them at all.

In Search of a Balanced View

Not all criticisms of tests can be deflected by claiming that they merely reflect misuses of tests. There are also apparent weaknesses in many tests, partly because we have yet a good deal to learn about measurement. We know enough already, however, to state unequivocally that uncertainty and error will always be with us, and no test of learning or mental ability or other characteristics can ever be presumed absolutely precise in its measurements. The professional judgments of teachers and other educators will continue to be essential in sound educational decision making. But we also assert—as do test advocates—that tests are often a great deal better than the

alternatives. Thus, we find ourselves caught in the middle of the debate between testing critics and enthusiasts.

The stridency of that debate occasionally calls to mind the old rhyme "When in danger or in doubt, run in circles, scream, and shout!" In more recent years, however, there has been some softening on both sides. Measurement experts spend less time defending tests and deriding their detractors and more time working to improve the science of measurement. At the same time, they have become more comfortable in acknowledging that test scores are approximations and less obsessed with claiming unflinching scientific support for every test they devise.

Meanwhile, critics seem less intent on diagnosing psychometric pimples as terminal acne. They seem more aware that many testing problems stem from misuse, and their calls for "testing reform" have quieted somewhat as they have recognized that even the best tests, if subjected to the same sorts of misuse, would prove no more helpful. Further, most critics are beginning to acknowledge that abolishing testing would leave us with many decisions still to make—and even less defensible bases on which to make them.

But even if there are no quick-fix answers to the testing dilemma, there are things we can do. We can: (1) scrupulously avoid any misuses of tests or test results; (2) educate ourselves and our colleagues about tests so that we understand their capabilities and limitations and do not ask them to tell us more than they can; (3) stretch to the limit our creative talents in test design, teaching ourselves to develop test items that not only resound with our own thoughtful understanding of critical content but that encourage students to think; and (4) recall, even when pressed for hasty or expedient decisions, that no matter how much any test may tell us, there is always so much more to be known.

---

[1]G. V. Glass, (1986), "Testing Old, Testing New: Schoolboy Psychology and the Allocation of Intellectual Resources," in *The Future of Testing*, Buros-Nebraska Symposium on Measurement and Testing, Vol. 2, p. 14, edited by B. S. Plake, J. C. Witt, and J. V. Mitchell, (Hillsdale, N.J.: Lawrence Erlbaum Associates).

Index

Credits/Acknowledgments

Cover design by Charles Vitelli

1. Perspectives on Teaching
Facing overview—A. Reininger/Woodfin Camp.

2. Development
Facing overview—Courtesy of Cheryl Greenleaf.

3. Exceptional and Culturally Diverse Students
Facing overview—Ed Keating/NYT Pictures.

4. Learning and Instruction
Facing overview—Sara Krulwich/NYT Pictures. 114-115—Figures © Innovative Learning Group, 975 Walnut Street, Suite 342, Cary, NC 27511.

5. Motivation and Classroom Management
Facing overview—Dushkin/McGraw-Hill photo.

6. Assessment
Facing overview—Dushkin/McGraw-Hill photo.

ANNUAL EDITIONS ARTICLE REVIEW FORM

■ NAME: _____ DATE: _____

■ TITLE AND NUMBER OF ARTICLE: _____

■ BRIEFLY STATE THE MAIN IDEA OF THIS ARTICLE: _____

_____

■ LIST THREE IMPORTANT FACTS THAT THE AUTHOR USES TO SUPPORT THE MAIN IDEA:

_____

_____

_____

_____

■ WHAT INFORMATION OR IDEAS DISCUSSED IN THIS ARTICLE ARE ALSO DISCUSSED IN YOUR TEXTBOOK OR OTHER READINGS THAT YOU HAVE DONE? LIST THE TEXTBOOK CHAPTERS AND PAGE NUMBERS:

_____

_____

_____

_____

■ LIST ANY EXAMPLES OF BIAS OR FAULTY REASONING THAT YOU FOUND IN THE ARTICLE:

_____

_____

_____

_____

■ LIST ANY NEW TERMS/CONCEPTS THAT WERE DISCUSSED IN THE ARTICLE, AND WRITE A SHORT DEFINITION:

_____

_____

_____

_____

*Your instructor may require you to use this ANNUAL EDITIONS Article Review Form in any number of ways: for articles that are assigned, for extra credit, as a tool to assist in developing assigned papers, or simply for your own reference. Even if it is not required, we encourage you to photocopy and use this page; you will find that reflecting on the articles will greatly enhance the information from your text.

We Want Your Advice

ANNUAL EDITIONS revisions depend on two major opinion sources: one is our Advisory Board, listed in the front of this volume, which works with us in scanning the thousands of articles published in the public press each year; the other is you—the person actually using the book. Please help us and the users of the next edition by completing the prepaid article rating form on this page and returning it to us. Thank you for your help!

ANNUAL EDITIONS: EDUCATIONAL PSYCHOLOGY 97/98
Article Rating Form

Here is an opportunity for you to have direct input into the next revision of this volume. We would like you to rate each of the 44 articles listed below, using the following scale:

1. **Excellent: should definitely be retained**
2. **Above average: should probably be retained**
3. **Below average: should probably be deleted**
4. **Poor: should definitely be deleted**

Your ratings will play a vital part in the next revision. So please mail this prepaid form to us just as soon as you complete it.
Thanks for your help!

Rating	Article	Rating	Article
	1. A Piece of Cake		21. Reflections on Multiple Intelligences: Myths and Messages
	2. The Six National Goals: A Road to Disappointment		22. Thinking Maps: Seeing Is Understanding
	3. Using Action Research to Assess Instruction		23. The Rewards of Learning
	4. Reflection and Teaching: The Challenge of Thinking beyond the Doing		24. Rewards versus Learning: A Response to Paul Chance
	5. Learning through "Play" as Well as "Work" in the Primary Grades		25. Sticking Up for Rewards
	6. The Moral Child		26. The Tyranny of Self-Oriented Self-Esteem
	7. Early Childhood Programs That Work for Children from Economically Disadvantaged Families		27. The Caring Classroom's Academic Edge
	8. Helping Children Become More Prosocial: Ideas for Classrooms, Families, Schools, and Communities		28. A Framework for Culturally Responsive Teaching
	9. Caring for Others and Being Cared For: Students Talk Caring in School		29. Problem Based Learning: An Instructional Model and Its Constructivist Framework
	10. Developmental Tasks of Early Adolescence: How Adult Awareness Can Reduce At-Risk Behavior		30. Investing in Creativity: Many Happy Returns
	11. At-Risk Students and Resiliency: Factors Contributing to Academic Success		31. How K–12 Teachers Are Using Computer Networks
	12. When Your Child Is Special		32. Choices for Children: Why and How to Let Students Decide
	13. A Holistic Approach to Attention Deficit Disorder		33. Motivating Underachievers: Make Them *Want* to Try
	14. Is It Acceleration or Simply Appropriate Instruction for Precocious Youth?		34. Using Motivational Theory with At-Risk Children
	15. Meeting the Needs of Your High-Ability Students		35. From Negation to Negotiation: Moving Away from the Management Metaphor
	16. Ability Grouping: Geared for the Gifted		36. Images of Management for Learner-Centered Classrooms
	17. What We Can Learn from Multicultural Education Research		37. Creating a Constructivist Classroom Atmosphere
	18. "All Kids Can Learn": Masking Diversity in Middle School		38. Why Violence Prevention Programs Don't Work—and What Does
	19. Multiculturalism: Practical Considerations for Curricular Change		39. The Challenges of Assessing Young Children Appropriately
	20. Remembering the Forgotten Art of Memory		40. Making the Grade: What Benefits Students?
			41. Creating Tests Worth Taking
			42. Performance Assessment: The Realities That Will Influence the Rewards
			43. Planning for Classroom Portfolio Assessment
			44. Putting the Standardized Test Debate in Perspective

(Continued on next page)

ABOUT YOU

Name _____ Date _____

Are you a teacher? ❏ Or a student? ❏

Your school name _____

Department _____

Address _____

City _____ State _____ Zip _____

School telephone # _____

YOUR COMMENTS ARE IMPORTANT TO US !

Please fill in the following information:

For which course did you use this book? _____

Did you use a text with this *ANNUAL EDITION*? ❏ yes ❏ no

What was the title of the text? _____

What are your general reactions to the *Annual Editions* concept?

Have you read any particular articles recently that you think should be included in the next edition?

Are there any articles you feel should be replaced in the next edition? Why?

Are there other areas of study that you feel would utilize an *ANNUAL EDITION?*

May we contact you for editorial input?

May we quote your comments?

ANNUAL EDITIONS: EDUCATIONAL PSYCHOLOGY 97/98

BUSINESS REPLY MAIL

First Class   Permit No. 84   Guilford, CT

Postage will be paid by addressee

Dushkin/McGraw·Hill
Sluice Dock
Guilford, Connecticut 06437

No Postage
Necessary
if Mailed
in the
United States